American Cinema's Transitional Era

American Cinema's Transitional Era

Audiences, Institutions, Practices

EDITED BY

Charlie Keil and Shelley Stamp

UNIVERSITY OF CALIFORNIA PRESS
Berkeley   Los Angeles   London

University of California Press
Berkeley and Los Angeles, California

University of California Press, Ltd.
London, England

Library of Congress Cataloging-in-Publication Data

American cinema's transitional era : audiences, institutions,
practices / edited by Charlie Keil and Shelley Stamp.
     p.   cm.
Includes bibliographical references and index.
ISBN 0-520-24025-1 (alk. paper).
—ISBN 0-520-24027-8 (pbk. : alk. paper)
     1. Motion pictures—United States.   2. Keil, Charlie.
3. Stamp, Shelley.

PN1993.5.U6A858   2004
791.43'0973—dc22   2003017216

Manufactured in the United States of America
13   12   11   10   09   08   07   06   05   04
10   9   8   7   6   5   4   3   2   1

The paper used in this publication is both acid-free and totally
chlorine-free (TCF). It meets the minimum requirements of
ANSI/NISO Z39.48–1992 (R 1997) *(Permanence of Paper)*.⊗

CONTENTS

LIST OF ILLUSTRATIONS AND TABLES / *vii*
ACKNOWLEDGMENTS / *ix*
INTRODUCTION / *1*

PART 1. DEFINING TRANSITION: REVISION AND DEBATE

1. Systematizing the Electric Message: Narrative Form, Gender,
   and Modernity in *The Lonedale Operator*
   Tom Gunning / *15*

2. "To Here from Modernity": Style, Historiography,
   and Transitional Cinema
   Charlie Keil / *51*

3. Periodization of Early Cinema
   Ben Brewster / *66*

4. Feature Films, Variety Programs, and the Crisis of the Small
   Exhibitor
   Ben Singer / *76*

PART 2. THE TRANSITIONAL SCREEN: NEW GENRES,
CULTURAL SHIFTS

5. What Happened in the Transition? Reading Race, Gender,
   and Labor between the Shots
   Jacqueline Stewart / *103*

6. The "Imagined Community" of the Western, 1910–1913
   Richard Abel / *131*

7. The Coney Island Comedies: Bodies and Slapstick
   at the Amusement Park and the Movies
   Lauren Rabinovitz / 171

8. Travelogues and Early Nonfiction Film: Education
   in the School of Dreams
   Jennifer Lynn Peterson / 191

PART 3. THE INDUSTRY IN TRANSITION:
CHANGING INSTITUTIONS AND AUDIENCES

9. Where Development Has Just Begun: Nickelodeon Location,
   Moving Picture Audiences, and Neighborhood Development
   in Chicago
   J. A. Lindstrom / 217

10. A House Divided: The MPPC in Transition
    Scott Curtis / 239

11. Not Harmless Entertainment: State Censorship and Cinema
    in the Transitional Era
    Lee Grieveson / 265

12. Cinema under the Sign of Money: Commercialized Leisure,
    Economies of Abundance, and Pecuniary Madness, 1905–1915
    Constance Balides / 285

13. The Menace of the Movies: Cinema's Challenge to the Theater
    in the Transitional Period
    Roberta E. Pearson / 315

14. "It's a Long Way to Filmland": Starlets, Screen Hopefuls,
    and Extras in Early Hollywood
    Shelley Stamp / 332

LIST OF CONTRIBUTORS / *353*
INDEX / *357*

ILLUSTRATIONS AND TABLES

ILLUSTRATIONS

1.1. Frame enlargement from *The Lonedale Operator* (Biograph, 1911) / *24*

1.2. Frame enlargement from *The Lonedale Operator* (Biograph, 1911) / *26*

1.3. Frame enlargement from *The Lonedale Operator* (Biograph, 1911) / *28*

1.4. Frame enlargement from *The Lonedale Operator* (Biograph, 1911) / *30*

1.5. Frame enlargement from *The Lonedale Operator* (Biograph, 1911) / *31*

4.1. American films by reel, 1908–1920 / *79*

4.2. U.S. feature films, shorts versus features, 1908–1920 / *80*

4.3. U.S. feature films, percentage of shorts versus features, 1908–1920 / *81*

4.4. U.S. feature films, total reels, shorts versus features, 1908–1920 / *82*

4.5. U.S. feature films, total reels, percentage of shorts versus features, 1908–1920 / *83*

6.1. American Film ad / *135*

6.2. Essanay ad / *137*

6.3. Production still from *The Indian Massacre* / *139*

6.4. New York Motion Picture ad / *142*

6.5. Production still from *The Invaders* / *148*

6.6. Pauline Garfield Bush / *152*

6.7. Essanay ad / *154*

8.1. Pamphlet advertising *A Trip to Yosemite* (1909) / *194*

8.2. January 1913 program from the Prince's Hall in Hull, England / *199*

8.3. Frame enlargement from *Loetschberg* (Eclipse, 1913) / *206*

9.1. Sanborn Fire Insurance map of West North Avenue, Chicago, 1910 / *225*

9.2. Urban Areas, Chicago, 1925 / *229*

11.1. Graphic from D. W. Griffith's *The Rise and Fall of Free Speech* / *267*

12.1. The symptomatic street: moral respectability or crass sensationalism? / *293*

12.2. Film under the sign of money / *302*

12.3. The star under the sign of money / *302*

12.4. Promissory note: visualizing the logic of exchange / *303*

14.1. Souvenir postcard showing tourists gathered outside Universal City, 1915 / *336*

14.2. Women socializing inside the Hollywood Studio Club, c. 1917 / *346*

TABLE

9.1. Percentages of Residents with Occupations of Various Skill Levels / *223*

ACKNOWLEDGMENTS

This project was nurtured under the enthusiastic support of Eric Smoodin and brought to fruition as a result of the diligent and insightful efforts of Mary Francis. The editors thank both of them, along with Cindy Fulton and Colette DeDonato, for their help in shepherding the manuscript through the production process at the University of California Press. We are grateful for the help Kass Banning provided when she was far too busy to do so; and Dick Abel, James Latham, Madeline Matz, and Sean Rogers supplied some greatly appreciated aid with illustrations at the eleventh hour. Jennifer Campbell deserves special thanks for providing invaluable assistance in the final stages. We also extend thanks to our contributors, who made putting together a collection of new material much easier than either of us had any right to expect and every bit as satisfying as we might have predicted.

Charlie Keil wishes to give special thanks to Shelley Stamp, who defines the role of ideal coeditor. Well organized and efficient beyond known human capability, but also collegial, helpful, and incisive, Shelley has been instrumental in navigating this anthology through its various stages. For a project that began much in the spirit of a Rooney-Garland musical ("Why don't we put together an anthology?"), it has assumed a gratifying coherence and internal logic resulting in large part from Shelley's efforts. I would work with her again in a second. I also want to thank two friends, Ben Singer and Scott Curtis, for sage advice and admirable listening skills. Finally, my family, especially Houston and Emma Keil-Vine and, as always, Cathy Vine, have demonstrated the patience, understanding and love that have enabled me to complete this project while maintaining a smile.

Shelley Stamp gratefully acknowledges the nimble footwork and seasoned chops of her coeditor, Charlie Keil, who kept us dancing in step and singing in unison throughout the project, despite the separation of two countries, three time zones, and one major power outage. Beto Byram, my offscreen song-and-dance partner, provided much of the joy to life outside the show.

Introduction

Charlie Keil and Shelley Stamp

Scholars of early cinema have worked diligently to distinguish film's earliest years from the previously monolithic notion of "silent cinema," a misnomer that conflated more than three decades of impressively diverse motion picture practice. We now have a far greater understanding of the complexity, uniqueness, and variety of filmmaking trends, moviegoing habits, screening venues, and production models at work prior to 1908. And we understand now that 1917, rather than the transition to sound in 1927, better marks the rise of classical Hollywood practices. But what of the years in between?

This volume offers the first collection of essays devoted to the so-called transitional era of U.S. filmmaking poised between the earliest motion picture work at the turn of the twentieth century and the rise of classical filmmaking models in the late 1910s. Often ignored in film scholarship, the years between 1908 and 1917 arguably witness the most profound transformation in American film history to date. It was during these years that cinema initiated the visual grammar and industrial structures it would retain well into the post–World War II era. Films gained mounting formal complexity as codes of continuity editing and narrative storytelling developed, first in the single-reel format, then quickly in multireel features. These years also saw the consolidation of film production companies in Southern California and an increased concentration of industrial power within a limited number of distribution concerns. Filmmaking techniques were increasingly rationalized in a studio system of mass production, a mode of standardization also facilitated by an emerging trade press discourse. As moviegoing became the nation's favored entertainment pastime during these years, motion picture audiences expanded and diversified, and the cult of celebrity turned picture players into full-fledged stars. Yet cinema's new prominence invited concern about its role within the cultural landscape, and the medium faced the growing challenge of state-controlled censorship and film regulation during this era. No other decade in U.S. film history encompasses such broad-ranging transformation. The sheer diversity of representational, institutional, and exhibition practices that coexist in this moment of transition point as much to the eventual shape that Hollywood filmmaking would assume in the classical era as to other possibilities and other models lost in the wake of consolidation and standardization that marked the studio era.

Although we want to make a case for the singularity of the transitional era, essays in this collection also interrogate the very parameters of the period they attempt to define. Difficulties begin with the name itself: *transitional* implies a move from one stable state of affairs to another. But is there anything distinctive about this period beyond its end point signaling the arrival of a "mature" classical cinema associated with the studio era? What aspects of early film practice linger during these years and why? How can we arrive at an accurate periodization? The last question seems particularly pertinent given that not all scholars delineate this era in the same terms. If one is studying formal change, then what becomes the more appropriate end point, the demise of one-reel films or the instantiation of classicism? If industrial transformation is at issue, and the period commences with the formation of the Motion Picture Patents Company, then does the Trust's legal elimination signal the end of the era, or the MPPC's effective displacement by Independent distribution outfits? And how do we reasonably assess when casual viewers of moving pictures became ardent movie fans, a process abetted by the emergence of trade journals, the construction of a star system, and the gradual shift of film production to the regions surrounding Los Angeles? If we have selected the years between 1908 and 1917 to mark the transitional era, it is not to insist that all relevant phenomena fit neatly within such a time frame but rather to suggest the significance of so many notable changes occurring in rough synchronicity.

By identifying a distinctive period within American cinema through a series of linked phenomena, we seek to question especially the assumption that transitional cinema did nothing save pave the way for classical Hollywood practice in the late 1910s. Instead, these essays collectively demonstrate this era's volatility and heterogeneity. As Ben Singer writes in his contribution, "transition is, almost by definition, a complex dynamic process in which disparate forces—competing paradigms and practices—overlap and interact." Charting the rich variety of material produced during these years, along with the wide-ranging production methods and screening contexts available, these essays seek to complicate our understanding of the very notion of transformation itself.

The sheer diversity of changes experienced by the American film industry and within American filmgoing culture during these years renders any attempt to encompass such developments within a uniform historical narrative problematic at best. Thus, the project of this anthology involves less an attempt to corral the various phenomena associated with transitional cinema into one all-purpose explanatory category than to provide a multifaceted exploration of the period's propensity for change. This investigation entails a contestation of previously held wisdom in concert with expanded thinking about this pivotal decade, when stylistic norms varied enormously, when habits of moviegoing and modes of viewing practice remained in flux, and when the cultural values of cinema were debated most openly and forcefully.

To prove this point, we begin with a series of essays that reveal in different ways the difficulties inherent in defining the nature of transition. One such hurdle involves properly understanding how we might link shifts that occur after 1907 to trends evident in the preceding years. Notions of change, or, more precisely, cultural dislocation, already inform many attempts to relate film at the turn of the century to broader social currents, usually under the rubric of modernity. Tied to spatiotemporal shifts wrought by such epoch-defining inventions as technologies of travel and communication (telephones, telegraphs, locomotives, and automobiles, to name but a few), visually oriented vehicles of display (billboards, department stores, and mass-circulation magazines), and the increasingly distractive quality of an urban environment defined by speed and sensation, cinema takes on added cultural significance. An accordance between features of the cinema of attractions (direct address, discontinuities produced by editing and lack of overarching narrational devices, and appeal to pure sensorial response) and this culture of modernity has cemented the connection. But if the transitional period brings a change to film form, how does this change affect the medium's relationship to sustaining currents of modernity? A sense of modernity's enduring impact on transitional cinema informs several of the essays in the collection but none more explicitly than Tom Gunning's "Systematizing the Electric Message: Narrative Form, Gender, and Modernity in *The Lonedale Operator*."

Using one of the era's best-known single-reelers to prove his point, Gunning demonstrates how modernity's reconfiguration of space and time was not arrested by the increased narrativization of transitional cinema (as some critics have claimed); instead, he argues, modern technologies of transportation and communication were foregrounded in early narrational devices of these years. Moreover, the film's attention to the particularities of gender embodied by the "girl telegrapher" offered audiences a complex guide to negotiating changing roles of women occasioned by modernity. Rather than merely anticipating the formal and ideological patterns of later classical practices, films like *The Lonedale Operator* offer a distinctive form of storytelling dependent on a concentrated version of repetition and alternation occasioned by the one-reel format. In fact, Gunning eschews the term *transitional* when defining this era, preferring instead *single-reel*, because he believes a dependency on this standardized format characterized the operations of the era.

If Gunning argues that storytelling efforts in the transitional period were bounded by the imposition of a one-reel standard, he still sees those efforts as ineluctably fostered by modernity. In this way he counters charges that the reduced force of the cinema of attractions during the transitional years throws into question the centrality of modernity's influence. Charlie Keil's essay, "'To Here from Modernity': Style, Historiography, and Transitional Cinema," pursues just such questions by examining the premises behind what he labels "the modernity thesis." Assessing the central claims made by proponents of this thesis, Keil finds that transitional cinema offers limited justification for seeing modernity's impact as paramount and posits that insistence on such influence can lead to historiographical distortions. His essay pushes beyond the transitional era proper to see how the ramifications of the modernity thesis may also prompt an alteration of our view of classicism. In conclusion Keil calls for a more moderate stance in advancing arguments about how film relates to cultural trends of the period. Taken together, Gunning's and Keil's essays allow readers to understand the topical issue of transitional cinema's links to modernity from two different perspectives and thus encourage further examination of how we relate the period to its surrounding culture.

Much like Tom Gunning, Ben Brewster, in his essay, "Periodization of Early Cinema," expresses dissatisfaction with how prevailing notions of the term *transitional* ignore certain particularities of the era. Arguing, instead, for a model that sees shorts and feature filmmaking coexisting as "parallel institutions," Brewster urges us to reexamine how exhibition contexts and formal developments affected one another and to question the relatively neat dissections of historical phenomena that current periodizations promote. Moreover, Brewster's survey of filmmaking and filmgoing trends outside of the United States reminds us that American-based typologies are not always applicable internationally. Finally, Brewster's comments might well lead to a more thorough investigation of other assumptions regarding the transitional era, primarily the notion that 1908 ushers in a new kind of cinema often typified by the decreased influence of a "cinema of attractions" and the advent of a "cinema of narrative integration," a typology most fully elaborated by Gunning. Few would dispute that the transitional period witnesses an increased narrativization, with many filmic devices enlisted to promote viewer involvement and the creation of a self-sufficient diegetic universe; but how might we best reconcile such changes to the wide range of exhibition contexts, audience reactions, and industrial upheavals typifying the period?

Both Gunning and Brewster isolate the introduction of the single-reel format as a signal development. Industry efforts aimed at standardizing the presentational format of film at the outset of the transitional period counterbalanced the multitude of diverse forces of change. By 1908 the industry had adopted single, one-thousand-foot reels as a norm in order to facilitate distribution, but increasingly complex story material demanded lengthier narratives within a matter of years. By 1912 multireel films, often two or three reels in length, began to appear, allowing for greater narrative development. By 1913 American companies began producing "feature" films of up to an hour's length or more, designed to hold an audience's sustained interest over the development of a complicated narrative. At first many theater owners were reluctant to abandon the familiar release pattern of single reels, since one-reelers had allowed them considerable control over their own pro-gramming and catered to nickelodeon markets, whose profits depended on high audience turnover. But the construction of larger theaters in the early teens, more reliant on audience volume for each screening than a constantly changing clientele, ultimately aided the shift to multireel releases.

Ben Singer's essay, "Feature Films, Variety Programs, and the Crisis of the Small Exhibitor," sustains the revisionist caste of Brewster's work while also extending its examination of exhibition contexts chronologically. By syn-thesizing preexisting data on production trends, Singer is able to describe with great precision the trajectory of two of the period's prominent changes, namely the shift to feature length and the demise of storefront theaters re-liant on a changing program of short films. Rather than overturning earlier broad claims about historical developments within this period, Singer seeks to interrogate how fully these claims should define its contours. If some of the shifts defining this era were less pervasive or dramatic than we have been led to believe, and vestiges of earlier practices and forms persisted longer than we have assumed, it could force a reevaluation of our sense of the pe-riod and its claims to ongoing change. At the very least, careful studies such as Singer's help us to focus on the rate of change during the transitional years and to recognize transition as multivalent and subject to flux.

Transformations in cinema's production, exhibition, and reception con-texts throughout this era were matched by broader changes in American cul-ture during the Progressive Era. It was during these transitional years that motion pictures asserted their place in the cultural landscape by providing commentary on all manner of social upheaval besetting the nation, from evolving gender and marital norms to the shifting ethnic and racial makeup of many cities and the rise of an urban-industrial economy and consumer culture. As the transitional era progressed, various film genres staked their claims to popularity by elaborating scenarios that negotiated these cultural concerns, thereby stoking public interest. Increasingly complex modes of narration, improvements in film technology, and standardized methods of production all helped filmmakers enlarge the range of means and material from which generic formulae and cinematic representations were derived.

As Jacqueline Stewart demonstrates in her essay, "What Happened in the

Transition? Reading Race, Gender, and Labor between the Shots," the advent of classical modes of narration and address marked an important moment of instability in cinema's developing racial and stylistic codes. In representations of Black female domestics, in particular, Stewart finds boisterous, aggressive women whose free circulation within public space breached social and racial hierarchies. No longer objects of one-shot visual gags, these female characters develop motivations that propel narratives forward, much as their physical actions organize diegetic space across multiple shots. The transgressive political and sexual implications of such representations of black mobility and interracial interaction were increasingly policed, she argues, as the film industry worked to transform itself into a legitimate entertainment for a multiclass, heterosocial, ethnically diverse but emphatically white moviegoing public. Stewart's essay illustrates the fruitfulness of looking closely at instances of instability in transitional cinema in order to understand the relationships among film form, social history, and industrial practice.

Like Stewart, Richard Abel looks at transitional film genres through a wider cultural lens, examining the ideological work of early westerns in forging a version of "American" identity both in the United States and abroad. In "The 'Imagined Community' of the Western" Abel charts the fortunes of one of the most popular transitional genres, exploring how the western's exploitation of action and landscape created a formula immensely appealing to audiences of the day. Although Abel uses the western to explore a variety of related phenomena—the function of the burgeoning trade press as critical arbiter, the limitations of distribution systems tied to single-reel features—his essay returns repeatedly to the question of how genre figures in the exercise of "nation building" to which American cinema contributed significantly during the Progressive Era.

Both Abel and Stewart maintain that transitional cinema engages its audiences in particular and often unexpected ways tied directly to the uncertainties of the period. Similarly, in "The Coney Island Comedies: Bodies and Slapstick at the Amusement Park and the Movies" Lauren Rabinovitz argues that the passive, visually oriented spectatorship associated with the rise of classical cinema was challenged by slapstick films that furnished pleasure through the visceral engagement of a good belly laugh and the "multifaceted fascination" of physical spectacle. Nowhere is this more obvious, she suggests, than in the series of comedies shot on location at Coney Island. Here the delights of early amusement parks, based in a celebration of speed, kineticism, and modern industry, overlap with those of physical comedy. Site of leisure and casual heterosexual interaction, the amusement park also licensed sexual expression, particularly for women, inviting a mockery of Victorian codes of marriage. In this transitional genre Rabinovitz finds novel models of viewing pleasure largely lost in the classical era.

Like Rabinovitz, Jennifer Lynn Peterson, in her essay, "Travelogues and Early Nonfiction Film: Education in the School of Dreams," notes the persistence of nonclassical modes of filmic construction and audience engagement throughout the transitional era. Organized around a "logic of collection," which emphasized exoticism and visual spectacle over narrative progression, travelogues eschewed continuity editing techniques increasingly common in story films of this period. In doing so they inspired a dreamlike mode of reception that ran counter to the sober educational rhetoric used to promote them. Like slapstick, travelogues were well suited to a variety programming format that stressed variation and fostered an accumulation of discrete pleasures, a mode of exhibition that would soon die out.

The emergence of new genres like the western alongside older forms like the travelogue reflects an industry adjusting to a growing and increasingly diversified audience, as do challenging new depictions of race, nationality, gender, and sexuality. Motion pictures achieved remarkable popularity during these years, becoming for the first time the nation's favored entertainment pastime. Cinema's audience base, chiefly centered on urban, working-class, and immigrant communities at the turn of the century, was now expanding to include more middle-class patrons and more small-town residents. Women, especially, were an increasingly prominent, and desirable, segment of the viewing public. Older, married women, encouraged to attend afternoon matinees or to come to theaters with their families in the evening, gave the medium an aura of respectability coveted by exhibitors, and younger women fueled an ardent fan culture.

Changing audience demographics were mirrored by developments in the exhibition context as well. Americans viewed movies in a wide assortment of venues during these years, venues heavily dependent on regional, ethnic, and class variables. But nickelodeon theaters, those hastily converted storefront operations of a few years earlier, were quickly being replaced by larger, more permanent, and oftentimes more elegant screening spaces, some converted from "legitimate" theaters, others new, purpose-built structures designed solely for the presentation of motion pictures. Sumptuous architectural and design features, together with a novel array of amenities and services, catered openly to middle-class patrons, especially women, accustomed to such features at Broadway playhouses, retail emporiums, and other spaces of upscale leisure. The culture inside those structures was also of enormous importance to the moviegoing experience. Revolving admission policies at most theaters, boisterous crowds not yet trained to remain silently attentive, and live music, often tailored to the particular cultural or ethnic makeup of audiences, ensured that interactions among patrons inside theaters remained equally important to what they were viewing onscreen. Black audiences, often segregated in "colored" theaters or inferior balcony seats, benefited from a growing number of black-owned cinemas, venues that catered to African American clientele with live jazz and community-based events. Such variety of moviegoing experience remains unprecedented in American film history.

Understanding how patterns of moviegoing evolved during these years is an important part of the equation. In her investigation of Chicago-area nickelodeons, "Where Development Has Just Begun: Nickelodeon Location, Moving Picture Audiences and Neighborhood Development in Chicago," J. A. Lindstrom proposes a more dynamic understanding of the relationship between moviegoing and broader processes of neighborhood and urban development. Forging what she calls an "urban geography" of moving picture theaters, Lindstrom reveals complex interactions between the working, living, and consumption patterns of the city's residents and the expansion of neighborhood-based film exhibition. In doing so she provides a nuanced portrait of the class and ethnicity of early Chicago audiences while also indicating how regional exhibition studies enhance our sense of the valence of change occurring within theaters throughout this period.

The expanding exhibition sector that Lindstrom charts helped fuel the move toward consolidation that defined the film industry during this period. At the end of 1908, in an effort to gain oligopolistic control, Edison joined with a select number of competitors to form a combine known as the Motion Picture Patents Company. Recognizing the need to incorporate distribution within the Trust it had formed, the MPPC moved to absorb all available film exchanges in 1910 through the General Film Company. Although the motives of the MPPC were to secure maximal profit for the participating companies, the organizational efforts of the Trust resulted in a variety of industry reforms, including standardized rental costs, rationalized release schedules, and prohibitions against duping and reselling prints already purchased. This, in turn, helped stabilize production by ensuring manufacturers of a predictable market for their films. Soon, producers sought out methods to facilitate regularized output, resulting in such innovations as continuity scripts, and, eventually, studios organized along departmental models of manufacturing efficiency. Nonetheless, many individual companies emerged and disappeared during this period. Some were victims of poor management; others were absorbed into larger concerns as competition between the MPPC and the Independents fostered an increased tendency toward consolidation. By the late 1910s a limited number of independent distribution combines, led by Universal and Mutual, pointed toward the model of industrial organization that would dominate in the decades to come.

Scott Curtis's study of the Trust, "A House Divided: The MPPC in Transition," sheds light on a set of internal tensions that informed and circumscribed the actions of this influential industrial force. Long characterized by historians as an inherently conservative and short-sighted group, the MPPC's actions indicate this portrait fails to acknowledge the often contradictory impulses guiding the Trust. Focusing on the MPPC's genesis, as well as its re-action to the advent of features, Curtis demonstrates that the upheaval cin-ema underwent during the transitional period could lead to the demise of its own architects.

Just as the forces transforming cinema during these years confounded its industrial leaders, so, too, did the medium's protean nature invite conster-nation on the part of lawmakers. Despite the film industry's efforts to ele-vate its cultural profile, and perhaps because of its increased economic suc-cess during the nickelodeon era, cinema attracted heightened scrutiny from society's gatekeepers from 1908 onward. Film industry leaders and mem-bers of New York's reform community came together in 1909 to form the National Board of Censorship, hoping to demonstrate that the business could regulate itself, free from the intervention of state and municipal agencies. Chicago had been the first municipality to establish a police censorship board in 1907, and by the early 1910s several states also began to regulate motion pictures. Scrutiny often focused on questions of sexuality and race relations, especially any combination of these two subjects, a phenomenon evident in scandals surrounding white slave pictures, fight films, and *The Birth of a Na-tion*. The latter case, which traveled all the way to the Supreme Court, re-sulted in the landmark 1915 decision declaring the legality of film censor-ship. Although the National Board of Censorship lacked legal authority to enforce its regulations, the model of industry self-regulation it pioneered would remain in place for another four decades.

Using the *Birth of a Nation* controversy as a focal point, Lee Grieveson, in his essay, "Not Harmless Entertainment: State Censorship and Cinema in the Transitional Era," examines the development of government efforts to con-trol film content. Arguing that censorship was always designed to regulate spectatorial response as much as images onscreen, Grieveson believes that the ideal way for the state to achieve its end was to push cinema toward pur-veying "culturally affirmative" entertainment to the exclusion of other func-tions. Tracing this effort through its various manifestations at the munici-pal, state, and federal levels, Grieveson finds that negotiating cinema's proper social role was a hallmark of the transitional period, resulting in the eventual equation of American film with the mainstream products of the stu-dio era.

Cinema's fluctuating social currency also figures in Constance Balides' essay "Cinema under the Sign of Money: Commercialized Leisure, Econo-mies of Abundance, and Pecuniary Madness," where she investigates debates about nickel theaters and cheap amusements against the broader struggle to define the new medium. In Simon Patten, Balides finds a sociologist fa-vorably inclined toward nickelodeons and commercial film culture. For him the vitality and passion that moving pictures engendered in their viewers could be harnessed for "a new morality" in the context of expanding consumption and a society of abundance. Patten's ideas resonated onscreen, Balides argues, in representations of borrowing, spending, accumulation, and the general circulation of capital.

Another facet of cinema's drive for respectability was its desire to compare favorably to other more legitimate art forms like photography, literature, and theater. In "The Menace of the Movies: Cinema's Challenge to the Theater in the Transitional Period," Roberta E. Pearson traces the interaction between theatrical and cinematic practices during these years, arguing that there was a greater cross-fertilization between these two arenas than has previously been thought. Like Balides, she finds buried within debates about the two media a considerable struggle to articulate cinema's aesthetic credentials. Did the medium's realist aesthetic and its capacity for visual spectacle cater to "unrefined" tastes? Could the cinema offer the transcendent experience that defines true art?

As Pearson points out, cinema's rivalry with spoken drama fueled efforts to entice theatrical stars to perform on film, but the results were rarely successful. Although the interchange between film and theater never ceased entirely, of course, its pertinence to cinema's cultural status receded somewhat as a movie star system developed in the early 1910s. Propelled by closer camera positions and a performance style based on facial expression, the star system found reinforcement in the promotional efforts of participating studios, along with fan magazines like *Motion Picture Story* and *Photoplay,* which debuted in 1911 and 1912, providing readers with information about performers' careers, as well as their lives offscreen. Although cinema was not the first entertainment medium to spawn a celebrity culture—theater, music, and sports all had comparable "stars" at the turn of the century—the particular characteristics of cinema, which promised both intimacy and absence, lent a unique edge to its star worship. Valuable though dedicated moviegoers were to the industry, many worried about the depth of their investment in this new medium and its storied performers. Alarmist reports about "movie-struck girls" bent on traveling to Southern California to achieve stardom on the "silver sheet" filled popular newspapers and magazines, as Shelley Stamp demonstrates in her essay, "'It's a Long Way to Filmland': Starlets, Screen Hopefuls, and Extras in Early Hollywood."

The consolidation of production companies in and around Los Angeles in the midteens, together with a growing romanticization of the city, its new state-of-the-art production facilities, and its celebrity inhabitants, drew many hopefuls to the area in search of work. Examining the derisive portraits of would-be starlets that emerge in contemporary coverage of this phenomenon, Stamp finds that such reports obscured the multifaceted nature of women's contributions to cinema during these years and disarmed the considerable impact that hundreds of unmarried, casually employed, recently transplanted young women posed to both the filmmaking industry and the greater Los Angeles community.

Debates of this kind provide an indication of the film industry's enormous impact on American culture throughout the transitional era, as well as the skepticism with which movie culture continued to be viewed. Much about cinema during these years remained up for debate: the safety of its screening venues, the saliency of its content, the value of its voice in popular debates, the social caliber of its clientele, its status as an art form—even its most rudimentary visual syntax. As the essays in this volume make clear, there was enormous concern during the transitional period about cinema's social standing, whether in relation to more traditional art forms like the theater or more suspect commercial entertainments like amusement parks, dance halls, and saloons—a concern manifest in ongoing regulation of film content, viewing modes, moviegoing culture, and industry labor. Ambivalence over changing relationships between men and women, people of varied racial and ethnic backgrounds, and people of different classes was also evident in both onscreen narratives and offscreen debates about film culture and industry practice.

If, in fact, the transitional period defines itself by the instability it introduces—into film form, industrial structure, production practices, screening venues, and spectatorial pleasures—these essays bear witness to the diversity of practices this instability fostered. If dissatisfaction remains with the vagueness associated with the term *transitional,* and disagreement persists over whether one periodization can adequately incorporate all relevant phenomena, perhaps we can satisfy ourselves somewhat with the knowledge that continued examination of the period can contribute to an increasingly detailed portrait of one of the most significant decades in U.S. film history.

PART ONE

Defining Transition

Revision and Debate

Systematizing the Electric Message

Narrative Form, Gender, and Modernity *in* The Lonedale Operator

Tom Gunning

FOR SOPHIA MOXIE

Open the story by bringing two strongly contrasted places and strongly contrasted sets of people, into the connexion necessary for the story, by means of an electric message. Describe the message—be the message—flashing along through space—over the earth and under the sea.
    CHARLES DICKENS, *Book of Memoranda Begun in January 1855*

"How can you tell a story jumping about like that? The people won't know what it's about."
    "Well," said Mr. Griffith, "doesn't Dickens write that way?"
    LINDA ARVIDSON, *When the Movies Were Young*

The Lonedale Operator (1911) may be D. W. Griffith's most frequently viewed and best-known film from the "transitional" era. Indeed, the film's star, Blanche Sweet, whose winsome charm and plucky moxie dominate the film, told me in later years that she finally refused to appear with it anymore because she had gotten so weary of its constant screenings. The film became available readily by the 1960s in 16 mm prints. VHS versions now are easy to rent or purchase, and most recently a DVD version appeared as part of the Treasures from American Film Archives set, presenting a Museum of Modern Art restoration of the film that gives us a tinted version, an aspect long missing from most modern prints and essential not only to the aesthetics but even the narrative logic of this film.

THE SYSTEM OF THE SINGLE-REEL FILM

As Kristin Thompson has pointed out,[1] *The Lonedale Operator* provides a perfect example of Griffith's Biograph style, or at least of his race-to-the-rescue melodramas, and of his use of parallel editing with the effect Griffith termed "sustained suspense."[2] Could the film stand, as well, as representative of the "transitional" era, defined by Charlie Keil as existing between 1907 and 1913,[3] that point between what has become known as "early cinema" and the later classical mode supposedly instituted around 1917?[4] Here the thicket of problems becomes tangled, involving not only the issue of typicality but also the term *transitional* itself. Although I have used the term, increasingly I feel it begs many questions, not the least of which is the implication that American cinema accommodated only one transitional period. Further, the term seems to indicate that this period's significance lies less in itself than in the eras it comes from and leads to. Serving as a bridge between an earlier cinema that was somehow different and a later classical cinema in which difference was repressed in favor of a fairly static and consistent pattern of both stylistic norms and production modes, the transitional era would serve mainly as a way station, a pit stop on the course of history.

Questioning the monolithic nature of Hollywood cinema between 1917 and 1960 lies beyond the scope of this essay. I would theorize provisionally that every period of American cinema could be seen as a "transitional" one, but acknowledging this fact does not invalidate the investigation of this key period of early film history. Seeing this period as more than "preclassical" may help us discover its unique qualities, revealing more than a period of apprenticeship in which the regimens of classical narrative structure were rehearsed and tested with an aim toward perfection. If anything typifies the period between 1907 and 1913, it would seem to be the rapid rate at which film style changes during the period so that the films from 1907 seem radically different from those released in 1913. This period may distinguish itself from others primarily through its protean nature. It might be better named a period of transformation than a period of transition.

In my own work on Griffith I have defined this period as one of "narrative integration" in which the various devices of the cinema were worked over with an eye to creating narratives that were not only easily comprehensible but also fully engaging. To make stories move quickly and clearly, Griffith (and other directors during the transitional period) clarified temporal and spatial relations between shots, working out the logic of such editing figures as parallel editing, reverse-angle cuts, and "sight links" or point of view shots. But these devices were not introduced simply to render stories more comprehensible (after all, *The Great Train Robbery,* from 1903, conveyed the basic action of its story without any of these devices) but more complex and involving as well. Character motivation and psychology, moral judgments, and devices of suspense were all introduced through editing and other means in order to transform film stories from distanced chronicles of action-dominated events to emotionally meaningful and exciting narratives, often carrying a moral message.

Charlie Keil's important new work, *Early American Cinema in Transition,* and my book on Griffith's early Biograph films both see 1913 as the end point of this era, largely because after this year the dominance of the single reel begins to give way in favor of the multiple-reel feature film.[5] Longer films led to new conceptions of narrative form, as filmmakers more frequently looked to the theater or the novel as models. The one-reel film understood itself in relation to the short plays presented in vaudeville and, especially, the short story.[6] Important as these models were, however, the sort of narrative condensation found in the films of the transitional period created new conventions, a sort of narrative shorthand unique to motion pictures. This condensed format rendered narrative strategies especially visible.

Thus, the "transitional" period feeds off a dialectical energy, as opposing forces rub against each other. On the one hand, the brevity necessitated by the limited length of the one-reel film, which was the industry standard during the transitional period, posed an inflexible format. This set length ran up against the expanding ambitions of the film industry, calling for more complex story lines and characterizations.[7] Instead of simply leading to an artistic standoff, however, this conflict inspired filmmakers such as Griffith to generate complex and very noticeable narrative conventions and formal systems. Combined with other constraints (such as limited budgets, extremely short shooting schedules, reliance on stock acting troupes and compressed multipurpose film studios, and release schedules that demanded a set number of films be completed each week), this tension between ambition and limitation led not only to an almost factory-like mode of production but also shaped stylistic aspects of the films, promoting highly systematic and schematic approaches. This system revolved around the standardization of the single reel as the basic industry product, the basis on which the industry was organized.[8] Thus I would propose calling this period "the single-reel era" to avoid the assumptions implied by calling it "transitional." The best films of the single-reel era, such as *The Lonedale Operator*, demonstrate the way art can thrive in the midst of constraints and triumph creatively over formulas, even as it employs them.

SYSTEMS OF NARRATION: REPETITION AND ALTERNATION

I must create a system or be enslaved by another man's.
WILLIAM BLAKE, *Jerusalem, the Emanation of the Giant Albion*

I have described Griffith's style as a "narrator-system."[9] By this term I wished to express that Griffith approached the process of narration systematically, working on the various levels of cinematic expression in order to create the narrative effects of suspense, characterization, and moral lessons. Such narrative devices were appearing in the films of other American production companies in this era as well. The conflict between narrative ambition and the one-reel format yielded differing outcomes. These conflicting demands could end in a fatal collision, exemplified, as Ben Singer has pointed out, in an episode from the Thanhouser 1914–15 serial *Zudora*, in which narrative coherence and characterization remain, as he puts it, "baffling."[10] But films by other production companies did employ systematic devices of repetition, alternation, and rhyming that guaranteed not only narrative clarity but also an aesthetic sense of coherence and unity. For instance, Ben Brewster has shown that Vitagraph one-reel films were often structured around a single object whose exchange unites the film, providing not only an economic narrative flow but a device that literally pulls the film together.[11] This interaction among constraints, clarity, and stylistic ambition could even, as in the case of *The Lonedale Operator*, produce a film in which formal systems interpenetrate narration to such a degree that the film not only achieves narrative clarity and emotional involvement of the audience but also attracts the viewer's attention to the film's systematic approach.

What does the term *system* contribute to this discussion of early film narration? In many ways I use it as a synonym for *structure* and indicate by it the way the individual elements of the film are arranged into clear patterns. I prefer *system* to *structure* because *structure* often carries a connotation of something static and rigid, whereas *system* seems to denote a process, the way something is done, rather than simply how it ends up. *System* is also the term used during the strongest period of film semiotics, in the analyses of Raymond Bellour (as in "The System of the Fragment") and Christian Metz's *Language and Cinema*, in which Metz examines not only the cinematic language system generally (that is, the codes of cinema) but also the unique system of a single cinematic text.[12] Indeed, in Bellour's magisterial analysis of *The Lonedale Operator*, "To Alternate/To Narrate," Bellour seeks to demonstrate "the systematicity at the heart of American high classicism."[13]

In Griffith's Biograph films action is channeled and funneled by devices of alternation and repetition in such a way as to make them orderly and clear. My analysis in many ways supplements Bellour's but seeks to explore *The Lonedale Operator* less as an exemplar of a larger system (such as the classicism Bellour seeks to highlight), or even as preparatory to a later system (the "Classical Hollywood Cinema" that the transitional era supposedly anticipates), and more as fashioning a unique system. I do, however, reach beyond the singular here to speculate on a somewhat smaller system than the classical: the unique qualities of the period of single-reel production.

Let me begin by relating the systematic nature of a film's editing with the organization of its actual filming, relating narrative form to the exigencies of production. After 1908 the single-reel film became the standard and basically unvarying commodity sold to exchanges and exhibitors by film production companies. The single-reel forms a unit in a grand scheme that embraces and controls the entire film market. The Motion Picture Patents

Company was founded in 1909 not only to protect the patents of its members but also to regulate the motion picture industry, uniting production, distribution, and exhibition of films in a predictable flow of product. Every production company had a determined number of single-reel films it was required to place on the market on fixed release dates. Film exchanges, the distribution agents of the era, placed a set number of "standing orders" with the companies, guaranteeing they would take a constant amount of the company's reels every week. Exhibitors had slightly more freedom in deciding how many films they would rent from the exchanges, but almost every film theater presented a program that included more than one film, and most of them changed their bills daily. A constant flow of films had to be guaranteed for these voracious exhibition outlets and the production of any single film could not slow down the process. Each film had to be carefully planned and, in effect, standardized, in terms of days devoted to its shooting, the locations in which it was shot, and even the camera setups used in order. Predetermined systems of filming had to be in place to guarantee the smooth operation of systems of exchanges and exhibition.

At the same time, however, filmmakers during this period gradually increased the number of shots used in a single reel. Before 1907 films rarely consisted of more than a dozen shots. According to Charlie Keil's sampling of American film up to 1911, the average number of shots per reel had doubled.[14] From 1908 to 1913 Biograph led the way in hyperediting, and *The Lonedale Operator* set a formidable standard. Griffith squeezed ninety-eight shots into its seventeen-minute length, as well as six intertitles, one main title, and two written inserts! Since this is the largest number of shots found in any of Griffith's films to this date (the film was released on 23 March 1911), and Griffith was the leader in hyperediting, it is unlikely any film released before *The Lonedale Operator* contained more shots. Yet Griffith and his cameraman, Billy Bitzer, shot this film in only four days! Only a systematic plan of shooting could mediate between the industry's demand for quickly made films and Griffith's desire to make his film more exciting through hyperediting.

Preplanning shooting through carefully constructed shooting scripts introduced a new economy of shooting and editing during the single-reel era, allowing cameramen to shoot films out of order. This meant every scenario had to be broken down into shots and the camera setups for these shots predetermined. In this way many shots could be taken from one camera setup and the process of shooting streamlined. *The Lonedale Operator* consists of ninety-eight shots[15] but uses only twenty-three camera setups. On average a single setup yielded four shots. Some setups were used for only one shot (nine, mostly shots of the train rushing down the track during the climactic race to the rescue), whereas others (such as the doorway to the station and the telegraph operator's office) were used for a dozen shots or more.

This system of camera setups yielding multiple shots also meant that a series of repetitions would appear across the film because of these recurring locations. Besides the obvious benefit of efficiency on the production level, on the level of narrative form such repetitions would anchor spatial relations in the minds of viewers. By always seeing the doorway to the Lonedale station from the same camera setup, the viewer quickly learns to recognize it. In addition to the recurrence of individual setups, Griffith employs repeated trajectories of spatially linked shots. Early in the film we follow the heroine from the exterior doorway through the interior ticket office and into the office of the telegraph operator. The trajectory of movement lays out the space of the station, setting up not only the primary location of the film but also the basic action (will the tramps penetrate from this exterior door to the operator's inner office?). Griffith repeats this three-shot trajectory through the office space four times over the film, fixing it in the viewer's memory.

Repetition structures *The Lonedale Operator* on both the level of single shots and multishot segments. But other forms of repetition stand out in the film through patterns of alternation. Parallel editing plays a key role in single-reel films and especially in the Biograph films. Parallel editing first appeared at the beginning of the single-reel era, primarily in films produced by the French film company Pathé Frères. In its simplest form parallel editing alternates between shots of two threads of action in different locations in order to indicate that they are interrelated, usually that they are simultaneous. The best example of this simple form of parallel editing in *The Lonedale Operator* occurs during the sequence in which the heroine, having seen the tramps skulking around the station, telegraphs for help. Eleven shots alternate between a closely framed shot of the heroine telegraphing and a medium shot of another telegraph office as a male operator first dozes then responds to the message, transcribes it, then rushes out. The telegraph connection underscores the effect of simultaneity (supplying narrative clarity), and the parsing of the action and the movement back and forth also creates suspense, provoking the questions: will the male operator wake up? Will he get the message? How will he react? Will he act in time?

Lonedale's major sequence of parallel editing adds a further complication. In the dramatic race to the rescue, which brings the film to its climax, Griffith introduces a three-pronged editing pattern. Instead of simply alternating between two threads of action, the film rotates among three different actions: the locomotive rushing to save the heroine, the tramps breaking through the various doorways of the station, and the heroine in her inner office.[16] This three-pronged rotation allows *Lonedale* to maximize all the effects of suspense the simpler form of alternation creates but also avoids the predictability an extended sequence of simple back-and-forth cutting entails.

Although each shot returns to one of the three elements (thieves, rescuers on locomotive, or heroine), Griffith also introduces variations. First, the thieves themselves are mobile, progressing into and through the station. Second, the series of shots devoted to the rescuers alternates among three views: a medium shot of the engineer from inside the engine cab (dynamically framed to reveal the landscape slipping by the window), a shot from outside the train showing the tracks as the engine barrels toward the camera, and a less frequent wider shot of the engine cab from the tender.[17] Thus, in moving among thieves, rescuers, and heroine the editing pattern, rather than simply stuttering, endows its repetition with variations, highlighting a complex system of alterations within set parameters.

The restoration of the film's original tinting pattern reveals another system of repetition and variation. A review of *The Lonedale Operator* in the *New York Dramatic Mirror* commented on the blue tint of the latter part of the film as "really looking like night." The reviewer added, "Tinted scenes in a Biograph is enough of a novelty to call for special praise anyway."[18] Tinted scenes appear in a number of 1911 Biograph films, usually the conventional blue for night, but sometimes with symbolic overtones, such as the golden tint for *The Broken Cross*. More unusual would be the red cast given to the shots within the engine cab in *The Lonedale Operator*. The realistic motivation for the tint comes from the glow of the overstoked boiler of the steam engine. As with most "red for fire" tints in early silent film, however, the monochrome carries as much abstraction as realism.

The rotation among the tints provides another formal system. As in the intercutting of action elements, the shots again rotate three possibilities: red (the engine cab), blue (darkness, including the train tracks, the exterior of the station, and the telegraph office, once the heroine turns off the lamp), and no tint at all (used as the equivalent of sunlight or lamplight and restricted to interiors in this section of the film). The tints do not change with every cut, since several dark shots might appear in succession. But they do change frequently and underscore the pace of the editing; after the heroine recovers from her faint, nearly every shot changes tint. Given the relative brevity of these shots (most less than five seconds, none more than fifteen seconds), one almost has the impression of an abstract color flicker film rhythmically moving between red, blue, and black and white. Although for the most part the change in tinting comes on a cut, in two instances the tinting changes during the shot (when the lamp is turned off and when it is turned on again), indicating tinting's relative independence from editing as a system of variation.

Kristin Thompson has also discovered other symmetrical patterns, less immediately apparent. Describing the race-to-the-rescue sequence as an alternation between shots of the train and shots of the station, she points out that the sequence returns to the station six times. Fascinatingly, the number of shots in each of these returns sets up a symmetrical order. The first return consists of a single shot (the thieves at the exterior door); the second return consists of four shots, the next return of two, the following return of two shots again; the penultimate return swells again to four shots, and the final return (before the engine arrives, that is) consists of a single shot of the heroine holding the tramps at bay with the wrench. As Thompson concludes, "Whether Griffith deliberately made his shots of the station balance symmetrically in this fashion or simply intuited the optimum rhythm for the presentation of the action cannot be known. Either way the rescue scene in *The Lonedale Operator* demonstrates Griffith's mastery of this technique."[19]

All these patterns serve the narrative—either through clarifying spatial and temporal relations between shots or by creating suspense and increasing audience involvement. Thompson points out that the number of shots in each of the station sequences fits the action being portrayed. In addition, the sensual rhythm of the editing, the brevity of shots combined with intense action (the speeding locomotive, thieves breaking through doorways), and the rotation of the tints create a visual experience of sharp alternations triggering a heightened sensual, physical excitement. The system of strong formal devices—repetition, symmetry, alternation, and variation on several levels—supports the film's obvious commercial purpose of telling a story in a clear and exciting manner.

I would claim that this impression of a strong formal system subtending the narrative operates as a key feature of the single-reel era, albeit one developed most fully by Griffith at Biograph. The brevity of the one-reel films dictated a limited number of elements, allowing spectators to notice repetitions that might be missed in a longer film. Devices of symmetry, alternation, or repetition were encouraged by the need to maximize the number of shots obtained from a single camera setup. Production efficiency and economy led to formal economy, a systematic use of elements that could take on artistic or poetic overtones. The coherence of the single-reel form (its use of symmetries and resolved asymmetries, as Raymond Bellour would put it) certainly gives these films a "classical" appearance, if by this we mean a formal unity and coherence. This foregrounded formal system contrasts sharply, however, with the classicism attributed to the Hollywood film that requires not only narrative coherence but also formal transparency, as narration as a self-conscious or noticeable aspect of the film tends to "fade out," in deference to the apparently unmediated unfolding of the story.[20] Although I believe the transparency of later Hollywood cinema has been asserted more than it has been analyzed, a unique aspect of the single-reel era may lie in the foregrounding of editing, tinting, and other means of narration by an emphasis on their formal as well as expressive qualities.

SYSTEMS: BEYOND ALTERNATION AND REPETITION

Time—the time appropriate to the production of exchangeable goods, to their transport, delivery and sale, to payment and the placing of capital—now served to measure space. But it was space which regulated time, because the movement of merchandise, of money and nascent capital, presupposed places of production, boats and carts for transport, ports, storehouses, banks and money brokers.
HENRI LEFEBVRE, *The Production of Space*

The Lonedale Operator not only is systematic in telling its story but also foregrounds its formal system through repetition, alternation, and rotation. But the film's system also includes shots that stand out by *not* being repeated or alternated. Figures of alternation or rotation are obviously systematic because they organize individual shots into larger patterns. But in a film like *The Lonedale Operator*, where so many shots can be absorbed into figures of alternation or rotation and in which most shots are filmed from camera setups that are repeated multiple times, one might neglect the special role played by shots whose camera position appears only once and is never repeated. Searching out such a unique camera setup to be used in only a single shot indicates a special role for the shot that overrides the economy gained by shooting multiple shots from one camera setup. It is likely, therefore, that each of these shots plays a key role in both the film's narrative and its formal system. In addition, thematic elements, systems of oppositions and tensions that link the film to historical issues of the era of its production and reception, such as class and gender, are welded to the film's narrative by these unique shots. Analyzing these images and patterns will allow us to move beyond the film as a closed formal system, to relate the film to the systems of society and history in which it was formed, as well as to us as viewers, living in the wake of that history.

The largest group of unique shots in *The Lonedale Operator* doesn't seem to carry special significance, however: the long shots of the train barreling toward the camera as it passes through various landscapes. But these shots do not really operate as independent shots. Although photographed from a series of unique camera setups,[21] the shots are similar in their depiction of action and in their composition, and this similarity clearly inscribes them as part of a series rather than as independent pivotal shots. The remaining four shots that are taken from unique camera setups, however, do mark out highly significant points within both the narrative and the referential systems of the film. The earliest unique shot provides the simplest, and perhaps the most elegant, example. The heroine and her engineer boyfriend enter a bucolic location dominated by the backlit foliage of a willow tree that frames the image (figure 1.1). In the background we see a hilly country path with rustic buildings in the distance. The couple approach from the background right until they are embraced by the foliage. Framed at the hip, they act out

Figure 1.1. The telegraph operator (Blanche Sweet) and her engineer sweetheart (Frank Grandin) meet before his run. *The Lonedale Operator* (Biograph, 1911; dir. D. W. Griffith), frame enlargement.

a flirtatious scene: the heroine shakes her head "no" to some plea from her beau; he pouts at this rejection, but she reassures him, and they hold hands. When he tries to kiss her, she playfully twists his ear. Then, pulling out his railway watch, she reminds him of his schedule. They exit happily toward the camera on the left.

For this love scene Griffith and cameraman Billy Bitzer selected a unique location with a diffused natural light that enfolds the tender scene and expresses a romantic mood. Ensconced in a natural landscape, it is the only shot in the film in which the world of technology is truly absent (with the exception of the engineer's watch, produced at the shot's end and motivating the characters' exit from this romantic locale). The composition fuses actors and landscape into an expressive unity. In this little oasis of nature the lovers enact their romance, as this lyrical setting contrasts with the modern environment (represented by the railway and the telegraph office).

Unique setups next appear in a pair of consecutive shots that introduce the central object of the film: the mine payroll. In the first the payroll is gathered from a cashier; in the next shot it is loaded on the train that will transport it to Lonedale. These two shots in some distant station remain isolated from the rest of the film. None of the characters we encounter here (the delivery boy who picks up and loads the payroll, the official who gives it to him, the typist in the office) appear again. Only the object, the money-laden payroll bag, will make the journey from this central station to the center of the story—distant Lonedale. Money, however, is the object that is no object, merely the medium of exchange.[22] Early in the system of telegraphy, the possibility of "wiring" money could eliminate its actual transport, opening up the information age.[23] *The Lonedale Operator* does not penetrate that far into the systems of modernity, however; its "MacGuffin" remains tangible.[24]

Why include these shots at all? The narrative introduction of the film's "MacGuffin" or, to use the contemporary term mischievously reintroduced into scholarly discourse by Ben Singer, the "weenie," the object of desire that motivates the film's action,[25] could be conveyed by the telegraph message the heroine receives in the following shot or, even more simply, by its delivery at Lonedale. Such repetition may anticipate the redundancy of later classical Hollywood cinema that repeats key information (it even follows the "rule of three," since we learn about the payroll shipment three ways: seeing it loaded, seeing the telegraph message that announces its arrival, and finally seeing it being taken from the train by the heroine).[26] But these shots of the shipping station also anchor Lonedale within a larger railway system.

These two shots stand out by being loaded with detail and a strong use of background action. The office in which the payroll is picked up teems with incidental details and explanatory inscriptions (figure 1.2). Two complementary desks (one closer to the foreground on the right with an elderly man facing right, the other a bit further back on the left, with a woman typist facing left, busily at work) split the rather cramped and shallow space. On the back wall above the head of the typist a large clock marks time with a continually swaying pendulum, and on the right edge of the frame a calendar decorates a partition. At each desk a man gives or takes orders from the cashier and the typist. Both these incidental characters exit when the delivery boy enters. After a moment a door on the left opens, and a delivery boy enters, bearing with him a panoply of written signs. The opened door reveals the word *Office;* the delivery boy carries a placard reading "Wells Fargo Express," which he puts down after he enters; the canvas bag he carries is emblazoned with "Return to Money Dept. S. F. Depot." Even the back of his ledger, which he gives to the elderly man to sign, briefly shows the words, "W. F. C. Express." The whole environment tells us we are in the realm of business, of words and messages, of records and carefully measured time.

Griffith was strongly influenced by naturalistic stagecraft, the ideal represented by David Belasco of recreating a world in miniature onstage, complete in all its details.[27] More than anything else in *The Lonedale Operator,* this office embodies that naturalistic ideal. But the constriction of space here, the cramming in of so much information and detail, gives the composition an excessive quality. The symmetry of the shot also strikes one: two desks fac-

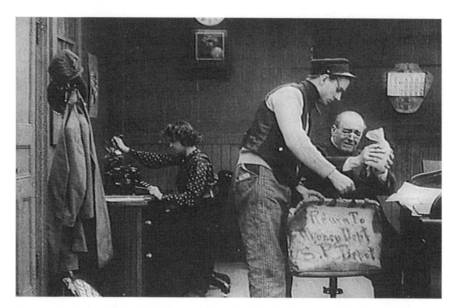

Figure 1.2. The Central Office, a bustle of activity as the payroll is dispatched to Lonedale. *The Lonedale Operator* (Biograph, 1911; dir. D. W. Griffith), frame enlargement.

ing opposite directions in two separate planes of action, the complementary men standing before each desk. While foreground position and extended interaction with the delivery boy marks the exchange of the payroll as the key action, we can hardly help our eye's wandering over to the woman's energetic typing, the rapid movement of her fingers matching the swaying of the clock pendulum above her. Griffith encourages our divided attention (without subverting the hierarchy of action that contributes to narrative clarity) by choreographing contrasting actions across the screen. As the delivery boy and the elderly man bend over the desk, signing and countersigning the ledger, the typist pauses, leans forward, and erases a word from her text.

The office presents a realm of money but also of words, order, and routines. The delivery boy gathers the money, but mutual signing of a record closes the deal, while in the background another written record is prepared and corrected. The clock and the calendar watch over these orderly and symmetrical actions, marking time and schedules. Although we are more likely to recall the charging locomotive and the heroine fervently clicking her telegraph key, such actions depend on this realm of business, words, and order. The systematic order of *The Lonedale Operator* extends beyond its narration and becomes part of its diegetic world, the modern environment of similarly systematic networks in which time and space are connected through technology, just as Griffith connects them via new patterns of editing. In effect, by bringing this systematic narration to a story about modern systems of transportation and communication, Griffith bares the device, accenting the modern nature of his style. Griffith edits his film as if inspired by the telegraph, constructs his dramaturgy as if mirroring the railway networks of interconnecting speed and urgency.

The railway and the telegraph were essential technologies in creating a new topography of space and time in the modern world.[28] This new topography overturned previous conceptions of space and time through new thresholds of speed. The railway not only transported people and goods from one place to another in drastically shortened periods, but it absorbed the points along its route—the individual stations such as Lonedale or the depot shown in these shots—into a single network. The telegraph sprouted along railway routes as means of letting stations communicate (as both other stations in this film communicate with the Lonedale operator). This network not only interrelated spaces but transformed time as well, as schedules were devised to regulate the speed and direction of trains (thus the innovation of the pocket watch, known originally as the railway watch, such as the one the heroine pulls out, keeping her engineer lover on schedule).[29] Standardized "railway time" maintained along a railway network preceded (and prepared the way for) Standard Time, overcoming the tyranny of individual town clocks, each with its own, often quite different, time.[30]

Led by Lynne Kirby, film historians have noted the congruence between the mastery of space and time by new technologies and the establishment of flexible but systematic spatial and temporal relations in cinema during the era of the single-reel film. Even Charlie Keil, although critical of making "correlations between formal change and large scale social observations,"[31] claims that "the moving picture stood as the culmination of a series of inventions that emphasized the capacities of technology to collapse conventional boundaries of time and space . . . that stretched from the telegraph and the telephone . . . through to the locomotive and automobile."[32] Thus, *The Lonedale Operator* not only displays the most advanced devices of film narration—its systematic use of editing, tinting, and composition—it also ties them directly to a story that foregrounds the systematic nature of the modern world.

The systematic nature of modernity in *The Lonedale Operator* does not appear only in the parallel edited sequences of telegraphic communication or the race of the speeding locomotive to "get there *in time*" that forms the film's climax. The overloaded accumulation of significant objects (typewriter, money bags, clock, calendar, ledger), actions (transfer, transcription, correction, signing, conferring), and written messages found in this shot, as well as the formal and symmetrical arrangement of all this, portrays the modern systems that subtend the action of the film. The publicity bulletin that the

Figure 1.3. The Central Station depot also teems with activity as the payroll is loaded onto the departing train. *The Lonedale Operator* (Biograph, 1911; dir. D. W. Griffith), frame enlargement.

Biograph company issued for this film emphasized Lonedale's ("the most isolated spot in the Western country") direct relation to "the city office," describing the run the engineer makes as stretching "between Lonedale and civilization." Within the network of the railway and telegraph, even a remote rural station participates in the topography of modernity (a point that should be brought home to those who assume modernity could only be experienced in crowded city streets).

The second unique shot portraying the bustling central station uses depth of composition to contrast it with isolated Lonedale (figure 1.3). A wide shot shows a train pulling in, moving past another train idling on a sidetrack (as opposed to Lonedale's single track). In contrast to the nearly deserted platform at Lonedale, the train yard here teems with activity. Griffith utilizes three separate planes: conductors help passengers on and off the train in the background, while a large crate is unloaded from a freight car onto a cart in midground, and in the narratively privileged foreground the delivery boy entrusts the payroll to an attendant on the train, getting him to sign for it in the ledger. The attendant writes a message on another form, which the delivery boy places in his hat as the train pulls out.

The intertitle that follows informs us, "The Operator is Notified of the

Money Shipment." The following shot shows the heroine tapping the telegraph key, transcribing the message she has just received. The cut joining these shots indicates the form that the delivery boy put in his hat contained the telegraph message the heroine received. Thus these three shots trace not only the process of sending off the payroll but also its paper trail, the information sent to precede and announce it. *The Lonedale Operator* traces a spatial and temporal drama in which not only does the engineer race to rescue his sweetheart, but telegraph messages always outstrip locomotives, as the communication of information jockeys with the transport of objects and people. Like an "electric message," Griffith's editing moves as swiftly as thought itself, tracing a parallel not only between film and telegraphy but between the telegraph operator and the film narrator. Even outside a pattern of parallel editing or repetition Griffith reveals the film's basis in the modern network of transportation and communication; from the center to far-flung reaches, all locations and events are connected by technology as well as by narration.

THE CLOSE-UP: DRAMAS OF VISIBILITY AND INVISIBILITY

My primary task is to make you see.
D. W. GRIFFITH *(paraphrasing Joseph Conrad)*

Our fourth and final shot from a nonrepeated camera setup unquestionably plays a pivotal, indeed resolving, role in the film, performing the film's essential revelation, and provides one of the strongest uses of close-ups in American cinema to this point. The penultimate shot of the film, this shot presents a close-up of the nickel-plated wrench with which the heroine holds off the tramps. From several points of view this shot pushes the envelope of the style of the single-reel era, but it also stays within the systematic foregrounding of techniques that marks the era rather than the routinization and naturalization of techniques that seem to typify the classical period that follows. As a close-up it uses a form of editing less common in this period and different from the parallel editing that dominates the film: editing within a single space, or intrascene editing (see figures 1.4 and 1.5).

Parallel editing serves as Griffith's primary narrative device during his Biograph years. Griffith most frequently cuts from one space to a different space. In addition he frequently uses patterns of alternation between spaces that are contiguous, often from one side of a door to the other, as in the cuts between the heroine in the telegraph office and the tramps forcing the door in the ticket office. Whether the shots are distant or proximate, all but three cuts (out of ninety-seven!) in *The Lonedale Operator* cut from one space to an entirely different one.[33] In these three cuts the spaces overlap, and we move from one view of a single space to another view of the same space, with the

Figure 1.4. The action is resolved, the romantic couple united, and the miscreants subdued. *The Lonedale Operator* (Biograph, 1911; dir. D. W. Griffith), frame enlargement.

camera setup either closer or farther back and with a change of angle. The first example of these overlapping shots switches from a medium close-up of the heroine as she first receives the message about the payroll to a subsequent shot filmed from a more distant position, showing the telegraph office in long shot. This "cut-back" from medium close-up to long shot is motivated by the heroine's rising to get out a large canvas bag.[34] The second overlapping cut repeats and reverses these camera positions. After the heroine glimpses the tramps outside, a long shot first shows her huddled against the door. Then, as she sits down at the telegraph to send her message, we cut to the medium-close framing. This "cut-in" plays a dramatic role. Although the switch to a closer view may be motivated by the need to enlarge a small object (telegraph key), the cut-in also intensifies the action, supplying an exclamation point and building suspense. Further, the closer position focuses our concern for the heroine, anticipating a practice in classical cinema, in which closer shots often express alignment or sympathy with a character.

During the single-reel era, cutting within a single space, overlapping or intrascene cutting, remained relatively underdeveloped compared with patterns of alternation across distant or proximate spaces. The emergence of intrascene cutting as the dominant form of editing marks the end of the

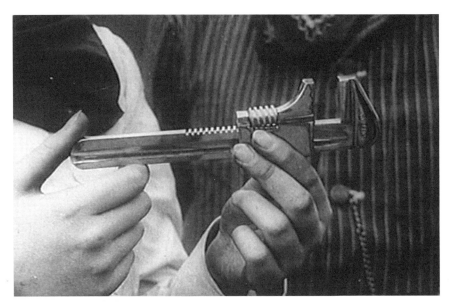

Figure 1.5. The "pistol" the operator held is revealed in close-up to be a monkey wrench. *The Lonedale Operator* (Biograph, 1911; dir. D. W. Griffith), frame enlargement.

single-reel era. Increased emphasis on character psychology, which the facial close-up supplies by highlighting expressions and reactions, motivates this change. This increased focus on characters naturalizes filmic narration—anthropomorphizes it—by directing viewer attention toward human emotions rather than formal systems. The new mode of facial close-ups also anchored cutting more closely to interaction between characters, giving rise to shot/countershot editing as the means of expressing a conversation or/and exchange of glances between characters. In contrast to the more character based cutting of the later period, during the single-reel era space took priority over character. Although in this era of narrative integration the focus became increasingly tied to character, spatial environment plays a more fundamental narrative role than emotional reactions conveyed by facial close-ups.

If we divide the narrative use of close-ups between those focused on objects (intended to reveal or emphasize a detail) and those focused on a face (intended usually to indicate a psychological reaction) in the single-reel era, objects appear much more frequently, especially before 1911. The close shots of the heroine at the telegraph desk in *The Lonedale Operator* move toward increased audience investment in characters. But the lack of such a facial close-up at its climax marks this film as belonging to an earlier paradigm. The close-up of the wrench that does supply the climax of the film pivots on visibility and on the film's displaying its own devices rather than focusing on character psychology. It fulfills the most frequent role of the closer view in single-reel films: the enlargement of a small object. Serving as a revelation and the denouement of the film, the wrench necessarily appears in a unique shot, showing something not seen before.

Nonetheless, Griffith uses this object-revealing close-up in an uncommon manner, tailored to supply the film's second climax. In most films of the single-reel era such close-ups appear at the moment the object is introduced, as in the close-up of the syringe injecting a chocolate with poison in Griffith's *The Drive for Life* (1909). In *The Lonedale Operator* the wrench had been introduced earlier, but our attention was not directed to it. Early in the film, framed in long shot, the heroine picks the wrench up after her father has gone home and she has refused his offer of a revolver. Although she handles the wrench for an extended time (she even waves it in her hand as she bids farewell to her engineer sweetheart), the shot's wide angle renders the object very small, almost unrecognizable. It remains part of an incidental action, sandwiched between two major events (her father's and her sweetheart's departure), although it clearly has been "placed" for its later dramatic use. The wrench reappears later in the film, again in long shot, as the tramps batter the door to the telegraph office. Moving away from the door, desperate, the heroine looks around and sees it on the table. She grasps it excitedly and then almost immediately turns off the lamp. Since the climax of the film takes place at night, extinguishing the lamp plunges the telegraph office into darkness, rendered dramatically through the blue tint that immediately suffuses the image, obscuring our vision. Griffith fashions the film's climax around issues of invisibility/visibility through the convergence of filmic devices (close-up and tinting).

The climactic close-up of the wrench, therefore, stands out in a number of ways. First, its delayed revelation creates a narrative strategy not common in the single-reel film: withholding key information from the audience.[35] The heroine's second discovery of the wrench, although strongly marked by Sweet's performance, still does not receive a close-up. A sharp-eyed viewer, remembering the earlier scene where the wrench was placed on the desk, might recognize and correctly identify the object.[36] But by filming the action in long shot and compromising our view almost immediately through tinting Griffith intentionally obscures recognition of the wrench. Like a good mystery writer, he has not prevented any possibility of identification. Hence he cannot be accused of breaking faith with the viewer; all the pieces are there if we watch the film carefully. But they are not emphasized.[37] Earlier in the single-reel era (and, as Singer has shown, even later) filmmakers do not always make narratively important elements visually salient, leading to unintentional obscurities in the narrative. In this penultimate close-up, however, Griffith flaunts his ability to display a privileged object clearly and unambiguously. In contrast, his refusal of a close-up earlier intentionally keeps visual certainty from the audience.

In the film's play with visibility the close-up of the wrench reverses the obscurity of the blue-tinted long shot. The unarmed heroine protects the payroll through subterfuge and cleverness, staging a scenario of visual trickery. Keeping her back to the window (from which, the Publicity Bulletin emphasizes, the moonlight glints off the metal in her hand), she deftly uses the cover of darkness and an ambiguous object to realize her performance of threatening the tramps with a pistol.[38] On their arrival her engineer sweetheart and his fireman produce a real pistol and turn the lamp back on, flooding the room with light. The heroine steps forward and dramatically flourishes the "pistol" in her outstretched arm. The succeeding shot, our climactic close-up, similarly displays its object, the light gleaming from the highly polished nickel-plated wrench. As Bellour puts it, "The unseen or badly seen objet appears in its true colors."[39] This triumph of visual clarity celebrates both the heroine's and Griffith's expert manipulation of concealment and revelation.

A review in *Moving Picture World* praised Griffith's use of the locomotive's rush to the rescue but notes that "such scenes had been enacted before"; the added plot twist of the pistol constituted the film's "novelty," its distinctive feature.[40] This final nonrepeated shot not only demonstrates the systematic nature of *The Lonedale Operator* but flaunts its devices, not only the close-up but the suspenseful withholding, then revealing, of an object. The close-up, the actors' performance, and the narrative structure all chorus, "Look at this!" in this final revelation. Griffith's climax exemplifies that "prominence of . . . deployment" of particular devices that Charlie Keil finds typical of the transitional period and that he attributes to the experimental process of introducing new devices. Keil interprets this style as primarily anticipating, through trial and error, a classical style in which such devices, far from being flaunted, would become automatic and conventional.[41] The teleology of this interpretation defines it, assuming filmmakers were always striving toward the classical ideal of stylistic transparency, sometimes with success, sometimes in failure. But Griffith's delight in this moment does not resemble a stab in the dark groping toward a device he would naturalize and render transparent if only he knew how. Other assumptions operate here: this narrative style flaunts not simply a single device as a novelty but its whole system. Rather than absorbing this happy ending into the beaming face of the heroine, as might happen in a later era, Griffith favors an object and in so doing demonstrates how the trick was done.

GENDER IN THE SPACE OF MODERNITY

They [women telegraph operators] are more or less public, and this is a disadvantage. Instead of meeting employers only (like a typist) the telegraph operator is thrown directly with the public.

HELEN CHURCHILL CANDEE, *How Women May Earn a Living*

Earlier filmmakers frequently shot close-ups against dark or neutral backgrounds, abstracting the enlarged view from the diegetic world of the film. But Griffith clearly strives to place the wrench within the space of the action. Behind the wrench, instead of a neutral background, we see the heroine's white blouse and part of her decorative bow and the engineer's striped uniform, part of his bandanna and even the watch chain that hangs from his button. These costumes are meticulously matched with the ones the characters have worn throughout and immediately identify the couple, even without showing their faces. This background detail serves other purposes than diegetic realism. As Raymond Bellour interprets it: "it unites the couple, as if over and above the action that re-forms it, by isolating fragments of their body which suddenly seem made, despite the contrast in clothes . . . of a continuous material."[42] The close-up of the wrench does seem to bolt together the romantic couple of the film.

Bellour tends to privilege alternation in his analysis of this film, founding the systematicity he seeks in "the reduction of a fundamental form of cinematographic discourse—alternation."[43] Noting figures of repetition and symmetry/asymmetry, Bellour pays careful attention to the opposition between shots, tracing their patterns of alternation in terms of time and space as I have. However, a larger semantic figure of alternation regulates the film, especially its resolution: gender. The initial four shots of the film alternate between the heroine and her sweetheart (a pattern Bellour describes as "He/She/He/She"). The couple are joined in the fourth shot and fifth shot (the unique nonrepeated camera setup at the willow tree I analyzed earlier), stroll together in the next shot, then separate, shaking hands at the station's exterior doorway. The departure of the engineer sets up an alternation between them, as Griffith cuts from the train leaving Lonedale station to the heroine waving from her telegraph office.

Bellour sees the alternation that subtends the race to the rescue not only as a suspenseful temporal/spatial articulation but as a gendered figure. The conclusion of the film not only rescues the heroine from danger but also rejoins the romantic couple parted near the film's beginning. Bellour summarizes the gender and narrative logic of the film: "the diegetic couple scarcely formed ([shots] 4–7), apparently only separates in order to meet again, to strengthen its image by the test of a dramatized separation whose internal form is alternation."[44] *The Lonedale Operator* conforms to one aspect of classicism Bellour finds in the American cinema: the creation of a romantic

couple (whose symmetry of union is interrupted by the asymmetry of separation, followed by the resolution of reunion and triumph over obstacles)
provides both story logic and narrative form in American cinema. Later
American films work out patterns of alternation, not only on the shot level
but also on the level of sequences or even diegetic actions.[45] Lynne Kirby, in
her commentary on Bellour's analysis and its particular relevance to early
railway films, refers to this type of resolution as "coupling."[46]

To lose sight of the key role Bellour ascribes to gender would gravely im-
poverish our understanding of this film. Gender, as Bellour demonstrates,
creates essential terms for the film's use of alternation. Although I claim alternation (and rotation) represent only one aspect (albeit a key one) of the
film's system, analysis of my other axis, the significance of unique nonrepeated camera positions, also reveals the central role of gender and the romantic couple. The initial and final unique camera positions are given to
the couple: the first position presents their tryst beneath the willow tree, and
their reunion serves as background for the revelation and display of the
wrench in the penultimate close-up. Gender roles, their definition and
redefinition, their establishment and their subversion, play an essential role
in the era of the single-reel film, both in terms of narrative structure and—
the issue, I maintain, cannot be ignored in early cinema—the accommodation and acting out of modernity's beginning. A great benefit to the study
of early cinema has come from paying attention to the role of gender in the
first two decades of cinema history.[47]

However, the analysis of gender in relation to early film narration as offered by Bellour and some analysts following him has sometimes been limited by approaching these films through the lens of later classical cinema,
focusing on the pernicious seeds of an insidious patriarchy. I would not deny
these seeds are there, but I would encourage attention to differences, as well,
and the way these films (or at least some of them) rehearsed new modern
forms of gender, engaging with the polyvalent figure of the New Woman.
This approach was initiated by Ben Singer's seminal essay on the Serial
Queen, work expanded in his recent book *Melodrama and Modernity*, as well
as Lynne Kirby's *Parallel Tracks*.[48] An emerging group of scholars has expanded this issue into a new paradigm, as in Jennifer Bean's essay on female
action stars or Vicki Callahan's work on Musidora.[49] That this work has often centered on the serial or series films seems to me significant, since these
forms mediated between the multireel feature and the single-reel film, in
many ways maintaining the earlier form through episodes consisting of one
or two reels.

Any intelligent undergraduate can probably produce an immediate
Freudian reading of *The Lonedale Operator* that would seem to address feminist issues. Our heroine takes over her father's place in command of technology; however, she does not take on true phallic authority, as imaged in

her refusal of the revolver he offers her. When she and her trust are threatened by males outside society, she enacts a series of traditionally feminine
defenses: she hides her treasure (the conflation of robbery and rape recurs
in Griffith's melodramas) in a chest; she locks the door, taking refuge in the
most interior room and, with the aid of the telegraph, calls for help. Her call
is heard by a male telegrapher who passes it on to her engineer lover, who
races to rescue her (the conflation of rescue and "coupling" is also constant
in Griffith), as control of the truly mobile apparatus, the locomotive, remains
in the hands of the male hero. Her cry for help accomplished, the heroine
dutifully performs Victorian femininity and faints. However, when the
tramps continue their invasion of her space, clever girl that she is, in effect
she performs masculinity and pretends to have a revolver in her hand. But
order is restored, first, when the male lover arrives in the nick of time, bringing a real phallus—or real revolver. Final resolution is achieved and gender
roles restored as the heroine's implement is proved not to be a revolver but
a *faux de mieux*. This joke of her brief inversion of gender roles restores traditional authority, as she embraces her lover and presses her face shyly into
his chest.[50]

I would not deny this interpretation explicates the dynamics of the film
in a coherent manner, but it also leaves energies unaccounted for. What appears as a critical ideological reading reproduces, rather than explores, the
strictures of patriarchy. The possibility that the film might be telling another
story seems foreclosed. In place of such an interpretation, I am not pleading for a "resistant reading." Rather I believe that a historical reading of *The
Lonedale Operator,* onc that places it not only within a logic of the development of narrative and filmic systems but also into larger cultural systems,
helps us determine what is at stake here. A consideration of the way the
women in this film (and there are more than one) find their place within
the film's stylistic narrative and cultural system does not necessarily produce
a positive or redemptive reading but, hopefully, a more complex one.

Historicizing the role of the telegraph operator within labor history complicates the view of gender and technology offered in the reading above. Like
the locomotive engineer, the telegraph "operator"[51] possessed specialized
technological skills and training, was difficult to replace on short notice, and
therefore could be a powerful labor force difficult to control.[52] Although
the failed Great Strike against Western Union broke the telegraph union in
1883 and operators' wages began to fall, telegraphy remained an attractive
alternative to factory labor, and telegraph schools turned out graduates eager to join the profession. Even though women operators were loyal supporters of the Great Strike, there is no question Western Union systematically hired women as telegraph operators as a means to drive down wages.[53]
Women promised not only lower wages, employers believed, but, as Katherine Stubbs puts it, a putative docility, a perceived willingness to be servants

of the technology and the company. The "feminization" of telegraphy (like the parallel feminization of clerical work) was not fully accomplished until the twentieth century and was at points strongly resisted by the previously dominating male operators.[54] Although largely a *fait accompli* by 1911, what Stubbs calls the "crisis of feminization" constitutes an important background for *The Lonedale Operator.*

The male resistance to female operators, although primarily based in economic issues—competition for the same jobs and fear women would work for lower wages—largely took the form of sexist claims about women's technological incompetence. Executive officer of the telegraph union, Eugene J. O'Connor, even testified before the Senate in 1883 that the "nervous system of women would not allow" them to handle the most demanding assignments.[55] Women operators denied these claims, however, asserting females in the job possessed superior skills.[56] The bulk of stories written during the close of the nineteenth century portraying female operators, primarily written by male operators, argued that women operators could or would cause disasters. The small amount of telegraphic fiction published by women operators, in contrast, celebrates, or at least explores with levity and enthusiasm, the possibilities the new technology opened to women, including new gender roles. As Stubbs summarizes her study of this material: "In the space of the circuit, then, the female operator experiences a different relation with her self; she earns the right to speak. Rendered invisible, temporarily freed from her body, she is also freed from conventional rules of female behavior, and seems no longer subject to the traditional forms of discipline, prejudice, and violence that exploit corporeal difference."[57] Stubbs wisely cautions against reading utopian achievement into this experience (temporary liberation primarily attests to permanent systems of containment). Nonetheless, at the beginning of the century, however exploited and controlled it may ultimately have been, the position of operator offered women a glimpse of a new world of work and technological mastery.

Observed against this background, the gender drama of *The Lonedale Operator* shifts a bit. Far from demonstrating female incapacity to deal with technology, the parallel-edited sequence of telegraphy demonstrates the heroine's competence, albeit with a major qualification: the heroine's faint, precisely the sort of overwhelmed emotional reaction male operators claimed women were subject to and that rendered them incompetent in the performance of their duty.[58] But the place of the heroine's loss of consciousness within the narrative logic of the film reveals the inherently contradictory nature of this film ideologically. Rather than letting it interfere with her duty, the heroine seems to willfully fight off her syncope until not only has she sent her message, but she has been assured it has been received. Thus the sequence seems to superimpose (almost in the form of a dream condensation in which contradictions cohabit within an image rather than being resolved) different views of female operators, as competent but also as liable to be overwhelmed by dangerous situations. The sequence, as Bellour indicates, involves a curious symmetry along gender lines as it alternates between male and female operators.[59] The opening suspense of this sequence derives from the unconsciousness of the *male* operator sleeping on the job (ordinary incompetence or lack of professionalism as a result of boredom), which delays communicating the message. In contrast, the heroine's fainting plays no key narrative role, delays no action. The fainting resembles a residual appendage, a souvenir of a traditional heroine, passive and incapable of protecting herself, grafted briefly onto a resourceful New Woman. This badly spliced-on character trait undoubtedly expresses the film's anxiety about fully acknowledging the heroine's autonomy and cues us not to deny the conservative aspects of the film's resolution but also not to ignore its struggle against older forms.

The climax displays a similar doubling, with two solutions to the thieves' threat provided: the traditional rescue by the male hero but also the New Woman's solution, achieved through pluck and cleverness. It is the latter that *Moving Picture World* found to be the film's real claim on audience interest. Rather than exclusively delivering a balanced resolution (and who would deny Bellour's demonstration of this?), the film could also be seen as duplicating solutions, offering less a convergent alternation than a systematic exploration of competing options, even ones that seem contradictory. Obviously, the imaginary resolution of contradictions, as opposed to their rational sorting out, is one definition of the operation of ideology. But contradictory terms unreconciled also indicate condensation, expressing not only the repression but also the signification of desire and the unconscious. The narrative doubling in *The Lonedale Operator* does not simply exemplify a rush toward classical order but rather juggles contradictory attitudes toward gender roles—projecting fantasies that are both reactionary and progressive.

The nature of the female telegrapher's work, the particular technology with which she engaged, also forms part of *The Lonedale Operator*'s system. Historians of early cinema, including Eileen Bowser, Jan Olsson, Yuri Tsivian, and myself,[60] claim that early narrative cinema mastered cutting freely through space and time and rendered it comprehensible to audiences partly through portraying telephone calls, the alternation between the communicating parties expressing the essence of modern communication technology: instantaneity over long distances. The use of the telegraph in *The Lonedale Operator* recalls the portrayal of telephone calls through parallel editing in other single-reel films. In a recent essay, however, Paul Young has questioned equating the two technologies, pointing out key differences that are vital for understanding *The Lonedale Operator*.[61]

The telephone primarily puts domestic and private spaces in communication, supplying as well the intimacy of the voice. The telegraph shows a much more public face, as a place of publicly conducted business, carrying news and information for large public entities such as the railway, businesses, and newspapers, as well as individuals, and translating all messages into the professional Morse code.[62] According to Stubbs, one resistance to women serving as operators was the claim that the job was "too public."[63] Although both the telephone and telegraph overcome spatial distance through instantaneous electronic communication, the spaces each medium opened up and put into communication differ.

This contrast can be explored by comparing *The Lonedale Operator* with the Griffith Biograph film that rivals it as exemplary of Griffith's narrative and editing style, *The Lonely Villa,* from 1909. *Lonedale* has frequently been approached as an elaboration of the parallel-edited suspenseful race-to-the-rescue plot of the earlier film. As Shelley Stamp has shown in her careful reading of *The Lonely Villa,* the earlier film exemplifies a melodramatic situation of the threatened female/family (a mother and her three daughters) and the invasion of domestic space by alien male intruders. The female family retreats before the male intruders into ever deeper and (as Stamp points out) ever more confining interior spaces, moving from room to room and barricading doors, whereas exterior space seems restricted to male characters—the thieves, and the husband racing to the rescue.[64] The vulnerable domestic space is not effectively protected by technology, which balances its successes in this film (such as communicating the danger that faces his family to the husband) with its failures and breakdowns (the cutting of the phone wire, the automobile's engine problems, the unloaded pistol).[65] In *The Lonedale Operator,* on the other hand, technology functions smoothly (the only glitch being the sleeping male operator), and the spaces invaded are public offices. Although the scenario of spatial retreat seems identical in the two films, the female operator's active defiance of the thieves with her ersatz pistol sharply contrasts with the action of the earlier film.[66] The wife is directed to a revolver left by her husband, but when she realizes it is unloaded, she abandons it, quite a different action from the operator's redefinition of a seemingly irrelevant tool.

The character traits of ingenuity, clear thinking, improvisation, and the ability to create a convincing scenario of defiance that the Lonedale operator displays match her profession and the technology over which she maintains control. The wife in *The Lonely Villa* can make use of the telephone and call for help, but she does not master technology in any manner. Whereas the Lonedale operator persists and gets her message through in spite of the initial glitch in communication, the wife can do nothing when the telephone line is cut, except retreat more deeply into her domestic space. The telephone link directly connects the wife with her husband, whereas the Lonedale operator's connection plugs her into a whole system of messages and transportation, as the male operator she contacts not only conveys the message to her lover but supplies him with a revolver and clears the tracks for his race to the rescue "with right of way over all trains," as an intertitle informs us. Rather than a simple alternation between the domestic space of the threatened house and the space of the husband attempting to get home offered by *The Lonely Villa,* the spatial world of *The Lonedale Operator* operates as a nexus of points, embodying the modern interconnection of spaces that the telegraph enabled. The bourgeois ideology of domesticity seeks to exclude the outside world, providing a private haven ruled over by traditional gender roles (*The Lonely Villa* dramatizes the breakdown of this ideology). The Lonedale operator introduces a modern New Woman heroine whose action in protecting herself and her professional trust lies partly in her ability to plug into that nexus of spaces and information and to master its technology, codes, and discourses.

If the unique shots of the trysting couple beneath the willow and the close-up of the wrench that connects them after the threat of narrative disruption has been resolved embody the classical order of the couple as described by Bellour, the shots of the central station marshal the forces of modernity—especially the shot of the office that dispatches the payroll. This space has also been penetrated by working women, the typist in the left midground of the office reminding us of the feminization of clerical work that occurred around the same time as the feminization of telegraphy. The "pretty typewriter" (the term referred originally to the operator of the machine rather than the machine itself) replaced male secretaries in the late nineteenth century, following the change from handwriting to technological inscription. As the term *typewriter* seems to predict, these women appeared to merge with, rather than dominate, their technology.[67]

This subordinated presence of the typist pictures other futures for the working woman that might curtail the fantasies inspired by the "girl operator." Both are employed to manage new apparatuses of language, technologies that resolve messages into mechanical units.[68] But to what extent does their mastery of technology allow them to function as masters of discourse? If the woman operator opens a portal of liberation, placing working women in public space with skills that provide them with employment while making them a nexus of the flow and transfer of information through new modern space, nonetheless the question of agency persists. The heroine in *The Lonedale Operator* enacts a fantasy that balances threat with agency, mastery with dependence, but primarily displays female competence and imagination. But does she find her dark twin, and possibly her future (or even unglamorous present), in this typist blocked into a subordinate position, staring only at her apparatus with the clock pendulum pressing down upon her? What agency does she possess? Irony rears its head as we recognize this bit actress as Jeanie Macpherson, a regular member of the Biograph stock troupe who (in spite of her beauty and strong sense of presence) never was able to become a featured player in Griffith's company but was to become one of the major Hollywood scenarists during the feature period, working especially for Cecil B. DeMille. Friedrich Kittler claims the introduction of the typewriter transformed the idea of authorship, undoing the traditional author's hand and authority.[69] The cinema, too, has made the question of authorship problematic (who was the author of *King of Kings*? Cecil B. De-Mille or Jeanie Macpherson? Is it authored at all?). Within the networks, systems, and circuits of modernity the issue of agency becomes redefined, as does gender.

INSIDE OR OUTSIDE THE CAGE?
GENDER, AUTHORSHIP, AGENCY, AND TECHNOLOGY

> *Most of the elements swam straight away, lost themselves in the bottomless common,*
> *and by so doing really kept the page clear. On the clearness, therefore, what she did*
> *retain stood sharply out; she nipped and caught it, turned it over and interwove it.*
> HENRY JAMES, *In the Cage*

In search of relations connecting the systematic nature of narration in the single-reel film, the systems of modernity, and the role of gender is it permissible to make a telegraphic leap from popular culture to high culture, from cinema to literature? Rubbing D. W. Griffith's *The Lonedale Operator* against Henry James's 1898 novella *In the Cage* may produce sparks of illumination. As has frequently been pointed out, James was one of the first major authors to compose texts by dictating to a typewriter, moving enthusiastically into the circuits of modernity after 1897.[70] Yet few texts seem more different than this action-packed single-reel film produced for nickelodeon audiences and James's elegant and ambiguous, extremely interiorized novella published by the progressive Chicago house of Herbert S. Stone (whose literary magazine *The Chapbook* two years earlier had denounced motion pictures as the acme of vulgarity).[71] Operating from very different assumptions about the fantasies of a working girl and providing distinct conclusions, both works address the limits and possibilities of female agency within modern technological employment.

The operator at Lonedale and the telegraphist at Crocker's who serves as heroine for James's tale contrast as sharply as their respective stations at the global wire. Only sending messages electronically links isolated Lonedale and the corner of Crocker's London grocery given over to a telegraph office. Although placed in the midst of a metropolis and its ebb and flow of activity, James's heroine experiences rigid separation between the class of people that send telegrams and her confinement within the cage of her occupation. Yet like her American counterpart's, her corner of the world abuts onto greater systems: "There were times when all the wires of the country seemed to start from the little hole-and-corner from which she plied for a livelihood."[72] A gentlewoman of declined fortunes, she has taken an occupation open to respectable young women. Gifted with imagination, insight, and a powerful memory, she also embodies the anxiety many held about the telegraph as the conveyer of information, that a conscious human being read the message before sending it. Such knowledge threatened the "violation of all secrecy" a writer in the British magazine the *Quarterly Review* quailed: "The clerks . . . are sworn to secrecy, but we often write things that it would be intolerable to see strangers read before our eyes."[73]

Rather than simply serving as the mechanical transfer of messages she is given to transmit, James's heroine reads, remembers, and speculates on them. In this era writers of telegrams, both personal and commercial, devised unique codes that served either to shorten the message via conventional abbreviations or to conceal meanings from prying eyes.[74] James's telegraphist cracks the code of a pair of her upper-class customers and discovers their romantic affair. But rather than use this knowledge as the basis for blackmail, as the *Quarterly Review* writer feared, she elaborates the fragmentary aspect of the texts available to her to construct a novelistic entertainment for herself. As Richard Menke, following James's own lead in his preface, demonstrates, the telegraphist operates like a novelist, following the clue of her impressions, weaving her threads into a romance.[75] Becoming a participant observer of this affair, she actually performs a significant service to the couple by remembering the encoded text of one of their messages. Exactly what this accomplishes for the couple James leaves ambiguous (as though we, the readers, remained outside the code), but the death of the woman's husband and the couple's marriage follow, as well as the telegraphist's disillusionment with her romance, whose sordid nature becomes clear to her.

Where do these very different telegraphic texts converge? Clearly on the figure of the female operator and the degree of her agency. Employed to fit within a system, to understand a technology and master its coded discourse, the female telegraphist maintains an ambiguous relation to the medium within which she operates. Transmitter and reader of private messages, James's character indulges in fantasies of authorship until she is reminded of her truly marginal role. Her American cousin moves within the realm of telegraphic melodrama rather than novelistic realism, the arena of action cinema rather than the domain of interiority and consciousness probed by James. Operating from her remote station, her office briefly becomes the convergent center of the whole system in a drama in which she plays the central role. Her agency pivots on her skill as an operator, her ability to perform clever substitutions, and her pluck in the face of danger. Griffith's heroine enacts a romance, whereas James's romantic telegraphist descends into realist disillusionment.[76] But both dramas imagine a fantasy that could be described with the terms Menke uses to discuss James's heroine: "she represents telegraphy not just as a mode of communication but also as a social practice, a medium of discourse come to life, an information exchange no longer transparent."[77] But can this medium remain lively and visible and not fade back into the automatic and transparent? In James's novella, after her telegraphic memory has somehow saved the adulterous couple, the heroine watches the hero of her imagined romance leave her behind in her cage "without another look."[78] Provided with the final bits of the true story, and deeply reflective about her own role in this sordid business, James's heroine walks off in a deep London fog, coming after several "sightless turns" to the edge of the Paddington canal, while she contemplates her life, "perhaps still sightlessly looking down on to it."[79] Resignedly, she decides to marry her grocer fiancé and leave the telegraph cage.

The Lonedale operator, in contrast, ends her romance in a blaze of visual display, flourishing her wrench and her triumph so theatrically (and so cinematically!) that her villainous thieves seemed cowed into being polite schoolboys, doffing their hats (marking that she is still a lady, deserving of good manners). Much more than James's fog-shrouded, sightless consciousness, she is telegraphy made visible, her triumph within the public arena and before an audience. But we can see a split trajectory looming. As Lynne Kirby has claimed, one path pulls our filmic heroines into ever more active scenarios and public action. One year later when Griffith remakes *The Lonedale Operator* as *The Girl and Her Trust,* Grace the heroic telegraphist will actually follow the safe she guards out onto the railway tracks when the thieves attempt a getaway, severing the relation of women to interior space still lingering in *The Lonedale Operator* and preparing the way for Helen Holmes and the railway and girl telegraphist serial queens of the later teens.[80] But another path recalls the forlorn typist in the central station office, remaining in the background, taking dictation from her male superiors, apparently more in thrall to her apparatus than master of it.

In his essay on the telegraph and early cinema Paul Young finds another way the telegraph system works as a figure for early cinema, related to, but not restricted to, their common ability to coordinate space and time. Young draws on a neglected claim by America's first film theorist, poet Vachel Lindsay. Lindsay spoke of the narrative structure of film in the midteens not simply as the switching about within space and time but as presenting "a conversation between two places."[81] Working Lindsay's metaphor, Young recognizes a link between cinematic narration and the telegraph, describing editing in terms of a transfer of messages rather than a transparent switch in spatial viewpoints. Developing this idea of a cinematic conversation, Lindsay commented, "And as to jumping over geographical spaces, the photoplay dialogue that technically replaces the old stage interchange of words is a conversation between places, not individuals."[82] Young terms this style, which he sees as functioning during most of the 1910s, as "communicative realism," a narrative style that counts on the spectator's actively reading and decoding the film—entering into a conversation with it—as opposed to the transparency of later classical conventions. Young describes this style as well understood to be a code, a lattice work for "conversations" between producers and viewers "that had to be self-consciously invented, taught, and learned before it could become naturalized."[83]

"Communicative realism" could describe the blatantly systematic aspect of the style of the single-reel era, in which systematic alternations, rotations, repetitions (and even unique shots) not only aided narrative comprehension but also made narration a palpable relation between audience and film. Rather than an automatic, naturalized, or transparent style of self-effacing narration, this style drew attention to its processes. Griffith's *The Lonedale Operator* may serve as an extreme example. Not every single-reel film displayed systematic relation between shots to the same degree. But the conditions of production of the single-reel era made such systematic construction a feasible option and, indeed, encouraged it. Lindsay's presentation of his theory of cinematic conversation in 1917 extends this style into the feature era, and many early feature films seem to maintain aspects of the single-reel style. Indeed, one should resist erecting an absolute barrier between different periods. Analysis of style after the single-reel period demands a less unified approach, one that takes notice of the styles used by different genres. My description of the single-reel era style as visibly systematic narration should not immediately assume the transparency and naturalization of all film narration across the board after 1917. As Jennifer Bean has claimed, genres such as the serial action film, slapstick, and mystery thrillers play their own games, balancing narration and spectacular effects. Bean's revisionist work on these orphan genres also asks that we reexamine the way gender is negotiated in American cinema of the silent era.[84]

Cinema, as a major form of mass entertainment employing technological representation and narrative, always engaged the experience of modernity. Critics of what they term the "modernity thesis" may shake their heads at such a broad pronouncement, claiming that if all eras of cinema engage modernity, then that relation becomes a commonplace that offers us nothing to investigate.[85] But as the exploration of early cinema demonstrates (and research into the 1910s and 1920s also shows), engagement with modernity differs in each period. If the cinema of attractions dealt with the shocks of modernity, the cinema of the period of narrative integration and the single-reel film seem rather to subordinate those shocks to larger systems, generating thrilling narratives, in which shocks and spectacles interpenetrate a logic of story development, sometimes propelling it, sometimes derailing it (as in many early slapstick films).[86]

If the cinema of attractions resembles a series of shocks, we might compare a single-reel film like *The Lonedale Operator* to an internal combustion engine, in which the systematic triggering of contained explosions is harnessed to produce a forward drive. The development of narration during the single-reel period responds in a complex manner to many factors: economic organization, modes of production, changing audiences, new contexts of viewing, and the experiences of modern life audience members brought into the theaters. To try to describe the development of film style in terms of a linear conception of singular cause and effect is simply foolish. To claim the style(s) of early film were "caused" by the demands of modern life surrounding them is to speak in a naive fashion. But one should not ignore the way these films and their formal operations portrayed and made use of the modern systems that surrounded them. Nor can one deny that these films were consumed and enjoyed by audience members who were living through the new demands made by the transformations of modern life. To do so would sever cinema from its life world, reducing it to a series of formal plays. As I hope I have shown, the formal systems of early cinema in the single-reel era provided more than occasions for academic exercises. They were the means by which new systems of space and time were processed, were made the basis for both insight and fantasy, and provided schemata through which changing gender roles could be rehearsed. Through these films audiences could recognize, laugh at, confront, and even enjoy images of the world they lived in and its challenges and novelties.

NOTES

This essay was probably conceived decades ago during conversations with Lynne Kirby, whom I miss; was gestated through arguments with Charlie Keil, my friend; and brought to term through discussions with Jennifer M. Bean, whom I am glad I met, finally. I want to thank Charlie Keil and Shelley Stamp for their patience.

1. Kristin Thompson, "*The Lonedale Operator*," in *The Griffith Project*, vol. 5, *Films Produced in 1911*, ed. Paolo Cherchi Usai (London: British Film Institute, 2002), 18.

2. D. W Griffith, advertisement, *New York Dramatic Mirror,* 13 December 1913, 36.

3. Charlie Keil, *Early American Cinema in Transition: Story, Style, and Filmmaking, 1907–1913* (Madison: University of Wisconsin Press, 2001).

4. David Bordwell, Janet Staiger, and Kristin Thompson, *The Classical Hollywood Cinema: Film Style and Mode of Production to 1960* (New York: Columbia University Press, 1985).

5. Keil, *Early American Cinema;* Tom Gunning, *D. W. Griffith and the Origins of American Narrative Film: The Early Years at Biograph* (Urbana: University of Illinois Press, 1991).

6. Bordwell, Staiger, and Thompson, *Classical Hollywood Cinema,* 163–66.

7. Keil, *Early American Cinema,* 43 and 45, notes the conflicts within the transitional period in somewhat similar terms.

8. Although this standardization was first formalized by the MPPC, it was widely

adopted by the Independent production companies and exchanges that grew up in opposition to the Trust.

9. Gunning, *D. W. Griffith.*

10. Ben Singer, *Melodrama and Modernity: Early Sensational Cinema and Its Contexts* (New York: Columbia University Press, 2001), 281–87. This is surprising for a film this late. Singer relates the lack of narrative clarity to the fact that this serial had a tie-in to a written serial published simultaneously in newspapers, which could have aided the viewer in following the film version.

11. Ben Brewster, "A Bunch of Violets" (paper presented at the Society for Cinema Studies Conference, Los Angeles, 1991). Brewster's discussion of other Vitagraph films shows their systematic use of alternation, an element I have explored as well; see Tom Gunning, "Il film Vitagraph e il cinema dell'integrazione narrativa," in *Vitagraph Co. of America*, ed Paolo Cherchi Usai (Pordenone: Studio Tesi, 1987), 225–40. Keil, *Early American Cinema*, 57, also discusses recurring objects.

12. Raymond Bellour, *The Analysis of Film*, ed. Constance Penley (Bloomington: Indiana University Press, 2000); Christian Metz, *Language and Cinema* (The Hague: Mouton, 1974).

13. Bellour, *Analysis of Film*, 262.

14. Keil, *Early American Cinema*, 173.

15. The Blackhawk print that I analyzed at the Library of Congress has ninety-seven shots. Raymond Bellour's analysis, illustrated by photograms of each shot, also has ninety-seven shots and seems to correspond to the Blackhawk print. The MoMA restoration has ninety-eight shots and has some minor differences in shot position from the Blackhawk print. Kristin Thompson seems to indicate the Blackhawk print she viewed had ninety-two shots, since she numbers the penultimate shot (the close-up of the wrench) as shot ninety-one.

16. Bellour, in his analysis, resolves most of these figures into alternation. Although his analysis is brilliant, I feel it tends to privilege polar and dichotomous relations, which Griffith likes to complicate into triadic relations. I don't think, however, that my change in emphasis undermines or contradicts Bellour's analysis.

17. This shot occurs only once in the Blackhawk version but twice in the MoMA restoration.

18. *New York Dramatic Mirror*, 29 March 1911, 31.

19. Thompson *"The Lonedale Operator,"* 20.

20. This aspect of classical narration is described in Bordwell, Staiger, and Thompson, *Classical Hollywood Cinema*, 27–36.

21. In the MoMA restoration there is one exception: the first two long shots of the train are actually filmed from the same setup, splitting the action of the train moving toward the camera into two shots. Likewise in the MoMA restoration the wider shot of the engine taken from the tender appears twice, whereas it appears only once in the Blackhawk print.

22. For a discussion of money and modernity see Georg Simmel, *The Philosophy of Money*, ed. David Frisby, trans. Tom Bottomore and David Frisby (London: Routledge, 1990).

23. Tom Standage, *The Victorian Internet* (New York: Walker, 1998), 119–20.

24. Alfred Hitchcock introduced the term *MacGuffin* in numerous interviews. See Francois Truffaut, *Hitchcock* (New York: Simon and Schuster, 1967), 98–100.

25. Singer introduces the weenie via Pearl White; see Singer, *Melodrama and Modernity*, 208.

26. Bordwell, Staiger, and Thompson, *Classical Hollywood Cinema*, 31.

27. Gunning, *D. W. Griffith*, 139–41.

28. Stephen Kern, *The Culture of Space and Time, 1880–1918* (Cambridge, Mass.: Harvard University Press, 1983), 12–14; Wolfgang Schivelbusch, *The Railway Journey: Trains and Travel in the Nineteenth Century* (New York: Urizen Books, 1979), 41–49; Lynne Kirby, *Parallel Tracks: The Railroad in Silent Cinema* (Durham, N.C.: Duke University Press, 1997), 48–57.

29. Michael O'Malley, *Keeping Watch: A History of American Time* (Washington, D.C.: Smithsonian Institution Press, 1990), 141–42.

30. Kern, *Culture of Space*, 12–14. Lynne Kirby brilliantly discusses the relation between time and both the railway and early cinema; see Kirby, *Parallel Tracks*, 48–57.

31. Keil, *Early American Cinema*, 16.

32. Ibid., 84.

33. One could argue that the cuts between different views of the locomotive engine exemplify cutting within a single space, especially the cuts between the engineer climbing onto the engine and settling in the cab and, later, the engine coming into Lonedale station and the shot of the engineer leaping from the cab. I think, however, that any viewer would agree that the examples I give form the only indisputable examples of spatially overlapping cuts.

34. In the MoMA restoration an insert of the telegraph message intervenes here, not present in the Blackhawk print. Thus, one could deny this is an example of a spatial overlap.

35. See David Bordwell's analysis of this sequence in *On the History of Film Style* (Cambridge, Mass.: Harvard University Press, 1997), 131.

36. Thompson, *"The Lonedale Operator,"* 22, quotes a reviewer in the trade journal *Motography* who complains that the wrench is made too obvious early in the film. This may indicate a greater degree of perspicacity on the part of contemporaneous audiences. I suspect, however, that this was not the majority's viewing experience and indicates carping by one critic.

37. David Bordwell discusses the withholding of narrative information and incommunicative narration, especially in terms of the mystery genre, in his *Narration in the Fiction Film* (Madison: University of Wisconsin Press, 1985), 64–70.

38. Biograph Bulletin, *"The Lonedale Operator,"* in *The Biograph Bulletins*, ed. Eileen Bowser (New York: Farrar, Straus and Giroux, 1973), 284.

39. Bellour, *Analysis of Film*, 277.

40. *Moving Picture World*, 8 April 1911, 780. Edison had released a film in 1910, apparently now lost, entitled *The Engineer's Romance*, whose plot *Moving Picture World* summarizes as follows: "A girl station agent in a lonely station is beset by thieves. She wires to a distance for help. Her sweetheart jumps on his locomotive and goes to her assistance. The last part of the film, showing alternately the progress of the locomotive and the steady retreat of the girl as the robbers force door after door is thrilling" (*Moving Picture World*, 22 January 1910, 91). Clearly Mack Sennett, the author of the film story for *The Lonedale Operator*, took careful notes of the films he viewed! The wrench seems to be *Lonedale*'s contribution to the Edison plot. The indication of alternation makes one wish the Edison film were available for a detailed comparison,

but it also indicates the commonality of narrative structures as well as plots during the single-reel era.

41. Keil, *Early American Cinema*, 81–82.

42. Bellour, *Analysis of Film*, 277.

43. Ibid.

44. Ibid.

45. See the various essays included in Bellour, *Analysis of Film*.

46. Kirby, *Parallel Tracks*.

47. Exemplary works—especially Shelley Stamp's *Movie-Struck Girls: Women and Motion Picture Culture after the Nickelodeon* (Princeton, N.J.: Princeton University Press, 2000); Lauren Rabinovitz's *For the Love of Pleasure: Women, Movies, and Culture in Turn-of-the-Century Chicago* (New Brunswick, N.J.: Rutgers University Press, 1998); and Miriam Hansen's pioneering *Babel and Babylon: Spectatorship in American Silent Film* (Cambridge, Mass.: Harvard University Press, 1991)—have tried to understand the development of early cinema in relation to female audiences well-known to have flocked to the movies, especially during the single-reel film era.

48. Singer, *Melodrama and Modernity*, 221–62; Kirby, *Parallel Tracks*.

49. Jennifer M. Bean, "Technologies of Early Stardom and the Extraordinary Body," *Camera Obscura* 48 (January 2002): 9–56; Vicki Callahan, "Screening Musidora, Inscribing Indeterminacy in Film History," *Camera Obscura* 48 (January 2002): 57–81. These essays and other extremely relevant ones also appear in the anthology *A Feminist Reader in Early Cinema*, ed. Jennifer M. Bean and Diane Negra (Durham, N.C.: Duke University Press, 2002).

50. I might note here that both Bellour, *Analysis of Film*, 277, and Kirby, *Parallel Tracks*, 107, indicate the film ends with a kiss, but I see only this shy embrace. Am I missing something?

51. This term, which was only retained for the telephone, was widely used at the turn of the century for skilled manipulators of technology. It was also the early term for both film projectionists and those running the cameras.

52. See Edwin Gabler, *The American Telegrapher: A Social History, 1860–1900* (New Brunswick, N.J.: Rutgers University Press, 1988); also Katherine Stubbs, "Telegraphy's Corporeal Fictions," in *New Media, 1740–1914*, ed. Lisa Gitelman and Geoffrey B. Pingree (Cambridge, Mass.: MIT Press, 2002), 91–111.

53. Gabler, *American Telegrapher*, estimates women were paid 50 percent of male wages, and average wages for operators declined steadily (134–35). One of the demands of the 1883 strike was equal pay regardless of gender.

54. Stubbs, "Telegraphy's Corporeal Fictions," 95–96. The whole-hearted support by women operators of the Great Strike belies this, but there are other indications that women operators frequently did not support more local strikes and were used as scabs; see Gabler, *American Telegrapher*, 38.

55. Gabler, *American Telegrapher*, 135.

56. Ibid., 136–37.

57. Stubbs, "Telegraphy's Corporeal Fictions," 103.

58. Gabler, *American Telegrapher*, 106, cites the *Boston Globe*'s report that four operators at Western Union's main office fainted at the commencement of the Great Strike, which he points out may have had more to do with the July weather and the constricting clothing required of women in the 1880s than with any lack of fortitude.

However, like the report that women fainted on seeing the Biograph film of an on-coming locomotive in 1896, this account indicates a myth about female conscious-ness worth exploring further.

59. Bellour, *Analysis of Film,* 270.

60. Eileen Bowser, "Le coup de téléphone dans le primitifs du cinéma," in *Les premiers ans du cinéma français,* ed. Pierre Guibbert (Perpignan: Institute Jean Vigo, 1985), 218–24; Gunning, "Heard over the 'Phone: *The Lonely Villa* and the De Lorde Tradition of the Terrors of Technology," *Screen* 32, no. 2 (summer 1991): 184–96; Jan Olsson, "Framing Silent Calls," in *Allegories of Communication: Intermedial Concerns from Cinema to the Digital,* ed. Jan Olsson (London: John Libbey, forthcoming). Yuri Tsivian's work on telephone films remains unpublished.

61. Paul Young, "Media on Display: A Telegraphic History of Early American Cin-ema," in *New Media, 1740–1915,* ed. Lisa Gitelman and Geoffrey B. Pingree (Cam-bridge, Mass.: MIT Press, 2003), 229–64.

62. Young, "Media on Display," 230–31.

63. Stubbs, "Telegraphy's Corporeal Fictions," 98–99.

64. Shelley Stamp [Lindsey], "Screening Spaces: Women and Motion Pictures in America, 1908–1917" (Ph.D. diss., New York University, 1994), 59–62.

65. Gunning, "Heard over the 'Phone."

66. That this retreat into successive rooms appears in the description of Edison's *The Engineer's Romance,* the apparent prototype of *The Lonedale Operator,* marks it as a device of the single-reel era rather than simply one of Griffith's inventions.

67. Friedrich A. Kittler, *Gramophone, Film, Typewriter,* trans. Geoffrey Winthrop-Young and Michael Wutz (Stanford, Calif.: Stanford University Press, 1999), 183. Kit-tler states oracularly, "The convergence of a profession, a machine and a sex speak *[sic]* the truth."

68. Ibid., 183–263.

69. Ibid., 196–200.

70. Kittler, *Gramophone, Film, Typewriter,* 216; Richard Menke, "Telegraphic Real-ism: Henry James: *In the Cage,*" *PMLA* 115, no. 5 (October 2000): 977.

71. Henry James, *Eight Tales from the Major Phase* (New York: Norton, 1958); *The Chapbook*'s denunciation of the Vitascope is quoted in Terry Ramsaye's *A Million and One Nights: A History of the Motion Picture* (London: Cass, 1926), 259–60. I want to thank Jonathan Auerbach for drawing my attention to James's novella and to Menke's article.

72. James, *Eight Tales,* 187.

73. Quoted in Standage, *Victorian Internet,* 110.

74. On telegraph codes see Standage, *Victorian Internet,* 105–26. Commercial codes whose main purpose was to save money by shortening word counts were a com-mon part of business. The telegraphic code for exchanges wishing to order prints of *The Lonedale Operator,* for instance, was "Rhinastre"; see Bowser, *Biograph Bulletins,* 284.

75. Menke, "Telegraphic Realism," 975–90.

76. Ibid., 985–86.

77. Ibid., 976.

78. James, *Eight Tales,* 251.

79. Ibid., 265–66.

80. Kirby, *Parallel Tracks,* 105–16.

81. Young, "Media on Display," 254, quoting an address by Lindsay reprinted and commented on in *Moving Picture World*, 10 March 1917, 1583.

82. Vachel Lindsay, "Photoplay Progress," originally published in *The New Republic*, 17 February 1917, 76–77, repr. in *Spellbound in Darkness*, ed. George C. Pratt (Greenwich, Conn.: New York Graphic Society, 1970), 225. Curiously, this article is a review of *The Photoplay: A Psychological Study*, by Hugo Münsterberg, the other pioneering American film theorist—and associate of Henry James's brother, William, as well as teacher of female author Gertrude Stein.

83. Young, "Media on Display," 255.

84. Bean, "Technologies of Early Stardom," 12; see also Jennifer M. Bean, "Towards a Feminist Historiography of Early Cinema," in *A Feminist Reader in Early Cinema*, ed. Jennifer M. Bean and Diane Negra (Durham, N.C.: Duke University Press, 2002), esp. 6–9.

85. The term "modernity thesis" appears simultaneously in Charlie Keil, "'Visualised Narratives,' Transitional Cinema, and the Modernity Thesis," in *Le Cinéma au tournant du siècle/Cinema at the Turn of the Century*, ed. Claire Dupré la Tour, André Gaudreault, and Roberta Pearson (Lausanne/Québec: Éditions Payot Lausanne/Éditions Nota bene, 1998), 123–37; and Bordwell, *History of Film Style*. The latter supplies an intriguing critique on 142–47, largely directed against my work. To some extent Charlie Keil continues this in *Early American Cinema in Transition*. Ben Singer has responded to many of the arguments offered by Bordwell and Keil in defending his own version of the modernity thesis in *Melodrama and Modernity*.

86. Don Crafton, "Pie and Chase: Gag, Spectacle, and Narrative in Slapstick Comedy," in *Classical Hollywood Comedy*, ed. Kristine Brunovska Karnick and Henry Jenkins (New York: Routledge, 1994), 106–19. Linda Williams's groundbreaking discussion of melodrama as the major dramatic mode of American cinema provides an important related argument; see *Playing the Race Card: Melodramas of Black and White from Uncle Tom to O. J. Simpson* (Princeton, N.J.: Princeton University Press, 2001), esp. 16–23.

CHAPTER TWO

"To Here from Modernity"

Style, Historiography, and Transitional Cinema

Charlie Keil

Debate on the efficacy of the phrase "transitional period" to identify the years when narrative cinema began to hold sway will continue unabated for some time, a strong indication that we are still working through the historiographical implications of periodizing the preclassical era.[1] Nonetheless, extensive research into the formal and industrial changes marking this period have confirmed for many that cinema underwent a significant upheaval a dozen or so years after its commercial debut and that such changes warrant recognition as a distinct phenomenon. How we characterize and label this period will influence the approach of future film historians, as will the terms under which efforts at definition take place. For this reason we must demand methodological precision of all attempts to examine the transitional period, particularly as scholars of early cinema continue to grapple with the issue of how to integrate observation of formal change into the formidable currents of broader cultural flux. More specifically, I question whether ongoing efforts to link early cinema to a preexistent culture of modernity can easily accommodate the contours of stylistic change afforded by a study of the transitional years. What that process of accommodation might entail and how it will shape our sense of the medium's development into and beyond the classical era constitute my primary concerns in this essay, but my initial focus will rest on efforts to reconcile the claims of modernity to the formal developments of the transitional period.

The general project of relating cinema to a cultural context defined by modernity has gained critical momentum over the years, propelled by the scholarship of Guiliana Bruno, Anne Friedberg, Tom Gunning, Miriam Hansen, Lynne Kirby, Lauren Rabinovitz, and others, developing into "a fairly cohesive focus of inquiry," to borrow the words of Ben Singer. Singer provides a cogent definition of what David Bordwell and I have both chosen to label the modernity thesis: "unearthing or rethinking cinema's emergence within the sensory environment of urban modernity, its relationship to late nine-teenth-century technologies of space and time, and its interactions with ad-jacent elements in the new visual culture of advanced capitalism."[2] The moder-nity thesis is not a negligible idea, and it derives from a reasonable query; namely, if cinema arose and developed during a time of significant cultural change, how did the medium respond to and exist within that cultural con-text? If I have reservations regarding the persuasiveness of the modernity the-sis, they reside primarily in its underdeveloped sensitivity to the formal qual-ities of early cinema and its limited capacity to explain formal change. In what follows I will elaborate on my qualms while indicating how these perceived inadequacies of the modernity thesis translate into a potentially diminished sense of the transitional (and ultimately the classical) era.

Broadly stated, our current purchase on the transitional period sees a re-lated set of formal developments (causally based narratives, increased em-ployment of editing tied to spatial and temporal articulation, mise-en-scène elements devised for the enhancement of verisimilitude and viewer en-gagement) gradually elaborated by filmmakers within a context of industrial maturation and attempts at standardizing production practices. In my own work on this period I have been inclined to look to proximate forces (the trade press, production companies competing for prestige and a share of a growing marketplace) for causal explanations rather than to the broad cul-tural pull of modernity.[3] But if we did look to modernity to explain how the transitional period assumes the shape it does, what could it tell us? Ideally, say its advocates, modernity animates imagery depicting new forms of ex-perience and communication cinema is uniquely suited to envision. The question remains whether modernity can tell us enough about how films de-vised the methods they did to justify designating this period as transitional. I think this question is of fundamental importance because it speaks to the issue of what degree of explanatory power the modernity thesis possesses in equipping us to address transition in specific terms. When applied to tran-sitional works, the modernity thesis may confirm its central premises—that one can find the influence of modernity marking its cultural products—but beyond that general task of elaboration, I am not sure how it will deepen our appreciation of the transitional period's particularities. To prove that point, I will begin by rehearsing four different arguments that proponents of the modernity thesis tend to employ when queried about the nature and extent of modernity's influence during the transitional period.[4]

WHITHER ATTRACTIONS? MODERNITY
AND THE TRANSITIONAL PERIOD

Early cinema's consonance with modernity has become a commonplace within film study, to the extent that the term recurs in the titles of various recent publications on preclassical cinema.[5] In most such studies modernity's influence continues unchecked throughout the midteens despite noticeable changes to the medium around 1907–8. But cinema's retreat from an attractions-based aesthetic, once storytelling becomes a more pressing concern for filmmakers, should create an obvious conundrum for advocates of the modernity thesis. One could put it this way: if attractions are born out of modernity and modernity continues unabated (and in some accounts, accelerates) after the turn of the century, then why would cinema, an avatar of modernity, move away from an aesthetic so clearly indebted to modernity?

Replies to this query occasionally shift focus away from the ostensible problems cinema's development might cause for the modernity thesis, preferring instead to challenge the grounds on which critics make the charge. Supporters of the thesis suspect either that the nature of modernity's relationship to cinema has been (deliberately?) misunderstood or that critics of the thesis believe that cinema and modernity must cooperate in a lockstep fashion. (Ben Singer, for example, in his carefully elaborated reply to David Bordwell's and my own earlier criticism of the modernity thesis, refers to our position on this matter as "a very naïve conception of historical determinism").[6] Such responses indicate that critics of the thesis have erred by overstating the scope and range of modernity's influence on cinema. Those subscribing to the modernity thesis, it is suggested, have *not* claimed a causal relationship between modernity's existence and cinema's development as a medium. And even if they did, they would never embrace the notion that modernity's influence is all encompassing and fully determinant. This I label the "causality counterclaim."

The first issue to address here is whether critics of the modernity thesis have "gotten it wrong" when it comes to the issue of causality. Do proponents of the thesis claim that modernity's effect on cinema is of a singularly causal nature? Both Singer and Gunning say no, arguing instead that modernity is but one of many forces shaping cinema at this time and that the modernity thesis merely suggests a cultural development as significant as modernity must have had some degree of influence. On the surface such a position strikes one as quite reasonable, but on closer inspection the influence posited assumes the quality of inescapability because most advocates of the modernity thesis tend to characterize the advent (and by extension the potential influence) of modernity in fairly grandiose terms. When modernity is described as an epochal change that sweeps up all before it, one becomes hard-pressed to understand how it could *not* prove the most influential of forces on cinema's development. Singer is correct when he says no proponent of the modernity thesis isolates modernity "as the only historical force governing cinema,"[7] but the obvious rejoinder would be that none of them needs to—the collective thrust of their valorization of modernity as the defining cultural moment achieves the result of relegating all other determinants to second-class status.

Moreover, the championing of modernity as the principal cultural force at work in the early twentieth century leads more than a few commentators to make statements whose causal emphasis is hard to ignore: "The culture of modernity rendered inevitable something like cinema, since cinema's characteristics evolved from the traits that defined modern life in general. . . . [Cinema] arose from and existed in the intertwining of modernity's component parts. . . . [T]hese elements created sufficient epistemological pressure to produce cinema."[8] One might ask how a medium rendered "inevitable" by modernity could then sidestep modernity's influence in even a limited fashion? Why would the favored child of modernity, described by Leo Charney and Vanessa Schwartz as "the fullest expression and combination of modernity's attributes,"[9] abandon its parentage? And if it did, then how could it still serve as modernity's "fullest expression"? Here is another: "The cinema was not just one among a number of perceptual technologies. . . . [I]t was above all . . . the single most expansive discursive horizon in which the effects of modernity were reflected."[10] This notion of cinema as a privileged repository for all of modernity's effects makes it difficult to accept the explanation that modernity is "merely" one factor among many influencing the medium.

In summation, were the advocates of the modernity thesis putting forward what Noel Carroll describes as "the obviously true, but uninteresting [claim that] cinema arose during the period identified as modernity and reflects modernity by being an example of it,"[11] and leaving it at that, it is unlikely anyone (even the staunchest of anticulturalists) would do more than stifle a yawn. Yet the arguments of many scholars exploring cinema as a function of modernity make it clear not only that they want to tie this observation to headier claims about concomitant changes to perception but that they also privilege modernity within any list of influential forces.[12] They do so in part because of the perceptual argument, but this in turn leads them to promote certain qualities of the medium, thereby reinforcing cinema's indebtedness to modernity's influence.

Advocates of the modernity thesis also dispute how the nature of transition has been conceived, particularly as it relates to the role of attractions. First, attractions did not disappear, as the naysayers would claim; instead, they were absorbed into an altered paradigm. This paradigm emphasizes narrative but scarcely reduces the overall effectiveness (the potential for shock and astonishment) of attractions. Second, in some accounts of transition too much attention is devoted to narrational economy and not enough given to the sustained appeal of attractions. A corollary to this argument involves the assertion that transitional films actually enhance attractions by enveloping the short bursts of unadorned sensorial shock from earlier years within an array of involving plots designed to enhance spectatorial involvement. This I call "sustaining attractions during transition."

To my knowledge critics of the modernity thesis do not believe that attractions completely disappear post-1906, nor do they believe all films prior to that year exhibit attractions-like qualities to the same degree. The question is whether the modernity thesis logically leads one to believe an attractions-based aesthetic *should* dominate early cinema from its inception. Were it not for the identification of so many early films fulfilling the general attributes of the cinema of attractions, would film be tied as strongly to modernity as it has been? If any party "shackles the modernity thesis to the most limited definition of the cinema of attractions,"[13] it is the architects of the modernity thesis themselves, who need that definition in order to mount a compelling case for cinema as the privileged medium of the modern era.

As for the notion that critics of the thesis create a "false dichotomy between attractions and the cinema of narrative integration,"[14] that dichotomy only arises because the dominance of attractions has been oversold in the campaign of justification. This, in turn, has led to a modernity-spawned canon for cinema's early years, which privileges films made prior to the transitional period. Ideally, the ones elected to the canon will feature sensation, visual display, or variations of sensorial shock. The favored choices tend to be kinesthetic motion films, which take their viewer on a ride that mimics the fast-paced existence of the urban traveler; or shock docs, like the oft-cited *Electrocuting an Elephant* (1902), which inflicts technology on an outsized animal body to sensationalistically illustrate and exploit the anxiety experienced by the urban subject; or transformation films, where editing effects substitutions in a parody of the quick-change nature of urban existence. The untold number of pedestrian comic episodes, staged vaudeville turns, or confusing brief dramas from the earliest years are virtually never mentioned, and their omission is not simply a function of their being unmemorable. These films serve no illustrative purpose. Although many films from the period embody the prized aspects of attractions—emphatic visuality, self-conscious employment of cinematic technique, solicitation of a direct and occasionally visceral response—probably even more do not. And the reason these ordinary films tend to be ignored dictates that a potentially larger number of films from the transitional period will also be overlooked, as their formal features do not help substantiate the modernity thesis either. A fragmentary mode of existence requires films exhibiting an aesthetic of fragmentation.

One could argue, as Tom Gunning does, that perhaps style has been improperly inserted into this debate, but as I stated before, it was precisely the distinct stylistic features of the cinema of attractions that recommended the films to the broader arguments of those advancing the modernity thesis. Anyone doubting this can find confirmation in Gunning's own aims to link the formal attributes of attractions to their function as an embodiment of urban experience:

> For my continued writing and research in early cinema, however, the attraction serves not only as a cornerstone of formal analysis but as a window that opens up the study of the origins of cinema to broader cultural dimensions. . . . Investigating the cinema of attractions illuminates the changes in environment brought about by the growth of capitalism in the 19th and early 20th centuries and its consequent technological transformations of daily life. It seems to me that attractions provide a key concept for exploring . . . "modernity." . . . If the experience of modernity finds its locus classicus in big city streets and their crowds, the unique stimulus offered by this new environment discovers its aesthetic form in attractions.[15]

In another essay I traced the lineage of the attractions model and its transformation from a method of analyzing the unique and noncontinuous style of early cinema to the chief way in which modernity gets read back out of film form.[16] Close stylistic observation laid the groundwork for attractions-based claims about modernity, but now such observation is refused proper consideration. To say that cinema's formal features prove valuable for their representation of modernity, but at the same time do not constitute relevant grounds for critics questioning whether such representation operates consistently, emerges as contradictory—either style is relevant to the consideration of modernity's relationship to cinema or it is not. One cannot point to style as corroboration only when the evidence supports one's contention, ruling it inappropriate at other times. Gunning has said that "Bordwell's and Keil's claim that the modernity thesis cannot explain stylistic change is probably correct, but seems to defeat a claim that no scholar of early cinema ever made."[17] This statement substitutes avoidance of a logical outcome for its systematic refutation.

The flip side of this problem is the vexed question of how transitional films function: as the polar opposite of the cinema of attractions (Singer's version of our claim) or as a more sophisticated and compelling version of attractions, with the shock neatly wrapped in a satisfying wrapper of narrative? Insofar as critics of the modernity thesis subscribe to the usefulness of the attractions model, we do not pretend that attractions are decimated by a principle of integration. However, their function is typically transformed: the close-up used in *Grandma's Reading Glass* (1900) differs in purpose from that employed in *Musketeers of Pig Alley* (1912), and one would be hard pressed to argue that even a favored transitional film like *The Lonedale Operator* (1911) has more in common with, say, *Explosions of a Motor Car* (1900) than the other narratively driven one-reelers being made with predictable regularity by 1911. The modernity thesis advocates don't go so far as to claim that, but they are drawing a continuity in purpose for the attraction that is a bit disquieting. If editing in the attractions era often serves as an attraction, should one say that it still does in the transitional period, even when efforts are already being expended to cover over editing's effects? The fragmentary force of editing, which purportedly defines the attractions era, is largely vitiated by the move toward continuity editing. If the attraction was the dominant in the years prior to 1906, it is definitely a submerged and subordinated element by the mid-1910s, and the modernity thesis has not provided a very compelling explanation for why this happens. For me the fact that cinema's formal development paradoxically refuses to conform to the contours of modernity as a cultural context remains a vexing issue. Even more troubling, however, is a tendency of many proponents of the modernity thesis to pretend that the kind of cinema they equate with modernity never goes out of fashion, because to admit that it does might weaken their contentions about the pervasive cultural prominence of modernity.

Keeping in mind the proviso of the causality counterclaim, proponents of the modernity thesis can prove a sustained and even increasing influence of modernity on and through film during the transitional era, especially if they study *reactions* to the cinema more so than the medium's formal contours. As Tom Gunning has explained, "What need to be made more precise are the social mediations of experience, observable not only in works or art, but in the scientific and political discourse of the period."[18] Singer reminds us that "the large majority of early observations [that link cinema to urban modernity] date from after the transition."[19] This I call the "discourse defense."

It would be dogmatic in the extreme to refuse the evidence supplied by various contemporaneous commentators as to the wide-ranging effects of modernity. But that differs from saying that the statements made at the time tying cinema to urban modernity should then convince us that film consistently (even progressively) reinforced such observations. What strikes me when reading these modernity-minded commentators from the 1910s is how they tend to talk about the phenomenon of cinema rather than particulars. In direct contrast to these figures one can put forward numerous contemporaneous writers who approach cinema with matter-of-fact acceptance as a fairly conventional narrative medium. The countless critics and editorialists in the trade press of the time, for instance, tend to concentrate their efforts on how to render cinema more comprehensible for the average nickelodeon-goer or more palatable for a middle-class patron. Rarely do these writers suggest that cinema reflects a fast-paced urban environment or a technology-ridden culture dependent on endless sensorial shocks. In fact, trade press writers tend to suggest the opposite: when they write about cinema being "close to life," it is typically in appreciation of how cinema captures emotional truths or the recognizable particulars of the external world. If they speak negatively of "realism," it is to criticize producers for crudely inserting stunts without properly contextualizing them within the ongoing narrative. Tellingly, trade press critics tended to see such latter-day attractions as tedious, not stimulating or revelatory of a defining cultural moment. I will quote one critic from *Moving Picture World* at length for a representative comment:

> The "tank drama" should not be revived through the medium of the silent stage [i.e., cinema]; or if revived, should be properly labeled as such. Let the titles be candid and announce "a phenomenal dive of 100 feet," or "a wonderful jump" or "a most realistic fire." The plot, written around the cleverness of some trained animal or around a "dive" or a "jump" may go once or twice, but it gets tiresome after that. Realism, as an integral part growing directly and naturally out of the plot, is much to be commended. The silent stage has a great advantage in being able to tell a story without natural settings. Realism for the sake of realism and the subordination of the plot to some feat of realism, is to be rejected and can be safely left to outdoor vaudeville.[20]

Now of course one could claim that such commentators were not sufficiently attentive to the commonalities shared by cinema and the outside world or that their inherent aesthetic conservatism kept them from noticing such affinities. One could also say that any comparisons between social critics and trade press writers simply reveal how differently these two groups approached the same phenomenon. The concerns of trade press writers simply do not lead them to contemplate how cinema might approximate modern urban life in the same way that sociologists like Simmel fail to think about narrative structure. All of these statements might be true,[21] but there is another possible explanation: cultural commentators were still responding to the novelty of cinema, not the weekly deluge of repetitive narratives reviewers had to contend with. This does not obviate the fact that cultural commentators perceived a link between urban modernity and cinema that the trade press did not, but it does suggest that a steady diet of film would not produce in its observers the inevitable conclusion that watching motion pictures was tantamount to a crash course in perceptual realignment. This leads one to wonder how much the average film induced in its viewer the destabilizing shock associated with urban modernity.

Finally, if one yearns to find proof of modernity's influence on transitional cinema, one need not concern oneself with the potentially contradictory evidence offered through stylistic analysis; instead, direct your attention to the *subject matter* of well-known examples from these years. The locus classicus here would appear to be *The Lonedale Operator,* but any film dependent on thrills, particularly the cinematic translations of Grand Guignol or the somewhat later serial queen melodramas, will fit the bill. Films featuring trains, automobiles, telephones, or other technologies of modernity also deserve attention. This I label "modernity as cinematic subject matter."

Perhaps even from the outset, and certainly by the transitional years, films did not simulate or embody the operations of modernity to the same extent that they depicted its most obvious manifestations. In other words films may not have contributed to the formation of a modern subject by bombarding her or him with sensorial overload as much as they revisited the epiphenomena of modernity and duplicated them on the screen. Trains, telegraphs, and a host of other modern inventions populate films of the period so extensively that watching them plunges the viewer into the imagery of modernity in an intensified fashion. Moreover, the anxiety that typically attends the appearance of these machines of modernity is redoubled when the narrative places them at the heart of a suspenseful plot, whether it be to speed the hero toward the endangered heroine or to carry supplies to needy Confederate troops.

Two distinct problems emerge within this line of argumentation. First, it overstates the prevalence of imagery directly relevant to modernity. For every film set in a modern urban environment trading on identifiable icons of modernity, several more have no tangible link to this imagery whatsoever. This calls into question just how much the average film avails itself of a connection to modernity. I would say very little. As part of the research for my book, I watched more than six hundred American films with release dates from 1907 to 1913. I tried to be representative in terms of both studio and genre. Based on my viewing sample, I would argue that the average film does not fortify the modernity thesis even on this weakened level of subject matter. There is a predictable repetition of narrative material in many films from the period, hardly surprising given the rapid rate of production. For that reason stories involving trains, telephones, and the like are at the center of a fair number of transitional films; however, far more make no concession to either urban life or modern technology. Bucolic rural comedies, housebound dramas, and western tales of stoic Indians and vengeful ranch hands are the order of the day. Moreover, if one is to suggest that even certain forms of writing constitute iconic representations of modernity, then nearly all films from the period become exemplary. But if writing is indicative of modernity because letters (eventually) help collapse spatiotemporal gaps dividing sender and recipient, then virtually any form of aided communication proves the influence of modernity, and the context of modernity functions as self-fulfilling prophecy. This reinforces my sense that modernity possesses far too strong a causal role when the modernity thesis is engaged for the purposes of analysis, in the same way that any instance of looking in painting can exemplify a "distracted modern gaze" if one determines that all modern subjects have been rendered distracted by their environment.[22] Second, when technology from modernity does appear, such as the telephone, its appearance is rather prosaic, a means to a narrative end rather than cinematic testimony to a pervasive spatiotemporal disruption. In other words if one looks at the average film, modernity does not loom large, and examples like *The Lonedale Operator,* which fuse technology with propulsive film form, are the exceptions that prove the rule.

What of the action-packed serial, which Ben Singer equates with modernity so convincingly in his book? Although popular, the serial does not strike me as representative of the typical film—its unique structure and dependency on convoluted action set it apart from more conventional films. Besides, by the admission of its own champions, the serial does little to prepare for the feature films that will dominate the production slates of majors for the next several decades. Even if one were to make a convincing case for the serial as the successor to attractions as the chief cinematic repository for modernity, the serial's anomalous nature would still lead that line of argumentation to a historical dead end. But I would also caution against the temptation to equate action sequences themselves with modernity, as such a move risks diluting the specific qualities of modernity to the point where any instance of rapid movement onscreen serves as modernity's functional equivalent. Modernity cannot be behind every fistfight or race to the rescue on horseback, or else modernity does become the vague all-purpose determinant defenders of the modernity thesis have been at pains to depict as the crude construction of its critics.

In summation, if one wishes to persist in the reading of transitional films as somehow formed by modernity, and one is beholden to a definition of cinema dictated by the attractions model, one can pursue numerous options. First, one can locate modernity not in attractions per se but in the plotlines and imagery of these later films. This has the benefit of recognizing the increased narrativization that defines post-attractions cinema but can lead to a tendency to read all such films as thematizations of modernity. One can foresee the likely prospect of a narrowly conceived transitional canon being combed over for endless examples of "circulation," "mechanization," and their modernity-bred kin. (Already, *Traffic in Souls* [1913] has been revisited several times precisely on such grounds.) Second, one might claim attractions persist more strongly than has been allowed. I addressed this in an earlier section but reiterate that it places its proponents in the odd position of arguing against the textual evidence pointing toward the eventual establishment (by the late teens) of a cinema governed by classical principles. Perhaps in recognition of this the inevitable corollary to the claim that critics of the modernity thesis underplay the persistence of attractions is that they also overstate the role of classicism. This leads, then, to a third option: challenging the hegemony of the classical model. This moves us beyond the period of early cinema proper but derives logically from some of the arguments I have rehearsed thus far. As far back as 1995 Linda Williams lauded the concept of attractions because "in addition to being [an] apt description of early cinema it describes aspects of all cinema that have also been undervalued in the classical paradigm."[23] The attractions concept had already been enlisted by critics eager for a model of spectatorship suitable to describe the postmodern experience.[24] Dislodging the obstinate historical fact of classicism would permit them to draw a through line from modernity to postmodernity. To do so would prove one of the central tenets of the modernity thesis: that modernity's influence continues unabated until the arrival of the postmodern moment.

MODERNITY TRIUMPHANT: DISLODGING CLASSICISM

Laying the groundwork most systematically for the act of reclassifying classicism has been Miriam Hansen, particularly in her development of the concept of "vernacular modernism." Hansen has laid out her ambitious project in a series of articles, its cornerstone imposingly entitled "The Mass Production of the Senses: Classical Cinema as Vernacular Modernism."[25] This project extends beyond the debunking of prevailing models of classicism to investigate the meaning of Americanism within an international marketplace and to chart how other national cinemas fostered within a context of modernity developed their own versions of popular modernism. For the purposes of this essay I will restrict myself to her arguments concerning modernism and classicism.

Hansen finds current notions of both classicism and modernism too limiting; as one might suspect, she seeks a methodological pathway that enables her to bring the terms closer together. Citing "David Bordwell, Janet Staiger and Kristin Thompson's monumental and impressive study, *The Classical Hollywood Cinema: Film Style and Mode of Production to 1960*," Hansen explains that the "authors conceive of classical cinema as an integral, coherent system, a system that interrelates a specific mode of production (based on Fordist principles of industrial organisation) and a set of interdependent stylistic norms that were elaborated by 1917 and remained more or less in place until about 1960."[26] By choosing to describe this system as classical, Hansen says, the authors deliberately invoke eighteenth-century aesthetics, thereby emphasizing "tradition and continuity rather than newness as difference, disruption, and change."[27] Mirroring the efforts of modernity thesis critics who push for a more attractions-oriented reading of transitional cinema, Hansen directs her attention to the excessive genres—the musical, melodrama, and horror films—so as to discredit the *Classical Hollywood Cinema* version of classicism as both too restrictive and "totalizing" an account. In a parallel move she relies on discursive evidence to upend received notions of Hollywood's conventionality. Quoting pertinent spokespeople from the modern era like Gertrude Stein, Hansen argues that "for contemporaries, Hollywood at its presumably most classical figured as the very symbol of contemporaneity, the present, modern times."[28]

Inasmuch as the dominant models of classicism have failed to account for its indebtedness to modernity, favored definitions of modernism have over-stated its distinctions from classicism. According to Hansen an appropriate understanding of both terms has been shackled by the binary thinking that has kept the concepts of classicism and modernism separate. She sees no reason why the term *modernism* should refer only to alternative forms of film practice, as it bespeaks an affiliation with the modern that the term *classicism* denies. Hansen would support a definition of *modernism* that collapses the distinctions the understood qualifier *high* has conferred on it. As she says, "the scope of modernist aesthetics [should] include the cultural manifestations of mass-produced, mass-mediated and mass-consumed modernity."[29] Because we are accustomed to thinking of modernism in terms of rarefied culture, Hansen bestows the adjective *vernacular* to signify a break with previous limited conceptions of the term.

In many ways this is a move one could have predicted. As the modernity thesis has always subscribed to the powerful influence of modernity as a cultural force, it only makes sense that its advocates would propose a revised description of its products to match the correspondence achieved within the postmodernity/postmodernism dyad. Once modernism is expanded to include cultural activity of a sufficiently broad nature, the only step left is to dispense with any nomenclature that still refers to outdated frames of thought. But how to convince skeptics that classicism has to go, especially since it has been applied to Hollywood cinema of the studio era with consistency for about the same amount of time as classicism itself persisted? Aside from the arguments rooted in genre deviations and contemporary discourse already cited, Hansen's chief rationale involves, ironically enough, the claim that a rethinking of the term will help to "restore historical specificity to the concept of classical Hollywood cinema,"[30] One welcomes research that will contribute to increased conceptual rigor, but many cinema historians have attempted to do just that without abandoning the framework proper.[31] My confidence in Hansen's project, which, in its attention to the international appeal of classical works, demonstrates the potential to inventively extend and redirect the insights of *The Classical Hollywood Cinema,* still stalls in the face of the preferred definition of classicism she produces: "less a system of functionally interrelated norms and a corresponding set of empirical objects than a scaffold, matrix or web that allows for a wide range of aesthetic effects and experiences—that is, for cultural configurations that are more complex and dynamic than the most accurate account of their function within any single system may convey."[32] Although Hansen presents her model of vernacular modernism as improving on the ahistorical obsession with stability she perceives in the dominant conception of classicism, one finds little evidence of the vaunted historical specificity. For example, when one surveys the articles for a notion of what her model will reveal that classicism has not, we learn this: "the new medium offered an alternative because it engaged the contradictions of modernity at the level of the senses, the level at which the impact of modern technology on human experience was most palpable and irreversible."[33] Sensory reflexivity is to vernacular modernism what formal reflexivity was to high modernism, minus the precision lent by artistic motivation.

If one looks for filmic examples to clarify matters, the results are no more encouraging. Within the American context Hansen's privileged example is the slapstick comedy. Stressing comedy's affective dimension, she argues that the "reason slapstick comedy hit home and flourished worldwide was not critical reason but the films' propulsion of their viewers' bodies into laughter."[34] Leaving aside the question of why this universal appeal ebbs and flows throughout the classical period, manifesting itself in a variety of forms, some featuring extreme physical violence (as in silent knockabout) and others more subdued interplay (as in sound-era screwball), one wonders how this can serve as a functional replacement for the insights of classicism. Classicism explains how an industrial system structures and repeats the diverse appeals of different generic materials in a sufficiently predictable way to ensure repeated audience interest. Hansen substitutes a vague invocation of reflexivity, ostensibly linking classical films to their more avant-garde counterparts by virtue of "the ways in which they allow their viewers to confront the constitutive ambivalence of modernity."[35]

A number of years ago I wrote that "certain tendencies within the modernity thesis risk sacrificing the fine-grained sense of historical change early cinema study has been cultivating over the past fifteen years."[36] Despite Singer's and Gunning's protestations to the contrary, I see nothing to convince me that the risk has been averted. On the contrary, if Hansen's rhetorical moves are any indication, modernity-thesis advocates are staking their claims on the basis of an improved historical understanding of cinema's development. Perhaps this is merely a case of irreconcilable values, with critics of the thesis adopting a microanalytical methodology that doesn't suit the large-scale cultural aspirations of those they are criticizing. But if the modernity thesis is to be pursued with anything more than lip service given to the need for exacting explanatory frameworks, it will require a renewed commitment to exploring how film emerged out of an era of modernity. Tom Gunning has admitted "that there is no question that the relations drawn between the structures of modernity and those of early film frequently lack specificity and remain on the level of vague analogies."[37] But rather than responding to that challenge by reconciling their visions of modernity to preexisting models of film's development, some champions of the thesis appear to be heading in the opposite direction, discrediting previously accepted terms and substituting contentious new concepts of their own. If the study of modernity is to successfully enrich our knowledge of cinema while connecting it meaningfully to a larger cultural context, its advocates must never lose sight of their original point of entry, lest the vibrant diversity of film and its history be eclipsed by the growing attraction of modernity.

NOTES

1. For essays questioning the usefulness of this phrase see the entries by Ben Brewster and Tom Gunning in this volume.

2. Ben Singer, *Melodrama and Modernity: Early Sensational Cinema and Its Contexts* (New York: Columbia University Press, 2001), 102. My list of central proponents of the modernity thesis largely coincides with that provided by Singer. Critiques of the modernity thesis appear in David Bordwell, *On the History of Film Style* (Cambridge, Mass.: Harvard University Press, 1997), 141–46; and Charlie Keil, "'Visualised Narratives,' Transitional Cinema, and the Modernity Thesis," *in Le Cinéma au tournant du siècle/Cinema at the Turn of the Century*, ed. Claire Dupré la Tour, André Gaudreault, and Roberta Pearson (Lausanne/Québec: Éditions Payot Lausanne/Éditions nota bene, 1998), 123–37.

3. Charlie Keil, *Early American Cinema in Transition: Story, Style, and Filmmaking, 1907–1913* (Madison: University of Wisconsin Press, 2001).

4. My summation of responses to criticism of the modernity thesis (and, in particular, claims that the thesis cannot adequately address the transitional period) derives primarily from the work of the two scholars cited most consistently in this text, Tom Gunning and Ben Singer. Many scholars have adopted versions of the modernity thesis in their work, but few have reflected on the validity of the assumptions guiding that work with the consistency and rigor of these two writers. I thank both of them for the stimulating but always cordial exchanges on this topic we have enjoyed over the years; Ben also graciously provided helpful feedback on a version of this article, as did David Bordwell, Scott Curtis, and Shelley Stamp.

5. A representative sampling includes *Cinema and the Invention of Modern Life*, ed. Leo Charney and Vanessa Schwartz (Berkeley: University of California Press, 1995); Singer, *Melodrama and Modernity;* Mary Ann Doane, *The Emergence of Cinematic Time: Modernity, Contingency, the Archive* (Cambridge, Mass.: Harvard University Press, 2002); Jennifer Bean, *Bodies in Shock: Gender, Genre, and the Cinema of Modernity* (forthcoming); see also Mark B. Sandberg, *Living Pictures, Missing Persons: Mannequins, Museums, and Modernity* (Princeton, N.J.: Princeton University Press, 2003).

6. Singer, *Melodrama and Modernity*, 127.

7. Ibid.

8. Charney and Schwartz, *Invention of Modern Life*, 1, 10.

9. Ibid., 10.

10. Miriam Bratu Hansen, "America, Paris, the Alps: Kracauer (and Benjamin) on Cinema and Modernity," in *Cinema and the Invention of Modern Life*, ed. Leo Charney and Vanessa Schwartz (Berkeley: University of California Press, 1995), 365.

11. Noel Carroll, "Modernity and the Plasticity of Perception," *Journal of Aesthetics and Art Criticism* 59, no. 1 (2001): 15.

12. For detailed critiques of the claim that modernity witnessed an actual change

to the faculty of perception see Bordwell, *History of Film Style;* and Carroll, "Modernity," 11–18.

13. Singer, *Melodrama and Modernity,* 129.

14. Ibid.

15. Tom Gunning, "The Whole Town's Gawking: Early Cinema and the Visual Experience of Modernity," *Yale Journal of Criticism* 7, no. 2 (1994): 189–201.

16. See Charlie Keil, "'Fatal Attractions': The Problems Transitional Cinema Poses for Spectatorship" (paper delivered at the Society for Cinema Studies Conference, Dallas, 1996).

17. Tom Gunning, "Early American Film," in *The Oxford Guide to Film Studies,* ed. John Hill and Pamela Church Gibson (Oxford, U.K.: Oxford University Press, 1998), 268.

18. Ibid.

19. Singer, *Melodrama and Modernity,* 129.

20. *Moving Picture World,* 26 August 1911, 520.

21. If modernity thesis proponents accept these caveats, however, it would be inconsistent to then enlist other trade press writers to support their case unless they can prove these writers *were* in tune with modernity. I thank David Bordwell for pointing this out to me.

22. For examples of this tendency see Patricia McDonnell, *On the Edge of Your Seat: Popular Theater and Film in Early Twentieth-Century American Art* (New Haven, Conn.: Yale University Press, 2002).

23. Linda Williams, ed., *Viewing Positions: Ways of Seeing Film* (New Brunswick, N.J.: Rutgers University Press, 1995), 12.

24. One such example would be Anne Friedberg, *Window Shopping: Cinema and the Postmodern* (Berkeley: University of California Press, 1993).

25. Miriam Bratu Hansen, "The Mass Production of the Senses: Classical Cinema as Vernacular Modernism," *Modernism/Modernity* 6, no. 2 (1999): 59–77.

26. Ibid., 63.

27. Ibid., 64.

28. Ibid., 65.

29. Miriam Bratu Hansen, "Fallen Women, Rising Stars, New Horizons: Shanghai Silent Film as Vernacular Modernism," *Film Quarterly* 54, no. 1 (2000): 11.

30. Hansen, "Mass Production of the Senses," 66.

31. Two exemplary instances of critical amendments to the classical paradigm rooted in extensive research are Henry Jenkins III, *What Made Pistachio Nuts? Early Sound Comedy and the Vaudeville Aesthetic* (New York: Columbia University Press, 1992); and Matthew Bernstein, "Hollywood's Semi-Independent Production," *Cinema Journal* 32, no. 3 (spring 1993): 41–54.

32. Hansen, "Mass Production of the Senses," 67.

33. Ibid., 70.

34. Ibid., 71.

35. Ibid.

36. Keil, "'Fatal Attractions.'"

37. Gunning, "Early American Film," 268.

CHAPTER THREE

Periodization of Early Cinema

Ben Brewster

In the introduction to her book on the early history of the film market in Germany, Corinna Müller remarks that "recent research in film history distinguishes between an early 'cinema of attractions' and a subsequent period of 'narrative film'; without saying so, these terms in fact imply the short film on the one hand and the long film on the other."[1] By contrast, American sources that make the distinction between a cinema of attractions and a cinema of narrative integration place the transition between them five years or more before the origin of the feature-length film.[2] This seems to be more than a misunderstanding of American usage on Müller's part, or a difference between the United States and Germany. There is here a discrepancy between two kinds of distinction: an essentially stylistic one between a cinema of attractions and a cinema of narrative integration, and an essentially economic or institutional one between a cinema of short films and one of features (for Müller—and I am convinced she is correct—the emergence of the long film is indissolubly linked with changes in the film market). An exploration of this discrepancy is informative for the periodization of the cinema before about 1917, not just in Germany but throughout the film-producing world, including the United States of America.

A closer look at Müller's study reveals, in fact, that she does not simply distinguish between two phases in the early German cinema, one of short films, the other of features. Rather she makes three distinctions: a period when films were screened as part of a mixed bill in a variety theater or in a fairground booth, a period of permanent cinemas showing programs of short films, and a period of permanent cinemas showing programs built around a feature-length film.[3]

In the earliest period the main exhibition outlets for German film producers were variety theaters and fairgrounds. Only around 1906–7 did this change, with the rapid rise of small shop-front moving picture theaters. These permanent sites showed film more or less exclusively, but the variety format persisted in their mixed programs of short films. The first ones were very successful, and, as there were virtually no barriers to entry, their numbers multiplied, giving rise to a highly competitive exhibition market in which theaters, often located more or less next door to one another, competed for customers by showing the latest films at the lowest prices. This resulted in the characteristic problem called by the contemporary trade press "excess competition." Exhibitors could not differentiate between their own offerings and their competitors' other than by price and novelty, and the premium commanded by novelty was easily eroded thanks to the universal availability of films as soon as they went onto the market. Ticket prices thus had to be as low as possible, exhibitors could not pay distributors or manufacturers anything but rock-bottom prices for the films they showed, and manufacturers had no incentive to raise the cost of production of their films. Meanwhile French and American producers, with more lucrative domestic markets (as we will see below), could export films to Germany at prices that undercut anything local producers could afford to offer. German film production was almost driven out of existence.

This situation changed with the emergence of what was called the *"Monopol-Film,"* the monopoly film or exclusive. Hitherto films had been sold or rented on the open market; that is, anyone could buy any film offered and screen it anytime and anywhere. Given the impossibility of differentiating among films, a more expensive film had no takers in this market. Another system of booking entertainment acts had long existed: the exclusive contract, where the manager of the act—for example, the production of a stage play—agreed with the theater that the act would not appear elsewhere in a given territory for a certain period of time, giving that theater exclusive local rights to that act and thus allowing a monopoly price to be charged. Exclusive contracts became significant in the German film market around the end of 1910. The exclusive contract allowed the exhibitor to charge whatever price he or she thought the prospective audience would pay without fear of being undercut for that title by nearby theaters; it allowed the exhibitor to play the film for as long as it would draw an audience up to the limit of the clearance allowed in the contract; and, within the same limits, it allowed him or her to delay the opening as long as necessary to conduct an effective publicity campaign for the film. The first monopoly films usually shared two qualities: they were longer than other films, and they were imported. The first characteristic derives from the need to be able to sell the particular exclusive subject as special and a draw for an audience in itself; it thus had to constitute a substantial part of the film program offered. The second follows from the first; for the reasons already adduced, no one in Germany was making "special" films of any type, let alone long films, and the films therefore had to come from abroad (some reasons as to why they could do so will be discussed later in this study). Apart from one early boxing film imported from the United States, the first German monopoly films were Danish and featured Asta Nielsen. Italian subjects soon followed. Once the principle of the monopoly film was well established, indigenous versions could be made, and, of course, Nielsen moved to Germany in 1911 and began the successful series of short features (usually four-reelers) made for Deutsche Bioscop from that year to the outbreak of the World War I.

The situation in Britain was essentially similar to that in Germany.[4] Initially films were screened in music halls and fairgrounds. From 1906 there was a rapid growth in the number of permanent small cinemas. Films were sold on an open market, with the same inhibiting effect on domestic production as in Germany; from one of the most advanced and prolific of filmmaking countries, Britain very rapidly saw its production decline and stagnate formally (an important factor here, as well as in the domestic market situation, was the loss of outlets in America with the foundation of the Motion Picture Patents Company there). In Britain the monopoly film was called an "exclusive." Whether the rise of the exclusive film resulted from borrowing from Germany, or vice versa, or the two developments were independent, I do not know; in neither country was there anything startlingly new about the concept. In Britain, too, the first exclusives were from abroad and were usually longer than one reel; and in Britain, too, the rise of the exclusive gave the domestic production industry a new lease on life but nothing like such a vigorous life as the German (in 1914 German domestic producers were effectively protected by the war, whereas their British equivalents remained as vulnerable as before to American imports).

France was somewhat different. Richard Abel divides the prewar years into four periods.[5] First was the founding period up to 1902, when film companies were essentially producers of equipment. Second was the period from 1902 to 1907, dominated by exhibition in variety shows and fairgrounds. The third period, from 1907 to 1911, saw a rapid rise of permanent movie houses, with Pathé owning a substantial share of them and instituting its own distribution system to serve them. The large market share and vertical integration Pathé enjoyed and its strong position on the world market allowed it to sustain relatively high production costs and hence compete in quality with its rivals, without the ruinous competition characteristic of England and Germany. The relative control of the film programs in its own theaters also enabled Pathé to extend the length of the films it made fairly freely (in contrast to American producers, as we will see). Nevertheless, the real impetus to much longer films in France came from the import by firms outside the Pathé circle of films from abroad, particularly Italy, which were distributed as exclusives, thus establishing the basis for the fourth period, beginning in 1911. Pathé and its rivals Gaumont and Éclair were in a position to match these productions with long films of their own, and by 1914 it was the well-established companies of the third period who also dominated the production and distribution of features in France in the fourth (although from that year American features became serious competitors).

If England and Germany were similar, so, too, were France and the United States. As is well known, before 1906 the predominant exhibition site for films in the United States was the vaudeville house. There were traveling projectionists—Charles Musser and Carol Nelson have chronicled the career of one of them, Lyman Howe[6]—but in the United States fairgrounds as such do not seem to have had the importance they had all over Europe. After 1906 the crucial site became the nickelodeon, the small permanent theater offering a relatively short program of short films screened continuously a number of times each day. The high competition among these theaters did not drive down production costs, however, because producers grouped themselves, voluntarily or involuntarily, into cartels: first into the Motion Picture Patents Company (MPPC); then into the MPPC and its distribution arm, the General Film Company, on the one hand, and a small number of rival combines of so-called Independent producers and their distribution firms on the other.[7] As in France, the strong international position of American film producers, but even more the ability their cartelization assured them to close the domestic short-film market to almost all imports, helped sustain production-cost levels.[8] Enjoying the advantages of monopoly through membership in a cartel, however, is not the same as having a preponderant position in the market by oneself, as Pathé had in France. Cartel members agree to abandon price competition, and each attempts to extend its market share by other means—but this can only happen within limits, or the members unable to compete by those means will break ranks and cut their prices. Central to the way the MPPC and the General Film Company handled this problem is the modular program: each company contracted to produce a certain number of films in each week's release schedule, totaling two or three times the footage any one theater would need. Local exchanges, affiliates or branches of the General Film Company, made up programs from these offerings and assigned those programs to theaters according to zoning and clearance agreements and the relative bargaining power of each theater. Mutual and the Motion Picture Sales Company, the distribution arms of the other American film cartels, acted in the same way. The possibility of modular assemblage of films, with all the participating producers thereby guaranteed a reasonable number of screenings of their output, produced the extreme standardization of film length characteristic of the American industry and of no other. Hence it proved impossible (despite several attempts) for the established short-film producers to extend the length of films in the way Pathé was able to. However, there was an alternative market for film, the "states' rights" system. This was the American equivalent of the exclusive contract, the territory within which the contract guaranteed the exhibitor a period of monopoly being a state or a traditionally associated group of states. In the United States, too, states' rights booking was a preexisting system used for theatrical and variety acts. By the beginning of the 1910s, longer films produced abroad were being imported and released through the states' rights system. By 1912 American producers were making feature-length films, mostly as underfinanced speculative ventures for states' rights distribution. Not until 1914 and W. W. Hodkinson's organization of Paramount, the distributor of a complete program of features produced by an alliance of film manufacturers, and hence an equivalent of the General Film Company for features, did feature production begin to dominate the American market.[9] On the other hand, the very high quality (i.e., the very high cost of production made possible by monopoly pricing) of American short films in the early 1910s gave American producers the power to penetrate European markets, with the result that, well before the United States was producing substantial numbers of feature films, American production had come to predominate in almost every European market.

About other countries I do not know enough to say very much. Italy and Denmark are clearly crucial, given that it was films produced in those countries that brought about the shift to feature-length production everywhere else. I have seen no satisfactory explanation for how Italian producers avoided the fate of their English and German counterparts. Corinna Müller suggests that the Danish exception may be explained by the very strict regulation of movie theaters, and particularly of the numbers of such theaters, by Danish municipalities. Given their monopoly position and their elite catchments, it was possible for Copenhagen theaters to charge high prices and present films in long runs; this encouraged production of identifiably high-quality films targeting well-off patrons and generated the excess profits to finance such production, and the metropolitan Danish cinemas invested in filmmaking in just this way. Kosmorama, the company that made *Afgrunden,* the film that launched Asta Nielsen and the genre that became known as "erotic melodrama," was the outgrowth of a Copenhagen movie house.[10]

Despite the variations from country to country that I have indicated so far, there is a remarkable uniformity in these accounts of the development of the cinema. There seem to be three broad phases. The first (although probably in all countries it was preceded by an equivalent of Abel's first phase for France—essentially a period in which film-related activity was still too new and too incoherent to qualify for the name "film industry") can be called the variety-theater/fairground period; the second the permanent-movie-house/short-film period; the third the feature-film period. And in all countries the first period gives place to the second around 1906–7 and the second to the third around 1912–14.

Were there corresponding stylistic phases? And if so, do they correspond to such stylistic descriptions as "cinema of attractions" and "cinema of narrative integration"? A first point to be made in relation to these questions is that the phases are not watertight. Fairground cinema did not end in 1907—itinerant booths showing films were still seen in European fairgrounds in the 1930s and later. Although in the United States moving pictures were abandoned by major vaudeville chains with the rise of the nickelodeon, some nickelodeons rapidly became "small-time vaudeville" houses, showing a combined program of second-class live acts and films, thus perpetuating a mixed show in the cinema, and this practice persisted to the end of the silent era (and much later in big U.S. cities and in some European countries more widely).[11] And cartoon and newsreel cinemas showing hour-long programs of short films similar in format to the nickelodeon program survived in London railway termini until at least the 1960s. What is at issue is the economically preponderant form. If there were exhibitors who persisted in a form that was no longer preponderant, they were to some extent served by producers and distributors who still provided suitable wares for their enterprises, although some items made for the preponderant institution would also serve their needs; thus the British railway terminus cinemas mentioned above showed cartoons and newsreels manufactured to provide the lower end of the bill in the dominant feature cinema.

Moreover, some characteristics of the format are carried over from phase to phase. Although it was much more exclusively a film-centered entertainment, the nickelodeon program allowed space for some live acts (most notably the song slide), and in its film program it retained the idea of a series of contrasting acts that dominated variety entertainment as a whole. Even the feature cinemas rarely showed just one film, so although one or, at most, two films clearly occupied the top of the bill and were the basis for the advertising of the evening's entertainment, the rest still constituted a variety program and retained the anonymity characteristic of the open-market nickelodeon cinema—audiences paid for the feature (although some patrons seem to have gone more for the live acts) but had expectations about the quality and variety of the rest of the bill, and exhibitors increasingly paid distributors a percentage of the box-office take for the feature and flat-rate rentals for the rest of the program.

A more important point concerns the vagueness of the characterization of the first phase. Demographically, the "variety theater" market is so broad as to encompass the whole urban population, and if "fairground" is coupled with it, towns and villages accessible even to remote rural populations are included. These venues, however, did not each cater to the whole social and geographical spectrum. Metropolitan variety theaters were luxurious and expensive and catered to elites, suburban ones to the respectable working class, and fairs to the urban and rural poor. Individuals who attended variety shows selected the venue that was appropriate to their pockets and their self-esteem. The managers of the venues booked the acts (and the film programs) that they thought would be appreciated by the clientele they hoped to attract. Given this situation it is not surprising that the standard way of selling films in this period is via the classified catalog. There is no reason to assume that someone who regularly attended a particular variety theater that showed Pathé films saw all or even a random cross section of the films in the latest Pathé catalog. As far as I know, little work has been done on the question of which films showed where in this period, although Abel remarks that Méliès' long *féeries* were made for a metropolitan variety theater,[12] and it is often claimed that, until the rise of the specialized film theater, Pathé films were especially directed at the fairground. If a variety program is the only common characteristic of all these different venues, then it would seem the only characteristic of the films appropriate to this market would be that they should be of all sorts, the negation of a stylistic category. One is left with Müller's suggestion that they are also all short, but even this is only relatively true: passion films could be assembled that were half an hour or more in length, and the longest films produced by the regular producers as single entities could be a full reel. Nevertheless, there were far more films of three to five minutes than became typical in the nickelodeon phase, despite the survival there of the split reel.

This seems to leave the notion of a "cinema of attractions" rather empty, but one characteristic of fairground cinema is that it was a showman's cinema, one where a presenter, whether actually present as a barker or lecturer or merely implicit in the name on the booth, offered an audience a sensational view or act. The same could be said of variety-theater cinema in those instances when the film program was booked as an "act," where an independent entrepreneur, often the filmmaker or his agent, presented a specially constructed program as a unit in the variety show. This "showmanship" aspect seems to accord well with the idea of explicit narration and direct address to the audience that Gunning and others have seen as central to the "cinema of attractions." This, however, is only one strand of exhibition in a cinematic period that could really be defined as one in which films have no character other than their variousness.

Much of the showmanship was lost in the succeeding nickelodeon period because the program was assembled for the theater by the exchange from what it got week by week and even day by day from the producers via the central distribution agency; the theater manager had little knowledge of what he or she was going to obtain and could thus have little control over its presentation. Films had to become much more self-explanatory and independent of context to work, and this is, again, a characteristic of the notion of "narrative integration." In the American situation the extremely standardized modular format with the relatively long unit of a quarter of an hour in a sense changed the problem of making a film from one of finding something to show the audience to one of filling a time slot in a way that would be interesting and novel, thus calling forth the institution and then elaboration of modes of narration that is such a strong characteristic of American filmmaking at the beginning of the 1910s. Although the slots were less predetermined by the program format in the rest of the world, it is still fair to say that duration became the central concern of filmmakers everywhere.

Although the feature-length film could be, and was, presented with showmanship, because the exclusive contract allowed extensive local advertising campaigns and lobby presentation, its increased length added to the problem of how to fill the allotted time and also brought films into parallel with nonvariety forms of entertainment, in particular, the stage play. This period saw the development of new narrative devices to accommodate the longer form. Some of these were elaborations of short-film devices (but some short-film devices were abandoned, notably narration by flashbacks),[13] whereas others represented a wholesale borrowing from other media, particularly from the live theater. The result was a cinema little removed from the one we have now, although the significance of theatrical models in this account runs counter to the currently prevailing conception of the feature film as built around cinematically specific devices.

Thus, the discrepancy noted at the beginning of this article between a stylistic opposition between attraction and narrative, on the one hand, and an institutional opposition between short and long films, on the other, can be resolved, with some reservations, by suggesting three periods: the variety-fairground period, which accommodates if it is not coterminous with the cinema of attractions; the nickelodeon period, characterized by the development of sophisticated film narrative in a short format; and the feature cinema, which adopted forms and subject matter from the established narrative and dramatic arts and developed the battery of devices we know as classical cinema. The reservations concern the dates of the transitions, which are vague. This is not because it took a certain amount of time to make the transition from one phase to another but because, the institutions for each type of cinema being essentially different from one another, they could and did exist side by side for quite long periods. Eventually, one or other form became so economically preponderant as to marginalize the others, and the marginalization affected the kinds of films that were made, distributed, and seen in the marginal cinemas.

The main novelty of this account thus centers on the second period, that of the one-reel film. If it has been given serious consideration hitherto, it has been conceived as a decade-long transition between the early cinema, however characterized, and the classical cinema.[14] But as historians often point out, the designation "transitional period" is an oxymoron, simply draining the years it covers of any particular characteristics. A failure to recognize that short-film cinema and feature cinema in the early 1910s were essentially parallel institutions has obscured the specificity of the former. Thus, if you calculate the average length of films released between 1910 and 1915 by adding up the total footage released and dividing by the number of titles, you get a steadily growing length. But this does not mean that producers were adding a few feet here and there to their productions so that films gradually got longer (which is a reasonable description of what happened between 1905 and 1910); rather, it is because more and more much longer films were released into the market in the parallel institution of feature cinema. In the short-film cinema, meanwhile, although there were ways to accommodate some films longer than a reel, most films adhered to a fairly constant length (and the longer exceptions were executed as multiples of that length).[15]

Periodization is a dubious enterprise; everything is always changing into something else. Its value is that it indicates what in the mass of data can be aggregated together, what averages and what comparisons are revealing and what misleading. Understanding film production, distribution, and exhibition everywhere in the 1910s is impossible unless it is realized that one phase of the cinema, that of the one-reel film, coexisted with another, that of the feature, at the same time that it was giving way to it.

NOTES

1. Corinna Müller, *Frühe deutsche Kinematographie: Formale, wirtschaftliche und kulturelle Entwicklungen* (Stuttgart: J. B. Metzler, 1994), 4–5. Müller cites Heide Schlüpmann as introducing the opposition into German film historiography but dating the transition in Germany to 1911.

2. In the locus classicus, "The Cinema of Attractions: Early Film, Its Spectator, and the Avant-Garde" (*Wide Angle* 8, no. 3/4 [1986]: 64), Tom Gunning dated the end of the cinema he characterizes as a "cinema of attractions" to 1906–7. I know of American scholars who feel this date is too late but none who suggest it is too early. In this study I use *feature* to mean a film of four reels or more. This is anachronistic because for most of the period I am covering the term meant simply that the film was "special" and hence could be the featured item in a program. But from around 1910 length became such a constant characteristic of feature films that the term gradually came to imply nothing else. See Michael Quinn, "Early Feature Distribution and the Development of the Motion Picture Industry: Famous Players and Paramount, 1912–1921" (Ph.D. diss., University of Wisconsin–Madison, 1998).

3. In a later study, "Variationen des Kinoprogramms. Filmform und Filmgeschichte," in *Die Modellierung des Kinofilms. Zur Geschichte des Kinoprogramms zwischen Kurzfilm und Langfilm (1905/6–1918)*, ed. Corinna Müller and Harro Segeberg, vol. 2 of *Mediengeschichte des Films* (Munich: Wilhelm Fink Verlag, 1998), 43–75, Müller

tries to extend "periodization by length" to include a fourth stage, characterized by the *"abendfüllende Film,"* the film that by itself provides an evening's entertainment (i.e., runs about three hours, including intervals). She dates this transition to after the war, so it is beyond the scope of this study, but I would like to indicate that I am skeptical. Films that constituted a full evening's program existed by 1913; *Germinal* (165 minutes) was the only item on the bill at the Omnia Pathé in Paris in October 1913. On the other hand, they never became standard. There was never an annual program of three-hour movies, and such films were usually road-showed—a form of exhibition by exclusive contract—rather than regularly released, or they were only regularly released in a cut-down form after their initial road-show run. It is not length as such but the distribution system that determines periodization.

4. See Rachael Low, *The History of the British Film,* vol. 1, *1896–1906,* and vol. 2, *1906–1914* (London: Allen and Unwin, 1948–49).

5. Richard Abel, *The Ciné Goes to Town, French Cinema, 1896–1914* (Berkeley: University of California Press, 1994).

6. See Charles Musser and Carol Nelson, *High-Class Moving Pictures: Lyman H. Howe and the Forgotten Era of Traveling Exhibition, 1880–1920* (Princeton, N.J.: Princeton University Press, 1991).

7. We are not dealing here with a struggle between brave "Independents" and a sclerotic "Trust," as American film historians from Ramsaye to Hampton liked to picture it, but with a relatively stable market dominated by a small number of competing cartels. The American film industry was already an oligopoly in 1910.

8. See Kristin Thompson, *Exporting Entertainment: America in the World Film Market, 1907–34* (London: British Film Institute, 1985), esp. chap. 1.

9. See Quinn, "Early Feature Distribution."

10. See Müller, *Frühe deutsche Kinematographie,* 124–25, esp. note 74.

11. See Robert Allen, *Vaudeville and Film, 1895–1915: A Study in Media Interaction* (New York: Arno Press, 1980); and Richard Abel, *The Red Rooster Scare: Making Cinema American, 1900–1910* (Berkeley: University of California Press, 1999).

12. Abel, *Ciné Goes to Town,* 160.

13. See Ben Brewster, *"Traffic in Souls:* An Experiment in Feature-Length Narrative Construction," *Cinema Journal* 31, no. 1 (fall 1991): 48–49.

14. See esp. Kristin Thompson, "The Formulation of the Classical Style, 1909–28," pt. 3 of David Bordwell, Janet Staiger, and Kristin Thompson, *The Classical Hollywood Cinema: Film Style and Mode of Production to 1960* (London: Routledge and Kegan Paul, 1985), 155–240. (Admittedly, Thompson is writing a prehistory of classical cinema rather than an account of preclassical cinema as such, so she is legitimately indifferent to the latter's specificities.) See also Charlie Keil, *Early American Cinema in Transition: Story, Style, and Filmmaking, 1907–1913* (Madison: University of Wisconsin Press, 2001).

15. See Brewster, *"Traffic in Souls,"* 39.

CHAPTER FOUR

Feature Films, Variety Programs, and the Crisis of the Small Exhibitor

Ben Singer

The phrase "transitional era" is almost too tame, too measured, to adequately capture the momentous upheavals—one might legitimately call them revolutions—that took place within the span of ten or fifteen years following the onset of the nickelodeon boom. Perhaps "transformational era," although still lacking appropriate punch, might better convey the sense in which this period involved fundamental and far-reaching redefinitions and expansions of cinema. The first revolution was the nickelodeon boom itself, and the motion picture's concomitant development as an effective story-telling medium. From a far-flung subsidiary attraction displaying very short (part-reel) non- or quasi-narrative films, cinema became the principal attraction presenting a series of short (one-reel) narratives in predominantly small storefront theaters. The second epochal shift, like the first, redefined cinema by altering its dominant venue and central commodity. Nickelodeons and short-film variety programs were eclipsed by grand purpose-built theaters and long films—feature films of four reels and longer. With both revolutions virtually every practice of production, distribution, exploitation, and exhibition underwent profound change.

The challenge posed by such phenomena is to figure out how to reconcile two essentially incompatible, but in this case equally legitimate, historiographical impulses: on the one hand, the need to accentuate radical transformation—to stress the fact that momentous, pivotal, hugely consequential historical shifts did indeed take place during this period—and on the other hand, the need to recognize that transitions are never succinct or definitive shifts from one state of affairs to another. Transition is, almost by definition, a complex dynamic process in which disparate forces—competing paradigms and practices—overlap and interact. Historians usually favor the first impulse, focusing on vivid, interesting, novel phenomena. Discussions of the transitional period therefore are more likely to emphasize "the rise of the feature film and the picture palace" than "the continuing coexistence and eventual decline of the short film and small theater." Both need attention, because it is the shifting dynamic between them—the complex interrelationships between the feature program and the variety program and between the picture palace and the nickelodeon—that makes this period so intriguing.

The first essential step to understanding that dynamic is to work toward something that has been largely absent in historical discussions of the rise of the feature film, namely, a "macro" model of its unfolding. Recent scholarship has productively investigated issues of stylistic development, specific genres, exhibition contexts, and social discourses, but more basic and all-encompassing questions about the exact timing, rapidity, and scope of the feature's emergence and the short's erosion have proved difficult to answer except in a vague way. One tendency in survey histories has been to stress the speed and decisiveness of the transition. A typical example maintains that, very soon after the success of Italian superspectacles like *Quo Vadis?* (mid-1913) and *Cabiria* (early 1914), "a feature craze was sweeping over the country and the industry, challenging . . . the very existence of its one- and two-reel films. The year 1914 was a crucial one for the American film industry. The feature had by this time triumphed almost completely over the one and two-reeler, which survived only in the cartoon, newsreel, serial installment . . . and comedy."[1] This summary may sound unobjectionable enough: there is no shortage of evidence indicating a boom in the popularity of features, and 1914 legitimately could be identified as the crucial year when it became absolutely clear that feature films were not just a passing fad but a powerful force that would permanently reconfigure the industry and the amusement landscape. The situation begins to look more ambiguous, however, when one analyzes production data and finds that in 1914 shorts composed no less than 94 percent of all titles produced by the American industry. "The very existence of its one- and two-reel films" could hardly have been in question when features accounted for only one-sixteenth of U.S. releases.

Creating a perfect macromodel of the relationship between shorts and features would require taking stock of the number and lengths of all the films exhibited, with information on how often the films were screened. This is, of course, beyond our grasp. What we are able to do, however, is analyze domestic production statistics from the explosion of mass-produced mass-market motion pictures around 1908 to 1920, a point at which the feature-centered exhibition model was universal. Such an inventory would have been virtually inconceivable until recently, since the task entails compiling information on roughly forty-two thousand films. Thanks to ambitious cataloging programs and computerization, however, a comprehensive inventory is now possible.

This statistical overview I have generated is the work of others—I simply have brought together data from several sources. Information on feature films was derived from *The American Film Institute Catalog of Feature Films, 1911–1920*, or, to be more precise, from a statistical table summarizing that catalog created by Alan Gevinson.[2] As yet, no AFI catalog is available for short films in the 1910s, so I used data derived from Einar Lauritzen and Gunnar Lundquist's two-volume *American Film-Index* (which covers 1908 to 1920, although I only used its data for 1911 to 1920).[3] For the years 1908 to 1910 I was able to use the volume of the AFI catalog entitled *Film Beginnings, 1893–1910*.[4] For newsreels and cartoons, two important varieties of short film, I used the comprehensive inventories available in Raymond Fielding's survey, *The American Newsreel, 1911–1967*, and Denis Gifford's catalog, *American Animated Films: The Silent Era, 1897–1929*.[5] Taken together, the data from these sources account for the vast majority of American films made between 1908 and 1920. Some proportion of films surely slipped through the cracks but probably not enough to significantly affect the overall picture of shorts versus features.

Figure 4.1 provides an overview of film production in the United States between 1908 and 1920. It shows year-by-year statistics on films of every length, from half-reel shorts to thirteen-reel superfeatures.[6] Figure 4.2 aggregates the data into shorts (films three reels and less) and features (four reels and longer). The relative percentage of shorts versus features for each year is compared in figure 4.3. Figure 4.4 and 4.5 provide more detail by showing the numbers and percentages of total reels produced rather than just titles.

I should also reiterate that simple data on the number of titles and reels produced are not the best possible indicators of trends in the industry. Statistics on the number of prints sold or the number of actual screenings of shorts vs. features would provide a more accurate picture of the commercial situation.[7] Nevertheless, on the principle that in a free market supply follows demand, I believe it is fair to proceed on the provisional assumption that an enumeration of titles and reels does serve as at least a rough index of market conditions.[8] Another methodological issue that must be acknowledged is that the data only cover domestic film production and therefore do not perfectly reflect the actual numbers of films distributed in the United States. European films were incredibly important for several years during the initial flourishing of mass-market cinema in America. In 1908, for example, over three-quarters of the films distributed in the United States were imports.[9] This fact must be underscored for the sake of historical accuracy, but for our purposes—analyzing the ratio of shorts to features from

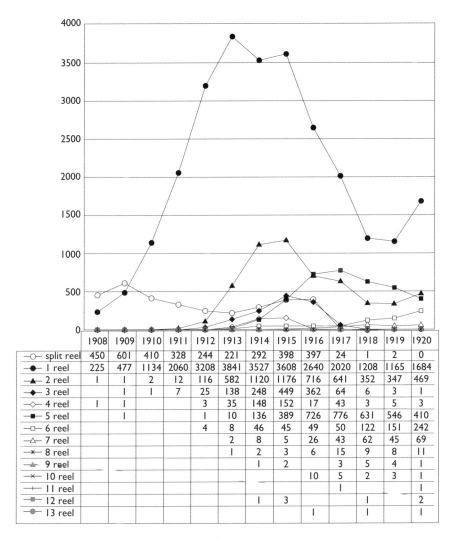

	1908	1909	1910	1911	1912	1913	1914	1915	1916	1917	1918	1919	1920
—○— split reel	450	601	410	328	244	221	292	398	397	24	1	2	0
—●— 1 reel	225	477	1134	2060	3208	3841	3527	3608	2640	2020	1208	1165	1684
—▲— 2 reel	1	1	2	12	116	582	1120	1176	716	641	352	347	469
—◆— 3 reel		1	1	7	25	138	248	449	362	64	6	3	1
—◇— 4 reel	1	1			3	35	148	152	17	43	3	5	3
—■— 5 reel		1			1	10	136	389	726	776	631	546	410
—□— 6 reel					4	8	46	45	49	50	122	151	242
—△— 7 reel					2	8	5	26	43	62	45	69
—✳— 8 reel					1	2	3	6	15	9	8	11
—✦— 9 reel						1	2		3	5	4	1
—✕— 10 reel								10	5	2	3	1
—+— 11 reel									1			1
—■— 12 reel						1	3			1		2
—●— 13 reel								1		1		1

Figure 4.1 American films by reel, 1908–1920.

year to year—it is adequate to focus exclusively on domestic production (as we must, given the data currently available for the 1910s), since inclusion of data on imports would not significantly alter the statistical profile.[10]

The statistics reveal that the feature craze was not a tidal-wave phenomenon that instantly wiped out the short film as soon as it hit the industry. The feature's trajectory of growth was indeed remarkably steady and steep, but it was not as immediately overwhelming as we are used to thinking. We see

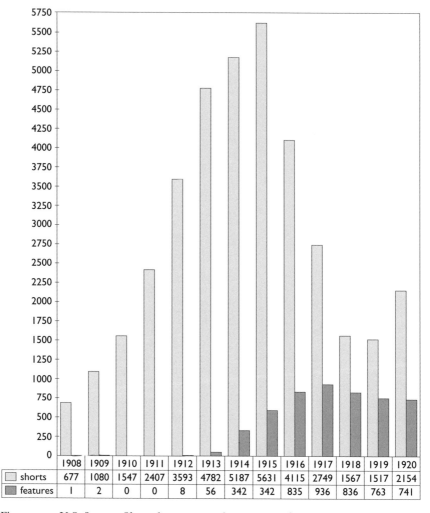

	1908	1909	1910	1911	1912	1913	1914	1915	1916	1917	1918	1919	1920
shorts	677	1080	1547	2407	3593	4782	5187	5631	4115	2749	1567	1517	2154
features	1	2	0	0	8	56	342	342	835	936	836	763	741

Figure 4.2   U.S. feature films, shorts versus features, 1908–1920.

that American feature production increased more than sevenfold from 1912 to 1913, but features nevertheless accounted for only one film in one hundred. Features increased again by over 500 percent in 1914, but as impressive as that sounds, they still constituted only one film out of sixteen, a mere 6 percent of the total. And in 1915 a full 90 percent of American productions were short films. Production of features was escalating sharply, but—and this is perhaps the most intriguing discovery—short films also main-

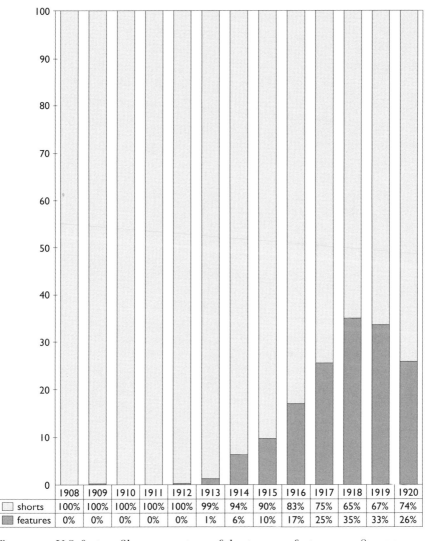

Figure 4.3 U.S. feature films, percentage of shorts versus features, 1908–1920.

tained a solid rate of growth. The production of shorts did not nose-dive during the high-profile feature-craze years of 1913, 1914, and 1915—on the contrary, it showed a respectable increase. This is an unexpected finding. It certainly complicates the usual assumption that features rapidly killed off shorts except for the few needed as fillers.

Granted, the 1913–1915 increase in shorts was not as spectacular as their

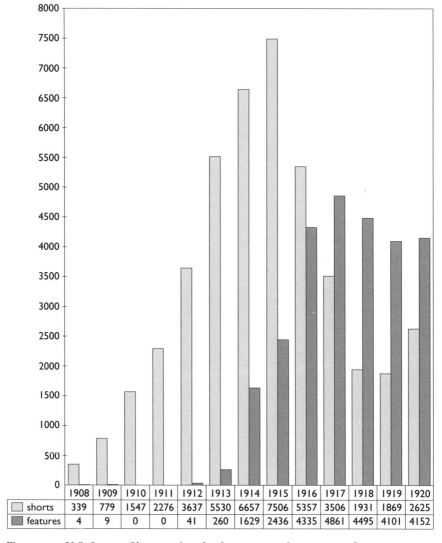

	1908	1909	1910	1911	1912	1913	1914	1915	1916	1917	1918	1919	1920
☐ shorts	339	779	1547	2276	3637	5530	6657	7506	5357	3506	1931	1869	2625
■ features	4	9	0	0	41	260	1629	2436	4335	4861	4495	4101	4152

Figure 4.4 U.S. feature films, total reels, shorts versus features, 1908–1920.

literally exponential annual growth between 1908 and 1912, during the nickelodeon boom and the rationalization of production and distribution by the Motion Picture Patents Company and the Independents.[11] (Figure 4.2 illustrates just how remarkably close to an exact exponential curve the 1908–1912 production numbers conform.) The number of shorts had grown by 60 percent in 1909 and then by about 50 percent a year, give or

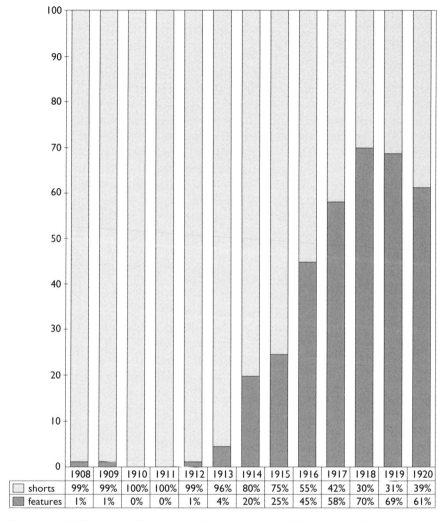

Figure 4.5 U.S. feature films, total reels, percentage of shorts versus features, 1908–1920.

take, for the next three years. In 1913, a year marked by a number of feature-film blockbusters, shorts increased about 33 percent. In both 1914 and 1915, by which time the feature had supposedly "triumphed almost completely," the production of shorts continued to grow at 8.5 percent each year—not nearly as strong as before but still a growth rate most industries would consider excellent.

One might object that some of the increase is attributable to a boost in the production of three-reelers. This length was a half-measure that the short-film producers hoped would stave off demand for features without disrupting their ensconced system of distribution and sales. Three-reelers had an ambiguous status: "They are too long for regular service, but not long enough to be features," one exchange man complained in late 1914.[12] "The line on three reels is a close one between 'feature' and 'daily release,'" concurred a *Variety* columnist. But, he continued, there was no ambiguity about what constituted a bona fide feature: "'Features' are now accounted as four reels or more."[13] Before long, three-reelers were invariably grouped with shorts. As Essanay's president affirmed in mid-1916, "The feature of more than three reels in length—the most gigantic development in the business—is here to stay, but it shall never completely obliterate the one, two and three reel pictures from which it sprang."[14]

In any case even if we disregard three-reelers, the production of shorts still grew at a decent rate during the "feature craze." This finding suggests that two different models of exhibition—the "variety program" and the feature program—both flourished, or at least shared an expanding market, for several years after the introduction of the feature film. This may sound odd to us today, but at the time, many voices in the industry downplayed the notion that the two models were in direct competition with each other. There was a belief (or at least a hope articulated as a belief) that these were simply two separate and parallel modes of exhibition, each with its own distinct niche. They both had a purpose and place; there was room enough for both to coexist and prosper, just as vaudeville and legitimate drama—their prototypes—had done for decades.[15] "Each has its place," stated the head of Essanay (who, of course, had a vested interest in the matter), "and each is going to occupy that place in the picture play world. . . . Each will settle into its rightful field without encroaching upon the other."[16]

Such a view would have been most viable before around 1915. Until then, features had not made much of an incursion into mainstream movie-theater exhibition. They belonged, for the most part, to an essentially different circuit comprising playhouses, concert halls, and general-purpose auditoriums. Moreover, features usually were not regular or permanent fare but rather occasional short-term offerings. They often played just on Sundays or in the summer theatrical off-season, filling some of the "dark" gaps in the schedules of legitimate theaters.

The separateness of feature exhibition was reinforced on a cultural level: its posh venues were the traditional domain of middle- and upper-class clienteles; its ticket prices reflected the comfortable means of that primary target audience; and its intertextual emphasis on prestigious works of literature and drama played by celebrated stage actors signaled high-culture credentials not found in run-of-the-mill films playing in run-of-the-mill variety-program movie theaters. The primary audience of these nickelodeons and "slightly advanced store theaters" (i.e., moderately upgraded late nick-elodeons) were members of the blue-collar and low-white-collar working class. The predilections, expectations, and means of "the masses" or "common people" obviously differed from those of the "classes" that frequented legitimate theater.[17]

Features and shorts also presupposed fundamentally different practices of moviegoing and spectatorship. Variety-program producers and exhibitors championed the "transient" spectator—someone who had a limited amount of spare time and wanted to drop into a picture show without having to worry about missing scheduled show times, arriving in the middle of a film, or having to leave before the end. As a Kalem spokesperson argued in early 1915:

> In most theaters a considerable proportion of the receipts are derived from people who drop in at odd times and for short stays—men with an hour between engagements, women who want to rest after a tour of the shops. The pleasure of these members of an audience is not to be ignored, yet what is more meaningless than a picture when one misses essential facts in the exposition of a plot? The surest way to alienate transients of this description is to draw them into a theater and keep them for the best part of an hour guessing at a story they can't comprehend.[18]

The transient audience, exhibitors were reassured, preferred the convenience and economy of the "informal come-and-go-as-you-please theater" that offered a brief, continuously running, refreshed-daily, low-cost variety program.[19] An added advantage of the variety bill, producers and trade journals told exhibitors, was that it afforded the protection of diversification. The exhibitor did not put all his eggs in one basket: one bad movie would not spoil an entire program or run, and the multiplicity of narratives and genres ensured that a broad range of customer preferences could be satisfied.[20]

Shorts also enjoyed a number of logistical advantages. With a full-service program contract with one of the three established short-film distributors (General Film Co., Mutual, or Universal), booking was easy, supply reliable, and expenses stable and predictable. With feature films, on the other hand—at least before the establishment of feature program services at the end of 1914—supply was more erratic, and booking a full schedule of features usually involved the hassle of dealing with a number of different distributors, with new price negotiations and contracts for every film. And because features generally ran for three days or a week (with big hits staying in first-run theaters for weeks and months on end), advertising required more attention and expense than it did with shorts.

The ultimate advantage of the variety program was the low cost of film rental. A week's worth of short films that changed daily would cost a typical exhibitor around $50 or $60. Nickelodeons with the lowest earning power might pay only $10 to $15 a week. Principal cinemas in big cities would pay as much as $100 to $150. In comparison a Paramount feature screened in a big-city first-run house would cost between $500 and $700 a week. With Paramount's zone/clearance system, small-town (hence fourth- or fifth-run) theaters did pay considerably less but still would have to spend at least three or four times what they would for shorts.[21]

There were, in short, a number of compelling reasons—sociocultural, logistical, economic—why exhibitors might regard the variety-program and feature-program formats as sufficiently differentiated and autonomous to allow both to prosper. It is not surprising that many exhibitors wanted to stick with shorts. The fact that short-film releases increased between 1912 and 1915, at the same time that feature production was also increasing by leaps and bounds, reflected the continuing, if perhaps somewhat tentative, viability of the variety program for the large majority of movie theaters throughout the country.

A couple of other factors might also help explain why the feature craze did not send the number of shorts spiraling downward right away. Although it may sound ironic, the rise of features actually may have spurred demand for shorts for a few years, at least. First, the introduction of features prompted variety-program exhibitors to increase the number of reels in their programs in order to remain competitive. Although their theaters may have occupied a separate niche, as I have argued, features still represented competition in the larger amusement marketplace. The phenomenon of twelve-reel blockbusters undoubtedly altered the public's sense of what a movie show could be, making standard variety bills comprising two to four one-reelers and a song-slide sing-along seem just too skimpy.[22] A second reason features might have increased demand for shorts is that the spread of features created an auxiliary demand for shorts by virtue of the fact that two or three shorts were required to accompany the main attraction. The need for "fillers" expanded the market for shorts. Of course, that bonus would soon be greatly outweighed by the decline in overall demand, as more and more theaters switched to the feature-program format.

The decline, as figures 4.2 and 4.3 show, was stunningly severe and rapid. The short's free fall lasted for three years, 1916 through 1918. The production of shorts fell off 37 percent in 1916, then 50 percent in 1917, and another 57 percent in 1918. It stabilized for a couple of years (which I will discuss later) and then headed upward again by 42 percent in 1920. I am not sure how to explain the 1920 upswing, but it may have had something to do with stronger demand for all kinds of films during American cinema's postwar boom and (more hypothetically) perhaps also reflected a trend toward enhanced programs, with more added-attraction shorts, resulting from increasing competition between Paramount and First National.

The sharp decline between 1916 and 1918 corresponded to a steady erosion in the key differences (described earlier) that previously had separated the original feature-film circuit and the broader mainstream of movie exhibition. No longer booked primarily into legitimate playhouses, features spread rapidly into full-time movie theaters across the country. A number of developments catalyzed this migration. A crucial element was the regularization of the supply of feature films. Mainstream exhibitors needed to be able to count on a sufficient and reliable supply of feature subjects that could be booked efficiently from just a few sources or, if possible, from a single supplier. Beginning around mid-1914, the feature distribution business underwent a major transfiguration from a haphazard regional enterprise fragmented among hundreds of state rights firms to a national enterprise dominated by about ten big companies.[23] The organizations that had already controlled the distribution of shorts—Universal, Mutual, the General Film Co., and Pathé—adapted their operations to handle features alongside their usual programs of shorts. More significant was the rapid proliferation of new nationwide exchange networks devoted to features, including Paramount (formed mid-1914); World (mid-1914); Fox (early 1915); Metro (early 1915); V-L-S-E (mid-1915), and Triangle (late 1915).

These new national distributors represented an important departure from the state rights system, in which producers sold their films outright to sundry independent regional distributors scattered across the country. Although this system survived (since it gave unaffiliated European studios and small startup producers a channel into the market), it was inefficient and costly for larger producers because it required an army of salesmen and myriad negotiations and contracts. It was also financially disadvantageous for producers, since state rights distributors often drove hard bargains, recognizing that they had the upper hand: studios needed cash to recoup production expenses, and without the assistance of regional distributors films would sit idle. A more important reason producers disliked the state rights system was that the practice of selling films outright to distributors meant that studios made only so much from a film, regardless of its box-office success. State rights firms reaped all the benefit from big hits—a situation obviously distasteful to those responsible for manufacturing the hits. This problem was solved through partial vertical integration—combining production and distribution under one roof—and through profit-sharing agreements between producers and distributors.

In the vertically integrated firms the production branch of the company supplied the distribution branch (usually set up as a subsidiary company) with most of the films to be distributed. However, most of the new national distributors—including studio-owned subsidiaries—formed alliances with an array of producers. In exchange for exclusive distribution rights, the distributor would provide producers assured nationwide saturation and a set percentage (typically two-thirds) of the booking profits. This new single-distributor/profit-sharing model proved considerably more efficient and lucrative for producers. With their increased revenues, combined, in many cases, with set advances fronted by the distributor to help finance each film, studios were able to expand their production of features.

Now, with an adequate supply of features and a rationalized system of distribution, it became increasingly plausible for ordinary movie theaters to begin offering feature programs. Paramount—by far the biggest and most influential distributor—made the switch particularly easy for exhibitors by introducing, in late 1914, the first full-service program of features. It was the feature-film equivalent of the full-service program-package booking system long used for shorts. Exhibitors contracted for a year's worth of films and received two features per week (each one playing for three or four days). Exhibitors that signed on assumed a long-term commitment, were prohibited from acquiring films from other distributors, had no say in what titles they received, and had to follow Paramount's dictates concerning minimum ticket prices and length of runs. In return, however, exhibitors benefited from the security and efficiency of a carefree standing-order booking service, strong clearance protection (i.e., no competing theaters could show the same films), and access to big films with superior production values and the most popular stars.[24]

Feature programs, however, were expensive to rent, as noted earlier. They made the most financial sense for venues that were able to justify charging three or four times—and up to ten or twenty times—more than the standard nickel and that possessed large seating capacity to allow high-volume sales of these more-expensive tickets. The theaters that fit those requirements most readily were the legitimate theaters of the sort that had first showcased big features: they were suitably grand—both with respect to opulence and size—and they were patronized by a clientele that was already accustomed to paying premium prices for high-quality entertainment. The feature's mid-decade spread into mainstream exhibition was spearheaded by the widespread adoption by legitimate theaters of full-time motion picture policies. There was also a boom in the construction of fancy new large theaters, many with seating for between fifteen hundred and three thousand patrons. These "picture palaces" were a direct outgrowth of cinema's new feature-centered commercial calculus: higher quality films and higher quality viewing environments generated greater public demand for cinema, which, in conjunction with higher admissions and higher seating capacities, ultimately yielded higher profit. In short, costs were much greater, but so were the returns.

The feature's domination of mainstream exhibition, however, would require its adoption beyond just top-echelon big theaters. The vast majority of theaters in the country remained small or middling unpretentious theaters—rural theaters, "neighborhood theaters," vestigial downtown nickelodeons, and worn-out larger venues. As the data on the rise of features and decline of shorts suggest, by 1918 the feature-program had succeeded in colonizing all these venues, forcing the unfit out of business. It was a painful transition for many rank-and-file exhibitors. With their small capacities, low admissions, humble trappings, and modest socioeconomic demographics, many small theaters had great difficulty affording the expensive feature services. Competition from grander houses further intensified their plight. As one fretful exhibitor proclaimed in an early 1917 trade journal article appropriately titled "Is the Small Theatre Utterly Doomed?": "We cannot compete with the big house by paying the prices demanded for first-run features; then, too, is the atmosphere, music, etc. of the big house, appealing directly to the classes."[25]

Small theaters had a number of options available to them as they tried to deal with the commercial upheaval wrought by the feature-film revolution:

1. They could stick with the inexpensive variety program and hope that all the trade journal reassurances about the fundamental soundness of that paradigm (the transient market, the advantages of diversification, etc.) were valid. Maybe an occasional feature, perhaps on Sundays, could embellish the regular offerings.
2. In an enhanced version of option one, they could maintain the variety program but try to compete with the picture palaces by upgrading their houses—adding ushers, expanding the orchestra, putting in plusher seats, etc.—praying that customer loyalty and raised ticket prices would keep them afloat.
3. They could try to put together feature programs culled from cheap state rights suppliers or discount national distributors and undercut the bigger theaters on price.
4. They could try to "live off the crumbs the big fellow leaves" (i.e., wait for second-run [or third-, fourth- and fifth-run] features from the major studios).[26]
5. They could go out of business.

It was not an easy choice, and small exhibitors often vacillated. A case study shows this vividly. The Colonial Theater in Lexington, Kentucky—one of the venues that Gregory Waller examines in his valuable study *Main Street Amusements*—illustrates the exhibitors' quandary.[27] A purpose-built 400-seat movie house, the Colonial opened in mid-1911, screening short films from 10 A.M. to 11 P.M. and charging a nickel. Richly decorated, and boasting two doormen and five ushers in uniform, the theater touted itself as a "picture palace." "Fancy nickelodeon" would probably be more apt: it certainly was a much more commodious and self-consciously well-heeled outfit than the makeshift storefront theaters associated with the early nickelodeon boom, but its size, admission, operating hours, and programs were essentially the same as any standard nickelodeon. The Colonial's shows consisted of just two (and, rarely, three) reels, changed daily, along with an illustrated song accompanied by a pianist. After adding one hundred seats in early 1913, the theater raised admission to a dime, and programs were expanded to four reels, with three singers, a pianist, and a six-piece orchestra. In response to the opening, in late 1913, of two much larger and grander theaters nearby (one a 930-seat vaudeville house that screened film programs on Sundays; the other a 1,400-seat multipurpose legitimate theater that intermittently presented big road-show features like *Quo Vadis?*, *Les Miserables*, and *Neptune's Daughter* before switching over entirely to feature programs in mid-1915), the Colonial increased its program, once more, to six reels. A short while later it changed its exhibition policy entirely and tried to compete head-to-head with the larger theaters by offering "all feature bills," with films from Paramount, World, or Alco changed four times a week. The orchestra was also enlarged again, first to nine then to twelve pieces. These ambitious upgrades soon proved financially untenable. "The cost of booking feature films and maintaining a good-sized orchestra," Waller notes, "was economically feasible only for those Lexington theaters that were double or triple the size of the Colonial."[28] Consequently, the exhibitor switched back to variety programs and maintained that policy for a couple of years. In 1916 the owner took another stab at an "all features" policy, but that tack quickly failed once again. Outclassed, or, more accurately, outsized, by its competition, the Colonial went out of business for good in January 1917. A more run-of-the-mill nickelodeon owned by the same exhibitor (the 350-seat Star) had already closed down a year earlier. The exhibitor did not quit the business, however. Adapting to the new reality, he became part owner and general manager of a newly constructed picture palace, the 1,600-seat Strand. A grand purpose-built cinema completed in late 1915, the Strand was part of the wave of picture-palace construction following the epochal opening of New York's impressive 3,500-seat Strand Theater the year before.

With respect to the above list of strategies, the Colonial started out trying a combination of options 1 and 2, then changed course and adopted option 4, then reverted to option 1, then tried option 4 again, and finally acquiesced to option 5. Option 3—showing cheap, low-quality features—presumably was ruled out for both commercial and temperamental reasons. There simply may not have been an adequate market for cheap features. By definition, the feature film was (or was supposed to be) something special, something promising exceptional quality. Given the choice, probably most people would have been willing to pay a bit more to see better films, with more alluring stars, in nicer theaters. And the better shows might not even require paying more, since large theaters generally offered three ticket prices (typically ten, fifteen, and twenty-five cents), with the lowest admission generally comparable to all but the cheapest nickelodeons. As for temperamental reasons for eschewing the lowbrow option 3, the owner of the Colonial had worked hard to decorate and staff his theater like a miniature opera house. He clearly embraced bourgeois inclinations and aspirations. It would have been difficult for him to pursue a deliberate strategy of downward mobility, particularly since he had entrepreneurial ambitions and undoubtedly perceived that Lexington's three large theaters all grew out of alliances among members of the status-conscious local business elite—a club he very much wanted to join.

Option 4—renting second- or later-run films—was the tack that most small theaters ultimately followed. Several national distributors—especially Universal, Pathé, and Fox—catered to smaller downtown, neighborhood, and rural theaters, providing films at somewhat lower prices than first-tier distributors like Paramount. Even with reasonably priced subsequent-run titles, however, renting features was a big expense, one that kept profit margins slim—much slimmer than had been possible in the halcyon days before the rise of the feature.[29] And this solution still left small exhibitors vulnerable to debilitating competition from big theaters. Seeking advice from *Motion Picture News* in early 1917, the owner of the three-hundred-seat Orpheum Theater in a city of forty thousand people recounted this scenario, described by the trade journal as "typical of hundreds, yes, thousands of small theaters":

> I always ran short pictures until last June, when I found that my patronage was gradually leaving. . . . I reflected what to do and finally decided to offer second-run features. . . . I was successful for a time . . . but then I witnessed a gradual falling off, due to the fact that the "big" house offered a daily change, first-run, with fine orchestras, at the same admission. I had to charge on account of capacity [i.e., had to raise ticket prices to pay for the second-run features], and now I find that I am still a "filler" [i.e., a peripheral subordinate entity, like the short-film "filler" is to the feature]. Will someone tell me what to do?[30]

Motion Picture News had little to offer by way of advice. It expressed the hope that *high-quality* short subjects might attract an audience, but "for the meantime" it suggested that the exhibitor find second-run features that he was sure would not be "over the heads" of the "common people"—films that ordinary people would not find "flat." In other words, as I interpret this, it nudged the exhibitor toward films that were somewhat more popular and sensational (seemingly hinting toward option 3). But there was little conviction in the answer, and the journal ended the article by begging, "Will not some exhibitor who has solved this problem speak up and come to the rescue of brother exhibitors in the same fix?"

Option 1—keeping the variety program—was, from the very beginning of the feature revolution, the strategy preferred by a number of trade journals. *Motion Picture News* consistently supported the variety format, no doubt because it echoed the sentiments of the small exhibitors who made up the journal's primary readership. Small exhibitors were acutely aware that they could not compete with big-theater feature programs, and they needed reassurance that the exhibition system that had sustained them in the past would continue to do so in the future.

The *New York Dramatic Mirror* also supported the variety program but apparently for a different reason. Its columnists seemed less concerned with the well-being of the little guy than with preventing the little guy from jeopardizing the success of the big guy. The *Mirror* feared option 3—the prospect that small exhibitors would try to compete by screening whatever cheap, padded, poor-quality features they could afford. Bad features would tarnish the reputation of features as a whole and thwart cinema's campaign of bourgeois market expansion. The *Mirror* told small exhibitors to calm down and stay in their proper place:

> The irresponsible "feature" is at present one of the most pernicious evils with which the motion picture has to deal. The foreign film, with its antecedents unknown, or the domestic pictures made overnight, are doing more to blur the reputation of the motion picture than many of its obvious enemies. They are the first thought of a certain class of exhibitors when competition becomes keen. "Get me a feature," is the cry, and three or more reels of "fillum" are passed over the counter. Also a large assortment of the ever-precious "paper" [gaudy posters]. . . . To the neighborhood theater owner, whose house is too small to allow him to pay the cost of the real "big" features, the cheapness of the price of the "unknown" has, of course, its immediate appeal, especially when it is thought necessary to compete with the larger theater nearby. But it is doubtful even here if the small exhibitor would not be following a wiser course by giving a carefully chosen programme of regular releases, even if the programme is a trifle shorter than the competitor's. Let the variety make up for the lack of reel length, for variety is something you can give and he cannot.
>
> Where is Mr. Exhibitor with a house of moderate capacity to find his place in competition with the [emergence of powerful] larger interests? We have nothing to fear for the wise exhibitor, for the man who is a close student of his business. But there is a class of exhibitor for whom we see some exceedingly unpleasant moments ahead. This is the exhibitor who . . . at the sight of stiff competition immediately turns pale, and decides that in order to fight his rival he must immediately fall in line with him, and adopt the same methods. The coming condition will do more than anything in the past to draw the line between the different classes of motion picture theatres and it will be the fortunate exhibitor who can see his proper class, and aim for success in that class. There is room and a place for all lengths of pictures, all types of pictures, but pick out your particular field and don't attempt to embrace all.[31]

This position, subtly inflected by undertones of patronizing classism, called for a tidily stratified cinema: feature programs for big theaters (and, by implication, cultivated audiences), short programs for small theaters (and common audiences).

Many small exhibitors would have been perfectly content with such a division of the market were it at all viable. Option 1 was certainly the simplest and most affordable strategy. Shorts were inexpensive and demanded nothing more from exhibitors but that they maintain their usual mode of operation. In some cases theaters might even benefit from increased product differentiation and price appeal and decreased immediate competition (i.e., from other variety programs) as surrounding theaters shifted to features and raised ticket prices.[32]

Unfortunately, those advantages could not counter the one crucial problem with the variety program. The problem was simply that there was not very much interest in short films (with the exception of Chaplin comedies and a few other attractions) once audiences got a taste of spectacular features and glamorous stars. As the head of one short-reel studio conceded in 1916, "The country suddenly went feature mad."[33] No one could even think of claiming the public was "shorts mad."

Studios specializing in shorts tried hard to convince exhibitors that the "the doom of the long feature" was inevitable[34] and that "one reel films are distinctly in vogue again."[35] *Motion Picture News* maintained that a core market for shorts prevailed in small towns: "[Our] survey of demand . . . among the exhibitors of the great Middle West indicates clearly that the mixed program rules a favorite in the smaller towns and that short pictures are consequently in wide demand."[36] But it was a lost cause. By 1916 no one could deny that features had relegated shorts to a distinctly and irreversibly inferior status.[37] Shorts had to "bow to the multiple-reel feature with more complete humility than ever before."[38] Their producers soon revised their marketing pitch from "Stick with shorts!" to "Why not screen shorts two nights a week?"[39] By early 1917 *Motion Picture News* could offer little more than half-hearted optimism that the good old days would return: "We think the time is coming when there will be a reflex action, and the little pictures will come into their own again."[40]

Some exhibitors opted to stay with the variety program—option 1—despite its marginalization, not because they put faith in such hollow prognostications but because their particular size limitations and contexts of competition left them no other choice except to go out of business. The desperate owner of the Orpheum who had written to *Motion Picture News* for advice decided to revert to the variety program and offered daily changes of one- and two-reel comedies, westerns, and sensational-melodrama serials. With such a small house he had no choice but to avoid head-to-head competition with big-theater feature programs. The Orpheum settled into a humble niche as a second-rank (or lower) house, eking out an existence through such measures as using teenaged nonunion projectionists who were paid only half of what every other projectionist in town earned.[41] It is hard to imagine that the Orpheum provided its owner anything more than a meager subsistence income. The audience simply was not there. "Time was," he grumbled, "when I played to more people on my two worst days than I am able to get during an entire week now."[42]

The crucial factor undermining the viability of the variety program was the increasing commercial salience of the star system.[43] Features became the sole showcase for stars. Variety-program exhibitors complained bitterly that they had been disenfranchised, robbed of the most essential element for attracting customers. As one small-theater owner protested:

> Time is not so far distant when the General, Universal, and Mutual made only subjects of one, two and three reels, which, if they had been maintained in their entirety would have always left a clientele for the small house. But all of a sudden they conceived the idea that they must make features, which was perfectly all right, but why take the stars that meant the very existence of the small house, and, with the taking of each one, a certain percentage of its clientele? . . . Mr. Laemmle [head of Universal] has issued more than 150 "Straight from the Shoulder Talks" urging us thousands of exhibitors to stick to the program, but every time one of his players became well enough known, they were taken away from me, and my patrons went with them.[44]

When a columnist for *Motion Picture News* discussed this grievance, and the industry's general abandonment of shorts, in an interview with an unnamed studio executive, the executive's stance was a telling mixture of "it's not our fault—blame the talent" and "that's the way it is—get used to it": "The writers want to write features, the stars want to act in them, the directors want to produce them. Only two of our directors are willing . . . to produce short length subjects, and they are our most capable and far-seeing; we need them on features. As for the stars, we can do nothing with them. They simply will not act in short subjects."[45]

With their talent raided, their products lacking box-office appeal, orders evaporating, and their financial resources dwarfed by those of savvier competitors, many shorts manufacturers—especially former members of the MPPC (which recently had been ruled illegal on antitrust grounds)—went out of business. Kalem and Lubin ceased production in 1916. Edison and Biograph quit in 1917. Essanay and Selig closed down in 1918. Universal terminated its full-service program of shorts in mid-1917, although it continued making two-reel westerns and comedies.

As for the vagaries of the variety program, we know very little about the precise trajectory of its decline. We know that it fell off rapidly after 1915 (but not earlier, as I discussed above), but that is still a pretty vague delineation. To my knowledge no one has unearthed any hard data surveying the actual number of variety programs that survived throughout the country in specific years. It is probably fair to assume, however, that the decline of this format more or less mirrored the decline in the production of shorts. I propose to use that data—or, more specifically, data on the number of *reels* produced (figures 4.4 and 4.5) to gain a more detailed understanding of the variety program's decline.

We can start by asking in what year *did* the variety program finally become extinct (or all but extinct)? At what point were all film exhibitors (or let us say 99 percent of them) running feature programs exclusively? To answer this question using production data, we need to find out at what point manufacturers produced only as many reels of film as would have been needed to make up feature programs *only*—that is, without any "extra" supply produced for the needs of variety programs. Of course, this method cannot purport to be anything but an academic exercise. There are far too many unknown variables that one would need to factor in (such as the number of prints produced or the number of times the prints were screened). The results yielded by looking simply at production data, however, appear strikingly on target.

In the late 1910s the typical feature program was composed of a five- or six-reel feature plus two or three reels of shorts.[46] For our purposes we will average these: feature-film programs contained an average of 5.5 feature-film reels and 2.5 short-film reels. That translates into a percentage ratio of 69 percent feature-film reels and 31 percent short-film reels. The question, then, is this: at what point did manufacturers produce about 69 percent feature reels and 31 percent shorts? The assumption is that the production of features vs. shorts would stabilize at something very close to that ratio once the feature program had become the universal norm and variety shows had all but disappeared. If we look at the data in figure 5, we see that this is *precisely* (!) the ratio of feature-film reels to short-film reels released in 1918 and 1919. I believe we can infer from this perfect correspondence that the variety program had virtually vanished by 1918.

The data also enable us to calculate the number of variety programs that lingered on during the previous years of rapid decline, assuming, again, that the "excess" production of short reels—that is, those short reels over and above the amount needed for feature programs—represents reels needed for variety-program theaters. By this measure we find that in 1915 almost two out of three movie theaters employed the variety-program format; in 1916 more than one third did so; and about one theater in six maintained that policy through 1917.[47] These are depleted but not utterly insignificant portions of the exhibition market. It means that almost ten thousand theaters across the country were presenting all-shorts programs in 1915; more than five thousand kept with the variety program through 1916; and almost twenty-five hundred theaters persevered showing just shorts for another year after that.

A very small number of theaters continued running variety programs into the 1920s. In fact, the Orpheum Theater described earlier managed to subsist showing virtually nothing but shorts all the way to 1930. It is hard to imagine that more than a few dozen such holdovers from the nickelodeon era (if that many) survived until the dawn of sound. But this remains an open question, one that scholars researching rural exhibition might help answer. However many variety-program theaters may have lingered on through the 1920s, there is no question that they were already anachronisms by the late 1910s. For the vast majority of moviegoers a cinema of short films—films without big stories, grand spectacles, and charismatic stars—simply fell short.

NOTES

1. David A. Cook, *A History of Narrative Film*, 3d ed. (New York: Norton, 1996), 38.

2. Alan Gevinson, "The Birth of the American Feature Film," *The Path to Hollywood, 1911–1920*, ed. Paolo Cherchi Usai and Lorenzo Codelli (Pordenone: Edizioni Biblioteca dell'Immagine, 1988), 132–55. *The American Film Institute Catalog of Motion Pictures Produced in the United States: Feature Films, 1911–1920* (Berkeley: University of California Press, 1988).

3. Einar Lauritzen and Gunnar Lundquist, *American Film-Index 1908–1915* (Stockholm: University of Stockholm Akademiebokhandeln, 1976); Lauritzen and Lundquist, *American Film-Index, 1916–1920* (Stockholm: Huddinge/Tonnheims, 1984). Paul Spehr has transposed that index into a computer database, enabling one to extract year-by-year statistics on film output and lengths (by number of reels). I would like to thank Paul and Larry Karr for their willingness to generate statistical breakdowns by year and reel especially for this essay. (Spehr used the database in a different way, grouping the data according to personal and corporate names, to generate a reference volume entitled *American Film Personnel and Company Credits, 1908–1920* (Jefferson, N.C.: McFarland, 1996).

4. *The American Film Institute Catalog of Motion Pictures Produced in the United States: Film Beginnings, 1893–1910; A Work in Progress* (Metuchen, N.J.: Scarecrow Press, 1995). An online version is available from Chadwyck-Healey (www.chadwyck.com). I used the AFI data for the years 1908, 1909, and 1910 because even though the *Film Beginnings* volume is described as a work in progress, it is more exhaustive than *American Film Index*. Lauritzen and Lundquist relied almost entirely on information found in just one trade journal, *Moving Picture World*, whereas the AFI catalog drew from many sources. I would not have been able to use the *AFI Catalog* data if not for the searchable online version. However, the search fields provided are not ideally suited for my research. With a bit of ingenuity one is able to determine the number of American films released, although they don't make it easy, since there are no search tags for U.S.-produced films, although there are for foreign films. Unfortunately, it is not possible to extract summary data on film lengths. To get information on film lengths, one must slog through all the film entries individually. *Film Beginnings, 1893–1910* differs from later AFI catalog volumes in that it includes entries not only for domestic productions but also for foreign films distributed in the United States. (The poorly annotated online version fails to indicate this.) My samples for 1908 to 1910 only include American films in order to maintain consistency with the data for later years. The implications of leaving out foreign films in this study are discussed in note 10.

5. Raymond Fielding, *The American Newsreel, 1911–1967* (Norman: University of Oklahoma Press, 1972). Fielding supplies data on newsreels per year (one reel each): 25 in 1911; 114 in 1912; 191 in 1913; 514 in 1914; 714 in 1915; 592 in 1916; 413 in 1917; 238 in 1918; 290 in 1919; 482 in 1920. Denis Gifford, *American Animated Films: The Silent Era, 1897–1929* (Jefferson, N.C.: McFarland, 1990). Gifford gives data on animated films per year: 1 in 1909; 1 in 1911; 1 in 1912; 78 in 1913; 44 in 1914; 130 in 1915; 346 in 1916; 273 in 1917; 201 in 1918; 193 in 1919; 387 in 1920.

6. One reel became standardized around 1910 as consisting of roughly one thousand feet of film. However, in 1908 and 1909 very few films were a thousand feet long, so I have allowed a slightly looser definition of a reel to include any film over 750 feet. A "split reel" would be anything shorter than 750 feet. In my statistical tables counting total reels of production, split reels are averaged as equivalent to half a reel.

7. An illustration makes this point clear: if a studio's production numbers showed that shorts increased by, say, 30 percent in a given year, it would look like an impressive gain, suggesting an increase in demand. But if the number of *prints* sold of each film dropped by fifty percent, then that inference would be mistaken.

8. This assumption is somewhat problematic since many factors other than demand hypothetically could affect the numbers of titles produced. Intangible human and institutional factors such as inertia, indecision, pride, denial, etc. might influence a studio's decisions. Using production numbers as an indication of demand could also be problematic in the case of increased consolidation in the industry. With increased consolidation one could expect the number of competing titles to decrease, yet this probably would not reflect any decrease in demand (as measured by the total number of prints, not titles, generated). One could even imagine a scenario in which the number of titles produced might be inversely proportionate to demand. This would happen if a studio *increased* production to try to compensate for a declining number of prints ordered of each title. If a studio were no longer able to sell thirty copies of ten films, perhaps it might try to stabilize income by selling ten copies of thirty films. (I thank Charlie Musser for mentioning this hypothetical to me in an e-mail correspondence.) I am not aware of any instances of such a strategy, however. When, in late 1914, the Edison studio found orders for its short films decreasing rapidly, it sought to revive profit by, on the one hand, cutting costs and, on the other, instituting quality-control evaluation systems designed to improve the appeal of their films. Neither measure was successful, which is not surprising given that the clampdown on budgets made it even more difficult for directors to make appealing films. On the cost-cutting measures see Charles Musser, *Before the Nickelodeon: Edwin S. Porter and the Edison Manufacturing Company* (Berkeley: University of California Press, 1991), 471–73.

9. Statistics for 1908 to 1910 (and before) can be calculated using the online version of the *AFI Catalog*.

10. As far as I am aware, no one has as yet compiled comprehensive data on the number and lengths of imported films exhibited in the United States between 1911 and 1920. In *Exporting Entertainment* Kristin Thompson samples film-release schedules that were printed in *Moving Picture World* in 1907 through 1914. Using that analysis of the market share of imports, one can see that adding imported films ultimately would have little effect on a statistical overview. Including imports would mean that there would be many more shorts to take into account before 1914 but since shorts

already accounted for such a vast majority of films, the percentage of shorts would simply edge slightly nearer to 100. The number of pre-1914 features would also increase considerably if foreign films were taken into account, but, again, features were so overwhelmingly outnumbered by shorts that the ratio of features to shorts would hardly change at all. After 1914 one might expect imported features to have a much larger impact, given the great escalation in feature-film production. But by that time, imported films possessed a much smaller share of the American market than in earlier years because of the rationalization and expansion of domestic production and the disruption of European production by World War I. Thompson found that foreign shorts released in the United States fell from 50–70 percent in 1907 and 1908 to a mere 5 percent by the end of 1914. No statistics are given for feature films, but the decline was probably similar. In October 1914 a *Variety* columnist noted "the practical elimination of the foreign feature as a competitor." See Kristin Thompson, *Exporting Entertainment: America in the World Film Market, 1907–34* (London: British Film Institute, 1985), 213–14; "Bright Outlook for Features with Shortage of Supply," *Variety*, 10 October 1914, 23.

11. On the rationalization of production and distribution see Eileen Bowser, *The Transformation of Cinema, 1907–1915* (New York: Scribner, 1990), chaps. 2 and 5.

12. Manager of the Cleveland Branch of the General Film Co., quoted by L. C. McChesney in an internal memo of the Edison Manufacturing Company dated 24 October 1914. Box 1914 MP (2 of 6), Edison National Historic Site, West Orange, N.J.

13. "Features for Ten Cent Houses," *Variety*, 3 October 1914, 19.

14. George K. Spoor, "Short Films to Stay," *New York Dramatic Mirror*, 8 July 1916, 33.

15. The comparison with vaudeville and legitimate drama was made, for example, by a *Variety* columnist in 1914: "The feature picture occupies the same relative position to the moving picture form of entertainment as a legitimate playhouse does to a vaudeville show" ("General Film Show," *Variety*, 1 May 1914, 21).

16. Spoor, "Short Films to Stay," 33.

17. For the phrase "slightly advanced store theaters" and a discussion of the different audiences drawing the familiar "mass vs. class" distinction see "Comment and Suggestion," *New York Dramatic Mirror*, 8 April 1914, 31; see also "Is the Small Theatre Utterly Doomed?" *Motion Picture News*, 10 March 1917, 1530.

18. William Wright, "Short Films the Best," *New York Dramatic Mirror*, 27 January 1915, 42.

19. Spoor, "Short Films to Stay," 33.

20. For an articulation of this view see William N. Selig, "Present Day Trend in Film Lengths," *Moving Picture World*, 11 July 1914, 81.

21. On film rental costs see Benjamin Hampton, *History of the American Film Industry: From Its Beginnings to 1931* (1931; repr., New York: Dover, 1970), 122; Richard Koszarski, *An Evening's Entertainment: The Age of the Silent Feature Picture, 1915–1928* (New York: Scribner, 1990), 10, 15; Bowser, *Transformation of Cinema*, 33; Michael Joseph Quinn, "Early Feature Distribution and the Development of the Motion Picture Industry: Famous Players and Paramount, 1912–1921" (Ph.D. diss., University of Wisconsin–Madison, 1998), appendix 2.

22. An example of a variety-program theater increasing the number of shorts of-

fered in the face of competition from features is the Colonial Theater in Lexington, Kentucky, discussed later in this essay.

23. My discussion of distribution is informed especially by Quinn, "Early Feature Distribution"; and Hampton, *American Film Industry*, chap. 9. A very minor note on nomenclature: film historians today generally use the term *states' rights*. However, the period sources I have come across use the labels "state rights" or "state right." See, e.g., "State Rights Men Combine," *New York Dramatic Mirror*, 1 September 1917, 17; "State Right Bargains," *New York Dramatic Mirror*, 1 April 1914, 33; Joseph F. Lee, "The State Right Matter," *Variety*, 28 December 1917, 234.

24. This "program service" was the first of several distribution models that Paramount employed in the 1910s. Others included "selective booking" (or "open market" booking), which permitted exhibitors to pick and choose any number of films; "star series booking," which involved packages of films all featuring a given star; and "block booking," which, like the program service, required contracting for large packages of titles but involved groups of twenty-five films or so rather than an annual contract. See Quinn, "Early Feature Distribution."

25. "Small Theatre Utterly Doomed?" 1530.

26. Ibid.

27. Gregory Waller, *Main Street Amusements: Movies and Commercial Entertainment in a Southern City, 1896–1930* (Washington, D.C.: Smithsonian Institution Press, 1995), 86–98, 138–42.

28. Ibid., 89.

29. An interesting comparison of one exhibitor's operating costs in 1912 and 1922, originally published in *Film Daily Yearbook of Motion Pictures* (1922–23) is presented in Koszarski, *An Evening's Entertainment*, 14. It shows a gross weekly profit of $170 in 1912 and $12 in 1922. Adjusting for inflation, the 1912 figure would be worth about $85 in 1922 dollars.

30. "Small Theatre Utterly Doomed?" 1530. The author of this letter, I discovered, was none other than John Stamper, one of the Lexington, Kentucky, exhibitors whose career Gregory Waller chronicled in *Main Street Amusements*. Waller was not aware of the *Motion Picture News* article, so it is a wonderful coincidence and a helpful one since it enables us to match up Stamper's first-person testimonial with the information Waller unearthed.

31. "Comment and Suggestion," *New York Dramatic Mirror*, 22 April 1914, 27; "Comment and Suggestion," *New York Dramatic Mirror*, 15 April 1914, 32.

32. For examples of theaters positioning themselves to take advantage of such benefits see "B'way Features to Herald Sq." and "Does Advertising Pay?" *Variety*, 1 May 1914, 18, 20.

33. Spoor, "Short Films to Stay," 33.

34. Carl Laemmle, "Doom of Long Features Predicted," *Moving Picture World*, 11 July 1914, 185.

35. Wright, "Short Films the Best," 42.

36. William A. Johnston, "Small House and Short Film," *Motion Picture News*, 21 October 1916, 1. It makes sense that small-town theaters would favor mixed programs. In locales with more competition big theaters put small variety-program theaters at a disadvantage, but in small towns, with little competition and a preponderance of small theaters, that problem was not so pressing.

37. Carl Laemmle, "Doom of Long Features Predicted," *Moving Picture World*, 11 July 1914, 185; see also Wright, "Short Films the Best."

38. Tom Ince, "The Feature Has a Future," *Moving Picture World*, 14 August 1915, 1166.

39. "George K. Spoor Urges Varied Program Use," *Motion Picture News*, 25 August 1917, 1262.

40. "Small Theatre Utterly Doomed?" 1530.

41. The detail about nonunion projectionists is from Waller, *Main Street Amusements*, 197.

42. "Small Theatre Utterly Doomed?" 1530.

43. On the star system "revolution" see Hampton, *American Film Industry*, chaps. 5 and 8; Tino Balio, ed., *The American Film Industry*, rev. ed. (Madison: University of Wisconsin Press, 1985), 113–16; Richard deCordova, *Picture Personalities: The Emergence of the Star System in America* (Urbana: University of Illinois Press, 1990).

44. "Small Theatre Utterly Doomed?" 1530.

45. William A. Johnston, "Small House and Short Film," *Motion Picture News*, 21 October 1916, 1.

46. "Statistics of the Motion Picture Industry," *Motion Picture News*, 18 November 1922, 2527. This source presents information from a survey mailed to ten thousand exhibitors. The number of actual respondents is not indicated.

47. The estimate works like this: For any given year, we have a figure for the total number of feature-film reels produced (using the data from table 4.1), and we know that that figure represents 69 percent of the reels presented within feature-film programs. We can then calculate the remaining 31 percent—the short reels filling out the feature program. That number of shorts is then subtracted from the *total* number of shorts produced in that year. What remains is, according to my hypothesis, the number of short reels slated for variety-program theaters.

PART TWO

The Transitional Screen

New Genres, Cultural Shifts

What Happened in the Transition?

Reading Race, Gender, and Labor between the Shots

Jacqueline Stewart

Black images in transitional cinema are, not surprisingly, heavily informed by stereotypes prevalent in turn-of-the-century American popular culture. They reflect the kinds of racist imagery that had found its way into the earliest footage of Blacks, even ostensibly nonfiction films, dating back to the 1890s.[1] They also feature Black stereotypes that would be developed further within the classical narrative paradigm as codified by the late 1910s. However, the ways in which film historians have described the familiar figures of "tom," "coon," "mulatto," "mammy," and "buck" do not fully account for the significant and often surprising manner in which many Black representations are constructed in American cinema during the shift from early attractions to narrative integration.[2] In fact, with the exception of the comic "coon," the stock Black types enumerated above make rare and rather inconsistent appearances until the rise of the multishot narrative film (between roughly 1903 and 1907), making the subsequent transitional years a crucial period in their cinematic elaboration. Unfortunately, developments in Black film images in preclassical cinema tend to be overlooked because of a general lack of discussion of race by historians of early cinema[3] and assumptions by scholars interested in Black representation that a monolithic racist sensibility dictates all Black images in mainstream silent film, epitomized by the African American stereotypes presented in D. W. Griffith's epic *The Birth of a Nation* (1915).[4]

The few critics who have surveyed Black images in films produced before *The Birth of a Nation* cannot help but note a seemingly anomalous film like Biograph's *A Bucket of Cream Ale* (1904), in which a Black maid dumps a foamy beverage over the head of her white employer.[5] Similar figures continue to transgress codes of behavior that would seem to be dictated by prevailing racial, gender, and class hierarchies in films produced over the next few years, clustered at the start of the transitional era: a laughing Black maid drops a bowl of soup all over a white man (her boss?) during a dinner party (*Laughing Gas*, Edison 1907, dir. Edwin S. Porter); a Black woman shopper at a department store bargain sale snatches items from the hands of white competitors (*Mixed Babies* [American Mutoscope and Biograph, 1908]); a Black woman applies for a job as a housekeeper where clearly a white woman is desired (*Nellie, the Beautiful Housemaid* [Vitagraph, 1908]).[6] These boisterous, aggressive, assuming Black female figures are not entirely without precedent in early cinema (as well as in minstrelsy and vaudeville), and they share characteristics with similar classical-era characters. What is significant about them is the degree to which narrative styles and structures, particularly editing, are organized around them. As Black female figures shift from objects of visual gags contained within one shot toward subjects with motivation and mobility elaborated across multiple shots, their presence frequently establishes the terms of continuity in narrative space and time, not to mention the terms of interracial interaction, as pictured onscreen. How can we understand the short-lived but striking appearance of these Black women in transitional cinema who are infused with agency that had been denied in early films and formal powers that do not survive into the classical period?

In this essay I explore how a sampling of Black female figures in transitional cinema perform visual and narrative functions that can complicate our understanding of the relationships between Black stereotypes and white audiences and between U.S. social/racial arrangements and the cinema's institutional and stylistic development. Produced by/at the intersection of historical shifts—in modes of cinematic address and in Black female laborer mobility—these figures allow us to see the layers of complexity beneath seemingly stable racial caricatures, as well as the use of different racial types for catering to and cultivating diverse white viewers. Unlike other frequently used Black types, Black female figures presented during the transitional era—typically portrayed as domestic workers—enjoy a unique and visible mobility across genres and between shots. Diverging from their male counterparts, the so-called "toms," these Black female domestics are presented as more overtly self-serving, autonomous, and sexually potent than their antebellum prototype. They also move relatively freely through (multiple) public spaces, frequently in contemporary, nonrural settings. In these ways transitional films make use of the cultural history of these Black female figures as traditional, known/knowable types, while also exploiting their roles as features of an unpredictable, modern landscape.

The mobility of Black female figures is particularly notable between 1907 and 1909, when their cultural identities and their sexuality frequently occupy center stage as they are reworked through developing cinematic narrative styles—from one-shot films to continuity editing techniques found in chase and linked-episode films. For a short time these figures produce in-novative (usually humorous) scenarios, and variations on familiar scenes, as they breech social hierarchies and boundaries, such as the relationship be-tween employer and employee, and the division between public and private spheres. I will describe how the transgressive political and sexual implica-tions of such representations of Black mobility and interracial interaction are increasingly highlighted and policed as the film industry works to trans-form itself into a legitimate and legitimizing entertainment for a multiclass, heterosocial, ethnically diverse but emphatically *white* moviegoing public. I trace the appearances of Black female domestics to consider how this set of representations demarcates an important moment of instability in the cin-ema's developing racial and stylistic codes; a moment when Black women continue to function as colored gags but also, very briefly, to migrate within transitional cinema's expanding boundaries of story, setting, and character construction.

The figures I describe might be called "mammies," since they are coded as Black and female, usually dark-skinned, usually large, and usually em-ployed as servants. Although they are clearly intended to evoke the mammy stereotype, even when housework is not explicitly represented, I resist using this term here because it obscures the overtly transgressive qualities these char-acters display in transitional films, qualities that are always present but more systematically suppressed and disavowed in other instantiations (from Stowe's Aunt Chloe to Aunt Jemima, from cookie jars to greeting cards, from the "faithful soul" in *The Birth of a Nation* to Hattie McDaniel in *Gone with the Wind*).[7] By describing them instead as Black female domestics, I want to call attention to the intersections of race, gender, and labor that condition their cinematic representations, particularly their sexuality as a locus of formal and thematic interest and anxiety. I refer to them as "domestics" to foreground the disrup-tions that their mobile bodies pose to notions of white domesticity (sanctity of the home, marriage, and family), the continued project of domesticating Black people (control of Black labor and behavior), and the construction of a domestic national identity (Blackness as synthesizing agent for a dominant white American culture). My discussion aims to illustrate that Black repre-sentations resonate beyond their effects on Black viewers or a narrow under-standing of "minority" images in film history. Instead, we should recognize the crucial function race has played alongside the more frequently explored categories of gender, class, white ethnicity, and even age in the dominant cin-ema's developing modes of representation and address.

BLACKNESS IN TRANSITION

The transition from early to classical cinema has been described by film his-torians as a set of interrelated changes in the ways films were produced, distributed, exhibited, and consumed during the medium's second decade.[8] Although rarely acknowledged, race played an important role in the cinema's changing modes of representation and address as the film industry revised its understanding of its audience.[9] One long-standing assumption about Black representation during the shift from a "cinema of attractions" (in which films primarily presented spectacles or curiosities) to a "cinema of narrative integration" (in which telling stories became the primary task of dominant cinematic discourse) is that Black figures lag behind white ones in terms of character development as increasing emphasis was being placed on conveying psychological individuation and motivation in order to weave characters more securely into an overall effect of narrative unity.[10] On the other hand, some critics have argued that Black representations were more "authentic" *before* the transition to narrative coherence. Thomas Cripps suggests that early nonfiction "actualities," like Edison's *Colored Troops Disembarking* (1898), present more realistic Black portraits than later narrative films because at the time they were produced, "moviemaking consisted of no more than a single camera upon a tripod, recording the objective reality before it without artifice, staging or editing."[11] Whether we read the transitional era as merely another episode in an unbroken history of racist representation or as the beginning of a more systematic and sophisticated approach to racial misrepresentation, we tend to overlook how the transitional era opened up some insurgent possibilities of surprise and variation between "primitive" cinema's claims to "actuality" and the rigorous fictionalized stereotyping we find during the classical era.

The transition to prioritizing narrative was motivated not simply by audience desires for longer and more complicated stories but also by a massive reorganization and consolidation of the moving picture industry in an effort to expand and legitimize the cinema's appeal to a diverse white viewing public. To enlist the audience's attention and emotions more systematically, and to guide viewers through the narrative without extradiegetic interruption, production companies began to assume editorial control over the wide range of local variables that had characterized early film exhibition, such as the inclusion of live music and ethnic performance. By standardizing film lengths and developing techniques like continuity editing, tight chains of cause and effect, and thorough character motivation, the industry also addressed concerns raised by religious leaders and social reformers regarding the suitability of film entertainment (not to mention moral and physical cleanliness of cheap, darkened public spaces in which films were shown), particularly for recent immigrants, youth, and women. One way to read the transition from early to classical representational practices, then, is to note the industry's efforts to uplift its impressionable and working-class audiences with stories designed to edify and educate, as well as entertain, while simultaneously attracting ostensibly more sophisticated middle-class viewers with stories organized to correspond with stylistic features found in literature and legitimate theater, such as coherent spatiotemporal relations, engaging characters, and the production of a self-enclosed aesthetic/entertainment experience.

Like class and white ethnicity the question of where race fits into these processes of standardization—in terms of the rendering of racial difference or the experiences of nonwhite audiences—is crucial to our understanding more fully the complex appeals that cinema was making during this transitional period in American film culture. For instance, we might explore how the use of racist imagery and the rigorous segregation of film exhibition venues worked in tandem with the move to carefully guide the viewer through an uninterrupted, self-contained, and universally intelligible diegetic experience. As the major film producers attempted to regulate film narration and address and thereby determine a textually prescribed spectatorship experience, they sought to bridge class and ethnic differences by effectively standardizing the ideal spectator as a "white" spectator.

Although African Americans made up part of the national moviegoing audience during the nickelodeon era, they are rarely acknowledged in discussions surrounding the cinema's transition (e.g., in trade publications or reformer investigations).[12] Although it is difficult to assess the size of the Black moviegoing audience during this period, the conditions of de jure and de facto segregation that structured American social life also clearly marginalized Black viewers from the official institutional discourses guiding the expansion of film production and distribution and the systematization of modes of representation and address. Throughout the transitional era African American audiences protested what they believed to be offensive representations of Blacks onscreen and restrictive segregationist practices of white theater owners.[13] These efforts alone, however, had little direct impact on the activities of production companies and distributors or on exhibitors beyond the local (neighborhood) level. I do not mean to minimize the importance of the Black presence in film audiences or of Black protest against racist images and segregated exhibition (not to mention the efforts of pioneer African American filmmakers to produce alternative Black film images).[14] On the contrary, I want to consider how African Americans exerted a more profound and far-reaching set of pressures on dominant cinema and the culture that shaped its institutional and representational practices.

Although Black representations in early and transitional cinema might seem to be transparently offensive and resistant to close analysis, they can be read productively as figures that are polyphonic in nature, "speaking of" and "speaking to" constructions of Blackness produced by whites and African Americans at the turn of the twentieth century.[15] As whites produced images of Black subservience, ignorance, and inferiority in a wide variety of media, African Americans responded by refuting limiting stereotypes and by constructing new images for themselves and their white observers. Black film images are influenced by many kinds of representations, both visual (e.g., postcards, illustrations, artifacts, live performance) and nonvisual (e.g., literature and journalism; political, legal, religious, and scientific discourses). In the various media in which "Black images" circulated during this period Blackness is structured by claims about the progress of the race, on the one hand, and the stasis, or even regression, of Black people, on the other. Preclassical films place Black figures within these competing discourses.

During the 1890s and early 1900s African Americans responded to intensified Jim Crow segregation, lynching, and disfranchisement, as well as inadequate wages, housing, and educational opportunities by emphasizing self-help and racial solidarity, migrating to southern and then northern cities, and organizing for racial advancement. In light of these African American geographical and political movements early and transitional cinema participate in a larger effort on the part of dominant white culture to suppress and ignore rising Black voices of self-determination, politicization, and protest. These films (along with newspapers, novels, the stage, and other media) register both fears about Black empowerment and assurances that racial hierarchies will remain firmly in place. But these films do not simply respond by representing Black people as familiar, negative stereotypes. Rather, early and transitional cinema display numerous approaches to addressing the increased presence and circulation of African Americans in various settings at the levels of form, genre, and performance style (e.g., nonfiction, fiction, comedy, drama, "genuine Negroes," whites in blackface).

Tropes of visibility and mobility work hand in hand in the representations of African Americans in early and transitional cinema. Many of these representations illustrate the unexpected entrance of Black bodies into previously closed or highly regulated white spaces, where they are not properly recognized or monitored (trains, offices, department stores, parks). Films staging such scenes are often set in urban environments, where long-standing racial hierarchies risked being refigured as African Americans migrated to cities with a new, postbellum, post-Reconstruction measure of social confidence and independence. This growing Black presence created increased opportunities for interracial mixing, as well as interracial mix-ups. By 1907 the competing discourses on Black character and the meaning of Black circulation across public and private spaces, along with changes in film form, created striking variations in Black cinematic imagery.

Much like the buried "Africanist" presence Toni Morrison has identified in literary works by white American writers, Blackness in American cinema provides an epistemological framework to enable white psychological, familial, and national coherence. This presence provides white cultural producers and consumers with the backdrop that enables the "gathering of identity unto [themselves] from the wholly available and serviceable lives of Africanist others."[16] Although this presence is at work in early, transitional, and classical films, during the transitional era we can read how Blackness is put to service specifically to unify the gaze of an increasingly diverse "white" audience and, at least early on, to explore formal and stylistic variations on representations of racial difference.

During the transitional era filmmakers were under pressure to shift away from "attractions" toward narrative, to diversify film product by altering and developing previous character types and story lines. In early cinema a film could be organized around the sheer visual curiosity that a Black figure could incite for white audiences (e.g., dark skin color, "characteristic" dance, or ethnographic performance). But in the move toward narrative integration even stereotypical figures are expected to perform in narratively motivated ways. The fluctuation between Black figures as curiosities and characters, known and unknown, predictable and surprising is more pronounced *during* the transitional era than either before or after classical narrative style is codified. As the cinema develops techniques to coherently connect characters and actions, to build a narrative logic across time and space, we can examine how Black representations are used to bridge shots as well as the formal space between attractions and narrative.

DOMESTIC COMEDIES

Black female domestics are a natural choice for such an inquiry because they are among the most common Black types featured in early and transitional cinema, as indicated by the number of surviving examples along with catalog descriptions of films that are not extant.[17] Unlike the "mulatto" figures who do not make significant appearances until the transitional period, when their parentage and (light-skinned) appearance can be narratively explained (e.g., *The Octoroon* [Kalem, 1909]; *The Debt* [Rex, 1912]), we can analyze Black female domestics as they develop before, during, and after the transitional era. Unlike the violent, renegade Black "buck" figures who appear primarily in dramatic stories (e.g., *Avenging a Crime; or, Burned at the Stake* [Crescent, 1904]; *The Slave, a Story of the South before the War* [a.k.a. *The Slave Hunt* (Vitagraph, 1907)]), Black female domestics have mobility across multiple genres (comedies, dramas, actualities). Unlike the abundance of "coon" figures who consistently perform in a highly self-conscious, exhibitionist manner throughout the transition to classical narrative (typically engaged in dancing, eating, and/or stealing), Black female domestics are represented in a range of performative styles—from broad gestures toward the camera to understated motions addressed to diegetic characters—depending on the context. Black female domestics are variously positioned as brief comic relief or extended screen presences, as tangential witnesses to white dramas or the pivots around which comic plots turn, playing alternately safe, suggestive, and surprising roles.

Black female domestics clearly share many attributes and narrative functions with the "tom," or Black male domestic figures. As fixtures in white homes and families Black male and female domestics reflect social and economic relationships between Blacks and whites, and they both proliferate in the spate of antebellum and Civil War dramas that were produced in the early 1910s. However, Black female domestics appear in a wider range of narrative scenarios than the "toms," who are almost always cast in dramatic films set in the past (*Uncle Tom's Cabin* [Edison, 1903, dir. Edwin S. Porter], and other versions; *His Trust* and *His Trust Fulfilled* [Biograph, 1911, dir. D. W. Griffith]). Continuing the tradition of representations begun in Stowe's novel and developed through nineteenth-century theatrical adaptations, representations of "Uncle Tom" figures in preclassical cinema are often constructed to enlist white viewer sympathy. Therefore, their sexuality (particularly suggestions of sexual contact with white women) is routinely downplayed, and they are typically constructed as nostalgic portraits of the docile "Old Negro" who is quickly fading from the American landscape.[18]

Actually, many preclassical representations of Black female domestics evoke the provocative figure of boxer Jack Johnson (who appeared in fight films during the transitional era) more than Uncle Tom. Like the flamboyant Johnson, who engaged in sexual relationships with white women and defeated white competitors in the ring, some Black female domestics are represented as troublesome "New" Negroes breaking the rules of interracial social and sexual decorum.[19] Since the domestics are female and fictional figures, however, they are not taken as seriously or monitored as rigorously as were Johnson's films; and whereas the distribution of Johnson's fight films was debated and restricted, films of Black female domestics consistently circulated widely.

Although all of the Black types named above can be explored for the ways in which race, class, gender, sexuality, and setting (North or South, rural or urban, old plantation or modern city) intersect in their presentation, reflecting a range of white presumptions, fantasies, and anxieties, the Black female domestic offers a particularly fruitful field for exploring the overlapping tensions between racial representational politics and contemporaneous transitions in film style. She is the one who is regularly rendered as a contemporary Black subject and consistently foregrounded by the stylistic techniques used to organize narrative time and space in longer, multiple-shot films. None of the other types motivate narrative logic in the ways that Black female domestics do, thereby illuminating how dominant film style constructed the relations between race, gender, and class and modern American life and culture.

By the time these films were produced, domestic work had become a kind of cultural shorthand for Black women and their social position in the United States. According to historian Elizabeth Clark-Lewis, "within the first two decades of the twentieth century, household work lost its importance as an occupation for white women. By contrast, the number of African-American female household workers *increased* by 43 percent. . . . African-American women were forced into a 'servant caste.'"[20] Black female domestics experienced and represented the deeply contradictory nature of turn-of-the-century interracial relations. For example, Black women could live in the homes of white employers (particularly the affluent classes), at the same time that cities passed ordinances promoting residential segregation by race when upwardly mobile African Americans sought to move into white neighborhoods. Historian Tera W. Hunter points out that "Jim Crow and domestic labor thus represented contradictory desires among urban whites striving to distance themselves from an 'inferior race,' but dependent on the very same people they despised to perform the most intimate labor in their homes."[21] Many African American women felt constrained by the limitations of domestic service—long hours, intense physical labor, separation from their own families, restricted access to other forms of wage work. The economic and sexual exploitation many Black female domestics experienced when they worked in white homes (whether they lived-in or performed day work) suggested that little progress had been made since the days of slavery.

At the same time, domestic service could provide Black women with economic self-sufficiency and a license to travel—to move away from home and/ or to circulate through otherwise restricted public spaces. During the years before the massive Great Migration of southern Blacks to northern cities around the time of World War I, African Americans began a slow but substantial migration to cities south and north. John Hope Franklin notes that although African American men often had difficulty finding employment in cities during this period, Black women "easily found employment as household servants," which "attract[ed] a larger number of women than men to the cities."[22] The Black maid, then, was a common if not conspicuous figure in the turn-of-the-century urban landscape. Therefore, it is not surprising that she surfaces in a number of early films characterizing contemporary city life.

For example, to return to *A Bucket of Cream Ale* (discussed above), a Black maid (played by a white actor in blackface) pours a glass of ale for her white male employer (a Dutchman according to the studio description), but it is all froth. As he expresses his dissatisfaction with her pouring, she sneaks a few sips from the bucket behind his back. When he catches her, he throws his glass of ale in her face. While he enjoys a hearty laugh, she responds by dumping the bucket of ale over his head. This short comedy pokes fun at both ethnic types—Dutchmen and colored maids—and does not evoke antebellum relations or a southern setting in action or mise-en-scène. Instead, the film plays with viewer expectations about how interracial relations might play out in a modern context. The film contains a generally popular slapstick display, but it is also intended to be humorous to a white audience because the Black maid's behavior is so surprising, given her subordinate status as employee, and so unlikely, given her social identity as a Black woman. Her behavior takes the antiauthoritarian premise of many early comedies (children vs. adults; wives vs. husbands) a step further by suggesting the possibility that Blacks—a subordinate population these films never directly address—are forgetting their proper, subservient place. Her employer (and presumably the viewer) is so busy laughing at her, expecting her to accept her role as the butt of the joke, that he fails to see her vengeance coming. This one-shot gag film provides a useful backdrop for understanding the operations of later Black female domestics as they are elaborated in longer, multiple-shot films of the transitional era, when the cinema vacillates between integrating Black women into more complex narrative logics and continuing to exploit their appeal as visual gags. Both moves suggest an acknowledgment of the implications of Black mobility, even if transitional films try to contain or disavow African American insurgency through narrativization or the recycling of familiar genres and scenarios.

My discussion focuses primarily on comedy films, and it is important to note that the narrative integration toward which comedy films shift during the transitional era does not necessarily entail the same development of deep character psychology, realistic motivation, or complete viewer absorption that would be required for dramatic films. Instead, transitional-era comedies retain many "exhibitionist" features (e.g., gags, shallow and outrageous characters and plots) while building a logic of spatial and temporal coherence that provides the viewer with a more complex diegetic world, increasingly constructed across multiple shots. Unlike melodrama, which, as Linda Williams argues, serves as a predominant mode in which American mass culture has staged and negotiated "the enduring moral dilemma of race" (particularly Black-white relations), comedy does not necessarily reinforce the cultural power and legitimacy of the various media in which it is staged.[23] Comedy, however, is minted on the opposite side of the melodrama coin, playing an important role in evolving definitions of American mass culture and national identity. Although comedy may not be geared toward eliciting white viewer sympathy for racial Others, it enjoys consistent popularity and takes risks melodrama cannot in its representations of interracial social and moral questions precisely because its Black figures seem to be contained by comedy's casual, superficial treatment of its subjects. It is this dialectic of risk and containment that structures representations of Black female domestics in transitional cinema at the levels of content and form, setting and structure.

WHAT HAPPENS IN THE TUNNEL

As film lengths increase during the transitional era, films featuring Black female domestics increasingly complicate the terms of interracial interaction by extending and highlighting moments of Black character agency and pleasure, even at the expense of white characters. This is evident in the way many transitional films open up the range of spaces—and the degree of publicness of those spaces—that Black characters inhabit. Whereas, as Constance Balides argues, early cinema regularly uses scenarios of the "everyday" (walking down the street, hanging laundry, shopping) as narrative pretexts to turn white working-class women into sexualized visual spectacles, the public visibility of Black female domestics is more problematic.[24] To what degree can exposure, desire, and/or intimacy be represented in the various "everyday" spaces Black women share with whites, particularly as narratives expand beyond short gags? For example, in the early one-shot film *A Bucket of Cream Ale* all of the action takes place in one setting—the Dutchman's living quarters. The gag takes very little time to play out (the film is only twenty-six feet long), and his "humiliation" stays within the home. However, a one-shot film produced toward the start of the transitional period, *Under the Old Apple Tree* (American Mutoscope and Biograph, 1907), is longer (378 feet) and takes place in a setting that blurs the boundary between public and private. These shifts suggest some of the ways in which the sexual and political implications of Black women's mobility in (to) the public sphere are both highlighted and blunted by developing techniques of narrative integration.

Under the Old Apple Tree presents a series of activities that take place in the yard outside of a large house situated in what appears to be a nonurban area.[25] A young sailor tries to romance his girl on a bench beneath the apple tree, but he is interrupted by the arrival of several rival (white male) suitors. The sailor gets rid of them by climbing the tree and throwing apples down on them. At the film's conclusion the girl's elderly father sits on the bench and, as a result of his poor eyesight, mistakenly kisses the hand of a large black woman who comes to sit on the bench (presumably the family maid). When he puts on his glasses and discovers his error, he is shocked and embarrassed.

Under the Old Apple Tree recalls an important set of early films in which white men accidentally kiss Black female domestics instead of the white women they serve. In films like *What Happened in the Tunnel* (Edison, 1903), *The Misdirected Kiss* (American Mutoscope and Biograph, 1904), and *A Kiss in the Dark* (American Mutoscope and Biograph, 1904), the white men react with disgust, as Black women are clearly inferior and completely undesirable substitutes for white women.[26] The white women, in turn, laugh at their suitors' embarrassment. Although the proximity of these Black domestics to whites is supposed to be rigidly circumscribed by their labor function, as it had been for centuries under slavery, these early films set up the transgressive joke by obscuring the white men's vision (lack of glasses, darkness in a tunnel, etc.). This device not only underscores the accidental nature of the interracial kiss but also heightens the absurdity of the notion that these white men cannot see the overdetermined markers of Blackness (darkness of skin, costume) that are immediately apparent to the spectator.

For obvious reasons these films have attracted much critical attention from feminist film scholars, who emphasize their politics of the gaze—the reversals of the male gaze at the woman as object, the maids' looks into the camera.[27] But in addition to looking relations we have a staging of public and social relations in these films in which Black women are not playing clearly subservient roles.[28] They look at and laugh into the camera, openly enjoying the white men's embarrassment.[29] The transgressive Black female domestics in *What Happened* and other early films perform and are performed upon in ways that suggest that African Americans, like white women, are falling out of the personal and social control of white men and, therefore, pose threats to traditional gender and racial hierarchies.[30] Although the Black female domestics in these films are supposed to function simply as vehicles for a joke between white men and women, their assertive mediating presence puts the problems of Black visibility and mobility squarely within their discourses on white female empowerment, white male sexual desire, and the maintenance of a white-controlled social order and public sphere.[31]

The threat of miscegenation that underwrites the comic operations of these early films repeatedly raises the problem of how publicly this threat can be illustrated. For example, many of the interracial kissing films take place in settings in which intimate exchanges are protected by an aura of privacy, even though a larger public world is implied just beyond the frame. *A Kiss in the Dark* details the Romeo-like courtship of a man on the street and a woman inside her home via the window. *What Happened in the Tunnel* takes place on a sparse-looking train, a public space where the white couple—or, rather, the interracial trio—is not observed by any other diegetic characters.[32] These films suggest how Blacks are both transgressing and blurring the boundaries between white public and private spaces, and much of their comic appeal derives from the exposure of interracial kissing to the viewing public in the theater rather than to a diegetic public onscreen. As this gag develops in later transitional films, the crisis/joke of visibility is expanded, but so are strategies to resolve and disavow them by pushing these interactions into more public spaces.

In *Under the Old Apple Tree* this transitional-era variation echoes *A Kiss in the Dark* and *What Happened in the Tunnel* by staging its action in a setting that is somewhere between public and private. The boughs of the apple tree (situated on the left side of the frame) cover a semisecluded space for romance, but this space remains open for observation, pranks, and interruptions from inside the tree (above) the road (at the back of the set), the home (on the right of the frame), and the audience (behind the camera, so to speak). Unlike the earlier films, however, there is an audience placed within the frame—a crowd of young white characters gathers around to laugh, along with the Black female domestic, at the elderly white man who does not share in the joke. In addition, the man's love interest, the Widow Jones, is portrayed as an older white woman who is quite disturbed by her lover's embarrassing mistake.[33] The interaction between a Black female domestic and a white man is made public by the witnessing (and judgment) of other whites. *Under the Old Apple Tree* continues the early cinematic tradition of expressing anxieties about miscegenation as a joke. But unlike earlier films set in urban contexts (e.g., the streets) and/or on trains, where such mix-ups are staged as risks of unregulated modern life, this film takes place in a nostalgic space (the old apple tree next to the old family home) where the breech of traditional social and racial hierarchies is, according to the film's logic, less likely and also less acceptable.

By this time the presentation of the misdirected kiss gag is foregrounded—and cushioned—by a series of parallel, heightening actions and disruptions (performed by white characters). *Under the Old Apple Tree* presents a much slower elaboration of its narrative than *A Bucket of Cream Ale* and offers a wider range of characters. The film establishes a longer rhythmic pattern of character movements (between bench and road, bench and home, bench and tree) to condition the viewer's expectation of the kind of variation (a narrative/comic payoff) at the end of the film. Thus the film diffuses the racial joke by drawing out the action (providing a much longer preparatory phase) and inserts the disapproving Widow Jones as a moral observer to mediate between the misdirected kisser and the audience(s), thereby policing the illicit possibilities of the interracial kiss.

WHAT HAPPENS BETWEEN THE SHOTS

Although *Under the Old Apple Tree* may retain early cinematic qualities because it is elaborated in one shot and employs distant framing, it illustrates a clear transition away from the spectacularity of an early film like *What Happened in the Tunnel*, which emphasizes the racial joke with a closer framing of the characters, among other techniques. This is what we might expect—the transitional era entails a gradual containment of racial figures via narrative integration after the "primitive" freedom of the early aesthetic of display. However, although *Under The Old Apple Tree* delays and mediates the impact of the potentially transgressive joke inherited from early cinema (to narrativize the spectacle), it continues to acknowledge and stage the Black female domestic's intimate relationship with white employers, her location between private and public spheres, and her status as a sexual threat and as sexually available. Comparing *What Happened in the Tunnel* and *Under the Old Apple Tree,* we can see the gradual and sporadic nature of the transition from early to classical styles as indicated by the shifting but overlapping narrative strategies employed to represent Blackness before and after pivotal year 1907. One of the most significant of these shifts is the use of editing.

What Happened in the Tunnel is an early three-shot film in which the dissolves to and from black leader represent the train entering and emerging from the darkness of a tunnel. Tom Gunning identifies this editing pattern as noncontinuous, in which a disruption caused by editing is used to express disruption on the film's story level.[34] In *What Happened in the Tunnel* the edits mark diegetic shifts in which the white and Black women change positions, surprising both the white male suitor and the viewer. Although the noncontinuous genre comes after the one-shot film in Gunning's preliminary genealogy of film genres, they overlap historically in their usage— one-shot films persist after examples of noncontinuous editing appear. The evolution Gunning traces from one-shot films to editing patterns he describes as governed by principles of noncontinuity, then continuity and discontinuity, is not intended to illustrate inevitable steps toward classical coherence (a genealogy he challenges). Rather, Gunning wants to suggest how a "diachronic comparison of filmic systems within history" can help us to see how different methods of constructing temporal and spatial relations between shots succeed (but do not necessarily eradicate) each other in achieving dominance. I will now consider the editing techniques of continuity and discontinuity as they emerged during the transitional era to explore how dialectical relations in both film form (presenting attractions and telling stories) and audience expectations (familiar stereotypes and refreshing variations) produce Black female figures that structure narrative economies even as they seem to exceed or be contained by them.

In contrast to the sometimes jarring visual gags and tricks performed in the noncontinuity genre, Black female domestics appear across different shots in films Gunning would classify within the continuity genre, a narrative editing system in which the disruption caused by edits is deemphasized by a bridging of continuous action at the story level. A prime example of this genre is the "chase" film, a heavily exploited technique used to tie different settings together from shot to shot. In a succession of locations, the same characters enter, pass through, and exit the frame, often moving in the same screen direction (left to right, background to foreground).[35] Another example of the continuity genre is the linked vignette film, a variation on the chase in which the same character appears in a series of settings represented in different shots, engaged in corresponding actions.[36] Chase and linked vignette films make significant modifications to racial types and interracial interactions as they had been represented in earlier films, placing an individual Black spectacle within a larger structure of narrative coherence or attaching a series of gags together into a narrative chain.

For example, the comedy *Jack The Kisser* (Edison, 1907) illustrates the exploits of a white man who goes around town "stealing" kisses.[37] After kissing several unsuspecting white women in different shots/locations, he comes on a white woman and her Black maid walking down the street. The women incidentally switch places when Jack is not looking, and he mistakenly kisses the Black woman. She is delighted; he is appalled. The second half of the film consists of a chase in which Jack's "victims" pursue him in several shots. At the end of the film Jack is apprehended, and as a punishment the white townspeople (mostly women) tie Jack to a tree and allow the Black female domestic to kiss him repeatedly, much to his consternation.

The Black female domestic plays an important narrative role in this film beyond the basic gag of misdirected kissing. In fact, the timing of her appearance and her positioning in relation to public space and white characters are pivotal elements of the film's structure. *Jack the Kisser* combines the linked vignette and chase subgenres, one after the other. In addition, chase elements are introduced during the linked-vignette opening of the film, as several shots end with women chasing Jack—a victim pursues him in anger in one shot, then the town's lusty Old Maid comes after Jack at the conclusion of four shots. In this way the viewer is not only led through a narratively linked series of spaces (what Gunning terms, a "synthetic geography") but also enjoys an overlapping alternation of continuity techniques that mirrors Jack's activities as agent-turned-victim. The domestic's episode with Jack precedes the introduction of the Old Maid so that the Black woman is the first to posit him as not just a predator but a desirable object; thus she sets up the narrative's reversal from Jack's kissing escapades to his retribution.

Although in some ways the Black female domestic is narratively integrated into the film (she joins the chase from shot to shot), she is segregated by other techniques. She is held out as a comic figure of a different order in her gaudy clothing (a dark dress with white polka dots) and her inability to keep up with the rest of the (conservatively dressed) women in the chase (in one scene she is so fat she has difficulty descending a rocky hill). Then at the end of the film we see that she wants to kiss Jack; her desires run in the opposite direction of his white "victims." But if her difference seems to be singled out as a gag by these factors, she is repeatedly compared to the Old Maid, who is also garishly dressed (in black and white stripes) and who runs last in the chase pack in several shots. Also, the Old Maid *really* wants to be the one to kiss Jack when he is caught at the film's conclusion—so much so that she and the Black female domestic engage in a physical fight as the film ends. As in *Under the Old Apple Tree, Jack the Kisser* guards against the transgressive implications of interracial romance by presenting one white female character that is distinctly unamused by the white man's exchange of kisses with a Black woman.

The Black female domestic is both spectacularized and narrativized in other ways in this film. The scenes of interracial kissing in *Jack the Kisser* are among the most explicitly public of the numerous stagings of this recurring joke, as the entire film is set outdoors. The depiction of the Black woman's pleasure is overt in this version, not a potentially unscripted effect of the actor's behavior. By removing the potential of interracial sexual contact from the private to the public realm and amplifying the Black woman's pleasure, the film plays up the absurdity of such activity; clandestine affairs and forced sexual encounters between Black women and white men may happen in private, "in the tunnel," but could never really happen in the street in broad daylight. What is more, unlike the early misdirected kiss films, in *Jack the Kisser* the Black female domestic becomes not merely an unthinkable replacement for beautiful young white women but an ongoing competitor with the undesirable white Old Maid in her desire for Jack. Here we see a further development in the narrativization of the Black female domestic, which does not preclude her exaggerated visual presentation (blackface, garish dress, broad gestures), emphasizing her spectacular qualities. Her status as sexual threat is simultaneously displayed and disavowed. The film's ultimate moral lesson—chastising Jack for not keeping white romance private (for taking his lust into the streets)—is conveyed, in part, through the presentation of the Black female domestic as false love object and then lusty pursuer across multiple shots linked by two different continuity editing techniques.

Another example of how Black female domestics are interpolated into developing narrative styles is the linked vignette film *Laughing Gas,* which demonstrates more agency on the part of the Black female domestic but also more effort toward containing the implications of her mobility. In many ways *Laughing Gas* is anomalous in the degree to which the film's entire structure depends on the movements of a Black female character. In this film a large Black woman (named "Mandy" in the Edison catalog) goes to the dentist to have a tooth pulled. In great pain she insists on receiving nitrous oxide, and after the tooth is removed, she begins to laugh uncontrollably. Her laughter is infections, and the dentist and his assistant begin to laugh as well. She proceeds to move through a series of public spaces in which she continues to laugh and spreads her laughter to everyone she encounters.

The representation of the Black female domestic in this film is striking in comparison to earlier films for many reasons. She is played by a Black actress, not a white actor in blackface. Before we see her working as a domestic, we see her at the dentist, on a streetcar, and in several street scenes in which she travels unaccompanied. She carries no groceries or basket of laundry to mark her occupation or to motivate her circulation in white public spaces. The seeming independence of this character becomes the central tension in reading the film. In many ways she appears to enjoy a considerable amount of autonomy we might not expect for a Black woman in turn-of-the-century America. She travels alone in the same section of public conveyances as whites; she patronizes a white dentist and presses him to administer the laughing gas; she causes a series of accidents and disruptions— causes an artist to drop his sculptures, pours soup in the lap of one of the white diners, and even ends up at the police station in the middle of the film—only to laugh herself out of trouble every time. One interpretation of the film might suggest that the representation of this Black female domestic in a leading role is a radical break from the brief, seemingly marginalizing, representations of most Black female domestics, even the ones discussed in this essay. The inclusion of two close-ups of Mandy—emblematic shots at the beginning and end of the film—might further indicate a rare effort to bring this character closer to the (white) viewer, to enlist audience sympathy for and/or identification with a Black subject.

On the other hand, each of the qualities that would seem to indicate that Mandy is a progressive departure from previous portrayals of Black female domestics can be read in the opposite direction to suggest how the film uses continuity and other techniques to extend and rework long-standing stereotypes, producing a character that unifies a white spectatorial gaze at her expense. For example, the fact that her persistent laughter is produced by the nitrous oxide administered by the dentist suggests that Black/female bodies are particularly susceptible to intoxication, and it potentially undermines her role as agent of goodwill, since she is not in control of her own faculties. The emblematic shots—first a close-up of her bandaged face writhing in pain, last a close-up of her continuous laughter—may not bring us closer to her consciousness but instead highlight her function as spectacle disconnected from the white world in which she circulates in the main body of the film.[38]

This sense of Mandy's disconnection from the whites who observe her can also be read diegetically in her travels across shots, where she creates or discovers a series of social disruptions among whites from different national backgrounds, including run-ins with a German street band, an Italian artist, and two arguing Irishmen. Through her laughter she brings disorder then harmony to each of these white ethnic types, enabling a kind of melting pot reconciliation via her boisterous Blackness. Does she disrupt assimilationist ideologies here and/or facilitate them? Can she partake in the spirit of camaraderie she cultivates among a variety of white male characters? These questions demarcate the contradictory, undertheorized space created by and for Black representations during the first steps toward narrative integration. These transitional films are still bound up with early cinematic traditions of racial stereotyping, and they foreshadow a classical conflation of representational modes for nonwhite characters, even as they use those very subjects to mediate the gaps among diverse white audiences and between two stylistic systems.

The stakes of representing racial difference in shifting modes of address— from presentation to narration—are outlined again in *Laughing Gas* through the links made between Black circulation in public space and Black female sexuality. These links are set in motion in the opening scene at the dentist. The removal of the Black female domestic's tooth is presented as a visual gag—the dentist has to sit on her lap to pull out the stubborn tooth, with his assistant helping to pull from behind. When, after much effort, the dentist finally dislodges the offending tooth, we see that it is gigantic, as if pulled from a large animal. The visual presentation of the white male dentist mounting the Black female domestic (indeed, the need for two white men to complete the job) clearly taps into discourses on interracial sex (voluntary and forced) and black women's "bestial" sexuality.[39] This scene is followed by her physical interactions with a number of other white men (e.g., falling into the laps of white men on the streetcar; delighting clusters of white men on the street, in the police station, in the home where she works). This series of spectacular moments of contact with white men is disrupted, however, toward the film's end.

After her escapades with whites, it is evening, and Mandy is approached by, and rejects, an ostentatious Black male "masher." Then the film's penultimate shot completes the folding of Mandy into an all-Black world after she has been established as moving confidently through white society. After dismissing the Black dandy, she goes to an African American church service where the congregation is swaying back and forth to the minister's sermon.[40] By showing that this Black female domestic is, at day's end, a member of a Black community, the film segregates her safely away to achieve narrative closure.

At church Mandy's laughter rocks her fellow Black worshipers out of their pews, disrupting the service. The culminating joke of the church scene— that Mandy's uncontrollable laughter is virtually indistinguishable from the gesticulations associated with Black religious ecstasy—suggests a connection between sexual and spiritual pleasures as registered by Black bodies. The wild physical motions she displays throughout the film (rolling on the floor, bumping into whites, kicking into the air) come to be naturalized by her cultural difference and, at the very end, to be disruptive within her own community. In the final close-up, when Mandy laughs into the camera, the film's diverse theatrical viewers are invited to unify as a white audience through her mirth and otherness, completing the pattern established for white characters in the film's vignettes. Mandy might be read as a potentially autonomous (and anomalous) Black subject, but she is also presented as a member of a primitive Black culture held up for display and ridicule to an ostensibly more modern and cosmopolitan white viewing public.

The continuity genre does not survive into the classical period, as audiences became more adept at bridging the spatial and temporal relations between shots. Instead, cinematic narrative came to be governed by principles of discontinuity, in which storytelling remains continuous through a disruption caused by editing on the plot level, which interpolates one or more lines of action. When Black characters appear in transitional and classical films of the discontinuity genre, the multiple lines of action sometimes stage interracial relations, such as in the popular comic plot of Black-white switching. In films like *Mixed Babies* and *Mixed Colors* (Pathé, 1913), white babies and Black babies are switched when their caretakers are distracted. Like the other films discussed in this essay, the comic, surprising appearance of a Black person where a white one is expected gives the general impression that social controls are not working properly and that embarrassing interracial mix-ups are waiting to happen, particularly in modern, urban contexts.[41] Although Black female domestics continue to subvert traditional racial and gender roles in films of the discontinuity genre, these films conclude with a more emphatic sense of order and closure as the separate lines of action are brought together.

In *Mixed Babies,* for instance, mothers check their babies at the door of a New York City department store as they enter to shop. All of the mothers are so preoccupied with their purchases (so consumed by consumer culture) that they do not notice that the claim tags have been switched on their baby carriages (by a young prankster), and they take the wrong infants home. One notable element in *Mixed Babies* is the extreme confidence displayed by the Black female shopper (played by a white actor in blackface). This character aggressively grabs for bargains and clearly holds her own in a predominantly white environment. Despite this display of modern Black female circulation, in the end all of the female characters are returned to their proper social places and visual spaces. The babies are returned to the right mothers, a conclusion reinforced by an emblematic shot in which white and Black mothers, seated in an isolated setting, hold the appropriate babies in their laps.

Black-white switches are also set in the workplace. As we have already seen, early and transitional cinema frequently figures the "problem" of modern, urbanized Blacks around their changing and/or improper relation to their roles as laborers. In several films discontinuous editing is used to play up the tensions between the type of female worker white men solicit (white, attractive) and the woman they receive (Black, undesirable) after placing public calls for employees. In Edison's *The Colored Stenographer* (1909), for instance, the skirt-chasing white boss switches the beautiful white typist he has recently hired with the Black scrubwoman in order to make his wife believe that he has given up his womanizing ways.[42] But the Black woman's reluctance to give up her newly acquired position at the film's conclusion suggests the problems that can arise when Blacks display increased assertiveness in the workplace. In *Nellie, the Beautiful Housemaid* three elderly white men place an ad in the newspaper for a maid; their ad is answered, much to their surprise, by a Black woman.[43]

These domestics stand in sharp contrast to the devoted Black maids and butlers who appear in antebellum and Civil War films of the transitional period. In those films Black domestics display undying loyalty and a commitment to preserving white families, facilitating white romances, and defending white supremacy, sometimes sacrificing their lives for the Confederacy.[44] Although many of these nostalgic films illustrate a deep level of intimacy between Black and white characters, films set at the contemporary moment illustrate the dangers of the interracial intimacy of servant/employer relationships now that African Americans no longer feel tied to a subservient place in American society, particularly Black women, who were seeking increased social and occupational opportunities.

In *Nellie, the Beautiful Housemaid* the alternation of shots builds suspense as the excited old white men write their ad ("Wanted a pleasant young woman as housekeeper") and receive a response ("I am a young girl, 23 yrs of age, brunette, good looking . . . first class cook and laundress"); as they groom themselves in anticipation of Nellie's arrival at their home; and the revelation at the train station (where the men are not present) that Nellie White is actually a large, gaudily dressed Black woman.[45] In both *Stenographer* and *Housemaid* the dangers of modern public space and public discourse are made quite clear: if you are not careful, you may unwittingly bring an aggressive Black female worker into your office or home. In both cases the white male characters are held at fault: the white businessman should not try to deceive his wife; the three elderly bachelors should not have designs on a young female employee. These films present aggressive Black characters alongside white characters with little moral authority, making fun of the vanity, sexuality, and self-absorption of the white figures. They indicate a brief but important moment of disruption, in which a Black presence challenges—at thematic and stylistic levels—the expectations of white characters and audiences across separate lines of action.

Nellie, the Beautiful Housemaid uses discontinuity editing to weave jokes/anxieties about Black female desirability, body size, skin color, train travel, fashion sense, and language in ways that suggest how Black figures fluctuate between freestanding visual gag and narrativized spectacle as devices of narrative integration (such as parallel editing) are developed. However, as discontinuity editing achieved dominance over continuity editing—ushering in a "narrator system" of integrated space and time beyond the physical movement of characters—Black female domestics play less and less significant structural roles.[46] It is not surprising that as spectators are enlisted more deeply into synthesizing separate lines of action, and sympathizing and identifying with characters, Black images would not figure as prominently in narrative logic, even if they continue to function in highly visible, thematically significant ways.

White men continue to misdirect romantic attentions toward Black women later during the transitional era and beyond. In Alice Guy Blaché's

Matrimony's Speed Limit (1913), a white man under a tight deadline to find a wife kneels and proposes to a woman wearing a white veil and gloves, who turns out to be Black.[47] He has already unsuccessfully proposed to a white woman on the street, and when this one reveals her face he responds with shock and flees. His search is intercut with his white girlfriend's search for him, and in the end the right, white marriage takes place. The well-dressed, rather stoic, Black woman in this film, placed in a public space for a short visual gag, points backward and forward in the ways her presence is both provocative and contained. She is the last diversion in the young white man's quest for a bride, just as other Black female figures are posited as the most unlikely and outrageous variations on a theme. As narrative integration reorganizes the terms of film-viewer relations—narratively, socially, and ideologically—Black female characters less frequently structure narrative organization, even if they continue to pop up in unexpected places. For a brief moment, though, Black female domestics suggest how the cinema, in its pursuit of cross-class popularity and cultural legitimacy, did not simply marginalize people of color but experimented with the formal and stylistic possibilities of figures that seemed to occupy the lowest rungs of modern American culture.

NOTES

1. The earliest film images of Blacks are heavily informed by popular Black representations in literature, vaudeville, newspapers, cartoons, and Black iconography on postcards and other commercial products, among other sources. Early cinema immediately adapted "Black" activities like the cakewalk, buck and wing, and other dances, as well as broad grinning, watermelon eating, and chicken stealing to the screen because theaters sought to provide their (white) audiences with proven, familiar forms of entertainment, and with confirmation of their beliefs about Black people and what they do (e.g., *The Pickaninny Dance—From the "Passing Show"/The Pickaninnies* [Edison, 1894], *A Coon Cake Walk* [American Mutoscope, 1897], *Who Said Watermelon?* [Lubin 1902], *Laughing Ben* [American Mutoscope and Biograph, 1902]). Many of these very early films are often classified as "nonfiction" because they are ostensibly shot on location or because they lack formal plot structures. However, the subjects selected for these films, the settings in which they are shot, and the ways they are framed are all conscious choices made by the producers, creating images that are never simply natural or authentic.

2. These terms for recurring Black stereotypes have long been in wide circulation, but the best known discussion of their recurrence in American cinema is elaborated in Donald Bogle, *Toms, Coons, Mulattoes, Mammies, and Bucks: An Interpretive History of Blacks in American Films* (New York: Continuum, 1990).

3. Important exceptions to these general trends in early film historiography are the writings of Charles Musser and Daniel Bernardi. Musser is consistently careful to provide cultural and historical context when discussing the appearance of racist

stereotypes in the works of early American filmmakers. See, e.g., Charles Musser, *Edison Motion Pictures, 1890–1900: An Annotated Bibliography* (Italy: Smithsonian/Le Giornate del Cinema Muto, 1997). Bernardi's work on silent cinema carefully traces how race functions not just as a biological classification or individual/group identity marker but as a sociohistorical formation, a hegemonic way of knowing and seeing. He then names white supremacy as a founding ideology and preoccupation of early filmmakers and audiences, linked to discourses on biological determinism, immigration, and U.S. imperialism in the late nineteenth and early twentieth centuries. See Daniel Bernardi, introduction to *The Birth of Whiteness: Race and the Emergence of U.S. Cinema*, ed. Daniel Bernardi (New Brunswick, N.J.: Rutgers University Press, 1996), 1–11.

4. For example, Manthia Diawara states that "[t]he release of D. W. Griffith's *The Birth of a Nation* in 1915 defined for the first time the side that Hollywood was to take in the war to represent Black people in America" (Manthia Diawara, "Black American Cinema: The New Realism," in *Black American Cinema*, ed. Manthia Diawara [New York: Routledge, 1993], 3). In his historically and institutionally grounded study of Black representation in commercial narrative films, Ed Guerrero opens with a discussion of the centrality of the "plantation genre" in "the cinematic devaluation of African Americans," citing *The Birth of a Nation* as its "original hegemonic impulse." See *Framing Blackness: The African American Image in Film* (Philadelphia, Pa.: Temple University Press, 1993), 10. Image-based analyses predominate in Black film criticism, and often these studies trace a history of negative stereotyping. Such studies include Peter Noble, *The Negro in Film* (London: Skelton Robinson, 1948); V. J. Jerome, *The Negro in Hollywood Films* (New York: Masses and Mainstream, 1950); Edward Mapp, *Blacks in American Films: Yesterday and Today* (Metuchen, N.J.: Scarecrow, 1971); James P. Murray, *To Find an Image: Black Films from Uncle Tom to Super Fly* (Indianapolis, Ind.: Bobbs-Merrill, 1973); Daniel J. Leab, *From Sambo to Superspade: The Black Experience in Motion Pictures* (Boston, Md.: Houghton Mifflin, 1975); Gary Null, *Black Hollywood: The Negro in Motion Pictures* (Secaucus, N.J.: Citadel, 1975); Lindsay Patterson, *Black Films and Film-Makers* (New York: Dodd, Mead, 1975); Jim Pines, *Blacks in Films: A Survey of Racial Themes and Images in the American Film* (London: Studio Vista, 1975).

5. Thomas Cripps, *Slow Fade to Black: The Negro in American Film, 1900–1942* (Oxford: Oxford University Press, 1977), 17; James R. Nestcby, *Black Images in American Films, 1896–1954* (Washington, D.C.: University Press of America, 1982), 16; Henry T. Sampson, *Blacks in Black and White: A Source Book on Black Films*, 2d ed. (Metuchen, N.J.: Scarecrow, 1995), 41; Phyllis R. Klotman, *Frame by Frame I: A Black Filmography* (1979; repr., Bloomington: Indiana University Press, 1997), 84. *A Bucket of Cream Ale* is extant in the Motion Picture, Broadcasting, and Recorded Sound Collection at the Library of Congress (hereafter abbreviated LOC).

6. My discussion of these films is based on my viewing of extant prints of *Laughing Gas* at the Film Study Center, Museum of Modern Art; *Mixed Babies* at LOC; and *Nellie, the Beautiful Housemaid* at LOC.

7. Bogle describes the "mammy" type as "so closely related to the comic coons that she is usually relegated to their ranks. Mammy is distinguished, however, by her sex and her fierce independence. She is usually big, fat, and cantankerous" (Bogle, *Toms*, 9). My discussion will focus on comic representations of the Black female domestic, but I will describe figures that appear before Bogle says this type "made her

debut" in the 1914 Lubin film *Coon Town Suffragettes.* See also Patricia A. Turner, *Ceramic Uncles and Celluloid Mammies: Black Images and Their Influence on Culture* (New York: Anchor, 1994), 41–62.

8. My summary of the relationships among industrial shifts in the production, distribution, and exhibition of films; the transition to the set of film-viewer relations that came to be associated with classical narrative style and modes of representation and address; and debates about the makeup of preclassical audiences is drawn from Eileen Bowser, *The Transformation of Cinema, 1907–1915* (Berkeley: University of California Press, 1990); David Bordwell, Janet Staiger, and Kristin Thompson, *The Classical Hollywood Cinema: Film Style and Mode of Production to 1960* (New York: Columbia University Press, 1985); Ben Brewster, "A Scene at the 'Movies,'"in *Early Cinema: Space, Frame, Narrative,* ed. Thomas Elsaesser (London: British Film Institute, 1990), 318–25; Charles Musser, "The Nickelodeon Era Begins: Establishing the Framework for Hollywood's Mode of Representation," in ibid., 256–73; and Miriam Hansen, *Babel and Babylon: Spectatorship in American Silent Film* (Cambridge, Mass.: Harvard University Press, 1991).

9. An exceptional discussion of the intersection of class, ethnic, and racial politics in the development of preclassical film culture is Alison Griffiths and James Latham, "Film and Ethnic Identity in Harlem, 1896–1915," in *American Movie Audiences: From the Turn of the Century to the Early Sound Era,* ed. Melvyn Stokes and Richard Maltby (London: British Film Institute, 1999), 46–63.

10. Tom Gunning's account of the transition from the "cinema of attractions" to a "cinema of narrative integration" is outlined in, among other places, *D. W. Griffith and the Origins of American Narrative Film: The Early Years at Biograph* (Urbana: University of Illinois Press, 1991), 6. Daniel J. Leab, like most of the pioneering scholars of Black film images, influenced subsequent interpretations of the silent era when he suggested that there were no differences between preclassical and classical representations of Blackness: "by 1915, the story film of feature length was well-established. These changes in the American film industry, however, made little difference in the treatment of black characters" (Leab, *Sambo to Superspade,* 11).

11. Cripps, *Slow Fade to Black,* 11. Charles Musser argues, however, that the publicity materials for many early nonfiction films demonstrate that racist discourses regularly made their way into ostensibly "objective" Black cinematic representations:

Although Thomas Cripps in *Slow Fade to Black* sees these early films as relatively free of offensive stereotyping in their depiction of African Americans, the catalog descriptions help to show how racial prejudices were assumed and perpetuated. Cripps' assessment of entry no. 559, *Colored Troops Disembarking* ("black men with weapons in hand marched down a gangplank on their way to Cuba"), as affirming black dignity is contradicted by the catalog description which sees their behavior as "laughable." (Musser, *Edison,* 54–55)

12. I discuss early evidence of Black moviegoing in my forthcoming book, *Migrating to the Movies: Cinema and Black Urban Modernity* (University of California Press). Among the rare mentions of Black audiences in the trade press during the nickelodeon era is an item cited by Greg Waller in his carefully researched chapter on African American moviegoing in Lexington, Ky. Reflecting the casual marginalization of Blacks in preclassical film culture, an "unnamed showman" remarks in the trade publication *Moving Picture World* in 1907: "Strange thing that moving pictures do not appeal to the masses of Negroes," in part because the Negro "doesn't seem

to grasp the idea of moving pictures" *(Moving Picture World,* 8 June 1907, 216–17, quoted in Gregory Waller, *Main Street Amusements: Movies and Commercial Entertainment in a Southern City, 1896–1930* [Washington, D.C.: Smithsonian Institution Press, 1995], 161). See also Mary Carbine's revelatory discussion of Black reception practices during the silent era, "'The Finest Outside the Loop': Motion Picture Exhibition in Chicago's Black Metropolis, 1905–1928," *Camera Obscura* 23 (May 1990): 9–41.

13. Anna Everett discusses the early history of African Americans' critical responses to the cinema in *Returning the Gaze: A Genealogy of Black Film Criticism, 1909–1949* (Durham, N.C.: Duke University Press, 2001). African American critics and moviegoers in Chicago occasionally registered complaints in the Black press about films shown in their neighborhood theaters that they found to be racially offensive. For example, in 1914 the *Defender* reported that Stroll patrons were fuming because the States Theatre was showing Lubin's *The Tale of a Chicken,* featuring "an illiterate going into a coop and stealing a chicken," and *Mother of Men,* which shows "a slave stealing a white child." See "States Theatre Displays Vile Race Pictures," *Defender,* 30 May 1914, n.p. The *Defender* also reported numerous cases during the early 1910s in which African Americans were discriminated against in downtown (white) theaters. See "Mr. George A. Wilson," *Defender,* 4 June 1910, 1; and Frank S. Heffron, "Colonial Theater Refuses Colored Gentlemen—Fined," *Defender,* 11 June 1910, 1.

14. For example, William Foster founded his Foster Photoplay Company in Chicago in order to specialize in nondegrading films about urban Black life. In comedies like *The Railroad Porter* (1913) and newsreels such as *The Colored Championship Base Ball Game* (1914), Foster tried to represent elements of the Black urban lifestyles that African Americans had cultivated in northern cities. None of Foster's films are extant.

15. The notion of a discursive approach to analyzing racial stereotypes comes from Ella Shohat and Robert Stam, *Unthinking Eurocentrism: Multiculturalism and the Media* (London: Routledge, 1994).

16. Toni Morrison, *Playing in the Dark: Whiteness and the Literary Imagination* (New York: Vintage, 1993), 20, 25.

17. This long list of titles includes films as varied as *The Seeress* (AM & B, 1904), a short tableau in which an elderly Black woman sits with a young white woman at a table and reads her fortune using a deck of cards; *The Stolen Pig* (Vitagraph, 1907), a comedy about "Mammy" and "Rastus" stealing a pig and disguising it as their baby; *Mammy's Ghost* [a.k.a. *Between the Lines of Battle*] (Vitagraph, 1911), in which a Black female domestic helps a Confederate officer and his son chase a Union soldier out of their home by making him believe there is a ghost in the attic; and *Old Mammy's Charge* (Majestic, 1913), a drama in which a Black female domestic raises the orphaned daughter of a white southern couple in the North following the Civil War.

18. For example, in Griffith's two-reelers *His Trust* (Biograph, 1910) and *His Trust Fulfilled* (Biograph, 1911) faithful servant George cares for the white widow and daughter of his slain master. Although he takes on the fallen white patriarch's role in this family in some ways (spending his savings to put the girl through school), he maintains an increasing physical distance from them—from giving the daughter horseback rides at the start of the film to giving up his cabin for them when they have no other home. See Michael Rogin's "'The Sword Became a Flashing Vision': D. W. Griffith's *Birth of a Nation,*" in *Ronald Reagan, the Movie, and Other Episodes in Political*

Demonology (Berkeley: University of California Press, 1984), 190–235, for a discussion of the *His Trust* films as precursors to Griffith's staging of white patriarchal power and fears about miscegenation and Black political insurgency in *The Birth of a Nation*.

19. For excellent discussions of the controversies surrounding Jack Johnson's fight films—their production, distribution, exhibition, and censorship—and the films' larger relationships to white supremacist ideology, Progressive Era politics, nonfiction film history, and evolving definitions of American film culture, see Dan Streible, "Race and the Reception of Jack Johnson Fight Films," in *The Birth of Whiteness: Race and the Emergence of U.S. Cinema,* ed. Daniel Bernardi (New Brunswick, N.J.: Rutgers University Press, 1996), 170–200; and Lee Grieveson, "Fighting Films: Race, Morality, and the Governing of Cinema, 1912–1915," *Cinema Journal* 38, no. 1 (fall 1998): 40–72.

20. Elizabeth Clark-Lewis, "'This Work Had a End': African-American Domestic Workers in Washington, D.C., 1910–1940," in *"To Toil the Livelong Day": America's Women at Work, 1780–1980,* ed. Carol Groneman and Mary Beth Norton (Ithaca, N.Y.: Cornell University Press, 1987), 197–98.

21. See Tera W. Hunter's exemplary study of the work, resistance, and leisure activities of Black women in Atlanta, *To 'Joy My Freedom: Southern Black Women's Lives and Labors after the Civil War* (Cambridge, Mass.: Harvard University Press, 1997), 105.

22. John Hope Franklin and Alfred A. Moss Jr., *From Slavery to Freedom: A History of Negro Americans,* 6th ed. (New York: McGraw-Hill, 1988), 279.

23. Linda Williams, *Playing the Race Card: Melodramas of Black and White from Uncle Tom to O. J. Simpson* (Princeton, N.J.: Princeton University Press, 2001), xiv. Williams observes that audiences of "Tom shows" in the mid nineteenth century and of *The Birth of a Nation* in 1915 would have been "converted to the new power, unprecedented length, and legitimacy of media that had not previously been taken seriously: the morally serious stage melodrama in the case of *Tom,* the 'two-dollar movie' in the case of *Birth.* In both instances the thrill to the power of a new medium and the thrill to the experience of new racial sympathy are linked. Both became integral to the very formation of national identity" (7).

24. Constance Balides discusses films such as *What Happened on Twenty-Third Street, New York City* (Edison, 1901), in which a woman's skirt is blown up by air from a vent in the sidewalk; *A Windy Day on the Roof* (American Mutoscope and Biograph, 1904), in which a man looks up a woman's skirt when it is lifted by the wind while she hangs laundry; and *The Gay Shoe Clerk* (Edison, 1903), in which a female shopper exposes her ankle (in close-up) to a male shoe salesman. See Constance Balides, "Scenarios of Exposure in the Practice of Everyday Life: Women in the Cinema of Attractions," *Screen* 34, no. 1 (spring 1993): 19–37.

25. *Under the Old Apple Tree* is extant at LOC.

26. *What Happened in the Tunnel, The Mis-Directed Kiss,* and *A Kiss in the Dark* are extant at LOC.

27. Hansen, *Babel and Babylon,* 39; Judith Mayne, "Uncovering the Female Body," in *Before Hollywood: Turn-of-the-Century Film from American Archives,* ed. Charles Musser and Jay Leyda (New York: American Federation of the Arts, 1987), 63–67; Lynne Kirby, *Parallel Tracks: The Railroad and Silent Cinema* (Durham, N.C.: Duke University Press, 1997), 99; Lauren Rabinovitz, *For the Love of Pleasure: Women, Movies, and Culture in Turn-of-the-Century Chicago* (New Brunswick, N.J.: Rutgers University Press, 1998), 85–87.

28. Hansen notes, e.g., that *What Happened in the Tunnel* ends with "the maid's direct glance at the camera suggest[ing] not only that she was not merely a prop but that she, rather than her mistress, might have authorized the substitution" (Hansen, *Babel and Babylon,* 39). The catalog descriptions of these films, however, stress the agency of the white women, not the Black women, in these substitutions. The Edison summary of *What Happened in the Tunnel* states, "Upon emerging he is hugging and kissing the colored maid, *the [white] young lady having changed seats with her* while in the tunnel, much to the young man's disgust" (emphasis mine). The description of *A Kiss in the Dark* points out, "She [the white woman] plays a joke on him [the suitor] by *causing a colored maid to take her place*" (*Biograph Bulletin* no. 55, 27 November 1905, 12; repr. in *Biograph Bulletins, 1896–1908,* comp. Kemp Niver [Los Angeles, Calif.: Locare Research Group, 1971], 202, emphasis mine). Although catalog descriptions rarely correspond exactly with what we see in the films, these extrafilmic materials tell us a great deal about how these films were expected to be read. In these cases we must ask why it is that these filmmakers seem willing to stage reversals of white male-female looking relations but are reluctant to ascribe agency to the Black women who enable these substitutions, especially when this agency seems to be so apparent in the films themselves.

29. We see the same dynamic at work at the end of *Under the Old Apple Tree,* when the Black female domestic giggles at the white man's mistake. Eileen Bowser observes, in her extensive viewing of racial identity gag films, that "the black woman is usually quite amused at the consternation of the white person who has made the mistake. If not amused, the black woman may be indignant. I have not seen one example in which the black woman appears to have been embarrassed or humiliated by the error" (Eileen Bowser, "Racial/Racist Jokes in American Silent Slapstick Comedy," *Griffithiana* 53 [1995]: 41). Bowser provides a long list of films (produced between 1903 and 1924) in which white men mistake Black women for white women in their lustful pursuits.

30. The dangers of collusion between Black and white women are also demonstrated in Lubin's comedy *Coon Town Suffragettes* (1914), in which Black women (led by washerwoman Mandy Jackson) ape white feminist activism (e.g., for temperance, gender equality) by raiding a gin mill and forcing their lazy husbands to work. These aggressive Black women subdue not only (stereotypically) their ineffectual husbands but the "coon town" police as well. The film uses Black women (the ridiculous notion of any sort of Black feminism) to mock white women's political organization. But it also suggests that alliances between white and Black women could result in a dangerous empowerment of those lowest on the social ladder. See descriptions in Sampson, *Blacks in Black and White,* 52; and *Moving Picture World,* 21 Feb 1914.

31. I would also argue that the representation of Black women as willing participants in these interracial switches further masks any possibility of white male desire for Black women. In this way these films help to deflect claims that white men, not Black men, used interracial rape as a tool of political terrorism, as maintained by activists like Ida B. Wells and artists like Oscar Micheaux (in the film *Within Our Gates* [1920]), who sought to set the record straight about the practice of sexual violence, particularly in the South. By illustrating that Black women are the ones who instigate and/or knowingly participate in interracial kisses and by characterizing them as inherently "unattractive" (fat, dark-skinned), these films insist that white men would

never deliberately pursue Black women. Rather, any romantic or sexual interactions between Black women and white men would have to be initiated by the Black female.

32. In her reading of *What Happened in the Tunnel* Susan Courtney points out the significance of the action taking place on a train, which served as both the locus for the legalized segregation of public accommodations (*Plessy v. Ferguson, 1896*) and the primary mode of transportation of southern Black migrants to northern cities. Thus, like the cinema itself, the train as a public space and as a relatively new technology "come[s] to signify mobility and constraint, play and rigidification" (Susan Courtney, "*What Happened in the Tunnel* and Other American Scenes," unpublished manuscript, 1999).

33. See description in *Biograph Bulletin* no. 112, 4 November 1907; repr. in Niver, *Biograph Bulletins, 1896–1908*, 314.

34. Gunning describes *What Happened in the Tunnel* in his discussion of noncontinuity and mentions that this editing technique is used to represent other kinds of disruptive ellipses, such as dreams and explosions. See Tom Gunning, "Non-Continuity, Continuity, Discontinuity: A Theory of Genres in Early Films," in *Early Cinema: Space, Frame, Narrative,* ed. Thomas Elsaesser (London: British Film Institute, 1990), 86–94.

35. Chase films feature Black subjects as both pursued (*The Watermelon Patch* [Edison, 1905]) and pursuers (*The Snowman* [American Mutoscope and Biograph, 1908]).

36. On linked vignettes see Bowser, *Transformation,* 57; and Gunning,, "Non-Continuity," 92.

37. *Jack the Kisser* is distributed by the Museum of Modern Art.

38. The final emblematic shot of "Mandy" is not unlike the early film *Laughing Ben* (American Mutoscope and Biograph, 1901), which presents an elderly Black man in close-up (shot as an "old plantation" type at the Pan-American Exposition in Buffalo, N.Y.) repeatedly spreading a toothless grin, presented as an entertaining spectacle in himself.

39. Michael Rogin notes that actress Hattie McDaniel, "before she was turned into the most famous motion picture mammy of all time," wrote and performed a song called "Dentist Chair Blues," which uses a trip to the dentist as an extended metaphor for describing a sexual encounter. See Rogin, *Blackface, White Noise: Jewish Immigrants in the Hollywood Melting Pot* (Berkeley: University of California Press, 1996), 111.

40. Clark-Lewis notes that live-in maids often could not attend Sunday "day services" because of their job obligations, so they frequently attended church services at night. See Clark-Lewis, "'This Work Had a End,'" 209.

41. *Mixed Babies* is extant at LOC. Susan Courtney has argued that the surprising appearance of a Black baby in a white household functions as the logical (and more explicit) extension of the miscegenation threat posed in interracial kissing films: "[W]e don't see interracial sexual contact as such, but its potential outcome" (Susan Courtney, "Hollywood's Fantasy of Miscegenation" [Ph.D. diss., University of California, Berkeley, 1997], 38). See also *How Charlie Lost the Heiress* (American Mutoscope and Biograph, 1903).

42. I have not found a surviving print of *The Colored Stenographer;* this discussion is based on summaries in Sampson, *Blacks in Black and White,* 48; Cripps, *Slow Fade to Black,* 22; Nesteby, *Black Images,* 16; and a review in *Moving Picture World,* 13 April

1909 (quoted in Sampson). Although stenography opened up new professional opportunities for women, both white and Black women struggled with the presumptions of white male employers. Balides observes that stenographers were susceptible to sexual harassment (Balides, "Scenarios of Exposure," 35); W. E. B. Du Bois recounts the difficulties two Black stenographers faced in trying to find employment because of their race (W. E. B. Du Bois, *The Philadelphia Negro*, 1899, quoted in *The City Reader*, 2d ed., ed. Richard T. LeGates and Frederic Stout [London: Routledge, 2000], 61).

43. The comic potential of modern Black labor problems seems to have international relevance. In the Italian-produced film *Wanted: A Colored Servant* (Italia, 1908), a clerk is sent out to hire a Black servant, but when he places an advertisement, far too many applicants arrive for the job. Sampson describes the film's conclusion: "Pandemonium reigns supreme at the home of the proprietor, and when the clerk returns he is promptly evicted and the waiting tribe of Africans set upon him." See Sampson, *Blacks in Black and White*, 125; and production company information from American Film Institute, *The American Film Institute Catalog of Motion Pictures Produced in the United States: Film Beginnings, 1893–1910*, comp. Elias Savada (Metuchen, N.J.: Scarecrow, 1995), 1156.

44. Such films usually feature Black male servants; see, e.g., Griffith's *His Trust* and *His Trust Fulfilled*, as well as *The Confederate Spy* (Kalem, 1910), *A Slave's Devotion* (Broncho, 1913), and *For His Master's Sake* (a.k.a. *For Massa's Sake* [Pathé, 1911]), in which Uncle Joe sells himself and his family back into slavery to help pay off the gambling debts of his former master's son. Black female servant/martyrs appear in *Old Mammy's Charge* (described above) and *Old Mammy's Secret Code*, in which the loyal "old Mammy" is executed as a spy after using her clothesline, inside of Grant's headquarters, to send coded messages to the rebels. This description and the scant production information comes from Cripps, *Slow Fade to Black*, 32; and Nesteby, *Black Images*, 17.

45. The print of *Nellie, the Beautiful Housemaid* housed at LOC is incomplete and out of order, but I attempt here to reconstruct the narrative from the surviving shots.

46. For more on parallel editing as a key component of the "narrator system" as developed by Griffith see Gunning, *D. W. Griffith*, 76–81.

47. *Matrimony's Speed Limit* is included on the Library of Congress Video Collection, *Volume 6: America's First Women Filmmakers: Alice Guy-Blaché and Lois Weber.*

CHAPTER SIX

The "Imagined Community" of the Western, 1910–1913

Richard Abel

In April and May 1911 *Moving Picture News* ran a page titled "Film Charts" in which Independent films released weekly in New York City were categorized into four "tracks."[1] Two of those, *dramatic* and *comedy,* had long been used by the industry to broadly distinguish certain types of film product; a third, *educational,* was a more recent invention, born out of the general effort to "uplift" moving pictures, and included both fiction and nonfiction films. The fourth track, *western,* was the most specific and, in the handicapping metaphor of the charts, had entries that ran "the fastest kind of a race." They "abound," as the *News* put it, "in the life, snap, and vigor that mean so much to M. P. audiences." This is a vivid yet far from anomalous indication of just how important westerns were not only to the Independents but also to the U.S. moving picture industry as a whole. Just two months earlier, an exhibitor in Zanesville, Ohio, who also toured a "floating theater seating 1000" on the Ohio and Mississippi Rivers, reported that wherever he showed films, his audiences wanted "Wild West pictures."[2] At the same time, thousands of miles away in England, the trade weekly *Bioscope* published a feature article about Essanay's "cowboy pictures," not only to express its own enthusiasm but also to satisfy the alleged demands of its readers, because the company's "Western subjects . . . [had] become so popular" there.[3] Indeed, "so numerous" were westerns both here and abroad, *Billboard* noted, in reviewing Selig's *The Outbreak* (March 1911), that it now took "extraordinary strong situations," as well as marvelous scenery and "fine horsemanship," to make them interesting.[4]

These wide-ranging yet complementary texts offer a point of entry to study the western at a crucial juncture in its development as a production/marketing strategy and an "American product" highly suitable for internal consumption and export.[5] Specifically, I want to focus on the volatile years of

1910 to 1913, when westerns proliferated despite repeated trade press criticism, when competition between the MPPC and Independents became particularly fierce, and when changes began to occur—the development of multiple-reel and then feature films, as well as movie personalities or stars—that would transform the industry. In short, I will examine the moment when, as Rick Altman puts it, a range of possibilities for the genre "were being explored, sifted, and codified."[6] First, I will sketch several important stages of that exploration and codification, drawing on manufacturers' production strategies and commentary on those strategies in the trade press. Then, after highlighting a crisis in production and distribution, I will use the popularity of westerns abroad to help frame several perspectives for analyzing variations on the emerging genre's "imagined community of nationality" (a key concept borrowed from Benedict Anderson)[7] and glance at the "constellated communities" (the term is Altman's) that the western's "usable past" may well have served—what, in Herbert Blau's prescient words, was "commonly remembered and adhered to, or thought of as better forgotten."[8] Throughout I will draw on descriptions and analyses of selected archive prints as well as instances of promotion and reception in selected local newspapers.[9] My overall aim is to argue for the significance of the western—a crucial instance of what Miriam Hansen has called the "new sensibility" of "action" that characterized American modernity"[10]—to a discussion of the intersection of those long-contested cultural artifacts of historical consciousness—*genre* and *nation*—in the "transitional era" of cinema in the United States.

ATTACK/COUNTERATTACK

The "life, snap, and vigor" cited by the *News* had been associated with westerns as "quintessential American subjects" at least since 1909, particularly those that *Moving Picture World* dubbed the "school of action" westerns allegedly aimed at the "masses."[11] It was this kind of "wild and wooly" picture in which Selig and Essanay specialized and that Independents like New York Motion Picture (NYMP) exploited with its Bison films to secure a niche in the U.S. market. Occasionally, the trade press deigned to praise a "school of action" western, such as Essanay's *Under Western Skies* (August 1910), one of the first films G. M. Anderson shot in California.[12] Typically, however, they were dismissed as no better than dime novels. By late 1910 this attitude culminated in a spirited attack published in the *World* as "The Indian and the Cowboy (By One Who Does Not Like Them)."[13] Not content to argue that "there [were] far, far too many of these pictures," the author countered a claim from exchanges and exhibitors that "children demand them"—a claim that *Film Index* accepted, citing a New York Child Welfare Committee survey, asserting that "three-fourths of the boys" questioned liked "Cowboys and Indians" best.[14] Instead, this author imagined an "intelligent . . . small boy" who, much like himself, knew better: "Indians and Cowboys are nasty, dirty, uncomfortable, unpleasant people." At best, he argued, kids looked on "these . . . stupid . . . Indian and Cowboy subjects with a mixture of amusement and toleration." Soon after, *Nickelodeon* concluded: "the Western photoplay has outrun its course of usefulness and is slated for an early demise."[15] Why? "Film makers went West" simply "to find a stamping ground for melodrama, [and] western melodramas have lost their ability to create suspense. . . . [T]he old thrills are exhausted." In tongue-in-cheek support *Nickelodeon*, one month later, printed a full-page caricature sketch in which half of the stereotypes that manufacturers supposedly could not do without came from Indian and Cowboy pictures.[16]

That these charges were fired off to provoke better film product may be inferred from their disappearance (for the most part) throughout much of 1911.[17] One reason was that, despite the attacks, westerns continued to be popular for "authentic" landscapes, as well as for thrilling action, and with a wide audience—Indians themselves, of course, excepted.[18] In April several managers in Canton, Ohio, listed westerns as one of three kinds of films that their clientele favored; likewise, two downtown theaters in Lynn, Massachusetts, frequently used westerns to compete for customers.[19] Accordingly, in June Selig announced that one of the three reels it released every Tuesday would be "A WESTERN" because the company was "humbly acced[ing]" to public demand.[20] A month later the *News* cited several Essanay westerns (in which girls outwitted or outran Indians) as examples of what the "average audience" liked in its films.[21] By summer's end the *News* was claiming that a cowboy picture, a good comedy, and a good educational film were all that was needed to compose an ideal program—especially if a cowboy could perform "the most daring feats of horsemanship," as did rodeo rider Tom Mix in Selig's *Saved by the Pony Express* (July 1911).[22] Not only does Mix leap from one galloping horse to another, but he also ropes and breaks a bronco in order to deliver a letter that exonerates a friend on trial.[23] The claim held especially true, the *News* asserted, "in small towns and cities [where] the cowboy and Indian are as popular as when they first appeared."[24] An exhibitor just outside New York City, writing to the *World,* agreed: based on seeing "an average of twenty reels of licensed film a week for three years . . . cowboys and real comedy are popular everywhere and always."[25] Even Vitagraph, which at that time made very few westerns, played on their popularity by representing its audience, in one ad, as a posse of rootin', shootin' cowpunchers.[26]

The Indian pictures in which Pathé and Bison specialized were equally favored but not always for the same reasons. Some followed the "school of action" formula but with an Indian playing the hero. In Bison's *A Squaw's Retribution* (June 1911) Mona Darkfeather began to gain recognition for her "very good work" as a woman (with child) who, abandoned by her white lover, now that he has acquired a fortune, takes revenge by drowning the white woman with whom he has taken up.[27] In the same company's *Little Dove's Romance* (September 1911), which so impressed the *World* with its "imaginative quality," white trappers rescue Little Dove (Darkfeather again) from their treacherous half-breed cook; but it is a young man from her tribal village who pursues and kills the half-breed and then gently persuades her that she is better off with him than with the departing trapper with whom she has fallen in love.[28] The "more artistic" Indian pictures, wrote the *World,* closely aligned with efforts by white Americans not only to preserve the cultural artifacts and rituals of a people pushed to the verge of extermination but also to "exalt the Indian [and] depict the noble traits of his character."[29] Cloaked with a rhetoric of authenticity, such pictures served up the Indian as a no-longer-threatening Other for (white) consumption. The *New York Dramatic Mirror* had joined the *World* in praising this impulse for "preservation" in earlier films, from Kalem's *The White Captive of the Sioux* (July 1910) to Biograph's *The Song of the Wildwood Flute* (November 1910).[30] Not surprisingly, the "preservationist" attitude was especially evident in those Pathé films that involved Indians exclusively and were directed by James Young Deer, a Winnebago Indian who had come to head the company's western unit after long experience in Wild West shows and earlier westerns.[31] The most acclaimed of these, *The Legend of Lake Desolation* (August 1911), made its central character not the white girl who is raised by Indians and then convinced to return to her original family but the old chief whose heart is broken and who, with winter's coming, in a final tableau, drifts onto a lake and sets his canoe afire.[32]

If Essanay, Selig, Kalem, and Pathé all continued to make westerns a significant part of their weekly releases, at least three Independent companies made cowboy pictures nearly the exclusive province of their production, with Bison alternating between Indian and cowboy pictures.[33] By April American Film was releasing "Two Flying A Cowboy Pictures a Week," the same output as that of Bison and Champion and twice that of Nestor's (figure 6.1).[34] For several weeks in May and June *Billboard* promoted these films for their good stories, acting, scenic effects, photography, and horsemanship.[35] But the *World* also paid more attention to their cowboy pictures, reprinting letters from exhibitors praising "Flying A" films, for instance, and accepting American's own contention that it was "recording into film classics the romantic stories of the West."[36] One possible reason for this was that Allan Dwan had become the chief writer-director for American's western unit that spring, and the *World* heralded one of his early films, *The Ranchman's Nerve* (July 1911), as the most "notable film" of the week.[37] American soon was using a new logo to advertise its "Cowboy Films" in the trade press[38] and boldly proclaiming its El Cajon Valley location in Southern California as "the last West" left.[39] In early 1912 the company experimented with a unique publicity ploy, publishing stories of the "Flying A" pictures, in advance of their release as films, in dozens of newspapers across the country.[40] With many MPPC and

Figure 6.1. American Film ad, *Moving Picture News*, 13
May 1911, back cover.

Independent companies now locating more and more of their production
in Southern California, westerns increasingly could exploit the iconographic
tradition of Wild West landscapes already widespread in American popular
culture and, in Alan Trachtenberg's apt phrase, its myth of "unimaginable
wealth."[41]

Initially, it seems surprising that attacks cropped up again in late 1911 and
early 1912. Now it was the *News* that led the charge, in November, citing all
the letters from moviegoers who were "utterly sick and tired . . . of Wild West
pictures."[42] Specifically, the *News* called on the Independents to stop making
"such foolish pictures" or to "produce Western subjects . . . with an elevating, uplifting story." A month later the *World* took up the cry: did manufacturers really "imagine that two-thirds of the population [were] dime-novel-
reading boys between the ages of ten and sixteen?"[43] Yet these attacks
coincided with changes already underway that would transform the western

precisely in ways advocated by the trade press. The best evidence came in late 1911, with an announcement by NYMP, perhaps inspired by the new level of spectacle that D. W. Griffith had achieved in mounting battle scenes in *Fighting Blood* and *The Last Drop of Water* (July 1911), the first of which the Voyons in Lowell, Massachusetts, promoted as "the greatest western picture ever made."[44] The company would abandon its "regular style of Indian and cowboy pictures" (which too often were "travesties of Western life"), reorganize its production, and make "nothing but sensational, spectacular Western subjects, with enormous casts," drawn from the riders, horses, and stock of the famous Miller Brothers 101 Ranch Wild West Show.[45] Moreover, unlike Griffith's films these would be two-reel special features, directed by a former IMP filmmaker, Thomas Ince.[46]

"ELEVATING" THE WESTERN

That all this criticism evaporated can be attributed to several new production and marketing changes in the industry. Although identified with a different company, each confirmed the *World*'s conclusion, in reviewing *The Last Drop of Water*, that "to Americans pioneer stories must always be welcome, for not only have these humble heroes opened up a new and wonderful land, but they have transmitted to later and present generations the endurance and contempt for danger, which are to this day a heritage of the American character."[47] One such strategy was distinctive to Essanay. As early as October 1911, probably in a move to challenge the "Flying A" films, Essanay began running weekly strip ads that staked its claim as the "indisputable originators of Cowboy Films" (figure 6.2). To support that claim there is a surviving print of *The Sheriff's Chum* (April 1911), the main attraction one Sunday, according to a rare newspaper ad, at the Dome Theater in Youngstown, Ohio.[48] Here Anderson not only pursues and captures an escapee from jail but discovers that his visiting "best friend" has tried to seduce his wife and then bests him in a rousing fight that the *New York Morning Telegraph* found "as dramatic and well worked up as any heretofore seen in motion picture plays."[49] At the same time, there was the testimony of an experienced cowhand who, in a letter to the *Mirror*, described Anderson as by far "the best cowboy character delineator of any film concern."[50] By November Essanay was promoting its western leading man and director as the "most photographed man" in the business.[51] The timing made Anderson one of the first recognized movie personalities, or stars, for it coincided with Majestic Pictures' attempt to exploit Mary Pickford's departure from Biograph and promote "Little Mary" as its own, culminating with her smiling image gracing the *Mirror*'s cover (6 December 1911).[52] Anderson's appeal was unmistakable in several unique newspaper stories that circulated weeks before Essanay announced its promotional campaign, specifically in several

Figure 6.2. Essanay ad, *Moving Picture World,* 21 October 1911, 226.

northeastern Ohio steel towns, in the *Youngstown Vindicator* and *Canton News-Democrat.*[53] There fans took to calling Anderson "Bullets," a nickname that theater managers then frequently used to promote "Essanay's Great Western Thrillers" well into the summer of 1912.[54]

By early 1912 Essanay itself was singling out Anderson's "inimitable character of Broncho Billy" and deploying it like a brand name to sell some of the one-reel westerns in which he appeared.[55] As Broncho Billy, Anderson was often a "good badman," an outlaw with enough conscience to finally turn away from crime and lead an honorable life. An early surviving example is *A Pal's Oath* (October 1911), in which a "pal" promises to keep Anderson's secret—that he has stolen some money to pay a doctor for tending the friend's injuries—but then arranges his arrest in order to court and marry the woman Anderson loves.[56] Released from jail several years later, Anderson plans his revenge, only to peer through a cabin window and see the "pal" embrace his wife and young daughter—and find that he cannot fire his pistol. This redemptive character often had the benefit of strong stories, perhaps most notably in *Broncho Billy's Christmas Dinner* (December 1911). Expecting to rob a stagecoach, Broncho Billy has to save its passengers when the horses are spooked by drunken cowboys; a young woman on the stage then invites him home for dinner, and, when she turns out to be the sheriff's daughter, he confesses, is given immunity, and accepted at the table. The *Mirror* found the "thrilling ride on [the] stage coach . . . as exciting and realistic as anything of its character ever shown in pictures"—and the surviving print reveals some deft framing and editing, including an unusual high-angle medium shot/long shot taken from a camera mounted on the stagecoach behind Broncho Billy as he struggles with the horses' reins.[57] The *Mirror* was impressed as well by the acting "in the quieter moments," as when a pensive Broncho Billy is washing up in the foreground of a small room while the family and other guests cluster around the Christmas dinner table visible through a background doorway.

A second strategy emerged with the Bison-101 plan to make two-reel westerns. Special multiple-reel films had circulated before—Selig's *Ranch Life in the Southwest* (1910), *Buffalo Bill Wild West–Pawnee Bill Far East* (1910), Atlas's *The James Boys in Missouri* (1911)[58]—but this was the first attempt to produce fictional "features" on a regular weekly or biweekly basis. The company it-self promoted the first of these, *War on the Plains* (February 1912), as mark-ing a "new era in western pictures"; in a full page devoted to its release the *World* compared it favorably to the latest historical spectacular from Italy, Am-brosio's *The Golden Wedding*.[59] *Battle of the Red Men* (March 1912) similarly was called as "epical" as Itala's earlier *The Fall of Troy*.[60] The *World* and the *Mirror* gave even more attention, respectively, to *The Indian Massacre* (March 1912) and *Blazing the Trail* (April 1912).[61] In an unprecedented four pages in the *World* Louis Reeves Harrison told the story of *The Indian Massacre,* in which the struggle between Indians and white settlers is driven by parallel desires.[62] One involves food and escalates into an attack on a white settle-ment and the retaliatory massacre of an Indian village; the other involves offspring and leads to the seizing of a white child during the initial massacre to replace a dead Indian baby. Just before the retaliatory massacre, however, the Indian mother returns the white child and, in a final extreme long shot tableau, stands silhouetted on a bare hilltop before the platform that bears her own dead child (figure 6.3).[63] As for *Blazing the Trail,* the *Mirror* extolled the "magnitude of [its] backgrounds" and Ince's astute "management of the exceedingly large number of players" that bestowed "an air of reality" to an otherwise familiar story of white settlers threatened while crossing the plains.[64] The *Mirror* also lauded the craft and artistry of *The Deserter* (March 1912), noting especially its final extreme long shot tableau, in which an army deserter (Francis Ford), having exonerated himself by saving a wagon train from an Indian attack, is honored with a formal military burial, presented in graphic detail, in the empty desert.[65] The *Sunday Telegraph* added that "the toning . . . used consistently throughout" was especially "appropriate and most effective."[66]

The Bison-101 productions had a huge impact in exhibition and served not only to promote the Independents overall but also to establish the west-ern as a serious historical subject. In Cleveland, for instance, *War on the Plains,* along with *The Crisis,* received special attention in the *Cleveland Leader*'s pi-oneering Sunday page devoted to moving pictures: one in an ad for the down-town Mall theater, the other in a photo story that also included Sarah Bern-hardt's *Camille* and Biograph's *The Girl and Her Trust*.[67] A third title, *Battle of the Red Men,* circulated through at least three leading theaters, including the newly built Park National—and on a lucrative weekend program.[68] In Boston *The Indian Massacre* was given a special advance screening for exhibitors (and pronounced "'big' in every sense of the word"); in nearby Lynn all of the Bison-101 westerns played exclusively at the Central Square over a four-month period and were the sole feature attractions in late May and early June.[69] The *Lynn Daily Item* praised *The Lieutenant's Last Fight* (June 1912) not only for its "thrills" but also because "it is educational in its scenic re-production of American history now closed."[70] In Toledo, Ohio, in late March

Figure 6.3. *The Indian Massacre*, production still, *Moving Picture World*, 9 March 1912, 857.

"the big spectacular photo-play" *The Deserter* was given the largest newspaper ad to date for its two-day screening at the downtown Colonial.[71] Most of the Bison-101 westerns were shown at the Crown, however, and by April that theater was promising a "new, fresh, and entertaining 101 Ranch Bison every Saturday."[72] In Minneapolis, from late February through June, these "thrilling headliners" played first at the Crystal (usually in four-day runs) and then at the Isis (on weekends), where *The Lieutenant's Last Fight* "arouse[d] the most hardened of moving picture 'fans'" with its depiction of "war in all its realism."[73] That spring, in Des Moines, Iowa, the Family Theatre also placed a rare ad for *Blazing Trail*—the latest of the "famous Bison '101' Ranch Wild West, Two Reel Indian and Cowboy Features"—in both of the city's leading newspapers.[74]

A CRISIS LEADS TO COMPETING WAR SPECTACLES

Despite their critical success and popular appeal, Bison-101 westerns suffered because the industry's distribution system, pegged to one-reel and split-reel films, could not easily accommodate their regular release.[75] According to the *Mirror* these "really high-class" features were too expensive to be profitable "at the prevailing rate of 10 cents per foot paid by the exchanges," and the latter refused to pay a higher price.[76] The Sales Company tried to solve this

problem by setting up a special department to handle Bison-101 features
(and others) by granting exclusive territorial rights to exchanges and newly
formed states' rights companies willing to pay fifteen cents per foot for rental
prints.[77] This solution worked well enough but for no more than a month,
as growing divisions among the Independent manufacturers finally led to
Sales's breakup in May 1912.[78] Initially, NYMP entered into a contractual
agreement with one faction, Universal, but relations quickly soured between
the company and Carl Laemmle, who headed IMP and soon would become
the leading figure at Universal.[79] An acrimonious court case—and alleged
gun battles around the Bison-101 locations near Los Angeles—delayed the
release of further western features throughout the summer.[80] Yet even after
NYMP switched its allegiance in August to the other faction, Mutual/Film
Supply, it lost any claim to the Bison brand to Universal and had to reorganize its production of westerns under the new brand names of Broncho (with
Ford now as director) and Kay-Bee (with Ince).[81] As a result no new features
with either the Bison (Universal) or Broncho logo appeared until September, and none appeared with the Kay-Bee logo until October. This was especially detrimental to Ince's three-reel *Custer's Last Fight*, which, although
ready for release in July, did not reach theaters until October.[82]

The consequences of this crisis initially were mixed. For several months
most westerns in circulation were one-reelers. However popular, as Essanay's
Broncho Billy pictures in particular continued to be, these were promoted
not as "special attractions" but as regular weekly releases—in Cleveland the
downtown Orpheum booked Essanay westerns on Sundays, specifically for
a clientele of working men and their families.[83] Important exceptions were
the two-reel Indian pictures made by Dwan at American, beginning with *The
Fall of Black Hawk* (July 1912) and *Geronimo's Raid* (September 1912), and
Warner's three-reel *Peril of the Plains* (September 1912), which marked both
companies' first moves into "feature" production.[84] Moreover, imported two-
reel French "westerns" such as Gaumont's *Their Lives for Gold* (July 1912)
and Eclipse's *The Red Man's Honor,* starring Joë Hamman (December 1912),
now found a welcome market.[85] Although the *Mirror* castigated *Their Lives
for Gold* for being inauthentic and overly "crammed full of exciting captures,
struggles, and escapes," the film seems to have been quite successful in exhibition: in Toledo it was featured at the Empress one weekend in August
and then rebooked one week later.[86] In a similar vein the crisis opened up
the growing market for multiple-reel films to other sensational melodramas
that relied on thrilling action—namely, jungle or animal pictures and, especially, Civil War films. Whereas Selig and Gaumont specialized in the former, Kalem took the lead in the other with titles such as *The Siege of Petersburg* (July 1912).[87] That summer the two factions struggling over the "Bison"
brand also decided that "the Civil War [could] be exploited in the same careful manner," especially for subjects demanding spectacular battle scenes.[88]

When the Bison (Universal), Broncho, and Kay-Bee westerns finally did appear in the fall of 1912, however, the trade press seemed eager to embrace them. Both the *World* and the *Mirror* found much to like in Bison (Universal)'s *The Massacre of the Santa Fe Trail* (September 1912), "a big feature Indian story."[89] By contrast, the *World* claimed, *A White Indian* (September 1912) would "attract attention" only because Darkfeather played the main character.[90] For the next six months Bison (Universal) committed to releasing, on average, one multiple-reel western per week, and Darkfeather proved a crucial draw in a series of Indian pictures directed by Frank Montgomery, from *Star Eyes' Strategy* (October 1912) to *Mona of the Modocs* (February 1913).[91] So successful were these that in May 1913 the two risked forming their own company; when that venture collapsed, Darkfeather appeared briefly that summer in one-reel Nestor Indian pictures.[92] Some of the other Bison (Universal) westerns won praise from both the *World* and the *Mirror,* either for clarity of storytelling, as in *Early Days in the West* (October 1912), or for the novelty of staging an ambush, as in *The Massacre of the Fourth Cavalry* (November 1912).[93] Yet most came in for repeated criticism for their slight stories, illogical story construction, or inadequate acting. The trade press, for instance, criticized *The Flaming Arrow* (March 1913), the first of a promised series from melodrama playwright Lincoln J. Carter, for being too full of "trite," "well-worn" action.[94] The surviving print bears this out to some extent, in a story that aligns White Eagle (an orphaned college-educated half-breed) and a colonel's daughter against a revengeful white rival, a disreputable Mexican, and drunken Indian marauders.[95] The story is efficiently told, however, skillfully combining spectacular battle scenes with close shots, as in the cut-in close-up of White Eagle discovering muddy evidence of the rival's deception and the concluding shot of the couple coming forward into a medium close-up.

The trade press consistently found more to commend in the westerns released by NYMP. *Moving Picture News* proclaimed the long-delayed *Custer's Last Fight* "The Most Stupendous Production Ever Conceived" (figure 6.4), and the *Mirror* lauded the film for achieving "the most realistic battle . . . ever witnessed" in moving pictures.[96] Also highly praised in the *Mirror, The Sergeant's Boy* and *The Vengeance of Fate* (October 1912) risked telling stories that ended as ironically or grimly as did the company's earlier films. In one a colonel's daughter "stood silently by and watched the body of the man she loved carried to the grave," murmuring, "And he never knew"; in the other a traitorous rival is shot in an Indian attack (from which the hero saves his wife and child) and "left in the woods for the hungry wolves to feed upon."[97] One of the first films released under the Kay-Bee label, the three-reel *The Invaders* (November 1912), struck Louis Reeves Harrison in the *World* as "an absorbing picture of dramatic conflict . . . the top of its kind, from an artistic point of view," comparable "to the best photography as applied to still

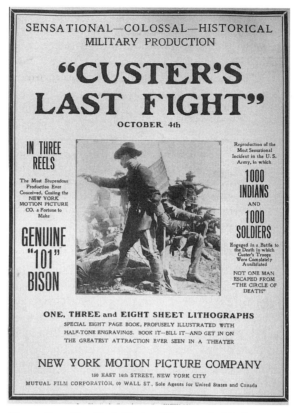

Figure 6.4. New York Motion Picture ad, *Moving Picture News*, 21 September 1912, back cover.

life, with far greater emotional effects."[98] *The Altar of Death* (November 1912) confirmed, for the *Mirror,* that the Kay-Bee production teams were "masters" in making such films.[99] That mastery continued in westerns that, unlike Bison (Universal) films, began to turn away from Indian stories, as in Broncho's *A Shadow of the Past* (January 1913)—in which a white renegade leading an Indian attack spares his former wife (now remarried) and her child, only to flee and be "killed by the officer whose family he protected"—or Kay-Bee's *The Wheels of Destiny* (February 1913), enhanced by "the delightful and convincing playing of [a] charming young actress," especially in a recognition scene between father and daughter.

The impact of the Broncho and Kay-Bee westerns in exhibition supported the *Mirror*'s claim that Ince, along with Anderson (but in a different way), had caught "the true vitality of the Western drama."[100] In Lynn the new Kay-

Bee and Broncho titles rivaled the earlier "famous Bison '101' westerns." Central Square promoted them as a weekly "special attraction," beginning in late November; Dreamland did the same with the Bison (Universal) westerns.[101] In Baltimore, between January and March 1913, westerns of all three brands figured prominently in downtown theater ads each week. In the second week of February there were no less than six playing, including *Mona of the Modocs* and *A Shadow of the Past;* a good number circulated on a regular basis from one theater to another, one night to the next, especially late in the week; and several Bison (Universal) features returned a month after their initial screening.[102] In Cleveland, where Lake Shore Film heavily promoted its Broncho and Kay-Bee westerns and where *Custer's Last Fight* served as the inaugural feature at the downtown Oxford Theater in October, the Doan Theater complemented its ad for *The Law of the West* with this claim: "there is no more popular film before the public today than the Kay-Bee western war pictures."[103] In Des Moines the Unique celebrated its contract with Mutual with an unusual half-page ad that included a weekly schedule highlighted by "the celebrated Kay-Bee western features" each Friday.[104] In Toledo Bison (Universal) westerns were a weekly attraction throughout the fall, and a unique weekend listing of neighborhood theaters, beginning in late January 1913, included a disproportionate number of Kay-Bee, Broncho, and Bison (Universal) westerns. By April the Wanda, a Polish neighborhood theater, was designating each Saturday a "WESTERN NIGHT."[105] Finally, Kay-Bee titles such as *A Shadow of the Past* and *The Wheels of Destiny* achieved an exceptionally long "shelf life," returning to downtown theaters from Lynn to Des Moines as much as six months after their initial release.

THE GREAT WEST

"Do you know The Great West as it was and is?" This question was just one of several rhetorical ploys to advertise "Flying A" westerns in Great Britain in early 1912,[106] where "Wild West dramas" were now such consistent hits that *Motography* could report that "phases of cowboy and Indian life are the most popular subjects for American films."[107] If *Bioscope* printed feature stories on such films as Flying A's *The Ranchman's Vengeance* or *The Poisoned Flume,* an Essanay ad illustrated the posters the company circulated, two of which boldly promoted "cowboy photoplays."[108] Indeed, throughout Europe, despite U.S. trade press misgivings, the fictitious Wild West of cowboy-and-Indian films was crystallizing into the American subject par excellence[109]— the one "doing most," as even the *Cleveland Leader* reported, "to make the American moving picture film popular abroad."[110] Yet the question also alludes to the West as a deeply embedded concept in American history, "the screen upon which [Thomas] Jefferson [first] projected his vision of a nation both democratic and enterprising . . . replete with accessible images."[111]

What, indeed, was the "Great West" that was "known" and represented in American westerns, however diverse? What "imagined community" did these films tend to produce? Who were the audiences invited to share this knowledge, and in what ways did they constitute (or not) a more or less "constellated community"? If "authentic" geographical landscapes of the West—an "empty land" of often arid, inhospitable spaces[112]—attracted a wide range of American audiences, did those landscapes always look and mean the same? Did the action-packed stories of "western life" and "larger-than-life" characters have the same mythological or ideological function, especially in a "New World" whose emerging sense of nationhood was far from inclusive? Together with certain points about the reception of westerns in the "Old World" of Europe, these questions prompt a closer examination of specific films, as well as the discourse around them, not only in the trade press but in local newspapers.

THE "IMAGINED COMMUNITY" OF THE "GREAT WEST": COWBOY PICTURES

So, what comes of looking again at Essanay's "cowboy pictures"? Although Anderson was well known in the USA as *the* "photoplay cowboy," either as "Bullets" or "Broncho Billy," it was in Great Britain and Germany that his films first coalesced into the "famous *Broncho Billy* series."[113] Although some reviews in the U.S. trade press began to refer to these "Broncho Billy pictures" in the summer of 1912, the series label did not become widespread until at least a year later.[114] On the one hand, Anderson's widespread appeal—what the British called the "irresistible charm of personality and the breezy, easy, infectious humour . . . of [this] magnetic man"—gave credence to Essanay's boast, furthered by certain newspapers, that Broncho Billy was the first American "world famous character-creation" or star.[115] On the other, the increasingly regular series in which his cowboy character appeared can be seen now as one of several efforts in the U.S. industry to emulate the production and marketing strategies of repetition and variation found not only in French films, such as Joë Hamman's *Arizona Bill* series,[116] but in serialized magazine stories and juvenile pulp fiction. Among them were Essanay's own comic western series, *Alkali Ike,* beginning in 1911; Nestor's forgotten attempt, in 1912, to revive the juvenile series, *Wild West Weekly,* with regular releases of one-reel films;[117] American's equally neglected 1913 comic western series, *Calamity Anne,* starring Louise Lester;[118] Edison's more familiar *The Adventures of Mary* (starring Mary Fuller), released in conjunction with monthly stories published in *The Ladies' World,* in 1912 and 1913;[119] and a slew of detective series throughout 1913 and into 1914 featuring Vitagraph's Maurice Costello as Lambert Chase, Edison's Laura Sawyer as Kate Kirby, and Edison's Ben Wilson as Cleek.[120] Essanay's Broncho Billy series simply proved the most successful.[121]

Yet the recurring story of Broncho Billy's redemption as an outlaw worthy of reintegration into an emergent social order also repressed or displaced other figures and stories. Ironically, Anderson had had to rename himself in order to mask his own Jewishness in the industry.[122] *Bioscope*'s special reviews of two "Flying A" westerns in 1911 highlight this repression/displacement and in different ways. *The Ranchman's Vengeance* (May 1911) offers a striking contrast to the films Dwan would soon shoot for the company.[123] Although cinematically conventional, the film tells an unconventional story in that its ranchman hero is a Mexican American, Lorenz Pedro, and his revenge is directed at a white man, Tom Flint, whom he had rescued from the desert and who had stolen away his wife and little daughter, only to abuse them and kill the woman. Pedro throws Flint off a cliff into the sea; then, at her mother's gravesite, the girl stops her father from shooting himself. Mexicans or Mexican Americans were the subject of a good number of earlier westerns, but they usually played villains—as in *Broncho Billy's Mexican Wife* (November 1912)[124]—victims, or characters who either gratefully were rescued by whites or sacrificed themselves for whites. *The Ranchman's Vengeance* is a revealing anomaly in its recasting of a figure typically seen as "racially inferior" and thus marginalized in the "imagined community" of the West.[125] The absence of U.S. trade press reviews of the film are suggestive, especially in contrast to its forthright acceptance by *Bioscope* as a "clean . . . popular" film with a strong plot and "excellent acting." On the one hand, the ending is more characteristic of European than American films—at least until the Bison-101 two-reelers of 1912—and this may have partly accounted for its popularity abroad. On the other hand, and more important, the lack of reviews (except for *Billboard*'s, which identifies only the "ranchman's servant" as Mexican)[126] means either that the film's circulation was limited to marginal areas of the U.S. social order—specifically in Southwest venues catering to Mexican Americans—or that the names in its intertitles had to be expunged from any ads elsewhere.

The other "Flying A" western is one of the earliest surviving films shot by Dwan, *The Poisoned Flume* (August 1911). Here a widow, Mrs. Napier, fears for her ranch's survival, and a neighbor, Martinez (J. Warren Kerrigan), tries to gain control of it by marrying her daughter. Rebuffed, he poisons the flume carrying water to the ranch but is discovered by her new foreman, who is wounded and then, with his fellow cowboys, kills Martinez in a gunfight. This story is accentuated by unusual framing—high-angle shots of the flume curving off into the distance, others that stage foreground action at the flume against expansive backgrounds—and by a climax in which Martinez tries to escape on a trestle carrying the flume over the valley.[127] The final image also is unusual but apt: his body falls into the flume and drifts slowly off in its current.[128] Although this film offers the "extraordinary strong situations" demanded by *Billboard*, it evokes and masks a significant factor in the West's development.[129] For the flume carrying water to the Napier ranch was but part of the vast system of irrigation that made the region a model, argues Donald Worster, of the "modern hydraulic society."[130] What is intriguing is that by the early 1900s an alliance of private and government capital and engineering expertise was necessary for this system to reach, as Worster puts it, a critical stage of *florescence.*[131] Yet what gets represented in a western such as *The Poisoned Flume* derives from an earlier period of *incipience,* in which individuals (including single women) and small communities living in relative isolation took the first steps toward what Worster dubs the "redemption of California."[132] In other words, in its depiction of the flume as both visual attraction and dramatic prop and of the cowboy hero who "gets the girl in the end" (not unlike Broncho Billy), the film asserts the frontier myth of socioeconomic individualism and mobility that would become a staple of the genre during the rest of the century.[133]

THE "IMAGINED COMMUNITY" OF THE "GREAT WEST": INDIAN PICTURES

A different trajectory of analysis results from looking again at the Bison-101 westerns, whose reception in Europe was as enthusiastic as it had been in the United States.[134] In Great Britain, according to *Bioscope,* these films were "a revelation—even to picture men . . . unequalled in the entire annals of Cinematography."[135] Not only "beautiful from a scenic point of view," they were "exceedingly well constructed" stories, consistently well acted by an ensemble of players (rather than relying on a star like Anderson), and often achieved a finish that was "dignified," "moving," and uniquely realistic—as in *The Deserter,* in which the hero's military funeral ended at a "lonely grave on the edge of the boundless prairie," with his comrades silhouetted against the sinking sun.[136] Other films' stories told of white men—weaklings, cowards, or "bad men"—who, through their experiences in the West, underwent testing and transformation; and one of the more intriguing (unfortunately, it seems not to have survived) is Broncho's *The Man They Scorned* (November 1912), which the *Mirror* described as "well-written, well-acted . . . and worthy of praise," and not only for its "wonderful battle scene."[137] Here the hero, a "tenderfoot" recruit sent to a western fort, is an anomaly, a "much-despised Jew," who quietly bears the taunts of his fellow soldiers and the unjust reprimands of the fort's colonel. By the end he has rescued the colonel from an Indian ambush, held off the attackers with a single rifle until reinforcements can arrive, and, recovering in a hospital, been cheered by "the soldiers that had so recently mocked him." *The Man They Scorned* may be no more unconventional than the earlier *Ranchman's Vengeance,* but it is far less ambiguous in representing Jewish (in contrast to Mexican) assimilation into an American social order—and not in an eastern city, but on the western frontier.[138]

Most of the Bison-101 films, however, were Indian pictures. For *Bioscope* they represented "the Redskin drama par excellence"; for the *World,* even if the Indian was recognized as "one of the most interesting and picturesque of elements in our national history," the films primarily were stories of "the pioneer as he was, one of the hardest fighters in the world."[139] So, what happens when we reconsider them as prime subjects for an analysis of the place and function of the "Indian" in the "imagined community" of the West? Of those discussed earlier, *The Lieutenant's Last Fight* is especially worthy of note. U.S. trade press ads described this film as a "military drama," in which "a troop of cavalry [is] entirely wiped out by Indians" and in which "the Lieutenant meets a heroic death" in a "heart-gripping, soul-stirring finale."[140] Yet as extensive trade reports attest, as does a surviving print,[141] the film's hero is actually a Sioux chief's son, Great Bear, who is commissioned as a U.S. Army officer at Fort Reno, scorned by all but a colonel's daughter, unfairly accused in a fight, court-martialed, and sent back to his tribe in dishonor. When circumstances lead the Sioux to declare war and attack a cavalry escort for the women leaving Fort Reno, Great Bear dons his uniform in order to save the white woman who trusted him. The ensuing battle favors the Sioux until he reaches a hillside above the encircled whites and begins shooting; the tide turns as he sounds a bugle call to halt the attack, and a rescue party of cavalry arrives—but he is killed by a retreating Sioux warrior. Unlike *The Deserter,* however, this film ends in a tableau of Great Bear's fallen body at twilight, "his heroism unknown even to the girl for whom he gave his life."[142]

A variation on this story occurred six months later in Kay-Bee's *The Invaders,* but here the heroine is a Sioux chief's daughter named Sky Star.[143] Two interrelated story lines drive this narrative. In one Sky Star rejects a suitor her father has accepted and then is attracted to a railway surveyor. In the other the Sioux protest to the colonel at a nearby fort that the surveyors are violating a recently signed treaty and then persuade the Cheyenne to join in an uprising. In alternating sequences Sky Star is injured in a fall, riding to warn the whites, but recovers just enough to reach the fort, while the Sioux attack and kill the survey crew. From then on the combined Indian forces ambush a cavalry detachment and lay siege to the fort, and, after the post telegrapher fails to signal another fort (the Indians cut the lines), a lieutenant proves himself worthy to the colonel (and his daughter) by escaping and returning with more troops—to rout the Indians. In the surviving print *The Invaders'* battle scenes remain impressive, marked by reverse-angle full shots/extreme long shots, some taken from a high-angle position.[144] Yet even more striking is the film's relative balance in depicting whites and Indians— the surveyor's POV shot of Sky Star through his scope is matched by POV shots of the Indian suitor viewing their exchange—and its refusal to celebrate one at the expense of the other—just as the killings of both whites and

Figure 6.5. *The Invaders,* production still, *Moving Picture World,* 9 November 1912, 521.

Indians resonated equally in an earlier title, *Indian Massacre.* The final tableau even offers a kind of "military funeral" for Sky Star, who dies of her injuries shortly before the siege is broken.[145] In a long shot of a darkened room, lit only by moonlight falling through a back window, the colonel's daughter kneels and weeps by her bed (frame left) then returns to the lieutenant at the closed door (frame right); and the colonel himself leans over the barely visible body, pauses, and finally closes the window shutters (figure 6.5).

In Europe Bison-101 Indian pictures were among the earliest imported American films that ran more than one reel and were far more regularly released than those of any other U.S. company.[146] That put them in the same league with all the Danish, Italian, and French multiple-reel films coming into vogue on the European market. And that, in turn, enhanced their status not only as an American product but also as a potential national epic, in which the conquest of the West offered a foundational story of national identity, a mythic narrative of origins.[147] Yet the Indian rather than the cowboy or horse soldier was the significant figure for Europeans. The U.S. industry considered "scenes of cowboys and Indians . . . [a] commodity of genuine commercial importance" for export, according to *Motography*, because they were "picturesque," that is, "bizarre, exciting, and unusual in American life."[148] For the British, by contrast, what appealed was the portrayal of "primeval man, with all his passions" confronting "the savage forces of Nature" and having to rely on his own resources.[149] The attraction was similar for the French, who were even more fascinated by Indians, for it confirmed their conception of America as a new mythic space of the primitive and barbaric.[150] In short, for both Americans and Europeans the "Vanishing American" was an especially salient figure of what Renato Rosaldo has called the "imperialist nostalgia" for the defeated heroic Other.[151] Yet if in Europe the "Redskin drama" symbolized an American barbarism that might revitalize their older civilizations,[152] in the United States the Indian served as a figure of exclusion from or assimilation into—and, either way, justified—a new "imperial" nation.[153] Perhaps even more than the historical pageants then so popular, Indian pictures enacted an ongoing ritual performance of "innovative nostalgia" that, in the new medium of moving pictures, "placed nostalgic imagery in a dynamic, future-oriented . . . context."[154]

In other words, the multiple-reel Indian pictures may have been particularly effective in binding disparate audiences in the United States into an "imagined community of nationality," whether within a single theater or across a variety of theaters, within a single city or across the country.[155] Here, in conjunction with the respectful attitude of most films, the shape-shifting identity of the Indian, more mythic figure than historical subject (especially since their numbers had dwindled so drastically in the late nineteenth century), would have been crucial. Unlike the usually fixed identity of the Mexican in other westerns or the African American in Civil War films—and more like the latter films' southern soldier whose sense of honor and sacrifice made him (or her, in the case of a "girl spy") suitable for assimilation—the "inbetween" figure of the Indian was open to multiple readings and interpretations. The specifics of those readings would have depended, in part, on an interested spectator's race/ethnicity, class, and/or gender; yet however different, it could have helped to elucidate and confirm that spectator's social position within the "nation." Drawing on the cities cited earlier,[156] could a French Canadian woman assembling shoes in Lynn, a Polish shop girl in Toledo, and a Scandinavian or Jewish stenographer in Des Moines have read an Indian such as Sky Star or one of Mona Darkfeather's heroines more or less similarly, as an honorable figure of their own assimilation? Could a Slovak steelworker in Youngstown and a Hungarian glassworker in Toledo have taken an Indian such as Great Bear (especially in contrast to the exceptional White Eagle in *The Flaming Arrow*), however differently, as a figure of doubt or warning in relation to their own assimilation? By contrast, could a second-generation German businessman in Cleveland have interpreted the figure as reason for finding one or even both of the others unfit for assimilation? Although written earlier, Mary Heaton Vorse's 1911 description of a Jewish immigrant audience in a lower East Side theater, even if fictionalized, offers an even more specific model of reading. There, enthralled by a one-reel Indian picture, sits a young woman Vorse describes as especially taken with Yellow Wing and her love for Dick the Trapper, murmuring out loud from time to time, "Surely, surely, she will save her beloved!" and "The poor child! How can she bear it? To see the *geliebte* wounded before one's very eyes!"[157]

In short, Indian pictures worked to forge, in Hansen's words, an *American* "mass public out of an ethnically and culturally heterogeneous society" yet one in which some degree of separation still marked their "constellated communities" or audiences.[158] In March 1913 the *Cleveland Leader* concisely summed up such films' ideological or "educational" function: "Bison, Broncho and Kay-Bee . . . are producing historic subjects that are worthy of exhibition in every school in the country."[159]

THE "IMAGINED COMMUNITY" OF THE "GREAT WEST": "COWBOY GIRL" PICTURES

Finally, a passing remark in Emilie Altenloh's 1913 dissertation on moving picture audiences in Germany—that women often were "at the center of the action" in American westerns—prompts a closer look at the many "cowboy girl" westerns of the period.[160] As I have argued before, cowboy girl westerns (from Selig, Essanay, and Bison) already were numerous by 1910, and they were no less so two years later—yet, unlike the Broncho Billy series and multiple-reel Indian pictures they were not the province of any one company.[161] Many of these, too, were "school of action" westerns. Vitagraph's *How States Are Made,* directed by Rollin S. Sturgeon,[162] "deal[t] with a well-known phase of Western life that everybody seems to have overlooked," the *World* wrote, "in the mad scramble to supply the demand for 'Western stuff'": the 1893 Oklahoma land rush.[163] Here, it is the wife (Anna Schaeffer) who has to ride furiously to stake a claim (after her husband has been injured) and beat out a villain in the bargain. In the same company's *A Girl of the West* (January 1912) the plucky sister of the hero's sweetheart does her own horseback riding to single-handedly foil a rustling plot.[164] In Alice Guy Blaché's *Two Little Rangers* (Solax, August 1912) a postmaster is robbed and a cowboy falsely accused of the crime until the postmaster's daughters track down the real criminal and, unable to get him to surrender, set fire to his shack (with him inside).[165] And, in a tribute to the "Kalem beauties" who performed in such westerns (among them Ruth Roland and Alice Joyce), the *Mirror* praised their daring, expert skills as horseback riders—even if specific films like *The Ranch Girls on the Rampage* (May 1912) upset one reviewer when those "beauties" played characters no better than "hoodlums."[166] Such cowboy girl westerns continued to be made at least for another year, as evidenced in Selig's *Sallie's Sure Shot* (July 1913), where, in a quickly edited sequence of close shots, the heroine (Kathlyn Williams) not only keeps two thieves at bay with a rifle but spins and fires, cutting the fuse on a stick of dynamite set to blow up her father's cabin.[167]

Yet not all cowboy girl westerns were "school of action" films. Take *The Craven* (April 1912), a "significant example," in the *Mirror's* words, "of the peculiarly strong type of Vitagraph Western picture."[168] Here a woman (Anna Schaeffer, again) discovers the boastful sheriff she has married is really a coward; when a man sought for murder shows up near town, she has to go out and kill him with a well-aimed rifle shot, then have her husband collect the body and take credit for the deed. As a "quality" film with strong social implications, *The Craven* not only focuses on the wife as a perceptive and skillful frontier woman but also ends with a close shot of her alone, dejected, revealing that her sacrificial heroism—not unlike that of Great Bear—goes unrecognized because never publicly voiced by her cowardly husband. A very different "character study" appears in Vitagraph's *Una of the Sierras* (November 1912).[169] This story sends an orphaned gold miner's daughter, unexpectedly left "enough gold to pay the national debt," to her aunt's city mansion, where she rapidly, and with zest, learns the ways of modern society—and ultimately saves her suitor's company from a rival's plot to corner its stock. Much like Selig's 1913 remake of *The Cowboy Millionaire* (1909),[170] this film plays as a comedy or satire, in which the behavior of an "uncivilized" character upsets all kinds of social norms. Yet its role reversals are far from frivolous, especially when the young woman outdoes the men as a sharp financier: at the climax she takes control of a stockholders' meeting—dominating the foreground space, with her back to the camera. Moreover, although the film barely hints at this, through her name and an intertitle describing her as "a child of nature" Una can be read as part Indian.[171] Indeed, her spontaneity, spunk, and "native" intelligence are so appealing that this "half-breed" figure puts a provocative spin on then current movie representations of the "New Woman."

Whether they wore the brand of "action" or "quality," cowboy girl westerns were far from anomalies at the time. Important contexts for their production included juvenile series for girls such as *The Ranch Girls,* which began publication in 1911,[172] and the commanding presence of women in Buffalo Bill's Wild West and especially the Miller Brothers' 101 Ranch Wild West. Edith Tantlinger and Lucille Mulhall, for instance, starred in the earliest 101 Ranch Wild West shows—one as a sharpshooter, the other as a champion steer roper[173]—and Lucille Parr and Bessie Herberg appeared as "poster girls" for the 1912 tour of 101 Ranch Wild West.[174] Indeed, in Toledo the 101 Ranch cowgirls openly described themselves as suffragists.[175] Newspapers, in particular, exploited the popularity of like-minded women in the movies. Begin-

Figure 6.6.   Pauline Garfield Bush, *Des Moines News,* 11
February 1913, 3.

ning in late 1912, Gertrude Price's many syndicated stories, in Scripps-McRae
papers, promoted western stars such as Mona Darkfeather, Ruth Roland,
Louise Lester, and Pauline Garfield Bush (Flying A) (figure 6.6).[176] If these
and other cowboy girls deserve a closer, serious look, it is not just because
they constitute a kind of "missing link" to later serial queens such as Kathlyn
Williams, whose own preserial promotional stories often highlighted their ad-
venturous roles.[177] It is because, as working women characters and actors
(some of whom were suffragettes), they embodied a healthy, active, even stren-
uous (and often single) way of life that had enormous appeal for young women
who, on the evidence of Price's widely distributed stories, even then were form-

ing the core of an emerging fan culture of "photoplay matinee girls."[178] Whatever the brand of cowboy girl western, Altenloh's remark is telling and contrasts sharply with what the *World* thought Europeans were learning about
American women from moving pictures: that they were treated with "delicate
courtesy" and a "universal chivalrous spirit."[179] Instead, what so many westerns, so popular here and abroad between 1911 and 1913, had at their center was a vigorously active heroine, a "Western species" of what the Europeans
perceived as a distinctly *American* "New Woman."[180]

A VANISHING MARKET FOR THE WESTERN?

According to some sources the western was fading by the summer of 1913.
The *Mirror* interviewed J. J. Raymond of Gordon Amusement, a major New
England exhibitor, who reported that "the Western picture has grown
stale."[181] In cartoons and reviews the *World* now tended to dismiss Anderson's cowboy hero as fit chiefly for "youthful admirers" (figure 6.7).[182] Fewer
cowboy girl westerns appeared in circulation, coinciding with a general movement that increasingly delinked working women from suffrage, after the failure of women that year to win the right to vote, and more closely aligned
them with mass consumption. Perhaps more important, as Kay-Bee, Broncho, and Bison (Universal) expanded production to include multiple-reel
films of the Civil War and Spanish-American War, so as to exploit the spectacle of large-scale battle scenes, the latter soon began to outnumber westerns. Indeed, none of these companies opted to make westerns of more than
three reels during the emergence of the feature-length film as a regular production and marketing strategy in 1913. Finally, according to Consulate Reports released in early 1914, "the cowboy picture had run its course in foreign lands," and "European picture goers," in particular, were "growing tired
[of] the cowboys and Indian fighters of Western America."[183] As Bush concluded, once "thought to be the foundation and hope of the motion picture," the western had come to its "destined end" of the trail.[184]

Yet news of the western's demise seemed much exaggerated. Essanay's
Broncho Billy series not only remained popular but, in the case of *Broncho
Billy's Mistake* (September 1913), received admiring trade press notices and,
with *Broncho Billy Gets Square* (October 1913), began to shift into multiple-
reel production.[185] Moreover, certain Essanay westerns such as *Episode at
Cloudy Canyon* (August 1913) told their stories so clearly in images that they
needed no intertitles.[186] Selig also increasingly featured the "skill, verve, and
nerve" of Tom Mix in multiple-reel cowboy pictures, beginning with *The
Law and the Outlaw* (June 1913) and *The Escape of Jim Dolan* (November
1913), and his westerns were not among those that European audiences
had "grown tired of," at least in Paris.[187] Encouraged by favorable trade press

Figure 6.7. Essanay ad, *Moving Picture World,* 5 April
1913, 40.

notices, Kalem made Indian pictures (now often starring Darkfeather) a
staple of its production, which, with *The Big Horn Massacre* (December 1913),
soon became regular multiple-reel releases.[188] When feature-length westerns finally did begin to appear in early 1914, they did not follow the "tradition" established by Kay-Bee and Broncho Indian pictures, which offered
leading roles to actual Indians;[189] instead, they turned back to adapt famous
stage plays from a decade earlier, such as Jesse Lasky's *The Squaw Man* (March
1914), directed by Cecil B. DeMille.[190] And one of these, Selig's nine-reel
The Spoilers (March 1914), featured on the inaugural program of the "picture palace" Strand in New York.[191] Whatever its ebbs and flows, the continuing popularity of westerns eventually would reach new heights several
years later—in the cowboy features of William S. Hart (for Triangle/
Artcraft), Mix (for Fox), and Francis Ford's brother Jack, later known as John
(for Universal).[192]

THE WESTERN AND AMERICAN MODERNITY

Even if the western did suffer a momentary fading or "vanishing," that does
not diminish the significance of all those cowboy, Indian, and cowboy girl

pictures so popular in the early 1910s. As I argued in *The Red Rooster Scare,* we can learn a great deal about how early cinema in the United States became an increasingly Americanized phenomenon just prior to 1910 by reexamining the emergence of the western in relation to the then dominant foreign films of Pathé. But we can learn just as much, as I argue here, about that Americanization process and the contingent development of a "New World" national identity by reexamining the shifting figures of inclusion and exclusion in the "imagined community" of the western in the early 1910s, in part by following the trails left by "Old World" as well as "New World" audiences and taking seriously their fascination with all those films that still remain unrecognized or even misrecognized. For if the cowboy (and cowboy girl) then registered as *the* figure of *American* modernity in early moving pictures—"the first living and breathing thing of modernity that was photographed in motion," wrote Harrison so presciently, in January 1914, remarkably anticipating Hansen[193]—the long vanquished and now vanishing Indian, more fictional than historical, played his (or her) ideological counterpart, either as the most noble foe and foil of that modernity or as its most inclusive, most assimilable figure of "otherness."

NOTES

This essay originated in a short paper given at the Society for Cinema Studies Conference (May 2000) and then in a longer paper delivered for an American Studies lecture series at the California Institute of Technology (October 2000). Thanks to Shawn Shimpach and Catherine Jurca, who organized the panel and lecture series, respectively, and for the comments and questions of those attending one or the other. The latter version appears in *France/Hollywood: Allers-retours et échanges,* ed. Martin Barnier and Raphaelle Moine (Paris: L'Harmattan, 2002). Thanks also to Charlie Keil and Shelley Stamp, whose valuable suggestions helped me tighten the essay and strengthen its argument.

   1. See, e.g., "Film Charts," *Moving Picture News* (hereafter *MPN*), 29 April 1911, 21; and *MPN*, 20 May 1911, 20. Nine months earlier the *New York Dramatic Mirror* did a survey of all films released on the market in July and came up with a similar set of categories, except for westerns, which it subsumed under the more general term *melodrama*—see "Pictures Need No Censoring," *New York Dramatic Mirror* (hereafter *NYDM*), 14 August 1910, 25. Six months earlier, in categorizing musical accompaniment for moving pictures, Clarence Sinn also subsumed "cowboy pictures" within melodrama, "more or less of a sensational order"—see "Music for the Picture," *Moving Picture World* (hereafter *MPW*), 3 December 1910, 1285.
   2. "Letters to the Editor," *MPW,* 11 February 1911, 314.
   3. "In the Far West," *Bioscope,* 9 February 1911, 11–12.
   4. "Motion Picture Reviews," *Billboard,* 11 March 1911, 15.
   5. This essay extends the argument developed in the last chapter of Richard Abel, *The Red Rooster Scare: Making Cinema American, 1900–1910* (Berkeley: University of California Press, 1999), 151–74; it will be expanded into two chapters in a forth-

coming book, *The "Imagined Community" of U.S. Cinema, 1910–1914* (Berkeley: University of California Press).

6. Although primarily interested in proposing a theoretical model of genre useful for cinema studies, Altman offers a relevant sketch of the western as a genre-in-the-state-of-becoming. See Rick Altman, *Film/Genre* (London: British Film Institute, 1999), 36–38.

7. The phrases "imagined community" and "cultural artefacts" come from an unusually instructive book on nationalism as a historical construct—Benedict Anderson, *Imagined Communities*, 2d ed. (London: Verso, 1991), 4.

8. Herbert Blau, *The Audience* (Baltimore, Md.: Johns Hopkins University Press, 1990), 21. For a definition of "constellated communities," particularly as distinct from Anderson's "imagined community," see Altman, *Film/Genre*, 161–62, 198, 199. The phrase "usable past" comes from Van Wyck Brooks's influential essay, "Creating a Usable Past," *Dial* 64 (11 April 1918): 337–41.

9. Here I draw largely on current research that involves a relatively systematic examination of local newspapers (1910–14) in three regions: northeastern Massachusetts, northern Ohio, and the upper Midwest. Initial results from that research can be found in Richard Abel, "A Marriage of Ephemeral Discourses: Newspapers and Moving Pictures," *Cinema et cie* 1 (2001): 59–83.

10. Miriam Bratu Hansen, "The Mass Production of the Senses: Classical Cinema as Vernacular Modernism," in *Re-Inventing Film Studies*, ed. Christine Gledhill and Linda Williams (London: Arnold, 2000), 340–44. See also Miriam Bratu Hansen, "Fallen Women, Rising Stars, New Horizons," *Film Quarterly* 54, no. 1 (2000): 12–13. Curiously, Hansen offers not westerns but "slapstick comedy, adventure serials, and detective films" as examples of that "new sensibility" of "Americanism" or American modernity during the 1910s.

11. See, e.g., Hans Leigh, "Acting and Action," *MPW*, 2 October 1909, 443; "Essanay Will Release Two Reels," *MPW*, 6 November 1909, 638; and "Comments on the Films," *MPW*, 8 January 1910, 17.

12. Anderson wrote, directed, and starred in most of these early Essanay westerns, which were filmed near Denver, El Paso, and Santa Barbara until he finally located a studio in Niles Canyon, thirty miles from Oakland, California, in the summer of 1912. See "The Essanay Story," probably written by Stuart Nixon, editor of the *Niles Township Register,* in March 1953, in the Hollywood Museum Collection, Margaret Herrick Library, American Motion Picture Arts and Sciences (hereafter AMPAS). A 35 mm viewing print of *Under Western Skies* (920 feet) is available at the Library of Congress.

13. "The Indian and the Cowboy," *MPW*, 17 December 1910, 1399. See also "Reviews of Independent Films," *NYDM*, 23 November 1910, 31; "Comments on the Films," *MPW*, 26 November 1910, 1238; and an article reprinted from the *Los Angeles Times* as "The Press and the Picture," *MPW*, 3 December 1910, 1290.

14. "Pictures That Children Like," *Film Index*, 21 January 1911, 3.

15. "The Passing of the Western Subject," *Nickelodeon*, 18 February 1911, 181–82.

16. "What Would the Film Producer Do without These?" *Nickelodeon*, 11 March 1911, 278.

17. Exceptions would include letters to "The Spectator" complaining about "the

awful flood of cowboy and Indian subjects that the film-makers still persist in turning out" (*NYDM,* 12 April 1911, 30; see also *NYDM,* 19 April 1911, 30).

18. Representatives of several tribes appeared in Washington, D.C., protesting the depiction of Indians in westerns. See "Those Indignant Indians [reprinted from the *New York World],*" *Nickelodeon,* 4 March 1911, 246; "The Indian and the Film," *Billboard,* 11 March 1911, 14; and "Indian War on Films," *MPW,* 18 March 1911, 581.

19. In Canton the managers of the Majestic and Dreamland were interviewed in "Picture Show Poor Man's Vacation Trip and Sure Cure for 'Blues' for All," *Canton News-Democrat,* 23 April 1911, 14. In Lynn the Comique and Central Square called particular attention to westerns, and Biograph films, in their ads in the *Lynn Daily Item* between December 1911 and February 1912.

20. See the Selig ad on the inside front cover of *Nickelodeon,* June 1911. Perhaps prompting Selig's strategy were reviews of such films as *The Outbreak;* see "Critical Reviews of Licensed Films," *New York Morning Telegraph* (hereafter *NYMT*), 5 March 1911, 4.1, 4.

21. "What an Audience Likes," *MPN,* 3 June 1911, 13. Even reputable critics such as W. Stephen Bush of the *World,* who usually preferred "art" films, occasionally recognized the "tragic power" of a western such as Kalem's *The Mexican Joan of Arc* (July 1911); see W. Stephen Bush, "The Mexican Joan of Arc," *MPW,* 15 July 1911, 19.

22. See the Selig ad in *MPW,* 29 July 1911, 227. Mix worked and trained at the Miller Brothers' 101 Ranch in Oklahoma before teaming up with Selig in 1910; see Paul Reddin, *Wild West Shows* (Urbana: University of Illinois Press, 1999), 190–91. See also Eileen Bowser, *The Transformation of Cinema, 1907–1915* (New York: Scribner's, 1990), 172.

23. A 35 mm viewing print of *Saved by the Pony Express* (920 feet) is available at the Library of Congress.

24. "Selecting the Programme," *MPN,* 9 September 1911, 14. See also "Comments on the Films," *MPW,* 12 August 1911, 377.

25. "Letters to the Editor: Cowboys Always Popular," *MPW,* 12 August 1911, 383. The only evidence of criticism that summer came in a letter from Cleveland, asking, "Why in the name of common sense are so many film producers Western mad?" and in Bush's diatribe against Indian stereotypes; see "Letters to the Editor," *MPW,* 22 July 1911, 132; and Bush, "Moving Picture Absurdities," *MPW,* 16 September 1911, 773.

26. See the Vitagraph ad in *NYDM,* 15 March 1911, 31.

27. "Reviews of Independent Films," *NYDM,* 21 June 1911, 32. Darkfeather was from "an old aristocratic Spanish family" in Los Angeles, but her study of Indian customs endeared her to many tribes and led to her being described as "the greatest exponent of Indian women in the motion picture business" ("Best 'Indian' in Films Is Not Real Redskin," *Cleveland Leader,* 22 December 1912, sec. S, p. 5).

28. "*Little Dove's Romance,*" *MPN,* 2 September 1911, 602. A 16 mm viewing print of *Little Dove's Romance* (388 feet), from the Paul Killiam Collection, is available at the Library of Congress.

29. "The Vogue of Western and Military Drama," *MPW,* 5 August 1911, 271. Edward S. Curtis, *The North American Indian: Being a Series of Volumes Picturing and Describing the Indians of the United States and Alaska* (Seattle, Wash.: published by the au-

thor, 1907–30). This preservationist impulse also was evident in several music collections published at the time: Alice C. Fletcher, *Indian Story and Song from North America* (Boston, Md.: Small, Maynard, 1900); Frederick R. Buton, *American Primitive Music* (New York: Moffat, Yard, 1909); and John A. Lomax, *Cowboy Songs and Other Frontier Ballads* (New York: Sturgis and Walton, 1910). See Charles C. Alexander, *Here Lies the Country: Nationalism and the Arts in Twentieth-Century America* (Bloomington: Indiana University Press, 1980), 58.

30. "'Spectator's' Comments," *NYDM*, 14 December 1910, 28. See also Sumiko Higashi, "The Song of the Wildwood Flute," in *The Griffith Project*, ed. Cherchi Usai (London: British Film Institute, 1999–2000), 4:218–19. The latter film allegedly depicted a harvest dance ritual. A 16 mm viewing print of *The Song of the Wildwood Flute* is available at the Library of Congress. Scholars still tend to focus on D. W. Griffith's Biograph westerns to the exclusion of others more popular and/or influential at the time, especially when they write about Indian pictures in the early 1910s: see, e.g., the otherwise excellent recent study by Alison Griffiths, "Playing at Being Indian: Spectatorship and the Early Western," *Journal of Popular Film and Television* 29, no. 3 (fall 2001): 100–111. An unusual variation on the first film occurs in Kalem's *Her Indian Mother* (December 1910), in which the daughter of an Indian and a Hudson Bay Company representative decides to remain in her mother's village rather than return with her father to Montreal. A 35 mm viewing print of *Her Indian Mother* is available at the Library of Congress.

31. Young Deer had performed with the 101 Ranch Wild West and then worked on western films for Kalem, Lubin, Biograph, Vitagraph, and Bison before being hired by Pathé in early 1910; later that year he was sent to Los Angeles to establish the company's western production unit near Selig's Edendale studio. Until the appearance of the Bison-101 westerns Pathé was the only company that consistently had Indians play Indian roles. See, e.g., "James Young Deer," *MPW*, 6 May 1911, 999; and the full-page Pathé ad for "Princess Red Wing," *NYDM*, 1 May 1912, 33. The earliest surviving film probably directed by Young Deer, but shot in New Jersey, is *White Fawn's Devotion* (June 1910), available on Program 3 of the *Treasures from American Film Archives* DVD (2000).

32. "*The Legend of Lake Desolation,*" *MPW*, 29 July 1911, 191. See also "Motion Picture Reviews," *Billboard*, 19 August 1911, 15.

33. In the summer and fall of 1911, according to its ads in *Billboard*, the Powers Company also manufactured at least one Indian picture a week.

34. See the American ad in *MPN*, 8 April 1911, 23. See also "Data from Manufacturers' List of Releases," *MPN*, 6 May 1911, 24.

35. See, e.g., "Motion Picture Reviews," *Billboard*, 20 May 1911, 50–51; and ibid., 27 May 1911, 51.

36. "Cowboy Pictures," *MPW*, 10 June 1911, 1304; "Progress of the Independent Product," *MPW*, 15 July 1911, 29.

37. "Reviews of Notable Films," *MPW*, 29 July 1911, 190–91. Bowser analyzes *The Ranchman's Nerve* in her *Transformation of Cinema*, 172.

38. See, e.g., the American ads in *MPN*, 26 August 1911, 17; *NYDM*, 6 September 1911, 24; and *MPW*, 16 September 1911, 770.

39. "Newsy Items from El Cajon Valley," *MPN*, 30 September 1911, 28.

40. See, e.g., the American ads in *MPN*, 9 March 1912, 51; and *MPW*, 16 March

1912, 980–81. At least three of these stories were published in the *Des Moines News:* "The Grub Stake Mortgage—A Moving Picture Short Story of Western Life," 17 January 1912, 10; "Where Broadway Meets the Mountains—A Moving Picture Story of the West," 27 January 1912, 3; and "How Lonesome Was Chased Off the Ranch," 9 April 1912, 4.

41. Alan Trachtenberg, *The Incorporation of America: Culture and Society in the Gilded Age* (New York: Hill and Wang, 1982), 17–18. At a Chicago "land show" in late 1911 the Union Pacific was still using moving pictures to entice people to settle in the western states; see "In the Moving Picture World," *Chicago Tribune,* 3 December 1911, sec. 2, pt. 2, p. 2. The catalog edited by William Truettner, *The West as America* (Washington, D.C.: Smithsonian Institute, 1991), includes extraordinary images from that iconographic tradition. For an analysis of earlier western films in the context of this tradition see Abel, *Red Rooster Scare,* 152–53.

42. "Wild West Pictures," *MPN,* 18 November 1911, 6. Even more letters agreeing with that article were cited in "Wild West Pictures," *MPN,* 25 November 1911, 7.

43. "Facts and Comments," *MPW,* 2 December 1911, 700. The diatribes lasted into February 1912, not only in the *News* but in the *Mirror,* where Frank Woods wrote that even if they were "better done" than before, there still were "too many melodramas and Wild West subjects" on the market; see "'Spectator's' Comments," *NYDM,* 7 February 1912, 28; and "The Wild West," *MPN,* 24 February 1912, 21. See also the remark that cowboy films, although "distinctly not criminal," were hardly "elevating in taste and generally worthless as examples of art," in "'Spectator's' Comments," *NYDM,* 6 December 1911, 28.

44. "At the Theatres," *Lowell Sunday Telegram,* 2 July 1911, 6. Both Biograph films also were among the first programs arranged by S. L. Rothapfel as the new manager of the seventeen-hundred-seat Lyric in Minneapolis; *Fighting Blood,* in particular, "held the audience spellbound and at its termination always evoked applause"; see "Vaudeville and Pictures," *Minneapolis Journal,* 15 October 1911, 8; and "Tag Day at the Lyric," *Minneapolis Journal,* 31 October 1911, 16. See also "Motion Picture Reviews," *Billboard,* 15 July 1911, 15.

45. "Bison Company Gets 101 Ranch Wild West," *MPN,* 2 December 1911, 24; "Bison Gets 101 Ranch," *NYDM,* 6 December 1911, 29; "Bison Company Gets 101 Ranch," *MPW,* 9 December 1911, 810; "Western Spectacles," *Billboard,* 9 December 1911, 46; "What Bison Wants," *MPW,* 13 January 1912, 119; and "Bison-101 Feature Pictures," *MPW,* 27 January 1912, 298. A solid reappraisal of Bison-101 and Thomas Ince can be found in Kevin Brownlow, *The War, the West, and the Wilderness* (New York: Knopf, 1978), 253–62. For a thorough, well-told story of the Miller Brothers' 101 Ranch see Michael Wallis, *The Real Wild West: The 101 Ranch and the Creation of the American West* (New York: St. Martin's, 1999).

46. "With the Western Producers," *MPW,* 18 November 1911, 41. See also "Mr. Thomas H. Ince," *MPN,* 26 October 1912, 21; and "Spectacular Pictures His Long Suit," *MPN,* 8 November 1913, 18. Later Ince would promote himself as a founder of the western genre in an article in *MPW* (5 July 1915, 225)—quoted in Brownlow, *The War,* 256. See also the column of articles later written by Ince, entitled "In the 'Movies'—Yesterday and Today," esp. numbers 4 and 5—in the Hollywood Museum Collection, AMPAS.

47. "Reviews of Notable Films," *MPW,* 29 July 1911, 193.

48. See the Dome Theater ad, *Youngstown Vindicator,* 9 April 1911, 14. A 35 mm viewing print of *The Sheriff's Chum* (750 feet) is available at the Library of Congress.

49. "Critical Reviews of Licensed Films," *NYMT,* 16 April 1911, 4.1, 7. Although praising the climactic fight, *Billboard* also found the film "entirely lacking in plot," with poorly connected events; see "Motion Picture Reviews," *Billboard,* 15 April 1911, 17.

50. "Letters to 'The Spectator,'" *NYDM,* 24 May 1911, 33.

51. "The 'Most Photographed Man,'" *Motography,* November 1911, 245; *NYDM,* 22 November 1911, 26; and "'Live' Advertising for Exhibitors," *MPN,* 2 December 1911, 714.

52. See also the Majestic ads for "Little Mary" in *NYDM,* 18 October 1911, 30; 25 October 1911, 30; and 15 November 1911, 29. Only a year later a second movie star, Pauline Garfield Bush, would appear on the *Mirror'*s cover (2 October 1912). In a popularity contest conducted by *Motion Picture Story Magazine* in early 1912 Anderson placed fifth among picture players (behind Maurice Costello, F. Dolores Cassenilli, Alice Joyce, and Florence Lawrence); Pickford placed tenth. See "Most Popular Picture Player," *Motography,* March 1912, 132.

53. "J. Max Anderson," *Youngstown Vindicator,* 15 October 1911, 14; and "This Man's Photo Seen Every Day for 300,000," *Canton News-Democrat,* 5 November 1911, 15. See also "Is Boys' Favorite," *Cleveland Leader,* 24 December 1911, sec. B, p. 7.

54. See, e.g., the Princess ads in *Youngstown Vindicator* (from 15 October 1911, 15, to 7 January 1912, 17); and the Orpheum ads in *Canton News-Democrat* (from 21 April 1912, 15, to 9 June 1912, 12). Several of these ads include a photo of "Bullets" Anderson.

55. See the Essanay ads in *MPW,* 23 December 1911, 951; and *MPW,* 2 March 1912, 739.

56. A 35 mm viewing print of *A Pal's Oath* (895 feet) is available at the Library of Congress. An ironic variation on this story, rather unusual in Anderson's westerns, occurs in *A Wife of the Hills* (July 1912), in which Anderson escapes jail to take revenge on a friend and his unfaithful wife, only to give himself up after a gunfight outside their cabin when he gratefully discovers that a stray shot from the sheriff or his posse has hit the friend, who dies in the wife's arms. A 35 mm viewing print of *A Wife of the Hills* is available at the Nederlands Filmmuseum. Another occurs in *Broncho Billy's Oath* (October 1913), in which Anderson does shoot his treacherous friend through a cabin window; see "Licensed Films," *NYDM,* 29 October 1913, 38.

57. "Reviews of Licensed Films," *NYDM,* 3 January 1912, 30. A 35 mm viewing print of *Broncho Billy's Christmas Dinner* is available at the Nederlands Filmmuseum.

58. See, e.g., James S. McQuade, "Famous Cowboys in Motion Pictures," *Film Index,* 25 June 1910, 9–10; the special poster for *Ranch Life in the Great Southwest* was reproduced in *Film Index,* 2 July 1910, 23; "Buffalo Bill Films," *Billboard,* 17 September 1910, 24; and for the Atlas ad see *MPN,* 30 September 1911, 18. The three-reel *James Boys in Missouri* was especially vilified in the trade press; see "The James Boys in Missouri," *MPN,* 2 September 1911, 8–9. An incomplete 35 mm viewing print of the Selig film (622 feet) is available at the National Film and Television Archive. A 16 mm viewing print of reel 1 of *Buffalo Bill Wild West–Pawnee Bill Far East* is available at the Library of Congress.

59. *War on the Plains* was given a special trade press screening in New York; see

"The New Home for the Bison Films," *MPN,* 20 January 1912, 22. See also "Bison-101 Feature Pictures," *MPW,* 27 January 1912, 298; the Bison-101 ads in *MPN,* 3 February 1912, 28; *MPW,* 10 February 1912, 449; *NYMT,* 17 March 1912, 4.2, 4; and *Film Fancies,* 24 February 1912—cited in Brownlow, *The War,* 256. *The Golden Wedding* received the gold medal at the 1911 Cinematograph Exposition in Turin, Italy, which a Cleveland theater, the Tabor, publicized when the film played there in late 1911; see "Reviews of Notable Films," *MPW,* 9 December 1911, 799; and "At Leading Theaters," *Cleveland Leader,* 31 December 1911, sec. B, p. 7.

60. "Comments on the Films," *MPW,* 23 March 1912, 1063.

61. See, e.g., the Bison-101 ads in *MPN,* 23 March 1912, 40; *MPW,* 30 March 1912, 1131; and *"Blazing the Trail," MPN,* 13 April 1912, 7. I have not yet viewed *Blazing the Trail,* which survives in a 35 mm viewing print at the Museum of Modern Art.

62. Louis Reeves Harrison, *"The Indian Massacre," MPW,* 9 March 1912, 854–56. A 35 mm viewing print of *The Indian Massacre* (1,716 feet) is available at the Library of Congress.

63. Biograph's better known, much praised *Iola's Promise* (March 1912) makes for an interesting comparison here, for its "dull and timid Indian girl," played by a quite recognizable Mary Pickford, is indebted to a white miner for rescuing her from a band of cutthroats and, in return, later rescues him and his wife from her own tribe (prompted by the latter's gesture making the sign of the Cross) and then dies—but not before revealing the source of the gold the miner is seeking in Indian territory. See, e.g., "Critical Reviews," *NYMT,* 17 March 1912, 4.2, 5; and "Reviews of Licensed Films," *NYDM,* 20 March 1912, 30. A 16 mm viewing print of *Iola's Promise* is available at the Library of Congress.

64. "Reviews of Special Feature Subjects," *NYDM,* 24 April 1912, 27.

65. "Reviews of Sales Company Films," *NYDM,* 20 March 1912, 33. See also "Critical Reviews," *NYMT,* 17 March 1912, 4.2, 4. A 35 mm viewing print of reel 2 of *The Deserter* (879 feet) is available at the Library of Congress. For an interesting column describing the choices of musical accompaniment for Bison-101 westerns, esp. "the climax of these beautiful plays," see Clarence E. Sinn, "Music for the Picture," *MPW,* 25 May 1912, 717.

66. "Critical Reviews," *NYMT,* 17 March 1912, sec. 4, pt. 2, p. 4.

67. For the Mall ad see *Cleveland Leader,* 10 March 1912, sec. S, p. 6; and "From Religious to Wild West, Range of Week's Films," *Cleveland Leader,* 7 April 1912, sec. S, p. 8.

68. "Programs of Leading Theaters," *Cleveland Leader,* 17 March 1912, sec. S, p. 6; 24 March 1912, sec. S, p. 6; and 2 April 1912, sec. W, p. 8.

69. "Correspondence," *MPW,* 23 March 1912, 1085. See the Central Square ads in the *Lynn Daily Item,* 23 March to 8 June 1912.

70. "The Critic's Comment," *Lynn Daily Item,* 4 June 1912, 5.

71. Colonial Theater ad, *Toledo News-Bee,* 27 March 1912, 7. With seating for one thousand patrons the Colonial was the largest Toledo theater.

72. "At the Photo Plays," *Toledo News-Bee,* 20 April 1912, 2. See the ads for the Crown Theater from early March to early June 1912. See also "Correspondence," *MPW,* 13 July 1912, 164.

73. "What's Offered This Week in the Local Show Shops," *Minneapolis Journal,* 2 June 1912, 8.8. See the ads for the Crystal and the Isis in the Sunday edition of the

Minneapolis Journal from 25 February through 6 June 1912. The Unique, which rarely advertised, even featured three Bison-101 westerns, one after the other, one week in June; see "'Movies' on a Ranch," *Minneapolis Journal,* 13 June 1912, 12.

74. See the Family Theatre ads in the *Des Moines Register and Leader,* 21 April 1912, 5; and the *Des Moines News,* 21 April 1912, 6. *Blazing the Trail* also played at the east side Elite Theater two months later; see the Elite Theater ad, *Des Moines News,* 30 June 1912, 6.

75. For a fine summary of how the distribution of multiple-reel and feature films created problems for both the MPPC and the Independents see Bowser, *Transformation of Cinema,* 218–24.

76. "Big Independent Developments," *NYDM,* 3 April 1912, 27.

77. "'101' Bison Problem Solved," *NYDM,* 10 April 1912, 25.

78. See, e.g., "New Corporation Enters Field of Film Exchange," *NYMT,* 24 March 1912, 4.2, 4; "Film Field Now Entered by Two New Rival Forces," *NYMT,* 19 May 1912, sec. 4, pt. 2, p. 1; "Independent Division?" *NYDM,* 22 May 1912, 27; "Break in Ranks of Sales Company," *MPW,* 25 May 1912, 707; and "Independent Split Complete," *NYDM,* 29 May 1912, 27.

79. See, e.g., the Universal ad in *NYDM,* 12 June 1912, 31; and "Laemmle Controls Universal," *MPW,* 21 June 1913, 1237.

80. See, e.g., the NYMP ad in *MPW,* 6 July 1912, 59; "Doings in Los Angeles," *MPW,* 20 July 1912, 235; and "Universal Bison Litigation," *NYDM,* 7 August 1912, 27. Throughout this essay, on the advice of Robert Birchard, I use Bison-101 to designate the westerns produced by Ince in 1912 and Bison (Universal) to designate those produced and released by Universal in 1912–13.

81. See, e.g., the Mutual ad in *MPN,* 10 August 1912, 38; the Broncho ad in *MPN,* 17 August 1912, 3; and the NYMP ad in *MPN,* 19 October 1912, 4–5. For Francis Ford's shift from acting to directing see "Doings in Los Angeles," *MPW,* 8 June 1912, 913; and *MPW,* 5 October 1912, 32.

82. See, e.g., the NYMP ad in *MPN,* 21 September 1912, back cover; "Custer Film at Oxford," *Cleveland Leader,* 13 October 1912, sec. W, p. 8; and the Kay-Bee and Broncho ads in *MPN,* 2 November 1912, 5.

83. See, e.g., "Anderson at Orpheum," *Cleveland Leader,* 10 November 1912, sec. B, p. 5; and the Orpheum ad in the labor weekly *Cleveland Citizen,* 28 December 1912, 2.

84. See, e.g., James S. McQuade, "The Fall of Black Hawk," *MPW,* 6 July 1912, 31–33; James S. McQuade, "Geronimo's Raid," *MPW,* 14 September 1912, 1054–55; and G. F. Blaisdell, "Peril of the Plains," *MPW,* 21 September 1912, 1167–68.

85. See, e.g., the favorable review by James S. McQuade, "The Red Man's Honor," *MPW,* 14 December 1912, 1064. Gaumont first had tried to break into this market with *Driven from the Ranch* (April 1912); see "Comments on the Films," *MPW,* 27 April 1912, 330.

86. "Reviews of Special Features," *NYDM,* 31 July 1912, 31; and "At the Photo Plays," *Toledo News-Bee,* 14 August 1912, 8, and 21 August 1912, 3. See also the more favorable review by G. F. Blaisdell, "Their Lives for Gold," *MPW,* 10 August 1912, 515. *Their Lives for Gold* was among the half dozen films seized in Cleveland when the authorities arrested several prominent theater managers for showing crime pictures on Sunday; see "Police Raid at Cleveland," *MPW,* 21 December 1912, 1192.

87. Louis Reeves Harrison, "The Siege of Petersburg," *MPW,* 13 July 1912, 151–52. The first Civil War film to be acclaimed was Biograph's *The Battle* (November 1911), with its "spectacular . . . displays of large and realistic battle scenes" ("Reviews of Licensed Films," *NYDM,* 15 November 1911, 28). See also W. Stephen Bush, "The Battle," *MPW,* 4 November 1911, 367.

88. The first inkling of this decision came in "Doings in Los Angeles," *MPW,* 6 July 1912, 35. It could be argued that the multiple-reel westerns and Civil War films both might be analyzed within a larger category of "war pictures" that were especially resonant just prior to World War I.

89. "Reviews of Universal Films," *NYDM,* 11 September 1912, 33; and "Comments on the Films," *MPW,* 21 September 1912, 1176–77.

90. "Comments on the Films," *MPW,* 21 September 1912, 1177.

91. See, e.g., "Reviews of Universal Films," *NYDM,* 16 October 1912, 33; 27 November 1912, 33; and 5 February 1913, 32; and "Feature Films," *NYDM,* 26 February 1913, 32.

92. "Mona Darkfeather Films," *NYDM,* 14 May 1913, 26; "Reviews of Universal Films," *NYDM,* 20 August 1913, 36.

93. "Comments on the Films," *MPW,* 26 October 1912, 343; and "Reviews of Universal Films," *NYDM,* 27 November 1912, 33.

94. "News and Reviews of Feature Films," *NYDM,* 12 March 1913, 29.

95. A 35 mm viewing print of *The Flaming Arrow* (1,800 feet) is available at the National Film and Television Archive.

96. "Reviews of Supply Co. Films," *NYDM,* 2 October 1912, 32.

97. "Reviews of Universal Films," *NYDM,* 16 October 1912, 33; and "Supply Co. Films," *NYDM,* 23 October 1912, 32.

98. Louis Reeves Harrison, "The Invaders," *MPW,* 9 November 1912, 542.

99. "Reviews of Supply Co. Films," *NYDM,* 20 November 1912, 36.

100. "Views of the Reviewer," *NYDM,* 2 October 1912, 24.

101. See, e.g., the large Central Square ad in the *Lynn Daily Item,* 23 November 1912, 2; and "The Critic's Comment," *Lynn Daily Item,* 10 December 1912, 13.

102. See, e.g., the ads for the Blue Mouse, Dixie, Lexington, Little Pickwick, and New Brodie theaters in the *Baltimore Sun,* 9 February 1913, sec. 4, p. 5.

103. "Where Best Shows Are Found Today," *Cleveland Leader,* 12 January 1913, sec. M, p. 5.

104. Unique Theatre/Mutual Films ad, *Des Moines News,* 26 January 1913, 6.

105. "Saturday's and Sunday's Moving Pictures and Where to See Them," *Toledo News-Bee,* 1 February 1913, 9, and 12 April 1913, 8.

106. American Film Company ad, *Bioscope,* 18 January 1912, 162.

107. "Moving-Picture Business Abroad," *Motography,* June 1911, 142. Nearly identical language appeared in J. D. Whelpley, "Moving Picture Business Abroad," *MPN,* 16 September 1911, 24.

108. "Two Great 'Flying A' Releases," *Bioscope,* 1 June 1911, 395; "The Poisoned Flume," *Bioscope,* 24 August 1911, 401; and the Essanay ad in *Bioscope,* 14 September 1911, xxviii. See also "London Likes Essanay Western Photoplays," *Nickelodeon,* 18 March 1911, 311; and "London Ramblings," *MPN,* 6 May 1911, 7.

109. In France, e.g., both MPPC and independent westerns were readily available; see, e.g., the "Nouveautés cinématographiques" listings in *Ciné-Journal* from July

1911 through August 1912. In Germany, according to censorship records found and analyzed by Deniz Göktürk, Essanay's *Broncho Billy* series was widely distributed; see Deniz Göktürk, "Moving Images of America in Early German Cinema," in *A Second Life: German Cinema's First Decades*, ed. Thomas Elsaesser (Amsterdam: Amsterdam University Press, 1996), 96. In Sweden, according to censorship records, surviving cinema programs, and Pathé archive records, "Wild West," "Indian," and "Cowboy" films also were quite popular; my thanks to Jon Fullerton, Mats Björkin, and Marina Dahlquist for helping me research this material in the Department of Cinema Studies at Stockholm University and at the Swedish Film Institute library.

110. "American Films Popular Abroad," *Cleveland Leader*, 11 February 1912, sec. S, p. 6. The trade press also was quick to quote from *Daily Consular Reports* when information gathered overseas began to mention American films; see, e.g., "Moving Picture Business Abroad," *MPN*, 16 September 1911, 24; "Moving Picture Preferences Abroad," *Motography*, November 1911, 214; J. H. Mayer, "The Picture Theatre in America and Abroad," *Billboard*, 3 February 1912, 5, 74–76; "The Motion Picture in European Countries," *MPW*, 10 February 1912, 494; and "'Spectator's' Comments," *NYDM*, 26 June 1912, 20.

111. Joyce Appleby, Lynn Hunt, and Margaret Jacob, *Telling the Truth about History* (New York: Norton, 1994), 108, 111.

112. The American West, not unlike much of Africa, tended to be depicted as "empty" or as a "clean slate" in many mid-nineteenth-century maps. Whereas Catlin and Buffalo Bill's images of the West maintained this protean inexactitude, the Miller Brothers initially, and unsuccessfully, sought to restrict their image of the West to the southern Great Plains, the location of their immense family ranch in Oklahoma; see Reddin, *Wild West Shows*, 8, 164.

113. See, e.g., the Essanay ads in *Bioscope*, 25 January 1912, xxii; 2 May 1912, vi; 2 June 1912, 734; and 18 July 1912, 1705. To be sure, Essanay sought to promote Anderson as "popularly known as Broncho Billy" as early as October 1911, just as he was being nicknamed "Bullets" in northeastern Ohio; see the Essanay ad in *MPW*, 7 October 1911, 60.

114. See, e.g., "Comments on the Films," *MPW*, 18 May 1912, 629. In July 1912, however, some of *MPW*'s reviews still were referring to "those typical Western dramas in which G. M. Anderson has won popular favor in the Old and the New World"; see James S. McQuade, "The Smuggler's Daughter," *MPW*, 20 July 1912, 233. For explicit references to the Broncho Billy pictures as a series see James S. McQuade, "Why Broncho Billy Left Bear County," *MPW*, 27 September 1913, 1371; "'Broncho Billy' Gets Square," *MPN*, 11 October 1913, 27; and the "new photograph," in *MPN*, 27 December 1913, 22.

115. See the review of *Broncho Billy's Narrow Escape* in "The Pick of the Programmes," *Bioscope*, 1 August 1912, 367; and Essanay ads in *MPW*, 29 June 1912, 1187; and in *NYDM*, 4 September 1912, 31. As a clear sign of his popularity, especially with boys, see Clyde Martin's doggerel, "I'm the Guy," *Motography*, 12 October 1912, 304. For remarks on Anderson as an appealing "personality" see "Reviews of Licensed Films," *NYDM*, 12 March 1913, 36. Although rarely as active as the cowboys in Buffalo Bill's Wild West, Anderson may have seemed to share with them, at least in the eyes of the British, a sense of hardened physicality and "natural" gentlemanliness; see Reddin, *Wild West Shows*, 93–94.

116. The *Arizona Bill* series was produced by Eclipse, first as one-reelers and then as multiple-reel films, from 1911 through 1913.

117. See, e.g., "Dramatizes Dime Novels," *Cleveland Leader,* 23 June 1912, sec. S, p. 6. The first of the Nestor series, *Young Wild West Leading a Raid* (June 1912), survives in a 35 mm viewing print (770 feet) at the National Film and Television Archive.

118. See, e.g., "Of Interest to the Trade," *Motography,* 4 January 1913, 25; and Mabel Condon, "Sans Grease Paint and Wig," *Motography,* 15 February 1913, 111.

119. See, e.g., "Edison-McClure," *MPW,* 29 June 1912, 1212.

120. See, e.g., "Reviews of Licensed Films," *NYDM,* 7 May 1913, 35, and 30 July 1913, 29; "Reviews of Licensed Films," *NYDM,* 10 December 1913, 43, and 7 January 1914, 36; and "Ben Wilson," *MPW,* 28 February 1914, 1069. One of Famous Players' earliest films featured Sawyer as Kate Kirby in *The Port of Doom;* see "Feature Films on the Market," *NYDM,* 26 November 1913, 33.

121. Broncho Billy films were released almost weekly from late November 1912 through March 1913, then settled into a biweekly release schedule for the rest of the year.

122. Anderson's real name was Max Aaronson; his "good badman" character thus offered a model of assimilation that stood in for another form of assimilation that could not be represented or at least publicized.

123. See "Two Great 'Flying A' Releases," *Bioscope,* 1 June 1911, 395. A 35 mm viewing print of *The Ranchman's Vengeance* is available at the Nederlands Filmmuseum

124. A 35 mm viewing print of *Broncho Billy's Mexican Wife* (767 feet) is available at the George Eastman House (Rochester, N.Y.).

125. *The Ranchman's Vengeance* is especially interesting because it was released during the initial years of the Mexican Revolution, which threatened to involve the United States. For an analysis of a contrasting jingoistic attitude toward Mexicans characteristic of the 101 Ranch Wild West shows see Reddin, *Wild West Shows,* 168–69.

126. See "Motion Picture Reviews," *Billboard,* 20 May 1911, 13.

127. Although *MPW's* reviewer found the film "very interesting," he also faintly objected to scenes like this as "too evidently 'being played'" ("Comments on the Films," *MPW,* 26 August 1911, 544). See also "Motion Picture Reviews," *Billboard,* 19 August 1911, 15.

128. The film submerges another story, the well-known homosexuality of Jack Kerrigan, the company's leading actor and a major star at the time. Decades later Dwan told Anthony Slide that he kept Kerrigan's face submerged in the flume as long as possible, as a joke for the rest of the crew and cast; see William J. Mann, *Behind the Screen: How Gays and Lesbians Shaped Hollywood* (New York: Viking, 2001), 2.

129. A 35 mm viewing print of *The Poisoned Flume* (972 feet) is available at the National Film and Television Archive (London). In an interview with Peter Bogdanovich Dwan seems to conflate this film with either *The Ranchman's Vengeance* or another later film; see Peter Bogdanovich, *Allan Dwan: The Last Pioneer* (New York: Praeger, 1971), 20.

130. The unusually arid environment of the American West, Worster argues, was developed chiefly by an intensive, efficient, large-scale manipulation of scarce water resources. Donald Worster, *Rivers of Empire: Water, Aridity, and the Growth of the American West* (New York: Oxford University Press, 1985), 6–7.

131. Worster encapsulates the development of the American West into three

stages: incipience (1847–1890s), florescence (1900–1940s), and empire (1940s on); see Worster, *Rivers of Empire*, 64.

132. Ibid., 96–111.

133. See, e.g., Richard Slotkin, *Gunfighter Nation: The Myth of the Frontier in Twentieth-Century America* (New York: Atheneum, 1992), 22–24.

134. "Notes d'Amérique," *Ciné-Journal*, 23 December 1911, 5; and the Cosmopolitan Film ads for Bison-101 films in *Bioscope*, 14 March 1912, 752; 28 March 1912, xii; and 6 June 1912, 722. See also the weekly listings of Bison-101 films, released through Paul Hodel, in "Nouveautés cinématographiques," *Ciné-Journal*, from April through September 1912.

135. "Pick of the Programmes," *Bioscope*, 25 April 1912, 289. See also "A First Rate Indian Film," *Bioscope*, 8 August 1912, 437.

136. "Pick of the Programmes," *Bioscope*, 25 April 1912, 291.

137. "Reviews of Film Supply Co. Films," *NYDM*, 6 November 1912, 33.

138. *The Man They Scorned* was one of the first films shown at the Central Square (Lynn), when it became an exclusive venue for Kay-Bee and Broncho films in November 1912; see the Central Square ad in the *Lynn Daily Item*, 30 November 1912, 2. It also played through the Thanksgiving weekend at the Star (Pawtucket) to large crowds; see the Star ad (27 November 1912) in Clippings Books, Series IV, Keith-Albee Collection, Special Collections, University of Iowa Library; and Star Theatre accounts book (p. 105), Box 10, Keith-Albee Collection. A possible variation on this story occurs in Broncho's *The Greenhorn* (October 1913), where the hero is described as Russian (usually a code word for Jewish); see "Feature Films on the Market," *NYDM*, 29 October 1913, 33.

139. "Pick of the Programmes," *Bioscope*, 25 April 1912, 289, 291; Louis Reeves Harrison, "The 'Bison-101' Headliners," *MPW*, 27 April 1912, 320–22.

140. See, e.g., the Bison-101 ads in *MPN*, 11 May 1912, 28; and *MPW*, 18 May 1912, 588.

141. "*Lieutenant's Last Fight*—Wonderful Military Film," *MPN*, 25 May 1912, 24–25; and "Stories of Licensed Films," *MPW*, 1 June 1912, 868–69. This analysis is based on an incomplete 35 mm viewing print of *The Lieutenant's Last Fight* available at the Nederlands Filmmuseum.

142. The quote, probably from a concluding intertitle (now missing), comes from "*Lieutenant's Last Fight*—Wonderful Military Film," *MPN*, 25 May 1912, 25.

143. Another variation can be seen in Broncho's *The Burning Brand* (January 1913), in which the son of an army chaplain discovers he is the adopted half-breed son of a chief's daughter (told in flashback); an outcast denied marriage to a colonel's daughter, he is rescued by his tribal ancestors and made their chief, leads them in an attack on the army outpost, and then tries to negotiate a peace but is killed. See "Reviews of Mutual Films," *NYDM*, 25 December 1912, 30. These films contrast sharply with 101-Bison's *The Flaming Arrow* (March 1913), in which a half-breed boy is adopted by an Indian chief and, once grown, not only aids both his adopted tribe and white soldiers in their battle against Apaches but foils a plot to kidnap a colonel's daughter, hatched by a rejected suitor and a Mexican, and then gets to marry her.

144. Harrison notes these changes in framing and editing in his review, "The Invaders," *MPW*, 9 November 1912, 542. This analysis is based on a 35 mm viewing print of *The Invaders* (2,741 feet) available at the Library of Congress.

145. The *Mirror*'s review of *The Invaders* is curiously muted, chiefly calling attention to several historical inaccuracies, perhaps reflecting its characteristically "mas-
culine" perspective on moving pictures; see "Reviews of Film Supply Co. Films," *NYDM,*
27 November 1912, 31.

146. Other two- and three-reel films such as Kalem's *Colleen Bawn* and Vitagraph's
Vanity Fair had appeared earlier in France in October 1911 and early March 1912,
respectively. Two of D. W. Griffith's first two-reel films were westerns, *A Pueblo Legend*
and *The Massacre,* but in France they were not released until September and November
1912, respectively.

147. John Burke had publicized Buffalo Bill's Wild West precisely in these terms,
as "the great epic of American history"; see John Burke, "Buffalo Bill's Wild West
and Congress of Rough Riders of the World," *Philadelphia Sunday Dispatch,* 12 September 1885—quoted in Reddin, *Wild West Shows,* xiii. Writers such as Owen Wister
and Frank Norris also had long argued that the Wild West could provide material
for a national epic; see, e.g., Owen Wister, "The Evolution of the Cow-Puncher,"
Harper's Monthly, September 1895, 602–17; and Frank Norris, "The Frontier Gone
at Last," *World's Work* 3 (1902)—repr. in *The Literary Criticism of Frank Norris,* ed. Donald Pizer (Austin: University of Texas Press, 1964), 111.

148. "Moving-Picture Business Abroad," *Motography,* June 1911, 142.

149. "Topics of the Week: The Popularity of Western Films," *Bioscope,* 18 August
1910, 4. See also Reddin, *Wild West Shows,* 94.

150. The French had expressed a similar fascination with the Indians of Buffalo
Bill's Wild West—see Reddin, *Wild West Shows,* 100. For a succinct analysis of the
French conception of American barbarism see Jody Blake, *Le Tumulte noir: Modernist
Art and Popular Entertainment in Jazz Age Paris, 1900–1930* (University Park: Pennsylvania State University Press, 1999). Interestingly, the French not only linked animal vitality and technological power in their view of the United States but subsumed
all kinds of different figures—"peaux rouges," "Negroes," cowboys, gauchos—within
the category of the "barbaric," especially in their fascination with "exotic" dances—
see Blake, *Le Tumulte noir,* 53–54.

151. Rosaldo's concept of "imperialist nostalgia" is discussed in Ann Fabian, "History for the Masses: Commercializing the Western Past," in *Under an Open Sky: Rethinking America's Western Past,* ed. William Cronon, George Miles, and Jay Gitlin (New
York: Norton, 1992), 232–33.

152. Buffalo Bill's Wild West served as a similar "object lesson in physical force,
exercise, and la jeunesse"; see Reddin, *Wild West Shows,* 101. See also Blake, *Le Tumulte
noir,* 56.

153. For an analysis of the Indian's ideological function in westerns produced
prior to the early 1910s see Abel, *Red Rooster Scare,* 167–71.

154. For an excellent study of historical pageantry see David Glassberg, *American
Historical Pageantry: The Uses of Tradition in the Twentieth Century* (Chapel Hill: University
of North Carolina Press, 1990), esp. 4–5. I appropriate the phrase "innovative nostalgia" from Robert Crunden, as cited (and criticized) in Michael Kammen, *The Mys-
tic Chords of Memory: The Transformation of Tradition in American Culture* (New York:
Knopf, 1991), 271.

155. Perhaps not unexpectedly, films that explicitly depicted immigrants and the
problems of assimilation were rare during the early 1910s. Exceptions included So-

lax's *The Making of an American Citizen* (1912), in which a male Russian peasant (in contrast to his wife) has to be taught by force how to behave as an American, and Kalem's *The Alien* (1913), in which an Italian family man and skilled mechanic (wrongly implicated in a ring of opium smugglers) "develops a wholesome respect for the laws of his new country and takes an oath of allegiance to the United States"; see "Licensed Film Stories," *MPW,* 3 May 1913, 508–9.

156. These hypothetical spectators are based on data gathered about each city from the 1910 census records, the 1914 *American Newspaper Annual and Directory,* and a survey of local newspapers.

157. Mary Heaton Vorse, "Some Picture Show Audiences," *Outlook,* 24 June 1911, 443, 445.

158. Hansen, "Fallen Women," 12.

159. "Latest Film Snapshots Local and Worldwide," *Cleveland Leader,* 2 March 1913, sec. M, p. 11.

160. "Emilie Altenloh, *Zur Soziologie des Kinos: Kie Kino-Unternehmung und die sozialen Schichten ihrer Besucher* (Jena: Eugen Diedrichs, 1914), 11–12 (paraphrased in Göktürk, "Moving Images," 99). The second part of Altenloh's dissertation is translated and printed as "A Sociology of Cinema" in *Screen* 42, no. 3 (autumn 2001): 249–93.

161. See Abel, *Red Rooster Scare,* 171–72.

162. Sturgeon was one of the first filmmakers to gain some kind of notoriety outside the industry; see "The Real Man Behind the Gun Is Director," *Des Moines News,* 23 May 1913, 4.

163. "How States Are Made," *MPW,* 17 February 1912, 565. See also "Critical Reviews," *NYMT,* 10 March 1912, sec. 4, pt. 2, p. 4; and "Reviews of Licensed Films," *NYDM,* 13 March 1912, 29. The importance of this film is signaled by newspaper stories about it; see, e.g., "How States Are Made," *Cleveland Leader,* 18 February 1912, sec. B, p. 6. A 35 mm viewing print of *How States Are Made* is available at the Nederlands Filmmuseum. A year later the *Mirror* cited this film in recognizing Sturgeon as a major filmmaker; see "From Harvard to Director's Place: Rollin S. Sturgeon Upsets Rules of the Game and Wins Out," *NYDM,* 15 January 1913, 42.

164. See the Vitagraph ad in *MPW,* 20 January 1912, 181; and "Reviews of Licensed Films," *NYDM,* 24 January 1912, 39.

165. See the Solax ad in *MPW,* 3 August 1912, 405; and "Licensed Film Stories," *MPW,* 3 August 1912, 482. A 35 mm viewing print of *Two Little Rangers* is available at the Nederlands Filmmuseum.

166. See "Ten Famous Kalem Beauties," *NYDM,* 31 January 1912, 53; and "Reviews of Independent Films," *NYDM,* 22 May 1912, 29. Occasionally in Essanay films it is a woman who "rides to the rescue," as in *Broncho Billy's Narrow Escape* (July 1912), a 35 mm viewing print of which is available at the Nederlands Filmmuseum. Louis Reeves Harrison also praises "Anna Little, a corking rider, full of vim in action," who "sweeps on the screen like a whirlwind" in Bison-101's *The Crisis* (Harrison, "The 'Bison-101' Headliners," *MPW,* 27 April 1912, 321).

167. A 35 mm viewing print of *Sallie's Sure Shot* (971 feet) is available at the National Film and Television Archive.

168. "Reviews of Licensed Films," *NYDM,* 24 April 1912, 29. A 35 mm viewing print of *The Craven* is available at the Nederlands Filmmuseum.

169. A 35 mm viewing print of *Una of the Sierras* (924 feet) is available at the National Film and Television Archive.

170. Selig's original version of *The Cowboy Millionaire* (December 1909) was so popular that in early 1913 the company released a two-reel remake, *The Millionaire Cowboy*, which expanded the stunt riding and roping at the beginning, as well as the high jinks of the cowboys who are invited to visit their now-wealthy friend in the city. See, e.g., James S. McQuade, "The Millionaire Cowboy," *MPW*, 25 January 1913, 344–45; and "Feature News and Reviews," *NYDM*, 12 February 1913, 31.

171. It may simply be the result of chance, but *Una of the Sierra* seems to have been ignored by the trade press: there are no reviews in the *World* or the *Mirror*.

172. See, e.g., Nancy Tillman Romalov, "Unearthing the Historical Reader, or Reading Girls' Reading," in *Pioneers, Passionate Ladies, and Private Eyes*, ed. Larry Sullivan and Lydia Cushman Schurman (New York: Hawthorne Press, 1996), 87–101.

173. See Wallis, *Real Wild West*, 4–5, 221–26, 229–31, 307–8. See also Reddin, *Wild West Shows*, 161, 171.

174. See, e.g., "Daring Girl Rider Coming," *Des Moines News*, 27 July 1912, 3; and "Summer Amusements," *Des Moines News*, 28 July 1912, 12. See also Wallis, *Real Wild West*, 358.

175. "Girls with Wild West Show to Help Women Gain Equal Suffrage," *Toledo Blade*, 17 August 1912, 7.

176. See, e.g., Gertrude Price, "The Great Spirit Took Mona, but in This Girl She Still Lives," *Des Moines News*, 6 February 1912, 12; "Western Girl You Love in the 'Movies' Is a Sure Enough Suffrager," *Des Moines News*, 11 February 1913, 3; and "Runs, Rides, Rows," *Des Moines News*, 16 April 1913, 6; and "Everyone Is for Busy Ann 'Calamity' Ann You Know!" *Des Moines News*, 29 April 1912, 10.

177. See, e.g., "Nervy as Ever to Act the Most Daring Things Ever Seen on The Stage!—Heroine of Movies," *Des Moines News*, 17 November 1912, 7; and "Sometimes the Beautiful Maiden Is REALLY Snatched from the Jaws of Death," *Des Moines News*, 13 March 1913, 10.

178. I develop this argument in "Fandom in the Heartland: Gertrude Price and the *Des Moines News*, 1912–1914" (paper delivered at the "Women and the Silent Screen" conference, University of California, Santa Cruz, 2 November 2001). The phrase "photoplay matinee girl" was circulating by 1911; see "The Photoplay Matinee Girl," *Film Index*, 3 June 1911, 11. The term "picture fan" first appears in "'Spectator's' Comments," *NYDM*, 7 August 1912, 24.

179. See "American Films Abroad," *MPW*, 4 November 1911, 357.

180. This was also the case with the New York reception of the 101 Ranch Wild West shows at Madison Square Garden in 1914; see Reddin, *Wild West Shows*, 170–72.

181. Gordon Amusement controlled ten theaters in New England, as well as the newly built Gordon in Rochester, and was then building a large theater in Boston; see "The Evolution of the Motion Picture IX: From the Standpoint of the Exhibitor," *NYDM*, 20 August 1913, 31.

182. See, e.g., James S. McQuade, "Why Broncho Billy Left Bear County," *MPW*, 27 September 1913, 1371. An incomplete 35 mm viewing print of *Why Broncho Billy Left Bear County* (537 feet), sans intertitles, is available at the George Eastman House.

183. "Valuable Consular Reports," *MPW*, 9 May 1914, 811.

184. W. Stephen Bush, "No Lowering of Standards," *MPW*, 24 January 1914, 389.

185. See "Reviews of Licensed Films," *NYDM*, 3 September 1913, 29; and the Essanay ad in *NYDM*, 8 October 1913, 35. *The Good-For Nothing*, Anderson's first four-reel western, did not appear until June 1914; see the Essanay ad in *MPW*, 27 June 1914, 1771.

186. "Reviews of Licensed Films," *NYDM*, 17 September 1913, 29. A surviving 35 mm print of *Episode at Cloudy Canyon* at the National Film and Television Archive, apparently complete and with its original title, also has no intertitles. This suggests that Essanay's one-reel westerns during this period may merit closer attention for their development of certain conventions of representation and narration—"tell[ing] their story unaided and without confusion"—that soon would become crucial to the "classical Hollywood cinema."

187. See "Selig Releasing Western Thriller," *Motography*, 31 May 1913, 395–96; "Feature Films," *NYDM*, 11 June 1913, 27; "Comments on the Films," *MPW*, 21 June 1913, 1251; "Reviews of Licensed Films," *NYDM*, 3 September 1913, 29; and "Feature Films on the Market," *NYDM*, 26 November 1913, 32.

188. See, e.g., Hanford C. Judson, "The Big Horn Massacre," *MPW*, 13 December 1913, 1261; "Reviews of Feature Films," *NYDM*, 24 December 1913, 39; "Feature Films of the Week," *NYDM*, 21 January 1914, 32; and "Reviews of Feature Films," *NYDM*, 18 February 1914, 42.

189. See, e.g., "An Indian Star," *Motography*, 26 July 1913, 24; and the prominence given the Indian actors in the Thomas H. Ince ad in *NYDM*, 24 December 1913, 26. By contrast, other companies such as Selig, Vitagraph, and even 101-Bison tended to have white actors play Indian or Mexican roles; see, e.g., Selig's *The Tie of Blood* (June 1913), Vitagraph's *When the West Was Young* (October 1913), and 101-Bison's *The White Vacquero* (October 1913). Alison Griffiths analyzes this white masquerade, focused on Griffith westerns, in "Playing at Being Indian." This practice also was widespread in historical pageants; see, e.g., David Glassberg's analysis of Percy Mackaye's *Pageant of St. Louis*, late May and early June 1914, in Glassberg, *American Historical Pageants*, 173–94.

190. "Feature Films of the Week," *NYDM*, 25 February 1914, 36; and Louis Reeves Harrison, "The Squaw Man," *MPW*, 28 February 1914, 1068.

191. James S. McQuade, "The Spoilers," *MPW*, 11 April 1914, 186–87; "Strand Theater Opens," *NYDM*, 15 April 1914, 31; and W. Stephen Bush, "Opening of the Strand," *MPW*, 18 April 1914, 371.

192. It is this period of Hart, Mix, and Ford westerns, which first reaches a high point in 1917, rather than the earlier prewar period that most interests George Fenin and William Everson, in *The Western: From the Silents to the Seventies*, rev. ed. (New York: Grossman, 1973), 74–129.

193. Louis Reeves Harrison, "Big Changes Taking Place," *MPW*, 3 January 1914, 24.

CHAPTER SEVEN

The Coney Island Comedies

Bodies and Slapstick at the Amusement Park and the Movies

Lauren Rabinovitz

The comic is that side of a person which reveals his likeness to a thing, that aspect of human events which, through its peculiar inelasticity, conveys the impression of pure mechanism, of automatism, of movement without life.
HENRI BERGSON, *"Laughter: An Essay on the Meaning of the Comic," 1911*

Silent American comedy developed a form which drew its inspiration from gags, rather than plotting. These gags have their origins in acts of anarchy, infantile revolts against authority and propriety. But their explosive counterlogic also found embodiment in devices of balance and trajectory, antimachines which harness the laws of physics to overturn the rules of behavior. Simultaneously revolts and engineering, these devices mine the fascination that spectators of the industrial age had with the way things work, the operational aesthetics.
TOM GUNNING, *"Crazy Machines in the Garden of Forking Paths: Mischief Gags and the Origins of American Film Comedy," 1995*

In their initial appearance early comedies full of power-driven pratfalls, repetitive gyrations, rhythmic punches, and elaborately staged brawls of intersecting parts provided the means for maintaining a particular inscription of the cinematic body in the transitional era. By cinematic body I mean both the body displayed in motion as a physical spectacle and the laughing spectator in all her or his presence. Bodies both onscreen and off were intertwined in those effects of cinema that produce celebration in the physicality of one's own body. But the history of cinema has unfairly ignored this comic carnal spirit, emphasizing Aristotelian categories associated with thought and consciousness as above those attached to the body. This essay writes the body back into the history of silent cinema and argues that slapstick in the transitional era provided an enlarged sense of corporeal delight—one associated with the mechanical modern—at just the moment when spectacle and narrative conjoined.

Slapstick comedy got its name from an old theatrical prop consisting of two slats of wood joined together so that they make a loud slapping sound when one actor hits another with the stick. Donald Crafton, in an important discussion on slapstick, likens the notion of "the slap" to the centrality of physical gags in slapstick movies that have a disruptive impact on the audience.[1] For Crafton the gags resist integration into the film's narrative and insist that the form remains a type of popular spectacle. Although Crafton's argument is an important critique of transitional era cinema treated as indistinct from classical cinema, he neither considers the implications of the palpable slap for theories of spectatorship or for the possibility that the cinema of attractions persists well into the transitional era.

In response to Crafton, Tom Gunning demonstrates that slapstick may indeed be understood as a continuation of the cinema of attractions, as the descendant of comic mischief films: slapstick gags provide a structure of "explosive interruptions" that often require mechanical devices so that "everything, both devices and human actants, seem to perform like interlocking gears in a grand machine."[2] Slapstick not only maintains early cinema's display of the human body as pure spectacle but accentuates it in relationship to the industrial through combination with gag devices. Both Crafton and Gunning are preoccupied with slapstick as a dual-focus narrative: they attempt to unlock the tensions between the "centrifugal energy" of the comic gag, best represented by the "pie in the face," and the "centripetal energy" of narrative, best represented by "the chase." Whereas Crafton seeks to differentiate slapstick from the classical cinema that succeeded it, Gunning blurs slapstick with the cinema that preceded it. Neither addresses specifically the distinctiveness of slapstick as a historical mode that not only synthesized early comic strategies and influenced later ones but that also maintained a unique integrity and function during the transitional era.

In addition, their analyses require the presence of not only a laughing, physically involved spectator but one whose pleasure derives from a multifaceted fascination rather than the production of knowledge through the linearity of cause-effect relations. Although they suggest that widespread familiarity with popular culture, especially the joke logic of contemporary comic strips, provided the cultural knowledge necessary for understanding slapstick's antinarrative force, they stop short of explaining that the very forms that made slapstick legible, so to speak, were also forms that depend on spectator positions quite antithetical to those of the classical cinema. In many respects the pleasures of slapstick comedy that Crafton and Gunning describe—the revelation of the loss of dignity, antinarrative corporeal involvement through violent explosive actions, interaction between devices and human motion that seems to resist laws of physics, and a vision of the world as "a crazy machine"—overlap with the pleasures of the popular turn-of-the-century amusement park. The amusement park's mechanical rides, displays of human and animal performances, pyrotechnics, and recreations were the most important model for training moviegoers to become *fascinated* rather than distracted spectators, to become pleasure seekers at the cinema. The more than fifteen hundred amusement parks across North America during the 1910s invited millions of people of varying classes, races, regions, and ethnicities to "learn with their bodies" a new concept of urban modernism—the celebration of kineticism and speed, the beauty of industrial technologies, and the physical experience of the crowd.[3] They made clear the importance of physical sensation in relationship to visual stimulation as a distinctly modern mode of perception. Inasmuch as Crafton and Gunning want to overturn film history's adjudication of silent cinema for how well it conforms to classical form, I want to overthrow the equally invalid assumption of a classical film spectator as the subject of these early films. By demonstrating cinema's participation in a new cultural mode of perception that gauged the bombardment of sight and sound in relationship to physical engagement, I claim that cinema's basis for pleasure lies not in the norms of passive spectatorship associated with the rise of Hollywood cinema, as has so often been assumed, but in its visceral engagement and *jouissance,* a decentered perceptual experience that occurs across the body and that has been more associated with feminine pleasure.

There is a special group of films that best illustrates this overlap between cinema and the amusement park, highlighting the invitation to *jouissance* available in both institutions. Between 1909 and 1917 various film companies periodically shot fictional films at Brooklyn's Coney Island, integrating action and the spectacle of bodies uniting with machinery in order to emphasize the body on display and increasingly flirtation, romance, and het-. erosexual pairing. Coney Island thus provides the cinema with a space of multiple valences: its mise-en-scène is a modern electrified and highly cinematic display of extravagant architectural shapes, lights, and movements; it temporally unfolds a series of machines in motion that engage bodies in comic contortions; it is a cultural space that seemingly authorizes more casual, intimate contact and courtship between relative strangers.

Representative titles of such films include *Jack Fat and Jim Slim at Coney Island* (Vitagraph, 1910), *Coney Island* (Comic Film Corp., 1917, dir. Fatty Arbuckle) and *Tillie Wakes Up* (Marie Dressler Film Corp., 1917, dir. Harry Davenport). These films, all comedies, interweave park views and parkgoers enjoying themselves in spatial rhythms demonstrating what unfettered physical enjoyment and self-pleasure signifies for relaxing Victorian codes of conduct, for gender roles, and for the institution of marriage. They signify an important refinement to the comic drive of early films shot at Coney Island before 1908 (e.g., *Rube and Mandy Go to Coney Island* [Edison, 1903]; *Boarding School Girls* [Edison, 1905]). The slapstick comedies of the transitional era foreground an exaggerated corporeal body while maintaining the spectacular display associated with the cinema of attractions in the background, and they delicately synchronize the antinarrative and narrative tendencies that Crafton and Gunning describe. These "Coney Island comedies" return movies to the fairgrounds, as it were, and stylize the "cinema of attractions" to create an alternative tradition to the more economic narrative storytelling that ascended during the teens.

THE SPECTATOR AS A PLEASURE SEEKER

Early slapstick cinema depended on reconciling bodily experience (and cognitive understanding) to the ascendancy of vision as the privileged self-sufficient source of perceptual knowledge. In other words, if cinema is—as so many have claimed—the paradigmatic Vision Machine of Modernism, it performs this reconciliation only by hyperbolizing vision in relationship to an embodied perceptual spectatorship. Cinema thus represents a complex interplay between embodied forms of subjectivity and arguments for disembodiment.

The history of cinema has always assumed that moviegoing affords a means of achieving a blissful state of disembodiment. Classical models of movie spectatorship presume that cinema produces modernist subjectivity through *being* a giant, disembodied set of eyes. Even when alternative views have surfaced, dominant film theories have perpetuated a belief in a single unitary viewing position—centered, distant, objectifying—that makes the spectator an effect of a linear technological evolution from the camera obscura to photography to cinema. Involvement in the cinema has always meant the fantasy of a despatialized, dematerialized self. As Linda Williams has noted, however, in a critique of spectator theory that shares my position, "Despite its focus on the visual pleasures of cinema, psychoanalytic film theory's preoccupation with the visual 'senses at a distance' has perpetuated this mind/body dualism by privileging the disembodied, centered gaze at an absent object over the embodied, decentered sensations of present observers."[4] Psychoanalytic, as well as feminist, theories, arguably the most powerful developments in the last twenty-five years, may critique and even vilify the *ideology* of the spectator position that promises an illusory power and coherence in subjugation to vision itself. But they do not challenge the assumption that the spectatorial process is essentially a disavowal of corporeal presence (embodiment) and an absorption into the distant world of image and sound.

Comedies in general bear a particular burden of the strain between the sensations felt by a present observer and the distracted gaze at a distant object because the physical sensation of embodiment threatens to overwhelm the spectator, who is supposed to laugh and even to lose bodily self-control in fits or convulsions of laughter. Jennifer Bean implicitly recognizes the stakes of the spectator's fully embodied subjectivity at the cinema in her discussion of slapstick comedy, noting that "the travesty of order on screen is little more than a prelude for the staggering loss of bodily integrity available to the viewer; one who succumbs first to a 'titter,' devolves toward a 'yowl,' cranks up for a stimulating 'bellylaugh,' and races on to laughter's apotheosis: the 'boffo,' or, 'the laugh that kills.'"[5] Here her definition of "the loss of bodily integrity" more accurately describes the loss of self-mastery over the corporeal once laughter "takes over." But what matters most is that this kind of physiologically engaged spectator negates the notion of a distracted, disembodied spectator that reigns as the ideal in spectator theory. Although it is not the project of this essay to lay out concepts of humor, the joke, or even the cognitive and psychological reasons that people laugh, it is necessary to note in passing that the laughing spectator is one fully conscious of the bodily pleasures of the cinematic experience (pleasures also available in such "bodily oriented genres" as pornography, action-adventure, horror, and melodrama).

More specifically, Coney Island comedies of the transitional era even *promised* bodily pleasure and *jouissance* in the very tag lines used to advertise the films. "We'll just simply rock 'em off their seats," promised Paramount Pictures' Fatty Arbuckle advertisements for 1917, instantiating that the lure of the comic is not only the "boffo" laugh that Bean describes but literally a physically active audience.[6] "Everybody rubbers, and everybody laughs themselves sick," said one summary of *Jack Fat and Jim Slim at Coney Island* (1910).[7] Another called *The Cook*, a 1918 Fatty Arbuckle comedy set at Los Angeles' Luna Park, a "mirth factory . . . [that produces] unconfined joy," applying industrial metaphors to the production of the fully embodied spectator.[8] Even *Moving Picture World* described a 1909 Coney Island comedy *(Cohen at Coney Island)* as "brimful of laughter from start to finish."[9] It is clearly the "gag" structure of these films and their incentive to laugh that provides the substance for the films' advertisements. Although the hyperbole may attribute "the laugh" to the film object itself, it quite willfully or naively conflates cinematic and spectatorial pleasure, promising not so much the disembodied spectator absorbed into the distant screen but the movie absorbed by the *body* of the spectator.

In addition, advertising for these Coney Island films also forwards the realism of the mise-en-scène itself. Integral to the sense of human motion and physical presence onscreen is the promise of a profilmic event in the real world, the promising continuity of the tradition of "actualité" associated with early cinema despite the fact that the photographic realism augments a clearly developed story space. As late as 1910 *Moving Picture World* asserted in its description of *Jack Fat and Jim Slim at Coney Island*, "Those who have seen Coney Island can rest assured they are looking upon an unusually faithful reproduction."[10] In short, there is a retrograde quality to the Coney Island comedies throughout the transition period: they not only provide continuity with the earliest spectacle displays, actualités, and mischievous gag, but they also nostalgically make the connection between the machine apparatus and its mechanical control over the individual in motion—both the object (on-screen) and subject (the audience's experience) of the film. In this way they reproduce the originary drive of cinema wherein the apparatus itself is organized, to quote Francesco Casetti, as a "snare ready to capture whoever enters its radius of activity."[11]

In fact, these films develop outwardly from the most primitive element of narrative: the chase. For Crafton, Gunning, and Charlie Keil the chase represents an important cinematic development between 1903 and 1908 as a means to connect action across disparate spaces and to link discrete shots through spatial and temporal continuity.[12] It is widely understood as an important building block for establishing a narrative sustained across individual shots. But the chase as the causal agent in 1910's *Jack Fat and Jim Slim at Coney Island* functions remarkably like the chase in *Boarding School Girls*, made five years earlier. By 1910 the chase element had supposedly been absorbed into more sophisticated storytelling techniques. Furthermore, *Jack Fat and Jim Slim*'s chase reemerges with few changes in *Coney Island* as late as 1917.

MOVIES AT THE AMUSEMENT PARK

In their spatial combination of mechanical thrill rides, animal shows, live performances, recreation, theaters, and cafes amusement parks asserted the euphoria of perceptual bombardment by sight, sound, and kinesthesia. The mechanical rides—scenic railways, velvet coasters, Ferris wheels, ticklers, shoot-the-chutes, and circle swings—were simulations of danger, providing a tenuous relationship between the perception of danger and the assurance of safety. They ran on a routinized schedule of starting and stopping, offering to patrons a precise rhythm not unlike the rhythm of industrialized labor: they consisted of waiting, boarding, riding, and disembarking organized around the purchase, anticipation, experience, and relief of risk, danger, and pleasure. As historian John Kasson has observed, "Riders could enjoy their own momentary fright and disorientation because they knew it would turn to comic relief; they could engage in what appeared dangerous adventure because ultimately they believed in its safety."[13]

These rides reversed the usual relations between the body and machinery in which the person controls and masters the machine: the person surrendered to the machine, which, in turn, liberated the body in some fashion from its normal limitations of placement and movement in daily life. Movies, which were featured at vaudeville theaters or nickelodeons in over 75 percent of the nation's amusement parks, were arguably another form of submission to a mechanized thrill. Cinema at the amusement park provided a mechanical means of liberation from everyday life similar to the other attractions: it granted men and women an imagined spatial and temporal freedom associated with the *flâneur*—the sense of being a wandering observer in scenes otherwise unattainable, from faraway exotic places to nearby illicit dens of iniquity. In the context of the amusement park space, movies were simply another variation of modern mechanically induced experience of speed, displacement, and the fantastic that liberated bodies from Victorian decorum, from rigid codes of social conduct and propriety, and from strict rules of sexual constraint.

In some instances movie exhibition constituted a mechanical thrill ride in and of itself that incorporated sound and motion effects. Hale's Tours and Scenes of the World, a popular amusement park attraction, consisted of theater railway cars that each seated seventy-two "passengers." The moving pictures that showed out the front end offered a filmed point of view from the front or rear of a moving train. The goal was to create the illusion of movement into or away from a scene, accentuated by mechanical apparatuses and levers that vibrated, rocked, and tilted the car. While steam whistles tooted and wheels clattered, air was blown into the travelers' faces. Imitators and variants of Hale's Tours also offered "virtual" tours by auto, hot air balloon, and steamboat.[14]

At the park, movies as shows or displays duplicated the other regularly featured entertainment. Acrobats, trapeze artists, animal tricks, and other similar circus acts were popular. Daredevil stunts were also common: aviators and auto drivers made loop the loops and other gyrations in their machines. Band concerts, ethnographic displays, dancing girls, infant incubators, and freak shows all counted among the offerings as well. Pyrotechnic displays combined with illuminated fountains and living statue displays. Disaster shows were a unique theater of spectacle during this period. These colossal shows relied on huge audience grandstand seating, elaborate painted stage sets, actors, and fireworks. The most popular of these were *Fighting the Flames,* the *Johnstown Flood, Mount Pelee,* and the *Battle of the Monitor and Merrimac,* each of which theatrically and spectacularly recreated disasters of urban tenement life, of nature, or of war. What is at stake throughout is that the park space and its rhythms established a kind of equivalency between cinema and these other spectacles. Long after feature films and purpose-built movie theaters claimed audiences for a more narratively driven cinema, audiences continued to experience movies within the confines of the attraction display.

In addition, the act of pleasurable and sexual looking, so tacitly a structure of cinematic experience, was likewise an implicit structure of the amusement park. Historian Kathy Peiss describes the situation at Coney Island: "The patrons were whirled through space and knocked off balance, their hats blown off, skirts lifted, senses of humor tried. The patrons themselves became the show, providing interest and hilarity to each other. . . . Audience participation, the interaction of strangers, and voyeurism were incorporated."[15] Both park owners and film manufacturers understood this fact. George Tilyou, owner of Coney Island's Steeplechase Park, even incorporated "the-patrons-as-show" in his famous Blowhole Theater, a theater adjacent to a funhouse where people exiting the funhouse were surprised by jets of air blowing up their legs, a "mischievous gag" that led to jumps, outbursts, and skirts being lifted. Whether victims of brief humiliation, comic contortions, or erotic revelations, the surprised patrons who exited onto a stage in front of an audience acted out the same scenario of surprise and humiliation that fills countless early films. They shifted easily between being the object-in-motion on display and being a member of the audience watching others assume their former place. The demarcation between being the surveyor and the surveyed was never clear at an amusement park. As one wandered from attraction to attraction (including cinemas), one was never far from being an object of fascination for others. Subjectivity at the amusement park—including in its cinemas—allowed for no tacit contract that grants one the fulfillment of voyeuristic desire without also subjugating one to others' voyeuristic gazes.

THE AMUSEMENT PARK AT THE MOVIES

From the beginning of cinema, movies not only showed at amusement parks but also depicted the parks, the mechanical rides, and the patrons' unrestrained behavior. In 1896 shooting-the-chutes at Coney Island was among the earliest Edison subjects, and New York film companies reshot it several times over the next ten years. Films like *Around the Flip-Flap Railroad* (American Mutoscope and Biograph, 1902) capitalized on the novelty of motion that was integral to both the ride and movies. Most early films depict Coney Island both because of its proximity to a number of early film producers and because Coney Island offered Thomas Edison's film company a chance for some additional advertising of electricity itself (e.g., *Coney Island at Night,* 1905).

But most of the movies display the riders, offering the moviegoer not only the voyeuristic privilege of looking at others as among the pleasures of both the amusement park and of the cinema but of the body connected to a device in order to produce moments of physically comical reactions and twists, turns, jolts, and tumbles. For example, in *Bamboo Slide* (American Mutoscope and Biograph, 1904) an all-male crowd of onlookers watch both the men and the women as they come down the slide and tumble into each other at the bottom; the onlookers alternate their glances between the riders and the camera.

Rube and Mandy Go to Coney Island follows two country bumpkins through their arrival and participation at the amusement park. Using two stock objects of ridicule in vaudeville, the film displays bodies that are caricaturized and clownish, not to mention unfamiliar with new technologies and technological procedures. The "bumpkin" or "rube" (short for Reuben) was a figure who unreasonably clung to anachronistic ways in a modern industrial, technologized world. Immediately recognizable as country bumpkins, Rube and Mandy arrive at Coney Island astride their dairy cow. This symbol of nineteenth-century rural farm life separates them from the urbanites who will arrive by train. Their exaggerated dress, makeup, and facial gestures further type them as comic outsiders. The film then follows them through the park as they try out the attractions. The film as an attraction offers up Rube and Mandy surrendering to a series of strange phenomena that physically disorient them. Backward and unsophisticated, they are more bewildered than pleased at the conclusion of each ride. On at least one occasion they are also punished: when Rube gets too close to Professor Wormwood's show of acrobatic dogs, the professor beats Rube over the head. (Of course, the film also advertises the park itself. Early on, several wide panoramic shots of the park establish the space of the profilmic event, documenting and inscribing Coney Island as the film's subject on a par with Rube and Mandy's antics.)

The film ends with an emblematic "waist-up" shot of Rube and Mandy in front of a studio interior flat (such a shot could be attached by the exhibitor at either the beginning or end of the film). The two stuff their faces with Coney Island hot dogs, a new and popular mass-produced food. It appears to be the only moment of real pleasure for the couple, whose grotesquery while eating now becomes the exhibition itself as they enact gluttony, stuffing their open mouths, shoving food in each other's faces, and smearing ketchup and mustard all over themselves. (The scene also borrows from contemporary facial-gesture films that illustrate close-ups of grimacing or laughing faces.)

Such overindulgence in consumption stands apart from the clean, rhythmic, mechanical pleasures of the amusement park. In this conclusion Rube and Mandy appear as rural peasants of a preindustrial era. Their bodies bridge the carnivalesque folk cultures of the past and the mechanical production of physical alienation in industrialized modern leisure. The film's comedy lies in the fact that they have not yet learned how to submit their bodies to the machines. Their reactions at the novelty of doing so throughout the film produce a series of moving poses, grimaces, and awkward motions that suggest it is already the normalization of bodies intertwined with machines that makes Rube and Mandy comic and other. Here, unlike Bergson's formulation, we laugh at their bodies making repetitive, mechanistic-type motions not so we can feel secure in our organic difference but because in failing to accept and understand their relationship to the machinery, they become all the more exaggerated automatons in their encounters. Mechanical motion has already won out, and this is merely an opportunity to mediate new technologies, urban leisure, and alienation through the display of the body.

One of the pleasures introduced in *Rube and Mandy*—the surveillance of bodies at the amusement park—combines with the visual pleasure of the female body displayed in motion in the comic chase film *Boarding School Girls*. There are two extant versions of this film (at the Library of Congress [LOC] and at the Museum of Modern Art [MOMA]), each slightly different from the other. Both versions begin in the same way, with the girls descending the stairs of their finishing school and boarding an omnibus, a shot that serves the narrative purpose of establishing the decorum, genteel deportment, and orderliness of the girls. (Only the LOC version includes a lengthy shot of the bus trip down the street while the girls daintily wave handkerchiefs at passersby.) Both versions depict the carriage's arrival at Coney Island, the girls disembarking, and their entering the park. However, the films handle the chase and space of Coney Island in subtly dissimilar ways.

Only the LOC version shows the girls breaking from their pack and running wildly out of the frame. After they run offscreen left, spatial continuity is preserved in the next shot, which shows them entering frame right and continuing from right to left as they clamber onto the miniature railroad. Their teacher, Miss Knapp, appears and runs after the departing train. Across two continuous shots the chase is motivated and established. The pattern continues for a sequence of ten shots in which the girls appear in the frame, try out a ride, and escape as Miss Knapp arrives to try to catch them.

In the MOMA version, however, the same ten shots appear in a different order and many have been trimmed so that the girls do not rush in from offscreen: they are already inside the frame, either getting on or already aboard a ride. The MOMA version preserves haptic space contained within each discrete shot rather than imagining a Coney Island landscape as a topography united by continuous action, something that is fundamental to the Coney Island comedies of the 1910s. The result is the heightening of the bodies on display in each shot or block as they engage with the mechanical attractions. The chase itself becomes more gratuitous than causal. It was thus not only possible at the time to treat the shots as discrete units but also to miss what the chase film has been understood as establishing in film aesthetics— a sense of narrative necessity from one shot to the next. Available to exhibitors who arranged and ordered the shots, the film of Coney Island bodies on display experiencing the mechanical rides triumphs over the development of a uniquely modernist cinematic syntax.

What is central to both versions is that the bodies are acted on, out of control, given over to shaking and jerking movements that produce a kind of unrestrained, sensual motion of the body rather than of individual will or subject control. Although the girls may be "costars" with the park, it is the concert of bodies and mechanically induced motion that offers up a physical antidote to the formality of Victorian deportment and manners, an antidote that also signifies the unleashing of repressed female sexuality.

Miss Knapp, on the other hand, is portrayed by a male actor in drag. Her stiff upright carriage and ungainly running (as opposed to the fluid, relaxed movement of the girls) are a caricature of the spinster and invert the expression of heightened sexuality. In the end of both versions (although with shots trimmed in the MOMA version) the girls dig a hole in the sand at the beach and cover it with a towel. Miss Knapp walks over it and clumsily falls down. It is the penultimate comic instance of watching her dignity deflated. Then the girls propel her toward the ocean and pull her into the waves.

Boarding School Girls established three types of bodily motion as more important than any development of narrative technique: the girls running, the girls on the rides, and Miss Knapp, whose actions, like Rube and Mandy's, are the most mechanical, jerky, lumbering, clumsy, and therefore laughable for their differentiation from "normal" human grace in motion. There is not necessarily anything awkward about the girls on the rides. The chief interest lies in the surveillance of both the rides and the reaction of the girls' otherwise relaxed, pleasure-seeking bodies to the mechanical attractions. Their bodies represent a kind of inversion of Rube and Mandy's—they are in harmony with the machines in which they engage. The surveillance of teenage girls, whose encounters with the mechanical rides produce a relaxation of Victorian codes of conduct, unrestrained self-pleasure, and celebration of their physical movement, offers up for the spectator a sexualized voyeurism in addition to comic pleasure. The incorporation of Miss Knapp's comic motions and her "difference" mediates open sexuality with the comic.

THE CONEY ISLAND COMEDIES OF THE TRANSITIONAL ERA

The Coney Island comedies of the transitional era preserve the chase subservient to the bodies being acted on by machines that dominated *Boarding School Girls*. In its protean form *Jack Fat and Jim Slim* introduces the theme of the amusement park as a carnivalesque space in which to escape the repressive bounds of matrimony, elaborating on *Boarding School Girls'* depiction of the topography as a cultural space for open expression of sexuality. Both *Tillie Wakes Up* and *Coney Island* also make this theme central for character motivation and behavior but provide this character justification as motivation for the display aesthetics of bodies in concert with the mechanical rides.

Jack Fat and Jim Slim has been easily overlooked in film discussions because although in its entirety it does develop character motivation, the logic of the chase, and even the narrative regulation of closure, the only extant copy of the film at the Museum of Modern Art is a partial print, with German intertitles, that has edited out all developing principles of narrative. In this version even the motivation for Jack and Jim to go to Coney Island, meet two girls, and then get chased by the girls' beau and their own wives is lost. The extant copy reduces the film to a cinema of attractions display, a Rube and Mandy–like series of experiences at Coney Island of a different shot for each individual ride that "uses up the space" before each shot ends. Even the chase itself is not legible. In this copy a chase film has been reedited into a length of discrete shots of body and machine encounters, suggesting the possibility of a retrograde reception and the success of display attractions well after transitional era films were developing narrative principles of storytelling.

In its full "story," according to *Moving Picture World*, intertitles appear after the first extant shot of Jack and Jim sitting coatless on their fire escapes: "Whew! Is it hot enough for you, Jim?" "Yes—plenty and a bit more!"[16] Jim looks at his newspaper and shows it to Jack. It is likely that an insert shot appears showing an advertisement of Coney Island. They tiptoe down the fire escape ladders, a "precaution" not made clear in the full version until their wives later appear on the fire escape and discover their absence. The extant version elides any cause and effect and simply establishes the two characters looking at a newspaper and departing for Coney Island, its location introduced by an intertitle.

In the next shot of the extant version Jack and Jim disembark arm in arm from a train and walk into the foreground. The next shot shows a number of people frolicking in the surf and, among them, Jack and Jim, who are playing with two girls. Ostensibly missing are any shots that the film summary describes: "The gay benedicts meet a couple of sporty ladies who visit the Island with a diminutive beau, whom they lose sight of in the company of Jack and Jim. . . . Their wives discover their absence, find the newspaper, and seeing the flaming announcement of Coney's allurements, guess the cause of their husbands' sudden disappearance and determine to follow them."[17] The implications of temporal discontinuity and crosscutting, as well as character and chase motivation, are lost.

Instead, what follows are fourteen shots of Jack, Jim, and the two girls trying out various attractions. In many of these a tiny man in white cap and full-length duster (the diminutive beau) follows on the ride, and he himself is followed by two women in exaggerated Victorian spinster-esque costumes who resist the machines and leave the shots raising their fists and waving their arms (the two wives). Yet no one in the half dozen audiences with whom I have seen this film recognized these "chasers" as continuing characters from frame to frame or even understood that they were following the two couples. With Jack, Jim, and the two girls foregrounded quite literally, the shots that dominate the film are about these bodies falling down, exhibiting fluid motion, and tumbling. Although most shots do not end with the departure of the two pleasure-seeker couples but with the next two or three "riders"— that is, the diminutive beau and the wives—the "chasers" serve as a punctuation mark and hyperbolic physical comedy in relationship to the central bodies on display.

The extant version simply fades to black after the last shot of Jack, Jim, and the two girls slipping on a rolling sidewalk. The film summary describes a more narratively satisfying conclusion in which the wives catch up to their errant husbands at a refreshment stand and then "march them to their homes, where we see them the next day seated on the fire escapes recounting their experiences and laughing."[18]

In addition, although the film's advertisements make numerous claims for the hilarity of their appearances on these rides, Jack and Jim's bodies in motion are, in fact, rather graceful. When they and the two girls try to walk through Steeplechase's rolling barrel, their repeated losses of balance are carried out in smooth, fluid movements. Although Jim may lurch forward as the camel he is astride stands up and Jack laughs at him, he gracefully carries his sweetheart from the surf to the sand, deftly helps her up the pitching "golden stairs," and otherwise maintains a relatively liquid ease while slipping and sliding and keeping his limbs gracefully moving in connection to his whole torso.

It is rather the diminutive beau and the wives who slam into the sand and fall over at the end of the helter-skelter slide because they try to maintain rigid spines. The wives' hats fall over their eyes, and they grimace in concern over the loss of their dignity. In short, they are not pleasure seekers, and they do not blend harmoniously with the rides—allowing themselves to lose control over decorum, proper carriage, and pride. If one observes it closely, the extant film establishes an important difference between bodies meshing fluidly with machinery so that the attraction of grace in motion contrasts with the clumsy recoveries, ungainliness, and quite mechanical movements of those who resist the rides. In this regard Jonathan Auerbach's description of the function of chase film bodily movement is inaccurate. He says, "[In the chase film, the pursued . . .] is less a man than a perpetual running machine, an automaton, at once rendered so by the cinematic chase itself, as well as the thing that makes unmotivated movement possible."[19] *Jack Fat and Jim Slim,* like *Boarding School Girls* before it, argues for more than one kind of motion in relationship to masterful machinery. Its comedy is rooted in the contrast between those who enter each shot *ready for action* and those who do not. Only the latter are rendered as automatons and likened to mechanical objects in their appearance and the depiction of their movements.

SLAPSTICK COMES OF AGE: *CONEY ISLAND* AND *TILLIE WAKES UP*

Tillie Wakes Up, although a feature-length film, seems to comprise two parts—in the first half a rather conventional comic drama satirizes the repressive nature of three marriages all within one apartment building, and in the second half a trip to Coney Island stalls the narrative and becomes a display of Marie Dressler's comic behavior and body in motion. *Tillie Wakes Up* is one of the series of feature-length "Tillie" films that Marie Dressler made in the midteens, all featuring the famous Broadway star in the character role that allowed her to show off, as Jennifer Bean says, her "extraordinary mobility [and] unflinching momentum."[20] Bean argues that the character of Tillie allows for the spectacular display of Dressler's "ability to mimic technology's sublime tics" in the way she brings repetitive motion, running, facial contortions, slips and slides, and a large girth to movements that are comic because they so depart from norms of femininity.[21] Throughout, the film's comedy depends less on anything that Tillie does or enacts than on the exhibition of her body being overtaken by the various machine devices. She synthesizes the oppositions established by Miss Knapp and the girls and by the men and their wives in the earlier comedies. Although she is not the direct descendant of Rube and Mandy, she is the crucible for mechanical motion, for automatism rendered because of her contact with modern machinery.

Tillie Wakes Up begins with a lengthy exposition introducing Tillie and her husband, Henry; the nosy neighbors; and the young married couple, J. Mortimer and Luella Pipkin. Both Henry and Luella are philanderers and go off together for a good time, leaving behind their sad spouses. The film crosscuts between Tillie and J. Mortimer, both of whom are in the marital doldrums and want to resuscitate their marriages. After reading an advice column in the newspaper Tillie decides to enlist J. Mortimer as her "Romeo" to make her husband jealous. They leave, noticed by the neighbors, for a day on the town.

The second half of the film records their outing. It begins with their taxicab colliding with another automobile, and Tillie and her beau flee the scene to avoid an afternoon in police court. They catch a ride on the back of an ice wagon and begin to slide back and forth on the ice, foreshadowing their encounter with the gag devices at Coney Island. Once they get off the wagon, so to speak, they are at Coney Island and stop at a beer garden to warm themselves up with a drink. Here they figuratively fall off the wagon as they proceed to get drunk. As they get increasingly tipsy, the film intercuts between them and their spouses, who are also having a good time.

Leaving the table, Tillie begins to waver and grimace. We next see her riding on "the Witching Waves" and then climbing into a vat of peanuts for a nap. J. Mortimer finds her, and they enter Steeplechase Park. The drunken Tillie and Mortimer try out several lurching and rolling rides, where the display of Tillie's weaving, laughing, relaxed body continues to be the subject. They then become victims of the Blowhole Theater. As her skirt is repeatedly lifted and her bloomers revealed, Tillie tries to lower her raised skirt.

The film cuts repeatedly to the reactions of the laughing audience. Ultimately, Tillie and her escort fall down on the wobbly platform beneath their feet, exit, and climb the lurching Golden Stairs.

In much the same way that earlier comedies simply advertise people on one attraction after another, Tillie does not *do* anything funny so much as simply submit to the rides. Unlike Rube and Mandy, however, Tillie expresses joy in her surrender to the machines of pleasure, authorizing the spectator to react likewise in his or her submission to the movie machine of the theater. Tillie's good-natured laugh at her own loss of dignity makes her less a victim of voyeuristic humiliation than a tacit partner with the audience for producing laughter.

The next section of the film offers parallel scenes—the attractions display of Tillie and J. Mortimer versus their spouses' dismayed reactions to the discovery of their absence. In this way the strict causal economy of the spouses' efforts to find the pair contrasts the nonnarrative energies of the spectacle of Tillie and J. Mortimer. After riding in succession the Human Whirlpool, the roulette wheel, the miniature railroad, and the Ferris wheel—where bird's-eye views of Coney Island are shown—J. Mortimer and Tillie finally confront their spouses. J. Mortimer punches Henry, and they flee on foot and then in a stolen automobile. Henry and Luella pursue them, and J. Mortimer drives the car into the ocean. Henry and Luella alert the lifeguards, and the lifeguards row out to rescue Tillie and J. Mortimer. Once they are rescued, Tillie and J. Mortimer are welcomed back into the open arms of their spouses, and they wink at each other.

In this instance the chase occurs not as the subject of the film across the grounds of the amusement park but merely as a coda to effect narrative closure and to reunite the four characters in one geographically continuous locale. Whereas chase films initially introduced the possibilities of action dispersed beyond the individual shot and allowed for a new geographic expansiveness unified by human action across topography, *Tillie*'s chase serves a conservative narrative function. It reins in parallel action occurring across distinctively different spaces in order to reunite all the principal characters in an interlocking set of spaces and, ultimately, in the film's final shot, showing them all together. The chase becomes the narrative's deus ex machina, a crudely motivated means for resolving the crisis introduced at the outset of the film. Its only climactic purpose is in relationship to what preceded it since it more importantly frees Tillie's and Mortimer's bodies from interaction with the machines of pleasure for display through action in the real world. In *Tillie Wakes Up* the binaristic antinarrative and narrative impulses of slapstick initially described by Crafton and Gunning cannot be so simply located in opposition to each other because elements like "the chase" that they categorize as centripetal narrative energy instead animate a relationship between humorous spectacle display and weak narrative resolution. The result can only be labeled a narrative comedy but one that is a highly stylized, sophisticated synthesis of elements borrowed from the cinema of attractions.

Coney Island replays the premise of *Jack Fat and Jim Slim* and *Tillie Wakes Up* in a more sophisticated synthesis of mischievous gags/display and forward direction of a story. It is a sublime example of physical motion as interlocking parts of a cosmic machine. The film introduces Fatty Arbuckle as a henpecked husband seated next to his wife on the beach, although he soon buries himself in the sand. Fatty's Coney Island is a far cry from the "actualité" beach of *Boarding School Girls* or even of *Jack Fat and Jim Slim.* Although the film was shot on location, the space is open, unpopulated, and there are no bystanders to look at the camera or obstruct our view of the performance. Action occurs centrally framed and closer to the camera than in the previous examples. The landscape of the beach functions, just as the park will, as an endlessly open topography for displaying Fatty's large girth against a kind of animated cartoon world. The mise-en-scène emphasizes openness so that his body is usually the largest object within the frame—his size becomes important—and competes with no randomly placed objects for attention or for showing off the nuances of his actions.

When Fatty's wife discovers that he is "missing" and runs off to find him, he heads for Coney Island's Luna Park. Skinny Buster Keaton, in his porkpie hat, and his girlfriend, who are introduced watching Coney Island's Mardi Gras parade, also go to Luna. Again, the film intercuts documentary footage of an actual parade, but Buster and his girl only react to it from a contiguous space that frames them and the lamppost that Buster shinnies up for a view. Although the film incorporates actual locations and documentary style, the photographic realism never functions as a subject in and of itself (an actualité) and instead cinematically serves character development and narrative legibility.

Since Buster does not have any money, he cannot get into the park. Al St. John, as the perennial rube, pays for Buster's girlfriend and makes off with her inside the park. The guy and the girl get on "the Witching Waves" ride, and Buster follows in classic chase form, but the display of the three on the ride represents the chase integrated into a new style. It occurs across multiple shots that allow for a variety of angles and for a close-up of the girl's face as she exhibits symptoms of motion sickness. Eventually, their cars collide, and the two men fight.

Al and the girl leave and, while he buys an ice cream for her, Buster tries his hand at "hitting the bell," and Fatty meets the girl, who is now trying desperately not to get sick. Again, the edited arrangement of shorts constructs contiguous spaces while foregrounding character action. In returning to the girl, St. John walks through the space where Buster is just getting ready to drop the sledgehammer, and St. John kicks him in the pants. When St. John returns to "his" girl, Fatty takes the two ice-cream cones. St. John punches Fatty, and Fatty sprays him with ice cream and pushes him offscreen, only for St. John to land in the next shot on top of Buster, who is still at the stand with the sledgehammer. Buster then knocks St. John out of the shot and into the next one of the ice-cream stand, where St. John retaliates by throwing scoops of ice cream that, in the next shot, hit Fatty in the face. St. John returns to Fatty and the girl, only to have Fatty cause his arrest by a passing policeman. This ballet of action occurring across contiguous spaces depends not only on editing, angles, and framing but on timing of performances and of the shot, as well as on unification of the spaces through eyeline matches. The beauty of this gag structure relies exclusively on a combination of expert acting, timing, and mastery of cinematic syntax associated with classical cinema.

Fatty makes off with Buster's girl, and they ride the shoot-the-chutes, depicted as a spatially and temporally fragmented series that occur in relationship to their close-up reactions. In a separate shot Buster looks offscreen at them and notices that the two have fallen out of their boat and into the lagoon. He rushes off to save the girl while Fatty is preoccupied with his own water ballet. Buster extends a hand to help Fatty out of the water but is rewarded by being pulled into the pond.

Fatty and the girl head for the bathhouse, where Fatty steals the attire of a nearby fat woman. (Interestingly, the two encounter a lifeguard who is a ringer for Jim Slim.) In this extended "middle" of the film a series of gags occur over Fatty dressing in drag and wandering through first the men's and then the women's dressing rooms. It is important here that the camera maintains a close or medium close relationship to Fatty. The sequence is about his performance, a star turning out "gender bender" antics as he performs to the camera. It is a self-conscious drag show, abetted by the onscreen presence of the girl who knows his true identity. Like Tillie, he expresses delight in his physical presence. Unlike Tillie, his is a deliberate bodily performance.

The film sets up its conclusion by first developing parallel actions intercut into this sequence: (1) Buster gets a job as a lifeguard and (2) at the police station Al St. John meets up with Fatty's wife, who is an old friend, and she pays his fine while enlisting his help to find Fatty. Back at the beach Fatty, in drag, and the girl are ready for fun. Just as *Tillie Wakes Up* effected a plot climax by bringing parallel actions into one geographic space, so does *Coney Island:* Buster begins his job as a lifeguard, St. John and Fatty's wife arrive at the beach, and Fatty recognizes his wife. In a series of close-ups and medium shots organized purely by sightlines, several actions occur: St. John abandons the woman in order to flirt with Fatty, the wife spies the two of them together, and Buster reveals Fatty's true identity to all. St. John fights with Fatty, and Buster runs off with his girl. Fatty's wife calls the police, who stumble, trip, and suffer a series of accidents before they finally arrive to arrest the brawling Fatty and St. John, who then join forces and lock up both the cops and Fatty's wife. In the last two shots, bridged by action and visual reaction, they reemerge from the station house vowing not to chase women, when St. John instantly spies a pretty girl and runs after her.

In *Coney Island* Fatty, centrally framed and emphasized throughout, revels in the pleasures of his own physical performance. He is never so much a character for identification as a model for corporeal self-delight, the site of production of the audience's laughs but also, like Tillie, a contractual partner in the titter, the belly laugh, the knee-slapper, and even rolling in the aisles. It is the relationship of the comic figure and his performance to the laughing spectator that is important here for establishing the spectator's synthesis of the film's visual spectacle, with the resulting sensory knowledge in one's own body, for that feel-good-all-over-sensation that can only be *jouissance.*

CONCLUSION

Later feature films in the 1920s, like Harold Lloyd's slapstick comedies *Why Worry?* (1923) and *Speedy* (1928), as well as the romantic comedy *Lonesome* (1929), continued to display actors on Coney Island's attractions. In these films, however, Coney Island's sexual significance altered as it became a backdrop for romance and courtship between sweethearts. In addition, the spectacle of bodies at Coney Island became only one sequence or insert into the narrative rather than the backbone for the film's entirety. Lloyd was a master at extending the spectacular logic of bodies encountering Coney Island, however, to the rest of the city as best exemplified in *Speedy*. But the narrative purpose and forward momentum of his films place them in a different category from those discussed here.

The Coney Island comedies depend on a pleasure that cannot be understood as a narrative one. Although such allowances are common in the first decade of cinema, these films demonstrate that there was a stylization of the "cinema of attractions" well into the teens despite more sophisticated storytelling techniques. Increasingly, the spectacular display of the body that interconnected with the pleasure machines of Coney Island became thematized for unleashing the sexual repression of the female body and the confinements of marriage. In this way the films also collectively map a satirical view of Victorian marriage and contrast it to the cultural space of the amusement park as its escape valve. The pleasures of Coney Island are depicted not so much as an accommodation to new technologies or a remedy for the alienating effects of modern industrial labor, as has so frequently been discussed, but as allowances for sexual expression in a society whose institutions are otherwise repressive. It is through the body—and especially the comedy of the body on display where modern machinery takes over the will of the person and instigates physical relaxation, spontaneity, the destruction of dignified bearing, and a fluid kineticism—that some individuals find grace.

NOTES

1. Donald Crafton, "Pie and Chase: Gag, Spectacle, and Narrative in Slapstick Comedy," in *Classical Hollywood Comedy*, ed. Kristine Brunovska Karnick and Henry Jenkins (New York: Routledge, 1995), 108.

2. Tom Gunning, "Crazy Machines in the Garden of Forking Paths: Mischief Gags and the Origins of American Film Comedy," in *Classical Hollywood Comedy*, ed. Kristine Brunovska Karnick and Henry Jenkins (New York: Routledge, 1995), 99.

3. For a more detailed discussion of this generalization see Lauren Rabinovitz, "Urban Wonderlands: Siting Modernity in Turn-of-the-Century Amusement Parks," *European Contributions to American Studies* 45 (2001): 85–97.

4. Linda Williams, "Corporealized Observers: Visual Pornographies and the 'Carnal Density of Vision,'" in *Fugitive Images: From Photography to Video*, ed. Patrice Petro (Bloomington: Indiana University Press, 1995), 15.

5. Jennifer Bean, "Early Cinema and the Philosophies of Laughter, or, Marie Dressler's Feature-Length Female Body," in *Women and the Silent Screen: Cultural and Historical Practices*, ed. Amelie Hastie and Shelley Stamp (forthcoming), 1.

6. "Fatty Arbuckle," Paramount Pictures Corporation advertisement, *Moving Picture World*, 7 April 1917, 31.

7. *"Jack Fat and Jim Slim at Coney Island,"* *Moving Picture World*, 17 December 1910, 1428.

8. *"The Cook,"* *Moving Picture World*, 14 September 1918, 1609.

9. *"Cohen at Coney Island,"* *Moving Picture World*, 9 October 1909, 489.

10. *"Jack Fat and Jim Slim at Coney Island,"* *Moving Picture World*, 1 December 1910, 1416.

11. Francesco Casetti, *Inside the Gaze: The Fiction Film and Its Spectator*, trans. Nell Andrew and Charles O'Brien (Bloomington: Indiana University Press, 1998), 8–9.

12. See Crafton, "Pie and Chase"; Gunning, "Crazy Machines"; and Charlie Keil, *Early American Cinema in Transition: Story, Style, and Filmmaking, 1907–1913* (Madison: University of Wisconsin Press, 2001), 47–49, 86–87.

13. John Kasson, *Amusing the Million: Coney Island at the Turn of the Century* (New York: Hill and Wang, 1978), 82.

14. For a more elaborate discussion of Hale's Tours see Lauren Rabinovitz, "'Bells and Whistles': The Sound of Meaning in Train Travel Film Rides," in *The Sounds of Early Cinema*, ed. Richard Abel and Rick Altman (Bloomington: Indiana University Press, 2001), 167–80; and Lauren Rabinovitz, "From *Hale's Tours* to *Star Tours:* Virtual Voyages and the Delirium of the Hyper-Real," *Iris* 25 (spring 1998): 133–52.

15. Kathy Peiss, *Cheap Amusements: Working Women and Leisure in Turn-of-the-Century New York* (Philadelphia, Pa.: Temple University Press, 1986), 134–35.

16. *"Jack Fat and Jim Slim at Coney Island," Moving Picture World,* 17 December 1910, 1428.

17. Ibid.

18. Ibid.

19. Jonathan Auerbach, "Chasing Film Narrative: Repetition, Recursion, and the Body in Early Cinema," *Critical Inquiry* 26 (summer 2000): 807.

20. Bean, "Early Cinema," 4.

21. Ibid.

CHAPTER EIGHT

Travelogues and Early Nonfiction Film

Education in the School of Dreams

Jennifer Lynn Peterson

"Everyone knows the value of travel in broadening the mind and enlarging the sympathies," wrote one film commentator in 1912. "To look at good pictures of distant peoples and scenes is to be a stay-at-home traveler, and to enjoy many of the advantages of real travel without its dangers and trials."[1] This kind of rhetoric was commonplace throughout the nickelodeon era. In the trade press and in general articles about the young motion picture medium it was pointed out that travelogues made it easy to tour places one would never otherwise visit. Travel films were compared with actual journeys, as though the two experiences were somehow equivalent. Of course, watching a film about another place is nothing like actually traveling to that locale, but the desire to compare the two experiences is significant. According to this logic travel films are both less and more than the real thing: the next-best-thing to real travel and, in some ways, even better than real travel because the stay-at-home tourist avoids the "dangers and trials" of actual expeditions. In this essay I want to play off this logic to explore the ways in which travelogues were not simply substitutes for tourism but, in fact, experiences in their own right. As the most prominent nonfiction genre of the silent film era, travelogues regularly provided filmgoers with visions of foreign lands that appealed both to their intellectual curiosity and to their exotic fantasies. Watching a travelogue film in the 1910s was a practice very different from real, physical travel, and it was an experience that was familiar to most moviegoers of the period.

Travelogues have existed throughout film history: from the first films of the Lumière brothers to the Travel Channel on cable TV, people have always found pleasure in looking at moving images of foreign lands. Travelogues were a common sight on movie screens from the 1920s through the 1960s as the short film before the main feature. But during the early years of silent cinema travel films existed in quite a different context. They were an important part of the variety film program, and they were one of the most recognizable film genres before the first World War. Travelogues and other nonfiction genres were promoted as "educational," and for a time it looked as though these films might have major commercial potential. Some even believed that educational films represented the future of the film industry, predicting that "some day they will be as common as slap-stick comedies."[2] Of course, we know now that nonfiction never became the cinema's dominant form. But early nonfiction films—and the debate surrounding them— reveal a great deal about the commercial and cultural aspirations of the early motion picture industry, which believed the way to maximize profits was to legitimate itself as a middle-class form of entertainment.

This essay examines travelogues exhibited commercially in the United States during silent film's transitional period, when the commercial and cultural value of nonfiction films was actively debated. After presenting an outline of early travelogue production and exhibition I will propose travelogues as a model for nonclassical film spectatorship. I ultimately argue that silent travel films may have inspired a dreamlike mode of reception that ran counter to the sober educational rhetoric used to promote them. Instead of providing a lesson about other nations and cultures, travelogues might alternatively have been experienced as a kind of hallucination, encouraging a spectator whose attention was less that of the rapt pupil and more that of a student lost in reverie.

EARLY NONFICTION FILM

Thanks to the renewal of interest in early cinema, it is now well-known that nonfiction dominated motion picture production for much of the first decade of film history.[3] Views of street scenes, sports events, parades, industrial processes, animals, and foreign lands greatly outnumbered story films on early motion picture screens, and some of these first films, especially those made by the Lumières and Edison, should be familiar to any student who has taken a class in silent cinema. It is less known, however, that nonfiction films *continued* to be a major presence in screening venues throughout the nickelodeon period and into the feature film era. Although it is true that nonfiction subjects became marginalized as the cinema shifted toward narrative by 1904, nonfiction genres such as travelogues persisted on film screens alongside comedies and melodramas well into the 1910s. In fact, during the first two decades of cinema, nonfiction was a more significant part of commercial film exhibition than at any other time in film history. It is perhaps surprising, then, that early nonfiction has been almost completely neglected by scholars of early cinema. In the last few years, however, nonfiction films have finally begun to receive some attention.[4]

As this rediscovery gets underway, one of the first things film historians have observed is that early nonfiction did not change much stylistically during silent cinema's transitional period. For example, Stephen Bottomore stated in a recent essay, "By the second decade of cinema, then, non-fiction may indeed be regarded as a relatively stagnant genre in terms of film style and technique."[5] I would argue, however, that *stagnant* is the wrong word to use here. It is true that once nonfiction had shifted from the single-shot actualities of early cinema into the multishot genre films of the cinema's second decade, there were no major new formal or stylistic developments. But calling the material "stagnant" seems to justify the decades of neglect these films have suffered, reinscribing the dismissive tone with which early nonfiction is mentioned in film histories published before the 1990s. Instead, we might look at this constancy as an element that makes early nonfiction all the more interesting. Since they did not change dramatically over a period of several years, we can assume that their form and style were entirely adequate to serve these films' rhetorical purposes. Thus it would seem all the more important to understand what was compelling about this nonfiction style during a period of rapid change in fiction film style. In addition, we must not forget to look outside the films to their social and historical context, for early nonfiction was a site of dynamic contestation for the various forces that were competing to shape the emergent film industry. What was "transitional" about nonfiction films during these years was not so much their style but their place within the film industry and their cultural status.

Even though nonfiction films no longer outnumbered story films in the nickelodeon era, as they had done in the 1890s, several factors guaranteed their persistence on cinema screens in the transitional era. First of all, by around 1907 the generic "actuality" of the early years had become organized into several distinct genres such as industrials, scientific films, sports films, newsreels, and travelogues. Although these genres were overlapping and unstable, they were more codified than the real-life "views" of the cinema's first decade, whose subjects ranged from the extremely generalized *Feeding the Doves* (Edison, 1896) to the hyperspecific *Searching Ruins on Broadway, Galveston, for Dead Bodies* (Edison, 1900). As early actualities were sifted into different genres, the cinema's initially euphoric function as a kind of reflexive cataloger-of-the-world in effect sobered up and began to follow the more streamlined classifications of natural history or the newspaper. Rather than the breathless sense one gets from watching early Biograph or Lumière films, which seem to proclaim, "Here is the world!," nonfiction from the nickelodeon era seems to say more calmly, "Here is Japan," or, "Here is a water-beetle." Through the creation of different genres nonfiction continued to appeal to the audience's curiosity about the world, but its subject matter was refined and targeted more efficiently.

The development of diverse nonfiction genres in turn fed into one of the

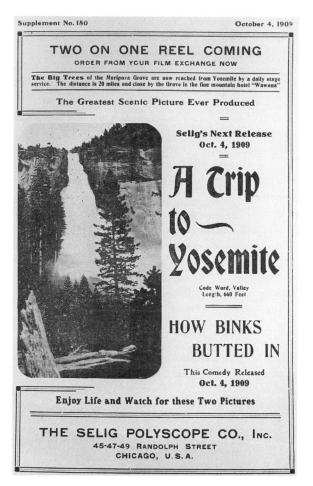

Figure 8.1. Pamphlet advertising Selig's travel film *A Trip to Yosemite* (1909). Courtesy of the Academy of Motion Picture Arts and Sciences.

most important (and least theorized) aspects of the nickelodeon era: the variety format.[6] The variety format required films of various genres to constitute each program. From about 1907 until the feature film era in the mid-1910s, motion picture shows were made up of several short films interspersed with song slides and accompanied by live musical entertainment, in a tradition carried over from vaudeville. The bulk of these variety programs comprised comedies and dramas, but usually there were one or two nonfiction films mixed into the program, depending on the theater. The variety format relied on generic diversity as part of its appeal, and multiplicity defined the experience of commercial film shows of this era. The nonfiction slot in a variety program could be filled by any one of several nonfiction genres, but travelogues were the most frequently shown.

In addition, nonfiction films were typically released as part of a split reel, which guaranteed their inclusion in film programs. By 1907 film reels had become standardized at one thousand feet. Nonfiction films averaged about five hundred feet (approximately five minutes) and were typically released to exhibitors on the same reel with a fiction film. For example, on 4 October 1909 the Selig Polyscope Company released a travelogue called *A Trip to Yosemite* on the same reel with a comedy called *How Binks Butted In* (figure 8.1). With variety literally built into the reel, split reels were obviously well-suited to the variety format. But by the mid-1910s split reels were becoming less common as fiction films lengthened into multiple reels. Likewise, it was the rise of the feature film that spelled the demise of the variety film show.

But there are other, less material, reasons for nonfiction's persistence on movie screens alongside comedies and melodramas of the day. Different nonfiction genres had different appeals, and at this point I will turn to the travelogue film in particular. Cinematic travel was broadly appealing to film audiences in ways that cut across the class and educational lines envisioned by early film manufacturers, exhibitors, and reformers. Specifically, travelogues could foster a kind of spectatorial reverie that encouraged exotic fantasies just as much as they served any educational purpose. Despite the utopian rhetoric about how such "armchair travel" could be a democratic substitution for real travel—travel made available to everyone for only five cents—it seems more useful to focus on travelogues as a unique experience in their own right. What was actually being made available to everyone was not travel but cinema.

THE TRAVELOGUE GENRE

Travelogues were called many things in the American press (such as "nature studies," "panoramas," and "natural scenic films"), but the most standard trade term for the early travel film was *scenic,* a term that emphasizes the intensely visual nature of the genre, as well as its pleasing, entertaining function as scenery. I emphasize the term *travelogue* rather than *scenic,* however, because the former word was used then and still persists in our vocabulary to this day—as indeed the travelogue genre still persists in various forms—whereas an archaic term such as *scenic* no longer carries the same resonance. The *Oxford English Dictionary* defines a travelogue as "An (illustrated) lecture about places and experiences encountered in the course of travel; hence a film, broadcast, book, etc., about travel; a travel documentary."[7] The term is often considered a neologism of travel lecturer Burton Holmes, and although I have not found evidence that Holmes was the one who coined the word, he was certainly the one who first popularized it.[8] Like the genre's variable terminology, boundaries between genres were also quite fluid; other genres such as industrials, scientific films, and even sports films often contained "scenic" elements.[9]

The idea that all the world's infinite variety could be recorded by the motion picture camera was still quite new in the years before World War I, and early travelogues seem almost as fascinated by the technology of motion pictures as by the places they documented. Travelogues were not systematic in their presentation of the world's scenery; rather, the choice of locations filmed often seems completely arbitrary. Films with titles such as *A Trip through Brazil* (Eclipse, 1910), *Motoring among the Cliffs and Gorges of France* (Gaumont, 1910), *Up the Thames to Westminster* (Kalem, 1910), and *In the Land of Monkeys and Snakes* (Pathé, 1911) were regularly shown in commercial theaters during these years, depicting places in all regions of the globe. Intertitles were sparse, the scenery presented flatly as a series of images that stand, synecdochically, for the larger place. The films typically feature sweeping landscape panoramas and shots of people performing everyday activities. Foreignness and otherness are the films' subject matter, and clichés abound: highlights of locations famous from the European grand tour were popular, and images of places less familiar to Western sensibilities tended to construct a generic exoticism.

A film called *Seeing Los Angeles,* for example, opens with a street scene of a bustling modern downtown filled with trolley cars, bicycles, and pedestrians.[10] This six-minute film proceeds to show some scenery of an unnamed park (now MacArthur Park), an alligator and ostrich farm, "the fastest trolley car in the world," and a hilltop panorama of the city's still-undeveloped landscape. The film concludes, as travelogues often do, with a shot of the ocean at sunset. This film was made in 1912 by the IMP company, which was bought by Universal later that same year. Manufacturer's descriptions of their films were regularly published in the trade press, and IMP's own description of this film explains: "Los Angeles, Cal., is counted one of the most beautiful and progressive cities in the United States. It is fortunate in its situation, being near the Pacific and under the shadow of picturesque mountain ranges. This picture gives a very good idea of the architectural and commercial features of the city."[11] Despite this description of the film, very little of the city's architectural features are actually shown. After a few city street shots in the beginning, the film works quite hard to exoticize Los Angeles with its focus on the alligator and ostrich farms. It seems, then, that IMP's description of the film was crafted to play up the image of Los Angeles as a bustling modern metropolis, whereas the film itself emphasizes the exotic and the unusual.

Audiences were free to make what they wanted out of the films they saw, of course, and at least one Los Angeles audience complained that this title was unrepresentative of their city. After a screening in a local theater, *Moving Picture World* reported that "the picture did not seem to fulfill the expectations it aroused. . . . [T]he chief criticism [was] that the particular scenes selected were neither the best nor the most characteristic that could have been obtained."[12] Today we can only speculate about what this audience objected to, but my guess is that they did not appreciate seeing so much of the alligator and ostrich farms.[13] Orange groves and lush gardens were the iconic images of Los Angeles at the time—the city had yet to become the capital of the film industry—and a local audience might have preferred to see these more pastoral images instead of unusual, foreign animals. Whatever the case, faraway audiences would have had no such sense of the actual Los Angeles to compare the film against. *Seeing Los Angeles* was shown in the Netherlands in 1913, for example, where the film met with a different set of audience expectations. Because they are at least nominally about geography, the geographical reception context of travelogue films has a great deal of significance, much more than for other genres.

Early travelogues and other nonfiction genres were indeed quite distinct from the melodramas and comedies of the era, which were now telling more complicated stories as classical narrative form was being developed. Nonfiction—and travelogues in particular—followed a different logic from fiction films, a logic of collection rather than of narrative progression. The basic formula for travelogues of this period is a series of single exterior shots of landscapes or people, punctuated by an occasional explanatory intertitle. The discrete, stand-alone quality of the shots is one of the genre's most notable formal elements, fostering what Tom Gunning has called the "view aesthetic."[14] Shots are almost always joined together in a disjunctive manner that preserves the integrity of each shot rather than making connections between shots using continuous space or matching on action. Neither are travel films usually organized with any sense of progression toward or away from a subject; instead, shots are typically arranged in a meandering, arbitrary fashion. This disjointed editing emphasizes that the film is a collection of images, a succession of views resembling a series of postcards or snapshots in a photo album—a rhetorical mode distinctly at odds with the strict narrative causality increasingly common in dramatic films of the era.

As I have already mentioned, commercial exhibition in the nickelodeon era offered variety-oriented entertainment. Rather than losing oneself in a single feature-length narrative, the moviegoer of the early 1910s was met with a wide array of short films, music, and live performance. (There is not space in this essay to discuss the important although erratic presence of the film lecturer.) The variety format stressed variation and fostered an accumulation of discrete pleasures. I believe that nonfiction films provided a rest in the program of films, a chance for spectators to catch their breath between story films. For example, a program presented at the Prince's Hall in Hull, England, during the week of 13 January 1913 comprised eight short films and a selection of music (figure 8.2). After a comedy, a drama, and another comedy, audiences saw a travel film about Norway called *The Sandmore District,* followed by a third comedy and an intermission. In the second half of the program there was another nonfiction film, this time Pathé's *Animated Newspaper.* In both cases the nonfiction film contrasts with the fiction films dominating the program, effectively serving as a break between stories. After three fiction films the spectators might well have been ready for a release from the demands of following so many narratives. Outdoor scenery described as "some of the wildest spots in Norway" would have provided a contrast to the indoor sets of the fiction films. And a few minutes of "a series of delightful views" would have provided a chance for the spectator to shift his or her attention, since nonfiction films encouraged a more disengaged mode of viewing.

In fact, reviewers in the trade press often pointed out how travel films and other nonfiction provided a rest in the screening program. One reviewer describes the experience of watching a travelogue of China called *Scenes in the Celestial Empire* (Eclipse, 1910): "This picture followed a series of films that had stirred one's sentimental nature and it was as welcome." Another reviewer had this to say about an industrial film called *Sabot Making* (Unique, 1908): "To those who have tired of the 'knock-down-and-drag-out' comedy film and the forced melodramatic stories, it is bound to be an interesting variation. The scenes are laid amid picturesque surroundings and the characteristic peasant workmen who turn the crude blocks of wood into shoes make up an odd and altogether interesting company. There are entirely too few subjects of this light but entertaining and educational sort." Still another reviewer described a film called *Sevres Porcelain* (Gaumont, 1909) by explaining: "The film runs only a few moments, but works in well among miscellaneous subjects."[15]

The task of regularly filling out a variety program was not an easy one, and exhibitors were constantly clamoring for more product. The term *filler* was used during this period to refer to films that were included on a program simply to fill some screen time. Often it was the educational films that were described as "fillers" or "filling out a reel," as in this review of the Vitagraph film *Montana State Fair* (1914): "On the same reel [as a comedy called *Their Interest in Common*] and a good filler."[16] Travelogues were not always the shortest film on the reel, however. A number of scenic films were longer than five hundred feet and thus longer than the film that accompanied them on the split reel, which would indicate that perhaps the fiction film was the filler on such a reel.[17] Even more, some travel films were a full reel in length, such as Ambrosio's *A Glimpse of Neapolitan Camorra* (1911). Such occasional travelogue "features" indicate that manufacturers were still experimenting to discover which kinds of films would be popular with the general audience. And

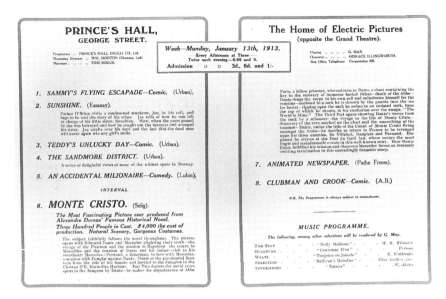

Figure 8.2. January 1913 program from the Prince's Hall in Hull, England.
Courtesy of the Academy of Motion Picture Arts and Sciences.

in the end there is not much difference between calling travel films "filler" and saying that they functioned as a break in the program. At this time the industry had not yet adopted the consumerist idea that each film should be equally valuable. Moviegoers were buying a full variety program with their nickel, after all, and not every film performed the same function within these programs. Often, going to the nickelodeon was simply a way to spend some time, and "fillers" occupied one's time just fine. On the other hand, the designation "filler" devalued travelogues, indicating the diminishing prestige of the disengaged mode of spectatorship they fostered in the wake of the absorbed viewing position increasingly demanded by more complicated multireel narrative films.

Although many early film companies made travelogue films, several manufacturers specialized in the genre. French companies, in particular, had a reputation for their scenic output: Eclipse, Gaumont, and especially Pathé Frères were renowned for their travel films. One reviewer remarked, "Between Gaumont, Pathé, and Eclipse it is hard to award the palm for scenics. If Pathé stirs a more intellectual pleasure, the others certainly stir a more esthetic."[18] Some of the other major producers of scenic films were Ambrisio and Cines in Italy, Warwick and Urban in England, Nordisk in Denmark, and Edison and Selig in the United States. In fact, most early film companies made at least a few scenic films at one point or another, even if they did not release as many as did these larger companies.[19] Scenics were relatively inexpensive and easy to make, after all. Some companies made "local" scenics, such as *Feeding Seals at Catalina Island,* which was shot by Essanay soon after the company established its California studio in 1910.[20] Another money-saving strategy was to shoot a scenic while a film crew was on location making fiction films, as was the case with Kalem's 1912 film *Ancient Temples of Egypt.*[21]

In 1907 European films dominated the general releases in the United States. In fact, there was an overall shortage of film prints, with exhibitors clamoring for more new material to satisfy their growing audiences. As Charles Musser has noted, this shortage "opened up tremendous opportunitiesfor foreign producers."[22] The French companies releasing the majority of scenics during this period were praised in the trade press for the high quality of their travel films, which were often color-tinted or, in the case of Pathé, even color-stenciled.[23] Referring to Pathé, a reviewer in *Variety* stated in 1909, "Depend upon these Frenchmen for at least one interesting travel view a week."[24] At this time Pathé was the largest film production company in the world, so it should come as no surprise that its scenic films were a common presence on U.S. film screens.[25] Although American film production gained market dominance by the early 1910s, European imports continued to play a major role in U.S. film exhibition throughout this period. Indeed, it seems likely that American travel film production was inspired by and modeled after the European scenic film.

Alongside Pathé, which distributed its own films, the most important distributor of European nonfiction films in the United States during this period was George Kleine. Based in Chicago, Kleine had been involved in the film business from the beginning, starting out in his father's optical shop, which was incorporated as the Kleine Optical Company in 1897.[26] The Kleine firm began importing films from Europe in 1903; by 1907 Kleine was distributing French and English films from Gaumont, Urban, and Eclipse. In January 1912, because of problems with Gaumont, Kleine switched to the Italian Cines company.[27] Gaumont subsequently opened up an American office and distributed its own films through the independent circuit. Kleine's importation of European films was brought to an abrupt halt in 1914 with the onset of World War I.

Kleine was a major figure in the early film industry, and he took it on himself to play the role of a cinema reformer. In 1910 Kleine issued a catalog of educational motion pictures he distributed in the United States.[28] Kleine's expressed objective in putting out this catalog was "to create a demand for these highly desirable films."[29] One commentator in *Nickelodeon* wrote soon after the catalog appeared:

> At last educational moving pictures are coming into their own. Whether it was Kleine's big catalogue that started it, or the numerous scientific shows which

have been held recently, is hard to tell; but the attitude of the exhibitor toward instructive subjects is certainly changing. Perhaps only the more astute exchange men have sensed the new order of things as yet; but those who have are acting upon their convictions, and will reap the first profits accordingly.[30]

Despite the efforts of cinema reformers such as Kleine, which I will expand on below, by the mid-1910s it was clear that nonfiction films were not going to have the commercial appeal that some had hoped for. World War I disrupted the production and distribution of educational films, and very few French scenics were imported to the United States by the end of 1914. Perhaps most important, the variety film program was superseded by feature films. As one commentator wrote in 1913, "While split reels, as an American institution, have not entirely disappeared, lingering still in the old combination of comedy and scenic, they have lost their importance to the manufacturer."[31] Features could combine all the disparate appeals of the variety program into one single narrative. More frequent location shooting in dramatic films could in some ways fulfill the "scenic" function that travelogues had performed, and stories set in foreign lands catered to the persistent audience fascination with exotic locales. In the later years of his career Kleine expressed his frustration that educational films were never as popular as he thought they should be. Speaking of his educational film catalog in a 1921 letter to Thomas Edison, Kleine wrote, "This catalogue brought little or no business and has been obsolete for many years."[32] Although travel films continued to be manufactured and exhibited commercially after the 1910s, the idea that they could become the most popular genre had been dashed for good.

Travelogues and certain other nonfiction genres could be reused over the years without much depreciation in value, however, and they found a second life after the nickelodeon era in schools. Unlike fiction films, and especially unlike topicals or newsreels, travelogues did not become outdated with time. After World War I the push to promote scenics, scientific films, and industrials for commercial exhibition was all but abandoned in favor of the nontheatrical market. Smaller-gauge film systems such as the Pathéscope were introduced, and educational films were rented to schools.[33] Travelogues were still shown in commercial movie theaters for decades—MGM released a series called "Fitzpatrick's Traveltalks" in the 1930s and 1940s, for example.[34] But after the 1910s travelogues clearly functioned as an added attraction to the main feature. Their years of being promoted as a primary commercial draw were over.

INSTRUCTIVE ENTERTAINMENT

The period in which nonfiction films were marketed for mainstream commercial audiences may have been brief, but the moment was significant, appearing now as the ghost of a road not taken in film history. Nonfiction films were caught up in the drive to legitimate the cinema as a respectable cultural form during the nickelodeon era. As soon as motion pictures became a major cultural force, social reformers stepped in with attempts to influence the kinds of films that were shown, in the name of "uplifting" the audience and promoting middle-class cultural values. In the United States and in Europe there was a vast campaign to "educate the masses" through moving pictures. Many within the industry made an effort to redefine moving pictures as a "high-class" form of entertainment. Unlike the social goals of the reform movement, however, the film industry's goals were commercial: the drive to legitimate the movies was a drive to broaden the audience and thus increase profits.

William Uricchio and Roberta Pearson have shown how the early film industry employed bourgeois subject matter such as Shakespearean plays as a strategy to promote the cinema as a respectable form of entertainment: "Although the high-art films, also known as 'quality films' . . . constituted a relatively small (though highly publicized) component of the industry's overall output, they represented one of the most visible markers of the film industry's desire to improve its cultural status, explicitly invoking 'high' culture referents but offering them in a 'low' culture venue, the moving picture shows."[35] The same could be said of nonfiction films during this period, when educators and reformers joined forces with the commercial film industry in a campaign to market nonfiction films as "educational." Although education would seem opposed to entertainment, it seems that nonfiction films were elastic enough to combine these seemingly opposite categories to function as something unique: instructive entertainment. Not only did travelogues function as spectacle, emphasizing and sensationalizing exoticism at every turn, but travel films were also laden with an educational function, tied to the discourses of reform and the ideologies of bourgeois taste.

Whereas some educators still looked askance at the cinema, then, a few were extremely enthusiastic about the cinema's potential as an educational tool. And more often than not, when an educator wanted to promote motion pictures, travelogues were the films singled out for praise. For example, in 1909 Frederick Starr, a University of Chicago anthropology professor, issued an endorsement of moving pictures that appeared in the *Chicago Tribune:*

> I have looked upon weird dances and outlandish frolics in every quarter of the globe, and I didn't have to leave Chicago for a moment. No books have taught me all these wonderful things—no lecturer has pictured them—I simply dropped in to a moving picture theater at various moments of leisure. . . . I have learned more than a traveler could see at the cost of thousands of dollars and years of journey.[36]

Starr's endorsement was an important one for reform-minded film businessmen, who reprinted it in the trade press and circulated it widely. It is significant, however, that Starr's words first appeared in public not as an editorial but as part of an expensive two-page advertisement for the Selig Polyscope Company, which suggests that Starr's opinion was perhaps not entirely disinterested.[37]

Although educators and reformers (those who were not opposed to film entirely) seemed to be in agreement about the educational value of travel films, those in the film industry were divided about the commercial potential of the genre. In the trade press writers debated publicly about the future of cinema, its commercial prospects, and its potential to become an educational tool rather than the dismissed, lowbrow entertainment form it had been at the beginning of the century. Trade journals such as *Nickelodeon* (which changed its name to *Motography* in April 1911) and *Moving Picture World* were especially reform-oriented. Scott Curtis observes that "the birth of trade magazines devoted exclusively to cinema coincides with the birth of the reform movement in 1907."[38] In these journals efforts were made to convince exhibitors that scenic and educational films were appealing not only to the "better classes" but also to the wider, more heterogeneous film audience made up of working-class and middle-class patrons. One writer in *The Nickelodeon* remarked that "we are still insisting that the educational subject is the most valuable and the most popular." Another claimed that "the average exhibitor does not realize what a tremendous demand there is for just such subjects as these."[39] Such reform-minded writers tried to use the logic of the marketplace to argue that educational films would be extremely popular if only they were given a chance. Educational film enthusiasts tended to blame what one writer called "bonehead exhibitors" for the fact that nonfiction films were not dominating the market.[40] Following a populist logic, audiences were said to want educational films. One editorial writer exclaimed, "*The preference of the public is for travel pictures.* Make no mistake about this. It is not merely the opinion of *Motography*'s editors, nor is it the theory of impractical students. It is the statement of the people themselves."[41]

These editorials in the trade press argued repeatedly for the marketability of instructive entertainment. Their logic was perhaps best summed up by Professor Starr, who explained that the cinema was "not only the greatest impulse of entertainment, but the mightiest force of instruction."[42] Perhaps this argument seemed all the more natural because instructive entertainment was essentially an Enlightenment ideal that had been around since the seventeenth century. But travelogue films engaged this contradictory notion on a grand scale: for the first time the cinema made it possible to engage a mass, global public in a popular form of education. For a time educational cinema seemed like a major triumph of social reform. But as other voices in the trade press indicate, it soon became clear that the forces of commerce were not so uniformly responsive to the educational ideal after all.

Despite the promotion of educational films, many exhibitors complained that scenics, industrial films, and scientific pictures were not popular with their audiences. One commentator explained, "A Chicago renter tells us that almost 90 per cent of his customers refused to take the film [Essanay's *Sensational Logging*]. The reason they gave was that it was a scenic subject, and 'scenics don't go.'"[43] For every exhibitor who complained about travel films, however, it seems there was another who praised them. An exhibitor at the Bell Theatre in Chicago wrote in a 1910 letter to George Kleine, "Your Urban Eclipse and Gaumont scenic subjects have certainly won a home with our audiences."[44] In another letter to Kleine the proprietor of the Majestic Theatre in Ault, Colorado, wrote, "I desire to thank you on behalf of my patrons for your importation of Gaumont's 'Vale of Aude.' It is the first and only picture that has ever been applauded in my M. P. Theatre here. My only regret is that it was too short by far. The applause last night was terrific & my business exceeded the night previous fifty percent."[45] It is clear, too, that there were a few bona fide nonfiction hits in this period. One film, *The Fly Pest* (Urban), garnered quite a bit of press during the spring of 1910. Classified as a scientific film, it was part of the effort made by reformers at the turn of the century to educate the public about health and sanitation, and it apparently struck a chord with audiences.[46]

Because evidence about the reception of these films is so scant and contradictory, it is extremely difficult to gauge the commercial popularity of early nonfiction films. And regardless, it seems that this debate about whether or not nonfiction films could be popular was insoluble. I would like to suggest that the reformers and exhibitors of early cinema were defining their debate along the wrong lines. Or rather, their debate about the *value* of travel films was entirely appropriate for their own needs: reforming the mass public, generating a profit from the mass public. In the early film period, as now, the film industry wanted more than anything to know what the audience wanted. In projecting its various hopes and fears onto the audience, however, the industry's discussion does not reveal much about the *experience* of watching a travelogue film. In fact, it seems clear now that the conflict was not actually between the forces of education and commerce; rather, the conflict was a fight to know and control the spectator. Reformers and exhibitors missed the point with their debate about what might be the most popular, and all the while film audiences may well have been viewing scenic films in quite different terms.

THE DREAM WORLD OF CINEMATIC TRAVEL

The travelogue genre has been characterized as a "cinema of reassurance," both for its old-fashioned aesthetics and for the way it apparently propagates bourgeois Western values.[47] The style seems old-fashioned now because travelogues follow many of the conventions of the old nineteenth-century travel lecture and often depend on antiquated picturesque aesthetics. This association with the "genteel" magic lantern lecture in turn gave travelogues a kind of "high-class" veneer, even though, as films, they were also associated with cheap entertainment. But more to the point, travelogues are often seen today as *ideologically* "reassuring." According to this kind of analysis travel films display images of the world's racial and cultural difference only to reassure the viewer that his or her lifestyle is truly the best: exoticism is produced only to be denigrated. Although there is clearly some truth in this assertion, I do not think it adequately accounts for the genre's appeal or complexity. Images of racial and cultural exoticism always contain a measure of ambivalence, after all, a mixture of both "desire and derision" for the otherness depicted.[48] Although there is not enough space in this essay to adequately discuss the travelogue's representation of racial and cultural difference, I do want to counter the accusation that these films were simply "reassuring."[49]

Although travel films were promoted for their middle-class educational values, the genre would seem to embody many of the qualities that reformers did not like. Travelogues were short, and they stressed discontinuity rather than the sanctioned bourgeois absorption of attention. They demonstrate no unity of action or unity of character, two elements that early film theorist Hugo Münsterberg believed were essential to cinema as an art form.[50] Indeed, as shown amid a disjunctive variety program to a heterogeneous public audience, it hardly seems accurate to call travelogues "reassuring" at all. The films appeared to fit into an educational agenda, yet they also clearly made appeals to popular tastes, presenting exotic spectacles of foreign lands. I want to suggest, therefore, that travelogues could induce a viewing experience that circumvented not only classical spectatorship but also the very educational uplift on which they were marketed.

Like real, physical travel, travelogue films are highly experiential. Take the film *Loetschberg*, for example. This "phantom ride" film of a railway line running through the mountains of Switzerland was made by Eclipse around 1913.[51] The film presents the viewer with images of railroad tracks, telephone poles, mountains, and Alpine cabins. The bulk of the film comprises motion-filled landscape shots taken from onboard a moving train, but there are some stationary shots of the train arriving at a station, reminiscent of the famous Lumière film. As the train passes through several tunnels, we experience the kinetic sensation of space moving away at the sides of the frame (figure 8.3). The film plays up the sensation of movement, as phantom rides had been doing since the 1890s. In the well-known Hale's Tours, which showed phantom rides inside stationary train cars, spectators were encouraged to imagine themselves onboard the train.[52] When shown in a regular nickelodeon theater, the effect would have been much the same. *Loetschberg* is more about the experience of movement than it is about the specificity of the Loetschberg railway. Although it is likely that this film was produced on

Figure 8.3.   Frame enlargement from *Loetschberg* (Eclipse, 1913). Courtesy of the
Nederlands Filmmuseum.

the occasion of the opening of a new railway line—probably with the full cooperation and encouragement of the railroad company—to a viewer unfamiliar with this landscape many of these images might just as well be pastoral scenes of any mountainous place in Europe. In picturing the world that
does exist, travelogues create a world that does not exist: a dream world of
cinematic geography.

Travel films produce geographies that can be found only on the screen.
Some contemporary commentators seem to have been aware of this, re-
marking for example that cinematic travel could be "superior to taking the
actual trip because the camera catches scenes impossible to the keenest observation of the traveler."[53] The implication here is significant: *superior to taking the actual trip*, the camera creates something new, something we might
call, following Walter Benjamin, an "optical unconscious."[54] In this sense
travel films are quite unlike actual travel, for they create an experience that
can only be had in the cinema.

If a film viewer had done some traveling in the early 1900s, perhaps as a
tourist but more likely as an immigrant, his or her experience would probably not have accorded with the idealized set of pictures displayed in the
scenic film. This dreamlike cinematic geography could have the effect of
putting the spectator into a state of reverie. And, in fact, I have found sev-

eral accounts of audiences who were so entranced by travel films that they fell silent in the theater. Here is an excerpt from a 1912 article defending travelogue films:

> Have you ever watched the average audience closely while the "weekly" or a beautiful travelogue picture was being exhibited? You do not hear the murmur of voices and exclamations that are generally audible during the exhibition of the ordinary program. The audience is perfectly quiet; you can hear a pin drop. This denotes attentiveness, which proves that the audience is interested.[55]

In another account a writer blames exhibitors for misreading the taste of the film audience:

> The average exhibitor has no more idea of what kind of pictures his patrons prefer than he has of their preference in literature between a dime novel and an encyclopedia. If he shows an alleged comic film of the slap-stick variety, and five people in the audience laugh, he concludes that he has found a winner. If he shows a scenic picture so beautiful that the whole audience sits almost breathless while it is run, he concludes from the absence of noise that the picture was no good.[56]

Another undercover observer—this time at a screening of the Paul Rainey African pictures—wrote, "There was found a large and seemingly breathless audience. Apart from the spokesman's voice there was not the faintest trace of sound."[57]

In each of these three accounts audiences were so enraptured by scenics that they fell silent. This response is apparently contrary to the usually vocal audience reaction to the material on the screen. Here I want to propose that travelogues encouraged spectatorship that resembles a kind of reverie. Of course, we can only speculate now about how early film audiences experienced these films. But when viewing them today, I certainly find myself sent off into daydreams inspired by the slow panning shots of landscapes and people posing stiffly for the camera. This dreamlike reception is certainly not the learning experience that educators envisioned; falling into a state of reverie is quite unlike learning an empirical lesson about the world's geography. Instead, the spectator in a state of reverie might experience a series of free-floating, subjective associations. Gaston Bachelard defines reverie as "a flight from out of the real."[58] Might we not say, then, that travelogues (and other early nonfiction) simulate the real world in order to allow the spectator to leave the real world? In fact, this dreamlike spectatorship would seem to produce something quite the opposite of knowledge: mystification. Exotic places and peoples tend to be presented in these films as though they are disappearing, as though these picturesque scenes of traditional crafts, natural landscapes, and "primitive" peoples might never exist again in such an idealized way. Travelogue reverie thus appears nostalgic, a dream of the premodern world viewed within a framework of loss.

Some intellectuals began to write about the cinema's dreamlike realism in the 1910s. French writer Jules Romains said this of the film audience: "They are no longer conscious of their bodies. Instead there are only passing images, a gliding and rustling of dreams. They no longer realize they are in a large square chamber, immobile, in parallel rows as in a ploughed field. A haze of visions which resemble life hovers before them. Things have a different appearance than they do outside."[59] Avant-garde artists and writers appreciated travel and scientific films for their magical, mysterious quality, not for the educational knowledge they were supposedly imparting. French film critic Louis Delluc wrote in 1917, "For a long time, I have realized that the cinema was destined to provide us with impressions of evanescent eternal beauty, since it alone offers us the spectacle of nature and sometimes even the spectacle of real human activity." Delluc singles out travelogues as films that excel in displaying this kind of beauty, although he complains that "they are far too short."[60]

We might say then—following Romains, Delluc, and a long tradition of avant-garde film criticism and spectatorship—that travelogues open up a dreamlike cinematic geography.[61] From this perspective travel films are more about desire than pedagogy, with all the perilous implications of fantasy and fetishism that implies. Travelogues cater to desires that lie to some extent behind all travel: a desire to experience someplace (anyplace) different, a desire to leave one's current conditions, a desire for new experiences. Herein lies the genre's appeal: travelogues presented images of the real world that allowed the spectator to experience a flight from out of the real, a flight toward exotic fantasy. Travelogues, therefore, encouraged a particular kind of spectator—perhaps not a spectator who watched in order to better educate herself or himself but a spectator who enjoyed the films because they provided a space apart for personal reverie. Rather than educating the audience in the traditional sense, early travel films functioned as a school of dreams, presenting strange and obscure pictures that teach lessons about desire.

NOTES

1. Professor W. T. Hewetson, "The Motion Picture Problem" (address delivered before the Women's Club in Freeport, Ill., quoted in *Moving Picture World,* 20 January 1912, 215).

2. James B. Crippen, "An Educational Innovation," *Nickelodeon,* 25 February 1911, 216.

3. See Charles Musser, "The Travel Genre in 1903–04: Moving Towards Fictional Narrative," in *Early Cinema: Space, Frame, Narrative,* ed. Thomas Elsaesser (London:

British Film Institute, 1990), 123–32. See also Musser's *The Emergence of Cinema: The American Screen to 1907* (Berkeley: University of California Press, 1990).

4. Until recently there was very little published work on early nonfiction, with a few important exceptions, such as Kevin Brownlow's *The War, the West, and the Wilderness* (New York: Knopf, 1979). In the last decade, however, there have been some new archival preservations and conferences that have facilitated the study of early nonfiction film. The Nederlands Filmmuseum in Amsterdam, which has preserved hundreds of early nonfiction films, held a workshop on silent nonfiction in 1994. Early nonfiction films were then screened at Bologna's "Cinema Ritrovato" and at the Pordenone Silent Film Festival in 1995. Silent nonfiction films have since been screened at other festivals and conferences, including the "Orphan Film" symposium at the University of South Carolina. Some publications dealing with silent nonfiction are Thierry Lefebvre, "The Scientia Production (1911–1914): Scientific Popularization through Pictures," *Griffithiana* 47 (May 1993): 137–52; Tom Gunning, "'The Whole World within Reach': Travel Images without Borders," in *Cinéma sans frontières, 1896–1918,* ed. Roland Cosandey and François Albera (Lausanne: Payot, 1995); *1895,* no. 18 (spring 1995), a special issue on French nonfiction, 1890–1930; Fatimah Tobing Rony, *The Third Eye: Race, Cinema, and Ethnographic Spectacle* (Durham, N.C.: Duke University Press, 1996); Daan Hertogs and Nico de Klerk, eds., *Uncharted Territory: Essays on Early Nonfiction Film* (Amsterdam: Stichting Nederlands Filmmuseum, 1997); Paula Amad, "Cinema's 'Sanctuary': From Pre-Documentary to Documentary Film in Albert Kahn's *Archive de la Planète,*" *Film History* 13 (2001): 138–59; Stephen Bottomore, "Rediscovering Early Non-Fiction Film," *Film History* 13 (2001): 160–73; Alison Griffiths, *Wondrous Difference: Cinema, Anthropology, and Turn-of-the-Century Visual Culture* (New York: Columbia University Press, 2002); and *Visual Anthropology* 15, no. 1 (January–March 2002), a special issue on "Travelogues and Travel Films." For an extended discussion of the topics raised in this essay see Jennifer Lynn Peterson, *Making the World Exotic: Travelogues and Silent Nonfiction Film* (Durham, N.C.: Duke University Press, forthcoming).

5. Bottomore, "Rediscovering Early Non-Fiction Film," 167.

6. On the variety format see Brooks McNamara, "The Scenography of Popular Entertainment," *Drama Review* 18, no. 1 (March 1974): 59–79; and Tom Gunning, *D. W. Griffith and the Origins of American Narrative Film* (Urbana: University of Illinois Press, 1994), 86. Nonfiction films were also exhibited in a different format by lecturers in nontheatrical venues, such as churches and lecture halls, during this period, but for the purposes of this essay I am concerned with only commercial exhibition in dedicated movie houses. For a history of one traveling lecturer who made his living showing nonfiction films outside the commercial movie houses see Charles Musser, in collaboration with Carol Nelson, *High-Class Moving Pictures: Lyman H. Howe and the Forgotten Era of Traveling Exhibition, 1880–1920* (Princeton, N.J.: Princeton University Press, 1991).

7. *Oxford English Dictionary,* s.v. "travelogue."

8. X. Theodore Barber writes, "in 1904, Holmes coined the term 'travelogue' to refer to his show, thereby giving it a greater air of novelty" (Barber, "The Roots of Travel Cinema: John L. Stoddard, E. Burton Holmes and the Nineteenth-Century Illustrated Travel Lecture," *Film History* 5, no. 1 [March 1993]: 82). Charles Musser,

however, has located a usage of the term as early as 1899 by someone other than Holmes. See Musser, *Emergence of Cinema,* 223.

9. On early film genre see Tom Gunning, "'Those Drawn with a Very Fine Camel's Hair Brush': The Origins of Film Genres," *Iris* 19 (1995): 49–61.

10. This film was released in the United States on 25 May 1912; it also apparently went by the title *Views of Los Angeles, Cal.* The film was distributed in France by Eclipse and released there on 2 August 1912 as *Une Promenade dans Los Angeles.* A color-tinted print of this film is held at the Nederlands Filmmuseum under the title of *Los Angelos.*

11. *Moving Picture World,* 18 May 1912, 664.

12. "Doings in Los Angeles," *Moving Picture World,* 29 June 1912, 1219.

13. Ostrich and alligator farming were sizable industries in Los Angeles at the time, and these animal farms were popular tourist attractions.

14. Tom Gunning, "Before Documentary: Early Nonfiction Films and the 'View' Aesthetic," in *Uncharted Territory: Essays on Early Nonfiction Film,* ed. Daan Hertogs and Nico de Klerk (Amsterdam: Stichting Nederlands Filmmuseum, 1997), 9–24.

15. Review of *Scenes in the Celestial Empire, Variety,* 24 September 1910; review of *Sabot Making, Variety,* 9 May 1908; review of *Sevres Porcelain, Variety,* 28 August 1909. All reviews cited here are from *Variety Film Reviews, 1907–1920,* vol. 1 (New York: Garland, 1983), unpaginated.

16. *Moving Picture World,* 24 January 1914, 412.

17. And not all "filler" was considered equal, as this review of a 1910 Gaumont comedy indicates: "'The Cheese Box' is a Gaumont comedy founded upon the substitution of an odoriferous cheese for a box of bon-bons. It has no particular qualities to recommend it, and although it draws a laugh, will be forgotten as soon as it is off the screen. It is short, however, and serves as a very good filler" (*Nickelodeon,* 15 May 1910, 259).

18. Review of *Jersey of the British Isles* (Eclipse), "Recent Films Reviewed," *Nickelodeon,* 4 February 1911, 138.

19. For a filmography listing over twelve hundred travelogues and related nonfiction films released in the United States between 1910 and 1914 see Jennifer Lynn Peterson, "World Pictures: Travelogue Films and the Lure of the Exotic, 1890–1920" (Ph.D. diss., University of Chicago, 1999). Some of the other companies that released one or more scenic films in the United States during the years 1910 to 1914 were Centaur, Eclair, Essanay, Itala, Kalem, Nestor, Powers, Rex, Solax, and Vitagraph. In effect, almost all film companies produced some nonfiction at this time. Biograph appears to be an important exception: I have found no evidence that Biograph made any nonfiction films after the mid-1900s, a drastic turnaround from the early days when nonfiction dominated Biograph's production.

20. A description of this film was published in *Nickelodeon* on 1 August 1910, 80: "This short educational subject was made on the beach at Catalina Island, off the coast of Southern California, and shows a party of tourists feeding the pet seals, famed to all tourists. These animals are very intelligent and absolutely fearless. Our picture shows Jupiter and Neptune, two of the largest of the herd, posing before the camera.—170 feet—Released August 10."

21. See the description of *Ancient Temples of Egypt* by Herbert Reynolds in *Before Hollywood: Turn-of-the-Century American Film,* ed. Jay Leyda and Charles Musser (New

York: Hudson Hills Press, 1987), 137. The George Eastman House holds a print of this film.

22. Musser, *Emergence of Cinema*, 488.

23. On color in early film see *Disorderly Order: Colours in Silent Film*, ed. Daan Hertogs and Nico de Klerk (Amsterdam: Stichting Nederlands Filmmuseum, 1996).

24. Review of Pathé's *Sports in Java, Variety*, 25 September 1909.

25. On the history of Pathé and early French cinema in general see Richard Abel, *The Ciné Goes to Town: French Cinema, 1896–1914* (Berkeley: University of California Press, 1994). On Pathé's dominance of the U.S. market and the cultural struggles that ensued see Abel, *The Red Rooster Scare: Making Cinema American, 1900–1910* (Berkeley: University of California Press, 1999).

26. For an overview of Kleine's career see Rita Horwitz, "George Kleine and the Early Motion Picture Industry," in *The George Kleine Collection of Early Motion Pictures in the Library of Congress: A Catalog*, prepared by Rita Horwitz and Harriet Harrison (Washington, D.C.: Library of Congress Motion Picture, Broadcasting, and Recorded Sound Division, 1980), xiii-xxv.

27. See "Kleine to Release Cines," *Motography*, January 1912, 34.

28. *Catalogue of Educational Motion Pictures Issued by George Kleine* (Chicago: George Kleine, 1910). Educational catalogs were also released by Charles Urban and the General Film Company. See *Urbanora: The World's Educator* (London: Charles Urban Trading Co., 1908); and *Catalogue of Educational Motion Pictures* (New York: General Film, 1912).

29. "Kleine's Big Educational Catalogue," *Nickelodeon*, 1 April 1910, 180.

30. "Educational Films Gaining Ground," *Nickelodeon*, 15 April 1910, 196.

31. *Motography*, 20 September 1913, 191.

32. George Kleine to Thomas Edison, 20 April 1921, George Kleine Papers, Library of Congress.

33. See *Descriptive Catalogue of Pathéscope Safety Standard Films*, 2d ed. (New York: Pathéscope Co. of America, 1920).

34. Paramount also released a series of travel films by Burton Holmes in the 1920s. Prints of some of these are held at the Library of Congress.

35. William Uricchio and Roberta E. Pearson, *Reframing Culture: The Case of the Vitagraph Quality Films* (Princeton, N.J.: Princeton University Press, 1993), 5.

36. Frederick Starr, "The World before Your Eyes," *Chicago Sunday Tribune,* 7 February 1909, unnumbered pages (part 7—Special Features). Starr's endorsement was reprinted as "Professor Starr's Valuable Contribution" in *Nickelodeon*, March 1909, 64. It was also reprinted, in slightly different form, in Kleine's *Catalogue of Educational Motion Pictures*.

37. The advertisement apparently cost more than twelve hundred dollars. See "Silly Press Items," *Nickelodeon*, 15 June 1910, 306. Professor Starr himself made some travelogue films that were released by the Selig Company.

38. Scott Curtis, "The Taste of a Nation: Training the Senses and Sensibility of Cinema Audiences in Imperial Germany," *Film History* 6, no. 4 (1994): 449; this article is specifically about German film exhibition, but the situation in the United States was similar. See also J. A. Lindstrom, "'Getting a Hold Deeper in the Life of the City': Chicago Nickelodeons, 1905–1914" (Ph.D. diss., Northwestern University, 1999); and J. A. Lindstrom, "'Almost Worse Than the Restrictive Measures':

Chicago Reformers and the Nickelodeons," *Cinema Journal* 39, no. 1 (1999): 90–112.

39. *Nickelodeon*, 1 November 1910, 245–46; and *Nickelodeon*, December 1909, 166.

40. "Bonehead Exhibitors," *Nickelodeon*, 15 March 1910, 140–41.

41. "Travel Pictures Again," *Motography*, 11 September 1911, 105 (emphasis in original).

42. Starr, "The World Before Your Eyes," in "Professor Starr's Valuable Contribution," 64.

43. "Bonehead Exhibitors," 139.

44. J. A. Bell to George Kleine, 26 September 1910, George Kleine Papers, Library of Congress.

45. J. R. Carter to George Kleine, 30 August 1910, George Kleine Papers, Library of Congress. *The Vale of Aude*, a scenic filmed in the south of France, was released in the United States in March 1910. One reviewer called the film "a perfect example of an ideal release" (*Variety*, 5 March 1910).

46. *The Fly Pest* was a 437-foot Urban film released by Kleine on 6 April 1910. See "Kleine Shows Scientific Pictures," *Nickelodeon*, 1 February 1910, 81; and "Roosevelt and the Fly," *Nickelodeon*, 1 May 1910, 223.

47. Musser, *High-Class Moving Pictures*, esp. 8–11. See also Rony, *Third Eye*, chap. 2.

48. Homi K. Bhabha, *The Location of Culture* (London: Routledge, 1994), 67.

49. For an extended discussion of racial and cultural difference in travelogue films see Peterson, *Making the World Exotic*.

50. Hugo Münsterberg, *The Film: A Psychological Study* (1916; repr., New York: Dover, 1970), 80–81.

51. Slightly different prints of this film are held at the Nederlands Filmmuseum and the Library of Congress. The former calls it *Loetschberg;* the Library of Congress's title is *From Spiez to Loetschberg, Switzerland;* and the original French title is *Chemin de fer du Loetschberg.* I have not been able to discover the film's U.S. release date.

52. See Raymond Fielding, "Hale's Tours: Ultrarealism in the pre-1910 Motion Picture," in *Film before Griffith*, ed. John Fell (Berkeley: University of California Press, 1983), 116–30.

53. Review of *One Thousand Miles through the Rockies* (Edison, 1912), *Moving Picture World*, 6 April 1912, 31.

54. Walter Benjamin, "A Short History of Photography," trans. Stanley Mitchell, *Screen* 13, no. 1 (spring 1972): 5–26. On Benjamin's "optical unconscious" see Miriam Hansen, "Benjamin, Cinema, and Experience: 'The Blue Flower' in the Land of Technology," *New German Critique* 40 (winter 1987). See also Susan Buck-Morss, "Dream World of Mass Culture," in her *The Dialectics of Seeing: Walter Benjamin and the Arcades Project* (Cambridge, Mass.: MIT Press, 1989), 253–86.

55. E. B. Lockwood, "Travelogues and Topicals," *Motography*, June 1912, 257.

56. "Bonehead Exhibitors," 139–40.

57. "Rainey African Pictures Making Good," *Moving Picture World*, 11 May 1912, 533. For a description of these films see "The Paul Rainey African Pictures," *Moving Picture World*, 20 April 1912, 214–15.

58. Gaston Bachelard, *The Poetics of Reverie: Childhood, Language, and the Cosmos*, trans. Daniel Russell (Boston: Beacon Press, 1969), 5.

59. Jules Romains, "The Crowd at the Cinematograph" (1911), trans. in Richard

Abel, *French Film Theory and Criticism* (Princeton, N.J.: Princeton University Press, 1988), 1:53.

60. Louis Delluc, "Beauty in the Cinema" (1917), trans. in Abel, *French Film Theory and Criticism,* 1:137.

61. This argument follows what Robert Ray has called the lost tradition of impressionist-surrealist film criticism. See Robert Ray, "Impressionism, Surrealism, and Film Theory: Path Dependence, or How a Tradition in Film Theory Gets Lost," in *The Oxford Guide to Film Studies,* ed. John Hill and Pamela Church Gibson (Oxford: Oxford University Press, 1998), 67–76.

PART THREE

The Industry in Transition

Changing Institutions and Audiences

Where Development Has Just Begun

Nickelodeon Location, Moving Picture Audiences, and Neighborhood Development in Chicago

J. A. Lindstrom

[A]s one continues into the city and observes the crowds of people hurrying to and fro past stores, theaters, banks, and other establishments, one naturally is struck by the contrast with the countryside. What supports this phenomenon? What do the people of the city do for a living? . . . Barbers, dry cleaners, shoe repairers, grocerymen, bakers, and movie operators serve others who are engaged in the principal activity of the city, which may be mining, manufacturing, trade, or some other activity.

CHAUNCY HARRIS AND EDWARD ULLMAN, "The Nature of Cities"

Two political scientists working forty years after the beginning of the nickelodeon era offer early film historians a suggestive starting point for thinking about early moving picture audiences. Chauncy Harris and Edward Ullman list movie theaters among the sine qua non of neighborhood services. More important, they situate the moving picture show in the everyday urban hustle and bustle of a street where all sorts of commerce and industry take place.[1] In addition to services and employers, any understanding of the urban vitality that Harris and Ullman describe must include information about housing stock, transportation infrastructure, and community population, as well as changes in the area over time. This picture implicitly contains a street-level view of the moving picture audience. Many elements of this picture have gone largely unaddressed in accounts of the early film exhibition. Work by film historians on the location of nickelodeons in urban centers has focused tightly on the ethnicity and socioeconomic class of the nickelodeon audience, but this research might also form the basis of a more dynamic understanding of the relationship between moving picture audiences and larger processes of neighborhood and urban development.

In this essay I argue for the kinds of research that will lead toward an urban geography of moving picture theaters. Specifically, this analysis offers both a sense of the everyday life in areas of Chicago where film exhibition flourished and an account of the development that these movie theaters fostered in the city. Looking at several neighborhoods in which the five- and ten-cent theaters flourished reveals that in Chicago the pattern of nickelodeon location was based not only on where the immigrant working-class lived but additionally—and, at the beginning of this time period, *primarily*—on where they worked.[2] Additionally, comparing these neighborhoods with early models of urban growth offers a new vocabulary for describing areas where nickelodeons thrived and highlights the characteristics that contributed to that success, especially diversified land use: the conjunction of tenement housing, transportation access, a variety of retail establishments, and many diverse commercial and manufacturing interests. A few years into the nickelodeon era five- and ten-cent theaters began to appear in new working-class neighborhoods, where they attracted an audience not only for the movies but also for the stores along new retail and commercial strips. Moving picture theaters thus contributed to important changes in the economic structure and prosperity of certain areas over time. Finally, although this analysis finds that the moving picture shows did not flourish in established middle-class and wealthy neighborhoods during these years, it shows that the audience was neither exclusively nor monolithically working class.

This very concrete sense of neighborhood and audience in the nickelodeon era is critical to our understanding of the rise of moving pictures in Chicago. Although the film industry did not escape the attention of the Chicago City Council in the years before World War I, exhibitors in most neighborhoods could find a location relatively free of regulatory interference.[3] This suggests that their choices reflected a combination of their estimation of the potential audience and the financial resources they had available for starting a moving picture theater. Additionally, the patterns of film exhibition in Chicago point to two divergent assessments of the duration of the nickelodeon era. On the one hand, the continuing popularity of storefront shows into the mid-1910s suggests that the nickelodeon era in Chicago was longer than some scholars argue. On the other hand, the opening of five- and ten-cent shows in new neighborhoods indicates that part of the nickelodeon audience was in transition well before the rise of features. Finally, and perhaps most important, the connection between moving picture theaters and commercial development in some areas indicates that film exhibition was not merely subject to the vicissitudes of urban development but was in some cases a causal element. Moving picture theaters in Chicago both fit into old neighborhoods and changed new ones.

THE "HOUSE OF DREAMS" AND THE NEIGHBORHOOD SNAPSHOT

In her insightful article about the continuity in advertising and exploitation practices between early moving pictures and precinema entertainments such

as the circus, Jane Gaines writes, "In the end, what counted was that moviegoing was integrated into the rhythms of local life and that commercially produced entertainment became embedded in the existing community life."[4]
Film scholars have described the nature of "the rhythms of local life," as well
as the processes by which film exhibition gained acceptance in a variety of
early-twentieth-century communities, from the rural to the urban, from the
great unwashed to the bourgeoisie, and, of course, among men, women, and
children. Early accounts of how movies fit into neighborhoods and communities often considered relatively powerless groups in an urban context,
showing that moving picture theaters allowed women, the working class, and
immigrants to negotiate new ways of being in the city and that this public
heterosociality, although fraught with difficulties, constituted a major component of modern culture. Kathy Peiss shows that the emergence of nickelodeons substantially increased the participation of working-class women
in commercial leisure, as families who otherwise frowned on amusements
outside the home permitted their daughters to attend five-cent shows.[5] Judith Mayne finds that in addition to escapism and acculturation the movies
offered immigrants and the working class the possibility of consumption or,
more accurately, "the image of an homogenous population pursuing the
same goals—'living well' and accumulating goods."[6] Miriam Hansen argues
that the immigrant movie audience allowed for "modes of reception reminiscent of older forms of working-class, immigrant culture," at the same time
as the films presented images of affluence onscreen and laid the groundwork for the audience's assimilation into commodity culture.[7] Thus, these
scholars note that the movies simultaneously satisfied existing needs for recreation and transformed those needs into more wide-ranging desires oriented
toward a burgeoning consumer culture.

Other scholars have focused on the arrival and reception of motion pictures in smaller cities and towns and have shown that in these communities
the acceptance of the moving picture shows depended less on notions of immigration and class than on notions of local standards. Kathryn Fuller's survey of small-town audiences shows that although they were sometimes more
conservative in taste than their urban counterparts, small-town audiences
were frequently knowledgeable and articulate about movie subjects.[8] Fuller
argues that the rise of fan culture helped make up for any deficiency in the
conditions of small-town exhibition and kept residents attending the shows.[9]
Gregory Waller demonstrates that acceptance of moving picture theaters in
Lexington, Kentucky—even with few immigrants or members of the industrial working class—was hardly less tentative and controversial than in larger
cities. Despite the limited success of Lexington's downtown, storefront nickelodeons emerged in the context of a variety of new commercial amusements
that eventually led to the construction of larger venues.[10] In their advertising most Lexington exhibitors emphasized the elegance of their theaters and

the quality of programming, seeking "the better class of patron"; this address largely excluded Lexington's substantial African American population, which was usually relegated to balcony seats accessible through separate doors.[11] Waller also shows that the citizens of Lexington sought local control over the more national and modern culture represented by commercial amusements; Lexingtonians used debates over amusement licensing, theater safety regulation, local censorship, and Sunday-closing laws, as well as policies of racial restriction, to consider the role they wanted the movies to play in their city.

The rhythms of local life included the consumer life of the city, and several scholars have focused on the address of the female audience as consumers. In her study of the social origins of the female cinema spectator, Lauren Rabinovitz writes, "Cinema benefited from the [female] shopper's and tourist's training to see and be seen through a complex set of subject-object relations."[12] Specifically she argues that although women's attendance at the moving picture shows allowed women a public role as consumers, it also fostered women's role as sexual spectacle to be looked at and ultimately commodified.[13] Shelley Stamp shows that although movies encouraged women to engage in commodity culture, this consumerism did not lead unequivocally to modes of classical spectatorship. Stamp writes that "serials self-consciously foregrounded the commodification of the motion picture experience, packaged to produce maximum calculable effect, and the potentially endless commercial reproduction of products in the new entertainment economy."[14] By encouraging viewers to consume, however—to read the newspaper installments and fan magazines, to buy star-image-bedecked decorative items and sheet music, to enter contests in which viewers wrote future plot turns, to form fan clubs—these tie-ins also fostered a heterogeneous and nonclassical mode of narrative engagement and cinema participation.

Other scholars have investigated the integration of movies and community life by looking more closely at the location of moving picture theaters. Douglas Gomery's work on film exhibition, on the one hand, describes a relationship between theater location and city shape and, on the other hand, understands film exhibition in historical context as a set of business practices.[15] Furthermore, in recent years the composition of the nickelodeon audience has been hotly contested, creating doubt about the characterization of "existing community life" in which the movies took hold. The main point of contention in the debate between Robert Allen and Ben Singer has been the socioeconomic class of the motion picture audience, about which there were two lines of inquiry: whether the Manhattan neighborhoods in which nickelodeons were most popular were largely middle class or working class or lower middle class—a possibility that both Allen and Singer eventually seem to cautiously consider[16]—and the role of small-time vaudeville in middle-class acceptance of the movies and the decline of the storefront nickelodeon. Adding to this debate Sumiko Higashi, William Uricchio, and Roberta Pearson point to competing definitions of *middle class* and the kinds of evidence that indicate socioeconomic class generally.[17] Furthermore, Allen, Singer, Uricchio, and Pearson all agree that any correlation between the nickelodeon audience and the ethnicity and social class of the surrounding neighborhood is tentative and incomplete.[18] Judith Thissen's work on *"muving piktshur pletzer"* in the Lower East Side uses a more diverse evidence to show that the failure rate of moving picture shows decreased over the course of the nickelodeon era.[19]

The nexus of social film audiences, film spectatorship, and consumer culture in the silent era is surely among the most engaging and contested terrains of film historical inquiry, and many scholars have contributed to our complex understanding of the aesthetic, social, and ideological contexts of early film exhibition. Even so, without a more detailed picture of the geographic and local economic contexts of early film exhibition, scholars are chasing a movable feast. Mapping an account of urban growth onto patterns of film exhibition highlights the factors that constitute class and quality of life in an area, on the one hand, and the variables involved citywide in the success of the moving pictures, on the other. This strategy presents a more viable possibility for tackling the elusive relationship between the socioeconomic class of a neighborhood and the constitution of the audience. Furthermore, movie patrons participated in the social and economic life of their communities in a variety of ways, as an analysis of neighborhood economic structures shows. Most important, film exhibition was integral to the economic development of some areas of the city. This kind of analysis begins with the effort to uncover where moving picture exhibitors set up shop.

MOVING PICTURE THEATERS
IN CHICAGO'S "INNER BELT" NEIGHBORHOODS

Nickelodeons in Chicago did not, on the whole, tend to cluster with the density of neighborhoods in Manhattan. In the most nickelodeon-rich neighborhoods half a dozen "nickel dumps" were spread out over as many blocks. Those locations that had a handful of moving picture theaters in close proximity were likely to be busy intersections, usually a transfer point for public transportation. Furthermore, many neighborhoods in Chicago were not stable or easily defined in the period before World War I, in terms of population, employment opportunities, or infrastructure; and five-cent shows were found exactly in those neighborhoods in the throes of transition. Initially moving picture theaters were most prevalent in neighborhoods with a variety of service and manufacturing jobs—unskilled, semiskilled, and skilled positions—as well as densely populated residential buildings inhabited by neighborhood workers and their families. Two of the neighborhoods with the most nickel shows were long-standing mixed-land-use immigrant neighborhoods.

In his classic 1978 comparative study of immigrant and race ghettos in Chicago Thomas Philpott notes that at the turn of the twentieth century Chicago's working class lived in a large arc that lay between the fire limits of the inner city and the subdivisions on the west, northwest, and southwest sides.[20] This "inner belt" of workers, poverty, and deteriorating housing was home to immigrants from the world over, as well as industries of all varieties. Most of these neighborhoods were high-population density, poor and working-class immigrant communities with mixed ethnicities, but they were usually characterized by a dominant ethnicity or language. Within the inner belt were several neighborhoods that had a relatively high concentration of five- and ten-cent theaters; included in the inner belt were the Little Italy/Jewish Ghetto neighborhood and the German north side.

LITTLE ITALY/JEWISH GHETTO

The Little Italy/Jewish Ghetto neighborhood occupied just over half of a square mile immediately west of Chicago's central business district. In Little Italy and the Jewish Ghetto moving picture patrons would find many choices in venues. From 1906 to 1915 forty-one nickelodeons opened at twenty different locations in the neighborhood.[21] Two five-cent theaters opened in the neighborhood in 1906, one of which, under owner George Friedman, remained in business until 1913. Five shows opened in 1907 and seven more in 1908. Of these fourteen venues only six lasted two or more years. New five- and ten-cent shows continued to open in the area throughout the period. In the period covered by this study there was an average of seven and a half nickel theaters in operation; this means that there was a theater for every 3,265 residents in Little Italy/Jewish Ghetto—over one-and-a-half times that of Chicago's 1909 average and more than three times the per capita rate of New York City.[22] Halsted Street, especially at Twelfth Street, was the focus of film exhibition in the neighborhood, but there were also theaters on other thoroughfares. Small retail establishments occupied most of the storefronts along Halsted, but there were also print shops, candy and ice-cream factories, a photography studio, paint and oil shops, and a department store.[23] On either side of Halsted the cross streets had a wide range of businesses and institutions, including a paper company, a trunk factory, stables and liveries, a stove repair company, foundries and metalworking shops, a bakery, a shirtmaking company, a furniture manufacturer, the Hull House complex, a school, and several synagogues and churches—and most blocks had housing between other buildings and flats on the top floors.

TABLE 9.1 Percentages of Residents with Occupations
of Various Skill Levels

	Italians	Jews	Czechs	Poles	Other
Unskilled	85	27	39	58	29
Skilled	10	47	52	37	51
Commercial	4	20	7	2	10
Special	1	7	2	2	10
Total	100	101	100	99	100

SOURCE: Data are based on Hunter, "Occupation by Nationalities," 196–97. "Special" included rabbis, teachers, retired owners, and a midwife. Percentages may not add up to one hundred because of rounding. The original data were based on 475 workers; presumably data were meant to be representative, but the report does not indicate how the sample was constituted.

The Little Italy/Jewish Ghetto was a busy but poor immigrant neighborhood. Jews and Italians, as well as Polish, Czech, and Greek immigrants, lived in the forty square blocks of the community. According to a 1901 City Homes Association study of three of the oldest immigrant settlements in Chicago, almost half of the households were headed by unskilled laborers.[24] Neighborhood workers were employed in textile factories, metal-smithies, bakeries, stables, and bookbinderies and as carpenters, machinists, masons, peddlers, laborers, tailors, saloonkeepers, and teachers (see table 9.1). Workers received, on average, ten dollars for a sixty-plus-hour workweek. They paid five to twelve dollars in monthly rent, and "the housing they received in return was crowded, dark, and filthy."[25] The neighborhood had many industrial concerns, and even the thriving ones had a negative effect on the housing stock:

> In a sense the whole territory . . . is awaiting the business invasion. Needed repairs on old houses, the proper building of new houses, improvements of every kind are postponed because of the current belief that this whole territory is in the near future to be taken over for commercial and industrial uses. In the meantime, while landlords and dealers wait, poor people continue to live in insanitary [sic] houses, tuberculosis breeds there, children grow up in dark, illventilated rooms, without proper space for play.[26]

Thus, the success (actual or anticipated) of commerce and industry contributed to the profit of some and the overcrowding of others. Furthermore, backyards were frequently supplanted by rear tenements and occasionally stables. Even sidewalks were a treacherous place to spend leisure time; few were paved, and garbage boxes sat on many of them.[27] Thus there were few open spaces and few opportunities to relieve the overcrowding of the neighborhood.

The majority of people who lived in the neighborhood worked in its many factories and workshops, but some workers and managers lived in communities nearby. The 1901 City Homes Association study found that some workers in each community walked or took streetcars to work from neighborhoods outside the immigrant ghettoes. Although some workers lived just west of Halsted Street, the most prosperous moved further west—many to North Lawndale, where Balaban and Katz would open their first picture palace in 1917. The Little Italy/Jewish Ghetto represents the traditional sense of the early moving picture audience, and this neighborhood had among the largest clusters of nickelodeons in the city. Although the fact that nickelodeons thrived in a Jewish/Italian neighborhood will not surprise film historians, the success of the movies in a predominantly German neighborhood may be more surprising.

GERMAN NORTH SIDE

At the northeast end of the "inner belt" was the German north side, where one might interact with neighbors, shopkeepers, and employers entirely in German. The popularity of nickel shows in the area indicates that Germans in Chicago participated in film culture.[28] Moving picture exhibition came to the neighborhood with two moving picture theaters, both owned by Hubert Daniels, in 1906; one stayed in business until 1908, the other until 1910 (although it was closed briefly in 1908 for violation of the city's fire code); Daniels would eventually own three moving picture theaters.[29] The years from 1906 to 1915 saw the launch of forty-one moving picture shows at twenty-two different locations in the area. Five nickel theaters opened in 1907 and two more in 1908. Of the eight moving picture venues that opened between 1906 and 1908, seven lasted at least two years, and four lasted at least three years. Here, too, new picture shows opened throughout the period. There was an average of seven and a half theaters in operation during the ten years of this study; this represents a per capita rate similar to the Jewish and Italian quarter and higher than most neighborhoods in Chicago. In 1910 the Sanborn Fire Insurance Company mapped the area from Chicago Avenue to Fullerton, which included the German north side. Their maps show seven moving picture theaters operating in 1910, of which only three were listed in the *Lakeside Annual Directory*. This suggests that the actual number of nickelodeons operating in the neighborhood was much higher than extant records reveal.[30] The neighborhood's main drag of moving picture shows was North Avenue. In the blocks on either side of the five-cent theater at 316 West North Avenue (seating capacity 136) in 1910 one would primarily find retail stores, but also a livery, a bakery, a sausage factory, an ice-cream factory, chocolate and candy factories, a soap factory, a feed and hay lot, a stable, and saloons (see figure 9.1). Many of these buildings had apartments

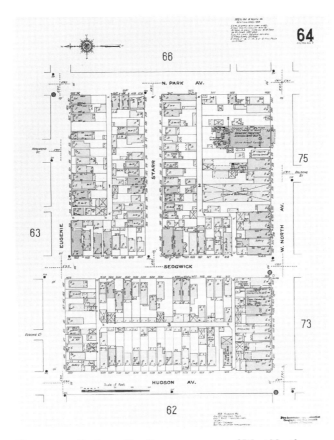

Figure 9.1. Sanborn Fire Insurance map of West North
Avenue. Copyright 1910, Sanborn Map Company, Sanborn
Library, LLC. All further reproductions prohibited without
written permission from The Sanborn Library, LLC. All
rights reserved.

on the second floor. Interestingly, the Comedy Theatre (seating capacity
twelve hundred) was next door to the moving picture show, and the Sittner's
Vaudeville Theatre (seating capacity circa six hundred, which probably
switched to a moving picture program in 1911) was across the street.[31]

These venues flourished in a community that was essentially a city unto
itself. "The variety and number of retail businesses and service facilities indicate that the area between Chicago and Fullerton avenues was practically
self-sufficient. Hospitals, schools, churches, and orphanages were spread
throughout the area," as were traditional places of amusement like clubs and
lodges.[32] Most of the north side Germans had semiskilled or skilled occu-

pations, and their jobs were mostly in the neighborhood. Many heads of households worked in trades where small shops of skilled laborers hired fellow Germans. By 1900 the number of heads of households who held white-collar positions was increasing. Of males other than heads of households, 46 percent were in commerce and trade positions; of females other than heads of households, 29 percent were in clerical and white-collar positions.[33] Commuting to the city center was still time-consuming, in spite of improvements in public transport on the north side; even young women in these families and the boarders—who were assumed to be more mobile in their choice of employment—tended to be "employed in neighborhood-based trades and low white-collar positions."[34]

The audience for the moving pictures among north side Germans developed by way of more ethnically specific forms of entertainment; saloons, beer gardens, and German popular theaters acted as springboards to movie culture.[35] In the late 1800s German saloons in Chicago began to offer cards and billiards, singers, even stand-up comedians and vaudeville acts. Beer gardens, too, started integrating vaudeville and comedians, signaling the decline of the specific Germanness of the beer garden.[36] German popular theaters offered comedies, burlesques, and musical sketches, as well as plays dealing with the German American (and usually the working-class) experience; tickets ranged from fifteen to fifty cents, and some theaters offered family tickets for a dollar.[37] German popular theaters as well as the voluntary associations where German men spent leisure time both suffered from the declining use of German among the second generation and from the availability of other commercialized amusements. "It is no accident that [German popular theaters] had completely disappeared by the turn of the century. The 'cultural industry' in America, with its vaudeville theaters—structurally similar to performances found in some popular theaters—and up-and-coming forms of entertainment like the nickelodeons and movies, had been taking over the function of the popular theaters."[38] The meeting places of the voluntary associations were also less popular with Chicago's second-generation German Americans: "traditional places of amusement, like clubs and lodge houses, had by 1900 been supplanted by newer varieties—five-cent theaters, coffee houses, palm gardens, and a natatorium."[39] Although the German labor press in Chicago initially decried this decline, the German-language labor daily *Chicagoer Arbeiter-Zeitung* eventually defended the five-cent theater against attacks by some reformers and took advertisements from some of them.[40] All evidence indicates that nickelodeons played a substantial role in the leisure of Germans in Chicago, especially for second-generation immigrants as a vehicle and evidence of Americanization.

In the early years of the nickelodeon era the Little Italy/Jewish Ghetto, the German north side, and the other old immigrant neighborhoods of Chicago had among the largest clusters of nickelodeons in the city. These communities represented a variety of different ethnic groups, but they had the qualities often associated with the early moving picture audience. The predominance of first- and second-generation immigrants is clear. Although the housing conditions in the German north side were less squalid and cramped than the Jewish/Italian quarter, both neighborhoods were mixed-use industrial, commercial, and residential areas whose residents were largely working-class or in the trades.

Half a decade into the rise of moving pictures, nickelodeons began to appear in new neighborhoods that were less defined by a dominant ethnicity or by industry and manufacturing. In the early 1900s the skilled and semi-skilled working class was increasingly moving into areas near their workplaces but where the housing was better than in immigrant ghettos. As noted above, some workers in the Jewish and Italian quarter moved west and northwest of the old neighborhood, and the German north side expanded north toward Fullerton Avenue. Residents of newer working-class districts along Milwaukee Avenue, Madison Street, West Twenty-sixth Street, and East Seventy-first Street started attending the moving picture shows closer to their new residences. Some families, however, moved to entirely new communities that were not adjacent to where the head-of-household worked. The new five- and ten-cent shows in these areas accelerated the development of new markets for exhibitors and new business districts. One of the most successful areas of film exhibition in Chicago after 1908 was a new working-class neighborhood, Englewood.

WORKER RESIDENTIAL NEIGHBORHOODS: ENGLEWOOD

The concentration of moving picture theaters in the south-side community of Englewood suggests a different chronological and developmental pattern than the older immigrant neighborhoods. I found no record of moving pictures in Englewood before 1908, when the Englewood elevated rail extension was completed. From 1908 to 1915, however, fifty-six nickelodeons went into business in Englewood at twenty different locations. John Brinkhouse opened his moving picture show at 817 West 63rd Street in 1908; it lasted through 1910 (the location was listed under the name of William Sweeney from 1911–13 and under James Chrissy in 1914). KayGee Amusement opened a nickel theater across the street in 1908 (it was cross-listed under Frank Kommers in 1908 and under Mrs. Rose Grapinski in 1909). KayGee owned as many as nine five- and ten-cent theaters from 1908 to 1910, mostly on the south side.[41] As in the old immigrant neighborhoods, moving picture theaters kept opening in Englewood through the 1910s. Between 1908 and 1915 there was an average of almost eleven and a half moving picture venues available to Englewood residents.

Before the turn of the century the area around 63rd and Halsted Streets had been slowly growing as a neighborhood of apartment buildings and two-flats. Although this housing was intended for middle-class buyers, they never arrived. As transportation facilities in the area improved, residential construction for the working class accelerated, especially west of Halsted.[42] Although many residents worked in new local stores serving the growing population of Englewood, most of the area's heads of household worked outside the neighborhood. Englewood is distinguished from many worker residential neighborhoods in that development was tied to the completion of an elevated line. In some worker residential communities the "old neighborhood" was more or less within walking distance; the hearty could walk to work or to the retail and commercial areas (with their moving picture shows). Yet the growth of new shopping areas and five- and ten-cent shows concurrent with residential development after the arrival of the elevated train makes Englewood an interesting case.

An increasing number of five- and ten-cent theaters in worker residential areas like Englewood indicates that film exhibition was expanding beyond the mixed-use industrial and immigrant areas in response to working-class residential developments. Furthermore, these worker residential areas had their own growing retail and commercial strips, and moving picture theaters were among the first businesses to open in these locations. Those who worked outside the neighborhood could return to their communities after work to see film shows, where wives and children might join them. More important, moving picture operators were on the front edge of this new urban development.

The growth in new communities, together with the established patterns from the mixed-use immigrant neighborhoods, brings us to the question of the relationship between urban expansion and moving picture shows. Models of urban geography bring the development of moving picture exhibition in Chicago into better focus—both in terms of the kinds of neighborhoods where nickelodeons flourished and how theaters expanded through the city. Furthermore, they also cast light on the persistent question of socioeconomic class and the moving picture audience.

NOT ALL WORK AND NO PLAY:
URBAN GEOGRAPHY AND EXHIBITION

In his 1925 prolegomena to urban geography and planning, "The Growth of the City," Ernest Burgess analyzes the processes of urban growth he had observed in Chicago. His model describes urban landscape as a series of concentric circles that circumscribe the various zones of the city, differentiated by use (figure 9.2). Zone 1, in the center of the figure, is the central business district—the Loop, in the case of Chicago. Zone 2, circling the central business district, is a "zone in transition" that contains land sought by man-

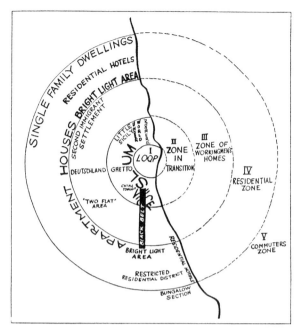

Figure 9.2. Urban Areas. Copyright 1925, Ernest
Burgess, "The Growth of the City," in Robert E. Park,
Ernest W. Burgess, and Roderick D. McKenzie, *The
City* (Chicago, Ill.: University of Chicago Press, 1925).

ufacturing concerns but that also contains overcrowded and overpriced housing for the workers in the nearby factories and in the central business district. The quality of housing stock and the amount of space increase as one
moves further out in zones 3 through 5. Zone 3, the second immigrant zone,
is the area where the workers moved who needed to live within walking distance of their jobs but who sought to relocate from the deteriorating housing in zone 2. Zone 4 has more single-family homes and nice apartment buildings. Zone 5 represents the suburban areas either outside of or on the fringes
of the city.[43]

In Burgess's model urban growth is the physical/geographic interaction
between these zones, the borders of which are in constant tension. Each area
expands outward, pushing into the next zone and forcing competition for
space between different uses of the land and facilities; Burgess calls this
process "succession."[44] Thus, growth means that some uses of urban land
move into new areas, taking over buildings or tearing them down, displac-
ing previous uses and tenants, and rebuilding infrastructure. Thus urban

growth moves people and businesses into contiguous areas and transforms those areas with new uses and populations.

But expansion is not only the slow creep outward. Burgess describes the process of "centralized decentralization" through which new communities spring up outside existing neighborhoods. These areas have their own business districts, which Burgess calls "satellite loops," and which area residents identify as the center of their neighborhood. Burgess points to land values as a measure of economic activity in these locations. He notes that although the land values in the Loop were still higher than in any other part of the city, they had been stagnant for ten years, whereas "in the same time they have doubled, quadrupled and even sextupled in the strategic corners of the 'satellite loops,' an accurate index of the changes which have occurred."[45] Burgess's account thus highlights two different patterns of growth: the succession of zones describes how different land uses tend to be stacked up almost on top of each other near the central areas of the city, and decentralization denotes the business districts that spring up at the center of new communities.

In his classic study of Chicago neighborhoods, *One Hundred Years of Land Values in Chicago,* Homer Hoyt elaborates on the growth of satellite loops. Hoyt outlines five factors that contributed to the formation of these outlying business centers. The first factor (which Burgess had also mentioned) is the new effort on the part of chain stores to locate near the homes of consumers. "The second factor was the building of theaters outside the Loop," Hoyt writes. "At first vaudeville houses, whose performances were inferior to the Loop theaters, and then showings of moving pictures that were the same as those displayed downtown induced people to seek their entertainment near their homes."[46] Banks and new factories, too, began to locate in outlying community centers. Finally Hoyt argues that the streetcar lines increasingly came into use not only as a means of getting to the Loop from outlying areas but as a way for people to get to the new business centers from surrounding residential areas.[47]

Hoyt's account offers two critical insights for understanding film exhibition in Chicago. He finds that people began using the streetcar or elevated train to get to new retail blocks—which frequently contained a moving picture theater—rather than going to the Loop. Furthermore, Hoyt underlines the role of moving pictures in the growth of new communities, arguing that they were integral to the rise of new business districts. Together Burgess's and Hoyt's accounts point to elements of the pattern of film exhibition that might otherwise be obscured.

FINDING THE NEIGHBORHOOD AUDIENCES

Putting evidence from the neighborhoods together with these models of urban geography offers additional insight into the communities where nickelodeons were a success. These models clarify that what the nickelodeon-rich neighborhoods of the inner belt shared was not simply a population of working-class immigrants. Neighborhoods withthe most five- and ten-cent theaters in the beginning of the nickelodeon era essentially exhibited the characteristics of Burgess's zone in transition. They had in common a mix of land uses, a wide range of employers and employment, high population density, and the infrastructural conditions that follow from diversified use. On many blocks were found small and medium-sized workshops, factories, and businesses that required an abundance of relatively cheap and variably skilled laborers, most of whom lived in the area. Those who commuted to work mostly did so on foot, although streetcar lines accommodated those who could afford to ride. Critically, although these communities were thought of as "old immigrant neighborhoods," factories, stores, and even schools were still being built, and more (and new groups of) immigrants were moving into these areas. Indeed, new five- and ten-cent theaters were open-ing in the inner belt communities through the mid-1910s. Burgess's account of growth supports the idea that the success of moving picture theaters in Chicago was tied to patterns of land use. Furthermore, his model helps dif-ferentiate these areas from neighborhoods with similar populations but fewer theaters.

There were immigrant, working-class neighborhoods in Chicago that did not have nearly as many nickelodeons as the inner belt neighborhoods. Neighborhoods such as Back of the Yards, Steeltown, and the vice districts each had a handful of nickelodeons. These neighborhoods were essentially company towns. Although they were populated by successive waves of poor immigrants, Back of the Yards and Steeltown were dominated by the stock-yards and the steel mills, respectively. The vice districts were, in a sense, com-pany towns as well, as they served a single industry: wine-room-based pros-titution in the Levee, burlesque on the Little White Way. Although these areas might superficially resemble other communities where film exhibition was successful, these neighborhoods lacked the new development in land use and industry that the zone in transition describes.

Burgess's and Hoyt's accounts of satellite loops illuminate the arrival of five- and ten-cent shows in new working-class neighborhoods. The success of the movies, as they were beginning to be known, suggests that part of the audience was moving up in the world (even if only incrementally). But they moved into new communities, not into the old middle-class residential neighborhoods.[48] In these relatively new communities entrepreneurs and more established businesses saw opportunities for new retail and commer-cial developments.[49] Residents had been accustomed to mixed-use neigh-borhoods where shopping was next door or around the corner—even down-stairs. For exhibitors, opening a moving picture show in Englewood, for example, was a sensible business decision. There was a built-in audience; residents had probably been film patrons in the immigrant ghettos. Further-more, land and rent in the newer communities were cheap. Although build-ings on high-traffic streets and corners cost more to rent than less strategic locations, these lots still cost much less than similar spaces in the Loop or in the industrial ghettos. And these satellite loops were successful. Both Burgess and Hoyt show that front footage rates along the new business districts rose in the early 1910s, and almost all of these satellite loops had nickelodeons.[50] For audiences the expansion of nickel theaters from the mixed-use, indus-trial, and tenement neighborhoods to newer working-class residential com-munities meant that their entertainment options were increasing: when work and home were no longer in the same neighborhood, audiences could find entertainment near work *or* near home.[51] Moving picture theaters were, thus, integral to the success of new business districts in developing working-class communities.

These different neighborhoods offer clues about the class composition of early film audiences. The popularity of five-cent shows in mixed-use, im-migrant, and industrial areas certainly underscores the presence of working-class, immigrant moviegoers. But this clientele was itself a diverse mix of people, and many people who did not live in the area passed through these neighborhoods every day, suggesting that nonresidents could easily stop in for an amusement lacking in their *own* communities. The appearance of mov-ing picture theaters in newer, better, but nonetheless working-class neigh-borhoods indicates that audiences were not as static as the earliest film his-tories suggested. Rather, part of the working-class audience was starting to move out of tenements and climb up the socioeconomic ladder. On the other hand, the appearance of film theaters in areas outside immigrant ghettos does not so much indicate the presence of a new, middle-class audience for moving picture shows as it does the movement of older audiences to less crowded areas in the city. Thus, to highlight this development in nickelodeon location is not to vote for one side or the other in the middle-class-audience versus working-class-audience debate but to suggest that a portion of the working-class audience for film was carving out a new class position for it-self in new neighborhoods.

CONCLUSION

Bringing together accounts of nickelodeon location and urban expansion produces some novel insights into where picture shows flourished and who was in attendance. Population growth, immigration, the development of the commercial and manufacturing base, infrastructural changes, new housing stock—indeed all of the factors involved in the growth of the city as a whole—influenced the patterns of exhibition in Chicago. Moving picture theaters participated in many overall trends in urban development; exhibitors in

Chicago behaved much as many other retailers and industries did: starting in the most crowded and dynamic industrial and tenement districts, then moving with a portion of the audience into new working-class areas. Land use, and specifically changing land use, turns out to be a critical variable in where five- and ten-cent shows thrived.

Following the success of five- and ten-cent theaters from the mixed-use immigrant neighborhoods to new working-class communities frustrates a simple account of the class composition of moving picture audiences. The first rounds of the middle-class versus working-class audience debate relied on terms too reified to accurately describe the audience. Additionally, that debate took place without the depth of geographic information that illuminates the changes occurring both within the working class and in the neighborhoods where new film theaters were cropping up. In Chicago these class relations were being negotiated on the land under the very feet of moving picture patrons. The exact duration of the nickelodeon era is also obscured by the success of moving picture theaters in different neighborhoods. In the years from 1905 to 1915 new five- and ten-cent theaters opened continuously in the inner belt neighborhoods and in new working-class communities. Indeed the rate at which new shows opened dropped off only slightly in most neighborhoods and stayed the same in others. However, the rise of the movies in new neighborhoods after 1908 shows that there were changes in the context of exhibition, even if the actual audience remained largely the same. Thus, the nickelodeon continued to be successful even as some of its contexts were in transition.

Finally, there was a close geographic relationship connecting film exhibition, work, home, and consumption in pre–World War I Chicago. The neighborhoods with the most nickelodeons contained all of these components of daily life.[52] In the inner belt neighborhoods five- and ten-cent theaters operated cheek by jowl with small retail shops and in the immediate vicinity of housing, commerce, and industrial production. Many patrons surely viewed five-cent shows in the midst of their household errands or on their way home from work, since they were frequently next door to each other. In this sense nickelodeons successfully fit into the "rhythms of local life" that already included consumption in the most everyday sense.[53] The success of film exhibition in new communities that largely lacked business and commercial blocks before the arrival of five- and ten-cent theaters illustrates rather dramatically that even as the neighborhood context of exhibition changed, the ties between home, consumption, and motion pictures remained strong. Five- and ten-cent shows, together with chain stores, branch banks, and public transportation, drew folks to new commercial developments in new communities where a growing number of consumers lived. Thus, moving picture theaters were a bellwether of changing patterns of residence and consumption, an indication not just of real estate developments but also of the terrain of peoples' daily lives: setting up household, going to work, shopping, and going to the show in new neighborhoods. Thus, moviegoing in most Chicago neighborhoods was geographically and economically connected to other kinds of consumption but also part of the vanguard of development in new areas of the city. Moving picture theaters thus contributed to the changing spatial experience of the city, while also helping to integrate people into its new communities.

NOTES

I take my title from F. Zeta Youmans, "Opportunity Night," *Survey Graphic Number* 18, no. 11 (1 September 1927): 485. Youmans's paragraph reads,

> Like other commercial enterprises, theatrical entertainment has become highly competitive. The building of the great new motion picture houses has resolved itself into a careful calculation not only of present population to be entertained but of possible future population. At every point of traffic intersection, even where the development has just begun, great new motion picture palaces have been built or are being built. In the mean time, there still exist the small neighborhood theaters which are driven into unequal and often losing competition with their magnificent rivals.

1. Chauncy Harris and Edward Ullman, "The Nature of Cities," in *Annals of the American Academy of Political and Social Sciences* 242 (November 1945): 7.

2. The chapters of my dissertation from which this essay is culled cover thirteen Chicago neighborhoods over the period from 1905 to 1915. This breadth is important in assessing where nickelodeons were successful, but because of allotted space I discuss only a few neighborhoods here. For accounts of other neighborhoods, as well as the regulatory environment, see J. A. Lindstrom, "'Getting a Hold Deeper in the Life of the City': Chicago Nickelodeons, 1905–1914" (Ph.D. diss., Northwestern University, 1998).

3. Although the city council did pass ordinances regulating the location of moving picture theaters beginning in late 1908, these laws dealt primarily with residential blocks and relied on the knowledge and interest of the neighbors for enforcement. They had a limited effect, therefore, on actual nickelodeon location.

4. Jane Gaines, "From Elephants to Lux Soap: The Programming and 'Flow' of Early Motion Picture Exploitation," *Velvet Light Trap* 25 (spring 1990): 39. On the "house of dreams" see Jane Addams, *The Spirit of Youth and City Streets* (New York: Macmillan, 1910), 76.

5. Kathy Peiss, *Cheap Amusements: Working Women and Leisure in Turn-of-the-Century New York* (Philadelphia, Pa.: Temple University Press, 1986), 148–53.

6. Judith Mayne, "Immigrants and Spectators," *Wide Angle* 5, no. 2 (1982): 34.

7. Miriam Hansen, *Babel and Babylon: Spectatorship in American Silent Film* (Cambridge, Mass.: Harvard University Press, 1991), 63.

8. Kathryn H. Fuller, *At the Picture Show: Small-town Audiences and the Creation of Movie Fan Culture* (Washington, D.C.: Smithsonian Institution Press, 1996).

9. Some audiences may not have experienced their theaters as inferior. Fuller writes, "The small-town theaters, exhibitors, audiences, programs, and the entire spirit

of the operation retained what might be called a nickelodeon flavor throughout the silent era" (Fuller, *At the Picture Show,* 48).

10. Waller writes, "Lexington's nickelodeon period . . . (1906–1912) saw the opening of not only more than ten different picture shows, but also the city's first successful vaudeville theater, amusement park, and skating rinks" (Gregory Waller, *Main Street Amusements: Movies and Commercial Entertainment in a Southern City, 1896–1930* [Washington, D.C.: Smithsonian Institution Press, 1995], 65–66).

11. Ibid., 111.

12. Lauren Rabinovitz, *For the Love of Pleasure: Women, Movies, and Culture in Turn-of-the-Century Chicago* (New Brunswick, N.J.: Rutgers University Press, 1998), 181.

13. Ibid., 121, 138.

14. Shelley Stamp, *Movie-Struck Girls: Women and Motion Picture Culture after the Nickelodeon* (Princeton, N.J.: Princeton University Press, 2000), 102.

15. Douglas Gomery, "Movie Audiences, Urban Geography, and the History of American Film," *Velvet Light Trap* 19 (1982): 23–29; and Douglas Gomery, *Shared Pleasures: A History of Movie Presentation in the United States* (Madison: University of Wisconsin Press, 1992).

16. Robert C. Allen, "Motion Picture Exhibition in Manhattan 1906–1912: Beyond the Nickelodeon," *Cinema Journal* 18, no. 2 (spring 1979): 2–15; Ben Singer, "Manhattan Nickelodeons: New Data on Audiences and Exhibitors," *Cinema Journal* 34, no. 3 (spring 1995): 5–35; Robert C. Allen, "Manhattan Myopia; or, Oh, Iowa!" *Cinema Journal* 35, no. 3 (spring 1996): 78–79; and Ben Singer, "New York, Just Like I Pictured It," *Cinema Journal* 35, no. 3 (spring 1996): 108–14. See also Robert Sklar, "Oh! Althusser! Historiography and the Rise of Cinema Studies," *Radical History Review* 41 (spring 1988): 21–23.

17. Sumiko Higashi, "Dialogue: Manhattan Nickelodeons" *Cinema Journal* 35, no. 3 (spring 1996): 72–74; and William Uricchio and Roberta Pearson, "New York? New York!" *Cinema Journal* 36, no. 4 (summer 1997): 98–102.

18. Singer, "Manhattan Nickelodeons," 21–22; Allen, "Manhattan Myopia," 78–79; Uricchio and Pearson, "New York? New York!" 98–102; and Ben Singer, "Manhattan Melodrama," *Cinema Journal* 36, no. 4 (summer 1997): 107–12.

19. Judith Thissen, "Oy! Myopia," *Cinema Journal* 36, no. 4 (summer 1997): 102–7; Judith Thissen, "Jewish Immigrant Audiences in New York City, 1905–1914," in *American Movie Audiences from the Turn of the Century to the Early Sound Era,* ed. Melvyn Stokes and Richard Maltby (London: British Film Institute, 1999), 15–28. Thissen also argues that the post-1909 revival of Yiddish vaudeville in Lower East Side nickelodeons constituted both a defense of *Yiddishkayt* in the neighborhood's popular culture and an effort to make exhibition more profitable, but it did not represent an appeal to an upwardly mobile audience; see Thissen, "Jewish Immigrant Audiences," 21–23.

20. Thomas Lee Philpott, *The Slum and the Ghetto: Neighborhood Deterioration and Middle-Class Reform, Chicago, 1880–1930* (New York: Oxford University Press, 1978).

21. The sources for these references include the Chicago city clerk's registries, the *Lakeside Annual Directory,* Sanborn Fire Insurance maps, reformers' surveys, and the trade press. Most of these numbers are probably quite low relative to the num-

ber of nickelodeons that were actually operating, but they are useful as a relative reference. For more about the joys and limitations of individual resources see Lindstrom, "'Getting a Hold.'"

22. In New York City there was one theater for every 11,250 residents. See Eileen Bowser, *The Transformation of Cinema, 1907–1915* (Berkeley: University of California Press, 1994), 6.

23. This information comes primarily from fire insurance maps of Chicago. Sanborn did not map the whole neighborhood in a single year, so it is harder to compare the map findings with *Lakeside* listings. See Sanborn maps of Chicago, 1W (1906): 100W, 107W, 114W; 8 (1914): 1, 2, 7; 7 (1917): 80, 96, 112, 114.

24. Robert Hunter, "Occupation by Nationalities," in *Tenement Conditions in Chicago: Report by the Investigating Committee of the City Homes Association* (Chicago, Ill.: City Homes Association, 1901), 196–97.

25. Philpott, *The Slum and the Ghetto*, 23–24; Philpott's assessment was based on information in *Hull-House Maps and Papers*, by the residents of Hull House (New York: Thomas Y. Crowell, 1895).

26. Sophonisba Breckinridge and Edith Abbott, "Chicago Housing Conditions, IV: The West Side Revisited," *American Journal of Sociology* 17, no. 1 (July 1911): 4. These conditions had been a problem since at least 1895, when the Hull House study of Little Italy noted that "as factories are built people crowd more and more closely into houses about them, and rear tenements fill up the open spaces left" (Residents of Hull House, *Hull-House Maps and Papers*, 117). This assessment is confirmed by Homer Hoyt, *One Hundred Years of Land Values in Chicago* (Chicago, Ill.: University of Chicago Press, 1933), 201.

27. Philpott, *The Slum and the Ghetto*, 40.

28. Germans were also among the ranks of Chicago exhibitors. Citywide, around 18 percent of Chicago's exhibitors had German or German-Jewish surnames. Curiously, only three German north side exhibitors listed in the *Lakeside* had German or German-Jewish last names, and the most common ethnicity was English. Several theaters in the area had nonfamily names, such as The Plaza, North Avenue Theatre, and The Park. I used several reference books on surnames and national origin to discern the ethnicity of exhibitors, including Alexander Beider, *A Dictionary of Jewish Surnames from the Russian Empire* (Teaneck, N.J.: Avolaynu, 1993); Heinrich W. Gugenheimer and Eva H. Gugenheimer, *Jewish Family Names and Their Origins* (New York: Ktav, 1992); Patrick Hanks and Flavia Hodges, *A Dictionary of Surnames* (New York: Oxford University Press, 1988); Eldon C. Smith, *New Dictionary of American Family Names* (New York: Harper and Row, 1973).

29. *Lakeside Annual Directory*, 1906–1911; *Billboard*, 15 December 1906, 32; 7 December 1907, 52; 21 March 1908, 96; 19 December 1908, 43; and *Moving Picture World*, 21 February 1908, 234.

30. Sanborn maps consistently showed more nickelodeons in a given neighborhood than other resources listed for that year. Citywide, over half of the nickelodeons shown in Sanborn maps were not in the *Lakeside* for the corresponding year.

31. Sittner's was listed among motograph users in *Motography*, November 1911, 242; cf. *Lakeside Annual Directory*, 1911.

32. Christiane Harzig, "Chicago's German North Side, 1880–1900: The Structure of a Gilded Age Neighborhood," in *German Workers in Chicago: A Documentary His-*

tory of Working-Class Culture from 1850 to WW I, ed. Hartmut Keil and John B. Jentz (Urbana: University of Illinois Press, 1988), 129.

33. Ibid., 136; Hartmut Keil, "Immigrant Neighborhoods and American Society: German Immigrants on Chicago's Northwest Side in the Late 19th Century," in *German Workers' Culture in the United States, 1850 to 1920*, ed. Hartmut Keil (Washington, D.C.: Smithsonian Institution Press, 1988), 36.

34. Harzig, "Chicago's German North Side," 135.

35. Klaus Ensslen argues that the blending of old and new came of the "syncretistic pressure exerted by mass culture in the expanding big city" on existing ethnic traditions. He cites the example of the transformation of Schützen Park into Riverview. See Klaus Ensslen, "German-American Working-Class Saloons in Chicago: Their Social Function in an Ethnic and Class-Specific Cultural Context," in *German Workers' Culture in the United States, 1850 to 1920*, ed. Hartmut Keil (Washington, D.C.: Smithsonian Institution Press, 1988), 173.

36. Ibid., 175.

37. Christine Heiss, "Popular and Working-Class German Theater in Chicago, 1870 to 1910," in *German Workers' Culture in the United States, 1850 to 1920*, ed. Hartmut Keil (Washington, D.C.: Smithsonian Institution Press, 1988), 186–88.

38. Ibid., 189. Heiss notes that many German popular theaters were converted to moving picture venues.

39. Harzig, "Chicago's German North Side," 129.

40. Heinz Ickstadt, "A Tale of Two Cities: Culture and Its Social Function in Chicago during the Progressive Period," in *German Workers' Culture in the United States, 1850 to 1920*, ed. Hartmut Keil (Washington, D.C.: Smithsonian Institution Press, 1988), 305–6; *Chicagoer Arbeiter-Zeitung*, 15 March 1909, 2.

41. *Lakeside Annual Directory*, 1908–14. Sanborn did not map the Englewood neighborhood in this period.

42. Gerald E. Sullivan, ed., *The Story of Englewood, 1835–1923* (Chicago, Ill.: Foster and McDonnell, 1924), 35–36.

43. Ernest W. Burgess, "The Growth of the City," in *The City*, by Robert E. Park, Ernest W. Burgess, Roderick D. McKenzie (1925; repr., Chicago, Ill.: University of Chicago Press, 1967), 50. Although this account dates from after the nickelodeon era, it describes phenomena occurring before and just after the turn of the century. Furthermore, this model has endured in urban geography and real estate economics as a basic conceptual account of urban growth around the turn of the century. See also *Internal Structure of the City: Readings on Urban Form, Growth, and Policy*, ed. Larry S. Bourne (New York: Oxford University Press, 1982); Martin Cadwaller, *Urban Geography: An Analytical Approach* (Upper Saddle River, N.J.: Prentice-Hall, 1996); Paul K. Knox, *Urbanization: An Introduction to Urban Geography* (Englewood Cliffs, N.J.: Prentice-Hall, 1994).

44. Burgess, "Growth of the City," 50–51.

45. Ibid., 61. Burgess cites Bridgeport, the Division-Ashland-Milwaukee intersection, Englewood, and Wilson Avenue. By 1910 each of these areas played a role in the expansion of film exhibition in Chicago except Bridgeport (which was an existing lower-middle-class neighborhood).

46. Hoyt, *One Hundred Years*, 225–26.

47. Hoyt cites the rise in front footage rates at the intersections of Sixty-third and

Cottage Grove, Sixty-third and Halsted (Englewood), Lawrence and Kimball, and the three-way intersections along Milwaukee Avenue as examples of this increase in activity. All of these intersections except Lawrence and Kimball had nickelodeons by 1910. See Hoyt, *One Hundred Years,* 226–27.

48. Five- and ten-cent theaters did not catch on in the older middle-class neighborhoods (such as Hermosa, Cragin, or Jefferson Park) that were not in the path of working-class relocation. Indeed, the movies would not arrive in middle-class residential neighborhoods until the rise of the picture palaces.

49. Historian Morris Janowitz confirms the changes created by satellite loops: "The community newspaper arose out of the development of satellite business centers in the metropolitan district, which made possible a base of advertising revenue. . . . The majority [of community newspapers] arose in areas where no village or small town antecedent could be found. The development of the satellite business district reflected changes in population distributions along community lines and created an audience which could be addressed in terms of local geographical identifications" (Morris Janowitz, *The Community Press in an Urban Setting,* 2d ed. [Chicago, Ill.: University of Chicago Press, 1967], 10).

50. Burgess, "Growth of the City," 61; Hoyt, *One Hundred Years,* 226–27.

51. For some groups entertainment choices had always been restricted. African Americans were largely limited to attending the (many) moving picture shows in the south-side Black Belt. In spite of Illinois' antidiscrimination ordinance African Americans were usually denied access to moving picture theaters in other areas of the city.

52. Although the Loop had more five- and ten-cent shows than most neighborhoods, it had less than 10 percent of the nickelodeon locations that I found.

53. Whether the proximity of moving pictures and retail stores contributed to a notion of shopping as a leisure activity in these neighborhoods is a vexing question, since there is little extant evidence that would illuminate the question.

CHAPTER TEN

A House Divided

The MPPC in Transition

Scott Curtis

That the single-reel photo-drama is the keystone of the motion picture industry be-
comes more apparent daily. Patrons of the film drama want their programs as di-
versified as possible. A program offering four or more productions is more apt to please
an entire audience than is a program offering one photo-play of four or five reels. Of
course, there are exceptions to this rule.

WILLIAM N. SELIG, *July 1914*

Although the one- or two-reel film was still an important part of the program in 1914, it is generally conceded that by 1917 films longer than four
reels dominated the market. In 1914 split-reels and one-, two-, and three-
reelers accounted for 80 percent of all reels released. In 1913 films of four
reels or longer made up barely 4 percent of the total number of reels, but
that number jumped to 20 percent the next year and continued to climb
steeply. By 1917 films longer than four reels made up 58 percent of the total, and by 1918 that number had increased to 70 percent.[1] If the sudden
statistical jump in the number of features in 1914 appeared to some as an
aberration, there was no denying the money to be made in the feature market. That much was clear.

Given this trend, apparent even in July 1914, Selig's statement sounds remarkably conservative if not downright obtuse. In fact, Selig's proclamation
is often cited as an example of the short-sightedness of the members of the
Motion Picture Patents Company (MPPC), as evidence that their inability to
adapt to changing market conditions and the rise of the feature led to their
downfall.[2] The story is well known: in 1907 Edison Manufacturing and several of the largest film companies join forces to control and regulate the
nascent film industry. Embroiled in bitter and costly litigation over patent
violations, the companies (Edison, Essanay, Kalem, Kleine, Lubin, Méliès,
Pathé Frères, Selig Polyscope, Vitagraph, and finally Biograph) eventually
form a trust—the MPPC—that will license and enforce several key patents.
The MPPC successfully regularizes and standardizes the industry, but cer-

tain key court decisions corrode the enforceability of its patent lawsuits and the legality of the Trust, while independent film companies, such as Famous Players-Lasky, find success with feature films and new forms of distribution. Unwilling to vary from the one- and two-reel format and legally impotent to enforce the patents, the members of the MPPC are eventually left in the dust, irrelevant by 1916 and out of business by 1918.

This story, which has become something of a capitalist cautionary tale, has an important place in all histories of the motion picture. Of course, the story is much more complicated than has been suggested by older, more traditional histories of American cinema.[3] For example, it is not often reported that, in the same issue of *Moving Picture World* that featured Selig's article, Carl Laemmle, a leader of the Independent movement, predicts the doom of long features in more vehement terms.[4] That is, the line between short films and longer films cannot be drawn simply between the MPPC and the Independents. Most histories that use Selig's quotation against him also leave out the significance of a June 1914 convention at which exhibitors passed a resolution that "expressed their disapproval of the production of reels of 1,000 feet and upward."[5] Owners of smaller theaters were especially anxious about the rising expense (and the impossibility of greater return, given the small number of seats) that features represented. Clearly, then, the trade journal became a stage from which Selig and Laemmle could play to the audience, placating nervous exchanges and exhibitors by reassuring them that they would not be abandoned in the changing times. Even in Selig's quotation we can see that he is trying to straddle the fence by coming down firmly on the side of one-reelers but not dismissing longer films entirely. No wonder: Selig, like many of his fellow MPPC members, was very busy making features and trying to cash in on this growing market.

Recent scholarship has done an excellent job of correcting older histories that paint the MPPC as a monolithic, conservative, lumbering dinosaur that did not have the sense to see the significance of features and thus was rightly phased out of the evolution of motion pictures. Anderson, Staiger, Bowser, and Quinn have pinpointed the issues that hindered the MPPC's entry into the feature market, even though many of its members were eager to try.[6] Most histories, however, focus on the battle between the MPPC and the Independents. As important as this skirmish is for the history of American cinema, the dissension within the MPPC, although evident at the time, has not been sufficiently emphasized.[7] The conflicts within the MPPC certainly make the story more interesting, but that is not the (only) reason to highlight them. Friction indicates where the stress points are; it can help identify the cracks in the system that would eventually widen to separate and isolate the members of the MPPC. In other words, studying the conflicts within the MPPC can help us better understand its decline. The rise of the feature film, in particular, put sufficient pressure on MPPC policy to make the cracks especially visible, even though they were evident from the very beginning.

This essay, therefore, will examine tension in three areas within the MPPC's domain: distribution (the tension between the MPPC and its licensed exchanges), exhibition (between the MPPC and its licensed theaters), and production (among the members of the MPPC). It is important to rehearse the early history of the MPPC—years before the rise of the feature—because the first friction at these spots would eventually grind down the finer, more successful, points of MPPC policy, rendering the organization ineffectual and immobile in the face of competition and innovation. In fact, I argue that the friction among the members of the MPPC, especially, is a principal cause of its decline, since the immobility of the group resulted primarily from their inherent mistrust of one another, coupled with self-interest at the expense of the organization. When discussing the MPPC and features, it is tempting to ask simply, why not? Why couldn't they adjust and enter the market as easily as their competitors? In order to understand the nature of the MPPC's immobility, or "executive paralysis," as Robert Anderson calls it,[8] we must understand the obstacles placed in front of them—as well as those they placed in front of themselves—with the very formation of the Trust.

After a March 1907 court decision[9] favoring Edison's patent claims made it clear that continued litigation (which had already gone on for a decade) would be costly and futile, several companies contacted Edison about the feasibility of a licensing agreement.[10] Edison was in a position of power (he had already started new cases against Selig and Vitagraph), but his patent suits discouraged native investment, thus facilitating foreign domination of American screens.[11] Legally strong but commercially vulnerable, Edison was ready to negotiate.[12] By May 1907 the representatives of Essanay Film Manufacturing Company (Chicago), Kalem Company (New York), George Kleine Optical Company (Chicago), Pathé Frères (France), Selig Polyscope (Chicago), and Vitagraph of America (New York) had come to an understanding with Edison.[13] By formally issuing licenses to these companies—as well as to Geo. Méliès (France) and S. Lubin (Philadelphia)—Edison formed the Association of Edison Licensees (AEL) in early 1908.[14] Although the American Mutoscope and Biograph Company seriously considered accepting an Edison license, it held important patents as well and was not willing to join the group until its claims were given parity with Edison's.[15] Edison was not willing to do this, so for the next year the industry was in turmoil as these two companies battled in the courts and negotiated in private. Biograph and George Kleine Optical Company, which was not granted a license, were the focal points for an Independent movement of manufacturers and (mostly) exchanges. This movement had its beginnings in Edison's attempt to organize the industry through a trade association.

In November 1907 all the manufacturers and renters—both the Biograph group and those affiliated with Edison—met in Pittsburgh "to remedy and improve the existing conditions and place the business upon the highest plane."[16] The nickelodeon boom of the previous two years had created an unprecedented demand for films, but the lawsuits and lack of investment kept the supply very tight. Furthermore, intense competition among exchanges created a chaotic and unreliable distribution network, even while profits for exchanges soared. To understand what was at stake, we need only to recall the incredible state of business at the beginning of the nickelodeon era. Since 1903 exchanges had been buying films directly from the manufacturer and then renting them at reduced rates to theater owners. This system made the prints cheaper for the exhibitors (who before had bought the films from the manufacturer), and it meant enormous profits for the distributor: if the rental price of a film was one-fifth the purchase price, the exchange needed to rent this print to only five exhibitors before subsequent rentals could be counted as pure profit. And since the demand was so high and the life of the print was, say, six months (before it became unprojectable), a print could generate at least fifteen to twenty more rentals beyond the original cost of purchase. Simple arithmetic shows that if nickelodeon owners were doing well in the boom years, owning a film exchange was nothing less than a license to print cash.

This kind of demand created an environment of cutthroat competition. Exchanges would shamelessly duplicate films, rent shoddy prints well past their life span, give preferential treatment to exhibitors who paid the most money, and they would resell a print to another exchange without paying the manufacturers a second time. Exhibitors would "bicycle" prints they already rented to another of their theaters, also without paying for the second rental; furthermore, the theaters would probably be cramped, dark, and poorly ventilated storefronts, which quickly became the target of reform campaigns. In short, the unscrupulous business practices of the exhibition and distribution wings of the industry threatened to ruin the business. But even more important than this was the plain and simple fact that the manufacturers were not getting what they considered to be their fair share of this money pie. So when the manufacturers and renters met in Pittsburgh "to improve existing conditions," the industry definitely needed improvement, but the manufacturers had a very strong financial incentive as well.

The AEL hoped to solve the supply problem by licensing and regularizing manufacture. Solving the chaotic distribution system required the participation of the 150 or so exchanges across the country. At the Pittsburgh conference the renters met separately from the manufacturers to create the United Film Service Protective Association, designed to work "in cooperation with manufacturers . . . to improve the service now furnished to the public, to protect each other in the manner of credits and all other con-

ditions affecting our mutual welfare."[17] Although the organization ostensibly represented the interests of the exchanges as an equal and separate partner in the task of improving existing conditions, the terms dictated by the
AEL (e.g., prohibiting film duplication, forbidding subrentals and resales of
prints, and banning the circulation of worn prints) were designed to redirect profits from the renters back to the manufacturers. Despite some resistance among the renters against the AEL, the ideals of the UFSPA were
ratified at the February 1908 Buffalo conference, where it was renamed the
Film Service Association, or FSA.[18]

Why would any renter even bother to join an association that was designed
to redirect profits back to the manufacturer? The stick, in this case, was the
possibility that the AEL would lock up the marketplace, and any renter who
did not join might be left without any films. The carrot was the possibility
that the AEL could coordinate the activities of the different branches of the
industry and thereby bring stability and standardization to an industry in
disarray. This possibility was particularly appealing to the smaller exchanges
and exhibitors, who were subject to price-cutting and other abuses. Smaller
exhibitors, especially, complained of preferential treatment given to larger
theaters. The FSA promised to standardize prices, initiate regular release
dates, remove dupes and old prints from the marketplace, and (through the
licensing program) eliminate backroom deals.[19]

As positive as these goals were, the policies of the AEL and FSA created
conflicts within the FSA that would come to haunt the combine throughout
its reign. First, the AEL assumed that by licensing the largest manufacturers, the others would either join or wither and die. This was decidedly not
the case. Biograph and Kleine led a combination of Independent manufacturers that, although initially not strong or representing the highest quality
in filmmaking, were large enough to provide an alternative to the AEL's
strong-arm tactics. Second, Edison Manufacturing pursued an aggressive,
hard-line policy of prosecuting any and all licensed exchanges or theaters
that rented or screened nonlicensed film, which only exacerbated feelings
of resentment among renters and exhibitors against the AEL.

These flaws in the plan led to cracks within the FSA. That the organization quickly dropped the terms *United* and *Protective* from its title indicates
the lack of unanimity among the members, which *Moving Picture World* called
"the rotten plank in the platform of the association."[20] Not only were there
internal rivalries, but the "Independent" combination, led by Biograph and
Kleine, made it difficult for the FSA to maintain discipline within its ranks.[21]
The high, even indiscriminate, demand for films meant that it was still
profitable, despite the threat of a revoked license or a lawsuit, to show both
licensed and nonlicensed product. Indeed, licensed exchanges were dependent on two companies, Pathé Frères and Edison, since at this early stage
Kalem, Selig, Lubin, and Vitagraph were not able to meet weekly demand.

Independent distributors advocated projecting licensed and nonlicensed films on the same program, and many theaters followed this advice, only to have their licenses revoked, causing further turmoil and animosity.[22]

Even the leadership of the FSA, such as William H. Swanson, a prominent Chicago renter who guided the FSA in its early incarnation, actively worked against AEL policy. A lightning rod for the exchange interests, Swanson was elected president pro tempore at the first FSA meeting in 1907 and officially at the January 1909 meeting.[23] In the interim he flouted AEL rules constantly by illegally opening branch offices of his exchange and price-cutting to gain entry to the territory.[24] Exchange men loyal to the AEL complained loudly about Swanson's tactics. Luke Mithen, an FSA representative and Swanson lackey, was particularly reviled for preferential treatment of some exchanges and exhibitors over others.[25] Swanson advocated allowing licensed exchanges to purchase unlicensed product and giving unlicensed exchanges permission to purchase licensed films, in direct opposition of the FSA's stated policy.[26] Swanson and Mithen even went so far as to try to organize exchanges against the manufacturers.[27] Swanson's dissatisfaction with his own organization became clear in a letter to a fellow exchange man:

> The entire Association matter in general has been a great detriment to me. I have lost a world of business since its inception, have gotten absolutely no advantage and have squandered a hat full of money and devoted my time and energy and it seems to be that it is an organization of very affable and easily led gentlemen organized for the purpose of benefiting a few manufacturers. The future may develop the fact that it may prove of benefit but judging by the past I am not very enthusiastic over it.[28]

His lack of enthusiasm was certainly economically motivated. In testimony for the MPPC antitrust suit Swanson declared that his exchanges in Chicago, New Orleans, and St. Louis grossed over $600,000 in 1907 and early 1908 but began to "rapidly" lose money when he "began to live up to the regulations and rules of the Edison license agreements."[29] When faced with the choice between following rules and making money, most large-volume exchanges had little trouble coming up with a solution: ignore the rules. Many exchanges rented both licensed and nonlicensed product, and virtually no exchange ever returned a single reel of film to the manufacturers as stipulated. The reason was obvious: the demand for film was too great, especially when the Keith and Proctor theaters in New York City moved from triweekly program changes to daily program changes, starting a trend in exhibition that lasted from 1909 to around 1914.[30] As Anderson notes, "Even though many FSA distributors called for the enforcement of the tenets of the licensing agreement, the abuses were too ingrained, wide-spread, and profitable to be rectified in a divided marketplace."[31]

Manufacturers did not stand by idly. Selig, for example, declared that

Swanson was "one of the worst offenders in the business, and that is no lie"[32] and assured offended exchange men that he would voice his displeasure with Swanson's tactics and lieutenants at meetings of the Executive Committee.[33] The rebellion of Swanson and others like him indicated to Edison and the AEL that full compliance with their policies would come only when the manufacturers could present a united front. Therefore, negotiations between Edison and Biograph proceeded apace, the two manufacturers having come to a preliminary agreement by July 1908.[34] By late 1908 the ground was cleared for a patent pool representing the major interests in the industry. As soon as Biograph and Kleine joined the Edison group, the members felt they had the industry locked up and that they could actually enforce the license agreements without the cooperation of the renters. So in January 1909 the Motion Picture Patents Company became official, and the FSA became superfluous. By electing Swanson their president, the exchanges of the FSA indicated their resistance to Edison's terms. But in a show of confidence the MPPC cancelled Swanson's license, thus ridding itself of a troublesome figure in the organization.[35] As long as important manufacturers and importers were outside the fold, the Edison group needed an organization like the FSA to negotiate terms with the exchanges and to persuade them to join. Once all the major manufacturers and importers were onboard, the exchanges had little choice: sign up or go Independent. The FSA became merely a fraternal organization after that. The MPPC did not license every manufacturer or every exchange, but it accomplished its goal: "to create a situation where 'Independent' meant a cheap theater, badly made films, and unreliable distribution."[36] Carl Laemmle, a Chicago renter who later founded Universal, wrote a letter to exhibitors explaining why he would not go Independent under these circumstances, which, considering that he did indeed jump ship in April 1909, seems somewhat disingenuous in retrospect:

> If you have any confidence in ME,—if you believe I am on the square—WHY do you suppose I decided not to join the so-called "Independents"? LISTEN to the answer:—It's because THEY HAVEN'T GOT A SINGLE LEG TO STAND ON. Their ONLY hope is that they can get their fight into the Courts and do business for perhaps half a year or so before they are thrown out by law altogether. . . . They expect you to help put up a losing fight, and in the meantime submit to all sorts of annoyance and nuisance.[37]

Of the 118 or so exchanges in the FSA in January 1909, the MPPC licensed 110.[38] Yet it licensed only nine of eighteen exchanges in Chicago, making it the de facto center of the Independent movement. Chicago had traditionally been the hotbed of anti-Trust sentiment, possibly because it was the first and largest center of new film exchanges in 1905 and 1906.[39] Exacerbating this inherent mistrust, between March and April 1908 Edison brought suit against thirty theater owners in the Chicago area for showing Biograph-licensed films.[40] A 1909 survey indicates that of the theaters in the Midwest, particularly Chicago, only 50 percent were licensed, as opposed to 90 percent in the East and a majority in the West.[41] In January 1909, after the MPPC dictated terms to the FSA, Independent manufacturers and exchanges met in Chicago to organize their response.[42] Max Lewis of the Chicago Film Exchange promised exhibitors, "We have not [signed] and will not sign the outrageous agreement offered to the Film Exchanges, and we positively refuse to connect ourselves with any movement intended to take the profits from you and others who have worked night and day and made the motion picture industry what it is today."[43] This typified the "Independent" battle cry shouted by such Chicago exchange men as Swanson and Laemmle. As the MPPC cancelled licenses right and left (especially when it moved to create its own distribution system in 1910), it only contributed to the competition.[44] But the pattern of rebellion against MPPC license policy began with the FSA. Even though the FSA was ostensibly controlled by the manufacturers, exchanges tried their best to regain their position in the industry by whatever means necessary. The MPPC's assumptions (e.g., that nonlicensed manufacturers, exchanges, and theaters would die off) were specious and its actions (e.g., redirecting profits) inflammatory, so it is not surprising that disagreements over license policy meant that the "Independent problem" came not only from outside the FSA but from *within* as well.

On the production side even the members of the MPPC had reason to grumble. For starters they could complain about profit percentage. As the patent holders, Edison and Biograph took the lion's share of the royalties from licensing: one-half and one-third, respectively. The other eight companies' tributes were pure gravy but still a pittance compared to Edison and Biograph's take. For example, in 1913 (the last year of royalty payments), of the over $1,000,000 in royalties, the other eight licensees received only $161,875 divided eight ways.[45] As litigation heated up again in 1913 (a result of the 1912 antitrust suit), Edison and Biograph expected the others to share legal costs equally, which raised eyebrows and voices. Receiving only a small share of the profits while paying for an equal share of costs did not sit well with the members. George Spoor of Essanay and George Kleine threatened to sue Edison for "past damages."[46]

Resentment toward Edison Manufacturing sometimes took the form of personal animosity between members of the MPPC. Selig, for example, felt that Frank Dyer, president of Thomas A. Edison, Inc., and later of the MPPC's General Film Company, was "the worst" GFC president the organization ever had. His report to Kleine of an annual meeting of the members indicates the level of hostility within the MPPC:

> We expected to learn the condition of the business, but even this he [Dyer] failed to disclose. Those whom he should stand by he has thrown down, and

is trying to make monkeys of us—only when he needs us for re-election he calls upon us as friends. Otherwise we are nothing. I am sick and tired of it and told him so and so did George Spoor. . . . In general he is incompetent to manage the General Film Co. and there is a general uproar against him, with the exception of Smith of the Vitagraph, who thinks he is just the right thing, because he will do just as Smith wants him to do. . . . In conclusion I will just simply state that if Dyer stays in another year, neither you nor I will be putting out very many films by the time the season is over, and I don't propose to stand for this double-crossing any longer.[47]

Other members had specific reasons to hold a grudge against other members of the MPPC. George Kleine, for example, had been a leader of the "Independents" in 1908 as Biograph and Edison fought it out in the courts and in the court of public opinion. In March 1908 Edison even filed suit against Kleine for infringing on a film patent that had not even been tested in the courts.[48] This after Kleine had gone to considerable trouble to negotiate an agreement between Edison and the other manufacturers in May 1907.[49] Such ingratitude, however, points to a troubled history between George Kleine Optical and Edison Manufacturing dating back to 1904. At that time Kleine had been Edison's Chicago sales agent, accounting for nearly 30 percent of Edison's film sales. As Biograph and Pathé appeared on the scene, Kleine started distributing their films as well, which did not sit well with William Gilmore, Edison's general manager, especially because Kleine chose to distribute original Pathé films rather than Edison dupes. Gilmore broke with Kleine on this point, but European manufacturers looked favorably on Kleine's stance, and he became the importer for a number of foreign manufacturers,[50] hence Gilmore and Edison's decision not to grant a license to Kleine in late 1907. But in an effort to mollify Kleine, they did give a license to Kalem Company, which Kleine had co-founded with Samuel Long and Frank Marion in early 1907, but only if Kleine resigned.[51] Further, Edison did not want to grant licenses to any importers because he had worked out a deal with Pathé to freeze out other foreign manufacturers, such as Éclair, Gaumont, and Urban-Eclipse, which imported their wares to the United States through Kleine.[52]

So Kleine was forced to join forces with Biograph in 1908, becoming the spokesman for the Independent movement during those years by taking his case to the press with strongly worded statements against the Edison group in *Moving Picture World, Show World,* and the *Chicago Tribune.*[53] *Moving Picture World* took care to point out that "in reference to the newspaper reports, [Kleine] informs us that he is not responsible for the statements appearing in reference to himself. In each case, he has refused to be interviewed and the remarks attributed to him are unfounded." Even so, Kleine sometimes came perilously close to burning his bridges: "There has been a contest between the Edison interests . . . for the Edison licensees and the Kleine Op-

tical Company, for the Independents. The public press as well as developments in the trade indicate how the contest is going. In a word, I would ad-
vise our friends to stand fast, to keep up their courage and to have absolute
faith in the independent movement winning this fight in the end."[54]

By July 1908 Biograph and Kleine had come to terms with Edison, and
Kleine was given a license in December. But it was a bitter victory for him.
In the July agreement Edison allowed Kleine to import five thousand feet a
week for all his manufacturers.[55] Licensed domestic manufacturers, however,
had no limit on the quantity they could produce.[56] But in December Edison
reduced that number and, over Kleine's objections, allowed him to import
only three reels (three thousand feet), two to be supplied by Gaumont and
one by Urban-Eclipse, which represented a significant reduction of revenue.[57]
The MPPC was a marriage of convenience that brought together former rivals who had a long history of mutual animosity. If contemporary publicity
and subsequent histories portrayed the organization as an efficient and happy
household, the pressures of money, continued antitrust litigation, and the
feature film would crack the corporate facade of unity.

Indeed, no issue put as much pressure on the tenuous bonds among
the MPPC members as the emerging market for features. Many of the
manufacturers—notably Lubin, Selig, Vitagraph, and importer Kleine—were
eager to enter this potentially lucrative market. In fact, by 1913 Kleine was
working outside the MPPC system to import Italian features much longer
than the limit imposed by Edison. In order to understand why it was such
an important issue and such a potentially lucrative market, we must first understand the system in place before the feature.

Until the mid-1910s the average nickelodeon exhibitor placed a lot of emphasis on the "variety" that he or she offered the audience. This "variety"
model of programming assumed a particular type of audience and a particular definition of cinema. A "show" consisted usually of three reels, each
of a different type (a western, a comedy, a drama, for example), repeated
throughout the day and changed the next. Patrons could enter and leave
the theater at any time, and with the show lasting only an hour or so, there
was little incentive to hang around. Nickelodeon owners relied on this "transient audience," as Michael Quinn calls it,[58] as both the basis of their programming decisions and as a profit generator. In fact, the average nickelodeon's low prices and small number of seats *required* high turnover in order
to make a profit. In many ways *variety* in this context is just a euphemism for
turnover. Exhibitors were creating an audience that would stop by anytime
and that craved the *experience* of cinema over any particular title. The shift
to a daily program change is a logical step in this direction and a way of increasing turnover (and, hence, profits). When exhibitors later complained
that longer films robbed their audience of the variety it craved, they really
meant that they were being robbed of the turnover they needed.

Furthermore, most nickelodeons had only one projector, so the breaks between reels seemed perfectly natural and allowed for a variety of types of entertainment, such as illustrated song slides. Many exhibitors relished their role as "producers" and resisted the loss of control that features (and the manufacturers who made them) imposed.[59] The variety model fit into a particular aesthetic of unity; a well-made show consisted of different reels with different emotional appeals, supplemented by live performance. It provided the basis for a carefully crafted program, one that conscientious theater owners were reluctant to change. The variety model of programming and the technical limitation of single-projector systems presented serious obstacles to the feature film. Distributors and exhibitors worked around these obstacles at first by splitting up multiple-reel films and showing them on separate weeks. This strategy worked well enough for a while, especially if the films, like, for example, *The Life of Napoleon* (Vitagraph, 1909), were made with this break in mind. But there were problems with advertising; people who had seen the first reel did not come back for the second because they thought they had already seen the film.[60] In fact, the whole system was designed for films of a standard length; anything beyond that length had trouble fitting in. Finding an appropriate day in the release schedule for a feature became a frustrating and troublesome pastime for the manufacturers.

These structural problems were fortified by the average exhibitor's resistance to change, even though the feature represented potentially more money. One-reelers had a very short life span within the distribution system at the time; exhibitors changed their program daily, so films were extremely "perishable." Manufacturers received a fixed amount per foot from the exchanges, around eleven cents per foot for a new release, discounted deeply as it aged.[61] Features, properly marketed and sold as "events," had a longer shelf life and could run for as long as the audiences came to see them. The potential for greater return was enormous compared to the price-per-foot limits under the current system, especially if combined with the economies of scale found in the larger "picture palaces."[62] "Properly marketed" is the key phrase here, however. When we say "feature" today, we mean "forty-five minutes or longer." But at the time, the meaning came from vaudeville, where *feature* connoted an act of greater appeal or importance than the rest of the program. A contemporary list of film trade terms defines *features* succinctly: "These are films of more than ordinary interest, of greater cost, and longer than the ordinary rental subject. Usually a subject of multiple reels."[63] So a feature may have been longer, or it may have had better-than-usual production values, but as Quinn points out, "Features were made special not only through production techniques or high budgets, but by a series of practices in distribution and exhibition which supported the differentiation of any individual feature from all other films."[64] In other words, films in the ordinary nickelodeon program were not differentiated from each other except in the broadest terms, such as name brand. If features could be marketed properly and shoehorned into the present system, film producers stood to make much more than with an ordinary one-reeler. MPPC manufacturers saw this as clearly as Independents, but structural barriers in exhibition and distribution hindered easy exploitation.

One of those problems was the MPPC's own pricing structure. Initially, exhibitors and exchanges were reluctant to accept longer films precisely because they had to pay more (eleven cents per foot for a two-thousand-foot reel rather than eleven cents per foot for a one-thousand-foot reel) without a chance to make more within the present system, which favored the manufacturers. Predictably, the manufacturers would sometimes try to take advantage of the standing-order system (exchanges were required to accept all of the licensed releases, regardless of length or content) by producing longer films, at which the exchanges would rightly balk. One typical exchange in San Francisco complained:

> Before the Film Service Association was in operation, we were getting goods of all makes; we received a great variety of subjects made up of lengths running from 300 to 500 feet, and we were thereby enabled to supply our customers with a variety of subjects, which is what they want. Now the manufacturers seem to aim to put out only lengthy subjects, in consequence of which our customers complain that they do not get the variety they previously did, which they say they must have.[65]

Selig Polyscope, for example, released *Damon and Pythias,* one of the first two-reelers, on 6 June 1908. Although Selig later claimed it as "the first feature,"[66] it was not differentiated at all in the Selig Polyscope catalog or given any special treatment and thus met with strong resistance:

> We were very much surprised yesterday on receipt of your latest film *Damon and Pythias* to find that it was two thousand feet long instead of one thousand feet. We cannot find that you ever advertised this film as being of extra length and we would kindly ask in the future [that you notify us] if the film is going to be of extra length, as it makes quite a difference with us in placing our orders for extra films. As you well know, we ordered extra prints of this film while owing to the fact that it is two thousand feet long instead of one thousand, we could not possibly afford to do. We have decided to keep these prints, however, but feel that we would have been justified in returning same to you. It is impossible for us to secure any more money out of this film than the regular rent owing to the dull condition of the business and considering the state of the film business at the present time it is very hard for us to put about $1000 into one subject, which is the case with *Damon and Pythias* owing to the length of the film.[67]

A June meeting of the FSA resulted in a resolution allowing exchanges to return prints of *Damon and Pythias* with impunity.[68] Selig Polyscope released other "features" in 1908, including *The Holy City* (25 April 1908, sixteen hundred feet) and the *Gans-Nelson Fight* (21 September 1908, four thousand feet), but with the exception of the occasional fight film Selig Polyscope did not make any more multiple-reel films for several years. In 1910 members of the MPPC exchanged letters about the possibility of a "conspiracy" among licensed Chicago exchanges to refuse "specials" altogether.[69] The distribution policy and structure simply could not accommodate them easily without significant change. As Eileen Bowser has noted, "the system that gave stability to the industry was also the system that resisted change."[70]

In 1908 the issue of features, or "specials," was clearly exceptional, but it became one of the more urgent problems confronting the MPPC, especially as it entered the distribution business. Between the emasculation of the FSA in 1909 and the debates about "specials" in 1910, the MPPC had established its own distribution arm, the General Film Company (GFC). Again, the primary reason for this move was to gain greater control for manufacturers. Even after the founding of the MPPC in late 1908 and early 1909, licensed exchanges continued to offer undependable service, to send out worn and damaged prints, and to provide preferential treatment to some theaters. In fact, the single most common complaint from exhibitors was distributor favoritism. The MPPC had assumed that licensed exchanges would divide the market equitably and amiably; unfortunately, capitalism being the pesky arrangement that it is, exchange managers were rather ruthless when competing for films and theaters. If the exchange men owned theaters (they often did), they would funnel the best films to their own houses, leaving the dregs for the rest of their customers.[71]

In an effort to rectify these problems the MPPC cancelled the licenses of dozens of exchanges between 1909 and June 1910. The Trust bought up whatever licensed exchanges were left, thereby creating a licensed distribution system completely under MPPC control, while simultaneously exacerbating the "Independent problem," since those exchanges with cancelled licenses had nowhere else to turn. If they did not sell, their license was promptly cancelled. J.J. Kennedy, the force behind Biograph and the president of the GFC, recalled, "[T]he object [of the General Film Company] was . . . to provide a means whereby the exhibitor could obtain a reliable and impartial supply of motion pictures. The intention was to try this experiment in localities where the abuses were greatest in an effort to help the exhibitor protect himself."[72] Although there is a grain of truth to this claim—distributor favoritism was a pressing issue in the industry—the title of a memo crafted by Kennedy, "Details of a Plan under Which Licensed Manufacturers and Importers Will Take Over the Licensed Rental Business of the United States," hints at the true, monopolistic intentions of the MPPC.[73] The idea that the GFC would work as a "model exchange" for the good of the industry was a mere pretext.

By putting the licensed exchanges directly under its control, the General Film Company did for distribution what the MPPC did for production. It eliminated wasteful competition among licensed exchanges and exhibitors, it regularized the release schedule, it handled film traffic much more efficiently, and it standardized film prices. But this very standardization discouraged quick responses to market pressures; an expensive production cost as much to rent as a cheaply made production, so a manufacturer received the same amount for both, and there was no incentive to improve. Films were rarely held over because they were due elsewhere, so there was no real way to make more money on popular films. The only way manufacturers could earn more was by selling more prints, but the efficient traffic system and schedule created a system where *fewer* prints were needed.[74] "Special" releases put extra pressure on the weak links of the GFC system. Manufacturers wanted a satisfactory return on their investment, which was usually higher for features, but the GFC could not accommodate such exceptions without changing the entire system, which was designed for one-reelers. By June 1910 Selig and Kleine were pleading with the MPPC to come up with a satisfactory policy regarding these "specials." Harry Marvin of Biograph promised them that the MPPC would come up with a "definite agreement" that would allow manufacturers to take advantage of this market.[75] But by October 1910 George F. Scull of Edison Manufacturing came to this position regarding an "aviation film," thus discouraging manufacturer hopes of working within the system: "While we disposed of a considerable number of prints all over the country, which helped to make it worthwhile possibly, from a money-making standpoint, I rather think our experience with this particular picture is such as to make us shy at any such proposition in the future. The amount of trouble and vexation always connected with these special things is not worth the result."[76]

By 1911 exhibitors were failing to renew their licenses yet still showing both licensed and unlicensed films.[77] The Independents by this time were strong enough to present a credible threat; if a license was cancelled, the exhibitor would go to the other side, and the GFC would lose a customer.[78] Independents were making inroads into licensed business; even their distribution companies, such as the Motion Picture Distributing and Sales Company (MPDSA), were modeled on the GFC.[79] Other modes of distribution, such as "states' rights" and road shows, sprang up to counter the reticence of the Sales Company and GFC regarding features. The "states' rights" system allowed a company to buy the exclusive rights to a film for a particular territory and exploit that film in whatever way it wished for as long as it wished: in special venues or ordinary movie houses or on the vaudeville circuit, for example. "Road shows" were modeled after touring stock companies: "numerous companies were sent out on the road with a print of the film, an advance man, a lecture-projectionist, and a manager. Features were shown as special attractions in the local opera houses and town halls and legitimate theaters at advanced prices and stayed for as long as there was enough business to support them."[80] Both of these strategies allowed exhibitors to milk a film until it was dry, something the GFC did not allow. Later in the decade Paramount arranged with its theaters to receive a percentage of a film's gross receipts—rather than a flat fee—which ensured healthy profits on popular films. Charles Musser points out that the "General Film Company's failure to pursue such innovative methods was a major reason for Edison's lack of profitability in the feature area."[81]

If Edison refused to make a timely transition to features,[82] we must not think that other MPPC manufacturers wanted no part of this pie. The members of the MPPC were irrevocably split on this issue, especially in the early 1910s, when features constituted a relatively small part of the market and could be dismissed as a passing fad. Furthermore, the MPPC had made its name and reputation on its "program service" of one-reelers, and many members saw no reason to move away from the "variety model" that so many exhibitors preferred. Generally speaking, Biograph, Essanay, Kleine Optical, Lubin, Selig Polyscope, and Vitagraph favored incorporating longer films, whereas Edison Manufacturing, Méliès, Kalem, and Pathé preferred shorter subjects. (None of them, of course, advocated abandoning shorts altogether.) Edison Manufacturing, especially, did not condone showing imported, unlicensed product (which early features usually were) in licensed theaters because it would eventually cut into the MPPC's profits. It certainly did: in 1911 licensed theaters were regularly showing unlicensed films; by 1913 the licensing agreement was universally disregarded as mixed programs became standard in licensed theaters.[83]

In 1912 Siegmund Lubin complained to Jacques Berst of Pathé (who was also treasurer of the GFC) of the urgent situation:

> Without going into the relative merits of the *quality* of the subjects released, I must point out to you the fact that the theatres which have the big reels and are enabled to advertise their theatre fronts accordingly, are the ones that make money and their competitors cannot remain idle in seeking an adequate program to combat this two-reel proposition.
>
> A great many of the Philadelphia and surrounding territory exhibitors have asked me what relief they might expect, stating frankly that they cannot see their competitors walk away with the crowds. They prefer the licensed pictures and wish to continue using them but they say that when it affects their pocketbooks, they must necessarily seek relief.[84]

Lubin advocated releasing more two- and three-reel subjects; he gladly volunteered one two-reeler a week. The GFC recognized that it had to act. It tested the waters with the release of Selig's three-reel *Coming of Columbus* in May 1912, which was very popular. With this film the GFC set up a "Special

Feature" service for its larger clients—economies of scale in larger theaters allowed greater return on features than was possible in small nickelodeons. It arranged a deal with the manufacturers to accept their multiple-reel films at the standard eleven cents per foot.[85] But there was still a lot to iron out. Lubin was displeased with the GFC's selection process: "Our system for examining multiple reel subjects is fair but I am positively not satisfied with this arrangement. . . . I have sent two multiple reels over for inspection and both were refused. . . . I think it is the duty of the Manufacturers to help me along instead of taking away my ambition to make the double reels."[86]

The larger problem, however, was fitting features into a system designed for one-reelers: the GFC found that changing one element of the system meant changing everything. Jacques Berst threw up his hands in frustration: "The last proposition which was adopted by the Board of Directors, regarding the placing on the market of multiple reels, has been carefully considered by us, and we find that it is not possible to work it out, as this would mean disturbing the booking service of each Branch and changing the booking for every one of our customers."[87] Berst offered another proposition to manufacturers: each exchange would receive "two multiple reel subjects a week (Monday and Friday) and if they find that they have too many reels they will cancel some of the regular reels."[88] This left it up to the exchange men to take what was needed to counter the Independents, but this arrangement was not entirely satisfactory because manufacturers did not receive extra revenues from their extra production costs, especially if their regular reels were cancelled.

To its credit the GFC tried to adjust. By 1913 even Frank Dyer, Edison executive and president of the GFC, could see that features were "the form of entertainment that is apparently developing."[89] So he outlined a plan to divide GFC service into four parts: "Regular" service would provide thirty one-reelers and six two-reelers a week; "Special Exclusive" offered eight one-reelers and two two-reelers; "Feature Films" service presented a feature of four to five reels every week or biweekly; and "Masterpieces" offered a feature of six to ten reels a few times a year. By offering different levels of service, the GFC hoped to accommodate the needs of different exhibitors (small and large), while permitting added revenue from a relatively fixed number of customers. This plan even included leasing films to larger theaters on a percentage basis, a lesson learned from the success of Kleine's import *Quo Vadis?* (Cines, Italy, 1913).[90] So once the writing was on the wall (and it spelled "Paramount," which offered an all-feature service), the GFC took up features fairly quickly.

But the problem, and the reason that the GFC continually lost money on its feature service, can be found in the booking and pricing structure that the GFC and the members of the MPPC tenaciously maintained. Dyer's percentage plan was never put in place, and the GFC sold its features the same way it sold its regular service of one-reelers—as a package at a certain price per level of service. So even if a film did well on the feature market, the GFC and the manufacturer would not see the extra profits except as demand for more prints. Albert Smith of Vitagraph complained, "We released eight feature pictures through General Film. Some were very good, but none made any money. General Film's method of handling was the reason for the loss in almost every instance."[91] George Kleine argued in 1914, "I think there is only one hope for the special feature department of General Film Co. and that is to separate it entirely from the regular service and let it enter the competition if it must. It can only prosper if handled alone and on its merits, considering the competition of Paramount, Alco, Warner, etc. There is every indication that these people are making progress."[92] Still committed to the "service" model, the GFC was simply not grabbing the profits from its feature service that other distribution systems were able to pull down.

And as late as 1917 Kleine, acting as president of the GFC, outlined a plan to "improve the condition of the General Film Company," in which he pleaded with the members to stop offering features at "service" prices:

> A radical change needs to be made in the method of booking and charging to the customer. I consider that the unsatisfactory nature of business at the present time is due to our persistence in booking service, a method efficient and satisfactory when exhibitors took their entire service from our exchange, but is no longer profitable when the average exhibitor is renting of us say 12 reels weekly and our average output is 28 reels. This condition permits the exhibitor to pick out his films at cheap service price. . . . Our figures prove inevitably that the service system reduces the price of the valuable film instead of elevating the less desirable. . . . [E]xhibitors are picking preferred subjects out of our weekly assortment . . . [and] our business is practically changed from a service to a feature basis, while our charges continue as under the service plan.[93]

So why *didn't* they institute a percentage plan or some other pricing and booking arrangement that would allow them to reap the profits from features as their competitors did? First, the service plan had always worked for them in the past. Their core customer was the small-time exhibitor committed to a variety model of one-reelers and the occasional feature. If Kleine had good reasons in 1917 to prompt a change in pricing, in 1913 no such compelling reason existed, given that features constituted only 4 percent of the market.

But there was another reason for their immobility on this issue: mistrust. None of the manufacturers wanted to give an edge to any of the others, so they were always at an impasse with regard to pricing. Frank Dyer, who also often complained of "the total lack of flexibility in the method of doing business by the General Film Co.," blamed dissension and the members' mutual mistrust:

> At the present time each manufacturer always looks out for his own interests, and never for the general interests of the Company. Whenever anything is pro-

posed, each manufacturer only considers it from his own narrow viewpoint. Each manufacturer is afraid that some of his associates are getting some special advantages. As a result of this situation, we have never been able to agree upon any plan by which films could be sold on merit and as a result a remarkably good film sells but little better than a poor one. A manufacturer can benefit himself only by making his average high. . . . Everyone admits that in merit the licensed pictures are far ahead of the Independent pictures, but because of the stupid and unscientific restrictions which are placed on the General Film Co. by the manufacturers, the situation apparently cannot be helped.[94]

This mistrust was not entirely unfounded. In the same 1912 memo to Edison, regarding a plan to reorganize the GFC, Dyer tipped his hand:

Another fact has just developed which will increase our difficulties. The several manufacturers [—] as directors of General Film Co. [—] now know the purchases for the last year. . . . These figures will certainly be disturbing. They show, for example, that the Biograph Co., with only two reels per week, sold practically as much as the Selig Co. with four reels; that the Biograph and Edison Companies, with a combined output of six reels sold more than 40% more than Kalem. . . . Of course I recognize that many of the manufacturers, including ourselves, increased the number of reels per week during the past year, but I doubt if the licensees take this into account. They think very superficially, and each one had an idea that he was doing better than the others. Now that they know the amount of the footage, they will not believe that any differences depend upon the popularity of their pictures but will assume that the Biograph and Edison Companies were specially favored because of their close affiliations with the Patents Company.[95]

Even if Edison and Biograph films were more popular, rest assured that, "superficial thinkers" they might have been, the other manufacturers knew very well which of them were "specially favored."

In a sense the members of the MPPC were trapped by their own pact. If they allowed films to be priced according to merit, popularity, or production cost, then by definition some members would do better than others. Although they considered the MPPC a marriage of convenience and nothing else, manufacturers were not willing to change the system for the good of the whole if such changes risked a loss of revenue for the individual firm. Who would allow themselves to be the patsy? If the films were priced according to merit, for example, who would decide which films merited higher prices? Furthermore, Dyer warned,

At the present time the Licensed manufacturers are practically assured of their fair share of the licensed business at a fair price for all. . . . Now if we are not very careful in reorganizing the Film Co.—if we take away from any particular licensed manufacturer the practical certainty that he will have a voice in the control of the Film Co.—if we take away the practical certainty he now has of getting his fair share of the business—and if we supplement licensed films by the purchase of Independent films so as to thereby curtail the demand for the licensed films, is there not danger that the respect for the Patents Co. will be lost?[96]

In other words, rather than risk a change in the system that would put them at the mercy of their partners or jeopardize the integrity of the MPPC brand name, they settled for their "fair share." So they could not agree on changes and maintained the status quo.

The danger that "the respect for the Patents Co. will be lost" was real. The expiration of the patents and the antitrust suit encouraged theaters to mix licensed and unlicensed film, which would eventually cut into MPPC revenues. Even within the MPPC this respect was tenuous, as several manufacturers decided to distribute their features outside of the GFC. Pathé quit the GFC to distribute its own product in 1914. Kleine distributed his imported features through his own system of exchanges. Selig Polyscope released two 1914 features through the GFC (*The Royal Box,* four reels, and *In the Days of the Thundering Herd,* five reels) but looked elsewhere to release two longer 1914 films, *The Spoilers* (nine reels) through "states' rights" and *Your Girl and Mine: A Woman Suffrage Play* (eight reels) through a major competitor, World Film Corp. Whether the GFC rejected these longer films for length or quality, or Selig hoped for greater profit from outside the MPPC system, both ways worked against the GFC in the long run. In 1915 Vitagraph, Lubin, Selig, and Essanay teamed up to distribute their features through their own company, V-L-S-E. This company did well enough in the first year to prompt Vitagraph to buy out the interests of the other companies. Essanay and Selig joined Kleine-Edison Film Service to distribute features through K-E-S-E in 1916.

There was a hint of desperation in the formation of V-L-S-E in 1915, which was a pivotal year for the MPPC and the GFC. Although most histories note this year because of the antitrust decision against the MPPC, the decree meant very little in terms of actual business practice. Basically, it demanded that the MPPC cease its licensing system, which it had already done in September 1913. The GFC lawyer was blunt:

> The decree in terms was as harmless and unobjectionable as it was possible for it to be, since it did not require the dissolution of the General Film Company, as had been seriously feared might be decreed, or require any other radical changes in the business of any of the defendants, except the abandonment of the licensing system, which, as a matter of fact, had already been abandoned for a substantial period of time.[97]

However, the decree did serve as prima facie evidence for treble-damage suits, which only hastened the demise of some manufacturers who were vulnerable.[98]

More damaging was the loss of revenue resulting from the precipitous decline in the demand for short films. In 1915 exhibitors and exchanges were canceling standing orders left and right.[99] According to Ben Singer the demand for shorts was off by 37 percent in 1916, 50 percent in 1917, and 57 percent in 1918, by which time the variety model was effectively dead.[100] If that wasn't bad enough, the loss of license royalties since 1914 had decimated profits, and the loss of the European market because of World War I hurt the MPPC much more than it hurt the Independents.[101] The attempt to switch to features and market them through V-L-S-E and other such mechanisms seems a severely hampered, last-ditch effort, since many of the MPPC stars and talent had been plundered by Independent firms.

The General Film Company continued to market shorts and features through 1919 but had been hemorrhaging cash badly since 1915. Those members still involved in the company (Edison, for one, got out as soon as he could) were actually propping it up, not only because of their investment in the company but also because of a number of stockholder suits against the GFC, demanding refunds to stockholders of large sums that had been distributed to manufacturers as profits. The appearance of stability helped maintain the stock price and forestall more suits of the same type. George Spoor of Essanay was pumping as much as four thousand dollars per week into the GFC to help keep it alive.[102] Transfusions of this sort only drained the donors, and the fiscal conservatism of the MPPC prevented them from accepting financing from Wall Street, which was eagerly funding the Independents.[103]

There were any number of reasons, then, for the demise of the MPPC, but it seems that most of the cracks were visible with the very formation of the company. On the distribution side the friction that generated the Independent movement came from within the FSA as a result of the MPPC's own (antagonistic) policies, even though those very policies helped to regularize an industry in disarray. In exhibition the MPPC's inability to enforce its licensed-film-only policy and the divided sentiments of the exhibitors toward features led to mixed programs in licensed theaters: shorts from the GFC, features usually from elsewhere. This eventually worked against the GFC and the manufacturers, especially with the decline in demand for shorts. Finally, the members of the MPPC, other than Edison and Biograph, did not feel beholden to the organization, except as a sanctuary against Edison's litigiousness. They would consistently put their own interests ahead of the group's and would actively work against it when it suited them. When we think of "the MPPC," we tend to picture it as a company with a single goal and voice, but it is best to think of it as an uneasy alliance of businessmen, some of whom joined out of a sense of self-preservation and would ignore the coalition for exactly the same reason. Once together, however, they could not work effectively as a group, and they eventually fell, a house divided.

NOTES

My thanks to Charlie Keil and Shelley Stamp for their finite patience and to Charlie and Ben Singer for their astute comments on an earlier draft.

1. See Ben Singer, "Feature Films, Variety Programs, and the Crisis of the Small Exhibitor," in this volume. My thanks to Ben for making a draft of his essay available to me. For statistics on 1914 see Eileen Bowser, *The Transformation of Cinema, 1907–1915* (New York: Macmillan, 1990), 213.

2. See Ralph Cassady Jr., "Monopoly in Motion Picture Production and Distribution: 1908–1915," in *The American Movie Industry,* ed. Gorham Kindem (Carbondale: Southern Illinois University Press, 1982), 62 (originally published in *Southern California Law Review* 32 [1959]); Janet Staiger, "Combination and Litigation: Structures of U.S. Film Distribution, 1896–1917," *Cinema Journal* 23, no. 2 (winter 1983): 60; and Bowser, *Transformation of Cinema,* 215.

3. Terry Ramsaye, *A Million and One Nights: A History of the Motion Picture through 1925* (New York: Simon and Schuster, 1926); Benjamin Hampton, *History of the American Film Industry from Its Beginnings to 1931* (1931; repr., New York: Dover, 1970); Lewis Jacobs, *The Rise of the American Film Industry* (1939; repr., New York: Teachers College Press, 1968).

4. Carl Laemmle, "Doom of Long Features Predicted," *Moving Picture World,* 11 July 1914, 185.

5. "Disapprove of Long Reels: Movies Exhibitors Decide to Reduce Unit to 500 Feet," *New York Times,* 12 June 1914, 13; see also Bowser, *Transformation of Cinema,* 214.

6. Robert Anderson, "The Motion Picture Patents Company" (Ph.D. diss., University of Wisconsin, 1983) (hereafter cited as Anderson, "MPPC"); see also Anderson, "The Motion Picture Patents Company: A Reevaluation," in *The American Film Industry,* rev. ed., ed. Tino Balio (Madison: University of Wisconsin Press, 1985), 133–52 (hereafter cited as Anderson, "Reevaluation"); Michael Quinn, "Early Feature Distribution and the Development of the Motion Picture Industry: Famous Players and Paramount, 1912–1921" (Ph.D. diss., University of Wisconsin, 1998); Staiger, "Combination and Litigation"; and Bowser, *Transformation of Cinema.* Other valuable tellings of the tale are Jeanne Thomas, "The Decay of the Motion Picture Patents Company," *Cinema Journal* 10, no. 2 (spring 1971): 34–40; Charles Musser, *Before the Nickelodeon: Edwin S. Porter and the Edison Manufacturing Company* (Berkeley: University of California Press, 1991); Tom Gunning, *D. W. Griffith and the Origins of the American Narrative Film* (Urbana: University of Illinois Press, 1991); and Charlie Keil, "Advertising Independence: Industrial Performance and Advertising Strategies of the Independent Movement, 1909–1910," *Film History* 5, no. 4 (1993): 472–88.

7. For a relatively contemporary overview of the MPPC's decline that stresses the internal conflicts see "How the 'Film Trust' Lost Its Hold," *Variety,* 31 December 1920, 4, 37; see also Anderson, "MPPC" and "Reevaluation"; and Bowser, *Transformation of Cinema.*

8. Anderson, "MPPC," 252.

9. "Moving Picture Men Hit," *New York Times,* 9 March 1907, 2.

10. Anderson, "Reevaluation," 135.

11. For a history of the struggle between American and such foreign manufac-

turers as Pathé see Richard Abel, *The Red Rooster Scare: Making Cinema American, 1900–1910* (Berkeley: University of California Press, 1999).

12. Musser, *Before the Nickelodeon*, 335–36, 375.

13. Anderson, "Reevaluation," 135; Kleine, both an importer and—as a founder of Kalem Company—a producer, was willing to work with the Edison group early on and acted as a liaison between Edison Manufacturing and the other firms. One suggestion from Kleine for the terms of the license agreement—"foreign films to be included"—indicates that he was hoping his importing company would be a part of the agreement. See letter dated 11 May 1907 from George Kleine to Mr. Pelzer, Edison Mfg. Co., folder 467, William N. Selig Collection, Margaret Herrick Library, Academy of Motion Picture Arts and Sciences, Beverly Hills, California (hereafter cited as "Selig Collection").

14. "The United Film Service Association and the Film Manufacturers," *Moving Picture World*, 15 February 1908, 111.

15. Musser, *Before the Nickelodeon*, 377.

16. "United Film Service Protective Association: Official Notice," *Moving Picture World*, 23 November 1907, 608.

17. Ibid., 609.

18. *Moving Picture World*, 15 February 1908, 111–12.

19. Anderson, "MPPC," 83–85.

20. "The Combine and Its Policy," *Moving Picture World*, 16 January 1909, 57.

21. Musser, *Before the Nickelodeon*, 381.

22. Anderson, "MPPC," 88.

23. James B. Clark of Pittsburgh Light and Calcium was elected president in January 1908. The other official of the FSA in 1907, D. MacDonald, later became general manager of the MPPC—not to say that anybody was in anyone's pocket or anything.

24. Musser, *Before the Nickelodeon*, 382.

25. James B. Clark to Selig, 11 and 23 September 1908, f. 459, Selig Collection.

26. See letter of complaint from H. H. Buckwalter, Denver Film Exchange, to William N. Selig, 12 August 1908, f. 458, Selig Collection.

27. Ibid.

28. William H. Swanson to H. H. Buckwalter, 22 August 1908, f. 460, Selig Collection. The exchange of letters among Buckwalter, Selig, and Swanson indicates that Buckwalter "tattled" to Selig on Swanson, who sent a somewhat contrite letter of explanation to Buckwalter.

29. *United States v. Motion Picture Patents Co.*, 225 F. 800 (District Court, E.D. Pa., 1915), quoted in Anderson, "MPPC," 90.

30. "Daily Changes of Films," *New York Dramatic Mirror*, 13 March 1909, 16.

31. Anderson, "MPPC," 91. Anderson also suggests that the MPPC's later decision to refuse stock to exchange men, excluding them from any substantial percentage of gross profits, contributed to their lasting resentment (see Anderson, "MPPC," 171).

32. Selig to P. L. Waters, Kinetograph Company, 8 September 1908, f. 459, Selig Collection. According to Musser, *Before the Nickelodeon*, 328, Selig financed Swanson's first exchange in 1906.

33. Selig to James B. Clark, 25 September 1908, f. 459, Selig Collection.

34. Musser, *Before the Nickelodeon*, 434.

35. Ibid., 444.

36. Quinn, "Early Feature Distribution," 52.

37. Carl Laemmle to Exhibitors, 5 February 1909, f. 459, Selig Collection.

38. Compare list of FSA members in *Moving Picture World,* 25 April 1908, 378, to list of licensed exchanges, *Moving Picture World,* 23 January 1909, 92.

39. Musser, *Before the Nickelodeon,* 328.

40. Ibid., 379–80.

41. Cassady, "Monopoly in Motion Picture Production," 50. Cassady does not cite the survey.

42. "Independents Meet in Chicago to Organize Response," *Moving Picture World,* 30 January 1909, 109.

43. Chicago Film Exchange to Exhibitors, 18 January 1909, Edison National Historic Site, West Orange, N.J.; quoted in Musser, *Before the Nickelodeon,* 443.

44. Cassady, "Monopoly in Motion Picture Production," 380n72.

45. Anderson, "MPPC," 284. Thomas Armat received one-sixth for his patent holdings.

46. Anderson, "Reevaluation," 149.

47. William Selig to George Kleine, 31 December 1913, William N. Selig (Selig Polyscope Company): General, 1911–30, Box 52, George F. Kleine Collection, Manuscripts Division, Library of Congress, Washington, D.C. (hereafter cited as "Kleine Collection"). It is perhaps only fair to indicate that Selig complained of *everything* with equal vehemence.

48. Musser, *Before the Nickelodeon,* 379.

49. That Kleine orchestrated the agreement between Edison and the other firms is evident from the correspondence between Kleine and William Gilmore, general manager of Edison Manufacturing, 5 May 1907, and, further, Edison Manufacturing, 1902–1908, Box 18, Kleine Collection.

50. Musser, *Before the Nickelodeon,* 278–79.

51. Musser, *Before the Nickelodeon,* 376–77; Bowser, *Transformation of Cinema,* 24–25.

52. Bowser, *Transformation of Cinema,* 23–26; Abel, *Red Rooster Scare,* 87–94.

53. Anderson, "Reevaluation," 136.

54. "Statement by Mr. Geo. Kleine," *Moving Picture World,* 14 March 1908, 205–6.

55. Musser, *Before the Nickelodeon,* 434.

56. Ibid., 440.

57. Ibid., 438.

58. Quinn, "Early Feature Distribution," 49. This paragraph is indebted to Quinn's interpretation.

59. For a history of the exhibitor's creative role see Charles Musser, *The Emergence of Cinema: The American Screen to 1907* (New York: Macmillan, 1990).

60. Bowser, *Transformation of Cinema,* 198.

61. The FSA instituted release-day pricing in July 1908; see Bowser, *Transformation of Cinema,* 28. Of course, these films were leased, not purchased outright.

62. For an excellent discussion of the small exhibitor's dilemmas see Ben Singer's article in this volume.

63. "Definition of Trade Terms," undated (probably c. 1914), General Film Co., Box 24, Kleine Collection.

64. Quinn, "Early Feature Distribution," 68.

65. Novelty Moving Picture Company to Selig Polyscope, 27 April 1908, f. 459, Selig Collection (grammar and punctuation corrected for readability).

66. Interview with Louella Parsons, 24 September 1916, f. 47, Selig Collection. Excerpt: "Did you ever know that I made the first feature film?" he asked. "On June 22, 1908, we produced 'Damon and Pythias.' It went big, and when I saw that the public was ready for features 'The Coming of Columbus' suggested itself to me as being something the great American public would like to see on the screen."

67. James. B. Clark to Selig Polyscope, 25 June 1908, f. 459, Selig Collection. In the same folder see also letters of complaint from William Steiner, Imperial Film Exchange, Troy, New York, undated (received 29 June 1908), and from the Novelty Moving Picture Company, San Francisco, 30 June 1908. Clark's figure of one thousand dollars for this film makes sense only if we consider that he leased several copies.

68. W. J. Watkins to Selig Polyscope, 29 June 1908, Charles G. Clarke Scrapbooks #2 of 3, p. 77, Margaret Herrick Library, Academy of Motion Picture Arts and Sciences, Beverly Hills, California.

69. George Kleine to George F. Scull (Edison Mfg.), 28 October 1910, Historical file: Motion Picture Patents Co., 1909–13, Box 26, Kleine Collection. See also complaints about scheduling in the Selig Collection: William T. Rock (American Vitagraph) to Selig Polyscope, 7 March 1908, f. 460; and Novelty Moving Picture Company, San Francisco to Selig Polyscope, 30 June 1908, f. 459.

70. Bowser, *Transformation of Cinema*, 192.

71. See "Uncover the Crooks," *Nickelodeon*, 1 March 1910, 115–16; and *United States v. Motion Picture Patents Co.*, 225 F. 800 (District Court, E.D. Pa., 1915), quoted in Anderson, "MPPC," 219, 223.

72. Jeremiah J. Kennedy, Record, vol. 6, 3161–3162, *United States v. Motion Picture Patents Co.*, 225 F. 800 (District Court, E.D. Pa., 1915), quoted in Cassady, "Monopoly in Motion Picture Production," 45.

73. Jeremiah J. Kennedy, "Details of a Plan under Which Licensed Manufacturers and Importers Will Take Over the Licensed Rental Business of the United States," undated [probably 1909], Historical file: Distribution, 1908–10, Box 26, Kleine Collection.

74. Bowser, *Transformation of Cinema*, 84.

75. H. N. Marvin, New York, to George Kleine, 16 June 1910, Historical file: Motion Picture Patents Co., 1909–13, Box 26, Kleine Collection:

> The questions raised by you are certainly somewhat intricate, and the position into which Mr. Selig has been forced is certainly unpleasant, and I regret very much the feeling that has been aroused. These special pictures have from time to time aroused more or less comment and controversy, and I hope that at the meeting of the Manufacturers next week it will be possible to arrive at a satisfactory solution of Mr. Selig's difficulty and reach a definite agreement about these special films.

76. George Scull to George Kleine, 1 November 1910, Historical file: Motion Picture Patents Co., 1909–13, Box 26, Kleine Collection.

77. Bowser, *Transformation of Cinema*, 84.

78. Even after the formation of the GFC the MPPC had trouble controlling its own exchanges. On the rather imperious and cavalier attitude GFC branch managers

had toward their customers, who often went Independent as a result of this antago-
nism, see Frank L. Hough Jr.'s report of such complaints to Frank Dyer, 12 December 1911, General Film Company: Records (1909–11), Motion Picture Patents Company Papers, Company Records Series, Thomas A. Edison Papers, Edison National
Historic Site, West Orange, N.J. (hereafter cited as "ENHS").

79. For similarities in tactics and structure between the MPPC and the Independents see Staiger, "Combination and Litigation"; and Keil, "Advertising Independence."

80. Bowser, *Transformation of Cinema,* 192.

81. Musser, *Before the Nickelodeon,* 472.

82. Ibid., 471.

83. Anderson, "MPPC," 253.

84. S. Lubin to J. A. Berst, 1 October 1912, Historical file: Motion Picture Patents
Co., 1909–13, Box 26, Kleine Collection (emphasis in original).

85. Telegram from General Film Company to George Kleine, 21 September 1912,
Historical file: Motion Picture Patents Co., 1909–13, Box 26, Kleine Collection. See
also Kleine's reply accepting the terms, dated 21 September 1912, in the same folder.

86. S. Lubin to Selig, 3 July 1912, f. 471, Selig Collection.

87. J. A. Berst, General Film Company to George Kleine, 21 October 1912, Historical file: Motion Picture Patents Co., 1909–13, Box 26, Kleine Collection.

88. Ibid.

89. *United States v. Motion Picture Patents Co.,* 225 F. 800 (District Court, E.D. Pa.,
1915) quoted in Anderson, "MPPC," 253.

90. Frank L. Dyer to Kleine, 24 June 1913, Historical file: Motion Picture Patents
Co., 1909–13, Box 26, Kleine Collection. See also *Moving Picture World,* 11 October
1913, 139; *Moving Picture World,* 25 October 1913, 385; and *Moving Picture World,* 13
December 1913, 1266.

91. Albert E. Smith and Phil Koury, *Two Reels and a Crank* (Garden City, N.Y.:
Doubleday, 1952), 259, quoted in Cassady, "Monopoly in Motion Picture Production,"
59.

92. Kleine to J. A. Berst, 2 October 1914, General Film Company, 1912–17, Box
24, Kleine Collection.

93. George Kleine, "A Plan Suggested to Improve the Condition of the General
Film Company" [1917], Distribution: Plans, Methods, and Improvements, 1917, Box
12, Kleine Collection.

94. Frank Dyer to Thomas Edison, 17 April 1912, General Film Company: Records (1912), ENHS.

95. Ibid.

96. Ibid.

97. W. M. Seabury, "Annual Report of Legal Matters Affecting General Film Company," 25 June 1918, 5, MPPC Litigation: Annual Summary of Litigation, 1918, Box
36, Kleine Collection.

98. Staiger, "Combination and Litigation," 62.

99. For a representative set of complaints see Leonard McChesney to Carl H. Wilson (then president of GFC), 5 January 1915, General Film Company: Records (1913–
15), ENHS.

100. See Singer in this volume.

101. Anderson, "Reevaluation," 150.

102. See Carl H. Wilson to Thomas A. Edison, 25 October 1916, General Film Company: Records (1916), ENHS; and George Kleine to Carl Wilson, 23 June 1917, General Film Company: Records (1917), ENHS.

103. Anderson, "Reevaluation," 150.

CHAPTER ELEVEN

Not Harmless Entertainment

State Censorship and Cinema in the Transitional Era

Lee Grieveson

In early 1915, when *The Birth of a Nation* (Epoch, 1915) played the city opera house in Lexington, Ky., Lexington police officers were directed by the commissioner of public safety to sit among the audience to control "demonstrations" and "enthusiastic outbursts," marking a curious conjuncture of film, highbrow culture, and state authority.[1] Likewise, police in Boston sought to prevent black people from buying tickets to the film when it played the Tremont Theater, although the concern there was less about the audience's enthusiasm than about their anger at the film's racism and was consistent with a broader policing of racially bifurcated public space.[2] Inside, Pinkerton detectives were scattered throughout the auditorium to stop demonstrations against the film like those that had taken place when the film was shown in the Liberty Theater in New York City. Protestors had thrown eggs at the Liberty's screen at the moment when a black man was shown chasing a young white woman with the intention of raping her.[3] In other locations the governmental policing of the film and of audiences led to the banning of the film. Local censor boards, councils, or mayors refused to allow it to be seen in cities like Cleveland, Ohio; Wilmington, Del.; St. Louis, Mo.; Topeka, Kans.; Louisville, Ky.; and San Antonio, Tex.[4] Likewise, the film was at least initially banned by statewide authorities in Illinois, Michigan, Kansas, and Ohio.[5] Ohio censors rejected the film in accordance with the remit of the state censor board established in 1913 that had granted the board authority to pass films of a "moral, educational or amusing and harmless character" and to ban films that were "sacrilegious, obscene, indecent or immoral."[6] The film was, they said, "not harmless."[7] Epoch appealed but the board restated its opinion that the film "was harmful and not of a harmless character."[8]

Local and state boards banned *The Birth of a Nation* in line principally with public nuisance and public disorder legislation, registering concerns about the responses of both black and white audiences and, more broadly, about the policing of vulnerable *and* potentially dangerous audiences as seen so vividly in Lexington, Boston, and New York City. Integral to the regulation of cinema and audiences was the rendering of the potentially *harmful* cinema *harmless,* a transition that I take to be one of the most important of the transitional era. Important to this transition, no doubt, was the censorship of content like the incendiary images of race hatred visible in *The Birth of a Nation* and also the shaping of filmic discourse into a narrative discourse intertwined with prevailing standards of morality.[9] Even more substantively, though, regulatory discourses, practices, and institutions in this period were linked to important debates about the *social functioning* of cinema—debates about how cinema should function in society, the uses to which it might be put, and thus effectively about what it could or would be. Here the issues revolved principally around conceptions of the cultural functions and relative weighting of "entertainment" and "education," issues played out frequently through discussions about narrative but also about the merits of fiction, nonfiction, indexicality, and "realism." Was it possible for cinema to represent issues of broader political import? Was cinema simply a commercial entertainment medium? Could cinema be a part of a public sphere of political debate, or was it to be configured differently?

Located in this context, *The Birth of a Nation* can stand as a useful starting point for an account of these debates about the function of cinema and their effects on censorship practices. The film was made to coincide with the fifty-year anniversary of the Civil War and was positioned by its producers and supporters as an intervention into broader public debates about the nation's history and about race and the necessity of racial hierarchies. It was widely praised by many precisely for this public intervention. Vice crusader the Reverend Dr. Charles Parkhurst wrote, "This drama is a telling illustration of the possibilities of motion pictures as an instrument of history," and the National Board of Censorship, a self-regulatory censorship body, passed the film with minor cuts because of its "historic significance."[10] Likewise, the film's director, D. W. Griffith, asserted that the film was true in its historical detail, and he backed this up by offering to pay the president of the National Association for the Advancement of Colored People ten thousand dollars if he could find a single historical inaccuracy in the film.[11] Later, after the controversy over the film, Griffith privately published a pamphlet called *The Rise and Fall of Free Speech,* in which he argued that film as "the pictorial press" deserved the constitutional guarantees of free speech enshrined in the First Amendment and in state constitutions (figure 11.1). If people "muzzle the 'movies,'" Griffith wrote, they will "defeat the educational purpose of this graphic art," for "[c]ensorship demands of the picture makers a sugar-coated and false version of life's truths." The central contention here was that film could make

Figure 11.1. Graphic from D. W. Griffith's *The Rise and Fall of Free Speech* (1915).

visible the "truths of history" or contemporary social problems "while at the same time bringing diversion to the masses."[12] Many people of different political persuasions argued for a similar sense of cinema's potential role in the public sphere.

Even so, state attention in the early 1910s to a series of controversial films about "white slavery," contraception, venereal disease, and labor/capital and race problems suggested that such a stance on the social role of cinema was increasingly contested.[13] Concerns about the potential effects of films on public order and on audiences made up of what was widely seen as the "light-minded" of the "lower middle classes" led many to argue for the necessity of a separation of the referential and the entertaining dimensions of cinema and hence the drawing of a distinction between mainstream cinema as a purveyor of "harmless" entertainment and the social role of the press.[14] Looked at in this way, then, the response of the municipal and state boards in banning *The Birth of a Nation*—and, as we will see, other films—was less a judgment simply of individual films than of the possible social role of cinema and its place in the public sphere, that common space in which members of society meet through a variety of media and discuss matters of common interest.

Legal decisions further mandated the gathering sense of the correct social functioning of cinema, culminating in a crucial Supreme Court decision in early 1915 on the validity of state censorship that was binding on the legal system throughout the nation. Legislating the legal status and function of cinema, the decision also insisted on the necessity of a split between the referential and pleasurable or entertaining functions of cinema. Even though the Supreme Court justices seemed to like *The Birth of a Nation* when it was screened specially for them—apparently the chief justice had been a former Klan member—the decision they rendered effectively disallowed the conception of the function of cinema that Griffith shared with many others.[15] Cinema was now to be conceived of as a business with a public role distinct from that of the press, becoming the only medium of communication in the history of the United States subject to legal prior restraint.

Legal discourse is, as Pierre Bourdieu has observed, peculiarly performative discourse.[16] Legal decisions thus enabled additional state intervention, effectively narrowing the definition of the function of cinema further by validating the stance that defined cinema as harmless entertainment to remove it from the contentious sphere of the political. Accordingly, what follows considers the formation and operation of municipal and state censor boards in the transitional era, before shifting to an account of the legal decisions following the censor board directives that reached the federal level in the Supreme Court and that had considerable effect on the shaping of cinema thereafter. Such an examination will allow me to attend to a crucial but underexplored dynamic in the transition to classicism, supplementing important work on the interrelation of the mode of production and representation with attention to the mode of regulation. This entails shifting attention away from the formal developments important in the transitional era toward an account of the establishment of a set of distinctions and definitions that were critical to the establishment of the discursive formation of mainstream cinema.

"LIMITED MEANS"

Late in 1907 a police censor board was established in Chicago, emerging as the first functioning censor board in the United States and paving the way for the plethora of municipal and later state boards that followed. The board was established after a number of reports were undertaken and published on the new phenomenon of nickelodeons that were in turn followed by a series of public discussions in the city about moving pictures and nickelodeons, including a "crusade" against them by the *Chicago Tribune*.[17] In the midst of these debates, an ordinance was proposed to the Chicago City Council that would require police censorship of all films to be shown in the city. It was initially regarded as an unusual extension of regulatory powers. "The question involved in this ordinance is a novel one," Assistant Corporation Counsel Cassels wrote to the proposer, Alderman Uhlir, for the ordinance "is in advance of the usual legislation regulating and controlling places of amusement"; and work on the police power of the states suggested that it "may be regarded as prohibited by the spirit of the Constitution."[18] Cassels, though, proceeded to downplay this potential constitutional problem by suggesting that "amusements" could not be protected on free speech grounds and furthermore by pointing to preexisting legislation that allowed the city council "[t]o license, tax, regulate, suppress and prohibit" amusements. Nickelodeons could, it was argued, be inscribed into these preexisting regulatory powers because they could be defined as "amusements," and moving pictures could thus not claim the protection of the free speech guarantees of the First Amendment and state constitutions.

Clearly this stance on the legal definition of the nascent cinema was widely supported, for the bill was voted on and overwhelmingly passed on 4 November 1907. A board of censors drawn from the police force was set up to view all films to be shown in the city and to prevent "the exhibition of obscene and immoral films . . . of the class commonly shown in mutoscopes, kinetoscopes, cinematographs and penny arcades."[19] Exhibitors or film exchanges had now to submit an application for a permit to screen a film for exhibition and then send a copy of the film to the police board of censors to be screened. A number of other municipal boards emerged from this moment, including ones initially in Detroit, Mich.; Cleveland, Ohio; Butte, Mon.; and later in the 1910s and early 1920s in Lexington, Ky.; San Francisco, Calif.; Kansas City, Mo.; Portland, Ore.; Seattle, Wash.; Dallas and Gainesville, Tex.; Pasadena and Palo Alto, Calif.; Camden, N.J.; and others.[20]

Extant records suggest the Chicago board focused particularly on films suggesting or representing sexual impropriety and/or political corruption. Exhibitors or distributors seeking a permit for the film *She Never Knew* (Buffalo, 1916), for example, were told to "transfer marriage ceremony to scene before showing baby."[21] Likewise, *Sapho* (Majestic, 1913) was rejected because it included "immoral scenes and adultery"; *Satan's Pawn* (1915) was rejected "because it features a wife's infidelity"; *Forbidden Fruit* (Ivan, 1916) was banned because it showed an illegitimate child; and a host of films showing white slavery were banned, including *Smashing the Vice Trust* (Progress Film Co., 1914), *The Eagle* (Universal, 1915), *Nobody Would Believe* (1915), *The Heart of New York* (Claridge, 1915), *The Bridesmaid's Secret* (Essanay, 1916), *It May Be Your Daughter* (Moral Uplift Society, 1916), and *Protect Your Daughter* (All Star, 1918).[22] Late in 1914 a film called *Forcing the Force* (Eclectic, 1914) was rejected "because of its slur on the police force" in the form of a story about how an "entire police force made love to two lady policewomen and neglect [sic] their duties," showing a concern again about sexuality but also now about the representation of the police that was not surprising for a board made up of police officers.[23] Further visible in relation to a host of other films that reflected poorly on the police, like *The Cooked Goose* (Thanhouser, 1914), *The Gilded Kid* (Edison, 1914), *The Hostage* (Lasky, 1914), and *Some Cop* (Crystal, 1914), the actions of the board segued into broader political concerns and interventions. Significant also was the excision of scenes of miners "rioting" from *The Mainspring* (Falcon, 1917), the excessive regulation of the films of the black filmmaker Oscar Micheaux, and the banning of a number of films representing the then European conflict in 1914 and 1915.[24] In these interventions the board made important judgments on the possible public role of cinema, particularly evident in relation to films that touched on questions of sexuality like the white slave films or on controversial themes of race and political corruption.

Late in 1908 a legal case sought to work out the constitutionality of the police censor board and in doing so drew questions of morality and political import together with those of public role and social function. Exhibitor Jake Block had been denied a permit for two films, *The James Boys in Missouri* (Essanay, 1908) and *Night Riders* (Kalem, 1908), and had appealed the decision to the Illinois Supreme Court. Lawyers working for Block argued that the censorship ordinance discriminated against the exhibitors of moving pictures, making a distinction between moving pictures and other forms of commercialized amusements. In particular they argued that the ordinance drew an unfair distinction between cinema and the theater, for whereas the films were disallowed, "certain plays and dramas were being performed in certain playhouses in the city of Chicago of which the pictures were reproductions of parts."[25] The lawyers went on to launch a further intriguing line of defense: the films, they claimed, were based on the "American historical experience" and thus could not be challenged on the grounds of immorality and obscenity. From this perspective the basis of the films in historical actuality, that is, in nonfictional discourse, protected them from concerns about morality and obscenity.

Early in 1909 Chief Justice James H. Cartwright dismissed these claims in the Illinois Supreme Court. It was the purpose of the law, Justice Cartwright asserted, "to secure decency and morality in the moving picture business, and that purpose falls within the police power," that power defined as the right (and duty) of the states to protect the health, morals, and safety of their citizens.[26] Even though the ordinance focused solely on moving pictures, Cartwright further observed, it did not necessarily license other immoral representations, and, furthermore, there is something specific to the regulation of moving pictures—the audience. Low admission prices, Cartwright claimed, meant that nickelodeons "are frequented and patronized by a large number of children, as well as by those of limited means who do not attend the productions of plays and dramas given in the regular theatres. The audiences include those classes whose age, education and situation in life especially entitle them to protection against the evil influence of obscene and immoral representations."[27] "Limited means" effectively translated here as lower-class immigrant groups, those groups that were commonly seen to make up the majority of the audience of nickelodeons and who also formed, the *Chicago Tribune* had suggested in the midst of fears about labor unrest and criminal activity in the city, "the early stage of that dangerous second generation which is finding such a place in the criminals of the city."[28] Vulnerable but also potentially dangerous audiences frequented nickelodeons more than the theater, Justice Cartwright suggested, so distinctions between the public roles afforded cinema and theater needed to be carefully drawn and policed.

Cartwright also responded to the claim that the films depicted "experiences connected with the history of the country" by observing that even if they did so, it did not follow that they were "not immoral" since they "necessarily portray exhibitions of crime."[29] Even though it is almost certain that the two films under consideration replayed historical actuality through fictional conventions, and that they were only retrospectively discursively positioned as straightforward representations of historical actuality, the decision took that positioning at its word and disallowed it.

Linking cinema to the theater and to nonfictional discourse—at least, the ostensibly nonfictional discourse of history—seemed to offer a way for Block to circumvent the powers of the police censor board. Yet these alliances were denied by the state supreme court, which insisted on a clear distinction among film, theater, and history amid fears about the effects of films on audiences and public order. Cartwright's decision had important ramifications for the definition of the uncertain social function of cinema, seemingly suggesting that mainstream cinema be disengaged from public debates about, for example, the history of the country and that it should occupy a fundamentally delimited place within the public sphere. Important precedents were set in a number of ways here, paving the way for the proliferation of municipal and state censor boards from this moment on and for future legal decisions on the public role of cinema.

"IMMORAL, SACRILEGIOUS, INDECENT AND OBSCENE"

Like the board in Chicago, the first statewide censor board set in place in Pennsylvania in 1911 was established with a clear distinction in mind between moving pictures, on the one hand, and the press and the stage, on the other. Initial discussions described the proposed bill as an "attempt to keep motion pictures attuned to public opinion and not necessarily in harmony with productions of the stage or newspapers, but rather to restrict the motion pictures to such as would afford clean entertainment or amusement and to eliminate everything which would tend to debase or inflame the mind to improper adventures or false standards of conduct."[30] Likewise, following the precedent of the board in Chicago, the Pennsylvania board was also set up to censor "immoral and obscene films."[31] No film could be sold, leased, lent or exhibited in the state until it had been inspected by the board, and films would not be passed if they were seen to be "sacrilegious, obscene, indecent or immoral" or if they tended "in the judgment of the board to debase or corrupt morals."[32]

Other states took this formulation as a precedent, including Ohio in 1913, Kansas in 1914, and Maryland in 1916. The state legislature in Ohio vowed to disallow films that were "sacrilegious, obscene, indecent or immoral" and would similarly not allow "an indecent subject, nor [one] representing lust"; the boards in Kansas and Maryland employed similar language, setting out to disapprove of films "such as are cruel, obscene, indecent or immoral, or such as tend to debase or corrupt morals" and those that are "sacrilegious, obscene, indecent or immoral."[33] *Immorality* and *obscenity* were keywords for practically all the municipal and state censor boards, then, as the declared reasons for the necessity of state interventions focused in the main on questions of sexuality. Here the history of moving picture censorship connects to a broader history of sexuality, particularly in relation to anxieties about the governance of individual bodies and the social body of a mass public.[34]

One of the first acts of the Pennsylvania state censor board was the banning of the white slave film *Smashing the Vice Trust* because of concerns both about the dissemination of images of urban vice to smaller towns and about the kind of public role that cinema might take. Like other white slave films, *Smashing the Vice Trust* was presented by its producers—although seemingly disingenuously—as a moral lesson and as an intervention into the broader public debates about white slavery, based, the *Variety* reviewer noted, on "newspaper stories" and including scenes featuring New York district attorney Charles Whitman.[35] White slave films like *Traffic in Souls* (Universal, 1913) and *The Inside of the White Slave Traffic* (Moral Feature Film Company, 1913) had occasioned considerable debate about the public role of cinema, in particular whether it was acceptable for cinema to represent pressing but distressing public problems. Earlier debates within the self-regulatory National Board of Censorship had produced a complicated stance that leaned toward the acceptance of a delimited social role for cinema but that still held out the possibility of cinema functioning as "propaganda" for pressing social issues.[36] Like the censor board in Chicago, the Pennsylvania board took a clearer stance here in banning all white slave films, a decision predicated on the fact that from the outset the board conceptualized film as having a distinct social role from that of the theater and the press. Even if the film was strictly a "propaganda" film produced for social betterment, it should not be allowed, for that role was beyond the one allotted to mainstream cinema.

Ellis Paxson Oberholtzer, longtime member of the Pennsylvania board, published a book-length treatment of the censorship question in 1922 that clarified the logic underpinning the board's decisions. He argued, in particular, that an educational remit was beyond the cinema as a "place of amusement" and that films about political issues, including, in particular, those relating to sexuality, were necessarily "contrary to public policy."[37] The municipal board in Minneapolis expressed similar logic in ruling that "as a general proposition the so-called educational and propaganda film for commercial use is to be condemned. . . . People go to the movies for recreation, amusement."[38] Other decisions by the boards in Pennsylvania and Ohio to entirely ban films followed this logic about the public role of cinema. Hence the film *Where Are My Children?* (Universal, 1916), covering the issues of abortion and contraception, was banned in Pennsylvania.[39] The prologue to the film *Prohibition* (Prohibition Production Company, 1916) was excised in Pennsylvania because it included a display of a number of public figures, including senators, who supported the temperance cause and so made a political statement that ran contrary to the board's conception of the social role of cinema.[40] Likewise, *The Iron Hand* (Universal, 1916), telling a story of political corruption, was rejected in Pennsylvania; *Stacked Cards* (Kay-Bee, 1914) and *Tracking the Government* (Warners Features, 1914) were banned in Ohio because of "scenes showing collusion between prostitute, policeman and corrupt politicians" and showing a "judge dividing ill-gotten money with moonshiners" respectively.[41] *The Strike at Coaldale* (1914), showing miners striking in Ohio, and *By Man's Law* (Biograph, 1913), critiquing Rockefeller's greed and manipulation of the police, were also banned in Ohio.[42] Important to the decisions of the municipal and state boards, then, was a careful policing of the public role of cinema, evident most clearly in the films that were banned outright and that entered either into broader political debates about sexuality and morality like *Smashing the Vice Trust* or *Where Are My Children?* or about other political questions like temperance, the Civil War, or official corruption. Like investigative journalism or "muckraking," these films sought to engage in public debates about pressing issues, sometimes no doubt for the commercial benefit that it was thought would accrue—but this public role was actively discouraged by state intervention.

Important here also in the state intervention into the definition and functioning of cinema were the distinctions drawn between the social role of cinema and that afforded to art, evident from Corporation Counsel Cassells's dismissal of the police power problems in regulating cinema in 1907, to Justice Cartwright's decision drawing a distinction between theatrical and filmic representations of historical events in early 1909, and to the establishment of the Pennsylvania board in 1911. In this context the banning of a number of films based on novels, operas, and plays helped further define the public role of cinema. *The Kreutzer Sonata* (Fox, 1915), for example, told a story based on a novel by Leo Tolstoy (and a play based on that novel) that ends with murder and suicide; the film was deemed unacceptable by censors in Pennsylvania and accordingly banned.[43] Likewise, the film *Carmen* (Fox, 1915), based on a story that was also a successful opera, was banned in Pennsylvania, as were the films *Sealed Lips* (Equitable Motion Pictures, 1915) and *The Easiest Way* (Clara Kimball Young Film Corp., 1917), based on a novel and play respectively.[44] The novels and the play on which *The Birth of a Nation* was based were considerably less controversial than the film. Long

accepted in postromantic cultural theory as a force of limited cultural negation like that seen in the conclusion to *The Kreutzer Sonata,* the social role of
art was evidently distinct from that afforded to cinema.[45]

Important though these decisions were in relation to the individual films
and the economic viability of their producers, their real importance lies more
in the way in which the underlying logic they manifested influenced the self-
definition of the film industry and, then, the production of films. The delimited public role of cinema was becoming ever more clear to those involved
in the industry. Films representing controversial issues of white slavery, eugenics, or birth control like *Is Any Girl Safe?* (Universal, 1916), *The Black Stork*
(Wharton, 1916), *Birth Control* (Message Photoplay, 1917), *The Hand That
Rocks the Cradle* (Universal, 1917), and others were increasingly condemned
in the trade press for being "too preachy."[46] Edward Weitzel of *Moving Picture World* argued that "the family photoplay theater, in the opinion of the
writer, is not the proper place" for the consideration of "serious ethical questions" and should therefore be reserved for "amusement and recreation,"
not "propaganda."[47] *Moving Picture World* condemned *The Black Stork,* about
eugenics and "defective" babies, noting, "The place to exploit [the subject]
is not the moving picture theater."[48] Likewise, the screenplay writing manuals that began to appear in the 1910s, further disseminating industry practice, frequently told prospective authors to avoid propaganda and controversy. "[H]eart interest must predominate," the authors of a manual called
Writing the Photoplay suggested, and "[t]hat form of journalism which is best
known as muckraking is also out of place in the picture."[49] Aspiring writers
were told "one may not use the screen for the aims of the proselyte," to avoid
tragedy and "morbidness," and to aim for a form of "art" that says "something worthwhile in a beautiful way."[50]

Increasingly, then, the effort to shift cinema from *harmful* to *harmless* became concentrated in pushing cinema away from an engagement with the
public sphere of political debate or cultural negation, rendering cinema ostensibly apolitical, as a provider of "harmless entertainment." Legal decisions
about the validity of state intervention further supported these definitions
of the public role of cinema.

A "PRETENSE TO WORTHY PURPOSE"

Lawyers for the interstate film exchange Mutual Film Corporation challenged
the Ohio state censorship ordinance in late 1913, gaining a temporary in-
junction against the state censorship board and halting its work after just
two months of censoring activity. Counsel for Mutual, Walter N. Seligsberg,
argued in the District Court of the United States for the Northern District
of Ohio that the censorship law imposed unconstitutional burdens on interstate commerce and thus had invidious effects on property rights.[51]

Linked to this was a secondary argument about free-speech rights, predicated on the definition of motion pictures as "publications" in line with a previous Supreme Court decision that held that a painting was a publication and was so protected by state and federal constitutions guaranteeing people the right to freely speak and publish their sentiments. Legislators in Ohio had no right to abridge or restrain the freedom of publication, Seligsberg argued, so "[u]nless this court is prepared to say that Ohio could pass a law providing for the censorship of newspapers and magazines, it cannot sustain the censorship of motion pictures."[52] The same arguments were mounted by Mutual's lawyers slightly later in separate cases challenging the constitutionality of the Chicago police censor board and the Pennsylvania and Kansas state boards.[53]

The decision rendered in April 1914 in the Ohio case denied Mutual's case, though, in line with the Ohio attorney general's arguments that the censorship law fell within the police power abrogated to the states, a precedent that was quoted in the subsequent denial of Mutual's cases in Chicago, Pennsylvania, and Kansas.[54] Judges in the various cases noted that the police power extends "to the making of regulations promotive of domestic order, health, morals and safety" and could be defined as the "principle of self-preservation of the body politic," indeed as the "chief function of government."[55] Even though lawyers for Mutual had described moving pictures as "harmless," the judges acted from the position that "it does not matter that the subject in the main is harmless; it does matter, however, if something associated with it that [sic] is *harmful*."[56] The free speech argument was denied on the grounds that corporations were not citizens and thus not included in constitutional guarantees of free speech. Even if they were, there is a clear distinction, the judges asserted, between the press and moving pictures. "Counsel overlook a broad distinction between the things they describe in their bills and the objects with which they make comparison," the judges noted, for moving pictures are aimed principally at "furnishing entertainment and amusement."[57]

Lawyers for Mutual duly filed an appeal with the Supreme Court, and the Court agreed to hear the cases together in January 1915. The legal strategy adopted by Mutual here differed from before, though, for now the free speech questions were given precedence over those involving the restraint of trade. Lawyers for Mutual argued that the company was entitled to invoke the protection of the state constitutional guarantees of free speech and freedom of publication because moving pictures were publications and thus "constitute part of 'the press' of Ohio within the comprehensive meaning of that word."[58] "The press" was defined by the lawyers with the help of a suitably inclusive dictionary definition as "a means of making or announcing publicly something that otherwise might have remained private and unknown."[59] Leading on from this, a description of the "use, object, and effect of motion pictures" by the lawyers was heavily skewed toward a sense of cinema's educative social function:

> They depict dramatizations of standard novels, exhibiting many subjects of scientific interest, the properties of matter, the growth of the various forms of animal and plant life, and explorations and travels; also events of historical and current interest,—the same events which are described in words and by photographs in newspapers, weekly periodicals, magazines, and other publications, of which photographs are promptly secured a few days after the events which they depict happen.[60]

Like the arguments mounted within the film industry about the white slave and "sex-problem" films and *The Birth of a Nation,* the critical argument here was about the proposed social function of cinema and its positioning in the cultural topography of America.

Lawyers for the state boards countered these arguments by arguing that "uncensored pictures were detrimental to the morals and perversive of true education" and should be restrained according to the police powers abrogated to the states.[61] This latter argument carried the most weight with the Supreme Court justices, for the decision rendered in late February 1915 denied Mutual's claims and the company's conception of the function of cinema. No doubt moving pictures had "many useful purposes as graphic expressions of opinion and sentiments, as exponents of policies, as teachers of science and history" and could be "useful, interesting, educational and moral," Justice Joseph McKenna wrote in the court's unanimous verdict,

> [b]ut they may be used for evil, and against that possibility the statute was enacted. Their power of amusement, and, it may be education, the audiences they assemble, not of women alone nor of men alone, but together, not of adults only, but of children, make them the more insidious in corruption by a pretense of worthy purpose. Indeed, we may go beyond that possibility. They take their attraction from the general interest, eager and wholesome it may be, in their subjects, but a prurient interest may be excited and appealed to.[62]

Moving pictures were "a business, pure and simple" that was in fact "capable of evil," even more so when they "pretended" to worthy purpose as films like the white slave films and *The Birth of a Nation* had done.[63] Entertainment, for the justices, was a category distinct from ideas and a boundary line between the two needed to be affirmed and policed. Keeping separate the referential from the prurient, the justices' comments made clear that their skepticism about referentiality was not simply a denigration of "prurient films," even if the concerns were frequently intertwined.[64] The logic of their argument suggested that the "pretense to worthy purpose" in film should be avoided, that cinema should be linked to fictional goals and nonpractical ends.

The *Mutual* decision was a vital and indeed "momentous" one that was binding on the entire legal system and that governed the validity of state censorship and the legal prior restraint of moving pictures until the Supreme Court reversed the decision in 1952.[65] The consequences of the decision were both specific and far-ranging, including the mandating of increased state regulation of cinema alongside a long-lasting and performative definition of the function of mainstream cinema as "entertainment" that should be divorced from the "pretense of worthy purpose." The decision effectively cemented the delimitation of cinema's role in the public sphere evident in earlier debates and legal decisions. In this sense a critical line in the sand was drawn here, divorcing the role of mainstream cinema from a function similar to the press or art and linking it to the goals of harmless and culturally affirmative entertainment. These distinctions and definitions were crucial to the establishment of the discursive formation of mainstream cinema, setting in place a set of basic assumptions and norms about the identity and parameters of that cinema that henceforth became hegemonic.

CONCLUSION

Legal decisions effectively backed up the judgments of municipal and state censors, and together they marked out the margins of what was acceptable in cinema, establishing the terrain of classical Hollywood cinema as that necessarily of harmless entertainment divorced from the broadly defined political. In the process these decisions marked a delimitation of the public role of cinema and, indeed, of the public sphere, of what Charles Taylor has recently called "metatopical common space," that broad space in which members of society meet through a variety of media and discuss matters of common interest.[66] Regulatory interventions extended the remit of governance in a liberal democracy and limited public discourse. Griffith's plea for First Amendment rights, shared by others of different political persuasions, was effectively a plea to be included in this common space—although it was a plea that was ultimately refused. *The Birth of a Nation*, so frequently regarded as the birth of classical Hollywood cinema, was in this sense a curious and complex birth, for the film manifested a conception of the function of cinema that concomitant censorship decisions refused. *Intolerance* (Triangle, 1916), following in the footsteps of *The Birth of a Nation* and *The Rise and Fall of Free Speech*, does not, then, mark simply a formally excessive deviation from classical norms—as the standard film historical narrative suggests—but together the two films mark a *functionally excessive* sense of mainstream cinema.[67]

Even so, this refusal of an engaged public role for cinema was not inevitable but was contingent. Cinema could be different, and revisions were possible in changed political circumstances, evident almost immediately after the *Mutual* decision when events in the wider geopolitical sphere culminated with the entry of the United States into the World War that led to a revised governmental sense of the possible public role of cinema. Immediately on entry into the war a Committee on Public Information was established by President Woodrow Wilson to help shape public opinion to support the war effort. Wilson and the head of the committee, George Creel, called on the film industry to undertake a propagandistic role in this context, and the film industry worked closely with the so-called Creel Committee, supporting the production of short instructional films and longer feature films, encouraging film stars to rally to the war effort and exhibitors to use the space of cinemas as communal meeting sites.[68]

Important though this reconfiguration of the relation between state and cinema was, it was partial and short-lived. Increased concerns during wartime about free speech, population strength, governance, and national security spilled over into an increased surveillance of cinema, visible, for example, in the new banning of *The Birth of a Nation* in a number of states where it had previously been shown because of its possible effects on race relations, in heightened concerns about films about birth control, and in the prosecution of at least one filmmaker under the terms of the 1917 Espionage Act.[69] The definition of the public role of cinema was reinforced in the immediate postwar period. *Fit to Fight* (American Social Hygiene Association, 1918), for example, was produced during the war period by the government to educate soldiers about the dangers and effects of venereal disease. Retitled *Fit to Win*, the film was released to a wider audience in the immediate postwar period but was caught up in considerable controversy, including the emergence of a Catholic-led campaign against the film that foreshadowed the later actions of the Catholic Legion of Decency.[70] *Moving Picture World* asserted that the film "does not belong in a family theater to be shown to a mixed audience of men and women" and the film was banned in New York City, a decision upheld by the U.S. Circuit Court of Appeals.[71] Evidently representations of the effects of sexuality could be imperative to state power in times of war but were quickly rebranded as "obscene" in the context of the resumption of normal business for the film industry in the immediate postwar period. Censorship was again tied to broad concerns about sexuality and the governance of populations. Even though the war period showed the malleability of the definition of the public role of cinema, then, the dominant framework set in place in the prewar period was quickly reestablished after the war and henceforth underpinned the definition and operations of classical cinema.

Excluded from the mainstream, alternative conceptions and practices of cinema flourished in the margins. Exploitation cinema, propaganda, documentary, and the avant-garde all emerged in this context, following the definition of the constitutional status of mainstream cinema and demonstrating not only stylistic deviations but, more critically, functional differences.[72] The critical distinction set in place in regulatory discourses and practices between entertainment and various alternatives was predicated on diverging conceptions of the function of cinema; this metageneric categorization—one of the most important in film history—was critical to the establishment of the terrain of classical Hollywood cinema and its alternatives. In this sense the study of censorship in the transitional era is crucial for our understanding both of the effects of censorship as a broad discursive and practical logic—tied to the broader sphere of the governmental—and for our efforts to precisely map the nature of the transition to classical Hollywood cinema. The narrowing of the definition of the function of cinema and its place in the public sphere was crucial to the formative shaping of American cinema.

NOTES

My thanks to the Arts and Humanities Research Board for a grant that enabled me to carry out the research for this article. Thanks also to the archivists and librarians at the Illinois Regional Archives Depositary, Ronald Williams Library, Northeastern Illinois University; Chicago Public Library; Ohio Historical Center; Pennsylvania State Archives; Rare Books and Manuscripts Division, New York Public Library; Academy of Motion Picture Arts and Sciences, Margaret Herrick Library, Los Angeles; and the Institute for Advanced Legal Study at the University of London. My thanks also to Charlie Keil for helpful editorial input and to Peter Kramer for a characteristically insightful reading of an earlier draft.

1. Gregory A. Waller, *Main Street Amusements: Movies and Commercial Entertainment in a Southern City, 1896–1930* (Washington, D.C.: Smithsonian Institution Press, 1995), 158.

2. Thomas Cripps, *Slow Fade to Black: The Negro in American Film, 1900–1942* (New York: Oxford University Press, 1977), 59–60.

3. Boston Branch of the NAACP, *Fighting a Vicious Film: Protest against "The Birth of a Nation,"* in *The Movies in Our Midst: Documents in the Cultural History of Film,* ed. Gerald Mast (Chicago, Ill.: University of Chicago Press, 1983), 129; *New York Times,* 15 April 1915, 1; *New York Times,* 18 April 1915, 15.

4. Nickieann Fleener-Marzec, *D. W. Griffith's "The Birth of a Nation": Controversy, Suppression, and the First Amendment as It Applies to Filmic Expression, 1915–1973* (New York: Arno Press, 1980), esp. 66–73, 94–99.

5. *Chicago Defender,* 22 May 1915, cited in Jane M. Gaines, *Fire and Desire: Mixed-Race Movies in the Silent Era* (Chicago, Ill.: University of Chicago Press, 2001), 233; Fleener-Marzec, *Griffith's "The Birth of a Nation,"* 265–68; *Record of Proceedings of the Industrial Commission of Ohio, Department of Film Censorship,* 6 January 1916, General Correspondence 1916–56, Box 50,736, Ohio Historical Center (hereafter OHC).

6. House Bill No. 322, 80th General Assembly, Ohio, 1913, in *General Assembly: Legislative Service Commission, Bills and Acts, 1835–1996,* Box 3552, OHC.

7. *Record of Proceedings of the Industrial Commission of Ohio, Department of Film Censorship,* 6 January 1916, General Correspondence 1916–56, Box 50,736, OHC.

8. *Record of Proceedings of the Industrial Commission of Ohio, Department of Film Censorship,* 11 January 1916, General Correspondence 1916–56, Box 50,736, OHC.

9. See Janet Staiger, *Bad Women: Regulating Sexuality in Early American Cinema* (Minneapolis: University of Minnesota Press, 1995), esp. 55–115; Tom Gunning, "From the Opium Den to the Theatre of Morality: Moral Discourse and Film Process in Early American Cinema," *Art and Text* 30 (1988), repr. in *Silent Cinema Reader,* ed. Lee Grieveson and Peter Kramer (London: Routledge, 2003); and Tom Gunning, *D. W. Griffith and the Origins of American Narrative Film: The Early Years at Biograph* (Urbana: University of Illinois Press, 1991), esp. 151–87.

10.* Rev. Dr. Charles Parkhurst, "*The Birth of a Nation,*" n.d. (review in numerous papers), repr. in *Focus on "The Birth of a Nation,"* ed. Fred Silva, (Englewood Cliffs, N.J.: Prentice-Hall, 1971), 102–3; "A Statement in Regard to the General Committee Meeting Held at the Liberty Theatre on March 1st at 2.30 P.M.," National Board of Review of Motion Pictures Collection, Rare Books and Manuscripts Division, New York Public Library (hereafter NBR).

11. Richard Schickel, *D. W. Griffith* (London: Pavilion, 1984), 294.

12. Griffith, *The Rise and Fall of Free Speech* (privately published pamphlet, n.p.).

13. On the debates about white slave films and other sex-problem films see Lee Grieveson, "Policing the Cinema: *Traffic in Souls* at Ellis Island, 1913," *Screen* 38, no. 2 (summer 1997): 149–71; Shelley Stamp, *Movie-Struck Girls: Women and Motion Picture Culture after the Nickelodeon* (Princeton, N.J.: Princeton University Press, 2000), 41–101; Shelley Stamp, "Taking Precautions, or Regulating Early Birth Control Films," in *A Feminist Reader in Early Cinema,* ed. Jennifer Bean and Diane Negra (Durham, N.C.: Duke University Press, 2002), 270–97. On labor filmmaking in the period and the ensuing controversies see Steven J. Ross, *Working-Class Hollywood: Silent Film and the Shaping of Class in America* (Princeton, N.J.: Princeton University Press, 1998).

14. Assistant Secretary of the National Board of Censorship to the Moral Feature Film Company, 22 December 1913, Box 171, NBR.

15. Edward D. White, the chief justice of the Supreme Court, is reported by Thomas Dixon to have told Dixon he was a Klan member and to have asked him if the film told "the true story of that uprising of outraged manhood" (Schickel, *D. W. Griffith,* 270).

16. Pierre Bourdieu, "The Force of Law: Toward a Sociology of the Juridical Field," *Hastings Law Journal* 38 (1987): 839.

17. *Chicago Tribune,* 3 May 1907, 2; Lee Grieveson, "Why the Audience Mattered in Chicago in 1907," in *American Movie Audiences from the Turn of the Century to the Early Sound Era,* ed. Melvyn Stokes and Richard Maltby (London: British Film Institute, 1999).

18. Assistant Corporation Counsel Edwin H. Cassels to Alderman Joseph Z. Uhlir, memorandum, 24 June 1907, 3 (quoted in J. A. Lindstrom, "'Getting a Hold Deeper in the Life of the City': Chicago Nickelodeons, 1905–1914" [Ph.D. diss., Northwestern University, 1998], 32).

19. *Proceedings of the City Council of the City of Chicago,* 4 November 1907, 3052.

20. *Moving Picture World,* 7 September 1907, 422; *Moving Picture World,* 21 September 1907, 454; *Moving Picture World,* 7 December 1907, 645; *Moving Picture World,* 14 December 1907, 665; *Views and Film Index,* 14 December 1907, 3; *Moving Picture World,* 21 September 1907, 454; *Moving Picture World,* 14 December 1907, 665; *Mo-*

tion Picture News, 6 June 1914, 39–40; Waller, *Main Street Amusements*, 139–43; 64 *American Law Review:* 505; Lucius H. Cannon, *Motion Pictures: Laws, Ordinances, and Regulations on Censorship, Minors, and Other Related Subjects* (St. Louis Public Library, July 1920); Ellis Paxson Oberholtzer, *The Morals of the Movie* (Philadelphia, Pa.: Penn Publishing, 1922), 117–18.

21. Illinois Regional Archives Depositary, Ronald Williams Library, Northeastern Illinois University (hereafter IRAD), Box 65a.

22. IRAD, Boxes 65a, 68, 72.

23. IRAD, Box 72.

24. IRAD, Boxes 72, 65b, 66a, 65b. The review of *The Mainspring* in *Moving Picture World* suggests the miners were actually striking: *Moving Picture World*, 2 December 1916, 1344. On the broader censorship problems besetting Micheaux see Charlene Regester, "Black Films, White Censors: Oscar Micheaux Confronts Censorship in New York, Virginia, and Chicago," in *Movie Censorship and American Culture*, ed. Francis G. Couvares (Washington, D.C.: Smithsonian Institution Press, 1996).

25. *Block v. City of Chicago*, 87 N.E. 1011, 239 Ill. 251 (1909), 1013.

26. Ibid.

27. Ibid.

28. *Chicago Tribune*, 15 April 1907, 1. On concerns about criminality and immorality in Chicago see George Kibbe Turner, "The City of Chicago: A Study of the Great Immoralities," *McClure's*, April 1907; and Sydney L. Harring, *Policing a Class Society: The Experience of American Cities, 1865–1915* (New Brunswick, N.J.: Rutgers University Press, 1983), 228–33.

29. *Block v. City of Chicago*, 87 N.E. 1011, 239 Ill. 251 (1909), 1016.

30. Pennsylvania State Board of Censors, Rules, and Standards passed 19 June 1911, Pennsylvania Session Laws for 1911, 1067–69, Pennsylvania State Archives, Box 3 (hereafter PSA). The board was established in 1911 but did not actually start functioning until 1914, initially because no appropriation of money was made in the bill and subsequently because producers sought a legal challenge to the bill. *Motion Picture News*, 6 June 1914, 23; *Moving Picture World*, 3 January 1914, 25–27; *Motion Picture News*, 9 May 1914, 21–24; *Motion Picture News*, 16 May 1914, 21–22.

31. *Journal of the House of Representatives of the Commonwealth of Pennsylvania*, Part 4 (1911), 3905–6; *Journal of the Senate of the Commonwealth of Pennsylvania*, Part 4 (1911), 3078; *Philadelphia Inquirer*, 20 June 1911, 2; *Smull's Legislative Handbook and Manual of the State of Pennsylvania* (Harrisburg: W. S. Ray, 1914), 66.

32. *Journal of the Senate of the Commonwealth of Pennsylvania*, Part 1 (1916), 73. For subsequent accounts of the function of the Pennsylvania board see Oberholtzer, *Morals of the Movie;* Michael G. Aronson, "'All Love Making Scenes Must Be Normal': Pennsylvania Movie Censorship in the Progressive Era," in *Turning the Century: Essays in Media and Cultural Studies*, ed. Carol A. Stabile (Boulder, Colo.: Westview Press, 1998); and Richard Carl Saylor, "The Pennsylvania State Board of Censors (Motion Pictures)" (Master's thesis, Pennsylvania State University at Harrisburg, 1999).

33. House Bill No. 322, 80th General Assembly, Ohio, *General Assembly: Legislative Service Commission, Bills, and Acts, 1835–1996*, Box 3552, OHC; *Journal of the House of Representatives of Ohio* (Columbus, Ohio: F. J. Heer Printing, 1913), 854; Senate Bill 367, *Kansas Senate Journal* (1913), 136; Maryland: Laws, 1916, c. 209, 411–16. On the formation and subsequent function of the Ohio Censorship Board see Ivan

Brychta, "The Ohio Film Censorship Law," *Ohio State Law Journal* 13, no. 2 (spring 1952).

34. See Michel Foucault, *The History of Sexuality, Volume 1: An Introduction*, trans. Robert Hurley (1976; repr., London: Penguin, 1990). I outline the relations among morality, governance, and the regulation of cinema in more detail in *Policing Cinema: Movies and Censorship in Early-Twentieth-Century America* (Berkeley: University of California Press, forthcoming).

35. *Variety*, 20 February 1914, 23. *Variety* regarded the film as a cheap imitation of *Traffic in Souls*.

36. *Moving Picture World*, 23 December 1916, 1792; Grieveson, "Policing the Cinema," 166–71. The board was effectively split over how to deal with the white slave films and, later, *The Birth of a Nation*. Its inability to resolve its stance on the social function of cinema drew considerable criticism, and this was one of the reasons behind the impetus for the creation of other municipal and state boards. For more on this see Grieveson, *Policing Cinema*, chap. 6.

37. Oberholtzer, *Morals of the Movie*, 41, 35.

38. Robbins Gilman to Executive Secretary, National Board of Review, 23 November 1916, Box 103, NBR.

39. PSA, Box 10.

40. PSA, Box 2; *Moving Picture World*, 17 April 1915, 399.

41. PSA, Box 3; OHC, Box 50,736.

42. Ross, *Working-Class Hollywood*, 109–10.

43. PSA, Box 3.

44. Ibid.

45. Peter Burger and Christa Burger, *The Institutions of Art*, trans. Loren Kruger (Lincoln: University of Nebraska Press, 1992).

46. *Wid's*, 31 May 1917, 349. Economic issues were critical here, of course, for the industry was increasingly becoming a national and, indeed, global one, and the mainstream industry was developing oligopolistic strategies of creating barriers to entry and of marginalizing maverick producers whose films could damage the long-term profitability of the industry.

47. *Moving Picture World*, 2 June 1917, 1458. Likewise, a survey of exhibitors by the national board showed that exhibitors tended to steer away from "sex pictures" and demand instead films that were suitable for family audiences. Box 145, NBR.

48. *Moving Picture World*, 24 February 1917, 1211, cited in Martin S. Pernick, *The Black Stork: Eugenics and the Death of "Defective" Babies in American Medicine and Motion Pictures since 1915* (New York: Oxford University Press, 1996), 124.

49. J. Berg Esenwein and Arthur Leeds, *Writing the Photoplay* (Springfield, Mass.: Home Correspondence School, 1913), 243–44.

50. Howard T. Dimick, *Photoplay Making* (Ridgewood, N.J.: Editor Company, 1915), 97; A. Van Buren Powell, *The Photoplay Synopsis* (Springfield, Mass.: Home Correspondence School, 1919), 26; Frederick Palmer, *Technique of the Photoplay* (Hollywood, Calif.: Palmer Institute of Authorship, 1924), 18. On the dissemination of censorship standards see also Eustace Hale Ball, *The Art of the Photoplay* (New York: Veritas, 1913), 44; William Lord Wright, *Photoplay Writing* (New York: Falk, 1922), 154–58; Wycliffe Aber Hill, *Ten Million Photoplay Plots* (Los Angeles, Calif.: Feature Photodrama, 1924), 89–92.

51. *Mutual Film Corp. v. Industrial Commission of Ohio et al.*, 215 *Federal Reporter* (September-October 1914); *Moving Picture World*, 27 December 1913, 1526–27; *Motion Picture News*, 18 April 1914, 17–18.

52. *Moving Picture World* (27 December 1913), 1527.

53. *Mutual Film Corporation v. City of Chicago*, 224 F. 101 (U.S.C.C.A. Ill. 1915); *Buffalo Branch, Mutual Film Corporation v. Breitinger*, 250 Pa. 225 (1915); *Mutual Film Corp. of Missouri v. Hodges*, 236 U.S. 230 (1915); John Wertheimer, "Mutual Film Reviewed: The Movies, Censorship, and Free Speech in Progressive America," *American Journal of Legal History* 37 (1993).

54. *Mutual Film Corp. v. Chicago* (1915) 139 C.C.A. 657, 224 Fed. 201; *Buffalo Branch, Mutual Film Corporation v. Breitinger*, 250 Pa. 225 (1915); *Motion Picture News*, 18 April 1914, 17–18.

55. *Mutual Film Corp. v. Industrial Commission of Ohio et al.*, 215 *Federal Reporter* (September-October 1914), 141; *Moving Picture World*, 27 December 1913, 1527; *Buffalo Branch, Mutual Film Corporation v. Breitinger*, 250 Pa. 231–32; *Motion Picture News*, 18 April 1914, 17–20, 44.

56. *Mutual Film Corp. v. Industrial Commission of Ohio et al.*, 215 *Federal Reporter* (September-October 1914), 141; *Motion Picture News*, 18 April 1914, 20 (my emphasis).

57. *Mutual Film Corp. v. Industrial Commission of Ohio et al.*, 215 *Federal Reporter* (September-October 1914), 142–43.

58. *Mutual Film Corporation v. Industrial Commission of Ohio*, 236 U.S. 230 (1915), 236.

59. Ibid., 243. Lawyers did not argue for First Amendment guarantees here but relied on the state constitutions' guarantees of free speech because it was not clear that the First Amendment was binding on the states.

60. Ibid., 232.

61. Ibid., 251.

62. Ibid., 242.

63. Ibid.

64. For example, a legal decision in 1922 following the logic of the *Mutual* decision denied that newsreels could be likened to the press. *Pathé Exch. v. Cobb* (1922) 202 App. Div. 450, 195 N.Y.

65. Garth S. Jowett, "'A Capacity for Evil': The 1915 Supreme Court *Mutual* Decision," *Historical Journal of Film, Radio, and Television* 9, no. 1 (1989): 59; *Burstyn v. Wilson* 343 U.S. 459 (1952). For a discussion of this case see Garth Jowett, "'A Significant Medium for the Communication of Ideas': The *Miracle* Decision and the Decline of Motion Picture Censorship, 1952–1968," in *Movie Censorship and American Culture*, ed. Francis G. Couvares (Washington, D.C.: Smithsonian Institution Press, 1996).

66. Charles Taylor, "Modern Social Imaginaries," *Public Culture* 14, no. 1 (2002): 114.

67. Philip Rosen has summarized this trope of film history: "The classical cinema has a genius father (Griffith), a first-born *(Birth of a Nation)* and a magnificent freak *(Intolerance)*" (Philip Rosen, "Securing the Historical: Historiography and the Classical Cinema," *Cinema Histories, Cinema Practices*, ed. Philip Rosen and Patricia Mellencamp [Frederick, Md.: University Publications of America, 1984], 22).

68. Leslie Midkiff DeBauche, *Reel Patriotism: The Movies and World War 1* (Madison: University of Wisconsin Press, 1997), 104–36.

69. Fleener-Marzec, *Griffith's "The Birth of a Nation,"* 265; *Message Photoplay Co. v Bell*, 167 N.Y.S. 129 (1917); *Moving Picture World*, 22 December 1917, 1786; *Moving Picture World*, 29 December 1917, 1947; *Moving Picture World*, 11 May 1918, 865; *Moving Picture World*, 25 May 1918, 1145; Richard Wood, ed., *Film and Propaganda in America: A Documentary History*, vol. 1, *World War I* (Westport, Conn.: Greenwood Press, 1990), 296.

70. *Variety*, 21 February 1919, 71; *Moving Picture World*, 24 May 1919, 1167; *Variety*, 18 July 1919, 46; Eric Schaefer, *Bold! Daring! Shocking! True! A History of Exploitation Films, 1919–1959* (Durham, N.C.: Duke University Press, 1999), 27–36.

71. *Moving Picture World*, 12 April 1919, 276; *Exhibitor's Trade Review*, 14 June 1919, 104, cited in Schaefer, *Bold! Daring! Shocking! True!*, 29.

72. See Annette Kuhn, *Cinema, Censorship, and Sexuality, 1909–1925* (London: Routledge, 1988), esp. 45–48; Schaefer, *Bold! Daring! Shocking! True!;* on the emergence and connections between documentary and avant-garde practices and institutions see, e.g., Charles Wolfe, "Straight Shots and Crooked Plots: Social Documentary and the Avant-Garde in the 1930s," in *Lovers of Cinema: The First American Film Avant-Garde, 1919–1945*, ed. Jan-Christopher Horak (Madison: University of Wisconsin Press, 1995); and Bill Nichols, "Documentary Film and the Modernist Avant-Garde," *Critical Inquiry* 27 (summer 2001): 580–611.

CHAPTER TWELVE

Cinema under the Sign of Money

Commercialized Leisure, Economies of Abundance, and Pecuniary Madness, 1905–1915

Constance Balides

Cheap *is an example of a word that has suffered peroration, the semantic process by which meaning degenerates over time. Before* cheap *could undergo this process, however, it had to become an adjective. Old English* cēap *and its Middle English descendant* chep, *from which our* cheap *derives, were nouns with neutral senses such as "bargain," "price." Middle English* chep *was commonly used in phrases:* god chepe, *"a favorable bargain,"* light chepe, *"at a favorable price,"* gret chepe, *"low-priced." From the shortening phrases like these came our adjective* cheap, *first recorded as standing by itself in 1509 and meaning simply "costing little." What costs little may not always be of good quality, and over time* cheap *also came to mean "of poor quality." This new, pejorative sense has not robbed* cheap *of all value: something that is cheap at half the regular price is a bargain and well worth having.*

Word Mysteries and Histories

Debates about the status of the nickel theater as a cheap amusement during the Progressive Era reiterate the etymological heritage of the word cheap. This semantic history includes the senses of exchange in the marketplace, a commodity both "costing little" and "of poor quality" and, by way of mitigating the term's peroration, something that is inexpensive but "well worth having."[1] For Progressive Era reformers in the United States the low-priced penny arcades, amusement parks, dance halls, excursion cruises, and nickel theaters offered tawdry commodified experiences exemplified by the risqué heterosexual dancing in unsupervised dance halls, films depicting criminal and immoral acts, and sensationalist advertising posters outside film theaters and indiscriminately visible from the street. More generally, these venues could also serve as a breeding ground for illicit behaviors in which young working-class women traded sex for money or treats such as liquor in dance halls or rides at Coney Island.[2] In this characterization of inexpensive commercialized leisure, or "cheap amusements," reformers foregrounded the connection between low cost and, more derisively, poor quality and dubious moral value.

At the same time, a number of reformers also made distinctions within the general category of commercialized leisure, and the cheap nickel theaters fared well in the comparison. As early as June 1907 Sherman C. Kingsley, superintendent of the Chicago Relief and Aid Society, argued that moving picture shows were "in the main . . . not objectionable" and "[answered] a real need in the community," in contrast to the unredeemable penny arcade and cheap theater. In April 1908 John Collier of the People's Institute in New York City characterized the nickelodeon as having substantially improved during the last five years to the extent that it could be called a "family theater," one that had "discovered a new and healthy cheap-amusement public," and he anticipated that cooperation with the film industry would result in "more elevated performances." In a detailed study of commercialized leisure in New York City published in 1911 Michael Davis Jr. characterized moving pictures, which he noted largely cost ten cents for adults and five cents for children, as "in the main a wholesome form of recreation."[3] In his view improvements in artistic, thematic, and educational aspects and a reputable audience gave moving pictures a social worthiness. In these assessments of leisure in urban centers the nickel theater involved an experience that was inexpensive and worth having.

Progressive reformers' views of the nickel phenomenon, both as a morally problematic incursion into the realm of recreation and as a "low-priced" but, nevertheless, socially valuable experience, draw on two key historical meanings of *cheap*. Before the term became an adjective with either derogatory or paradoxical connotations, however, it was a noun referring to bargain or price, a meaning associated with commercial transactions. My focus in this essay is on this initial marketplace implication of *cheap*, which I assess in relation to three issues, namely, reformers' and social observers' comments on the commercialized nature of new leisure activities, especially the critique of capitalism and the profit motive; cinema as it figured in debates by economists of the period, especially Simon Patten's positive view of the nickel audiences' vitality as a paradigmatic effect of an emerging modern consumer-oriented economy; and, finally, pecuniary culture, particularly as it was theorized by Georg Simmel in his analysis of modern experience associated with urban overstimulation and as it was represented in *Ready Money* (Apfel, Lasky, 1914), a farce about stock speculation.[4] Reformers' critiques of capitalist leisure, a capitalist economist's positive valorization of cinema, and the filmic representation of a mature money economy are key parameters that mark out a discursive terrain in which cinema existed under the sign of money during the transitional era.

Characterizing cinema in this way stems in part from an interest in thinking about this period in relation to the problematic of the economy and its relationship to culture, an issue that subtends various theoretical interventions in film studies, critical theory, and cultural studies.[5] In a discussion of

Western Marxism Eugene Lunn, for example, notes that key historical developments in the 1920s, including the political victories of fascism, constituted a crisis for an orthodox Marxism and resulted in the turn to "questions of 'consciousness' and culture . . . as a means of better understanding the stabilizing features of modern capitalism."[6] In a project of "historical semantics" Raymond Williams, in *Keywords,* assesses the way social and historical processes are embedded in the meanings of particular words. *Interest,* for example, evolved from an initial association with compensation or investment to a generalized sense of curiosity or attracting attention, a trajectory suggesting the extent to which the word is "saturated with the experience of a society based on money relationships."[7] Georg Simmel, in "The Metropolis and Mental Life," elaborates on his observation that "the metropolis has always been the seat of money economy" by pursuing connections between characteristic urban behaviors and the logic of exchange embedded in commercial transactions.[8] These arguments point to the imbrication of the economy and culture whether in terms of the staying power of a capitalist mode of production (Lunn), the extent to which words bear the trace of the economy (Williams), or the way early-twentieth-century urban experience rearticulated the logic of money (Simmel). The connection between the cheap amusement phenomenon and pecuniary culture of early-twentieth-century America is a good historical test case for analyzing the imbrication of the economy and culture, in part, because of the extent to which the relationship between commerce and cultural life was an explicit topic of public debate.[9]

The emphasis on this connection also relates more specifically to recent debates about the transitional period. A number of film scholars have assessed the bid for respectability on the part of the film industry during this time in relation to issues such as the emergence of censorship, the formal shift toward narrative integration and quality productions, and the difficulties of harnessing women's presence in the audience to the project of achieving a better tone in theaters.[10] An important strategy in this essay is to look at the discursive construction of cinema as an economic object,[11] particularly the way cinema figured both as a negative and a positive sign of a consumer-oriented capitalist economy. This focus on struggles over the specifically commercial aspect of the nickel and other leisure experiences adds another dimension to the picture of the transitional period as one during which the social currency of cinema was being established.

Finally, foregrounding the connection between the nickel theater experience and theories of the economy resonates with a characterization of the years from 1880 to 1920 in the United States as ones involving an intensification of the shift from a producer-oriented society to a consumer-oriented society. Dominant values of hard work, thrift, and restraint associated with a production ethos and the centrality of a work identity during the early to mid nineteenth century, at least for working- and middle-class men, were supplanted by a view of consumption as the sphere of life for expressing individual autonomy, the spectacular as a dominant mode of mass visual culture, the circulation of commodities linked to their visual display, and the importance of spending and pleasure.[12] This transformation provides a broader context for understanding tensions over the meaning of "the consumer"[13] and over the psychological implications of consumers' relationships to commodities discussed in this essay.

COMMERCIALIZED LEISURE

Has the play impulse in "our town" been coined at a nickel a thrill, a quarter for a real sensation?

RICHARD HENRY EDWARDS, *Popular Amusements (1915)*

How did moving pictures figure under the sign of commerce? During the early twentieth century there was a widespread debate about leisure as a business. A major characteristic of commercial recreations was their popularity, and the numbers of those attending were frequently cited by enthusiasts, detractors, and reformers of various persuasions. The Coney Island showman, Frederic Thompson, who opened Luna Park in 1903, boasted in 1908 that twenty-five million people had visited the park during that five-year period. Lewis B. Palmer in 1909 in *The Survey* cited daily audience figures of 250,000 and of 500,000 on Sundays in 350 motion picture theaters in New York City, of 200,000 in 345 theaters in Chicago, and of 150,000 in 158 theaters in Philadelphia. He also estimated that 4,000,000 patrons per day attended theaters in 118 cities across the country. In Manhattan alone, Davis reported in *The Exploitation of Pleasure,* there were one hundred dancing academies, which reached one hundred thousand paying pupils, and more than a hundred dance halls were attended by an estimated four to five million men and women during the winter season.[14] In addition to studies of major metropolitan areas smaller cities and towns were also investigated, and the results of a number of these local surveys are compiled in Richard Henry Edwards's *Popular Amusements* (1915). In Milwaukee 60.2 percent of the show-going public attended fifty motion picture theaters, which were filled to capacity eight to eleven times per week. In Detroit 73.1 percent of the show-going pubic attended motion picture theaters. In Cleveland "one in six . . . citizens attended a motion picture theater each week day, and one in every three" did so on weekends and holidays; and in Kansas City an average weekly attendance of 449,064 amounted to "almost twice the population of the city."[15] This level of popular appeal alone commended moving pictures and other amusements to public scrutiny.

The meaning of these large numbers had to be negotiated in relation to

various critiques: commercialized recreations were tawdry and sensationalist (especially penny arcades, amusement parks, and the posters outside
nickel theaters); admission by payment involved an undiscriminating attention to clientele (especially in dance halls and excursion cruises); consumers
and spectators were passive; and the profit motive diverted a healthy impulse
toward play.[16] Edwards, for example, characterizes spectatorship in a particularly pointed manner: "The disease of *spectatoritis* is abroad in the land.
Its germs are in every breath we draw and most of us are affected with that
paralysis of play activities which is its most striking symptom."[17] This social
disease of spectatoritis involves a passive relationship to leisure associated
with spectating, viewed as "the habit of being amused" as opposed to an active mode of participating. In Edwards's view this problematic development
has been exacerbated by the emergence of the professional entertainer, who
acts as an intermediary between the participant and an event. Spectatoritis
has also fueled a "jaded sensationalism" that is "the basis of appeal in an alarming proportion of our public spectacles."[18] These spectacles, which are associated with the commercialization of leisure in activities ranging from sports
to theatrical productions to dancing, have usurped the place of the amateur
in athletics, community drama, and ethnic dancing, which are characterized
by a direct, self-determining, and cooperative or team involvement.

A key issue both for Edwards and for Jane Addams, whose book, *The Spirit
of Youth and the City Street* (1909) informs the general critique in *Popular Amusements,* is that commercialized leisure has exploited a natural and fundamentally wholesome interest in play, which has a moralizing force. The business
promoter perverts this interest through the logic of monetary gain; that is,
"the love of fun in the human heart is a cold matter of dollars and cents." Allegiance to the "cash box" also predisposes the organizers of commercialized
leisure to adopt a cavalier attitude toward morality. Edwards notes that "the
substitution of cold profit-seeking amusements, artificial and often nasty, can
but exercise a correspondingly profound effect for demoralization."[19]

The necessity of leisure for working-class city dwellers was frequently emphasized by reformers, especially in light of crowded living conditions in tenements, an increasingly monotonous and routinized workday, and physical
debilitation associated with greater differentiation of tasks requiring small
repetitive movements in factory manufacture.[20] Indeed the social case for
recreation and the necessity to provide opportunities, whether through voluntary play organizations, charity efforts, social settlements, or municipal
facilities, were important to the progressive reform agenda.[21] In this context
the debate about the "so-thought 'superficial' question of cheap amusements" and the reform of leisure were linked, for some, to an explicit critique of capitalist business practices and, for others taking a more amelio-
rative view, to the need to regulate industrial practices in order to bring about
a more equitable democratic society.[22] Edwards, for example, relates the

"ruthless" exploitation of natural resources by "certain financial interests" to the exploitation of "the natural resource of the play instinct."[23]

A problem for Edwards's general polemic against profit as moral exploitation, however, is the fact that moving pictures are rated well in his own report. A cited study by Fred McClure on Kansas City (1911–12) indicates that 79 percent of motion pictures scored "good," as did 71.1 percent of amusement parks, as opposed to 23.1 percent of dance halls and 7.7 percent of riverboat excursions. Edwards also characterizes moving pictures in a positive vein, describing them as a "theater of the people," a phrase used throughout the transitional period, and he suggests that the qualities of "cheapness, their family and neighborhood character [and] their attractiveness to children" contribute to their popularity.[24]

There is a gap in logic in *Popular Amusements* between the negative label of *commercial* associated with morally suspect practices and the fairly sanguine evidence offered with regard to moving pictures. Edwards, pursuing the potential for possible problems, for example, suggests that local groups organize investigating forays in their own town to "study the moral attitude of the audience" as they watch a film; and, he adds, these groups should ask themselves whether the audience "applaud[s] the sensually suggestive when it is shown, or is the attitude one of decency and wholesomeness?" Groups should also be vigilant about the content of motion pictures and the social milieu of the theaters ("are low jokes and immoral suggestions tolerated?").[25] In this case the label of commercialization seems to overpower the evidence.

The strength of conviction that the critique of making profit from leisure carried during this period is reiterated in other studies and social commentaries across the spectrum of political and religious affiliations. Addams, in *The Spirit of Youth,* connects exploitation at work and exploitation in the realm of leisure, elaborating with specific reference to the subcultures of young women:

> We see thousands of girls walking up and down the streets on a pleasant evening with no chance to catch a sight of pleasure . . . save as these lurid places provide it. Apparently the modern city sees in these girls only two possibilities, both of them commercial: first, a chance to utilize by day their new and tender labor power in its factories and shops, and then another chance in the evening to extract from them their petty wages by pandering to their love of pleasure.[26]

Addams's sense of the homology between exploitation in the workplace and in the place of leisure is backed up by her participation in a wide range of reform causes affecting working conditions.[27] Although Davis has a more positive view of moving pictures than Addams, he makes a similar critique of commercial enterprises, which "[build] the gaudy structure of profit-paying recreation" on the justified impulse of the denizens of the street to avoid unpleasant environments and to embrace pleasurable ones. Davis also employs the language of political critique of business (reminiscent of muckraking arguments) when he argues for public responsibility over leisure: "*laissez faire*, in recreation as an industry, can no longer be the policy of the state."[28]

Maxim Gorky offers one of the most scathing critiques in his commentary on amusement parks published in *The Independent* in 1907. For Gorky the peeling paint on structures at Coney Island looks like a "skin disease," each building stands "like a dumbfounded fool with wide-open mouth," and flimsy structures are matched by trite moral injunctions. These vulgar displays are related to the fact that Coney Island is a "paying business" designed to get people to part with their money, and Gorky's description of capitalism invokes the imagery of a vile Moloch "fed by the passion for gold." He also makes a suggestive analogy between the golden sands of Coney's beach and the color of gold or, more precisely, "the cold, cynical whistle of the Yellow Devil."[29] In 1912 Walter Rauschenbusch similarly criticizes a capitalist logic in amusements although, unlike Gorky, he does so from the perspective of radical Christianity. The displays of tents and booths for carnival games on a small-town street suggest to Rauschenbusch a monotonous sensibility of "pay, pay, pay, and nothing but a gambling thrill or satisfied curiosity to show for it." He describes capitalism in terms of a relentless logic. "[L]ike Christianity, it is a missionary force. It is impatient of any moral restraint that hampers it in making profit. . . . It will maul ride down, and trample any force that interferes with its profits."[30]

In the end solutions posed varied in their attempt to steer the popularity of cheap amusements toward better ends. Edwards (optimistically) suggests avoiding activities that encourage "'the carnival spirit' or crowd consciousness," and he recommends "shunning" commercial recreations, thereby pitting wholesome against commercial activities.[31] Addams similarly extols the virtues of ethnic dancing against modern dancing in dance halls, makes paternalistic remarks about working-class women's subcultural fashion practices ("the huge hat with its wilderness of bedraggled feathers"), and is dismayed by the misplaced dedication of "a group of young girls accustomed to the life of a five-cent theater [who] reluctantly refused an invitation to go to the country for a day's outing because the return on a late train would compel them to miss one evening's performance."[32] At the same time, various hybrid solutions were also offered. During the summer of 1907 Hull House ran a nickel theater showing a range of films including actualities, travel scenes, fairy tales (including the adventures of Cinderella), and films with known stories such as *Uncle Tom's Cabin* in an attempt to compete with neighborhood theaters, and in 1908 Collier, referring to this experiment, suggests the possibility of the People's Institute starting "one or more model nickelodeons" aimed at "forcing up the standard through direct competition."[33] In a similar vein two municipal dance pavilions in Cleveland's public parks, which boasted chaperones, closing times just before those in commercial halls, and slightly lower rates, aimed to beat business at its own game. Newton Baker, former chief of police, recalls the result: "The price in the dance halls usually was five cents a dance, for a dance of three minutes. . . . [W]e charged . . . three cents for five minutes. And everybody came to dance with us!"[34]

Reformers were, to be sure, fighting a losing battle. Their critique of the profit motive, however, complicates the historiography of the transitional years of moving pictures. On the one hand, many reformers assessed commercialized recreation in terms of a moralism, a paternalistic attitude to audiences, and an outmoded sensibility with regard to new leisure forms. In addition, viewing social problems as being amenable to bureaucratic solutions, a key distinguishing feature of Progressive Era reform, ensured the authority of a professional middle class.[35] On the other hand, some of the same reformers viewed commercialized recreation as existing along a continuum with exploitative industry practices, arguing that leisure entrepreneurs were capitalizing on a need produced by insalubrious and debilitating home and work conditions. To the extent that reformers explicitly politicized the emerging realm of commercialized recreations, they made leisure visible in a way that undermines a sense of the period as one involving a simple opposition between reformers, viewed solely as purveyors of a respectable morality, and mass culture audiences, viewed as resisting this moral myopia in their cathexis to the new amusements. This point in no way challenges work both by social historians on the myriad ways in which subcultural groups did use new commercial spaces of leisure to negotiate class, gender, and racial identities on their own terms and by historians who theorize the potential of these new inclusive and heterosocial commercial public spheres for providing the structural conditions for imagining identity and community in ways that were not solely circumscribed by commercial imperatives.[36] Rather, I am arguing that the formative and contradictory nature of leisure during this period also finds expression in the discourses of reformers.

THE ARCADE SIDE OF THE STREET

In an article by Bennet Musson and Robert Grau in *McClure's Magazine* in 1912 the illustration shown here was accompanied by the following caption: "The moving-picture theater has become America's favorite family entertainment. Apparently even the babies attend the show"[37] (figure 12.1). This caption and the numerous baby carriages in the image imply the presence of mothers and families in the audience and are used to secure the point in the article that censorship initiatives have been successful, especially the voluntary submission of films by production companies to a censorship board associated with the People's Institute and with representatives of various so-

THE MOVING-PICTURE THEATER HAS BECOME AMERICA'S FAVORITE FAMILY ENTERTAINMENT   APPARENTLY EVEN THE
BABIES ATTEND THE SHOW

Figure 12.1. The symptomatic street: moral respectability or crass sensationalism?
Illustration from *McClure's Magazine*, November 1912.

cial, civic, and religious organizations in New York City (that is, the National
Board of Censorship). These efforts, Musson and Grau argue, have resulted
in "a great improvement in the character of the shows."[38] The illustration
from *McClure's*, with its well-appointed (if stucco) theater facade and its reliance on the authority of the domestic, does not simply support the claim,
however, that nickelodeons are now reputable. The narrative of uplift is belied by other elements in the image. Behind the hyperbolic (and possibly
staged) presence of the baby carriages lining the sidewalk stands a riot of
advertising posters. One large poster for the film that is "playing today" shows
a man with his hands tied behind his back surrounded by a crowd of men
who appear to be holding rifles, a woman standing beside the man, and the
tag line, "Marriage or Death." The poster alludes to a somewhat suggestive
scenario (why is the man being threatened with the ultimatum of marriage
or death?), and the insistent heralding of wares enticing the gaze of passersby
invites comparison with the ballyhoo mentality of Coney Island's sideshows.
That is, the image both rehearses the problematic elements of the commercialized street and marks its improvement.[39]

It was the look of the commercialized street, moreover, with its sensationalist advertising that visualized the problem of the profit motive for a

number of reformers. For Addams the posters produced an inexorable allure matched by the "gang" atmosphere in theaters. The young women who preferred their moving picture routine to a trip to the country "found it impossible to tear themselves away not only from the excitements of the theater itself but from the gaiety of the crowd of young men and girls invariably gathered outside discussing the sensational posters." Davis argues that the "poster evil" associated with displays in front of vaudeville, burlesque, and moving picture shows should be regulated. Although the moral content of these advertising vehicles, he suggests, varies with the specific film performance, they generally rely on an advertising logic in which "[the posters] always *exceed* the performance." In addition, the poster is assaultive in its attempt to "catch the eye of the street passenger; [the poster] must hold him up; it is . . . a psychological blow in the face." Gorky likewise describes the harsh electric lights at Coney Island, which "stun" the amusement seeker, whose "consciousness is withered by the intense gleam." Whereas for Thompson the "carnival spirit" is the goal of the entrepreneur as showman and gives the public what it wants, for Gorky this spirit is only a "contented *ennui*" in which pleasure seekers wander aimlessly in response to "nerves . . . racked by an intricate maze of motion and dazzling fire."[40]

This characterization of the sensory experience of the commercialized street as one of excess, assault, and enervation, which I return to later in this essay, stands in stark contrast to Patten's view of cheap amusements. In 1905 Patten extolled the stimulating and communal aspects of "Coney Islands" and department stores, and in 1909 he enthusiastically described the gaiety of streets festooned with lights where nickel theaters stood, as well as the vitality and enthusiasm of nickel audiences.[41] In *Product and Climax* he adopts the pose of the economist as *flâneur* as he reminisces about walking down the street of his New England town. On one side stood venerable cultural institutions such as the museum; the library, with "its spiked gateway fortifying the heavy doors" and notices of closing times; and the church, a "stagnant place" in which an evening prayer meeting had an air of "perfunctory . . . duty." In contrast to the monumental architecture, protective gates, and prohibitory ethos of this "dark" and "dull" side of the street was the other side, the "arcade side," which was "festooned with lights and cheap decorations" and where shop doors "stood wide open." Emblematic of this other side of the street is the nickel theater. Patten, the social observer, continues his stroll:

> Opposite the barren school there was the arcaded entrance to the Nickelodeon, finished in white stucco, with the ticket seller throned in a chariot drawn by an elephant trimmed with red, white and blue lights. A phonograph was going over and over its lingo, and a few picture machines were free to the absorbed crowd which circulated throughout the arcade as through the street. Here were groups of workings girls—now happy "summer girls"—because they

had left the grime, ugliness and dejections of their factories behind them, and were freshened and revived by doing what they like to do. There was nothing listless, nothing perfunctory here.[42]

The cheap appeal of the nickel theater's physical appearance and crass patriotism and the impermanence of its building ("white stucco") contribute to a convivial and enthusiastic ambience. Where Gorky saw cheap and tawdry, Patten saw gaiety. Where Addams saw exploitation in another guise, Patten saw vitality. Where reformers sought to usurp the place of commercialized activities with wholesome versions or with other activities unmediated by money, Patten saw in the "arcade side" the legitimate potential to fulfill the need for stimulating pleasures.[43] He extends his remarks to a critique of the supposed higher moral authority of instructive establishments, which he likens to "factories in the dull season," by charging them with a cultural myopia, noting that "the institutions of progress—the conserving moral agencies of a respectable town—have their shutters down and nobody needs their wares."[44]

The large numbers attending nickel theaters were a positive indication for Patten of the extent to which theaters were striking a fundamental chord with their audiences ("[they appeal] to the foundation qualities of men").[45] By contrast, Addams despaired of the undue influence suggested by high attendance figures. In the case of young boys, for example, she recounts a story of a gang of boys aged nine to eleven who were influenced by westerns to the extent that they adopted the expression, "'Dead Men Tell No Tales,'"as their "watchword," bought a revolver, and, wearing black cloths over their faces, held up the milkman.[46] For Addams film plots and the words of illustrated songs involved a trite moralism and a cheapening of sentiment. For Patten film adventures stimulated the imagination and as a result were "up-building"; the viewing of films involved a purposive concentration, whether in following the plot or watching unfamiliar cultures in travelogues; the experience of spectating enhanced vitality as opposed to drinking alcohol with its debilitating effect ("after the cheap show, the glow lasts"); and the audience atmosphere involved a positive sense of community ("the companionship of the like-minded").[47] Unlike Kingsley, Collier, and Davis, moreover, who stressed increasing respectability in films, Patten validates moving pictures in a way that acknowledges their "cheaper" aspects by commending the adventures and the thrill of rescues, and, contra Addams, even "the bad man's capture [which] is overlaid by new sensations." Patten is not, therefore, valorizing the immoral in moving pictures or asserting the primacy of mass culture or advocating unregulated commercial development. Rather, he makes a connection between commercial stimulations and the affective quality of vitality.

The significance of these sensations is elaborated in Patten's theory of

the economy. The overarching focus on making product, conducted in ap-
palling conditions in factories, depleting workers' energy, and resulting in
a debased citizenry, is associated with a nineteenth-century economy of
scarcity. The early twentieth century is more appropriately characterized as
an economy of abundance given the plethora of agricultural produce and
consumer products available. This economy involves a logic of climaxes, that
is, the direct connection between effort and result, rather than product. It
also enhances psychic values of "plasticity, efficiency, and vigor," sets the stage
for a committed citizenship, and supplants outdated values of "restraint and
discipline." In a society of abundance a plethora of goods provides the occasion for "expanding wants" for the working classes, requires an "economic
altruism" from capitalists in the form of a distribution of wealth through
taxes, and involves a "new morality" that consists "not in saving, but in expanding consumption; not in draining men of their energy, but in storing
up a surplus in the weak and young."[48] The experience of moving pictures
as a form of climax for Patten, to be sure, occupies a lower order of the new
morality than sports (as a voluntary group organization) and the summer
outings of social clubs, and at times Patten prevaricates; for example, he argues, negatively, that five-cent theaters should not be closed because it would
bolster the numbers attending saloons. Nevertheless, amusements such as
nickel theaters for him exist on a continuum with morality, religion, and culture (as the "lower rounds of the ladder of progress") and contribute to the
virtues of abundance and the authority of a burgeoning consumerism with
its potential to extend the logic of climax through consumption.[49]

Patten was a well-known figure in Progressive Era reform circles, and the
valorization of an economy based on abundance with its attendant sensibility of vitality supported an expressive approach to reform concerned with
effecting social change by providing opportunities for developing positive
behaviors as opposed to out-of-date methods employing repressive measures.[50] Kingsley, in his 1907 article on cheap amusements, praises the nickel
theater experiment at Hull House, as well as plans by the Catholic Church
to show moving pictures and a proposed study of playgrounds and field
houses in Chicago, and in a deferential nod he notes that these efforts are
supported by Patten's view that "to release virtues is better than to suppress
vice." In an editorial in the *Charities and the Commons* Patten is characterized
as "the ablest exponent of the new view of philanthropy" despite the fact that
he is a university professor not directly involved in settlement houses, legislative activism, or exposing graft and corruption, and social workers are
enjoined to take note of his writings and buy his book, *The New Basis of Civilization*.[51] A subsequent editorial looks to Patten as the key theorist behind
the journal's practical social work. Excerpts from Patten's *Product and Climax* appear in *The Survey* in 1909, and in the same volume Lewis E. Palmer
quotes the passage about the arcade side of the street in the context of his

own positive appraisal of moving pictures, suggesting Patten's views are a timely response to the question, "What should be the attitude of the social worker toward this new-found recreation?"[52] Even reformers sitting on the other side of the fence on the question of commercialized leisure construed Patten's work as an acknowledged frame of reference for the debate. Addams, commenting on Patten's argument about the importance of a direct connection between cause and effect (that is, between effort and climax) in commercialized entertainments, demurs, "the youth, of course, [are] quite unconscious of this psychology." In *Popular Amusements* Edwards quotes extensively from the street passage in *Product and Climax,* even though he goes on to take exception with it.[53]

Patten's positive assessment of nickel theaters is an important component in the wider debate about the status of the transitional period and the terms through which the authority of the new leisure activity was being established.[54] Not only was he a major figure in reform and economic circles at the time, but his views, like those of the reformers discussed earlier, complicate a sense of the period, particularly with regard to the relationship between an emerging consumer-oriented economy and cinema. On the one hand, Patten captures the importance of the affective resonance in the way subcultural groups were experiencing moving picture culture, namely, a genuine attachment encouraged by a nonauthoritarian institutional logic. He had a keen sense of the virtues of the arcade side of the street and of the pleasures of collective cinemagoing. In this regard he is perhaps best contrasted to Addams, who also observed the community feeling in nickel theaters but feared it could too easily dissipate into less savory activities.[55] On the other hand, Patten theorizes how the business of commercialized leisure could capitalize on those very qualities. His economic theories offer a contemporary rationale for industrial practices that linked cinema to other commodities during the transitional period, notably, tie-ins with songs, new fashions, and even food products discussed by Janet Staiger and others.[56] Although Patten did not theorize cinema industry practices per se, his notion of abundance suggests a connection between the experience of cinema and the experience of commodities. In linking abundance to the world of commodities and the nickel experience to the vitality engendered by that world, he placed the nickel experience within the orbit of a burgeoning consumer culture. His writings constitute an early statement of an economic logic that makes a constitutive connection between a consumer mentality, expressed through a relationship to commodities, and the sensibility of cinematic culture, which was becoming invested in its connection to commodities. In this sense, and with certain provisos, Patten could also be viewed as a de facto ideologue for commercial strategies of "late cinema" in that his theories look down the road to *Star Wars* (Lucas, Twentieth Century Fox/Lucasfilm, 1977; reissued 1997), *Jurassic Park* (Spielberg, MCA/Universal/Amblin, 1993), and the extensive merchandising, product placement, and tie-ins that are now a commonplace practice of blockbuster films.[57] As distinct from the present time, however, when profitability is often normalized as an index of public welfare, early public debate about commercialized leisure included a strong countervailing critique of profit.[58]

PECUNIARY MADNESS AND THE INDIFFERENCE TO THINGS

Prosperity, like depression, may be largely psychological.
New York Dramatic Mirror (1914)

The discursive framework of the economy puts stress marks in different places in an emerging historiography of the transitional period. Debates in reform circles ranged from a critique of capitalist self-interest to a valorization of capitalist production under the sign of a democracy of abundance. At the same time, a number of films during the same period represented money matters across the political spectrum. Films dealing with the thematics of spending, speculation, and economies of various kinds are by no means limited to the transitional years. *The Usurer's Grip* (Edison, 1904), *Greed* (Stroheim, Metro-Goldwyn, 1925) and *The Gold Diggers of 1933* (LeRoy, Warner Bros., 1933) are notable examples of films from earlier and later periods dealing with these topics and featuring money as a visual motif.[59] The formative nature of the debate in which cinema was being produced as an economic object during the transitional period, however, invites a consideration of how the economy was represented on the other side of the screen. Or more precisely, how did films from the period make pecuniary culture visible?

A number of these films feature economic types such as the usurer in *The Usurer* (Griffith, Biograph, 1910); the female spendthrift in *The Spendthrift* (Edwin, Kleine, 1915) and *When Justice Sleeps* (Harvey, Balboa Amusement Company, 1915); and the stock market speculator in *A Corner in Wheat* (Griffith, Biograph, 1909), *A Corner in Cotton* (Balshofer, Quality Pictures Corp., 1916), and *The Pit* (Tourneur, Brady Picture Plays, 1914). Films from the period also develop the thematics of borrowing, spending, and accumulation through specific issues, such as the problem of profit in the context of labor and capital relations in *Why?* (Eclair, 1913), *Money* (Keane, United Keanograph, 1915), and *The Dividend* (Edwards, New York Motion Picture Corp., 1916); women's extravagance in the context of domestic relationships in *Paid in Full* (Thomas, All Star Feature Corp., 1914) and *The Cheat* (DeMille, Lasky, 1915); retribution by a son for a father ruined by a capitalist in *Man of the Hour* (Tourneur, Brady Picture Plays, 1914); and the psychology of money in *Ready Money* (Apfel, Lasky, 1914). In line with the formal heterogeneity of the transitional period, films about money run the gamut and include social problem films, melodramas, serials, farces, and "modern photoplays," and they range from films such as *The Usurer*, with a didactic message achieved through the use of contrast editing that is associated with other early Biograph films discussed by Tom Gunning, to *Ready Money*, a feature with no explicit moral that uses formal strategies such as detail cut-ins to magnify actions and to repeat an element of the mise-en-scène for the purpose of narrative clarity, a strategy Charlie Keil associates with a transitional style.[60]

Publicity campaigns also reinforced the status of films about money by making them a vehicle for potential spectators to make money. An advertisement in *Moving Picture World* for *The Million Dollar Mystery* (Hansell, Thanhouser, 1914–15), a twenty-three-part serial with a story line involving international intrigue, kidnapping, and the attempted theft of a million dollars by Russian secret service agents, for example, boasted a contest with a reward: "Remember, $10,000 will be paid for the best 100-word solution of the mystery." In addition, visual effects included the use of documentary footage; for example, *The Dollar and the Law* (North, Vitagraph, 1916), which was made in cooperation with the American Banker's Association, contains a scene showing the printing process for a dollar bill filmed in the Bureau of Engraving and Printing.[61]

Ready Money, a "farce of frenzied finance," foregrounds the importance of appearances as a key factor in the psychology of a money economy.[62] In the film Steve flashes counterfeit bills that have been printed by Jackson Ives, who describes the speculative logic that motivates plot events in a dialogue intertitle: "If you have money, you don't have to spend it. All you need to do is show it. It takes money to get money." Both Ives and Steve escape prosecution, and the speculative investments in a mine with no gold are secured when gold is accidentally discovered at the end of the film. *Moving Picture World* forgives this lack of moral discourse in light of the film's entertainment value: "we may not have an altogether wholesome moral, judged from stricter standards, but we certainly have good entertainment. The theme may be said to be rather unmoral than immoral."[63] In *Ready Money* the profit motive is normalized as farce.

As contemporary reviews suggest, the film also had something timely to say about the psychology of a money culture. The *New York Dramatic Mirror* notes there is an "element of truth" regarding the depiction of how "a fat roll of bills . . . acts as a sort of money magnet." The review continues: "When Steve is reduced to one lonesome quarter and the stock in his Skyrocket mine is about as popular as a week-old newspaper, he learns the magic of flashing greenbacks. Straightway his friends draw optimistic conclusions. Steve has money, therefore he must have struck gold, and if the mine is producing gold, they must have a share of it. . . . Prosperity, like depression, may be largely psychological."[64] *Ready Money*, that is, depicts what happens to experience in a pecuniary culture. By way of elaborating this claim, I turn to writings by Simmel, who theorizes the connection between the modern experience of urban stimulations and the logic of a mature money economy. More generally, his work provides a useful context both for assessing films of the period and for extending the implications of debates about commercialized leisure discussed in this essay.[65]

A key factor in Simmel's analysis of money and the city experience is the connection between money as a medium of exchange and behaviors involving the capacity for abstraction. For Simmel the economic types of the miser and the spendthrift are particularly drawn to the abstraction of value inherent in money. These types appear to be different in their relationship to commodities; for example, the miser hoards money but does not spend it on things, and the spendthrift spends too much money on things. Simmel argues, however, that both types are invested in the "pure potentiality" of money rather than in its capacity to acquire actual commodities. The stock speculator, especially one who deals in futures rather than actual commodities, is an extreme version of the spendthrift and is hooked on a "pure money speculation" that involves a sense of the infinite potential of money. Unlike Edith, the spendthrift cum speculator who loves clothes in *The Cheat*, speculation for Steve and his friends in *Ready Money* is not directed toward acquiring goods. Steve's friends are so caught up in the speculative game that they insist Steve take their checks in order to buy shares in the mine, trusting the appearance of Steve's counterfeit money more than Steve's admonitions that he has not struck gold.

For Simmel these behaviors are related to the logic of the circulation of money. In *The Philosophy of Money* Simmel notes that money initially bore a connection to objects exchanged (for example, the stamp of a fish on bronze coins) or related size to value (for example, the first bank note from China was eighteen inches long and nine inches wide). By contrast, in modern times money is purely symbolic and involves both an abstraction from the physical qualities of commodities and a razing of the qualitative distinctions between things. Simmel's analysis of the history of currency draws on Marx's distinction between use value, in which the qualitative distinctions between things are foregrounded, and exchange value, which is concerned with quantitative distinctions.[66] Simmel also borrows a rhetorical strategy from Marx in *Capital*, where he anthropomorphizes commodities in the analysis of exchange value, which has the effect of emphasizing the inversion of terms between things and people in the logic of commodity fetishism. At the point when exchange is expressed through a series of equivalences between different commodities (that is, as expanded form of value), Marx comments that the commodity becomes "a citizen of the world."[67] Simmel similarly describes the agency of money in its capacity to act as a universal equivalent form of value: "To the extent that money, with its colorlessness and its indifferent quality, can become a common denominator of all values it becomes the frightful leveler—it hollows out the core of things, their peculiarities, their specific values and their uniqueness and incomparability in a way that is beyond repair. They all float with the same specific gravity in the constantly moving stream of money."[68] As a "common denominator" money eradicates the differences between things, becomes a "frightful leveler" of distinctions between them, and, in the "constantly moving stream" that characterizes exchange in the market place, drains things of their substantiality (they "float"). Money in its symbolic mode, moreover, depends on an "intellectualist" ability, which involves the capacity for abstract thinking, for example, making a connection between two objects based on how each relates to a third. As a result, Simmel notes that "the age in which money becomes more and more a mere symbol" is marked by "the growth of intellectual abilities and of abstract thought." This mentality is further extended in the logic of calculation, which becomes the order of the day when the "exactness, precision, and rigour" required in economic relationships become a way of negotiating social relationships and everyday life.[69]

The representation of money and its power to attract in *Ready Money* rehearses Simmel's delineation of a mature money economy. Frequent deadlines, which organize time according to a logic of unfolding suspense, reinforce a calculating logic in relation to time through key narrative questions: Will gold be found in the mine before Steve's note becomes due? Can Steve get investors to buy stocks so he can pay his debt even before gold is struck? During a New Year's Eve celebration suspense is enhanced by the placement of an illuminated sign with the date of the new year (1915) in the background of the shot, indicating both time for the revelers to mark the moment and the immanence of the due date of Steve's loan.[70] In addition, Simmel's imagery of things "float[ing] with the same specific gravity in the constantly moving stream of money" is visualized in the film through a striking motif of money and money equivalents in circulation. Currency, promissory notes, and checks appear in insert close-up shots throughout the film. This motif begins in the opening credit sequence with the first shot of a close-up of a facsimile of a one-thousand-dollar bill in which "Jesse L. Lasky Feature Film Co." humorously replaces the U.S. Treasury as authorizing organization and "One thousand feet of film" replaces the amount (figure 12.2). This shot is followed by five shots in which the bill remains in the same position in the frame while the film's actors replace the portrait of a forefather in a series of dissolves, including a shot of Edward Abeles playing Stephen Baird (figure 12.3). This strategy has the effect of literally placing the film under the sign of money. Later in the film a diegetically motivated insert close-up shot of a promissory note to James R. Morgan for twenty thousand dollars, signed by Stephen Baird to cover money he borrowed to buy the Skyrocket mine (figure 12.4), is followed by insert shots of checks for ten thousand,

Figure 12.2. Film under the sign of money. *Ready Money,* opening credit sequent. Frame enlargement from 35 mm print. Courtesy of the Library of Congress.

Figure 12.3. The star under the sign of money. *Ready Money,* opening credit sequent. Frame enlargement from 35 mm print. Courtesy of the Library of Congress.

seven thousand, and eight thousand dollars belonging to Steve's friends to be used to invest in the mine. These shots both convey narrative information and visualize the circulation of equivalent forms of value: promissory note for money, check for shares in the mine. Other insert close-ups of letters and telegrams commenting on money owed, money needed, and deadlines for repaying money contribute to the sense of calculation associated with the movement of money in the market place.

For Simmel a money logic is "marred by the curse of restlessness and transience," key tropes of experience in modernity, and in his view the "feverish

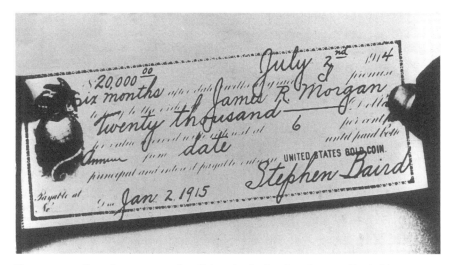

Figure 12.4. Promissory note: visualizing the logic of exchange. *Ready Money,* insert shot. Frame enlargement from 35 mm print. Courtesy of the Library of Congress.

commotion" of the stock market is a more extreme version of the "acceleration in the pace of life" in the city. More precisely, the stock market is a place in which "the specific influence of money upon the course of psychological life become[s] most clearly discernable."[71] *Ready Money* illustrates this sensibility of shock in its characterization of the volatility of fortunes gained and lost; for example, the deus ex machina of an explosion in the Skyrocket mine (an attempt to ruin Steve by Morgan, the man who lent Steve money to buy the mine) results in the discovery of gold and an abrupt reversal. Steve, who is on the verge of bankruptcy, is now suddenly wealthy.

Simmel also relates the intellectualist response associated with money in its symbolic mode to the blasé attitude that involves "an indifference toward the distinctions between things," one that results from the "intensification of emotional life" associated with metropolis.[72] This connection among shock, the circulation of money, and the blasé attitude also, finally, suggests a connection between the film, with its sensibility of money madness, and reformers' critiques of commercialized experience. Ben Singer notes the historical coincidence between Simmel's analysis in "The Metropolis and Mental Life" and Davis's use of the term *hyperstimulus* in *The Exploitation of Pleasure.*[73] This observation can be extended to other descriptions of the overstimulation of city streets including another by Davis, namely, his characterization of the "kaleidoscopic stimuli of New York life" unconducive to "*any* purposeful" theatrical experience, as well as Edwards's view of spectatoritis as involving "the path of a jaded sensationalism," Gorky's sense of the "racked" nerves of amusement park consumers, and even Addams's group of convivial young women congregating around sensational posters.[74] Although these writers suggest that the commercialized street involves the experience of thrill, agitation, and disquiet, they also describe a resulting enervation, similarly echoing Simmel's analysis of the connection between overstimulation and the blasé attitude. Edwards points to the "paralysis of play activities" as an effect of spectatoritis. Gorky describes the pleasure seeker's supposed pleasure as "the slavery of a varied boredom." Davis views penny arcades, with their suggestive posters and slot machines open to the street, as inviting "the listless 'hanging-round.'"[75]

It goes without saying that the cinema industry was organized along capitalist lines, and the transitional years saw the development of capitalist business arrangements and strategies.[76] The discourses assessed in this essay point to a somewhat different issue, namely, what happens to experience in a world ruled by a money logic? Both critical and sympathetic views of nickel theaters as a form of commercialized experience, as well as the cinematic representation of money, address this topical question. Taken together these disparate texts suggest a range of positions within a discursive formation broadly characterizable as economic. In this context Simmel's theoretical assessment of the connection of modernity, urban experience, and money is useful as a contemporary discourse that foregrounds key ways in which experience is mediated historically, in this case, by a mature money economy. Treating Simmel's writings in this way reiterates the focus on historical discourses and the importance of cinema as a cultural phenomenon in which experience is negotiated in the broader argument in film studies about the relationship linking modernity, shock, and cinema spectatorship.[77] Simmel's writings, moreover, usefully link the realms of the economy and culture by stressing the status of money as a form of representation and its consequences for modern subjectivity, particularly in the social space of the city.

In tracing out connections across various texts in this discursive formation I have also been interested in foregrounding a number of anomalies. Addams and Edwards criticize the profit motive in contemporary leisure but moralize about its commercialized experience in a way that looks to a nineteenth-century scenario of the economy based on restraint. Patten applauds the attachment of nickel audiences to the cinema experience in the name of abundance, vitality, and psychological health, but this positive assessment anticipates a later intensification of the commodification of experience. *Ready Money*, a lighthearted farce that celebrates pecuniary culture with no pretension to social critique, makes the historical experience of a mature money economy visible in ways that rearticulate Simmel's connection between urban stimulations and the circulation of money endemic to an early-twentieth-century economy.

The focus on economic discourses and representations in this essay points to a struggle over the role of cinema in the marketplace, and the views of Edwards, Addams, Patten, and Simmel delineate some of the parameters of this debate. Looking to the distant past, their various positions also suggest a lineage between nickel theaters and the term *cheap*, especially linguistic relics such as Cheap-Jack, a nineteenth-century term for "a traveling hawker who offers bargains" (Addams); *chep*, a Middle English term meaning "abundance of commodities, plenty" (Patten); and *Cheapside*, "a place of buying and selling" (cinema).[78] The transitional years were a period of struggle over the meaning of the social life of cinema spectators. Situating moving pictures under the sign of money highlights the social life of cinema in the company of the commodities it was keeping.

NOTES

A version of this essay was given at the Screen Conference, University of Glasgow, Glasgow, Scotland, June 2002. Thanks to Shelley Stamp for useful editorial suggestions and to both Shelley and Charlie Keil for their interest in this essay; to Madeline Matz, Rosemary Hanes, and Zoran Sinobad, Library of Congress, for their research assistance on the films; and particular thanks to the students participating in my "Culture and Commodity" seminar at Tulane for their enthusiastic engagement with issues informing the broad framework of concerns in this essay.

1. Robert Claiborne, foreword to *Word Mysteries and Histories: From Quiche to Humble Pie* (Boston: Houghton Mifflin, 1976), 40.

2. Belle Israels explains the problematic practices on excursion cruises in which staterooms could be rented by the day, or by the hour, or for the time it took to go from 129th Street to downtown Manhattan (for a cost of twenty-five cents). Richard Edwards, in *Popular Amusements*, quotes the *Report of the Vice Commission of Philadelphia* (1913), which puts moving picture shows in the same problematic category as public dance halls and "other amusement centers" as "breeding places of vice—the rendezvous of men who entrap girls and of girls who solicit men." Jane Addams, as I discuss below, viewed the gang mentality of youth with regard to neighborhood nickel theaters as problematic. See Belle Lindner Israels, "The Way of the Girl," *Survey* 22 (3 July 1909): 486–97; and Richard Henry Edwards, *Popular Amusements* (1915; repr., New York: Arno Press, 1976), 18.

3. Sherman C. Kingsley, "The Penny Arcade and the Cheap Theatre," *Charities and the Commons* 18 (5 June 1907): 295; John Collier, "Cheap Amusements," *Charities and the Commons* 20 (11 April 1908): 75; and Michael M. Davis Jr., *The Exploitation of Pleasure: A Study of Commercial Recreations in New York City* (New York: Russell Sage Foundations, 1911), 24. Collier's report was conducted shortly before the formation of the National Board of Censorship in 1909, an organization in which he was also involved.

4. The studies to which I refer deal with urban nickel theaters. On the importance of taking account of nickelodeon cultures outside the metropolis see Robert Allen, "Manhattan Myopia; or, Oh, Iowa!" *Cinema Journal* 35, no. 3 (spring 1996):

75–103, and for a study of nickel culture in Lexington, Kentucky, see Gregory A. Waller, *Main Street Amusements: Movies and Commercial Entertainment in a Southern City, 1896–1930* (Washington, D.C.: Smithsonian Institution Press, 1995). For a detailed elaboration of the meaning of *cheap* along these lines see *The Oxford English Dictionary*, 2d ed., s.v. "cheap." The reference to pecuniary culture as a way of characterizing late-nineteenth- and early-twentieth-century America is most closely associated with the writings of Thorstein Veblen. See esp. Thorstein Veblen, *The Theory of the Leisure Class: An Economic Study of Institutions*, with an introduction by C. Wright Mills (1899; repr., New York: New American Library, 1953).

5. Although I am not conflating different theoretical approaches within film studies or among film studies, critical theory, and cultural studies, I am suggesting the extent to which the relationship between the economy and culture has been an object of concern in these various fields of study. I discuss the general problem of how to negotiate this connection in the analysis of a contemporary film and in the context of contemporary film theory influenced by Louis Althusser's reworking of the base and superstructure model in his argument about the relative autonomy of ideological state apparatuses in Constance Balides, "Jurassic Post-Fordism: Tall Tales of Economics in the Theme Park," *Screen* 41, no. 2 (summer 2000): 139–60.

6. Eugene Lunn, introduction to *Marxism and Modernism: An Historical Study of Lukacs, Brecht, Benjamin, and Adorno* (Berkeley: University of California Press, 1982), 5.

7. Raymond Williams, introduction and "Interest," in *Keywords: A Vocabulary of Culture and Society*, rev. ed. (New York: Oxford University Press, 1983), 23, 173. I am indebted to Williams's project of "historical semantics" for the idea of turning to the marketplace implications of the word *cheap* as the framing device for this essay.

8. Georg Simmel, "The Metropolis and Mental Life [1903]," in *On Individuality and Social Forms*, ed. Donald Levine (Chicago, Ill.: University of Chicago Press, 1971), 326.

9. As I will discuss later, this point has a bearing on the debate about modernity as a historical and theoretical framework for analyzing early as well as transitional and early classical cinema. Tom Gunning usefully argues against limiting the connection between film and modernity to the cinema of attractions period, and by way of stressing the importance of historical discourses as a justification for turning to broader theoretical explanations on the particular question of the causes of film style, he includes the following in the mix of possible causes: "transformations in film's relation to society [which are] . . . traceable in contemporary discourse, and not a matter of a mystical reflection of a Zeitgeist." See Tom Gunning, "Early American Film," in *Oxford Guide to Film Studies*, ed. John Hill and Pamela Church Gibson (Oxford: Oxford University Press, 1998), 268.

10. For a useful overview of the transitional period see Roberta Pearson, "Transitional Cinema," in *The Oxford History of World Cinema: The Definitive History of Cinema Worldwide*, ed. Geoffrey Nowell-Smith (Oxford: Oxford University Press, 1996), 23–42. On the emergence of formal strategies during the transitional years—e.g., temporal continuity and spatial contiguity—see David Bordwell, Janet Staiger, and Kristin Thompson, *The Classical Hollywood Cinema: Film Style and Mode of Production to 1960* (New York: Columbia University Press, 1985); and Charlie Keil, *Early American Cinema in Transition: Story, Style, and Filmmaking, 1907–1913* (Madison: University of

Wisconsin Press, 2001). On early censorship see Robert Fisher, "Film Censorship and Progressive Reform: The National Board of Censorship of Motion Pictures, 1909–1922," *Journal of Popular Film* 5, no. 2 (1975): 143–56; Daniel Czitrom, "The Redemption of Leisure: The National Board of Censorship and the Rise of Motion Pictures in New York City, 1900–1920," *Studies in Visual Communication* 10, no. 4 (fall 1984): 2–6; Nancy J. Rosenbloom, "Between Reform and Regulation: The Struggle over Film Censorship in Progressive America, 1909–1922," *Film History* 1, no. 4 (1987): 307–25; Lee Grieveson, "Fighting Films: Race, Morality, and the Governing of Cinema, 1912–1915," *Cinema Journal* 38, no. 1 (fall 1998): 40–72; Lee Grieveson, "'A Kind of Recreative School for the Whole Family': Making Cinema Respectable, 1907–1909," *Screen* 42, no. 1 (spring 2001): 64–76; and Lee Grieveson, *Policing Cinema: Movies and Censorship in Early-Twentieth-Century America* (Berkeley: University of California Press, 2004). For work that relates censorship issues to formal and narrative elements in films see Tom Gunning, "From the Opium Den to the Theatre of Morality: Moral Discourse and the Film Process in Early American Cinema," *Art and Text* 30 (September–November 1988): 30–40; Eileen Bowser, *The Transformation of Cinema, 1907–1915* (Berkeley: University of California Press, 1990); Tom Gunning, *D. W. Griffith and the Origins of American Narrative Film: The Early Years at Biograph* (Urbana: University of Illinois, 1991); William Uricchio and Roberta E. Pearson, *Reframing Culture: The Case of the Vitagraph Quality Films* (Princeton, N.J.: Princeton University Press, 1993). On the project of addressing female spectators see Miriam Hansen, *Babel and Babylon: Spectatorship in American Silent Film* (Cambridge, Mass.: Harvard University Press, 1991); Lauren Rabinovitz, *For the Love of Pleasure: Women, Movies, and Culture in Turn-of-the-Century Chicago* (New Brunswick, N.J.: Rutgers University Press, 1998); and Shelley Stamp, *Movie-Struck Girls: Women and Motion Picture Culture after the Nickelodeon* (Princeton, N.J.: Princeton University Press, 2000).

11. In the introduction to *Policing Cinema* Grieveson offers an interesting analysis of negotiations over the term by which "cinema" as a discursive object was to be named. For a theoretical analysis of the historiographical intervention effected by an analysis of discursive formations see Michel Foucault, *The Archaeology of Knowledge and the Discourse on Language*, trans. A. M. Sheridan Smith (New York: Pantheon Books, 1972).

12. The argument about a shift from producer to consumer society is associated with T. J. Jackson Lears, "From Salvation to Self-Realization: Advertising and the Therapeutic Roots of the Consumer Culture, 1880–1930," in *The Culture of Consumption: Critical Essays in American History, 1880–1980*, ed. Richard Wightman Fox and T. J. Jackson Lears (New York: Pantheon, 1983), 3–38. See also William Leach, *Land of Desire: Merchants, Power, and the Rise of a New American Culture* (New York: Vintage, 1993); and for an analysis of the implications of this shift from changing conceptions of the meaning of the wage see Lawrence Glickman, *A Living Wage: American Workers and the Making of Consumer Society* (Ithaca, N.Y.: Cornell University Press, 1997).

13. Although in this essay I do not focus specifically on the gendering of spectators and consumers in reformers' discourses, this topic of the politics of leisure specifically for women is an important one for the period. Kathy Peiss makes a key argument in her study of urban working-class women's subcultures in the dance hall, nickel theater, and the like, noting the extent to which the meaning of these activities involved a new heterosocial public milieu in which women could develop a mod-

ern and Americanized identity at odds with a moralizing view of reformers such as Jane Addams. The general status of the commercial-industrial public sphere with its inclusive reach based on the ability to pay, coupled with the collective heterosocial reception context of nickel theaters, could also provide female spectators, as Miriam Hansen argues, with an opportunity to negotiate the contradictions in their experience of modernity. See Kathy Peiss, *Cheap Amusements: Working Women and Leisure in Turn-of-the-Century New York* (Philadelphia, Pa.: Temple University Press, 1986); and Hansen, *Babel and Babylon*. In these cases the cheap price of entry into the world of commercialized leisure is associated with a contradictory and potentially progressive implication. On female spectatorship see also Rabinovitz, *For the Love of Pleasure;* Stamp, *Movie-Struck Girls;* and Jennifer M. Bean and Diane Negra, eds., *A Feminist Reader in Early Cinema* (Durham, N.C.: Duke University Press, 2002). On the particular question of the construction of the female consumer in reformers' discourses see Constance Balides, "Making Ends Meet: 'Welfare Films' and the Politics of Consumption during the Progressive Era," in *A Feminist Reader in Early Cinema,* ed. Jennifer M. Bean and Diane Negra (Durham, N.C.: Duke University Press, 2002), 166–94.

14. Frederic Thompson, "Amusing the Million," *Everybody's Magazine,* September 1908, 378; Lewis E. Palmer, "The World in Motion," *Survey* 22 (5 June 1909): 356; Davis, *Exploitation of Pleasure,* 15–16. The figure on dance halls did not include figures for the summer at Coney Island.

15. Edwards, *Popular Amusements,* 50–51.

16. See, e.g., Davis, *Exploitation of Pleasure;* and Israels, "Way of the Girl."

17. Edwards, *Popular Amusements,* 134. The pathology of spectatorship was also discussed during this period in terms of neurasthenia, a nervous disorder, and "serialitis," which Shelley Stamp discusses in *Movie Struck Girls.* Stamp draws out the gender-specific implications of cinemagoing construed as pathology.

18. Edwards, *Popular Amusements,* 133, 135. On the specific issue of commercialization, Edwards notes that the businessman promoter "lies in wait for the spirit of youth," a phrase invoking the authority of Jane Addams and the title of her own book *The Spirit of Youth and the City Streets* (1909; repr., Urbana: University of Illinois Press, 1972).

19. Edwards, *Popular Amusements,* 140–41.

20. On the problems associated with working conditions see, e.g., Helen L. Sumner, *History of Women in Industry in the United States,* vol. 9 of *Report on the Condition of Woman and Child Wage-Earners in the United States,* 61st Cong., 2d sess., 1910, S. Doc. 645 (Washington D.C.: Government Printing Office, 1910).

21. A small sample of literature on activism in relation to parks and organized play includes the Reverend George L. McNutt, "Chicago's Ten-Million Dollar Experiment in Social Redemption," *Independent* 57, no. 2911 (15 September 1904): 612–17; Henry S. Curtis, "Relation of Playgrounds to Other Social Movements," *Survey* 22 (15 May 1909): 251–53; Graham Romeyn Taylor, "Ten Thousand at Play," *Survey* 22 (5 June 1909): 365–73; and Howard S. Braucher, "Play and Social Progress," *Annals of the American Academy of Political and Social Science* 35 (January–June 1910): 325–33. For a discussion of the importance of assessing Addams's relationship to moving pictures in terms of her views on the importance of a municipal responsibility for recreation see J. A. Lindstrom, "Almost Worse than the Restrictive Measures:

Chicago Reformers and the Nickelodeons," *Cinema Journal* 39, no. 1 (fall 1999): 90–112.

22. Edwards, *Popular Amusements,* 141.

23. Ibid., 140.

24. Ibid., 20, 55, 51.

25. Ibid., 56.

26. Addams, *Spirit of Youth,* 7–8.

27. Jane Addams (1860–1935) was a major figure in reform during the Progressive Era. She viewed environmental factors as key contributors to social problems. Addams worked for legal reforms ranging from factory inspection to protective legislation for women to the playground movement; held key positions in the National Woman's Trade Union League, the National Conference of Charities and Corrections, and the National American Woman Suffrage Association; and lectured widely and wrote prolifically on social and political issues. In 1889 she cofounded Hull House, a residential social settlement in an immigrant neighborhood in Chicago, offering neighborhood services (day nursery, cooking and sewing classes, playground) and clubs, including the Working People's Social Science Club, arts-based activities including an art gallery, little theater, and music school. She strongly argued for the importance of recreation in the lives of working people and for municipal responsibility for recreations. Although Addams was not a socialist, she was deeply committed to an equitable democratic society and struggled to reform the excesses of capitalist industrialization.

28. Davis, *Exploitation of Pleasure,* 4.

29. Maxim Gorky, "Boredom," *Independent* 63, no. 3062 (8 August 1907): 311, 314, 310. See also John F. Kasson, *Amusing the Million: Coney Island at the Turn of the Century* (New York: Hill and Wang, 1978).

30. Walter Rauschenbusch, *Christianizing the Social Order* (1912; repr., New York: Macmillan, 1915), 441, 240. Rauschenbusch was a major figure in the social gospel movement and studied socialism with the Webbs in England. Edwards, in *Popular Amusements,* cites the "pay, pay, pay" passage from Rauschenbusch's book (see Edwards, *Popular Amusements,* 139).

31. Edwards, *Popular Amusements,* 165, 106. Edwards cites his own set of impressive numbers of social settlements and YMCA/YWCAs that sponsor more wholesome activities, namely, 413 social settlements in the United States, 2,357 YMCAs in the United States and Canada, and 949 YWCAs in the United States (Edwards, *Popular Amusements,* 174–75).

32. Addams, *Spirit of Youth,* 8, 91. Addams has been criticized for an out-of-date sensibility with regard to working-class women's leisure and fashion sensibilities. See Peiss, *Cheap Amusements.* On reformers' problematic views of working women's subcultures see also Nan Enstad, *Ladies of Labor, Girls of Adventure: Working Women, Popular Culture, and Labor Politics at the Turn of the Twentieth Century* (New York: Columbia University Press, 1999).

33. On the program for the Hull House theater see "Hull House, Chicago," *Moving Picture World,* 29 June 1907, 262–63. See also Collier, "Cheap Amusements," 76.

34. Newton D. Baker, "Expression Versus Suppression," *Social Hygiene* 4, no. 3 (July 1918): 314.

35. Within Progressive Era historiography Robert H. Wiebe is a key figure asso-

ciated with the view of the period as one involving an organizational approach to reform, one in which a new professional middle class sought to effect social change through bureaucratic means. See Robert H. Wiebe, *The Search for Order, 1877–1920* (New York: Hill and Wang, 1967). For a more recent discussion of the implications of this dynamic in relation to women reformers and working-class women's subcultures see Mary E. Odem, *Delinquent Daughters: Protecting and Policing Adolescent Female Sexuality in the United States, 1885–1920* (Chapel Hill: University of North Carolina Press, 1995); and Ruth M. Alexander, *The 'Girl Problem': Female Delinquency in New York, 1900–1930* (Ithaca, N.Y.: Cornell University Press, 1995).

36. On social historians' assessments of these activities see Peiss, *Cheap Amusements;* and Enstad, *Ladies of Labor;* on working-class men's subcultures see Roy Rosenzweig, *Eight Hours for What We Will: Workers and Leisure in an Industrial City, 1870–1920* (Cambridge, U.K.: Cambridge University Press, 1983). On the theoretical lineage of debates about the public sphere, as well as an analysis of various ways of approaching the reception of U.S. silent film in terms of cinema's function as an alternative public sphere, see Hansen, *Babel and Babylon.*

37. Bennet Musson and Robert Grau, "Fortunes in Films: The Romance of Moving Pictures," *McClure's Magazine* 40, no. 1 (November 1912): 71. This article was followed in the next issue by Bennet Musson and Robert Grau, "Fortunes in Films: Moving Pictures in the Making," *McClure's Magazine* 40, no. 2 (December 1912): 193–202.

38. Musson and Grau, "Romance of Moving Pictures," 70.

39. In a similar vein Shelley Stamp explores tensions around the interpellation of female spectators as respectable in *Movie-Struck Girls.*

40. Addams, *Spirit of Youth,* 91; Davis, *Exploitation of Pleasure,* 54; Gorky, "Boredom," 310, 311–12.

41. Simon Nelson Patten, *Product and Climax* (New York: B. W. Huebsch, 1909), 13, 17. Although Patten is less known than Veblen in the present time, Patten was a major figure in economic circles. He was educated in Germany during the 1870s and was part of a cohort of young economists including John Bates Clark, Richard Ely, Henry Carter Adams, and Edwin R. A. Seligman, a group that formed the American Economic Association in 1885. Although there were differences among these economists, they were united in a critique of laissez-faire businessmen or others such as William Graham Sumner, who favored an economic system that was unregulated. Patten took up a teaching position in 1887 at the newly formed Wharton Business School, University of Pennsylvania, and Patten and Edmund James, senior professor at the school, founded the American Academy of Political and Social Science in 1889. For a useful overview of Patten's career and of his writings see Daniel M. Fox, *The Discovery of Abundance: Simon N. Patten and the Transformation of Social Theory* (Ithaca, N.Y.: Cornell University Press, 1967). Fox notes that "in contrast to Marx, with his emphasis on changing modes of production, Patten viewed social welfare in terms of the 'mode of consumption,' of men's utilization of the material, aesthetic, and spiritual goods available in their environment" (28).

42. Patten, *Product and Climax,* 13–14, 16, 18–19.

43. Kasson in *Amusing the Million* also discusses Patten and contrasts his views to those of reformers. See esp. Kasson, *Amusing the Million,* 87–112.

44. Patten, *Product and Climax,* 22, 19–20.

45. Ibid., 45.

46. Addams, *Spirit of Youth*, 93, 80.

47. Patten, *Product and Climax*, 45–46.

48. Ibid., 63; Simon N. Patten, *The New Basis of Civilization* (1907; repr., New York: Macmillan, 1915), 85–86, 215.

49. Patten, *Product and Climax*, 66. For Patten's comments on the saloon see 46.

50. For a discussion of the relationship between expressive and repressive tendencies in Progressive Era reform see Paul Boyer, *Urban Masses and Moral Order in America, 1820–1920* (Cambridge, Mass.: Harvard University Press, 1978). Jane Addams subscribed to an expressive approach, one that was also central to the logic of the social settlement movement.

51. Kingsley, "Penny Arcade," 357; "The New View," *Charities and the Commons* 18 (4 May 1907): 135.

52. Lewis E. Palmer, "The World in Motion," *Survey* 22 (5 June 1909): 357; and "Social Forces: A Program of Social Work," *Charities and the Commons* 21 (00 October 1908): 1–2. The social work journal *Charities and the Commons* became *The Survey* in 1909.

53. Addams, *Spirit of Youth*, 78; Edwards, *Popular Amusements*, 14–15.

54. Patten's writings, to my knowledge, have not been included in this debate. John F. Kasson, a notable exception, discusses Patten in the context of the debate about amusement parks. See Kasson, *Amusing the Million*.

55. See Addams, *Spirit of Youth*, esp. 75–103.

56. See Janet Staiger, "Announcing Wares, Winning Patrons, Voicing Ideals: Thinking about the History and Theory of Film Advertising," *Cinema Journal* 29, no. 3 (summer 1990): 3–31. For a discussion of the connections between serial melodramas and their simultaneous publication in popular magazines as serialized stories see Ben Singer, "Fiction Tie-Ins and Narrative Intelligibility, 1911–1918," *Film History* 5, no. 4 (1993): 489–504; Ben Singer, *Melodrama and Modernity: Early Sensational Cinema and Its Contexts* (New York: Columbia University Press, 2001), esp. 263–87; and Stamp, *Movie-Struck Girls*, esp. 102–53.

57. Patten's defense of capitalism includes a critique of exploitative practices in factories that operate according to a nineteenth-century sensibility of scarcity, a critique of conspicuous consumption, and the importance of an eventual restraint in consumption that would emerge once needs were satisfied and a scarcity mentality was left behind. See Patten's *A New Civilization* and *Product and Climax*. For a detailed discussion of the differences among product placements, merchandising, and tie-ins in contemporary film see Janet Wasko, *Hollywood in the Information Age: Beyond the Silver Screen* (Austin: University of Texas Press, 1994). Wasko also notes that in the contemporary period "popular films often initiate or continue an endless chain of other cultural products" (4). My use of the phrase "late cinema" comes from Miriam Hansen, "Early Cinema, Late Cinema: Permutations of the Public Sphere," *Screen* 34, no. 3 (1993): 197–210.

58. For example, I refer here to a celebratory mode in the common practice of announcing high box-office returns in national news broadcasts and newspapers, and, before the financial scandals regarding Enron, Arthur Anderson, and Worldcom, to the supposed "democratization" of the stock market with the dot-com phenomenon during the 1990s and pension funds invested in the stock market. Thomas Frank usefully describes the recent (however, pre-2002) faith in the stock market in terms

of a "market populism." See Thomas Frank, *One Market under God: Extreme Capitalism, Market Populism, and the End of Economic Democracy* (New York: Doubleday, 2000).

59. Eric Von Stroheim's *Greed* (1925) uses the imagery of sand and gold in a sharp critique of a money logic that is similar to Gorky's description of Coney Island noted above. The newly restored Kino video uses gold tinting to incredible effect. Also see the use of coin imagery in the well-known opening of *Gold Diggers of 1933.*

60. *When Justice Sleeps* is part of the *Who Pays* series directed by Harry Harvey at Balbao Amusement Company and distributed in 1915. For an ad for the film, which focuses on a woman's consumer desires without a thought for the consequences, see the *New York Dramatic Mirror,* 28 April 1915, 27. On stylistic issues mentioned see Gunning, *D. W. Griffith;* and Keil, *Early American Cinema in Transition.* See also Bordwell, Staiger, and Thompson, *Classical Hollywood Cinema,* 155–240. On social problem films that critique industrial and capitalist practices see Kevin Brownlow, *Behind the Mask of Innocence* (New York: Knopf, 1990).

61. Ad for *The Million Dollar Mystery, Moving Picture World,* 26 September 1914, 1714. The serial was reissued as a six-reel feature by the Randolph Film Corporation in 1918. For the details on *The Dollar and the Law* regarding the filming of making money see the entry on the film in King Hanson and Alan Gevinson, eds., *The American Film Institute Catalog of Motion Pictures Produced in the United States: Feature Films, 1911–1920* (Berkeley: University of California Press, 1988).

62. "Ready Money," *New York Dramatic Mirror,* 11 November 1914, 30.

63. Review of *Ready Money, Moving Picture World,* 26 September 1914, 1714.

64. "Ready Money," *New York Dramatic Mirror,* 11 November 1914, 30.

65. The texts by Simmel that I use here were written during the first decade of the twentieth century, namely, "The Metropolis and Mental Life" (1903); "The Miser and the Spendthrift" (1907), in *On Individuality and Social Forms,* ed. Donald Levine (Chicago, Ill.: University of Chicago Press, 1971); and *The Philosophy of Money,* ed. David Frisby, trans. Tom Bottomore and David Frisby (1907; 2d rev. ed., London: Routledge, 1990).

66. See Karl Marx, *Capital: A Critique of Political Economy,* vol. 1, trans. Ben Fowkes (London: Penguin, 1976), esp. 125–255.

67. Ibid., 155. For the analysis of the history of currency see Georg Simmel, *The Philosophy of Money,* ed. David Frisby, trans. Tom Bottomore and David Frisby, 2d ed. (London: Routledge, 1990), esp. 146–53.

68. Simmel, "The Metropolis and Mental Life," 330.

69. Simmel, *Philosophy of Money,* 152, 446.

70. Keil discusses the use of devices such as clocks in the mise-en-scène as one way of asserting the significance of time for the narrative in transitional films. See Keil, *Early American Cinema,* esp. 83–124.

71. Simmel, "The Miser and the Spendthrift," 185; and Simmel, *Philosophy of Money,* 506.

72. Simmel, "Metropolis and Mental Life," 329, 325.

73. See Singer, "Modernity, Hyperstimulus, and the Rise of Popular Sensationalism"; Singer, *Melodrama and Modernity;* and Gunning, "Early American Film," esp. 266–68.

74. Edwards, *Popular Amusements,* 135; Gorky, "Boredom," 312; Davis, *Exploitation of Pleasure,* 36.

75. Edwards, *Popular Amusements*, 134; Gorky, "Boredom," 311; Davis, *Exploitation of Pleasure*, 10.

76. For an analysis of the industrial developments see Staiger, "Announcing Wares"; and Bordwell, Staiger, and Thompson, *Classical Hollywood Cinema*, 121–41.

77. Simmel's writings anticipate the later theoretical writings about modernity and experience by Siegfried Kracauer and Walter Benjamin. David Frisby, for example, discusses the importance of Simmel—whom he characterizes as "the first sociologist to explicitly emphasize the analysis of social space"—on work on modernity by Kracauer and Benjamin. See David Frisby, *Fragments of Modernity: Theories of Modernity in the Work of Simmel, Kracauer, and Benjamin* (Cambridge, Mass.: MIT Press, 1986), 79. On the connection between Simmel and Kracauer see also Miriam Hansen, "America, Paris, the Alps: Kracauer (and Benjamin)," *Cinema and the Invention of Modern Life*, ed. Leo Charney and Vanessa R. Schwartz (Berkeley: University of California Press, 1995), 362–402; and Patrice Petro, *Aftershocks of the New: Feminism and Film History* (New Brunswick, N.J.: Rutgers University Press, 2002). Simmel's writings lend support to an important line of argument in film studies that draws on theoretical assessments of a modern urban sensibility to understand the way cinema refigured the experience of shock. On Simmel's analysis of the overstimulation of city streets in "Metropolis and Mental Life" see Ben Singer, "Modernity, Hyperstimulus, and the Rise of Popular Sensationalism," *Cinema and the Invention of Modern Life*, 72–99. Singer uses Simmel's essay to characterize the implications of the city experience as overstimulation effected through the presence of billboards on city streets, in illustrated press images, and in sensationalist serials during the transitional period. As the editors of the volume also suggest, Simmel's characterization of the city as "'the rapid crowding of changing images, the sharp discontinuity in the grasp of single glance, and the unexpectedness of onrushing impressions'" is also a description of cinema. See Leo Charney and Vanessa R. Schwartz, introduction to *Cinema and the Invention of Modern Life*, ed. Leo Charney and Vanessa R. Schwartz (Berkeley: University of California Press, 1995). For a discussion of the connection between theories of modernity and the cinema of attractions see Tom Gunning, "An Aesthetic of Astonishment: Early Film and the (In)credulous Spectator," *Art and Text* 34 (1989): 31–45. Gunning also relates temporality in the cinema of attractions, which is based on surprise and a "discontinuous succession of instants," to the experience of shock in Benjamin's assessment of modernity, and he contrasts this logic to classical cinema narrative with its unfolding of time associated with suspense. See Tom Gunning, "'Now You See It, Now You Don't': The Temporality of the Cinema of Attractions," *Velvet Light Trap* 32 (1993): 3–12. For a critique of the applicability of theories of modernity associated with Simmel, Kracauer, and Benjamin see David Bordwell, "La Nouvelle Mission de Feuillade; or, What Was Mise-en-Scène?" *Velvet Light Trap* 37 (1996): 10–29; and Charlie Keil, "'Visualized Narratives': Transitional Cinema and the Modernity Thesis," *Le cinéma au tournant du siècle/Cinema at the Turn of the Century*, ed. Claire Dupré la Tour, André Gaudreault, and Roberta Pearson (Lausanne/Québec: Editions Payot Lausanne, 1999), 133–47. Singer reasons through the applicability of a number of these critiques in his *Melodrama and Modernity*.

78. According to the *OED Cheap Jack* is used in this way by Mayhew ("The Cheap Jacks, or oratorical hucksters of hardware at fairs and other places") in 1851. *Cheap-John* is a synonymous term; for example, from 1875, the following usage is cited: "a

Cheap-John is retailing his rude witticisms . . . to induce people to purchase his Sheffield cutlery" (65, *OED*). The term was used in the United States from 1826 to refer to a peddler of cheap wares, in 1869 with reference to auctioneers shouting about the virtues of Cheap John clothing, and in 1880 in *Harper's Magazine*, with reference to a Jewish merchant: "Outside stood Isaac son—a traveling cheap-John who had opened a stock of second hand garments for ladies and gentlemen in a disused fish-house on the wharf." It is unclear from this reference to what extent the term was used in an anti-Semitic way. See Sir William Craigie and James R. Hulbert, *A Dictionary of American English, On Historical Principles*, vol. 1 (Chicago, Ill.: University of Chicago Press, 1938), 473. *Cheap John* could also be used to refer to a flophouse, cheap brothel, or a dirty and dilapidated saloon. See Harold Wentworth and Stuart Berg Flexner, eds., *Dictionary of American Slang* (New York: Thomas Y. Crowell, 1975), 95. In 1905 "cheap John" is reported as a phrase referring to poor taste, low breeding, and vulgarity, as in "We don't want any *cheap John shows* in this lecture course" (usage is from Northwest Arkansas); in 1912, as a merchant who does things in a cheap way, i.e., someone who sells goods on street corners (usage is from Western Indiana); and in 1915 "cheap John" is reported as a disparaging term linked to a vulgar show, namely, "'That was a *cheap John* show.'" See, respectively, *Dialect Notes* 3, pt. 1 (New Haven, Conn.: American Dialect Society, 1905): 74; *Dialect Notes* 3, pt. 8 (New Haven, Conn.: American Dialect Society, 1912): 573; and *Dialect Notes* 4, pt. 3 (New Haven, Conn.: American Dialect Society, 1915): 219. Cheapside, the market street in London, was given that name in 1559, the year of the coronation of Queen Elizabeth. In 1520 other streets in the vicinity had names bearing the trace of commerce, for example, Threadneedle (tailors), Milk (dairymen), and Friday (fishmongers) Streets. See Benjamin Woolley, *The Queen's Conjuror: The Life and Magic of Dr. Dee* (London: Flamingo, 2002), 64, 5. The term *amuse* similarly has origins in the marketplace, specifically, to practices intended to divert the attention of shopkeepers, as for example, "'to fling dust in the eyes.'" Amusers were people who filled their pockets with dust that they would throw into people's faces in order to divert and then rob them; it also applies to individuals who would draw people out of their shops under the pretense that someone they knew had drowned, and then the amusers' cohorts would steal from the shop. These usages originated in England in the eighteenth century but were current in the United States in 1859 and still current in 1903. See Eric Partridge, *A Dictionary of the Underworld: British and America* (London: Routledge and Kegan Paul, 1949; repr. with new addendum 1961), 7. Quotation in Partridge is from *A New Canting Dictionary* (1725).

CHAPTER THIRTEEN

The Menace of the Movies

Cinema's Challenge to the Theater in the Transitional Period

Roberta E. Pearson

New media must establish their audiences and their distinguishing characteristics relative to previously existing media—radio versus cinema, television versus radio, television versus cinema, the Internet versus television and cinema—and, during the first two decades of the twentieth century, cinema versus theater. In his 1949 book tracing the cinema's debt to the American theater, *Stage to Screen*, A. Nicholas Vardac stated that his goal was "to see how the film fits into the evolutionary pattern of world theater, how the blood stream of the screen was drawn from the stage, and how, under the pressure of this withdrawal, certain stage forms died upon the boards."[1] Vardac's book concerned only the two media's representational practices, but in this essay I will establish at least an association, if not a direct and provable causal relationship, between the migration of certain representational practices from stage to screen and the migration of certain audiences from theaters to cinemas. I will also demonstrate that, contra Vardac, the cinema had a positive as well as a negative influence on the theater. By the close of the transitional period's interplay between the two media, the theater had learned to appeal to a new minority elite audience, and the cinema had entrenched itself as the new mass medium.

In the early cinema period, circa 1895 to 1907, the new mechanical amusement remained dependent on the United States' then dominant mass medium in all its varied forms—vaudeville, burlesque, melodrama, and the "legitimate." The cinema borrowed performers from vaudeville, for example, the kinetoscopes that were shot at Edison's Black Maria studio. The cinema copied the theater's representational practices; for example, Edwin S. Porter drew on the melodrama's staging of simultaneous action.[2] The cinema was exhibited in vaudeville theaters and opera houses. This dependency continued to some extent during the initial years of the transitional period, roughly from 1908 to 1912, as the new medium struggled for economic stability and cultural respectability. The eight companies that in 1908 formed the Motion Picture Patents Company attempted to establish an oligopolistic control over the industry, resembling that exerted over the theater by Klaw and Erlanger's Syndicate. Studios allied with the so-called Trust employed and publicized theatrical stars such as Elita Proctor Otis, who appeared as Nancy in Vitagraph's *Oliver Twist* (1909), and Cecil Spooner, who played in Edison's *The Prince and the Pauper* (1909).[3] Seeking to establish its cultural bona fides, the cinema emulated theatrical performance style and filmed "great" stage plays and "great" dramatists, the American industry, for example, producing more than thirty Shakespeare films.[4]

As the cinema's drive for stability and respectability proved increasingly successful, the theater industry took notice of a potential rival. In July 1909 the *New York Dramatic Mirror* reported, "There is still a reluctance among the greater part of the prominent players to consider offers from the film manufacturers."[5] Klaw and Erlanger reinforced this reluctance a few months later, forbidding actors under contract with them to appear in films.[6] Perhaps the theatrical magnates had good reason for concern. Walter Prichard Eaton, one of the period's leading drama critics, said that same year, "Popular melodramas, since moving pictures became the rage, have decreased fifty percent in number."[7] According to William Lyon Phelps, another of the period's critics, the decrease in the number of melodramas, together with what he termed "pure" farces, began about 1907. Phelps believed the trend directly attributable to the cinema, which provided for ten cents what the theater offered for two dollars.[8] Despite Phelps's assertion, direct causality between the theater's fall and cinema's rise was much debated in period discourse. It is undeniable, however, that the theater entered a period of sustained economic downturn circa 1912, the decline heralded by the disastrous New York theatrical season of 1911–12, in which many of the legitimate houses remained closed for the entire season.[9] At this point theater began to experience the full force of the cinema's rivalry, as theaters were converted into moving picture houses and theatrical moguls were converted into moving picture moguls.

Drama critics despaired and the film trade press exulted as theaters became moving picture houses. In March 1912 Robert Grau said that "fully one-third of the theaters [in New York City] have been able to escape financial disaster only by resort[ing] to moving pictures. In fact, hardly a week goes by that some theater management . . . does not install a moving-picture machine, thereby avoiding bankruptcy."[10] The conversion of Broadway's Lyceum Theater, owned by theater impresario Daniel Frohman, had particular resonance. Reporting this event, the *Moving Picture World*'s Man About Town said that "Broadway types" held that "the invasion of the Broadway theaters by motion pictures" was a "freak venture." But the fact was that the shift to motion pictures occurred "during the regular season when all the houses had bookings that had several weeks to run. The conversion of these places was made because it is believed that from a business standpoint the pictures formed the best attraction."[11] By 1915 Harold Edwards, in one of two period pieces titled "The Menace of the Movies," reported that the new medium had made severe inroads on the old: theaters had converted to picture houses, pictures had replaced stock companies during the previous summer, and the stock companies' actors had migrated to Los Angeles in search of work in the motion pictures.[12] Economics dictated the continuation of the trend. Provincial theater managers had to meet fixed costs even while their houses remained dark in between bookings of touring drama companies. Managers could sometimes slot in touring vaudeville companies, but moving pictures, which meant that houses never had to be dark, were "a real godsend to theater owners in the first decade of [the twentieth] century." Even in the big cities "legitimate" theaters could offer only six evening and two matinee performances a week during a limited theater season. No wonder owners decided to show continuous performances of films, almost guaranteeing greater profits even at lower admission prices.[13]

By the end of 1913 Klaw and Erlanger, who had previously banned their actors from appearing in the new medium, capitulated, showing films in the New Amsterdam Theater, their most prestigious house, "every afternoon except on matinee days and on Sunday nights." Klaw and Erlanger's rivals, the Shubert brothers, Lee and Jacob (known as JJ or Jake), had decided to replace the Sunday night band concerts in their Hippodrome Theater with moving pictures. Said the *Motion Picture News,* "The utilization of their crack theaters by K&E and the Shuberts to show motion pictures during the spare moments is the entering wedge. It will go further because they are planning to show the right kind of pictures [big pictures, real features and educational subjects]."[14] Neither K&E nor the Shuberts opted for the one- and two-reelers playing in New York City's still numerous nickelodeons but rather for the new multireel features imported from Europe and beginning to be produced by the American studios. Sara Bernhardt's *Queen Elizabeth* (1912) had premiered at Frohman's Lyceum Theater prior to its permanent conversion to moving pictures. The Shuberts had formed the Shubert Feature Film Booking Company to book films for their theaters and achieved success with *Traffic in Souls* (1913).[15]

But these theatrical impresarios were not just going to show features; they were going to make them. In 1912 Daniel Frohman joined forces with Adolph Zukor to form the Famous Players Film Company.[16] In June 1913, as D. W. Griffith completed the California shooting of *Judith of Bethulia,* his New York–based Biograph bosses made a deal with K&E to produce films based on the 104 plays owned by the partners. Biograph would produce two films a week to be shown in legitimate theaters at Broadway prices.[17] By 1914 the World Film Corporation's general manager, Lewis J. Selznick, today most famous as the father of David, had exclusive distribution rights to plays owned by the Shuberts, William A. Brady, Charles E. Blaney, Owen Davis, and the Thomas McEnnery Syndicate.[18] In that same year Cecil B. DeMille, scion of a theatrical dynasty, abandoned the stage to join the Jesse L. Lasky Feature Play Company, which in 1916 merged with Zukor's Famous Players to form the company that soon would become Paramount Pictures. Sumiko Higashi observes that DeMille's going to Hollywood was "part of a wholesale importation of Broadway producers, actors, playwrights, art directors, and music composers."[19]

Period discourse substantiates Higashi's assertion. Said "TB" in an article about K&E's film ventures, "[Motion pictures are] absorbing dramatists, theatrical producers, painters, actors and actresses and the like. Instead of the stage annexing or absorbing the motion picture, it is the other way."[20] Robert Grau, speaking in 1912 of the entry of former Broadway players into the new industry, concluded, "Another year should witness so many well-known players into the newer field that the difference to the theater-going public between the real and the mechanical drama will tend to be visibly diminished."[21] "TB" and Grau both got it wrong. The motion pictures did not absorb the theater, partially because the differences between the two media were not "visibly diminished" but vastly accentuated, as can be seen in discourses concerning (1) each medium's essential or defining characteristics and (2) the nature of the reception and composition of the two media's audiences. During the transitional period the cinema became the medium judged to best suit the tastes of the mass of the American public. At the same time, the live theater, now primarily spoken drama rather than the melodrama, vaudeville, and burlesque of old, became a medium for the minority, its increased cultural status compensating for the loss of audiences. The cinema had achieved sufficient respectability to become mainstream fare for the majority, but it could never rival the cultural prestige of a theater now catering to minority tastes.

The American theater had not been perceived as culturally prestigious prior to the advent of the cinema. According to Richard Butsch drama critics had fulminated about the debased state of the American theater since the turn of the century, seeing it as "commercially successful but artistically bankrupt," with its "second rate" plays, "histrionic" acting and a theatrical syndicate that had driven out "independent producers devoted to art."[22] Such criticisms did not prevent those within the theatrical community from asserting their medium's aesthetic superiority to its new mechanical rival. Said playwright William DeMille, concerning his brother's desertion to Hollywood, "I cannot understand how you are willing to identify yourself with a cheap form of amusement . . . which no one will ever allude to as art. Surely you know the contempt with which the movie is regarded by every writer, actor and producer on Broadway."[23] Walter Prichard Eaton heartily agreed. For him the theater was "the most universal of fine arts," its "varied aesthetic appeal" providing its patrons with romance, poetry, and intellectual stimulation. The movies, by contrast, were a "semi-mechanical pantomime" falling short of every artistic criterion. "They are utterly incapable of intellectual content. . . . Only the skeleton of narrative is possible, and usually that narrative is utterly banal. All poetry, all music, all flash of wit, all dignity of spoken eloquence, they can never know."[24]

Some in the film industry conceded the argument, still looking to the theater for their cultural bona fides. Adolph Zukor, whose company promised the public "Famous Players in Famous Plays," had particular incentive to remain deferential to the older medium. Writing in the *Moving Picture World,* Zukor said, "The moving picture man must try to do as artistic, as high class, and as notable things in his line of entertainment as such men as . . . Charles and Daniel Frohman were doing in high-class Broadway theaters."[25] Others contested the theater industry's assertions of superiority. In 1918 the fan magazine *Photoplay* reported that eminent Broadway producer David Belasco had recently compared the cinema unfavorably to the theater. The magazine accused Belasco of "speaking in ponderous generalizations of things concerning which he has, obviously, almost no knowledge."[26] Stephen Bush, regular columnist for the *Moving Picture World,* argued that the cinema was closer to the originary fount of the drama than was the theater. "The playwright . . . must have a series of clear, strong, simple pictures in his mind before he begins to prepare his dialogue. . . . The screen is a unique power for the translation, the visualization and the plain interpretation of all dramatic values."[27]

In the same article Bush also said, "In all that pertains to the spectacular side and to scenic perfection the screen is the master of the stage."[28] Even the theater's passionate adherents, such as eminent critic and Columbia professor Brander Matthews, readily conceded the cinema's greater capacity for spectacle and photographic realism: "The moving-picture director can go into the open and maneuver in a vast and indefinite perspective. . . . There are a multitude of things which the drama can do only incompletely and with difficulty and which the movies can do easily and superbly. So far as mere pictorial story-telling is concerned the drama is simply outclassed."[29] But the cinema was hoist on its own petard, its detractors insisting that the medium's capacity for "pictorial story-telling" rendered it inherently inartistic. William A. Brady, theatrical producer, partner in the World Film Corporation, and by 1918 president of the National Association of Motion Picture Industry, said that adapting stage properties for the screen "made frequent artistic muddles of good plays." The cinema's need to "open the play up" as we would now put it, or the "struggle for good photography, or a struggle to transplant it from stage tradition to the open air" as Brady put it, was achieved at the expense of "artistic subtlety . . . intimate revelation of character."[30]

The debate over aesthetic value shaded into a debate over media effects. Did the cinema's realism and spectacle appeal to the spectators' finer emotions and imagination or stimulate their coarser sensibilities? Could the cinema offer spectators the transcendent experience that defines true art? Brady believed that it could not: "The big productions on the screen have pushed realism to the point where it has stimulated the popular imagination beyond measure. . . . The ideal dramatic effect in a theater is what we can throw upon the sensitive imagination by suggestion. An ideal sinks deeper when it is evolved from a suggestion than when from a compelling realism of fact."[31] Walter Prichard Eaton asserted that the moving pictures "have a cruel realism which at once dulls the imagination and destroys the illusive romance of art."[32] The film spectator could never experience "the deep emotional glow, the keen intellectual zest, the warm aesthetic satisfaction, which come from living, vital acting, from distinguished, witty speech," crucial elements of a good theatrical production.[33] Others thought that the cinema's impression of reality could offer the same emotional involvement and catharsis as older art forms. The moving pictures, said Day Allen Willey, were "true to life in every detail" since they originated from "that wonderful artificial eye, the camera lens. So we know that we are seeing actual occurrences—at least, we think we are—and they are so realistic that we may laugh or cry or watch the canvas with every thought centred on it, as we would read an absorbing novel."[34]

The debate formulated at the beginning of the twentieth century still structures critical reception at the beginning of the twenty-first century. Today's film critics, believing delight in visual pleasure to be a less legitimate spectatorial response than involvement in narrative, condemn blockbuster action/adventure and science fiction films for sacrificing character and story to the demands of spectacle. Cinema that provides visual stimulation is still seen as culturally deficient relative to other art forms. Another early-twenty-first-century debate echoes but reverses the terms of an early-twentieth-century debate. In the present, hugely popular film stars such as Nicole Kidman occasionally appear on Broadway and in the West End. Critics ask, "Can these film stars really act, that is, sustain a convincing live performance, or is their casting simply designed to attract punters who would otherwise never attend the live theater?" In the past, circa 1913, hugely popular theater stars began to appear in the moving pictures. Critics asked, "Would theatrical stars really contribute to the artistry of the new medium, or was their casting merely a cynical ploy to attract the punters who might otherwise never go to the movies?" Harold Edwards, in his "Menace of the Movies" article, asserted that the casting of theatrical stars had little to do with art. "There never was a more frankly commercial argument. The advertising value of the name of a star is rated at so much, the name of the play at so much, and if the star photographs well and the play lends itself to picture adaptation, why all the better, but these are secondary considerations."[35]

Did the theatrical stars succeed in attracting new patrons to the cinema? We have no hard empirical evidence, but, according to William Brady, regular filmgoers found the "great stars" disappointing. "The artistic failure of some of the big stars as motion picture actors has been generally admitted."[36] We cannot precisely ascertain the meaning of Brady's phrase "artistic failure," although it most likely hints at an incompatibility between theatrically trained actors and the new medium in terms of performance technique and audience appeal. A detailed study of theatrical actors in films of the transitional period would enhance our understanding of the manner in which the new medium superseded the old as America's mass entertainment, with regard to both audiences and signifying practices. I recommend the project to some ambitious doctoral student but will restrict myself here to a single case study. In 1916 the tercentenary of William Shakespeare's birth, English actor-manager Sir Herbert Beerbohm-Tree appeared in a film version of *Macbeth* produced by the Triangle-Reliance Film Company.[37] The tercentenary year saw three other American Shakespeare films, *Romeo and Juliet,* directed by J. Gordon Edwards, produced by the Fox Film Corporation, and starring Theda Bara; *Romeo and Juliet,* directed by John W. Noble, produced by Metro, and starring Francis X. Bushman; and *King Lear,* directed by Ernest Warde, produced by the Thanhouser Company, and starring stage actor Frederick Warde. Two of these productions, *Macbeth* and *King Lear,* featured well-known stage actors, whereas both *Romeo and Juliet*s featured very popular film stars. The film critics loved the spectacle of Tree's filmed *Macbeth,* singling out for praise that which the cinema undeniably did best, but audiences nonetheless stayed away in droves. The two productions of *Romeo and Juliet* seemed to have fared somewhat better at the box office, although neither was a resounding success, and both displeased the critics. The critical reception and box-office performance of these four films reflect the distinctions made by contemporary critics and audiences between the moving pictures and the spoken drama.[38]

Sir Herbert's own comments on his performance style indicate that he may not have been attuned to the requirements of silent film acting. By 1916 film actors externalized characters' thoughts and emotions through a combination of small, flowing gestures, facial expression, and the use of props, augmented by close-ups and editing patterns. Since performance style was not, as on the stage, the primary signifier of characters' mental processes, film acting, in a sense, required "less" of the performer than did theatrical acting.[39] Yet Sir Herbert insisted on the reverse, saying that screen acting demanded more energy than theatrical acting. "Acting before the camera . . . is much more exhausting than acting on the stage. . . . The lens cannot be cheated, and every second you must throw yourself into the part without letting down a moment."[40] Sir Herbert's throwing himself into the part was too much for some critics. *Photoplay* opined that *Macbeth* "fails of greatness because it relied upon stellar acting, and after the first few episodes, the acting consisted, on the part of Sir Herbert, of staring and wobbling, and that staring eye, when translated into black and white, becomes extremely monotonous."[41] Most reviewers of the Fox *Romeo and Juliet* considered it more a "Bara" film than a "Shakespeare" film and implied that audiences did also, a probable conclusion since the star was then at the height of her fame and popularity. The reviews also suggest that the Fox film tailored its cinematic signifying practices to its star, which is not surprising given that director Edwards had worked with the star on three previous films. Commented *Variety*:

> Theda Bara, of course, has an enormous following among the picture fans who will be interested in her Juliet, and the picture is put forward frankly to please them and without any great pretensions to artistic purpose. The whole film is highly flavored with Miss Bara. . . . [E]very artifice, such as "close ups" and holding Juliet in the conspicuous position of the picture to center attention upon her is employed to emphasize the star.[42]

Macbeth failed so badly that Triangle attempted to terminate its five-film contract with Sir Herbert, next casting him as an American farmer in the hopes that the actor would rebel;[43] meanwhile, the *Romeo and Juliets* seem to have done relatively well, at least in New York City. *Moving Picture World*'s Stephen Bush contrasted *Macbeth*'s uptown failure with the eager reception accorded the other two films in downtown Manhattan's poorer quarters:

> Shakespeare in motion pictures . . . failed at the Rialto. . . . I contrast this Broadway coldness toward the immortal bard with the exuberant welcome given him by Fourteenth Street. . . . In the Academy, for many years a hopeless morgue, huge crowds tread upon each others' heels to look at Fox's "Romeo and Juliet" while less than a block away Charley Steiner's big playhouse is playing to continued capacity with the Metro version of the immortal tragedy of love.[44]

Bush's observations regarding the fate of *Macbeth* hint at several factors determining the box-office performance of the Shakespeare tercentenary films. Economics provides the simplest explanation for *Macbeth*'s failure relative to the two *Romeo and Juliets*.[45] The Triangle-Reliance Company that produced and released *Macbeth* strove to put the cinema on a footing with the legitimate stage by making films with top stars, exhibiting them in select theaters such as the Rialto (one of the first movie palaces), and charging the standard theatrical admission fee of two dollars. The uptown crowd at whom *Macbeth* was aimed apparently resisted the lure of a well-known theatrical star, whose stage productions they had previously patronized, perhaps because they still considered the movies déclassé. The downtown crowd that did patronize films apparently preferred fifty-cent Shakespeare to two-dollar Shakespeare, most probably because the by then well-established cinematic star system predisposed audiences to respond more favorably to familiar performers performing in a familiar manner.

I will return to the issue of audiences by way of examining the assumption about the implicit nature of the film medium that underlay the debates concerning realism and theater/film stars. Day Allen Willey concluded that moving pictures had to be "true to life in every detail" since they originated from "that wonderful artificial eye, the camera lens." As long as the cinema's subjects remained primarily nonfictional, its technical basis advantaged it against its older competitors, for moving pictures provided spectators a more "realistic" view of the world than panoramas or stereographs and the like ever could. But as the cinema began to threaten the primacy of the spoken drama, its mechanical nature became a cultural disadvantage. According to Harold Edwards, the movies posed a menace precisely because "photographed pantomime reflected on the screen is not equivalent to human beings moving and speaking on the stage."[46] The moving pictures should conform to their essential nature and do what they do best rather than competing with the spoken drama: "As a recorder of news events and of mammoth spectacles, as a realistic medium for the presentation of facts and the furtherance of a propaganda, and as an entertainment in cheap theaters, the motion picture serves a beneficial purpose. But efforts to photograph the stage seem doomed to failure. The spirit, the meaning, the charm elude the coldly, exact eyed—the camera."[47] In his own assessment of the menace of the movies the prescient Walter Prichard Eaton foresaw a world where the mechanical reigned supreme. If you reduced plays to a motion picture screen, "the stage of Sophocles and Shakespeare and Moliere and Sheridan, of Garrick and Cibber and Kean and Booth, is dead and done for completely. We are entering the last phase of mechanical civilization. Everything from undershirts to art is now machine made. It only remains to hatch babies artificially; and no doubt that will come before very long. Science is king."[48]

For Eaton, and undoubtedly for others, the spoken drama's mechanical, artificial, and soulless rival fueled anxieties related to the Fordism and rationality of a rapidly advancing modernity. The economic decline that began circa 1912 must have intensified the fears of the theater's passionate devotees. The title of Anna Steese Richardson's 1915 *McClure's* article "Who Closed the Theater in Your Town?" attested to the extent of the crisis in the theater industry, assuming that many readers would take the question personally. Some blamed the movies, and some did not, but all agreed that the condition of the touring road shows had been a factor. Steese tells the apocryphal story of a man returning to his hometown after seven years in New York City. Finding the Grand Opera House shut, he asks a journalist friend for an explanation. The journalist responds, "Folks just got out of the habit of going to the theater." But it was the poor quality of the productions rather than the movies that undermined the theatergoing habit. The town had been getting "number two" companies, minus the original stars, cast, and sets, and even some of the scenes, since plays might be cut to enable the company to catch the last train out of town. Said the fictional journalist, "Our salaried men would rather see a good dramatic or musical show—if they were sure of getting a dollar's worth for a dollar. . . . But a seat for the movies costs fifteen cents at the most. . . . Your old neighbors patronize the movies because they get their money's worth, while at the Grand Opera House they didn't."[49] The mechanically reproduced motion picture delivered the money's worth that touring theater companies no longer guaranteed.

The cinema's mechanical nature may have culturally disadvantaged it vis-à-vis the theater, but the ability to strike numerous, identical prints of the same film gave it the economic advantage. Both Walter Prichard Eaton and Harold Edwards acknowledged the uncomfortable fact that a cinematic performance, unlike its theatrical counterpart, did not vary from city to town to country. Said Eaton, "The patron of the spoken drama, in any town except the few large centres, is generally taking chances with an unknown play and unknown players. The smallest town, however, sees the same motion-picture players as the largest—there are no second companies in the film world. John Bunny and Mary Pickford 'star' in a hundred towns at once."[50] Eaton's comment attested to the new economic stability the film industry enjoyed in the wake of the struggle between the Trust and the Independents. "A photoplay exhibited at the Knickerbocker in September may be seen a few months later in ten cent houses; then in five cent houses, and save that the film probably will be worn and accompanying music a bit ragged, the last entertainment will be as good as the first."[51] By 1915 the industry had already begun to establish the intricately designed system of first, second, and third runs that would form a crucial component of the classical Hollywood cinema's vertical integration. As the theater industry suffered unprecedented economic hardship, the film industry grew ever stronger. As Edwards remarked, "Motion pictures have become national and the stage local."[52]

The crisis in the theater industry, coupled with the film industry's continued growth, caused a fundamental shift in the American mediascape noted by contemporary commentators. The gloomy Walter Pritchard Eaton deplored what he saw as the growing rift between the theater and the moving pictures. "Already the spoken drama and the silent drama are far apart. Each is the amusement . . . of a separate and antagonistic class."[53] Eaton, taking his cue from Matthew Arnold, feared that this split in the audience would have a deleterious effect on the nation since the theater no longer served as an uplifting and civilizing influence on the lower orders. Others believed that the cinema, far from exacerbating class conflict, constituted a force for democracy and civilization. As early as 1907, at which point the film industry had barely begun its struggle for respectability, the *Saturday Evening Post* published an article that took a very sanguine view of the new medium, Joseph Medill Patterson's "The Nickelodeon: The Poor Man's Elementary Course in the Drama." "Today the moving-picture machine cannot be overlooked as an effective protagonist of democracy. For through it the drama, always a big fact in the lives of the people at the top, is now becoming a big fact in the lives of the people at the bottom."[54]

Was Eaton right? Was there no overlap between theater and cinema audiences? Exactly who went to the cinema, and who went to the theater? Was Patterson right? Would the moving pictures not only introduce the "people at the bottom" to the drama but perhaps induce them to patronize the real thing? Or would the new medium simply kill off the old one? These questions were hotly debated not only in the film and theater trade press but in more mainstream publications, such as the *Saturday Evening Post*. The majority of commentators thought that the cinema had to some extent contributed to the theater's woes by luring some of its erstwhile clientele to the nickelodeons. As early as 1909 Day Allen Willey, speaking of the decrease in box-office receipts at the legitimate and vaudeville theaters and the disbanding of theatrical companies, said that nearby nickelodeons often accounted not just for the empty seats in the gallery but for the absence of "every class of theater goer."[55] By 1911 the *New York Dramatic Mirror* reported this as conventional wisdom. "There is no doubt that the motion pictures have quite measurably injured the theater in some respects. . . . The cheaper seating in all theaters . . . have *[sic]* suffered from the picture competition."[56]

Walter Prichard Eaton disagreed. In articles dating from 1912 and 1913 he contended that the nickelodeon audience had never previously patronized the theater. In "What's the Matter with the Road?" he asserted that "[the motion picture's] appeal is . . . to a large class of the population who, hitherto, have not patronized the higher forms of drama at all, rather than to the former gallery patrons of that drama." Motion picture audiences bore a "much closer resemblance to the audiences at vaudeville, and they contain . . . a vastly greater proportion of children and young people. . . . Even in the smaller towns, many of the patrons of the canned drama, particularly the juvenile patrons, are not of the class which supports . . . the legitimate drama."[57] In his 1913 "Menace of the Movies" article Eaton asserted, "It is obvious that many of these twenty millions of canned theatergoers never were patrons of the conventional playhouse."[58] Eaton seems attuned to nuances of difference among theatrical forms and audiences missed by his contemporaries, although he did not advance hard empirical data to substantiate his assertions. Ninety years on such substantiation would be at best difficult, although the effort might prove a worthy task for my hypothetical ambitious doctoral student perhaps aware of archival sources unknown to me.

By 1915 even Eaton had accepted the prevailing view. The cinema had caused "not only the practical extinction of the cheaper melodramas which used to cater to 'the masses' . . . but also the practical desertion of the gallery seats for dramas of the better sort."[59] But did the cinema's impact on the older medium have to be entirely negative? Might it paradoxically, as some believed, prove the savior of the drama? The *New York Dramatic Mirror,* the flagship trade paper of the theatrical industry, had obvious reasons to hope that the cinema might eventually lure audiences to the live theater. "Those persons whose only knowledge of amusement at all related to the drama was originally gained in the smaller and cheaper motion picture places have risen in taste and appreciation to the better picture theaters, and from patronage of these theaters must develop a taste for the drama itself in its best circumstances."[60] Robert Grau, writing a year later, agreed: "The full houses of the cheaper theaters are, to a certain extent, composed of audiences to whom theater-going is entirely a novelty. These people, attracted to the photo-play by the cheap price of admission, become gradually possessed of the desire to see plays presented by live actors."[61]

The cinema may have replaced the theater as the majority's favorite medium, but elite critics still clung to their assumption of the theater's cultural superiority. Eaton shared this assumption but tempered it with an economic and sociological realism. People attracted to the photoplay because of the cheap price of admission may have desired to see live actors, but the theater's higher admission prices and price-discriminatory seating patterns would dissuade them. The working-class father at the cinema "will sit on the ground floor, with his own kind. . . . Here he is apart from his day-time distinctions of class. . . . He is paying as much as anybody else, and getting as good a seat." For this reason "in the larger towns, where the higher-priced drama co-exists with the motion-picture plays, the line of cleavage is sharply drawn in the character of the audience, and this line is the same line which marks the proletariat from the *bourgeoisie* and capitalist class."[62] In other words the movies' chief distinction from the theater was that "They are cheap."[63]

Yet some would have argued that the cinema's beneficial effect on the theater consisted not in educating new audiences for it but in freeing it from the demands of the mass audience. Even Eaton realized that theater had undergone an artistic renaissance at the same time as it hemorrhaged audiences. The 1910s saw a "new interest in serious drama, focused in the Drama League of America with its fifty thousand members, the course in dramatic composition and study in our colleges, the sudden new demand for plays in printed form, and finally the growth of native drama."[64] Jack Poggi, in the most complete economic history of the American theater yet written, argues that as long as American theatrical producers depended for the majority of their profits on the provinces rather than New York, plays had to appeal to the common interests of a mass audience scattered across the country, much as did the films of the classical Hollywood cinema. Only after the decline of the road and the initiation of the noncommercial theater movement through the establishment of companies such as the Provincetown Players, which first staged Eugene O'Neill's plays, could American playwrights write for a minority taste.[65] The same might be said of all those involved in the spoken drama, from directors to actors to set designers—no longer were they constrained by the taste of the majority.

In 1916, the same year that Sir Herbert Beerbohm-Tree made his cinematic *Macbeth,* he also appeared in *The Merchant of Venice* at Broadway's New Amsterdam Theater, the play staged in the spectacular, "realistic," and "historically authentic" style for which the actor-manager was famous. At the same time, the amateur Drama Society of New York offered a two-week run of *The Tempest* at the Century Theater, performed in accordance with contemporary understanding of the customs of Elizabethan stagecraft. New York's critics, who only a few years earlier had praised Tree's spectacular productions, now claimed that the Drama Society's *Tempest* approached much more closely the true spirit of Shakespeare than Tree's visually excessive *Merchant.* Said *Vogue*'s critic, "The production prepared by the Drama Society affords the poet an unimpeded appeal to the imaginations of the public, whereas the production provided by Sir Herbert Tree inhibits the enjoyment of imagination by a sedulous insistence on superfluous details of actuality."[66] Richard Silvester, in an article on Elizabethan staging published at precisely the time that Sir Herbert was performing his *Merchant of Venice* at the New Amsterdam, explained why a "sedulous insistence" on "actuality" should be deplored: "We have become weary of imitating actuality represented for itself alone, and have begun to look for an interpretation of the abstract through the medium of stage pictures and effects. Late in the nineteenth century, producers were satisfied if they succeeded in making their spectators believe what they saw. Now, by means of visual suggestions, they try to induce their audience to imagine more than they can actually see."[67] Appealing to the imagination by suggestive means, the province of the theater, was now much more culturally credible than satisfying the baser instincts through spectacle, the province of the cinema. Theater had lost the mass audience but stood at the top of the cultural hierarchy, whereas cinema had gained the mass audience but would for decades be relegated to the cultural outer darkness.

The rise of cinema as the country's mass medium and the consignment of the theater to a minority taste resonates in suggestive fashion with what happened roughly half a century later, when television displaced cinema as the most popular of media. As I noted just above, Eaton had written in 1913 of a new interest in serious drama, an interest he attributed to the not-so-convivial meeting of the theater with an upstart cinema. In the 1960s, as the classical Hollywood studio system fell apart and network television enjoyed its relatively brief hegemony, art house and revival cinemas sprang up, film production and cinema studies programs appeared in colleges around the country, serious film magazines began publication, and the American independent cinema flourished. As network television's hegemony fell apart in the multichannel, multimedia environment of the late twentieth century, television studies programs sprang up alongside film studies programs, critics and audiences engaged in serious debates about the medium's aesthetic and cultural value, and "good" television flourished outside the three traditional networks—*The Simpsons* at Fox, *The Sopranos* at HBO. Might the intermedial competition between cinema and theater at the beginning of the twentieth century tell us something about the competition between cinema and television in the second half of the twentieth century and perhaps even about the competition among cinema, television, and the Internet at the beginning of the twenty-first century? Can a mass medium appealing to a mass audience ever be perceived as having cultural value?

NOTES

1. A. Nicholas Vardac, *Stage to Screen: Theatrical Method from Garrick to Griffith* (Cambridge, Mass.: Harvard University Press, 1949), vii.

2. Ibid., 23.

3. Eileen Bowser, *The Transformation of Cinema, 1907–1915* (Berkeley: University of California Press, 1990), 107.

4. See Roberta E. Pearson, *Eloquent Gestures: The Transformation of Performance Style in the Griffith Biograph Films* (Berkeley: University of California Press, 1992); and William Uricchio and Roberta E. Pearson, *Reframing Culture: The Case of the Vitagraph Quality Films* (Princeton, N.J.: Princeton University Press, 1993).

5. "Spectator's Comments," *New York Dramatic Mirror,* 10 July 1909, 15, quoted in Bowser, *Transformation of Cinema,* 106.

6. Bowser, *Transformation of Cinema,* 106.

7. Walter Prichard Eaton, "The Canned Drama," *American Magazine,* September 1909, 500.

8. See Jack Poggi, *Theater in America: The Impact of Economic Forces, 1870–1967* (Ithaca, N.Y.: Cornell University Press, 1968), 263.

9. Kemp R. Niver, *Klaw and Erlanger Present Famous Plays in Pictures* (Los Angeles, Calif.: Locare Research Group, 1976), 33.

10. Robert Grau, "The Moving-Picture Show and the Living Drama," *American Monthly Review of Reviews* (March 1912): 329.

11. "Observations by Our Man About Town," *Moving Picture World,* 27 April 1912, 323.

12. Harold Edwards, "The Menace of the Movies," *The Theater* (October 1915): 176.

13. Niver, *Klaw and Erlanger,* 28–29.

14. George D. Proctor, "Oh, It's an Interesting Life!" *Motion Picture News,* 29 November 1913, quoted in Niver, *Klaw and Erlanger,* 49.

15. Kevin Lewis, "A World across from Broadway: The Shuberts and the Movies," *Film History* 1 (1987): 39.

16. Bowser, *Transformation of Cinema,* 226.

17. See Niver, *Klaw and Erlanger,* for a full accounting of this enterprise, including analysis of the surviving films.

18. Bowser, *Transformation of Cinema,* 226. For more on the World Film Company see Lewis, "World across from Broadway."

19. Sumiko Higashi, *Cecil B. DeMille and American Culture: The Silent Era* (Berkeley: University of California Press, 1994), 8.

20. TB, "Marc Klaw, The 'K' of K&E," *Motion Picture News,* 15 November 1913, cited in Niver, *Klaw and Erlanger,* 43.

21. Grau, "Moving-Picture Show," 332.

22. Richard Butsch, *The Making of American Audiences: From Stage to Television, 1750–1990* (Cambridge, U.K.: Cambridge University Press, 2000), 121–22.

23. Higashi, *Cecil B. DeMille,* 7.

24. Walter Prichard Eaton, "Class-Consciousness and the 'Movies,'" *Atlantic Monthly,* January 1915, 53, 52, 55.

25. Adolph Zukor, "Famous Players in Famous Plays," *Moving Picture World,* 11 July 1914, 186, quoted in Higashi, *Cecil B. DeMille,* 8.

26. "Close-ups," *Photoplay,* July 1918, 75, quoted in Higashi, *Cecil B. DeMille,* 17.

27. W. Stephen Bush, "Classics and the Screen," *Moving Picture World,* 11 November 1916, 863.

28. Ibid.

29. Brander Matthews, "Are the Movies a Menace to the Drama?" *North American Review* (March 1917): 449–50.

30. William A. Brady, "Have the Movies Ideals?" *Forum* (March 1918): 310.

31. Ibid., 313.

32. Eaton, "Class-Consciousness and the 'Movies,'" 55.

33. Walter Prichard Eaton, "The Theater: The Menace of the Movies," *American Magazine,* September 1913, 58.

34. Day Allen Willey, "The Theater's New Rival," *Lippincott's Monthly Magazine,* October 1909, 455. The debate over the value of realism and spectacle occurs during what Tom Gunning characterizes as the transition between the "cinema of attractions" and "the cinema of narrative integration" (Tom Gunning, "The Cinema of Attractions: Early Film, Its Spectator, and the Avant-Garde," in *Early Cinema: Space, Frame, Narrative,* ed. Thomas Elsaesser [London: British Film Institute, 1990], 45–55).The criticisms of cinema as too "realistic" and too "spectacular" illustrate the persistence of visual pleasure even in the new narratively integrated feature films. The realism/spectacle debate also relates to Lee Grieveson's work on censorship during the transitional period. The realist depiction of contemporary social problems such as prostitution and white slavery was acceptable in literature and even on the stage but objectionable in cinema because of the medium's perceived imagistic power over susceptible audiences. See Lee Grieveson, *Policing Cinema: Movies and Censorship in Early-Twentieth-Century America* (Berkeley: University of California Press, 2004).

35. Edwards, "Menace of the Movies," 178.

36. Brady, "Have the Movies Ideals?" 310.

37. Sir Herbert had made two other Shakespearean films, both in England: an excerpt from *King John* in 1899 and a thirty-minute *Henry VIII* in 1911. See Robert Hamilton Ball, "The Shakespeare Film as Record: Sir Herbert Beerbohm-Tree," *Shakespeare Quarterly* (July 1952): 230–32. See also Ball's *Shakespeare on Silent Film: A Strange Eventful History* (London: George Allen and Unwin, 1968).

38. Unfortunately, none of the four films survives, so my analysis is predicated entirely on period discourse, of which, for *King Lear,* there is very little. For a fuller discussion of these films see Roberta E. Pearson and William Uricchio, "'Shrieking from Below the Gratings': Sir Herbert Beerbohm-Tree's *Macbeth* and His Critics," in *Reclamations of Shakespeare,* ed. A.J. Hoenselaars (Amsterdam: Rodopi, 1994).

39. For a discussion of the transformation of cinematic acting immediately prior to this period see Pearson, *Eloquent Gestures.*

40. *Memphis (Tennessee) Appeal,* 12 March 1916, Herbert Beerbohm-Tree Scrapbooks, Robinson-Locke Collection, Billy Rose Theater Collection, New York Public Library for the Performing Arts at Lincoln Center (hereafter NYPL). A contemporary of Sir Herbert's, E. H. Southern, shared his opinion, saying that facial expression "must be exaggerated beyond anything he has ever permitted himself on the legitimate stage" (E. H. Southern, "The 'New Art' as Discovered by E. H. Southern," *Craftsman* [September 1916]: 579).

41. *Photoplay,* August 1916, Herbert Beerbohm-Tree Scrapbooks, NYPL.

42. "Romeo and Juliet," *Variety,* 27 October 1916, clipping files, NYPL.

43. Ball, "The Shakespeare Film as Record," 235.

44. Bush, "Classics and the Screen," 863. "The Academy" refers to the Academy of Music on Fourteenth Street.

45. I lack sufficient data on the Thanhouser *King Lear* to discuss its success or failure.

46. Edwards, "Menace of the Movies," 177.

47. Ibid., 178.

48. Eaton, "The Theater," 55.

49. Anna Steese Richardson, "Who Closed the Theater in Your Town?" *McClure's,* October 1915, 18, 19.

50. Eaton, "Class-Consciousness and the 'Movies,'" 49.

51. Edwards, "Menace of the Movies," 177.

52. Ibid.

53. Eaton, "Class-Consciousness and the 'Movies,'" 52.

54. Joseph Medill Patterson, "The Nickelodeon: The Poor Man's Elementary Course in the Drama," *Saturday Evening Post,* 23 November 1907, 11.

55. Willey, "Theater's New Rival," 58.

56. "A Matter of Evolution," *New York Dramatic Mirror,* 4 January 1911, 3.

57. Walter Prichard Eaton, "What's the Matter with the Road?" *American Magazine,* July 1912, 359.

58. Eaton, "The Theater," 58.

59. Eaton, "Class Consciousness and the 'Movies,'" 49.

60. "Matter of Evolution," *New York Dramatic Mirror,* 3.

61. Grau, "Moving-Picture Show," 322.

62. Eaton, "Class Consciousness and the 'Movies,'" 50, 51.

63. Eaton, "The Theater," 59.

64. Ibid., 58. Richard Butsch tells us, "The Drama League was founded in 1910 to educate middle class American audiences about good drama, by helping them select plays" (Butsch, *Making of American Audiences*, 122).

65. Jack Poggi, *Theater in America*, 260–62.

66. "The Merchant of Venice," *Vogue*, 15 June 1916, Herbert Beerbohm-Tree Scrapbooks, NYPL.

67. Richard Silvester, "The Shakespearean Stage and the Stage of To-day," *Review of Reviews* (May 1916): 591.

CHAPTER FOURTEEN

"It's a Long Way to Filmland"

Starlets, Screen Hopefuls, and Extras in Early Hollywood

Shelley Stamp

Here they come, extra girls, hordes and hordes of them flocking to the studios. Each one believes she is chosen. I pity them all.
ACTRESS IRENE WALLACE, *Green Book*, 1914

Just a word of warning here to the aspiring young girls all over the country who may believe that a trip to Los Angeles will put them in the pictures. The warning is: don't come.
Everybody's Magazine, October 1915

Beginning in the mid-1910s, trade papers, fan magazines, and general-interest publications reported, with mounting alarm, the long lines of young women waiting outside studio gates in Los Angeles hoping to find work as motion picture "extras." In its celebrated diagnosis of the "movie-struck girl" *Woman's Home Companion* noted "at eight o'clock every morning you may see a pathetic breadline of waiting actresses anxious for 'extra' work at a few dollars a day, hoping each time that the director will give them the opportunity to make a hit, and ultimately reach stardom."[1] Essanay, Lasky, and Reliance-Majestic all reported some thirty or forty applicants each day.[2] "Hundreds apply weekly at a film studio for employment," one 1916 witness recalled.[3] Another testified that "tens of thousands of film aspirants" flocked to the new filmmaking capital each year, "ranging from the fourteen-year-old school girl in love with a certain film hero to the grandmother of fifty-odd who has suddenly discovered her histrionic talent."[4] The tendency to describe all starstruck hopefuls as female, and to present them as silly creatures caught under the sway of overwrought emotion, was characteristic of most reports. Only three kinds of young women sought motion picture work, claimed another 1914 observer: "foolish chits" in love with matinee idols they have seen on the screen; "vain movie-struck girls who want only to see themselves on screen"; and, in much smaller numbers, a few young women with serious talents interested in working hard and earning a living. Most who made the trek were "shallow, without balance or serious interest, their main purpose in life being to be admired and flattered."[5] *Picture Progress* found among those eager to "break into motion pictures" a high school girl insisting that "all my friends say that I look like Mary Pickford" and a worn-out twenty year old, "her shoulders . . . stooped and her finger tips . . . roughened from the coarse thread of the sweatshop," who craved motion picture work because "'It must be such an easy life!'"[6] So prevalent was the phenomenon that Mae Marsh declared, "[S]ometimes I am given to the thought that every young girl in the United States wants to go into motion pictures."[7]

Young women lampooned in these accounts, said to arrive at studio gates bedecked in Mary Pickford curls or Theda Bara ear loops, pressing themselves on directors in the hopes of becoming an "onjewnew,"[8] were pursuing a particularly gendered version of the American dream, one that was driven by the unique transformations of transitional era filmmaking. As the film industry's new center of production, Los Angeles became the object of fascination in travel and lifestyle magazines during the early 1910s, as, more figuratively, the movie screen became a site of fantasy for young female fans encouraged to imagine their own image projected there. Colored by celebrity profiles that trumpeted the rise of early stars from very humble origins, fan magazines offered their readers advice on every aspect of the business—how to dress, how to style their hair, how to pose, along with more practical tips on how to find work as extras on studio lots. Yet, in the end, derisive and alarmist reports of fans and would-be actresses flocking to Los Angeles determined to find a place for themselves onscreen obscured the multifaceted nature of women's contributions to cinema during the early years of Hollywood and disarmed the considerable impact that hundreds of unmarried, casually employed, recently transplanted young women posed to both the filmmaking industry and the greater Los Angeles community.

THE LURE OF EARLY HOLLYWOOD

The extra "problem" was propelled by significant changes in the film industry beginning around 1913, chiefly the expansion of film production and the resulting rationalization of filmmaking techniques, the centralization of motion picture concerns around Los Angeles, and the growing cult of celebrity attached to movie stars. In an effort to streamline production methods and lower costs several production companies were decreasing their stock companies in the mid-1910s and relying with greater frequency on extras, or "jobbers," who could be paid by the day rather than receiving a fixed salary.[9] This marked a change from the early years of the transitional period when many outfits began hiring stock companies to fill the escalating demand for films and the new emphasis on fictional subjects. As Murray Ross demonstrated in his 1941 history of movie work, early studios needed an enormous range of "types" for varied projects, yet there was no way each company could provide regular or steady employment for such a large labor pool, let alone place performers on permanent salary. Without any protective organization these workers were left prey to various more-or-less-legitimate schemes promoting acting schools, placement agencies, and the like. Nor did the studios maintain any systemized procedure for hiring extras when needed, necessitating that those looking for work make the rounds of various outfits daily.[10]

Also around 1913 production companies, many of which had been scattered throughout the country, began to set up permanent facilities in and around Los Angeles, creating for the first time a geographical center for the industry. With early studios in Edendale, Pasadena, Santa Monica, and the San Fernando Valley, the Los Angeles area became a single, year-round destination for those in search of movie work, although the term *Hollywood* did not emerge until later in the teens to unify these disparate facilities.[11] "The pictures . . . have added and are adding uncounted thousands to the population of Los Angeles," western lifestyle magazine *Sunset* reported in 1915.[12] Indeed, the city's Chamber of Commerce estimated that spring that close to fifteen thousand residents earned their living in the film industry, drawing some five million dollars in wages annually.[13] Universal alone employed twelve hundred to two thousand actors, and even a smaller outfit like Inceville had over 250 performers on its payroll.[14] "Los Angeles has, of a sudden, become the motion picture center of the world," *Sunset* declared.[15] Even those working as extras, although largely anonymous onscreen and invisible in studio labor pools, became a notable element of the city's culture, regularly gathering during their off-hours to socialize near the corner of Hollywood Boulevard and Cahuenga—a phenomenon noted with interest by the *Los Angeles Times*.[16] Although *Everybody's Magazine* affirmed that "Los Angeles takes very kindly to the picture folk," another sentiment is audible in the slang terms Angelenos adopted to describe their new neighbors.[17] Studios were called "camps" and their inhabitants dubbed "the movie colony," leading historian Gordon De Marco to surmise that city residents considered this first rush of motion picture recruits a fleeting phenomenon at best, one with little lasting connection to the city itself.[18]

With Los Angeles now becoming identified as the locus of film production nationally, it became an object of fascination for those interested in seeing how and where films were made, in seeing that mythic space behind the screen. "Millions of persons in other states and other countries cannot sit before the screens every day without feeling the lure of the sunshine that mellows the picture," *Sunset* pronounced.[19] Spectacular motion picture studios built to accommodate the industry's newly streamlined, mass film production techniques—Inceville, Universal City, and the Lasky Studios—were profiled in widely circulated publications like *Everybody's, Scientific American,* and *Ladies' Home Journal* in features that stressed the vast tracts of land oc-cupied by the companies, their extraordinary facilities, and the enormous workforce they employed.[20]

These vicarious tours of "Motion-Picture Land" simultaneously demystified *and* reified the moviemaking process, for those looking behind the screen to see the "real" world of filmmaking beyond found only another layer of fantasy. "In the studios—behind the 'movie' screen—what a mystery-land lies there!" *Photoplay* proclaimed in one of many celebrations of Los Ange-les studios published in early fan magazines.[21] A desire to see past the screen, to learn the workings of an industry unfamiliar to most Americans at the time, was given a particularly feminine cast by writer Rufus Steele in his 1915 profile of Universal City for *Ladies' Home Journal.* His guide to the company's massive new San Fernando Valley complex was framed by a vignette featur-ing two young women whispering to one another at the cinema. "'Were you ever filled with a desire to go straight through the screen and see just what is behind it?' one says to the other. 'I mean did you never want to go through the screen, just as Alice went through the looking-glass? What we see is noth-ing but the shadow. Don't you realize that somewhere all these interesting and exciting things are actually taking place?'"[22] Enraptured fans here pos-sessed a curiosity to match the "shadows" they saw onscreen with the reality in Southern California studios. In a fascinating application of the *Alice in Wonderland* story—surely an "Ur" narrative of female curiosity—the young women would travel through the screen/mirror to see not reality but a whole new realm of make-believe. An actual location, the moviemaking capital was now frequently depicted as a fantastic space.

Alongside vicarious studio tours offered to readers of mass-circulation mag-azines, Los Angeles–based filmmaking outfits also began catering to a new breed of motion picture tourists eager to see the industry's inner-workings firsthand. Already dubbed "Mecca of the motion picture" in 1915, Los An-geles became an object of sacred pilgrimage for the devoted.[23] Perhaps the most adept at studio tourism was Universal, which mounted an enormous publicity campaign to mark the official opening of its Universal City facili-ties in March of 1915, offering special trolley expeditions from downtown Los Angeles and even arranging a tie-in with the Panama-Pacific Exposition in San Francisco so that visitors who had traveled to that city by rail would be entitled to a free trip to Los Angeles and Universal City.[24] The picture-making complex was simultaneously promoted as "just another municipal-ity," complete with post office, fire station, police force, and elected officials, *and* as a spectacle on par with anything on display at the Pan-Pacific Expo: a "wonder city of the world," a "fairyland where the craziest things in the world happen," and "a place to think about and talk about all the rest of your days!"[25] Enormously popular, the studio tours drew between five hundred and one thousand visitors per day, including, of course, many would-be star-

Figure 14.1. Souvenir postcard showing tourists gathered outside Universal City, 1915.

lets (figure 14.1). Indeed, actress Mary MacLaren recollected being lured to Universal City by just such a promotion. Traveling out to California where she would be performing at the Pan-Pacific Expo, MacLaren remembers, "I bought a magazine, *The Movie Magazine,* and in it was this article about Universal Studios. Well, from then on I could think of nothing but Universal."[26]

It was not only accounts of filmmaking feats that drew the curious to California but also news of the glamorous lives led by film personalities, for Los Angeles quickly garnered a reputation as the movie stars' playground. Unlike itinerant musical and stage performers of a generation earlier, motion picture players did not have to travel far beyond the newly centralized filmmaking facilities in Los Angeles and thus could establish permanent residences there, many of them lavish structures in keeping with the performers' burgeoning wealth and celebrity status—a phenomenon celebrated as early as 1915 with an elaborate *Photoplay* article on stars' homes.[27] As Richard deCordova demonstrated, the movie star system developing in 1913 and 1914 encouraged a new fascination with performers' offscreen lives—their marriages, divorces, children, and lovers; their homes, closets, bedrooms, and kitchens; indeed, their innermost thoughts, secrets, and desires. The star system, he said, led fans "toward that which is behind or beyond the image, hidden from sight."[28] Fan magazines wasted no time in romanticizing Los Angeles culture for readers eager for details of life outside studio gates. Film stars were to be found dining in fashionable cafes, walking down urban thoroughfares, and, of course, attending the movies. Reporting from the perspective of "we lucky Angelenos," *Motion Picture Classic* writer Fritzi Remont declared, "I don't want to make all you fans jealous, but I really do think we dwellers in the film capital of the world are just a little better off than you are."[29]

Celebrations of opulent living in the filmmaking community were part of a broader glamorization of Los Angeles fostered by an aggressive promotion of the city at the turn of the century. Indeed, swelling ranks of film personnel were part of a larger trend in westward migration, so much so that the city's population had increased fivefold since then, to include some 550,000 residents by 1914, and by 1916 had become the largest city, geographically, in the United States.[30] Southern California lifestyles had been romanticized for easterners for at least a decade prior to the expansion of film production there. The region's temperate climate, its emphasis on outdoor living, its varied foods, and its spectacular landscape were all touted. But perhaps most intriguingly, profiles also often stressed unique features of life there: "Southern California to the newcomer presents a new phase of existence, a different idea, which suggests deviation from the usual ways of seeing things," *Out West* magazine told its readers.[31] Here the possibility of self-transformation, already a powerful ingredient in star discourse, was linked still further with everyday life in California.

With Hollywood, both as a filmmaking center and an alluring offscreen community, painted in breathtaking terms, is it any wonder that eager movie hopefuls flocked there? A particularly powerful ingredient in this phenomenon were stories celebrating the "discovery" of young women pulled from the ranks of studio extras and elevated to the heights of stardom. Movie aficionados could read such narratives everywhere: *Motion Picture Classic* began a regular column devoted to "How They Got In" narratives in 1916, and top-drawer national publications started featuring testimonials from picture personalities like Mary Fuller, who reported on "My Adventures as a Motion Picture Heroine" for *Collier's* readers in 1911, and Mary Pickford, who followed suit with a *Ladies' Home Journal* piece describing "What It Means to Be a 'Movie' Actress."[32] Books like Mae Tinee's 1916 volume *Life Stories of the Movie Stars* also detailed the rise of a new generation of celebrities from the humblest of origins.[33]

Accounts of director Lois Weber's "discovery" of actress Mary MacLaren in 1915 provide just one example of this type of narrative. As a young woman MacLaren reportedly "got the fever" and became "eager to stand with the other girls in the crowds that waited to be called as 'extras.'"[34] According to a tale spun in promotional literature, Weber spotted MacLaren in a long line of hopefuls gathered at Universal gates. "It was one of those trifles which so often affect the whole course of life," *Green Book* pronounced. Weber "looked directly into the eyes of a girl whose face attracted and held her attention. There were other girls there, a bevy of them; but she saw only the one girl. In her face was 'something' magnetic. 'Are you looking for work?' the woman director asked the girl."[35] *Universal Weekly* proudly proclaimed, "Mary Mac-Laren is Lois Weber's discovery and it is entirely due to her chance meeting with the totally inexperienced girl that a new screen star has risen in the photoplay firmament. The story reads like a fairy tale, and in itself would make an extremely interesting photoplay if Lois Weber should ever be at a loss for a striking plot."[36] Another piece compared MacLaren's "fairy tale" rise to fame with that of Cinderella, casting Weber in the role of fairy godmother who "brought happiness to Cinderella through the wave of her magic wand."[37] "From Extra to Stardom," *Motion Picture Magazine* blared in its profile of the actress.[38] Stories of this kind presented the journey from obscurity to stardom as a model of class mobility and financial independence—especially for women—an imaginary trajectory that could be mapped onto the physical journey to Southern California.

Standing alongside such almost certainly embellished accounts of "how I got in," a host of novels, short fiction, and serialized stories also dramatized the road to stardom, providing first-person accounts to their female readers. "Peg O' the Movies," a serial that ran in *The Ladies' World* during late 1913 and early 1914, chronicled the heroine's pursuit of a motion picture career even over her fiancé's stubborn objections.[39] (Of course she becomes a star!) "My Experiences as a Film Favorite" offered *Photoplay* readers an "interesting and intimate inside story" of the exploits of one pseudonymous Polly Dean, recounting her journey to a California film studio and her (inevitable) rise to fame.[40] Novels such as 1915's *My Strange Life,* the story of a seventeen-year-old girl who leaves home in search of film work, were illustrated with photographs of leading players of the day—Mary Pickford, Grace Cunard, Clara Kimball Young—a strategy that tempted fans to trace these stories back onto the lives of actual celebrities.[41] More important still was the way these fictional narratives encouraged female readers to identify with the drama of rising stardom, to envision themselves in the same "role." Together with celebrity profiles, first-person narration in serialized stories fostered a mode of identification that allowed readers to project themselves into these potent fantasies of self-transformation.

So prevalent were these narratives that *McClure's* concluded the "modern malady" *filmitis,* that compulsive desire to appear onscreen, almost always materialized following "an announcement that some little lady with a winning smile, but unheralded and unsung, yea, even untrained and inexperienced in legitimate drama, has signed a contract for more or less thousands per week with the Glittering Glory Moving Picture Company."[42] Accordingly, fans besieged stars for advice on their own prospects. Mae Marsh reported that a significant portion of her fan mail, beginning in the midteens, was given over to the subject. Young women wrote her concerned about whether they were the correct physical type for film work, whether motion picture morals were "safe for the average girl," and how long they would have to work as an extra before receiving a starring role.[43] As early as 1912 *Photoplay*'s newly instituted "Answers to Inquiries" column asked readers to refrain from submitting questions related to their own prospects in film so besieged was the magazine by such requests.[44]

A host of advice columns in movie magazines and popular newspapers, along with booklets, correspondence lessons, and motion picture "schools," all catered to the burgeoning interest in film work with the promise of practical guidance. Louella Parsons began a series of syndicated newspaper articles for the Hearst circuit on "How to Become a Movie Actress" in 1915, for instance, trading on what she dubbed her "wide experiences in the world of the photoplay" as scenario writer, executive, and "intimate friend of practically all the great stars." Introducing the series, the *Chicago Herald* invited readers to indulge their own fantasies of stardom: "Do you dream of becoming a moving picture actress and actually plan to be one? Then think of this: Every day that dream is coming true. Not a day passes but some girl who has shared your fondest fancies is made exquisitely happy. Her long-cherished hopes are realized. She breaks into the movies!"[45] Frances Agnew's 1913 guide to *Motion Picture Acting* wove together interviews with those already famous, like Clara Kimball Young and Muriel Ostriche, with tips on the acting craft, encouraging fans to map their own imagined screen destiny onto those profiled in the book.[46]

Yet, with qualifications necessary for such positions kept extremely vague and lack of experience encouraged, much of the "advice" proved to be near universally applicable. One needed only elusive characteristics like "personality," "vitality," and "natural talent" to qualify for motion picture work, and in many cases those *without* prior experience were encouraged over more seasoned counterparts. "There is not a film studio in this country that would reject a woman whose natural gifts lend to artistic achievement, no matter if she has been on the stage or has even studied its techniques."[47] D. W. Griffith, screen hopefuls were told, "prefers to engage women who have, as he puts it, 'nothing to unlearn.'"[48] Articles on such topics as "Dressing for the Movies" and "Have You a Camera Face?" offered aspiring starlets little more than encouragement to study their own reflections in the mirror.[49]

Should one desire more than simple self-scrutiny, expert lessons were also available from outfits with impressive-sounding names like the International Photoplay Studio and Dramatic School.[50] "Don't trust to luck," an ad for one school warned. "The stakes are too big."[51] If advertisements such as these stressed the necessity of training for screen acting, seeming to debunk myths of overnight "discovery," they simultaneously pledged that such preparation would be effortless and readily attainable. "Any clever girl can easily master the art of moving picture acting," one ad promised.[52]

Not surprisingly, reports surfaced early on that many such "schools" were tendering little in the way of concrete help at quite steep prices. Screen hopefuls at one such enterprise were paraded in front of a camera, noisily cranked by an operator, unaware that it contained no film, furnishing "a bitter lesson to those who ached to become famous on the screen," *Moving Picture World* concluded.[53] Another company charged the considerable sum of five hundred dollars to make two-reel films of screen aspirants, assuring each one that her picture could later be sold to a distribution company, which, of course, it could not.[54] In one more popular ruse applicants paid a fee to have their particulars listed in a directory that they were told would be circulated to studios, when in fact few filmmaking outfits in the 1910s hired talent from such listings.[55] This latter scheme was exposed in a *Motion Picture Magazine* article highlighting "fakes and frauds" in the film industry, indicating that fans were being warned early on that their enthusiasm might be exploited—a distinct irony given that fans often read about such scams in publications that were themselves the chief advertising venue for their proponents.

Although an opportunist industry of motion picture schools, advice columns, and how-to manuals fueled the aspirations of movie hopefuls drawn to Los Angeles in the early 1910s, portraits of star-crazed young women that emerge in contemporary coverage of this phenomenon ironically circumscribed women's participation in the emergent film industry rather than espousing the many opportunities available to them there, as such reporting often pretended to do. By imagining that women's primary interest in motion pictures lay in a desire to see themselves onscreen, these caricatures resigned women to a wholly passive role of being discovered, noticed, and looked at. Elsewhere I have argued that accounts of such "movie-struck girls" pathologized and infantilized female film viewers at a time (paradoxically) when they were most courted as paying customers; in this context it becomes clear that characterizations of this sort also limited images of women's movie work during a crucial period of expansion in early Hollywood.[56]

THE EXTRA PROBLEM

Stories focused on long lines of women waiting outside studios to be hired as extras created an impression that women were shut out of the industry during these years, literally kept outside the gates behind which moviemaking took place, and that appearing onscreen was the sum total of their engagement with the cinema—images that belied the state of the field in the mid-1910s, when many women held positions as top-ranked directors and screenwriters. By Anthony Slide's count at least twenty production companies were controlled by women in the 1910s.[57] The tale of Mary MacLaren waiting woefully outside Universal, for instance, obscures the particular wealth of female talent housed within, for at the time the studio was home to perhaps the greatest concentration of female directors and screenwriters in the business, among them Cleo Madison, Ruth Stonehouse, Ida May Park, Lule Warrenton, Dorothy Davenport Reid, and Lois Weber.[58] Announcing "Woman's Conquest of Filmdom" in 1915, Robert Grau celebrated the unique opportunities that motion picture work held for women. "In no line of endeavor has woman made so emphatic an impress than in the amazing film industry," he declared. "The fair sex is represented as in no other calling to which women have harkened in the early years of the twentieth century."[59]

If reports of women lined up outside studio gates waiting to be discovered masked the breadth and scope of women's participation in early Hollywood, they also tended to conceal the actual labor involved in working as an extra. Paid by the day, rather than the hour, extras could count on long shifts if they found work. "Often after staying around all day we didn't start to work until late in the afternoon and had to work most of the night," one young woman reported, comparing her working hours to those of a night watchman. Calling the conditions under which they toiled "wholly vicious," *Motion Picture Magazine* also feared that extras could not "do their best when weighed down with poverty and the knowledge that next day, or the day after, they will again be hunting for work."[60] Extras often had to supply their own clothing and makeup, and working under mercury lamps for long hours irritated the eyes of those shooting indoors. Far-flung studios in Santa Monica, Pasadena, and the San Fernando Valley also posed travel obstacles for screen aspirants. One woman remembered having to walk two miles from the end of the streetcar line to reach the studio.[61] "The reason that they are called 'extra' girls is because of the extra amount of work that one has to do. The only thing that isn't extra is the pay," one writer quipped.[62]

Ironically, such poor working conditions actually quelled possible complaints according to Danae Clark, who emphasizes that "a constant pool of unemployed and underemployed workers (mostly extras) made it possible for studios to reduce labor dissension. The promise of moving up in the star system hierarchy kept hopefuls in line, while the fear of plummeting to the bottom was used to keep employed actors from challenging their employers and complaining about exploitive labor practices."[63] Press reports that stressed the vanity and naiveté of screen aspirants also ignored the fact that for many this was not a frivolous proposition; in fact, a significant number of women seeking work as extras were supporting other family members back home.[64] One such figure was ZaSu Pitts, who recalls leaving her home in Santa Cruz, some 350 miles north of Los Angeles, at age nineteen in order to provide for her widowed mother and two siblings. "Mother decided to send me to some friends in Hollywood who had written that young girls without any experience were being paid the enormous sum of three dollars a day by the moving picture studios," she remembered. "So off I went in Mother's best coat, dreading the ordeal that lay ahead of me."[65]

Tales of extras being "discovered" by famous directors also muted women's labor, of course, for they emphasized passive acts of waiting and being looked at over the skill and effort required to succeed in the industry. Some performers, like Mary MacLaren, sought to reclaim the talent and training hidden under myths of instant discovery by actively countering publicity accounts of their rise to stardom. In an article titled "How I Happened," published in 1917, just a year after she became famous, MacLaren rejected the ingenue guise that had been cast for her, emphasizing instead her own agency in the drive for professional success—her long years of training and experience—and insisting that her acting abilities be valued over the talents of others merely to recognize her skills. Working hard at Universal under Lois Weber's tutelage, MacLaren remembered, "[I] soon realized that I had 'found myself' at last."[66] Other actresses made a similar point to emphasize the great effort that stood behind their own accomplishments. Mae Marsh argued forcefully against the "myth of the 'overnight' star," stressing that those and others like her "had attained stardom only after years of rigorous training, self denial and hard work."[67] Mary Fuller's advice to screen aspirants: "work, work, work."[68]

Another factor ignored in derisive caricatures of silly, self-absorbed Hollywood hopefuls was the sizable appeal that motion picture work might have held for young women with few other avenues open to them for profitable, independent, and rewarding professions. Indeed, as early as 1908 *The Film Index* pronounced that "women's chances of making a living have been increased by the rise of the cinematograph machines."[69] Thus, there is good reason to presume that many ambitious women traveled to Los Angeles with the aim of living rather unconventional lives—outside of marriage, free from their families, economically self-sufficient, and creatively employed—lives that must have held tremendous appeal to those eager for models of behavior different from the Victorian standards by which their mothers had been raised. Two such young women, who migrated separately to Los Angeles in 1915, ended up pooling their financial and artistic resources, setting up house together, and establishing their own production company.[70] Unmarried and self-supporting, these "girl picture magnates" lived together in an alternative domestic model and pursued creative careers free from the need to follow the dictates of others in a male-controlled industry. The feasibility of such a plan for most American young women notwithstanding, one can imagine its idealistic appeal to those ready for life outside the bounds of conventional femininity.

Demeaning portraits of vain, deluded would-be starlets, then, served to obscure the multifaceted nature of women's contributions to filmmaking in the teens, not just as lowly, easily dispensable "extras" but as directors, writers, influential performers, critics, and commentators. And they obscured the economic and social advantages that movie work offered to young women. By infantilizing the "girls" who fell prey to delusions of stardom, these stories served yet another purpose: they disarmed the considerable threat that hundreds of unmarried, casually employed, recently transplanted young women posed to the filmmaking industry, to the Los Angeles community, and to ladylike codes of behavior.

Given its unpredictability and low wages, extra work prompted concern from many quarters. "Stability of employment makes for stability of character. Irregularity of work breeds irregularity in everything else," *Motion Picture Magazine* warned. Even when day work was available it did not pay well, a fact that led the magazine to conclude that "practically all" of those seeking work as extras went hungry. "It is easy to be honest with a well-filled stomach and a well-lined purse. It is hard to hold one's ideals of virtue when actual starvation is at your door and the rent collector is beckoning you to move out."[71] That young women migrated to Los Angeles on their own to pursue such work was cause for further alarm. Aspiring stage performers of a generation earlier might have found work with local stock companies and would not have had to leave their families. Now, "the girl who would be a film star" needed to relocate to New York or Los Angeles, often far from home, in order to seek work.[72]

"All those idle, mischief-filled hours" spent waiting for filming to begin also raised eyebrows, as the "freedom of the studio life" and the "lack of restraint one observes when a company is out on 'location'" became the object of unspoken apprehension.[73] Sexual and moral transgression appear the only likely outcome of motion picture work, with its extended hours, distant locales, and easy camaraderie. Trepidation about women's participation in the morally suspect world of filmmaking also surfaces in reports about the sexual exploitation of extras beginning as early as 1913. In one particularly scandalous case, widely discussed in the filmmaking community, a young screen hopeful was said to have been discovered wandering New York streets, "stupefied with liquor," after having been "betrayed" by the director of a famous company, an incident that, reportedly, kept her confined in an asylum for the better part of a week. *Variety*, which recounted the incident with pronounced unease, determined that similarly exploitive conditions existed for young women at three-quarters of the major production houses.[74] Euphemisms like "friend of the director," "protégée of the manager," and "favorite of the leading man" emerged to cloak the industry's sexual economy.[75] Actress Irene Wallace, providing an insider's exposé of the phenomenon, claimed that "the public cannot comprehend how many women are selling their ability and labor and brains at so many dollars a week, with their souls thrown in." Wallace's turn of phrase, introducing the specter of prostitution, is noteworthy, given that she was best known at the time for her role in the 1913 white slave picture *Traffic in Souls*. Girls who fancied themselves in love with matinee idols were the most vulnerable, she reported: "What more could an unscrupulous man ask?"[76]

By 1914 *Variety* reported that the practice of "loving up" attractive applicants was customary at many studios; indeed, it was so prevalent that the Screen Club considered adding a clause to its bylaws that would guarantee expulsion for any director caught abusing his authority.[77] After several young women provided sworn statements detailing "liberties" that studio managers and directors had taken with them, Los Angeles officials began a formal inquiry in 1915, an investigation that prompted stern condemnations of the Hollywood filmmaking community from local clergy.[78]

Although frequently portrayed as innocent victims, women sometimes willfully participated in Hollywood's sexual bartering, precisely for the chance it gave them to break free from the limited options awaiting them at home. As one screen hopeful put it in 1914, acquiescing to the system guaranteed her a good likelihood of success. Without it, she said, "I will have to keep on working for thirty-five dollars a week from now until doomsday, unless I get married. If I got married I would never be satisfied to become a mere dish-washing wife. Now what would you do?"[79] Reporting on Hollywood culture in 1921 Theodore Dreiser surmised that most women who pursued motion picture work knew "very well beforehand . . . the character of the conditions to be met." Those who came to Los Angeles had demonstrated by that very act, he argued, that they were "already mentally liberated from most of the binding taboos which govern in the social realms from which they emanate."[80] Even more than stories of innocents "betrayed" and exploited, reports of women's voluntary engagement in the industry's sexual marketplace highlight how fundamentally these unmarried, casually employed female "jobbers" threatened both the film industry and older codes of ladylike conduct.

Given concerns raised by the influx of movie hopefuls, it is not surprising to find that very quickly directives were issued warning women about the dangers of traveling westward in search of work. Stressing the difference between the physical journey to Los Angeles and the more mythic rise to stardom, *Motion Picture Supplement* cautioned its readers, "Yes, Maude Jones, it's a long, long way to Filmland!"[81] Many believed that a strong dose of reality would cure even the most starstruck hopeful. "If the movie-struck girl could foresee just a bit of the hard road to success as a film player," one writer surmised, "she would hesitate a long time before leaving home."[82] Following the same logic, *Photoplay* published a series of exposés on extra work, including one 1914 report on "breaking into the game," penned by "a girl who didn't break in."[83] Mary Pickford cautioned *Ladies' Home Journal* readers in

1915 that prospects were not good. Most studios had stock companies and long waiting lists, she explained, "so it is difficult for a girl without exceptional qualifications to find a place."[84] L. M. Goodstadt, casting director at Lasky, declared that "the best advice I can offer is for the pretty aspirant to stay home unless she has enough money to provide for her wants for at least a year."[85] *Everybody's Magazine* provided "just a word of warning here to the aspiring young girls all over the country who may believe that a trip to Los Angeles will put them in pictures. The warning is: don't come. The Los Angeles Welfare Committee is kept pretty busy right now taking care of young girls who failed to get work and are stranded."[86]

With high-profile involvement on the part of the city's Welfare Committee and prominent warnings in mass-circulation magazines, the phenomenon of young women flooding to Los Angeles became the focus of national attention. Indeed, many in Hollywood became increasingly concerned that an industry so reliant on female patronage should be seen to be endangering its very constituency. More tangible efforts, beyond mere warnings, were required. Perhaps the best, and most enduring, example of this effort was the Hollywood Studio Club, founded in 1916 to provide low-cost housing for women seeking work in the film industry. After female extras began gathering in the basement of the Hollywood Public Library to rehearse and socialize, a librarian concerned about the conditions under which many of them lived in boardinghouses and cheap hotels approached the YWCA about finding more suitable accommodations. Funds were then quickly raised to rent a house where some dozen women could live and many others could socialize. Meals were provided, and residents had access to a library, an outdoor gymnasium, acting lessons, Red Cross classes, and talks by notables from the filmmaking community, including director Lois Weber, who spoke to residents in late 1917. Along with Weber the Studio Club attracted such prominent backers as Mary Pickford, Nazimova, and the wives of studio executives Jesse Lasky and William DeMille.[87] With its notable patronage and generous amenities the Studio Club quickly became "a center of social life among the younger girls about the studios," according to the *Los Angeles Times* (figure 14.2).[88] Yet, as Heidi Kenaga argues in her excellent research on the club's activities in the 1920s, residences like the Studio Club, together with later agencies like Central Casting, furnished mechanisms of surveillance and regulation that aimed to curtail the sexually and economically threatening aspects of the film industry's transient, casual female workforce.[89]

Although statistics gathered by Central Casting in the 1920s revealed that men vastly outnumbered women among the ranks of those actually *hired* for extra work, the image of deluded "movie-struck girls" persisted as the primary face of Hollywood's unskilled talent pool for decades.[90] If anything,

Figure 14.2. Women socializing inside the Hollywood Studio Club, c. 1917.

warnings to screen hopefuls became even more alarmist after the celebrity scandals of 1921 and 1922 drew national attention to Hollywood's "decadent" inhabitants, as Kenaga and Victoria Sturtevant have demonstrated in their recent work.[91] So extreme was the mounting tenor of this discourse that Adela Rogers St. John famously dubbed Hollywood "the port of missing girls" in a series of 1927 *Photoplay* articles.[92]

Although concern over offscreen behavior in and around Hollywood is usually thought to begin with the 1920s star scandals and the resulting efforts to regulate actors' behavior, hiring practices, and film content, in fact, it is clear that such concern arose much earlier, well before scandalous headlines and economic downturn rocked Hollywood in the early 1920s. A confluence of changes unique to the transitional era, including the emergence of the star system, the rise of Los Angeles as a film production center, and the expansion of mass-production filmmaking techniques dependent on a vast labor pool, provided singular circumstances for the fantasy of instant stardom in a defined locale. One might go as far as to say that it was not until films provided narratives of a certain duration and complexity that female fans could envision themselves occupying roles within them. In effect, the trajectory of narrative-building the industry underwent in the transitional period provided the framework of fantasy actual viewers needed to transport themselves to the site of moviemaking. Young women's journeys to Los Angeles thus mirrored the "distance" film narrative had traveled by the rise of the feature film in the mid-1910s.[93] At the same time, press caricatures that mocked such aspirations show us just how radically women's marked presence altered early Hollywood, whether it was their flourishing creative influence, obscured in such accounts, or the pointed challenge their offscreen behavior posed to an industry newly self-conscious about its impact on American life.

By the early 1920s much of this had changed. Women who had held influential positions in early Hollywood lost considerable power with the consolidation of the major studios and the rise of exclusionary professional guilds. Those aspiring to movie work were now encouraged to seek employment as stenographers, rather than actresses, and certainly not as directors or screenwriters.[94] In Hollywood of the Will Hays era women were frequently held up as examples of moral respectability inside the tarnished filmmaking community, a portrayal that muted concerns about female sexual and economic independence prominent in earlier "movie-struck girl" controversies. "Refinement without undue prudishness—that is what the movies are waiting for the women to bring them," one observer claimed.[95] But when the phenomenon of Hollywood hopefuls was freshest, and most alarming, to the nation, in the mid-1910s, it served to illuminate the very possibilities of women's presence there.

NOTES

My thanks to Sirida Srisombati for her help in gathering materials used in this essay.

1. William A. Page, "The Movie-Struck Girl," *Woman's Home Companion*, June 1918, 18.

2. William Allen Johnston, "In Motion-Picture Land," *Everybody's Magazine*, October 1915, 445, 447; and Roy Somerville, "Breaking into Motion Pictures," *Picture Progress*, July 1915, 131.

3. Arthur Hornblow Jr., "Have You a Camera Face?" *Motion Picture Classic*, May 1916, 15.

4. Austin C. Lescarboura, *Behind the Motion Picture Screen* (New York: Scientific American, 1919), 46, 48.

5. Irene Wallace, "The Woman on the Screen," *Green Book*, December 1914, n.p.; repr. in *Taylorology* 41 (May 1996): http://silent-movies.com/Taylorology/Taylor41 .txt. Accessed 30 June 2003.

6. Somerville, "Breaking into Motion Pictures," 6.

7. Mae Marsh, *Screen Acting* (Los Angeles, Calif.: Photo-Star Publishing, 1921), 20.

8. Alfred A. Cohn, "What Every Girl Wants to Know," *Photoplay*, June 1919, 29; and Kenneth McGaffey, "Mollie of the Movies," *Photoplay*, November 1915, 124.

9. H. Sheridan-Bickers, "Extra Ladies and Gentlemen," *Motion Picture Magazine*, September 1917, 82.

10. Murray Ross, *Stars and Strikes: Unionization of Hollywood* (New York: Columbia University Press, 1941), 64–65.

11. Richard Koszarski, *An Evening's Entertainment: The Age of the Silent Feature Picture, 1915–1928* (New York: Scribner, 1990), 99.

12. Rufus Steele, "In the Sun Spot," *Sunset*, April 1915, 699.

13. George Blaisdell, "Mecca of the Motion Picture," *Moving Picture World*, 10 July 1915, 215; and Albert Marple, "Making Pictures in California," *Motion Picture Classic*, April 1916, 37.

14. Steele, "In the Sun Spot," 696; Marple, "Making Pictures in California," 39; and Johnston, "In Motion-Picture Land," 440–41.

15. Steele, "In the Sun Spot," 690.

16. Quoted in "In the Capital of Movie-Land," *Literary Digest* 55 (10 November 1917): 85.

17. Johnston, "In Motion-Picture Land," 441.

18. Gordon De Marco, *A Short History of Los Angeles* (San Francisco, Calif.: Lexikos, 1988), 107.

19. Steele, "In the Sun Spot," 699.

20. Johnston, "In Motion-Picture Land"; Steele, "In the Sun Spot"; "The Strangest City in the World," *Scientific American*, 17 April 1915, 365; and Rufus Steele, "Behind the Screen: How the 'Movie' Is Made in the Valley of the New Arabian Nights," *Ladies' Home Journal*, October 1915, 16, 80–81.

21. "The Glory Road," *Photoplay*, October 1916, 106. Cited in Richard deCordova, *Picture Personalities: The Emergence of the Star System in America* (Urbana: University of Illinois Press, 1990), 98.

22. Steele, "Behind the Screen," 16.

23. Blaisdell, "Mecca of the Motion Picture." Islamicist metaphors were common in descriptions of early Hollywood. Rufus Steele, for instance, describes Universal City's San Fernando Valley location as "the Valley of the New Arabian Nights" in "Behind the Screen."

24. I. G. Edmonds, *Big U: Universal in the Silent Days* (South Brunswick, N.J.: A. S. Barnes, 1977), 52–54; and Johnston, "In Motion-Picture Land," 440.

25. Quoted in Edmonds, *Big U*, 52–53.

26. Richard Koszarski, "Truth or Reality? A Few Thoughts on Mary MacLaren's *Shoes*," *Griffithiana* 40–42 (1991): 81. In the article Koszarski transcribes an interview he conducted with MacLaren in 1973.

27. Grace Kingsley, "Movie Royalty in California: Estates and Palatial Homes Bestowed on Photoplayers by Their Calling," *Photoplay*, June 1915, 123–27. See also Mary Dickerson Donahey, "Living Neighbor to the Movies: Adventures of a Home in Movieland," *Photoplay*, February 1916, 63–69; and "Some Palaces the Fans Built," *Photoplay*, June 1917, 77.

28. deCordova, *Picture Personalities*, 145.

29. Fritzi Remont, "Our Pacific Coast News-Letter," *Motion Picture Classic*, March 1917, 54, 55. See also "The Hidden Glory of California," *Photoplay*, June 1919, 28–34.

30. Norman M. Klein, "The Sunshine Strategy: Buying and Selling the Fantasy

of Los Angeles," in *20th Century Los Angeles: Power, Promotion and Social Conflict,* ed. Norman M. Klein and Martin J. Schiesl (Claremont, Calif.: Regina Books, 1990), 1–38; Jeffrey Charles and Jill Watts, "(Un)real Estate: Marketing Hollywood in the 1910s and 1920s," in *Hollywood Goes Shopping,* ed. David Desser and Garth S. Jowett (Minneapolis: University of Minnesota Press, 2000), 253–76; and "Los Angeles Becomes the Largest City in Area in the United States," *American City,* July 1916, 65–66.

31. "Here the Sun Rises and Sets," *Out West,* May 1913, 283.

32. Mary Fuller, "My Adventures as a Motion-Picture Heroine. Being the Account of Real Experiences in Unreal Life as Related by Mary Fuller to Bailey Millard," *Collier's,* 30 December 1911, 16–17; and "The Best-Known Girl in America. Mary Pickford Tells What It Means to Be a 'Movie' Actress," *Ladies' Home Journal,* January 1915, 9.

33. Mae Tinee, *Life Stories of the Movie Stars* (Hamilton, Ohio: Presto, 1916).

34. "Great Year for Mary MacLaren," *Moving Picture World,* 3 February 1917, 672.

35. "Discovering Mary McLaren *[sic].* How One Girl Got Her First Big Chance," *Green Book,* March 1917, 404–5, envelope 1280, Robinson Locke Collection, New York Public Library for the Performing Arts (hereafter RLC).

36. "The Strange Case of Mary MacLaren," *Moving Picture Weekly,* 24 June 1916, 9.

37. Unidentified article, *Theatre Magazine,* April 1919, n.p., envelope 1280, RLC.

38. "From Extra to Stardom," *Motion Picture Magazine,* September 1917, 39.

39. James Oppenheim, "Peg O' the Movies," *Ladies' World,* November 1913, 5–6, 31–32. Installments followed monthly.

40. "My Experiences as a Film Favorite," *Photoplay,* January 1914, 55. The story's first installment appeared in November 1913. Cited in deCordova, *Picture Personalities,* 99–100.

41. *My Strange Life: The Intimate Life Story of a Moving Picture Actress* (New York: Grosset and Dunlap, 1915).

42. Anne Steese Richardson, "'Filmitis,' the Modern Malady—Its Symptoms and Its Cure," *McClure's Magazine,* January 1916, 12.

43. Marsh, *Screen Acting,* 20.

44. *Photoplay,* March 1912, 72. Cited in deCordova, *Picture Personalities,* 106.

45. Louella Parsons, "How to Become a Movie Actress," *Chicago Herald,* 19 September 1915, n.p., Robinson Locke Scrapbook Collection, vol. 294, New York Public Library for the Performing Arts.

46. Frances Agnew, *Motion Picture Acting* (New York: Reliance Newspaper Syndicate, 1913).

47. Robert Grau, "Woman's Conquest of Filmdom," *Motion Picture Supplement,* September 1915, 44.

48. Ibid., 43.

49. Pearl Gaddis, "Dressing for the Movies," *Motion Picture Classic,* August 1916, 56–58.

50. Advertisement, *Motion Picture Supplement,* September 1915, 70.

51. Advertisements, *Motion Picture Classic,* April 1916, 3; and *Motion Picture Classic,* December 1915, 2.

52. Quoted in Page, "Movie-Struck Girl," 18.

53. *New York Dramatic Mirror,* 24 June 1914, 26.

54. Page, "Movie-Struck Girl," 64.

55. Horace A. Fuld, "The Fakes and Frauds in Motion Pictures," *Motion Picture Magazine*, November 1915, 111. Cited in Koszarski, *An Evening's Entertainment*, 98.

56. Shelley Stamp, *Movie-Struck Girls: Women and Motion Picture Culture after the Nickelodeon* (Princeton, N.J.: Princeton University Press, 2000), 37–40.

57. Anthony Slide, *The Silent Feminists: America's First Women Directors* (Landham, Md.: Scarecrow Press, 1996), 2.

58. On the impressive contingent of women working at Universal in the mid-1910s see Slide, *Silent Feminists*, 41–59.

59. Grau, "Woman's Conquest of Filmdom," 41.

60. Sheridan-Bickers, "Extra Ladies and Gentlemen," 82.

61. Cohn, "What Every Girl Wants to Know," 30; Johnston, "In Motion-Picture Land," 446; Sheridan-Bickers, "Extra Ladies and Gentlemen," 80, 84; Helen G. Smith, "The Extra Girl Is Handed a Few Snickers," *Photoplay*, March 1920, 107, 108; and "'Breaking into the Game'. Told by a Girl Who Didn't Break In," *Photoplay*, August 1914, 135.

62. Smith, "Extra Girl," 108.

63. Danae Clark, *Negotiating Hollywood: The Cultural Politics of Actors' Labor* (Minneapolis: University of Minnesota Press, 1995), 20.

64. Thoreau Cronyn, "The Truth about Hollywood. Part III. What Happens to a New Girl in Hollywood?" *New York Herald*, c. March 1922, n.p., repr. in *Taylorology* 13 (January 1994): http://silent-movies.com/Taylorology/Taylor13.txt. Accessed 30 June 2003.

65. ZaSu Pitts, *Candy Hits: The Famous Star's Own Candy Recipes* (New York: Duell, Sloan, and Pearce, 1963), 14. Thanks to Amelie Hastie for drawing my attention to this sweet little volume.

66. Mary MacLaren, "How I Happened," *Moving Picture World*, 21 July 1917, 427.

67. Marsh, *Screen Acting*, 24.

68. Fuller, "My Adventures," 17.

69. "Women Film Actors," *Film Index*, 3 October 1908, 9. Quoted in Slide, *Silent Feminists*, 1.

70. Joan Jordan, "The Girl Picture Magnates," *Photoplay*, August 1922, 22–23, 111.

71. Sheridan-Bickers, "Extra Ladies and Gentlemen," 82, 83.

72. Cohn, "What Every Girl Wants to Know," 29.

73. Wallace, "Woman on the Screen"; and Page, "Movie-Struck Girl," 18.

74. "Picture Stock Scandal May Carry Its Lesson," *Variety*, 21 February 1913, n.p.; repr. in *Taylorology* 41.

75. Wallace, "Woman on the Screen."

76. Ibid.

77. "Attention and Punishment for Flirtatious Directors," *Variety*, 13 March 1914, n.p.; repr. in *Taylorology* 41.

78. "Startling Immorality Charges," *Variety*, 29 December 1915, n.p.; repr. in *Taylorology* 41.

79. Quoted in Wallace, "Woman on the Screen."

80. Theodore Dreiser, "Hollywood: Its Morals and Manners," *Shadowland*, November 1921, n.p.; repr. in *Taylorology* 41.

81. "It's a Long Way to Filmland," *Motion Picture Supplement*, October 1915, 69.

82. Cohn, "What Every Girl Wants to Know," 31.

83. "'Breaking into the Game.'"

84. "Best-Known Girl in America," 9.

85. Cohn, "What Every Girl Wants to Know," 30.

86. Johnston, "In Motion-Picture Land," 445.

87. Cohn, "What Every Girl Wants to Know," 31, 33; "In the Capital of Movie-Land," 85–86; Cronyn, "The Truth about Hollywood"; Laurance L. Hill and Silas E. Snyder, *Can Anything Good Come Out of Hollywood?* (Hollywood, Calif.: Snyder Publications, 1923), 21; and Bruce T. Torrence, *Hollywood: The First 100 Years* (Hollywood, Calif.: Hollywood Chamber of Commerce, 1979), 79, 81.

88. "In the Capital of Movie-Land," 85.

89. Heidi Kenaga, "'Making the Studio Girl': The Hollywood Studio Club and Industry Regulation of Female Labor," in *Women and the Silent Screen: Cultural and Historical Practices,* ed. Amelie Hastie and Shelley Stamp (forthcoming).

90. Ross, *Stars and Strikes,* 74–75.

91. Kenaga, "'Making the Studio Girl'"; Victoria Sturtevant, "Sin and Stardom: Melodrama, History, and the Movie-Struck Girl" (paper presented at the Society for Cinema Studies Conference, Washington, D.C., 2001).

92. The articles ran from February to July 1927.

93. Thanks to Charlie Keil for this insight.

94. Lois Hutchinson, "A Stenographer's Chance in Pictures," *Photoplay,* March 1923, 42.

95. E. Leslie Gilliams, "Will Woman Leadership Change the Movies?" *Illustrated World,* February 1923, 860.

CONTRIBUTORS

Richard Abel is Robert Altman Collegiate Professor of Film Studies at the University of Michigan. His most recent books are *The Red Rooster Scare: Making Cinema American, 1900–1910* (University of California Press, 1999); and, coedited with Rick Altman, *The Sounds of Early Cinema* (Indiana University Press, 2001). Currently he is editing the Routledge *Encyclopedia of Early Cinema* and writing a book tentatively titled *The "Imagined Community" of U.S. Cinema, 1910–1914.*

Constance Balides, associate professor in the Department of Communication at Tulane University, has published on women and early cinema in various anthologies and journals, including *Screen,* and is completing a book entitled *Making Dust in the Archives,* which looks at U.S. silent cinema in relation to vice, thrift, and domestic management. The article in this volume is part of a new project on cinema and the economy in the early and late twentieth century.

Ben Brewster is the assistant director of the Wisconsin Center for Film and Theater Research, Madison, Wisconsin. He is the coauthor, with Lea Jacobs, of *Theatre to Cinema: Stage Pictorialism and the Early Feature Film* (Oxford University Press, 1997) and has published articles on the early cinema in *Screen, Cinema Journal,* and *Film History.*

Scott Curtis is assistant professor in the Department of Radio/Television/Film at Northwestern University, where he teaches film history and historiography. He has published a number of articles on early cinema, including "If It's Not Scottish, It's Crap: Harry Lauder Sings for Selig." He is interested primarily in cinema and modernity at the turn of the century, and his current projects are a history of German film culture before World War I and a history of scientific and medical cinema.

Lee Grieveson is a lecturer in cinema studies at King's College, University of London. He is the author of *Policing Cinema: Movies and Censorship in Early-Twentieth-Century America* (University of California Press, 2004) and coeditor, with Peter Krämer, of *The Silent Cinema Reader* (Routledge, 2003).

Tom Gunning is Edwin A. and Betty L. Bergman Distinguished Service Professor in the Department of Art History and the Cinema and Media Committee at the University of Chicago. Author of *D. W. Griffith and the Origins of American Narrative Film* (University of Illinois Press, 1991) and *The Films of Fritz Lang: Allegories of Modernity and Vision* (British Film Institute, 2000), he has written numerous essays on early and international silent cinema and on American cinema, including Hollywood genres and directors, as well as on the avant-garde film. He has lectured around the world, and his works have been published in a dozen different languages.

Charlie Keil is associate professor in the Graduate History Department and Cinema Studies Program at the University of Toronto. His work on early cinema includes *Early American Cinema in Transition: Story, Style, and Filmmaking, 1907–1913* (University of Wisconsin Press, 2001), as well as essays in *Iris, Cinema Journal,* and *Film History.* He has also published on documentary and contemporary cinema. His current project involves a study of early film marketing.

J. A. Lindstrom works as a film electrician and best boy electric in Chicago, Cleveland, and L.A. She is currently working on a book about film exhibition in Chicago during the silent era.

Roberta E. Pearson is a reader in the School of Journalism, Media, and Cultural Studies at Cardiff University. She has written extensively on the silent cinema, and her publications include *Eloquent Gestures: The Transformation of Performance Style in the Griffith Biograph Films* (University of California Press, 1992); and, coauthored with William Uricchio, *Reframing Culture: The Case of the Vitagraph Quality Films* (Princeton University Press, 1993).

Jennifer Lynn Peterson received her Ph.D. from the University of Chicago. Her book, *Making the World Exotic: Travelogues and Early Nonfiction Film,* is forthcoming from Duke University Press. A fan of travel amusements since her first visit to Disneyland, she is currently teaching at the University of California, Riverside.

Lauren Rabinovitz is chair of the American Studies Department and professor of American Studies and Cinema at the University of Iowa. She is the author of *For the Love of Pleasure: Women, Movies, and Culture in Turn-of-the-Century*

Chicago (Rutgers University Press, 1998), *Points of Resistance: Women, Power, and Politics in the New York Avant-Garde Cinema,* 2d ed. (University of Illinois Press, 2003), and other books, articles, and CD-ROMs on cinema, television, and cultural history.

Ben Singer is an associate professor in the Department of Communication Arts at the University of Wisconsin–Madison. His book *Melodrama and Modernity: Early Sensational Cinema and Its Contexts* was published by Columbia University Press in 2001.

Shelley Stamp is associate professor of Film and Digital Media at the University of California, Santa Cruz, where she won the Excellence in Teaching Award. Author of *Movie-Struck Girls: Women and Motion Picture Culture after the Nickelodeon* (Princeton University Press, 2000), a Choice Outstanding Academic Book, and coeditor (with Amelie Hastie) of *Women and the Silent Screen: Cultural and Historical Practices,* she is at work on a book about Lois Weber in early Hollywood.

Jacqueline Stewart is associate professor in the Department of English Language and Literature, the Committee on African and African American Studies, and the Committee on Cinema and Media Studies at the University of Chicago. Her book, *Migrating to the Movies: Cinema and Black Urban Modernity, 1893–1920* (University of California Press, forthcoming), examines how the massive African American urban migration produced Black subjects, spectators, and filmmakers who challenged and influenced the cinema's development as both a social space and a representational medium.

.

INDEX

Abel, Richard, 6, 68, 70, 72, 155
actors, 10, 15, 17, 24, 32, 33, 40–41, 43,
    46n10, 47n25, 68, 70, 84, 132–34, 136–
    38, 140–42, 144–46, 149–54, 156n12,
    157nn22,27, 160nn52,54,56, 161n63,
    164nn113,114,115, 165nn120,122,128,
    168n166, 170nn185,189, 192; as extras,
    10, 332–34; stock companies and, 333;
    transition from stage to screen, 316–17,
    320–23; wages and working conditions
    of, 332, 334, 340–45. *See also* perfor-
    mance style; star system
acting: guides to, 339–40
actualities. *See* nonfiction film; travelogues
Addams, Jane, 249 253, 289–90, 294–95,
    297, 298, 304–5, 308n13, 309n27;
    contests and, 297. *See also* Hull House
Adventures of Mary, The (Edison, 1912–1913),
    144
advertising and promotion, 7, 27–28, 33, 67,
    71–73, 85, 131–38, 142–43, 145, 147,
    152, 154, 157n19, 158n33, 160n54,
    161n59, 175–76, 183, 218–20; posters
    and, 285, 293–94; tie-ins and, 46n10,
    297
Afgrunden (Kosmorama, no date), 70
African Americans: in audiences, 7–8, 105,
    107–8, 220, 238n51, 265–66; as film-
    makers, 107, 269; history of, 108–9,
    111; representations of, 6, 103–23; as
    theater owners, 7; as vaudeville perform-
    ers, 104. *See also* National Association

for the Advancement of Colored People;
    race and ethnicity
Agnew, Frances, 339
Alco, 90, 255
Alien, The (Kalem, 1913), 168n155
Alkali Ike (Essanay, 1911), 144
Allen, Robert C., 220, 221
Altar of Death, The (Kay-Bee, 1912), 142
Althusser, Louis, 306n5
Altman, Rick, 132, 156n6
Ambrosio, 138, 199
American Film Manufacturing Company,
    134–35, 140, 144
American Mutoscope and Biograph
    Company, 24
amusement parks (fairgrounds), 6, 11, 66,
    68–73, 172–73, 175, 177–78, 180, 186,
    285, 288–89, 291, 304; film exhibition
    in, 176–77; representation of, 173–74,
    178–88. *See also* commercial recreation;
    Coney Island
Ancient Temples of Egypt (Kalem, 1912), 200
Anderson, Benedict, 132, 156n7
Anderson, G. M (aka "Bullets" Anderson),
    132, 136–37, 142, 144–46, 153, 156n12,
    160nn52,54,56, 164nn113,114,115,
    165n122, 170n185
Anderson, Robert, 240–41, 244, 260n31
Animated Newspaper (Pathé, 1913), 198
Arizona Bill (Eclipse, 1911–1913), 144,
    165n116
Armat, Thomas, 261n45

Arnold, Matthew, 324

Arbuckle, Roscoe (Fatty), 186

Around the Flip-Flip Railroad (American Muto-
    scope and Biograph, 1902), 178

Arvidson, Linda, 15

Association of Edison Licensees (AEL),
    241–45

Atlas Film Company, 137

audiences, 1, 3, 5–8, 10, 217–21; African
    Americans in, 7–8, 105, 107–8, 220,
    238n51, 265–66; children in, 106,
    132–33, 135, 270, 276, 278, 292–93,
    295, 325; class composition of, 7, 8,
    11, 23, 57, 72, 84–85, 88, 91, 92, 106,
    140, 192, 203, 205, 219–20, 222–32,
    238n48, 267, 270, 282n47, 325; immi-
    grants in, 106, 150, 206, 219, 222–32,
    270; mobility of, 85, 248; protests by,
    107–8; racial and ethnic composition
    of, 7, 8, 11, 104–1\5, 134, 149, 150, 155,
    222–32, 235n19, 270; reactions of, 4,
    5, 7, 23, 38, 45, 63, 197, 202–4, 206–8,
    239, 326; in small towns, 219, 234n9;
    vaudeville and, 325; women in, 6, 7, 23,
    48n47, 85, 106, 150, 219–20, 276, 278,
    287, 292–93, 345. *See also* moviegoing;
    spectatorship

Auerbach, Jonathan, 183

avant-garde film, 63, 278

Avenging a Crime; or, Burned at the Stake
    (Crescent, 1904), 109

Bachelard, Gaston, 207

Baker, Newton, 292

Balaban and Katz, 224

Balides, Constance, 9–10, 113

Bamboo Slide (American Mutoscope and
    Biograph, 1904), 178

Bara, Theda, 321–22, 333

Battle of the Red Men (Bison, 1912), 138

Battle, The (Biograph, 1911), 163n87

Bean, Jennifer, 35, 44, 174–75, 184

Beerbohm-Tree, Sir Herbert, 320, 322, 327

Belasco, David, 25, 319

Bellour, Raymond, 18, 22, 33–35, 38, 40,
    46nn15,16, 48n50

Benjamin, Walter, 206, 313n77

Bergson, Henri, 171, 179

Bernardi, Daniel, 123n3

Bernhardt, Sarah 138, 317

Berst, Jacques, 253–54

Birchard, Robert, 162n80

Big Horn Massacre, The (Kalem, 1913), 154

Biograph Company, 19–22, 28, 40, 49n58,
    94, 134, 136, 138, 158nn30,31, 159n44,
    161n63, 163n87, 193, 210n19, 239, 241,
    243, 245–48, 251–53, 256, 258, 299,
    317

Birth Control (Message Photoplay, 1917), 274

birth control films, 273–74

Birth of a Nation, The (Epoch, 1915), 9, 103,
    105, 124n4, 127nn18,23, 265–67, 273,
    276–78, 282n36, 283n67

Bison (Brand Name of NYMP and Univer-
    sal), 133–34, 137–43, 145–48, 150, 153,
    158n31, 161n65, 162nn73,80

Bitzer, Billy, 19, 24

Blaché, Alice Guy, 122, 150

Black Stork, The (Wharton, 1916), 274

Blake, William, 17

Blaney, Charles E., 318

Blau, Herbert, 132

Blazing the Trail (Bison, 1912), 138

Boarding School Girls (Edison, 1905), 173,
    176, 180–81, 183, 186

Bogle, Donald 124n7

Bottomore, Stephen, 193

Bordwell, David, 46n20, 47n37, 50n85, 51,
    53, 56, 61, 64n4, 65n21

Bourdieu, Pierre, 268

Bowser, Eileen, 38, 128n29, 240, 251

Brady, William A., 318–21

Brewster, Ben, 4, 18, 46n11

Bridesmaid's Secret, The (Essanay, 1916), 269

Britain: competition with foreign film mar-
    kets in, 68; distribution in, 69; domestic
    production in, 68–69; exhibition in, 68,
    71; reception of American film in, 143,
    145–46, 149, 164n115. *See also* Europe

Broken Cross, The (Biograph, 1911), 21

Broncho (Brand Name of NYMP), 140–
    43, 146, 150, 153–54, 166nn138,143

Broncho Billy Series (Essanay), 144, 150,
    153–54

Broncho Billy's Christmas Dinner (Essanay,
    1911), 137

Broncho Billy Gets Square (Essanay, 1913), 153

Broncho Billy's Mexican Wife (Essanay, 1912),
    145

Broncho Billy's Mistake (Essanay, 1913), 153

Broncho Billy's Narrow Escape (Essanay, 1913),
    169n166

Broncho Billy's Oath (Essanay, 1913), 160n56

Brownlow, Kevin, 159n46

Bruno, Guiliana, 51

Bucket of Cream Ale, A (Biograph, 1904), 103, 111, 113, 115

Buckwalter, H. H,

Buffalo Bill, 164n112

Buffalo Bill's Wild West, 151, 164n115, 167nn147,150,152

Buffalo Bill Wild West-Pawnee Bill Far East (Selig, 1910), 137

Bunny, John, 324

Burke, John, 167n147

Burgess, Ernest, 228–30, 231

Burning Brand, The (Broncho, 1913), 166n143

Bush, Pauline Garfield, 152, 160n52

Bush, Stephen W., 157nn21,23, 319, 322

Bushman, Francis X., 321

Butsch, Richard, 318

By Man's Law (Biograph, 1913), 273

Cabiria (Italia, 1914), 77

cable television: early film exhibition and, 191, 328

Calamity Anne (American, 1913), 144

Callahan, Vicki, 35

camera position and framing, 19–20, 22–24, 29–30, 115, 186. *See also* close-ups

Camille (Film d'Art, 1912), 138

Carmen (Fox, 1915), 273

Carroll, Noel, 54

Carter, Lincoln J., 141

Casetti, Francesco, 176

Cassenilli, F. Dolores, 160n52

Catholic Church, 296

Catholic Legion of Decency, 278

censorship and regulation, 2, 9, 11, 164n109, 220, 265 79, 281n30, 282nn36,47, 283nn59,64, 287, 292; of exhibition venues, 220, 234n3; industry self-regulation and, 9, 266, 272; lawsuits and, 9, 267–68, 270, 274–78, 283nn59,64; MPPC and, 82, 239, 242–58, 261n61, 262n78, 268–78; municipal censorship boards and, 271–73, 277, 282n36; police censor boards and, 269, 271, 275, 282n36; state censorship boards and, 271–77, 281n30, 282n36. *See also* National Board of Censorship; reformers

Centaur Film Manufacturing Company, 210n19

Central Casting, 345

Champion Film Company, 134

Chaplin, Charlie, 93

Charney, Leo, 54, 313n77

chase films, 182

Cheat, The (Lasky, 1915), 298, 300

Chicago: distributors in, 200; exhibition in, 217–34, 234n3, 296

Chicago Relief and Aid Society, 286

Cine, 199, 200

cinema of attractions, 3, 4, 44, 53–58, 60–61, 66, 71–73, 74n2, 103, 106, 109, 172, 174, 177, 182, 188, 329n34

cinema of narrative integration, 4, 26, 44, 55, 66, 71, 73, 103, 106, 109, 112, 329n34

cinematograph, 269

circus: cinema and, 218

cities, 7, 55–57, 59, 71, 272; ethnic make-up of, 5; exhibition of films in, 85–86, 150, 168n156, 268, 270; modernity in, 56–57. *See also* urban space

Civil War: films depicting, 122, 140, 149, 163nn87,88

Clark, Danae, 341

Clark, James B., 260n23, 262n67

Clark-Lewis, Elizabeth, 111

class: audience composition and, 7, 8, 11, 23, 57, 72, 84–85, 88, 91, 92, 106, 140, 192, 203, 205, 219–20, 222–32, 238n48, 267, 270, 282n47, 325; commercial recreation and, 289

classicism, 1–4, 6, 16, 18, 22, 29–30, 33–35, 38, 40, 44, 46n20, 51–52, 60–63, 73–74, 75n14, 268, 277–79

classical Hollywood cinema, 18, 62, 105–6, 172, 170n186, 277, 279; comedy and, 172; spectatorship and, 174, 192

Cleveland, Ohio: commercial recreation in, 288, 291–92

close-ups, 29–34, 40, 56, 119–20, 141, 179, 301–2. *See also* camera position and framing

Cohen at Coney Island (1909), 175

Colleen Bawn (Kalem, 1911), 167n146

Collier, John, 286, 291, 295

color. *See* tinting

Colored Stenographer, The (Edison, 1909), 121, 122

Colored Troops Disembarking (Edison, 1898), 105

comedy, 6, 55, 63, 77, 93–94, 131, 133, 144, 151, 171–89, 248; nonfiction film and, 192; racial representation in, 109, 111–12

comic strips: cinema and, 172

Coming of Columbus, The (Selig, 1912), 253, 262n66

commercial recreation: attendance at, 288; cinema and, 171–89, 219, 285–98; class and, 289; recreation studies and, 286, 288, 290; reformers and, 286, 289–90, 292, 294–98, 303; women and, 290–91, 294–95, 303, 307–308n13. *See also* amusement parks

Committee on Public Information, The, 278

Coney Island, 6, 173, 175, 177–80, 182, 184, 186, 188, 285, 288, 291, 293–94, 312n59. *See also* amusement parks

Coney Island (Comic Film Corp., 1917), 173, 176, 181, 186–88

Coney Island at Night (Edison, 1905), 178

Confederate Spy, The (Kalem, 1910), 130n44

Conrad, Joseph, 29

consumer culture, 287, 29; commercial recreation and, 286; film exhibition and, 218–19, 238n53, 297; spectatorship and, 220. *See also* department stores

Cook, The (1918), 175

Cooked Goose, The (Thanhouser, 1914), 269

Coon Cake Walk, A (American Mutoscope and Biograph, 1897), 123n1

Coon Town Suffragettes (Lubin 1914), 125n7, 128n30

Corner in Cotton, A (Quality Pictures, 1915), 298

Corner in Wheat, A (Biograph, 1909), 298

Costello, Maurice, 144, 160n52

Courtney, Susan, 129nn32,41

Cowboy Millionaire, The (Selig, 1909), 151, 169n170

Crafton, Donald, 172–74, 176, 185

Craven, The (Vitagraph, 1912), 151

Creel Committee, 278

Creel, George, 278

Cripps, Thomas, 105

Crisis, The (Bison, 1912), 138, 168n166

crosscutting. *See* parallel editing

cross-dressing, 181, 187

culture: film's reflection of, 1, 4, 36, 51,

53, 56–58, 62; significance of film's influence on, 3, 5, 9, 11, 265–68, 270–74, 276–79, 282n36; status of film within, 10–11, 285–98, 315–28

Cunard, Grace, 338

Curtis, Scott, 8–9, 64n4, 203

Custer's Last Fight (Kay-Bee, 1912), 140–41, 143

Damon and Pythias (Selig, 1908), 250, 262n66

Darkfeather, Mona, 133–34, 141, 149, 152, 154, 157n27

Davis, Michael, Jr., 286, 288, 290–91, 294–95, 303–4

Davis, Owen, 318

Debt, The (Rex, 1912), 109

deCordova, Richard, 336

Delluc, Louis, 208

De Marco, Gordon, 334

DeMille, Cecil B., 41, 154, 318

DeMille, William, 318

DeMille, Mrs. William, 345

Denmark: film industry in, 68; influence on American shift to feature-length production, 70, 148; regulation of theatres in, 70. *See also* Europe

department stores, 294; representation of, 108, 121. *See also* consumer culture

Deserter, The (Bison, 1912), 138–39, 146–47

Detroit: commercial recreation in, 288

Deutche Bioscop, 68

Diawara, Manthia, 124n4

Dickens, Charles, 15

distribution, 5, 8, 19, 68, 73–74, 87, 241–42, 246; agents of, 19, 67, 69, 70, 72, 85, 88, 200, 249, 269; independent outlets of, 2, 82, 87, 244; international films and, 199–201; outlets of, 18, 19, 46n8, 69, 72, 84, 132, 139–40, 240, 242–46, 249–52, 254–55, 257–58, 260n32, 261n38, 262nn67,78, 269, 274; split reels and, 72, 97n6, 139, 201, 239; systems of, 6, 19, 68–69, 71–72, 75n3, 76, 82, 84, 87–89, 91, 99nn23,24, 132, 139, 240, 242, 247, 249–52, 255, 257–58, 261n41; zoning and clearance rules of, 69, 86, 88. *See also* states' rights system

Dividend, The (New York Motion Picture Corp., 1916), 298

Dixon, Thomas, 28n15

Dollar and the Law, The (Vitagraph, 1916), 299

Drama League of America, 326, 331n64
Drama Society of New York, 327
Dreiser, Theodore, 344
Dressler, Marie, 184
Drive for Life, The (Biograph, 1909), 32
Driven From the Ranch (Gaumont, 1912),
    162n85
Dwan, Allan, 134, 140, 145, 165nn128,129
Dyer, Frank, 246–47, 254–56

Eagle, The (Universal, 1915), 269
Early Days in the West (Bison, 1912), 141
Easiest Way, The (Clara Kimball Young Film
    Corp., 1917), 273
Eaton, Walter Prichard, 316, 319, 323–26
Éclair, 68–69, 210n19, 247
Eclipse, 140, 165n116, 199, 200, 210n19,
    247. *See also* Urban-Eclipse
Edendale, Calif., 334
Edison Film Manufacturing Company, 94,
    97n8, 144, 178, 192, 199, 239, 241–
    43, 245–48, 252–53, 256–57, 260n13,
    261n49, 315. *See also* Thomas A. Edison
    Inc.
Edison, Thomas A., 8, 47n40, 49n66, 201,
    241, 245, 247–48, 253, 256, 258, 260n13.
    See also Thomas A. Edison Inc.
editing, 3, 16, 18–19, 21, 27, 29–30, 39, 43,
    46n11, 46n15, 47nn53,52,55,57, 104,
    116, 137, 147, 151, 182, 184–87, 297;
    continuity, 1, 7, 57, 104–6; intrascene,
    29–30, 47n33; parallel, 15–16, 20, 27,
    29, 33, 37–39, 182; sightlines and, 187;
    travelogues and, 197
Edwards, Harold, 316, 320, 323–24
Edwards, J. Gordon, 321–22
Edwards, Richard Henry, 288, 289–90, 297,
    304–5
Electrocuting an Elephant (Edison, 1902), 55
Engineer's Romance, The (Edison, 1910),
    47n40, 49n66
Ensslen, Klaus, 237n35
Episode at Cloudy Canyon (Essanay, 1913),
    153, 170n186
Epoch, 265
Escape of Jim Dolan, The (Selig, 1913), 153
Essanay Film Manufacturing Company,
    84, 94, 131–34, 136–37, 140, 143–44,
    150, 153–54, 156n12, 164nn109,113,
    168n166, 239, 246, 253, 257–58, 269–
    70, 332

Europe: American reception of films from,
    78, 87; effect of World War I on produc-
    tion of film in, 98n10; exhibition of film
    in, 71; importation of films from, 199–
    201; penetration by American film in,
    70; production in, 98n10; reception
    of U.S film in, 131, 143–44, 146, 148,
    153, 164n110; stylistic phases of film
    in, 71
Everett, Anna, 126n13
Everson, William, 170n192
exhibition: amusement parks and, 176–
    77; contexts of, 4, 5, 74, 77, 269, 293–
    95; expansion of, 8; music and, 86, 106,
    194, 249, 295; non-theatrical venues
    and, 201, 209n6; practices of, 2, 7, 19,
    66–69, 71–72, 74n2, 75n3, 76–77, 84–
    96, 98n22, 99n36, 100n47, 106–7, 142,
    180, 241–42, 244, 248–50, 252–53, 258,
    269, 271; racial segregation and, 107;
    theater location and, 217–34; travel-
    ogues and, 194–95, 197–99; venues of,
    1, 5, 7–9, 11, 19, 41, 45, 66–72, 74n2,
    76–78, 84–96, 98nn15,22, 99n30, 36,
    100n47, 131, 133, 138, 143–45, 153–54,
    157n19, 159n44, 161nn59,71, 162n86,
    166n138, 169n18, 240, 242–46, 248–
    49, 251–54, 257–58, 265–66, 268–70,
    274, 278. *See also* nickelodeons; theaters
    (motion picture)
exhibitors, 5, 7, 18–19, 70–71, 85–87,
    95, 99nn24,29, 100n46, 131–34, 138,
    162n86, 169n181, 240, 242–46, 248–55,
    258, 269, 270, 278, 282n47; competition
    among, 66, 69, 88–94, 99nn22,30,36;
    ethnic background of, 236n28
Explosion of a Motor Car (Hepworth, 1900),
    56

fairgrounds. *See* amusement parks
Fall of Black Hawk, The (American, 1912),
    140
Fall of Troy, The (Itala, 1912), 138
Famous Players Film Company, 165n120,
    317–19
Famous Players-Lasky, 240
fans, 2; culture of, 7, 153, 219–20, 334–40.
    See also star system
fan magazines, 10, 33, 160n52, 169n178,
    332; depiction of Hollywood in, 336–
    37

feature films, 1, 4–5, 9, 17, 60, 66, 69–71, 73–74, 74n2, 76–96, 98nn10,15, 99n22, 100n47, 132, 136–40, 153–54, 177, 183, 188, 194–95, 239–41, 249–55, 257–58, 262nn66,75, 278; era of, 41, 44, 70. *See also* multireel films

Feeding the Doves (Edison, 1896), 193

Feeding Seals at Catalina Island (Essanay, 1910), 200

Fenin, George, 170n192

Fielding, Raymond, 78

Fighting Blood (Biograph, 1911), 136, 159n44

Film Service Association (FSA), 243–46, 250–51, 258, 260n23, 261n61

First Amendment, 266, 269, 275, 277, 283n59

First National, 86

Fit to Fight (American Social Hygiene Association, 1918), 278

Fit to Win (American Social Hygiene Association, 1918), 278

Flaming Arrow, The (Bison, 1913), 141, 149, 166n143

Fly Pest, The (Urban, 1910), 204

"Flying A" Pictures (Brand Name of American Film Company), 134, 136, 143, 145, 152

For His Master's Sake (Pathé, 1911), 130n44

Forbidden Fruit (Ivan, 1916), 269

Forcing the Force (Eclectic, 1914), 269

Ford, Francis, 138, 140, 154, 170n192

Ford, Jack (John), 154

Fox Film Corporation, 87, 91, 154, 273, 321

France: distribution in, 69; exhibition in, 70, 72; film in, 69, 148; and its influence on American film, 144; production in, 68, 69; reception of American film in, 163n109, 167nn146,150. *See also* Europe

Frank, Thomas, 311n58

Franklin, John Hope, 111

Friedberg, Anne, 51

Frisby, David, 313n77

Frohman, Charles and Daniel, 316, 319

Fuller, Kathryn, 219, 234n9

Fuller, Mary, 144, 337, 342

Gabler, Edwin, 48nn52,58

Gaines, Jane, 219

Gans-Nelson Fight (Selig, 1908), 251

Gaumont, 68–69, 140, 162n85, 199, 200, 247–48

General Film Company, The, 8, 69–70, 85, 87, 94, 246–47, 251–56, 258, 262n78

George Kleine Optical Company, 239, 241, 243, 245, 247–48, 252–55, 257. *See also* Kleine, George

genre, 5–7, 44, 59, 62–63, 70, 77, 85, 132, 156n6; animal pictures, 140; aviation film, 252; birth control films, 274; cartoons, 71, 77–78; Civil War films, 122, 140, 149, 163nn87,88; comedy, 6, 55, 63, 77, 93–94, 131, 133, 144, 151, 171–89, 248; detective films, 144, 156n10; dramas, 55, 59, 131, 248; educational, 131, 133; exploitation cinema, 278; *Féeries*, 72; fight films, 9, 68; horror films, 61; instructional films, 278; jungle pictures, 140; kinesthetic motion films, 55; melodrama, 15, 36, 39, 42, 50n86, 58, 61, 70, 93, 112, 133, 140–41, 155n1, 159n43; mystery thrillers, 44, 47n37; musicals, 61; newsreels, 71, 77, 78, 198; nonfiction film, 175–76, 186, 191–208, 278, 291; passion films, 72; serials, 35, 44, 46n10, 58, 60, 77, 93, 152, 156n10, 220, 297; slapstick, 6–7, 44, 63, 156n10; transformation films, 55; travelogues, 7, 191–208; war pictures, 163n88; westerns, 131–55; white slave pictures, 9, 267, 269–70, 272, 274, 278, 282n36

Germany: competition with foreign markets and, 68; distribution in, 69; exhibition in, 66–67; production in, 66–67, 69; reception of American film in, 164n109. *See also* Europe

Geronimo's Raid (American, 1912), 140

Gevinson, Alan, 78

Gifford, Denis, 78

Gilded Kid, The (Edison, 1914), 269,

Gilmore, William, 247, 261n49

Girl and Her Trust, The (Biograph, 1912), 43, 138

Girl of the West, A (Vitagraph, 1912), 150

Glimpse of Neapolitan Camorra, A (Ambrosio, 1911), 198

Gold Diggers of 1933, The (Warner Bros., 1933), 298, 312n59

Golden Wedding, The (Ambrosia, 1912), 138

Gomery, Douglas, 220

Gone with the Wind (MGM, 1939), 105

Good-For-Nothing, The (Essanay, 1914), 170n185

Goodstadt, L. M., 345
Göktürk, Deniz, 164n109
Gorky, Maxim, 291, 294–95, 304, 312n59
Grandin, Frank, 24
Grandma's Reading Glass (Warwick, 1900), 56
Grau, Robert, 292–93, 316, 318, 326, 341
Great Train Robbery, The (Edison, 1903), 16
Greed (Metro-Goldwyn, 1925), 298, 312n59
Greenhorn, The (Broncho, 1913), 166n138
Grieveson, Lee, 9, 307n11, 329n34
Griffith, D. W., 49n66, 137, 158n30,
    167n146, 170n189, 283n67, 317;
    camera set-ups in films of, 19–20, 22–
    24, 29–30; characterization in films
    of, 16–17, 31–32, 38–39; censorship
    and, 266–68, 277; close-ups in films
    of, 29–34, 40; on directing actors, 339;
    editing in films of, 16–23, 25–27, 29–30,
    34–35, 37–40, 46n16, 47n33; gender
    representation in films of, 34–43; nar-
    ration in films of, 17, 23, 26–27, 29, 33–
    34; narrative form in films of, 16–17, 20,
    22–23, 26, 32–33, 37–39; suspense in
    films of, 16–17, 20, 22, 30, 38, 39; tint-
    ing in films of 21–22, 27, 32–33
Griffiths, Allison, 170n189
Guerrero, Ed, 124n4
Gunning, Tom, 3–4, 51, 53, 55–57, 63–
    64, 64n4, 72, 74n2, 116, 117, 171, 172–
    74, 176, 185, 197, 299, 306n9, 313n77,
    329n34

Hale's Tours, 176, 205
Hamman, Joë, 140, 144
Hampton, Benjamin, 75n7
Hand That Rocks the Cradle, The (Universal,
    1917), 274
Hansen, Miriam Bratu, 48n47, 51, 61–63,
    128n28, 132, 150, 155, 156n10, 219,
    308n13
Harris, Chauncey, 217
Harrison, Louis-Reeves, 138, 141, 155,
    166n144, 168n166
Hart, William S., 154, 170n92
Hastie, Amelie, 350n65
Hays, Will, 347
Heart of New York, The (Claridge, 1915), 269
Her Indian Mother (Kalem, 1910), 158n30
Higashi, Sumiko, 221, 318
His Trust (Biograph, 1911), 110, 126n18,
    130n44

His Trust Fulfilled (Biograph, 1911), 110,
    126n18, 130n44
historiography, 4, 51, 74n1, 76
Hitchcock, Alfred, 46n24
Hodkinson, W. W., 70
Hollywood. *See* Los Angeles, Calif.
Hollywood Studio Club, 345, 346
Holmes, Burton, 196, 211n34
Holmes, Helen, 43
Holy City, The (Selig, 1908), 251
Hostage, The (Lasky, 1914), 269
How Binks Butted In (Selig, 1909), 195
How States Are Made (Vitagraph, 1912), 150,
    168n163
Howe, Lyman, 69
Hoyt, Homer, 230
Hunter, Tera W., 111
Hull House (Chicago, Ill.), 222, 236n26,
    291, 296

immigrants: audiences of, 150, 206, 219,
    222–32, 270
importation of films, 199–201
In the Days of the Thundering Herd (Selig, 1914),
    257
In the Land of Monkeys and Snakes (Pathé, 1911),
    196
Ince, Thomas, 136, 138, 140, 142, 159n46,
    162n80
Inceville, 334
Independents, the, 2, 8, 46n8, 69, 75n7, 82,
    131–32, 134–35, 138, 140, 163n109,
    240–41, 243–48, 250–52, 254, 256–58,
    263n78, 324
Independent Motion Picture Company (IMP),
    136, 140
Indian Massacre, The (Bison, 1912), 138–39,
    148
Inside of the White Slave Traffic (The Moral
    Feature Film Company, 1913), 272
Itala, 138
Italy: distribution of film in, 68; film in,
    68, 148; influence on American shift
    to feature production and, 70, 77;
    production of spectaculars in, 138.
    See also Europe
internet, 315
Intolerance (Triangle, 1916), 277, 283n67
Invaders, The (Kay-Bee, 1912), 141, 148,
    166n144
Iola's Promise (Biograph, 1912), 161n63

Iron Hand, The (Universal, 1916), 273
Is Any Girl Safe? (Universal, 1916), 274
Israels, Belle Lindner, 305n2
It May Be Your Daughter (Moral Uplift Society, 1916), 269
Itala, 210n19

Jack Fat and Jim Slim at Coney Island (Vitagraph, 1910), 173, 175, 176, 181, 183, 186
Jack The Kisser (Edison, 1907), 117–18
James Boys in Missouri, The (Atlas, 1911), 137, 160n58
James Boys in Missouri, The (Essanay, 1908), 270
James, Henry, 41–43, 50n82
Janowitz, Morris, 238n49
Johnson, Jack, 110
Joyce, Alice, 150
Judith of Bethulia (Biograph, 1913), 317
Jurassic Park (MCA/Universal, 1993), 297

Kalem Company, 85, 94, 140, 150, 154, 157n21, 158nn30,31, 167n146, 210n19, 239, 241, 243, 247, 253, 256, 260n13
Kansas City: commercial recreation in, 288, 290
Karr, Larry, 96
Kasson, John, 176
Kay-Bee (Brand Name of NYMP), 140–43, 147, 150, 153–54, 166n138, 273
Keaton, Buster, 186
Keil, Charlie, 4, 16, 19, 27, 33, 45n7, 46n11, 50n85, 176, 199
Kenaga, Heidi, 345–46
Kennedy, J. J, 251
Kerrigan, Jack, 165n128
Kerrigan, J. Warren, 145
K-E-S-E, 257
Kidman, Nicole, 320
kinetoscope, 269, 315
King of Kings, The (Paramount, 1927), 41
King Lear (Thanhouser, 1916), 321
Kingsley, Sherman C., 286, 295–96
Kirby, Lynne, 27, 35, 43, 47n30, 48nn50,51
Kiss in the Dark, A (American Mutoscope and Biograph, 1904), 113–14, 128n28
Kittler, Friedrich, 41, 49n70
Klaw and Erlanger, 316, 318
Kleine-Edison Film Service, 257
Kleine, George, 200–201, 204, 246–48,

252, 255, 260n13, 261n49. *See also* George Kleine Optical Company
Kosmorama, 70
Koszarski, Richard, 99n29
Kracauer Siegfried, 313n77
Kreutzer Sonata, The (Fox, 1915), 273–74

Laemmle, Carl, 94, 140, 240, 245–46
Lake Shore Film, 143
Lasky Feature Play Company, 154, 269, 318, 332, 334, 345
Lasky, Mrs. Jesse L., 345
Last Drop of Water, The (Biograph, 1911), 136
last-minute rescue films. *See* race-to-the-rescue films
Laughing Ben (American Mutoscope and Biograph, 1902), 123n1
Laughing Gas (Edison, 1907), 104, 118–20
Lauritzen, Einar, 78, 96n4
Law and the Outlaw, The (Selig, 1913), 153
Law of the West, The (Kay-Bee, 1913), 143
Lawrence, Florence, 160n52
lawsuits: antitrust-based, 94, 240, 246, 257; censorship-based, 9, 267–68, 270, 274–78, 283nn59,64; contract-based, 140; patents-based, 241–45, 247–48
lecturer. *See* presenter
Lefebvre, Henri, 23
Legend of Lake Desolation, The (Pathé, 1911), 134
Lester, Louise, 144, 152
Lewis, Max, 246
Lieutenant's Last Fight, The (Bison, 1912), 138–39
Life of Napoleon, The (Vitagraph, 1909), 249
Little Dove's Romance, (Bison, 1911), 134
Lindsay, Vachel, 43, 44, 50n82
Lindstrom, J. A, 8
literature: influence on film of, 17, 84; relation to film, 41–43, 151; use as source material, 84, 273, 275
Little, Anna, 168n166
Lloyd, Harold, 188
Lonedale Operator, The (Biograph, 1911), 3, 15, 17–41, 43–45, 46nn15,16,21, 47nn33,34,36,40, 49nn66,74,56,58,60
Lonely Villa, The (Biograph, 1909), 39–40
Loetschberg (Eclipse, 1913), 205–6
Lonesome (Paramount, 1929), 188
Long, Samuel, 247
Los Angeles, Calif.: audiences in, 197;

emigration to, 317–18, 340, 342–45;
    as film production center, 317, 332–37;
    representation of, 175, 196–97
Lubin Film Manufacturing Company, 94,
    158n31, 239, 241, 243, 248, 253, 257
Lubin, Siegmund, 253–54
Lumière, Louis and Auguste; films of, 191,
    192, 193, 205
Luna Park (Coney Island), 186, 288
Luna Park (Los Angeles), 175
Lundquist, Gunnar, 78, 96n4
Lunn, Eugene, 287

Macbeth (Triangle-Reliance, 1916), 321–22,
    327
MacDonald, D., 260n23
MacLaren, Mary, 336–38, 341–42
Macpherson, Jeanie, 40–41
Madison, Cleo, 341
magic lantern shows, 205
Mainspring, The (Falcon, 1917), 269, 281n24
Majestic Pictures, 136
Making of an American Citizen, The (Solax,
    1912), 168n155
Mammy's Ghost (Vitagraph, 1911), 126n17
Man of the Hour (Brady Picture Plays, 1914),
    298
Man They Scorned, The (Broncho, 1912), 146,
    166n138
Manhattan: exhibition in, 220–21, 286, 288,
    317. *See also* New York City
Marion, Frank, 247
Marsh, Mae, 333, 338
Marvin, Harry, 252
Marx, Karl, 300
Marxism, 287
Massacre, The (Biograph, 1912), 167n146
Massacre of the Fourth Cavulry, The (Bison,
    1912), 141
Massacre of the Santa Fe Trail, The (Bison,
    1912), 141
Matthews, Brander, 319
Matrimony's Speed Limit (Solax, 1913), 123
Mayne, Judith, 219
McClure, Fred, 290
McDaniel, Hattie, 105, 129n39
Méliès. *See* Star Film Company
Méliès, Georges, 241
melodrama, 15, 36, 39, 42, 50n86, 58,
    61, 70, 93, 112, 133, 140–41, 155n1,
    159n43

Menke, Richard, 42–43
Metro Pictures, 87, 321
Metz, Christian, 18
Mexican Joan of Arc, The (Kalem, 1911),
    157n21
Micheaux, Oscar, 128n31, 269. *See also*
    African Americans, as filmmakers
Miller Brothers 101 Ranch Wild West Show,
    136–39, 151, 157n22, 158n31, 164n112,
    165n125, 169n180
Million Dollar Mystery, The (Thanhouser,
    1914–15), 299
Millionaire Cowboy, The (Selig, 1913),
    169n170
Milwaukee, Wisc.: commercial recreation
    in, 288
Mis-Directed Kiss, The (American Mutoscope
    and Biograph, 1904), 113
Miserables, Les (S.C.A.G.L., 1912), 90
Mithen, Luke, 244
Mix, Tom, 133, 153, 157n22
Mixed Babies (American Mutoscope and
    Biograph, 1908), 104, 121
Mixed Colors (Pathé, 1913), 121
modernism, 61–62. *See also* postmodernism;
    vernacular modernism
modernity, 3–4, 15, 27–28, 34–35, 40–41,
    44–45, 51–64, 65n21, 132, 154–55,
    156n10, 302–3, 313n77; cinematic
    representations of, 56, 58–59. *See also*
    technology
modernity thesis, 4, 44, 50n85, 51–57, 59–
    63, 64nn2,4, 65n21
Mona of the Modocs (Bison, 1913), 141, 143
Money (United Keanograph, 1915), 298
Montana State Fair (Vitagraph, 1914), 198
Montgomery, Frank, 141
Morrison, Toni, 108
Motion Picture Distributing and Sales Com-
    pany (MPDSA), 252
Motion Picture Patents Company (MPPC, or
    "The Trust"), 2, 8–9, 18–19, 45, 46n8,
    68–69, 75n7, 134–35, 163n109, 239–58,
    260nn13,23,31, 261nn41,45, 262n78,
    316, 324; AEL, and 241–45; antitrust
    suits against the, 94, 244, 248, 257; con-
    flicts within the, 239–41, 243, 245–46,
    248, 253, 255, 258; FSA and, 243–46,
    250–51, 258, 260n23, 261nn31,61; GFC
    and, 246–47, 251–58, 262n78; Indepen-
    dents versus the, 132, 240–41, 243–48,

Motion Picture Patents Company (MPPC, or "The Trust") (continued) 250–52, 254, 256–58, 263n78; lawsuits and, 240–43, 245–47, 258; licensing and, 161n38, 241–48, 250–53, 256–58, 260n13; regulation of the industry by the, 82, 239, 242–58, 261n61, 262n78, 268–78; reluctance to produce features by the, 239–41, 248, 250–55, 257–58, 262nn66,75; trade press and, 240, 247–48; UFSPA, and 242–43

Motion Picture Sales Company, The, 69, 139–40

Motoring among the Cliffs and Gorges of France (Gaumont, 1910), 196

moviegoing, 8, 57, 85, 96; culture of, 11; trends in, 3, 4, 71, 45, 85, 249. See also audiences; spectatorship

Müller, Corinna, 66, 70, 72, 74n1, 75n3

multireel films, 1, 5, 17, 35, 93, 100n47, 132, 137, 148–50, 153–54, 163n88, 165n116, 249, 251, 254. See also feature films

Münsterberg, Hugo, 50n82, 205

music: in theaters, 106, 194. See also song slides

Musketeers of Pig Alley (Biograph, 1912), 56

Musser, Charles, 69, 123n3, 125n11, 253, 260n32

Musson, Bennet, 292–93

mutoscope, 269

Mutual Film Corporation, 8, 69, 85, 87, 94, 143, 274–78, 283nn59,64

Mutual Film-Supply Company, 140

National Association for the Advancement of Colored People (NAACP), 266. See also African Americans

National Association of Motion Picture Industry, 319

National Board of Censorship, 9, 266, 272, 274, 282n47, 293. See also censorship and regulation

narration, 18, 22, 26–27, 29, 31, 47n37, 73

narrative: chase and, 105, 116, 176, 180–81, 183, 185–86; comprehensibility of, 18, 20, 22, 26, 33, 38, 44, 46n10; development of classical codes of, 5, 36, 45, 51, 52, 73, 170n186; forms of, 1, 3–5, 7, 15–18, 20, 22–23, 32–34, 37–38, 43–44, 47n37, 48n40, 53–54, 56, 58–60, 72–73,

76, 266; rise of, 103, 106–7; spectacle and, 116–18, 171–72. See also cinema of narrative integration; classical Hollywood cinema

Nazimova, Alla, 345

Nellie, the Beautiful Housemaid (Vitagraph, 1908), 104, 121–22

Nelson, Carol, 69

Neptune's Daughter (company, date unavailable), 90

Nestor Company, 134, 141, 144, 165n117, 210n19

New York City, 343. See also Manhattan

New York Motion Picture Company (NYMP), 132, 136, 140–42

newsreels, 71, 77, 78, 198. See also nonfiction film

nickelodeons, 5, 7–9, 41, 57, 69, 71–72, 76–77, 84–86, 88–89, 97n8, 242, 248, 249, 254, 268–70; audience composition in, 217–21; boom of, 76, 82, 89, 242; commercial recreation and, 285–86; descriptions of, 294–95; era of, 72–73, 96, 242; location of, 217–34, 176, 291; reformers and, 296–97, 304. See also exhibition; theaters

nickel theaters. See nickelodeons

Nielson, Asta, 68, 70

Night Riders (Kalem, 1908), 270

Noble, John W., 321

Nobody Would Believe (Universal, 1915), 269

nonfiction film, 175–76, 186, 191–208, 291; racial representation and, 103, 109, 205. See also newsreels; travelogues

Nordisk, 199

Norris, Frank, 167n147

Octoroon, The (Kalem, 1909), 109

Old Mammy's Charge (Majestic, 1913), 126n17, 130n44

Oliver Twist (Vitagraph, 1909), 316

Olsson, Jan, 38

one-reel films. See single-reel films

O'Neill, Eugene, 327

Ostriche, Muriel, 339

Otis, Elita Proctor, 316

Outbreak, The (Selig, 1911), 131, 157n20

Paid in Full (All Star Feature Corp., 1914), 298

Pal's Oath, A (Essanay, 1911), 137, 160n56

Palmer, Lewis E., 296
Panama-Pacific Exposition (San Francisco, Calif.), 335–36
parallel editing, 15–16, 20, 27, 29, 37–39, 122–23, 182, 184–85, 297. *See also* editing
Paramount Pictures, 87, 88, 90, 99n24, 211, 253–55, 318
Park, Ida May, 341
Parsons, Louella, 339
Pasadena, Calif., 334, 341
Pathé Frères, 20, 68–69, 87, 91, 133, 134, 155, 158n31, 164n109, 199, 200, 247, 253, 257
Pathéscope, 201
Patten, Simon, 9–10, 286, 294–97, 304–5, 310n41, 311n57
Patterson, Joseph Medill, 325
Pearson, Roberta E., 10, 202, 221
Peiss, Kathy, 177, 219, 307n13
penny arcades, 269
People's Institute (New York City), 286, 291, 292
performance style, 10, 32–33, 43; in "legitimate" theater, 316, 321; racial representation and, 109. *See also* acting
Perils of the Plains, The (Warners, 1912), 140
periodization, 2, 4–5, 11, 51, 66, 74, 75n3
Peterson, Jennifer Lynne, 7
Philppott, Thomas, 222
Phelps, William Lyon, 316
Pickaninny Dance, The—From the "Passing Show/ The Pickaninnies (Edison, 1894), 123n1
Pickford, Mary, 136, 160n52, 161n63, 324, 333, 337–38, 344–45
Pit, The (Brady Picture Plays, 1914), 298
Pitt, ZaSu, 341
Poggi, Jack, 326
Poisoned Flume, The (Flying A, 1912), 143, 145–46, 165n127, 128, 129
politics: representation of, 266, 268–70, 273–74, 277–78
Porter, Edwin S., 315
postmodernism, 61–62
Powers Company, 158n33, 210n19
presenter, 72
Price, Gertrude, 152
Prince and the Pauper, The (Edison, 1909), 316
production: Europe and, 66–69, 98n10, 138; independent, 69, 131–32, 134–

35, 138, 140, 163n109, 240–41, 243–48, 250–52, 254, 256–58, 263n78; trends and practices in, 1, 2, 5, 10–11, 17, 19, 61, 67–71, 76–84, 87–88, 93–94, 97nn6,7,8,10, 98n10, 239–58, 262n66, 268, 274, 278, 282n46. *See also* studios
Progressive Era, The, 5–6, 285, 292
Prohibition (Prohibition Production Company, 1916), 273
promotion. *See* advertising and promotion
propaganda, film as, 272, 278
prostitution and white slavery: representation of, 9, 267, 269–70, 272, 274, 278, 282n36, 329n34. *See also* sexuality
Protect Your Daughter (All Star, 1918), 269
Provincetown Players, 327
publicity. *See* advertising and promotion
Pueblo Legend, A (Biograph, 1912), 167n146

Queen Elizabeth (1912), 317
Quinn, Michael, 240, 248–49
Quo Vadis? (Cines, Italy, 1913), 77, 90

Rabinovitz, Lauren, 6–7, 48n47, 51, 220
race and ethnicity: of audiences, 7, 8, 11, 104–5, 134, 149, 150, 155, 222–32, 235n19, 270; representations of, 6, 7, 9, 11, 103–23, 133–34, 138, 141–42, 145–49, 151, 154–55, 157nn18,25,27, 165n125, 166n143, 168n155, 265–67, 270, 278, 205; of theater owners, 236n28. *See also* African Americans
race-to-the-rescue films, 15, 21, 34, 39–40, 60, 168n166
radio, 315
railway, 25, 27–29, 35–36, 39, 43, 59; representations of, 108, 205–6; mechanical rides and, 176–77. *See also* Hale's Tours
Rainey, Paul, 207
Ramsaye, Terry, 75n7
Ranch Girls on the Rampage, The (Kalem, 1912), 150
Ranch Life in the Southwest (Selig, 1910), 137
Ranchman's Nerve, The (American, 1911), 134
Ranchman's Vengeance, The (Flying A, 1912), 143, 145–46, 165nn125,129
Rauschenbusch, Walter, 291
Ray, Robert, 213n61
Ready Money (Lasky, 1914), 286, 298–304
realism, 21, 34, 42, 44, 52, 57–58, 139, 141, 146, 175, 266, 320, 329n34

Red Man's Honor (Eclipse, 1912), 140
reformers, 106, 202–5; commercial recrea-
   tion and, 286, 289–90, 292, 294–98,
   303; Hollywood culture and, 344–45
regulation. *See* censorship and regulation
Reid, Dorothy Davenport, 341
Reliance-Majestic, 332. *See also* Triangle-
   Reliance
Rex, 210n19
Richardson, Anna Steese, 323
road shows, 90, 252
Rogin, Michael, 129n39
Romains, Jules, 208
Romeo and Juliet (Fox, 1916), 321–22
Romeo and Juliet (Metro, 1916), 321–22
Rosaldo, Renato, 149
Rosen, Philip, 283n67
Ross, Murray, 333–34
Royal Box, The (Selig Polyscope, 1914),
   257
Royland, Ruth, 150–52
Rube and Mandy Go to Coney Island (Edison,
   1903), 173, 180

St. John, Adela Rogers, 346
Sallie's Sure Shot (Selig, 1913), 151
San Francisco, Calif., 335
Sandmore District, The (Urban, 1913), 198
Santa Cruz, Calif., 341
Santa Monica, Calif., 334, 341
Sapho (Majestic, 1913), 269
Satan's Pawn (Majestic, 1915), 269
Saved By the Pony Express (Selig, 1911), 133
Sawyer, Laura, 144, 165n120
Scenes in the Celestial Empire (Eclipse, 1910), 198
Schaeffer, Anna, 150–51
Schlüpmann, Heide, 74n1
Schwartz, Vanessa R., 54, 313n77
Scull, George F., 252
Sealed Lips (Equitable Motion Pictures,
   1915), 273
*Searching the Ruins on Broadway, Galveston,
   for Dead Bodies* (Edison, 1900), 193
Seeing Los Angeles (IMP, 1912), 196–97
Seeress, The (American Mutoscope and
   Biograph, 1904), 126n17
Selig, William N., 239–40, 244, 248, 250,
   252, 260n28, 32, 261n47, 262n66, 75
Selig Polyscope Company, 94, 131–34, 137,
   140, 150–51, 153, 157nn20,22, 158n31,

169n170, 170n189, 199, 239, 241, 243,
   250–51, 253, 256–57
Seligsberg, Walter N., 274–75
Selznick, David, 318
Selznick, Lewis J., 318
Sennett, Mack, 47n40
Sensational Logging (Essanay, 1910), 204
Sergeant's Boy, The (NYMP, 1912), 141
serials, 35, 46n10, 58, 60, 77, 93, 152, 220,
   297; serial queens and, 35, 43, 152
Sevres Porcelain (Gaumont, 1909), 198
sexuality: representation of, 7, 9, 105, 110,
   114–15, 117–18, 120–21, 173, 177,
   181, 183, 188–89, 269–70, 272, 274,
   276, 278, 282n47; extras and, 342–44.
   See also prostitution and white slavery
Shadow of the Past, A (Broncho, 1913),
   142–43
Shakespeare, William: film adaptations of,
   202, 321–23, 327; stage productions
   of, 321, 327
She Never Knew (Buffalo, 1916), 269
Sheriff's Chum, The (Essanay, 1911), 136,
   160n49,
short film, 4–5, 67–70, 73–74, 76–89, 91–
   96, 97nn7,10, 98nn10,22, 100n47, 240,
   258. *See also* single-reel films
Shubert, Lee and Jacob, 317–18
Shubert Feature Film Booking Company,
   317
Siege of St. Petersburg, The (Kalem, 1912), 140
single-reel films, 1, 3–6, 15, 17–20, 22, 27,
   32, 35, 38, 41, 44–45, 56, 73–74, 76–77,
   84, 86, 93–94, 97n6, 137, 139–41, 144,
   165n116, 170n186, 239–40, 249, 252–
   53, 255; era of, 3, 17, 19–20, 22, 29–32,
   44–45, 48nn40,47, 49n66
Silvester, Richard, 327
Simmel, Georg, 58, 286, 287, 300, 302–5,
   313n77
Singer, Ben, 2, 5, 18, 24, 32, 35, 46n10,
   47n25, 50n85, 51–53, 56–57, 60, 63,
   64nn2,4, 220, 221, 258, 303
The Slave, a Story of the South before the War
   (Vitagraph, 1907), 109
Slave's Devotion, A (Broncho, 1913), 130n44
Slide, Anthony, 165n128, 340
Smashing the Vice Trust (Progress Film Co.,
   1914), 269, 272–73, 282n35
Smith, Albert, 247, 255

Snowman, The (American Mutoscope and Biograph, 1908), 129n35

Solax, 167n155, 168n155, 210n19

Some Cop (Crystal, 1914), 269

Song of the Wildwood Flute, The (Biograph, 1910), 134, 158n30

song slides, 86, 249, 295. *See also* music

"specials," 251–54, 262n75

spectatorship, 6, 9, 22, 44, 55, 61, 85, 149, 289, 295, 303–4; comedy and, 171–75, 188; race and, 107, 120, 122; travelogues and, 192, 195, 197–98, 205–8; women and, 219–20, 308n13. *See also* audiences; moviegoing

Speedy (Paramount, 1928), 188

Spehr, Paul, 96n3

Spendthrift, The (Kleine, 1915), 298

split reel, 72, 97n6, 139, 201, 239

Spoilers, The (Selig Polygraph, 1914), 257

Spooner, Cecil, 316

Spoor, George, 246–47, 258

Squaw Man, The (Lasky, 1914), 154

Squaw's Retribution, A (Bison, 1911), 133

Stacked Cards (Kay-Bee, 1914), 273

stage plays. *See* theater ("legitimate")

Staiger, Janet, 46n20, 61, 240, 297

Stamp, Shelley, 10, 39, 48n47, 64n4, 220

stars: of film, 10, 88, 90, 93–94, 96, 99n23, 132, 136, 144, 152; of theater, 10, 84, 320–21. *See also* actors and acting

star system, 1–2, 10, 94, 323–33, 336–39, 346. *See also* fans

Star Eyes' Strategy (Bison, 1912), 141

Star Film Company, 72, 239, 253

Star Wars (Twentieth-Century Fox, 1977), 297

Starr, Frederick, 202–3

States' Rights System, 69–70, 87, 89, 99n23, 140, 252, 257

Steele, Rufus, 335

Stewart, Jacqueline, 5–6

Stolen Pig, The (Vitagraph, 1907), 126n17

Stonehouse, Ruth 341

storefront theaters. *See* exhibition; nickelodeons

Strand Theater, 90, 154

Strike at Coaldale, The (Warners, 1914), 273

Stubbs, Katherine, 36–38

studios: facilities at, 334–35; location of, 334–35; production methods in, 346; tourism at, 335–37; working conditions at, 332, 334, 340–45

Sturgeon, Rollin S., 150, 168nn162,163

Sturtevant, Victoria, 346

Swanson, William H., 244–46, 26onn28,32

Sweden: reception of American film in, 164n109. *See also* Europe

Sweet, Blanche, 15, 24, 32

Tale of a Chicken, The (Lubin, 1914), 126n13

Taylor, Charles, 277

technology, 3, 5, 24, 26–27, 29, 35–41, 48n51, 52, 55–57, 59–60, 63; amusement parks and, 172, 188; comedy and 171. *See also* modernity

telegraphy, 24–25, 27–29, 31, 36–43, 48nn58,59, 49n74

television, 315, 327–28

Thanhouser, 18

theater ("legitimate"), 7, 84, 85, 88, 90, 98n15; comparison to film, 10, 270–72, 315–28; influence on film, 17, 73, 154, 315–28; performance style in, 316, 321; stars of, 10, 84, 320–21

theaters (motion picture): attendance at, 288, 295; black-owned, 7; competition among, 69, 88–93, 98n22, 99nn22,36; conversion to motion picture exhibition, 316–17; location of, 217–34; picture palaces and, 77, 88–90, 154, 249, 322. *See also* exhibition; nickelodeons

Their Interest in Common (Vitagraph, 1914), 198

Their Lives For Gold (Gaumont, 1912), 140, 162n86

Thissen, Judith, 221, 235n19

Thomas A. Edison Inc., 246. *See also* Edison Film Manufacturing Company; Edison, Thomas

Thompson, Frederic, 288, 294

Thompson, Kristin 15, 21–22, 46nn15,20, 47n36, 61, 75n14, 97n10, 98n10

Tie of Blood, The (Selig, 1913), 170n189

Tillie Wakes Up (Marie Dressler Film Corp., 1917), 173, 181, 183–85, 186, 187

Tilyou, George, 178

Tinee, Mae, 337

tinting, 15, 21–22, 27, 32–33

Tolstoy, Leo, 273

Trachtenberg, Alan, 135

Tracking the Government (Warners Features, 1914), 273
trade press, 1, 2, 6, 52, 57–58, 65n21, 67, 85, 89, 91–94, 131–51, 153, 155n1, 156n17, 157n17, 159n43, 160nn49,52, 58–59, 161n59, 164nn110,114, 165n127, 166n144, 167n145, 168nn163,166, 169n171, 203, 247–48, 272, 274, 278, 316, 332
trade unions, 347
Traffic in Souls (Universal, 1913), 60, 272, 282n35, 317, 344
travelogues, 191–208, 291, 295; reception of 202–4. *See also* nonfiction film
Triangle, 87, 154
Triangle/Artcraft, 154
Triangle-Reliance, 322. *See also* Reliance-Majestic
Trip Through Brazil, A (Eclipse, 1910), 196
Trip to Yosemite, A (Selig, 1909), illus. 194, 195
Truettner, William, 159n41
Tsivian, Yuri, 38
Two Little Rangers (Solax, 1912), 150

Ullman, Edward, 217
Una of the Sierras (Vitagraph, 1912), 151, 169n171
Uncle Tom's Cabin (Edison, 1903), 110, 291
Under the Old Apple Tree (American Mutoscope and Biograph, 1907), 113, 114–15, 117, 128n29
Under Western Skies (Essanay, 1910), 132
United Film Service Protective Association (UFSPA), 242–43
Universal, 8, 85, 87, 91, 94, 140, 43, 153–54, 162n80, 334–37, 341–42; tourism at, 335–37; women working at, 340–41
Up the Thames to Westminster (Kalem, 1910), 196
Uricchio, William, 202, 221
Urban, 199, 200
Urban-Eclipse, 247–48. *See also* Eclipse
urban space: circulation of African Americans in, 108, 120; modernity and, 302–3; motion picture exhibition and, 217–34. *See also* cities
Usurer, The (Biograph, 1910), 298–99
Usurer's Grip, The (Edison, 1904), 298

Vanity Fair (Vitagraph, 1912), 167n146
Vardac, A. Nicholas, 315
Variety Theaters, 66

variety programming format, 7, 66–68, 71–72, 74n2, 76–77, 84–86, 89–96, 98n22, 99n36, 100n47, 248–49, 253, 258; nonfiction films and, 192, 194–95, 197–99. *See also* exhibition practices
vaudeville, 17, 55, 58, 69n71, 84, 89, 98n15, 104, 249, 252; cinema and, 176, 1179, 94, 220, 226, 230, 235nn10,19, 294, 315, 318, 325
Vengeance of Fate, The (NYMP, 1912), 141
verisimilitude. *See* realism
vernacular modernism, 61–63
vertical integration, 68, 87
Vitagraph of America, 18, 46n11, 133, 144, 150, 151, 158n31, 167n146, 170n189, 210n19, 239, 241, 243, 247–48, 253, 255, 257
V-L-S-E, 87, 257–58
Vorse, Mary Heaton, 150

Wallace, Irene, 332, 343–44
Waller, Gregory, 89–90, 99n30, 125n12, 219, 235n10
Wanted: A Colored Servant (Italia, 1908), 130n43
War on the Plains (Bison, 1912), 138, 160–61n59
War, The West, and the Wilderness, The 159n46
Warners Features, 140, 273
Warrenton, Lule, 341
Warwick, 199
Wasko, Janet, 311n57
Watermelon Patch, The (Edison, 1905), 129n35
Weber, Lois, 337–38, 341–42, 345; films of 273–74
Wells, Ida B., 128n31
westerns, 6–7, 59, 93–94, 131–55, 155n1, 156nn 6–7,9–10,12, 157nn17,18,19,20,21,22,25,27, 158nn30,31,33, 159nn41,43,44,46, 160nn49,52,54,56,58–59, 161n59,63,65,71, 162nn73,75,80,85,86, 163nn87,88,109, 164nn109,110,112,113,114, 165nn116,117,120,122,125,127,128,129, 130,131, 166nn138,142,143,144, 167nn145,146,147,150,152,154,155, 168nn155,156,162,163,166, 169nn170,171,178,180,181, 170nn185,186,189,192, 248; actors/

stars of, 132, 133, 136–38, 140–42, 144–
46, 149, 151–53, 156n12, 157nn22,27,
158n33, 160nn52,54,56, 161n63,
164nn113,114,115, 165nn120,122,
128, 168n166; advertising for, 131–38,
142–43, 145, 147, 152, 157n19, 158n33,
160n54, 161n59; audiences for, 131–35,
140, 144, 149–50, 155; nation-building
function of, 132, 135, 143–44, 146,
148–49, 155, 156n7, 159n41, 164n112,
165n131, 166n131, 167nn147,150;
reception of, 132–33, 139–40, 144–
47, 149, 153, 159n44; 163n109,
164nn109,110,114; representation
of gender in, 150–53, 155, 157n27;
169n78; representation of race in,
133–34, 138, 141–42, 145–51, 154–55,
157nn18,25,27, 158nn30,31, 160n63,
165nn122,125, 166nn138,143,
170n189; trade press response to, 131–
51, 153, 155n1, 157n17, 159n43,
160nn49,52,58,59, 161n59,
164nn110,114, 165n127, 166n144,
167n145, 168nn163,166, 169n171
What Happened in the Tunnel (Edison, 1903),
113, 114, 115, 116, 128n28, 129n32
Wheels of Destiny, The (Kay-Bee, 1913),
142–43
When Justice Sleeps (Balboa Amusement Co.,
1915), 298
When the West Was Young (Vitagraph, 1913),
170n189
Where Are My Children? (Universal, 1916), 273
White Captive of the Sioux, The (Kalem, 1910),
134
White Fawn's Devotion (Pathé, 1910), 158n31
White Indian, A (Bison [Universal], 1912), 141
White, Pearl, 47n25
white slavery. *See* prostitution and white
slavery
White Vacquero, The (101–Bison, 1913),
170n189
Who Said Watermelon? (Lubin, 1902), 123n1
Wife of the Hills, A (Essanay, 1912), 160n56

Wild West Weekly (Nestor, 1912), 144
Why? (Elclair, 1913), 298
Why Worry? (Paramount, 1923), 188
Wiebe, Robert H., 309n35
Willey, Day Allen, 320, 323, 325
Williams, Kathlyn, 151–52
Williams, Linda, 50n86, 60–61, 112,
127n23, 174
Williams, Raymond, 287
Wilson, Ben, 144
Wilson, Woodrow, 278
Wister, Owen, 167n147
Within Our Gates (Micheaux Film Corpora-
tion, 1920), 128n31
women: as audiences, 7, 23, 48n47, 85, 150–
52, 219–20, 276, 278, 287; changing
roles of, 3, 10–11, 35–44, 150–52,
169n78; commercial recreation and,
290–91, 294–95, 303; as filmmakers,
337–38, 340–41; New Woman and, 35,
38, 40, 151, 153; representation of, 6, 7,
34–44, 103–23, 150–53, 155, 157n27,
169n78, 173, 180–85; working in early
Hollywood, 10–11, 40–41, 332–47
World Film Corporation, 87, 90, 257,
318–19
World War I, 68, 75n3, 98n10, 163n88, 258,
278
Worster, Donald, 146, 165nn130,131,
166n131

Youmans, F. Zeta, 234
Young, Clara Kimball, 338–39
Young Deer, James, 134, 158n31
Young, Paul, 38, 43–44
Young Wild West Leading a Raid (Nestor,
1912), 165n117
Your Girl and Mine: A Woman Suffrage Play
(Selig, 1914), 257

zoning and clearance. *See* distribution,
zoning and clearance rules of
Zudora, (Thanhouser, 1914–15), 18
Zukor, Adolph, 317–19

Compositor:	Integrated Composition Systems
Text:	10/12 Baskerville
Display:	Baskerville
Printer and binder:	Thomson-Shore, Inc.